BEELZEBUB'S TALES TO HIS GRANDSON

Born in Alexandropol in 1866, in a region of the Czarist empire that could be viewed as the seam between Europe and Asia, George Ivanovitch Gurdjieff traveled throughout the Middle East, Central Asia, and North Africa in search of knowledge concerning the hidden possibilities of human beings and our place in the universe. On his return, he began to gather pupils in Moscow and St. Petersburg before the First World War. During the years of the Russian Revolution and civil war, he migrated with a small party of followers to Essentuki in the Caucasus, and then through Tiflis, Constantinople, and Berlin to what would become his home in Paris and its region. In 1922, he opened the Institute for the Harmonious Development of Man at the Château du Prieuré in Fontainebleau-Avon, near Paris. The following year, his pupils gave public demonstrations of his Sacred Dances in Paris and, early in 1924, in several cities of the United States. This was the first of Gurdjieff's visits to the United States.

After a near-fatal automobile accident in the summer of 1924, Gurdjieff closed the Institute and devoted himself to writing. The first chapters of *Beelzebub's Tales* were written in this period.

The Prieuré was sold in 1932 and Gurdjieff moved to Paris where he resumed his work with pupils and completed his writings. After World War II, pupils from many countries were able to study and work with him until his death in October 1949.

Gurdjieff's writings are contained in a three-part series: *Beezlebub's Tales to His Grandson, Meetings with Remarkable Men,* and *Life is Real Only Then, When 'I Am'.* Records of his lectures and talks, primarily from the early years at the Prieuré, are presented in *Views from the Real World: Early Talks of Gurdjieff.* All are published in Penguin Compass.

G. I. Gurdjieff

BEELZEBUB'S TALES TO HIS GRANDSON

An objectively impartial criticism of the life of man

PENGUIN COMPASS

PENGUIN BOOKS
Published by the Penguin Group
Penguin Group (USA) Inc., 375 Hudson Street, New York, New York 10014, U.S.A.
Penguin Books Ltd, 80 Strand, London WC2R 0RL, England
Penguin Books Australia Ltd, 250 Camberwell Road, Camberwell, Victoria 3124, Australia
Penguin Books Canada Ltd, 10 Alcorn Avenue, Toronto, Ontario, Canada M4V 3B2
Penguin Books India (P) Ltd, 11 Community Centre, Panchsheel Park, New Delhi – 110 017, India
Penguin Books (N.Z.) Ltd, Cnr Rosedale and Airborne Roads, Albany, Auckland, New Zealand
Penguin Books (South Africa) (Pty) Ltd, 24 Sturdee Avenue,
Rosebank, Johannesburg 2196, South Africa

Penguin Books Ltd, Registered Offices: 80 Strand, London WC2R 0RL, England

Published in the United States of America by E. P. Dutton
& Co., Inc., 1964
This edition published in Arkana 1999

7 9 10 8

Original written in Russian and Armenian. Translations into other languages have been made under the personal direction of the author, by a group of translators chosen by him and specially trained according to their defined individualities, in conformity with the text to be translated and in relation to the philological particularities of each language.

Library of Congress Catalog Card Number: 50–5848
ISBN 0-525-05222-4 (hc.)
ISBN 0 14 01.9473 8 (pbk.)

Printed in the United States of America
Set in Garamond

ALL AND EVERYTHING

Ten Books in Three Series

FIRST SERIES: *Three books under the title of "An Objectively Impartial Criticism of the Life of Man," or, "Beelzebub's Tales to His Grandson."*

SECOND SERIES: *Three books under the common title of "Meetings with Remarkable Men."*

THIRD SERIES: *Four books under the common title of "Life is Real Only Then, When 'I Am.'"*

All written according to entirely new principles of logical reasoning and strictly directed towards the solution of the following three cardinal problems:

FIRST SERIES: To destroy, mercilessly, without any compromises whatsoever, in the mentation and feelings of the reader, the beliefs and views, by centuries rooted in him, about everything existing in the world.

SECOND SERIES: To acquaint the reader with the material required for a new creation and to prove the soundness and good quality of it.

THIRD SERIES: To assist the arising, in the mentation and in the feelings of the reader, of a veritable, nonfantastic representation not of that illusory world which he now perceives, but of the world existing in reality.

Friendly Advice

[Written impromptu by the author on delivering this book, already prepared for publication, to the printer.]

ACCORDING TO the numerous deductions and conclusions made by me during experimental elucidations concerning the productivity of the perception by contemporary people of new impressions from what is heard and read, and also according to the thought of one of the sayings of popular wisdom I have just remembered, handed down to our days from very ancient times, which declares:

"Any prayer may be heard by the Higher Powers and a corresponding answer obtained only if it is uttered thrice:

Firstly—for the welfare or the peace of the souls of one's parents.

Secondly—for the welfare of one's neighbor.

And only thirdly—for oneself personally."

I find it necessary on the first page of this book, quite ready for publication, to give the following advice:

"Read each of my written expositions thrice:

Firstly—at least as you have already become mechanized to read all your contemporary books and newspapers.

Secondly—as if you were reading aloud to another person.

And only thirdly—try and fathom the gist of my writings."

Only then will you be able to count upon forming your own impartial judgment, proper to yourself alone, on my writings. And only then can my hope be actualized that according to your understanding you will obtain the specific benefit for yourself which I anticipate, and which I wish for you with all my being.

AUTHOR

Contents

FIRST BOOK

SECOND BOOK

THIRD BOOK

FIRST BOOK

CHAPTER 1

The Arousing of Thought

Among other convictions formed in my common presence during my responsible, peculiarly composed life, there is one such also—an indubitable conviction—that always and everywhere on the earth, among people of every degree of development of understanding and of every form of manifestation of the factors which engender in their individuality all kinds of ideals, there is acquired the tendency, when beginning anything new, unfailingly to pronounce aloud or, if not aloud, at least mentally, that definite utterance understandable to every even quite illiterate person, which in different epochs has been formulated variously and in our day is formulated in the following words: "In the name of the Father and of the Son and in the name of the Holy Ghost. Amen."

That is why I now, also, setting forth on this venture quite new for me, namely, authorship, begin by pronouncing this utterance and moreover pronounce it not only aloud, but even very distinctly and with a full, as the ancient Toulousites defined it, "wholly-manifested-intonation"—of course with that fullness which can arise in my entirety only from data already formed and thoroughly rooted in me for such a manifestation; data which are in general formed in the nature of man, by the way, during his preparatory age, and later, during his responsible life engender in him the ability for the manifestation of the nature and vivifyingness of such an intonation.

Having thus begun, I can now be quite at ease, and should even, according to the notions of religious morality existing among contemporary people, be beyond all doubt assured that everything further in this new venture of mine will now proceed, as is said, "like a pianola."

In any case I have begun just thus, and as to how the rest will go I can only say meanwhile, as the blind man once expressed it, "we shall see."

First and foremost, I shall place my own hand, moreover the right one, which—although at the moment it is slightly injured owing to the misfortune which recently befell me—is nevertheless really my own, and has never once failed me in all my life, on my heart, of course also my own—but on the inconstancy or constancy of this part of all my whole I do not find it necessary here to expatiate—and frankly confess that I myself have personally not the slightest wish to write, but attendant circumstances, quite independent of me, constrain me to do so—and whether these circumstances arose accidentally or were created intentionally by extraneous forces, I myself do not yet know. I know only that these circumstances bid me write not just anything "so-so," as, for instance, something of the kind for reading oneself to sleep, but weighty and bulky tomes.

However that may be, I begin . . .

But begin with what?

Oh, the devil! Will there indeed be repeated that same exceedingly unpleasant and highly strange sensation which it befell me to experience when about three weeks ago I was composing in my thoughts the scheme and sequence of the ideas destined by me for publication and did not know then how to begin either?

This sensation then experienced I might now formulate in words only thus: "the-fear-of-drowning-in-the-overflow-of-my-own-thoughts."

To stop this undesirable sensation I might then still have had recourse to the aid of that maleficent property existing also in me, as in contemporary man, which has become inherent in all of us, and which enables us, without experiencing any remorse of conscience whatever, to put off anything we wish to do "till tomorrow."

I could then have done this very easily because before beginning the actual writing, it was assumed that there was still lots of time; but this can now no longer be done, and I must, without fail, as is said, "even though I burst," begin.

But with what indeed begin . . . ?

Hurrah! . . . Eureka!

Almost all the books I have happened to read in my life have begun with a preface.

So in this case I also must begin with something of the kind.

I say "of the kind," because in general in the process of my life, from the moment I began to distinguish a boy from a girl, I have always done everything, absolutely everything, not as it is done by other, like myself, biped destroyers of Nature's good. Therefore, in writing now I ought, and perhaps am even on principle already obliged, to begin not as any other writer would.

In any case, instead of the conventional preface I shall begin quite simply with a Warning.

Beginning with a Warning will be very judicious of me, if only because it will not contradict any of my principles, either organic, psychic, or even "willful," and will at the same time be quite honest—of course, honest in the objective sense, because both I myself and all others who know me well, expect with indubitable certainty that owing to my writings there will entirely disappear in the majority of readers, immediately and not gradually, as must sooner or later, with time, occur to all people, all the "wealth" they have, which was either handed down to them by inheritance or obtained by their own labor, in the form of quieting notions evoking only naïve dreams, and also beautiful representations of their lives at present as well as of their prospects in the future.

Professional writers usually begin such introductions with an address to the reader, full of all kinds of bombastically magniloquent and so to say "honeyed" and "inflated" phrases.

Just in this alone I shall follow their example and also begin with such an address, but I shall try not to make it very "sugary" as they usually do, owing particularly to their evil wiseacring by which they titillate the sensibilities of the more or less normal reader.

Thus . . .

My dear, highly honored, strong-willed and of course very patient Sirs, and my much-esteemed, charming, and impartial Ladies—forgive me, I have omitted the most important—and my in no wise hysterical Ladies!

I have the honor to inform you that although owing to circumstances that have arisen at one of the last stages of the process of my life, I am now about to write books, yet during the whole of my life I have never written not only not books or various what are called "instructive-articles," but also not even a letter in which it has been unfailingly necessary to observe what is called "grammaticality," and in consequence, although I am now about to become a professional writer, yet having had no practice at all either in respect of all the established professional rules and procedures or in respect of what is called the "bon ton literary language," I am constrained to write not at all as ordinary "patented-writers" do, to the form of whose writing you have in all probability become as much accustomed as to your own smell.

In my opinion the trouble with you, in the present instance, is perhaps chiefly due to the fact that while still in childhood, there was implanted in you and has now become ideally well harmonized with your general psyche, an excellently working automatism for perceiving all kinds of new impressions, thanks to which "blessing" you have now, during your responsible life, no need of making any individual effort whatsoever.

Speaking frankly, I inwardly personally discern the center of my confession not in my lack of knowledge of all the rules and procedures of writers, but in my nonpossession of what I have called the "bon ton literary language," infallibly required in contemporary life not only from writers but also from every ordinary mortal.

As regards the former, that is to say, my lack of knowledge of the different rules and procedures of writers, I am not greatly disturbed.

And I am not greatly disturbed on this account, because such "ignorance" has already now become in the life of people also in the order of things. Such a blessing arose and now flourishes everywhere on Earth thanks to that extraordinary new disease of which for the last twenty to thirty years, for some reason or other, especially the majority of those persons from among all the three sexes fall ill, who sleep with half-open eyes and whose faces are in every respect fertile soil for the growth of every kind of pimple.

This strange disease is manifested by this, that if the invalid is somewhat literate and his rent is paid for three months in advance, he (she or it) unfailingly begins to write either some "instructive article" or a whole book.

Well knowing about this new human disease and its epidemical spread on Earth, I, as you should understand, have the right to assume that you have acquired, as the learned "medicos" would say, "immunity" to it, and that you will therefore not be palpably indignant at my ignorance of the rules and procedures of writers.

This understanding of mine bids me inwardly to make the center of gravity of my warning my ignorance of the literary language.

In self-justification, and also perhaps to diminish the

degree of the censure in your waking consciousness of my ignorance of this language indispensable for contemporary life, I consider it necessary to say, with a humble heart and cheeks flushed with shame, that although I too was taught this language in my childhood, and even though certain of my elders who prepared me for responsible life, constantly forced me "without sparing or economizing" any intimidatory means to "learn by rote" the host of various "nuances" which in their totality compose this contemporary "delight," yet, unfortunately of course for you, of all that I then learned by rote, nothing stuck and nothing whatsoever has survived for my present activities as a writer.

And nothing stuck, as it was quite recently made clear to me, not through any fault of mine, nor through the fault of my former respected and nonrespected teachers, but this human labor was spent in vain owing to one unexpected and quite exceptional event which occurred at the moment of my appearance on God's Earth, and which was—as a certain occultist well known in Europe explained to me after a very minute what is called "psycho-physico-astrological" investigation—that at that moment, through the hole made in the windowpane by our crazy lame goat, there poured the vibrations of sound which arose in the neighbor's house from an Edison phonograph, and the midwife had in her mouth a lozenge saturated with cocaine of German make, and moreover not "Ersatz," and was sucking this lozenge to these sounds without the proper enjoyment.

Besides from this event, rare in the everyday life of people, my present position also arose because later on in my preparatory and adult life—as, I must confess, I myself guessed after long reflections according to the method of the German professor, Herr Stumpsinschmausen—I always avoided instinctively as well as automatically and at times even consciously, that is, on principle, employing this language for intercourse with others. And from such a trifle, and perhaps not a trifle, I manifested thus again thanks to three data which were formed in my entirety during my preparatory age, about which data I intend to inform you a little later in this same first chapter of my writings.

However that may have been, yet the real fact, illuminated from every side like an American advertisement, and which fact cannot now be changed by any forces even with the knowledge of the experts in "monkey business," is that although I, who have lately been considered by very many people as a rather good teacher of temple dances, have now become today a professional writer and will of course write a great deal—as it has been proper to me since childhood whenever "I do anything to do a great deal of it"—nevertheless, not having, as you see, the automatically acquired and automatically manifested practice necessary for this, I shall be constrained to write all I have thought out in ordinary simple everyday language established by life, without any literary manipulations and without any "grammarian wiseacrings."

But the pot is not yet full! . . . For I have not yet decided the most important question of all—in which language to write.

Although I have begun to write in Russian, nevertheless, as the wisest of the wise, Mullah Nassr Eddin, would say, in that language you cannot go far.

(Mullah Nassr Eddin, or as he is also called, Hodja Nassr Eddin, is, it seems, little known in Europe and America, but he is very well known in all countries of the continent of Asia; this legendary personage corresponds to the American Uncle Sam or the German Till Eulenspiegel. Numerous tales popular in the East, akin to the wise sayings, some of long standing and others newly arisen, were ascribed and are still ascribed to this Nassr Eddin.)

The Russian language, it cannot be denied, is very good. I even like it, but . . . only for swapping anecdotes and for use in referring to someone's parentage.

The Russian language is like the English, which language is also very good, but only for discussing in "smoking rooms," while sitting on an easy chair with legs outstretched on another, the topic of Australian frozen meat or, sometimes, the Indian question.

Both these languages are like the dish which is called in Moscow "Solianka," and into which everything goes except you and me, in fact everything you wish, and even the "after-dinner *Cheshma*"* of Sheherazade.

It must also be said that owing to all kinds of accidentally and perhaps not accidentally formed conditions of my youth, I have had to learn, and moreover very seriously and of course always with self-compulsion, to speak, read, and write a great many languages, and to such a degree of fluency, that if, in following this profession unexpectedly forced on me by Fate, I decided not to take advantage of the "automatism" which is acquired by practice, then I could perhaps write in any one of them.

But if I set out to use judiciously this automatically acquired automatism which has become easy from long practice, then I should have to write either in Russian or in Armenian, because the circumstances of my life during the last two or three decades have been such that I have had for intercourse with others to use, and consequently to have more practice in, just these two languages and to acquire an automatism in respect to them.

O the dickens! . . . Even in such a case, one of the aspects of my peculiar psyche, unusual for the normal

* *Cheshma* means veil.

man, has now already begun to torment the whole of me.

And the chief reason for this unhappiness of mine in my almost already mellow age, results from the fact that since childhood there was implanted in my peculiar psyche, together with numerous other rubbish also unnecessary for contemporary life, such an inherency as always and in everything automatically enjoins the whole of me to act only according to popular wisdom.

In the present case, as always in similar as yet indefinite life cases, there immediately comes to my brain—which is for me, constructed unsuccessfully to the point of mockery—and is now as is said, "running through" it that saying of popular wisdom which existed in the life of people of very ancient times, and which has been handed down to our day formulated in the following words: "every stick always has two ends."

In trying first to understand the basic thought and real significance hidden in this strange verbal formulation, there must, in my opinion, first of all arise in the consciousness of every more or less sane-thinking man the supposition that, in the totality of ideas on which is based and from which must flow a sensible notion of this saying, lies the truth, cognized by people for centuries, which affirms that every cause occurring in the life of man, from whatever phenomenon it arises, as one of two opposite effects of other causes, is in its turn obligatorily molded also into two quite opposite effects, as for instance: if "something" obtained from two different causes engenders light, then it must inevitably engender a phenomenon opposite to it, that is to say, darkness; or a factor engendering in the organism of a living creature an impulse of palpable satisfaction also engenders without fail nonsatisfaction, of course also palpable, and so on and so forth, always and in everything.

Adopting in the same given instance this popular wisdom

formed by centuries and expressed by a stick, which, as was said, indeed has two ends, one end of which is considered good and the other bad, then if I use the aforesaid automatism which was acquired in me thanks only to long practice, it will be for me personally of course very good, but according to this saying, there must result for the reader just the opposite; and what the opposite of good is, even every nonpossessor of hemorrhoids must very easily understand.

Briefly, if I exercise my privilege and take the good end of the stick, then the bad end must inevitably fall "on the reader's head."

This may indeed happen, because in Russian the so to say "niceties" of philosophical questions cannot be expressed, which questions I intend to touch upon in my writings also rather fully, whereas in Armenian, although this is possible, yet to the misfortune of all contemporary Armenians, the employment of this language for contemporary notions has now already become quite impracticable.

In order to alleviate the bitterness of my inner hurt owing to this, I must say that in my early youth, when I became interested in and was greatly taken up with philological questions, I preferred the Armenian language to all others I then spoke, even to my native language.

This language was then my favorite chiefly because it was original and had nothing in common with the neighboring or kindred languages.

As the learned "philologists" say, all of its tonalities were peculiar to it alone, and according to my understanding even then, it corresponded perfectly to the psyche of the people composing that nation.

But the change I have witnessed in that language during the last thirty or forty years has been such, that instead of an original independent language coming to us from the remote past, there has resulted and now exists one, which though also original and independent, yet represents, as might be said, a "kind of clownish potpourri of languages," the totality of the consonances of which, falling on the ear of a more or less conscious and understanding listener, sounds just like the "tones" of Turkish, Persian, French, Kurd, and Russian words and still other "indigestible" and inarticulate noises.

Almost the same might be said about my native language, Greek, which I spoke in childhood and, as might be said, the "taste of the automatic associative power of which" I still retain. I could now, I dare say, express anything I wish in it, but to employ it for writing is for me impossible, for the simple and rather comical reason that someone must transcribe my writings and translate them into the other languages. And who can do this?

It could assuredly be said that even the best expert of modern Greek would understand simply nothing of what I should write in the native language I assimilated in childhood, because, my dear "compatriots," as they might be called, being also inflamed with the wish at all costs to be like the representatives of contemporary civilization also in their conversation, have during these thirty or forty years treated my dear native language just as the Armenians, anxious to become Russian intelligentsia, have treated theirs.

That Greek language, the spirit and essence of which were transmitted to me by heredity, and the language now spoken by contemporary Greeks, are as much alike as, according to the expression of Mullah Nassr Eddin, "a nail is like a requiem."

What is now to be done?

Ah . . . me! Never mind, esteemed buyer of my wiseacrings. If only there be plenty of French armagnac and "Khaizarian bastourma," I shall find a way out of even this difficult situation.

I am an old hand at this.

In life, I have so often got into difficult situations and out of them, that this has become almost a matter of habit for me.

Meanwhile in the present case, I shall write partly in Russian and partly in Armenian, the more readily because among those people always "hanging around" me there are several who "cerebrate" more or less easily in both these languages, and I meanwhile entertain the hope that they will be able to transcribe and translate from these languages fairly well for me.

In any case I again repeat—in order that you should well remember it, but not as you are in the habit of remembering other things and on the basis of which are accustomed to keeping your word of honor to others or to yourself—that no matter what language I shall use, always and in everything, I shall avoid what I have called the "bon ton literary language."

In this respect, the extraordinarily curious fact and one even in the highest degree worthy of your love of knowledge, perhaps even higher than your usual conception, is that from my earliest childhood, that is to say, since the birth in me of the need to destroy birds' nests, and to tease my friends' sisters, there arose in my, as the ancient theosophists called it, "planetary body," and moreover, why I don't know, chiefly in the "right half," an instinctively involuntary sensation, which right up to that period of my life when I became a teacher of dancing, was gradually formed into a definite feeling, and then, when thanks to this profession of mine I came in contact with many people of different "types," there began to arise in me also the conviction with what is called my "mind," that these languages are compiled by people, or rather "grammarians," who are in respect of knowledge of the given language exactly similar to those biped animals whom the esteemed Mullah Nassr Eddin characterizes by the words: "All they can do is to wrangle with pigs about the quality of oranges."

This kind of people among us who have been turned into, so to say, "moths" destroying the good prepared and left for us by our ancestors and by time, have not the slightest notion and have probably never even heard of the screamingly obvious fact that, during the preparatory age, there is acquired in the brain functioning of every creature, and of man also, a particular and definite property, the automatic actualization and manifestation of which the ancient Korkolans called the "law of association," and that the process of the mentation of every creature, especially man, flows exclusively in accordance with this law.

In view of the fact that I have happened here accidentally to touch upon a question which has lately become one of my so to speak "hobbies," namely, the process of human mentation, I consider it possible, without waiting for the corresponding place predetermined by me for the elucidation of this question, to state already now in this first chapter at least something concerning that axiom which has accidentally become known to me, that on Earth in the past it has been usual in every century that every man, in whom there arises the boldness to attain the right to be considered by others and to consider himself a "conscious thinker," should be informed while still in the early years of his responsible existence that man has in general two kinds of mentation: one kind, mentation by thought, in which words, always possessing a relative sense, are employed; and the other kind, which is proper to all animals as well as to man, which I would call "mentation by form."

The second kind of mentation, that is, "mentation by form," by which, strictly speaking, the exact sense of all writing must be also perceived, and after conscious confrontation with information already possessed, be assimilated, is formed in people in dependence upon the conditions of geographical locality, climate, time, and, in general, upon the whole environment in which the arising of the given man has proceeded and in which his existence has flowed up to manhood.

Accordingly, in the brains of people of different races and conditions dwelling in different geographical localities, there are formed about one and the same thing or even idea, a number of quite independent forms, which during functioning, that is to say, association, evoke in their being some sensation or other which subjectively conditions a definite picturing, and which picturing is expressed by this, that, or the other word, that serves only for its outer subjective expression.

That is why each word, for the same thing or idea, almost always acquires for people of different geographical locality and race a very definite and entirely different so to say "inner content."

In other words, if in the entirety of any man who has arisen and been formed in any locality, from the results of the specific local influences and impressions a certain "form" has been composed, and this form evokes in him by association the sensation of a definite "inner content," and consequently of a definite picturing or notion for the expression of which he employs one or another word which has eventually become habitual, and as I have said, subjective to him, then the hearer of that word, in whose being, owing to different conditions of his arising and growth, there has been formed concerning the given word a form of a different "inner content," will always perceive and of course infallibly understand that same word in quite another sense.

This fact, by the way, can with attentive and impartial

observation be very clearly established when one is present at an exchange of opinions between persons belonging to two different races or who arose and were formed in different geographical localities.

And so, cheerful and swaggering candidate for a buyer of my wiseacrings, having warned you that I am going to write not as "professional writers" usually write but quite otherwise, I advise you, before embarking on the reading of my further expositions, to reflect seriously and only then to undertake it. If not, I am afraid for your hearing and other perceptive and also digestive organs which may be already so thoroughly automatized to the "literary language of the intelligentsia" existing in the present period of time on Earth, that the reading of these writings of mine might affect you very, very cacophonously, and from this you might lose your . . . you know what? . . . your appetite for your favorite dish and for your psychic specificness which particularly titillates your "inside" and which proceeds in you on seeing your neighbor, the brunette.

For such a possibility, ensuing from my language, or rather, strictly speaking, from the form of my mentation, I am, thanks to oft-repeated past experiences, already quite as convinced with my whole being as a "thoroughbred donkey" is convinced of the right and justice of his obstinacy.

Now that I have warned you of what is most important, I am already tranquil about everything further. Even if any misunderstanding should arise on account of my writings, you alone will be entirely to blame, and my conscience will be as clear as for instance . . . the ex-Kaiser Wilhelm's.

In all probability you are now thinking that I am, of course, a young man with an auspicious exterior and, as some express it, a "suspicious interior," and that, as a novice in writing, I am evidently intentionally being eccentric in the hope of becoming famous and thereby rich.

If you indeed think so, then you are very, very mistaken.

First of all, I am not young; I have already lived so much that I have been in my life, as it is said, "not only through the mill but through all the grindstones"; and secondly, I am in general not writing so as to make a career for myself, or so as to plant myself, as is said, "firm-footedly," thanks to this profession, which, I must add, in my opinion provides many openings to become a candidate d-i-r-e-c-t for "Hell"—assuming of course that such people can in general by their Being, perfect themselves even to that extent, for the reason that knowing nothing whatsoever themselves, they write all kinds of "claptrap" and thereby automatically acquiring authority, they become almost one of the chief factors, the totality of which steadily continues year by year, still further to diminish the, without this, already extremely diminished psyche of people.

And as regards my personal career, then thanks to all forces high and low and, if you like, even right and left, I have actualized it long ago, and have already long been standing on "firm feet" and even maybe on very good feet, and I moreover am certain that their strength is sufficient for many more years, in spite of all my past, present, and future enemies.

Yes, I think you might as well be told also about an idea which has only just arisen in my madcap brain, and namely, specially to request the printer, to whom I shall give my first book, to print this first chapter of my writings in such a way that anybody may read it before cutting the pages of the book itself, whereupon, on learning that it is not written in the usual manner, that is to say, for helping to produce in one's mentation, very smoothly and easily, exciting images and lulling reveries, he may, if he wishes, without wasting words with the bookseller, return it and get his money back, money perhaps earned by the sweat of his own brow.

I shall do this without fail, moreover, because I just now again remember the story of what happened to a Transcaucasian Kurd, which story I heard in my quite early youth and which in subsequent years, whenever I recalled it in corresponding cases, engendered in me an enduring and inextinguishable impulse of tenderness. I think it will be very useful for me, and also for you, if I relate this story to you somewhat in detail.

It will be useful chiefly because I have decided already to make the "salt," or as contemporary pure-blooded Jewish businessmen would say, the "Tzimus" of this story, one of the basic principles of that new literary form which I intend to employ for the attainment of the aim I am now pursuing by means of this new profession of mine.

This Transcaucasian Kurd once set out from his village on some business or other to town, and there in the market he saw in a fruiterer's shop a handsomely arranged display of all kinds of fruit.

In this display, he noticed one "fruit," very beautiful in both color and form, and its appearance so took his fancy and he so longed to try it, that in spite of his having scarcely any money, he decided to buy without fail at least one of these gifts of Great Nature, and taste it.

Then, with intense eagerness, and with a courage not customary to him, he entered the shop and pointing with his horny finger to the "fruit" which had taken his fancy he asked the shopkeeper its price. The shopkeeper replied that a pound of the "fruit" would cost two cents.

Finding that the price was not at all high for what in his opinion was such a beautiful fruit, our Kurd decided to buy a whole pound.

Having finished his business in town, he set off again on foot for home the same day.

Walking at sunset over the hills and dales, and willy-nilly perceiving the exterior visibility of those enchanting parts of the bosom of Great Nature, the Common Mother, and involuntarily inhaling a pure air uncontaminated by the usual exhalations of industrial towns, our Kurd quite naturally suddenly felt a wish to gratify himself with some ordinary food also; so sitting down by the side of the road, he took from his provision bag some bread and the "fruit" he had bought which had looked so good to him, and leisurely began to eat.

But . . . horror of horrors! . . . very soon everything inside him began to burn. But in spite of this he kept on eating.

And this hapless biped creature of our planet kept on eating, thanks only to that particular human inherency which I mentioned at first, the principle of which I intended, when I decided to use it as the foundation of the new literary form I have created, to make, as it were, a "guiding beacon" leading me to one of my aims in view, and the sense and meaning of which moreover you will, I am sure, soon grasp—of course according to the degree of your comprehension—during the reading of any subsequent chapter of my writings, if, of course, you take the risk and read further, or, it may perhaps be that even at the end of this first chapter you will already "smell" something.

And so, just at the moment when our Kurd was overwhelmed by all the unusual sensations proceeding within him from this strange repast on the bosom of Nature, there came along the same road a fellow villager of his, one reputed by those who knew him to be very clever and experienced; and, seeing that the whole face of the Kurd was aflame, that his eyes were streaming with tears, and that in spite of this, as if intent upon the fulfillment of his most important duty, he was eating real "red pepper pods," he said to him:

"What are you doing, you Jericho jackass? You'll be burnt alive! Stop eating that extraordinary product, so unaccustomed for your nature."

But our Kurd replied: "No, for nothing on Earth will I stop. Didn't I pay my last two cents for them? Even if my soul departs from my body I shall still go on eating."

Whereupon our resolute Kurd—it must of course be assumed that he was such—did not stop, but continued eating the "red pepper pods."

After what you have just perceived, I hope there may already be arising in your mentation a corresponding mental association which should, as a result, effectuate in you, as it sometimes happens to contemporary people, that which you call, in general, understanding, and that in the present case you will understand just why I, well knowing and having many a time commiserated with this human inherency, the inevitable manifestation of which is that if anybody pays money for something, he is bound to use it to the end, was animated in the whole of my entirety with the idea, arisen in my mentation, to take every possible measure in order that you, as is said "my brother in appetite and in spirit"—in the event of your proving to be already accustomed to reading books, though of all kinds, yet nevertheless only those written exclusively in the aforesaid "language of the intelligentsia"—having already paid money for my writings and learning only afterwards that they are not written in the usual convenient and easily read language, should not be compelled as a consequence of the said human inherency, to read my writings through to the end at all costs, as our poor Transcaucasian Kurd was compelled to go on with his eating of what he had fancied for its appearance alone—that "not to be joked with" noble red pepper.

And so, for the purpose of avoiding any misunderstanding through this inherency, the data for which are formed in the entirety of contemporary man, thanks evidently to his frequenting of the cinema and thanks also to his never missing an opportunity of looking into the left eye of the other sex, I wish that this commencing chapter of mine should be printed in the said manner, so that everyone can read it through without cutting the pages of the book itself.

Otherwise the bookseller will, as is said, "cavil," and will without fail again turn out to act in accordance with the basic principle of booksellers in general, formulated by them in the words: "You'll be more of a simpleton than a fisherman if you let go of the fish which has swallowed the bait," and will decline to take back a book whose pages you have cut. I have no doubt of this possibility; indeed, I fully expect such lack of conscience on the part of the booksellers.

And the data for the engendering of my certainty as to this lack of conscience on the part of these booksellers were completely formed in me, when, while I was a professional "Indian Fakir," I needed, for the complete elucidation of a certain "ultraphilosophical" question also to become familiar, among other things, with the associative process for the manifestation of the automatically constructed psyche of contemporary booksellers and of their salesmen when palming off books on their buyers.

Knowing all this and having become, since the misfortune which befell me, habitually just and fastidious in the extreme, I cannot help repeating, or rather, I cannot help again warning you, and even imploringly advising you, before beginning to cut the pages of this first book of mine, to read through very attentively, and even more than once, this first chapter of my writings.

But in the event that notwithstanding this warning of mine, you should, nevertheless, wish to become acquainted with the further contents of my expositions, then there is already nothing else left for me to do but to wish you with all my "genuine soul" a very, very good appetite, and that you may "digest" all that you read, not only for your own health but for the health of all those near you.

I said "with my genuine soul" because recently living in Europe and coming in frequent contact with people who on every appropriate and inappropriate occasion are fond of taking in vain every sacred name which should belong only to man's inner life, that is to say, with people who swear to no purpose, I being, as I have already confessed, a follower in general not only of the theoretical—as contemporary people have become—but also of the practical sayings of popular wisdom which have become fixed by the centuries, and therefore of the saying which in the present case corresponds to what is expressed by the words: "When you are in Rome do as Rome does," decided, in order not to be out of harmony with the custom established here in Europe of swearing in ordinary conversation, and at the same time to act according to the commandment which was enunciated by the holy lips of Saint Moses "not to take the holy names in vain," to make use of one of those examples of the "newly baked" fashionable languages of the present time, namely English, and so from then on, I began on necessary occasions to swear by my "English soul."

The point is that in this fashionable language, the words "soul" and the bottom of your foot, also called "sole," are pronounced and even written almost alike.

I do not know how it is with you, who are already partly candidate for a buyer of my writings, but my peculiar nature cannot, even with a great mental desire, avoid being indignant at the fact manifested by people of contemporary civilization, that the very highest in man, particularly beloved by our COMMON FATHER CREATOR, can really be named, and indeed very often before even having made clear to oneself what it is, can be understood to be that which is lowest and dirtiest in man.

Well, enough of "philologizing." Let us return to the main task of this initial chapter, destined, among other things, on the one hand to stir up the drowsy thoughts in me as well as in the reader, and, on the other, to warn the reader about something.

And so, I have already composed in my head the plan and sequence of the intended expositions, but what form they will take on paper, I, speaking frankly, myself do not as yet know with my consciousness, but with my subconsciousness I already definitely feel that on the whole it will take the form of something which will be, so to say, "hot," and will have an effect on the entirety of every reader such as the red pepper pods had on the poor Transcaucasian Kurd.

Now that you have become familiar with the story of our common countryman, the Transcaucasian Kurd, I already consider it my duty to make a confession and hence before continuing this first chapter, which is by way of an introduction to all my further predetermined writings, I wish to bring to the knowledge of what is called your "pure waking consciousness" the fact that in the writings following this chapter of warning I shall expound my thoughts intentionally in such sequence and with such "logical confrontation," that the essence of certain real notions may of themselves automatically, so to say, go from this "waking consciousness"—which most people in their ignorance mistake for the real consciousness, but which I affirm and experimentally prove is the fictitious one—into what you call the subconscious, which ought to be in my opinion the real human consciousness, and there by themselves mechanically bring about that transformation which should in general proceed in the entirety of a man and give him, from his own conscious mentation, the results he ought to have, which are proper to man and not merely to single- or double-brained animals.

I decided to do this without fail so that this initial chapter of mine, predetermined as I have already said to awaken your consciousness, should fully justify its purpose, and reaching not only your, in my opinion, as yet only fictitious "consciousness," but also your real consciousness, that is to say, what you call your subconscious, might, for the first time, compel you to reflect actively.

In the entirety of every man, irrespective of his heredity and education, there are formed two independent consciousnesses which in their functioning as well as in their manifestations have almost nothing in common. One consciousness is formed from the perception of all kinds of accidental, or on the part of others intentionally produced, mechanical impressions, among which must also be counted the "consonances" of various words which are indeed as is said empty; and the other consciousness is formed from the so to say, "already previously formed material results" transmitted to him by heredity, which have become blended with the corresponding parts of the entirety of a man, as well as from the data arising from his intentional evoking of the associative confrontations of these "materialized data" already in him.

The whole totality of the formation as well as the manifestation of this second human consciousness, which is none other than what is called the "subconscious," and which is formed from the "materialized results" of heredity and the confrontations actualized by one's own intentions, should in my opinion, formed by many years of my experimental elucidations during exceptionally favorably arranged conditions, predominate in the common presence of a man.

As a result of this conviction of mine which as yet doubtlessly seems to you the fruit of the fantasies of an afflicted mind, I cannot now, as you yourself see, disregard this second consciousness and, compelled by my essence, am obliged to construct the general exposition even of this first chapter of my writings, namely, the chapter which should be the preface for everything further, calculating that it should reach and, in the manner required for my aim, "ruffle" the perceptions accumulated in both these consciousnesses of yours.

Continuing my expositions with this calculation, I must first of all inform your fictitious consciousness that, thanks to three definite peculiar data which were crystallized in my entirety during various periods of my preparatory age, I am really unique in respect of the so to say "muddling and befuddling" of all the notions and convictions supposedly firmly fixed in the entirety of people with whom I come in contact.

Tut! Tut! Tut! . . . I already feel that in your "false"—but according to you "real"—consciousness, there are beginning to be agitated, like "blinded flies," all the chief data transmitted to you by heredity from your uncle and mother, the totality of which data, always and in everything, at least engenders in you the impulse—nevertheless extremely good—of curiosity, as in the given case, to find out as quickly as possible why I, that is to say, a novice at writing, whose name has not even once been mentioned in the newspapers, have suddenly become so unique.

Never mind! I personally am very pleased with the arising of this curiosity even though only in your "false" consciousness, as I already know from experience that this impulse unworthy of man can sometimes even pass from this consciousness into one's nature and become a worthy impulse—the impulse of the desire for knowledge, which, in its turn, assists the better perception and even the closer understanding of the essence of any object on which, as it sometimes happens, the attention of a contemporary man might be concentrated, and therefore I am even willing, with pleasure, to satisfy this curiosity which has arisen in you at the present moment.

Now listen and try to justify, and not to disappoint, my expectations. This original personality of mine, already "smelled out" by certain definite individuals from both choirs of the Judgment Seat Above, whence Objective justice proceeds, and also here on Earth, by as yet a very limited number of people, is based, as I already said, on three secondary specific data formed in me at different times during my preparatory age. The first of these data, from the very beginning of its arising, became as it were the chief directing lever of my entire wholeness, and the other two, the "vivifying-sources," as it were, for the feeding and perfecting of this first datum.

The arising of this first datum proceeded when I was still only, as is said, a "chubby mite." My dear now deceased grandmother was then still living and was a hundred and some years old.

When my grandmother—may she attain the kingdom of Heaven—was dying, my mother, as was then the custom, took me to her bedside, and as I kissed her right hand, my dear now deceased grandmother placed her dying left hand on my head and in a whisper, yet very distinctly, said:

"Eldest of my grandsons! Listen and always remember my strict injunction to you: In life never do as others do."

Having said this, she gazed at the bridge of my nose and evidently noticing my perplexity and my obscure understanding of what she had said, added somewhat angrily and imposingly:

"Either do nothing—just go to school—or do something nobody else does."

Whereupon she immediately, without hesitation, and with a perceptible impulse of disdain for all around her, and with commendable self-cognizance, gave up her soul directly into the hands of His Truthfulness, the Archangel Gabriel.

I think it will be interesting and even instructive to you to know that all this made so powerful an impression on me at that time that I suddenly became unable to endure anyone around me, and therefore, as soon as we left the room where the mortal "planetary body" of the cause of the cause of my arising lay, I very quietly, trying not to attract attention, stole away to the pit where during Lent the bran and potato skins for our "sanitarians," that is to say, our pigs, were stored, and lay there, without food or drink, in a tempest of whirling and confused thoughts—of which, fortunately for me, I had then in my childish brain still only a very limited number—right until the return from the cemetery of my mother, whose weeping on finding me gone and after searching for me in vain, as it were "overwhelmed" me. I then immediately emerged from the pit and standing first of all on the edge, for some reason or other with outstretched hand, ran to her and clinging fast to her skirts, involuntarily began to stamp my feet and why, I don't know, to imitate the braying of the donkey belonging to our neighbor, a bailiff.

Why this produced such a strong impression on me just then, and why I almost automatically manifested so strangely, I cannot until now make out; though during recent years, particularly on the days called "Shrovetide," I pondered a good deal, trying chiefly to discover the reason for it.

I then had only the logical supposition that it was perhaps only because the room in which this sacred scene occurred, which was to have tremendous significance for the whole of my further life, was permeated through and through with the scent of a special incense brought from the monastery of "Old Athos" and very popular among followers of every shade of belief of the Christian religion. Whatever it may have been, this fact still now remains a bare fact.

During the days following this event, nothing particular happened in my general state, unless there might be connected with it the fact that during these days, I walked more often than usual with my feet in the air, that is to say, on my hands.

My first act, obviously in discordance with the manifestations of others, though truly without the participation not only of my consciousness but also of my subconsciousness, occurred on exactly the fortieth day after the death of my grandmother, when all our family, our relatives and all those by whom my dear grandmother, who was loved by everybody, had been held in esteem, gathered in the cemetery according to custom, to perform over her mortal remains, reposing in the grave, what is called the "requiem service," when suddenly without any rhyme or reason, instead of observing what was conventional among people of all degrees of tangible and intangible morality and of all material positions, that is to say, instead of standing quietly as if overwhelmed, with an expression of grief on one's face and even if possible with tears in one's eyes, I started skipping round the grave as if dancing, and sang:

"Let her with the saints repose,
Now that she's turned up her toes,
Oi! oi! oi!
Let her with the saints repose,
Now that she's turned up her toes."

. . . and so on and so forth.

And just from this it began, that in my entirety a "something" arose which in respect of any kind of so to say "aping," that is to say, imitating the ordinary automatized manifestations of those around me, always and in everything engendered what I should now call an "irresistible urge" to do things not as others do them.

At that age I committed acts such as the following.

If for example when learning to catch a ball with the right hand, my brother, sisters and the neighbors' children who came to play with us, threw the ball in the air, I, with the same aim in view, would first bounce the ball hard on the ground, and only when it rebounded would I, first doing a somersault, catch it, and then only with the thumb and middle finger of the left hand; or if all the other children slid down the hill head first, I tried to do it, and moreover each time better and better, as the children then called it, "backside-first"; or if we children were given various kinds of what are called "Abaranian pastries," then all the other children, before putting them in their mouths, would first of all lick them, evidently to try their taste and to protract the pleasure, but . . . I would first sniff one on all sides and perhaps even put it to my ear and listen intently, and then though only almost unconsciously, yet nevertheless seriously, muttering to myself "so and so and so you must, do not eat until you bust," and rhythmically humming correspondingly, I would only take one bite and without savoring it, would swallow it—and so on and so forth.

The first event during which there arose in me one of the two mentioned data which became the "vivifying sources" for the feeding and perfecting of the injunction of my deceased grandmother, occurred just at that age when I changed from a chubby mite into what is called a "young rascal" and had already begun to be, as is sometimes said, a "candidate for a young man of pleasing appearance and dubious content."

And this event occurred under the following circumstances which were perhaps even specially combined by Fate itself.

With a number of young rascals like myself, I was once laying snares for pigeons on the roof of a neighbor's house, when suddenly, one of the boys who was standing over me and watching me closely, said:

"I think the noose of the horsehair ought to be so arranged that the pigeon's big toe never gets caught in it, because, as our zoology teacher recently explained to us, during movement it is just in that toe that the pigeon's reserve strength is concentrated, and therefore if this big toe gets caught in the noose, the pigeon might of course easily break it."

Another boy, leaning just opposite me, from whose mouth, by the way, whenever he spoke saliva always splashed abundantly in all directions, snapped at this remark of the first boy and delivered himself, with a copious quantity of saliva, of the following words:

"Shut your trap, you hopeless mongrel offshoot of the Hottentots! What an abortion you are, just like your teacher! Suppose it is true that the greatest physical force of the pigeon is concentrated in that big toe, then all the more, what we've got to do is to see that just that toe will be caught in the noose. Only then will there be any sense to our aim—that is to say, for catching these unfortunate pigeon creatures—in that brain-particularity proper to all possessors of that soft and slippery 'something' which consists in this, that when, thanks to other actions, from which its insignificant manifestability depends, there arises a periodic requisite law-conformable what is called 'change of presence,' then this small so to say 'law-conformable confusion' which should proceed for the animation of other acts in its general functioning, immediately enables the center of gravity of the whole functioning, in which this slippery 'something' plays a very small part, to pass temporarily from its usual place to another place, owing to which there often obtains in the whole of this general functioning, unexpected results ridiculous to the point of absurdity."

He discharged the last words with such a shower of saliva that it was as if my face were exposed to the action of an "atomizer"—not of "Ersatz" production—invented by the Germans for dyeing material with aniline dyes.

This was more than I could endure, and without changing my squatting position, I flung myself at him, and my head, hitting him with full force in the pit of his stomach, immediately laid him out and made him as is said "lose consciousness."

I do not know and do not wish to know in what spirit the result will be formed in your mentation of the information about the extraordinary coincidence, in my opinion, of life circumstances, which I now intend to describe here, though for my mentation, this coincidence was excellent material for the assurance of the possibility of the fact that this event described by me, which occurred in my youth, proceeded not simply accidentally but was intentionally created by certain extraneous forces.

The point is that this dexterity was thoroughly taught me only a few days before this event by a Greek priest from Turkey, who, persecuted by Turks for his political convictions, had been compelled to flee from there, and having arrived in our town had been hired by my parents as a teacher for me of the modern Greek language.

I do not know on which data he based his political convictions and ideas, but I very well remember that in all the conversations of this Greek priest, even while explaining to me the difference between the words of exclamation in ancient and in modern Greek, there were indeed always very clearly discernible his dreams of getting as soon as possible to the island of Crete and there manifesting himself as befits a true patriot.

Well, then, on beholding the effect of my skill, I was, I must confess, extremely frightened, because, knowing nothing of any such reaction from a blow in that place, I quite thought I had killed him.

At the moment I was experiencing this fear, another boy, the cousin of him who had become the first victim of my so to say "skill in self-defense," seeing this, without a moment's pause, and obviously overcome with a feeling called "consanguinity," immediately leaped at me and with a full swing struck me in the face with his fist.

From this blow, I, as is said, "saw stars," and at the same time my mouth became as full as if it had been stuffed with the food necessary for the artificial fattening of a thousand chickens.

After a little time when both these strange sensations had calmed down within me, I then actually discovered that some foreign substance was in my mouth, and when I pulled it out with my fingers, it turned out to be nothing less than a tooth of large dimensions and strange form.

Seeing me staring at this extraordinary tooth, all the boys swarmed around me and also began to stare at it with great curiosity and in a strange silence.

By this time the boy who had been laid out flat recovered and, picking himself up, also began to stare at my tooth with the other boys, as if nothing had happened to him.

This strange tooth had seven shoots and at the end of each of them there stood out in relief a drop of blood, and through each separate drop there shone clearly and definitely one of the seven aspects of the manifestation of the white ray.

After this silence, unusual for us "young rascals," the usual hubbub broke out again, and in this hubbub it was decided to go immediately to the barber, a specialist in extracting teeth, and to ask him just why this tooth was like that.

So we all climbed down from the roof and went off to the barber's. And I, as the "hero of the day," stalked at the head of them all.

The barber, after a casual glance, said it was simply a "wisdom tooth" and that all those of the male sex have one like it, who until they first exclaim "papa" and "mamma" are fed on milk exclusively from their own mother, and who on first sight are able to distinguish among many other faces the face of their own father.

As a result of the whole totality of the effects of this happening, at which time my poor "wisdom tooth" became a complete sacrifice, not only did my consciousness begin, from that time on, constantly absorbing, in connection with everything, the very essence of the essence of my deceased grandmother's behest—God bless her soul—but also in me at that time, because I did not go to a "qualified dentist" to have the cavity of this tooth of mine treated, which as a matter of fact I could not do because our home was too far from any contemporary center of culture, there began to ooze chronically from this cavity a "something" which—as it was only recently explained to me by a very famous meteorologist with whom I chanced to become, as is said, "bosom friends" owing to frequent meetings in the Parisian night restaurants of Montmartre—had the property of arousing an interest in, and a tendency to seek out the causes of the arising of every suspicious "actual fact"; and this property, not transmitted to my entirety by heredity, gradually and automatically led to my ultimately becoming a specialist in the investigation of every suspicious phenomenon which, as it so often happened, came my way.

This property newly formed in me after this event—when I, of course with the co-operation of our ALL-COMMON MASTER THE MERCILESS HEROPASS, that is the "flow of time," was transformed into the young man already depicted by me—became for me a real inextinguishable hearth, always burning, of consciousness.

The second of the mentioned vivifying factors, this time for the complete fusion of my dear grandmother's injunction with all the data constituting my general individuality, was the totality of impressions received from information I chanced to acquire concerning the event which took place here among us on Earth, showing the origin of that "principle" which, as it turned out according to the elucidations of Mr. Alan Kardec during an "absolutely secret" spiritualistic seance, subsequently became everywhere among beings similar to ourselves, arising and existing on all the other planets of our Great Universe, one of the chief "life principles."

The formulation in words of this new "all-universal principle of living" is as follows:

"If you go on a spree then go the whole hog including the postage."

As this "principle," now already universal, arose on that same planet on which you too arose and on which, moreover, you exist almost always on a bed of roses and frequently dance the fox trot, I consider I have no right to withhold from you the information known to me, elucidating certain details of the arising of just that universal principle.

Soon after the definite inculcation into my nature of the said new inherency, that is, the unaccountable striving to elucidate the real reasons for the arising of all sorts of "actual facts," on my first arrival in the heart of Russia, the city of Moscow, where, finding nothing else for the satisfaction of my psychic needs, I occupied myself with the investigation of Russian legends and sayings, I once happened—whether accidentally or as a result of some objective sequence according to a law I do not know—to learn by the way the following:

Once upon a time a certain Russian, who in external appearance was to those around him a simple merchant, had to go from his provincial town on some business or other to this second capital of Russia, the city of Moscow, and his son, his favorite one—because he resembled only his mother—asked him to bring back a certain book.

When this great unconscious author of the "all-universal principle of living" arrived in Moscow, he together with a friend of his became—as was and still is usual there—"blind drunk" on genuine "Russian vodka."

And when these two inhabitants of this most great contemporary grouping of biped breathing creatures had drunk the proper number of glasses of this "Russian blessing" and were discussing what is called "public education," with which question it has long been customary always to begin one's conversation, then our merchant suddenly remembered by association his dear son's request, and decided to set off at once to a bookshop with his friend to buy the book.

In the shop, the merchant, looking through the book he had asked for and which the salesman handed him, asked its price.

The salesman replied that the book was sixty kopecks.

Noticing that the price marked on the cover of the book was only forty-five kopecks, our merchant first began pondering in a strange manner, in general unusual for Russians, and afterwards, making a certain movement with his shoulders, straightening himself up almost like a pillar and throwing out his chest like an officer of the guards, said after a little pause, very quietly but with an intonation in his voice expressing great authority:

"But it is marked here forty-five kopecks. Why do you ask sixty?"

Thereupon the salesman, making as is said the "oleaginous" face proper to all salesmen, replied that the book indeed cost only forty-five kopecks, but had to be sold at sixty because fifteen kopecks were added for postage.

After this reply to our Russian merchant who was perplexed by these two quite contradictory but obviously clearly reconcilable facts, it was visible that something began to proceed in him, and gazing up at the ceiling, he again pondered, this time like an English professor who has invented a capsule for castor oil, and then suddenly turned to his friend and delivered himself for the first time on Earth of the verbal formulation which, expressing in its essence an indubitable objective truth, has since assumed the character of a saying.

And he then put it to his friend as follows:

"Never mind, old fellow, we'll take the book. Anyway we're on a spree today, and 'if you go on a spree then go the whole hog including the postage.' "

As for me, unfortunately doomed, while still living, to experience the delights of "Hell," as soon as I had cognized all this, something very strange, that I have never experienced before or since, immediately began, and for a rather long time continued to proceed in me; it was as if all kinds of, as contemporary "Hivintzes" say, "competitive races" began to proceed in me between all the various-sourced associations and experiences usually occurring in me.

At the same time, in the whole region of my spine there began a strong almost unbearable itch, and a colic in the very center of my solar plexus, also unbearable, and all this, that is these dual, mutually stimulating sensations, after the lapse of some time suddenly were replaced by such a peaceful inner condition as I experienced in later life once only, when the ceremony of the great initiation into the Brotherhood of the "Originators of making butter from air" was performed over me; and later when "I," that is, this "something-unknown" of mine, which in ancient times one crank—called by those around him, as we now also call such persons, a "learned man"—defined as a "relatively transferable arising, depending on the quality of the functioning of thought, feeling, and organic automatism," and according to the definition of another also ancient and renowned learned man, the Arabian Mal-el-Lel, which definition by the way was in the course of time borrowed and repeated in a different way by a no less renowned and learned Greek, Xenophon, "the compound result of consciousness, subconsciousness, and instinct"; so when this same "I" in this condition turned my dazed attention inside myself, then firstly it very clearly constated that everything, even to each single word, elucidating this quotation that has become an "all-universal life principle" became transformed in me into some special cosmic substance, and merging with the data already crystallized in me long before from the behest of my deceased grandmother, changed these data into a "something" and this "something" flowing everywhere through my entirety settled forever in each atom composing this entirety of mine, and secondly, this my ill-fated "I" there and then definitely felt and, with an impulse of submission, became conscious of this, for me, sad fact, that already from that moment I should willy-nilly have to manifest myself always and in everything without exception, according to this inherency formed in me, not in accordance with the laws of heredity, nor even by the influence of surrounding circumstances, but arising in my entirety under the influence of three external accidental causes, having nothing in common, namely: thanks in the first place to the behest of a person who had become, without the slightest desire on my part, a passive cause of the cause of my arising; secondly, on account of a tooth of mine knocked out by some ragamuffin of a boy, mainly on account of somebody else's "slobberiness"; and thirdly, thanks to the verbal formulation delivered in a drunken state by a person quite alien to me—some merchant of "Moscovite brand."

If before my acquaintance with this "all-universal principle of living" I had actualized all manifestations differently from other biped animals similar to me, arising and vegetating with me on one and the same planet, then I did so automatically, and sometimes only half consciously, but after this event I began to do so consciously and moreover with an instinctive sensation of the two blended impulses of self-satisfaction and self-cognizance in correctly and honorably fulfilling my duty to Great Nature.

It must even be emphasized that although even before this event I already did everything not as others did, yet my manifestations were hardly thrust before the eyes of my fellow countrymen around me, but from the moment when the essence of this principle of living was assimilated in my nature, then on the one hand all my manifestations, those intentional for any aim and also those simply, as is said, "occurring out of sheer idleness," acquired vivifyingness and began to assist in the formation of "corns" on the organs of perception of every creature similar to me without exception who directed his attention directly or indirectly toward my actions, and on the other hand, I myself began to carry out all these actions of mine in accordance with the injunctions of my deceased grandmother to the utmost possible limits; and the practice was automatically acquired in me on beginning anything new and also at any change, of course on a large scale, always to utter silently or aloud:

"If you go on a spree then go the whole hog including the postage."

And now, for instance, in the present case also, since, owing to causes not dependent on me, but flowing from the strange and accidental circumstances of my life, I happen to be writing books, I am compelled to do this also in accordance with that same principle which has gradually become definite through various extraordinary combinations created by life itself, and which has blended with each atom of my entirety.

This psycho-organic principle of mine I shall this time begin to actualize not by following the practice of all writers, established from the remote past down to the present, of taking as the theme of their various writings the events which have supposedly taken place, or are taking place, on Earth, but shall take instead as the scale of events for my writings—the whole Universe. Thus in the present case also, "If you take then take!"—that is to say, "If you go on a spree then go the whole hog including the postage."

Any writer can write within the scale of the Earth, but I am not any writer.

Can I confine myself merely to this, in the objective sense, "paltry Earth" of ours? To do this, that is to say, to take for my writings the same themes as in general other writers do, I must not, even if only because what our learned spirits affirm might suddenly indeed prove true; and my grandmother might learn of this; and do you understand what might happen to her, to my dear beloved grandmother? Would she not turn in her grave, not once, as is usually said, but—as I understand her, especially now when I can already quite "skillfully" enter into the position of another—she would turn so many times that she would almost be transformed into an "Irish weathercock."

Please, reader, do not worry . . . I shall of course also write of the Earth, but with such an impartial attitude that this comparatively small planet itself and also everything on it shall correspond to that place which in fact it occupies and which, even according to your own sane logic, arrived at thanks of course to my guidance, it must occupy in our Great Universe.

I must, of course, also make the various what are called "heroes" of these writings of mine not such types as those which in general the writers of all ranks and epochs on Earth have drawn and exalted, that is to say, types such as any Tom, Dick, or Harry, who arise through a misunderstanding, and who fail to acquire during the process of their formation up to what is called "responsible life," anything at all which it is proper for an arising in the image of God, that is to say a man, to have, and who progressively develop in themselves to their last breath only such various charms as for instance: "lasciviousness," "slobberiness," "amorousness," "maliciousness," "chickenheartedness," "enviousness," and similar vices unworthy of man.

I intend to introduce in my writings heroes of such type as everybody must, as is said, "willy-nilly" sense with his whole being as real, and about whom in every reader data must inevitably be crystallized for the notion that they are indeed "somebody" and not merely "just anybody."

During the last weeks, while lying in bed, my body quite sick, I mentally drafted a summary of my future writings and thought out the form and sequence of their exposition, and I decided to make the chief hero of the first series of my writings . . . do you know whom? . . . the Great Beelzebub Himself—even in spite of the fact that this choice of mine might from the very beginning evoke in the mentation of most of my readers such mental associations as must engender in them all kinds of automatic contradictory impulses from the action of that totality of data infallibly formed in the psyche of people owing to all the established abnormal conditions of our external life, which data are in general crystallized in people owing to the famous what is called "religious morality" existing and rooted in their life, and in them, consequently, there must inevitably be formed data for an inexplicable hostility towards me personally.

But do you know what, reader?

In case you decide, despite this Warning, to risk continuing to familiarize yourself with my further writings, and you try to absorb them always with an impulse of impartiality and to understand the very essence of the questions I have decided to elucidate, and in view also of the particularity inherent in the human psyche, that there can be no opposition to the perception of good only exclusively when so to say a "contact of mutual frankness and confidence" is established, I now still wish to make a sincere confession to you about the associations arisen within me which as a result have precipitated in the corresponding sphere of my consciousness the data which have prompted the whole of my individuality to select as the chief hero for my writings just such an individual as is presented before your inner eyes by this same Mr. Beelzebub.

This I did, not without cunning. My cunning lies simply in the logical supposition that if I show him this attention he infallibly—as I already cannot doubt any more—has to show himself grateful and help me by all means in his command in my intended writings.

Although Mr. Beelzebub is made, as is said, "of a different grain," yet, since He also can think, and, what is most important, has—as I long ago learned, thanks to the treatise of the famous Catholic monk, Brother Foolon—a curly tail, then I, being thoroughly convinced from experience that curls are never natural but can be obtained only from various intentional manipulations, conclude, according to the "sane-logic" of hieromancy formed in my consciousness from reading books, that Mr. Beelzebub also must possess a good share of vanity, and will therefore find it extremely inconvenient not to help one who is going to advertise His name.

It is not for nothing that our renowned and incomparable teacher, Mullah Nassr Eddin, frequently says:

"Without greasing the palm not only is it impossible to live anywhere tolerably but even to breathe."

And another also terrestrial sage, who has become such, thanks to the crass stupidity of people, named Till Eulenspiegel, has expressed the same in the following words:

"If you don't grease the wheels the cart won't go."

Knowing these and many other sayings of popular wisdom formed by centuries in the collective life of people, I have decided to "grease the palm" precisely of Mr. Beelzebub, who, as everyone understands, has possibilities and knowledge enough and to spare for everything.

Enough, old fellow! All joking even philosophical joking aside, you, it seems, thanks to all these deviations, have transgressed one of the chief principles elaborated in you and put in the basis of a system planned previously for introducing your dreams into life by means of such a new profession, which principle consists in this, always to remember and take into account the fact of the weakening of the functioning of the mentation of the contemporary reader and not to fatigue him with the perception of numerous ideas over a short time.

Moreover, when I asked one of the people always around me who are "eager to enter Paradise without fail with their boots on," to read aloud straight through all that I have written in this introductory chapter, what is called my "I"—of course, with the participation of all the definite data formed in my original psyche during my past years, which data gave me among other things understanding of the psyche of creatures of different type but similar to me—constated and cognized with certainty that in the entirety of every reader without exception there must inevitably, thanks to this first chapter alone, arise a "something" automatically engendering definite unfriendliness towards me personally.

To tell the truth, it is not this which is now chiefly worrying me, but the fact that at the end of this reading I also constated that in the sum total of everything expounded in this chapter, the whole of my entirety in which the aforesaid "I" plays a very small part, manifested itself quite contrary to one of the fundamental commandments of that All-Common Teacher whom I particularly esteem, Mullah Nassr Eddin, and which he formulated in the words: "Never poke your stick into a hornets' nest."

The agitation which pervaded the whole system affecting my feelings, and which resulted from cognizing that in the reader there must necessarily arise an unfriendly feeling towards me, at once quieted down as soon as I remembered the ancient Russian proverb which states: "There is no offence which with time will not blow over."

But the agitation which arose in my system from realizing my negligence in obeying the commandment of Mullah Nassr Eddin, not only now seriously troubles me, but a very strange process, which began in both of my recently discovered "souls" and which assumed the form of an unusual itching immediately I understood this, began progressively to increase until it now evokes and produces an almost intolerable pain in the region a little below the right half of my already, without this, overexercised "solar plexus."

Wait! Wait! . . . This process, it seems, is also ceasing, and in all the depths of my consciousness, and let us meanwhile say "even beneath my subconsciousness," there already begins to arise everything requisite for the complete assurance that it will entirely cease, because I have remembered another fragment of life wisdom, the thought of which led my mentation to the reflection that if I indeed acted against the advice of the highly esteemed Mullah Nassr Eddin, I nevertheless acted without premeditation according to the principle of that extremely sympathetic—not so well known everywhere on earth, but never forgotten by all who have once met him—that precious jewel, Karapet of Tiflis.

It can't be helped. . . . Now that this introductory chapter of mine has turned out to be so long, it will not matter if I lengthen it a little more to tell you also about this extremely sympathetic Karapet of Tiflis.

First of all I must state that twenty or twenty-five years ago, the Tiflis railway station had a "steam whistle."

It was blown every morning to wake the railway workers and station hands, and as the Tiflis station stood on a hill, this whistle was heard almost all over the town and woke up not only the railway workers, but the inhabitants of the town of Tiflis itself.

The Tiflis local government, as I recall it, even entered into a correspondence with the railway authorities about the disturbance of the morning sleep of the peaceful citizens.

To release the steam into the whistle every morning was the job of this same Karapet who was employed in the station.

So when he would come in the morning to the rope with which he released the steam for the whistle, he would, before taking hold of the rope and pulling it, wave his hand in all directions and solemnly, like a Mohammedan mullah from a minaret, loudly cry:

"Your mother is a — —, your father is a — —, your grandfather is more than a — —; may your eyes, ears, nose, spleen, liver, corns . . ." and so on; in short, he pronounced in various keys all the curses he knew, and not until he had done so would he pull the rope.

When I heard about this Karapet and of this practice of his, I visited him one evening after the day's work, with a small *boordook* of Kahketeenian wine, and after performing this indispensable local solemn "toasting ritual," I asked him, of course in a suitable form and also according to the local complex of "amenities" established for mutual relationship, why he did this.

Having emptied his glass at a draught and having once sung the famous Georgian song, "Little did we tipple," inevitably sung when drinking, he leisurely began to answer as follows:

"As you drink wine not as people do today, that is to say, not merely for appearances but in fact honestly, then this already shows me that you do not wish to know about this practice of mine out of curiosity, like our engineers and technicians, but really owing to your desire for knowledge, and therefore I wish, and even consider it my duty, sincerely to confess to you the exact reason of these inner, so to say, 'scrupulous considerations' of mine, which led me to this, and which little by little instilled in me such a habit."

He then related the following:

"Formerly I used to work in this station at night cleaning the steam boilers, but when this steam whistle was brought here, the stationmaster, evidently considering my age and incapacity for the heavy work I was doing, ordered me to occupy myself only with releasing the steam into the whistle, for which I had to arrive punctually every morning and evening.

"The first week of this new service, I once noticed that after performing this duty of mine, I felt for an hour or two vaguely ill at ease. But when this strange feeling, increasing day by day, ultimately became a definite instinctive uneasiness from which even my appetite for 'Makhokh' disappeared, I began from then on always to think and think in order to find out the cause of this. I thought about it all particularly intensely for some reason or other while going to and coming from my work, but however hard I tried I could make nothing whatsoever, even approximately, clear to myself.

"It thus continued for almost two years and, finally, when the calluses on my palms had become quite hard from the rope of the steam whistle, I quite accidentally and suddenly understood why I experienced this uneasiness.

"The shock for my correct understanding, as a result of which there was formed in me concerning this an unshakable conviction, was a certain exclamation I accidentally heard under the following, rather peculiar, circumstances.

"One morning when I had not had enough sleep, having spent the first half of the night at the christening of my neighbor's ninth daughter and the other half in reading a very interesting and rare book I had by chance obtained and which was entitled *Dreams and Witchcraft*, as I was hurrying on my way to release the steam, I suddenly saw at the corner a barber-surgeon I knew, belonging to the local government service, who beckoned me to stop.

"The duty of this barber-surgeon friend of mine consisted in going at a certain time through the town accompanied by an assistant with a specially constructed carriage and seizing all the stray dogs whose collars were without the metal plates distributed by the local authorities on payment of the tax and taking these dogs to the municipal slaughterhouse where they were kept for two weeks at municipal expense, feeding on the slaughterhouse offal; if, on the expiration of this period, the owners of the dogs had not claimed them and paid the established tax, then these dogs were, with a certain solemnity, driven down a certain passageway which led directly to a specially built oven.

"After a short time, from the other end of this famous salutary oven, there flowed, with a delightful gurgling sound, a definite quantity of pellucid and ideally clean fat to the profit of the fathers of our town for the manufacture of soap and also perhaps of something else, and, with a purling sound, no less delightful to the ear, there poured out also a fair quantity of very useful substance for fertilizing.

"This barber-surgeon friend of mine proceeded in the following simple and admirably skillful manner to catch the dogs.

"He somewhere obtained a large, old, and ordinary fishing net, which, during these peculiar excursions of his for the general human welfare through the slums of our town, he carried, arranged in a suitable manner on his strong shoulders, and when a dog without its 'passport' came within the sphere of his all-seeing and, for all the canine species, terrible eye, he without haste and with the softness of a panther, would steal up closely to it and seizing a favorable moment when the dog was interested and attracted by something it noticed, cast his net on it and quickly entangled it, and later, rolling up the carriage, he disentangled the dog in such a way that it found itself in the cage attached to the carriage.

"Just when my friend the barber-surgeon beckoned me to stop, he was aiming to throw his net, at the opportune moment, at his next victim, which at that moment was standing wagging his tail and looking at a bitch. My friend was just about to throw his net, when suddenly the bells of a neighboring church rang out, calling the people to early morning prayers. At such an unexpected ringing in the morning quiet, the dog took fright and springing aside flew off like a shot down the empty street at his full canine velocity.

"Then the barber-surgeon so infuriated by this that his hair, even beneath his armpits, stood on end, flung his net on the pavement and spitting over his left shoulder, loudly exclaimed:

"'Oh, Hell! What a time to ring!'

"As soon as the exclamation of the barber-surgeon reached my reflecting apparatus, there began to swarm in it various thoughts which ultimately led, in my view, to the correct understanding of just why there proceeded in me the aforesaid instinctive uneasiness.

"The first moment after I had understood this there even arose a feeling of being offended at myself that such a simple and clear thought had not entered my head before.

"I sensed with the whole of my being that my effect on the general life could produce no other result than that process which had all along proceeded in me.

"And indeed, everyone awakened by the noise I make with the steam whistle, which disturbs his sweet morning slumbers, must without doubt curse me 'by everything under the sun,' just me, the cause of this hellish row, and thanks to this, there must of course certainly flow towards my person from all directions, vibrations of all kinds of malice.

"On that significant morning, when, after performing my duties, I, in my customary mood of depression, was sitting in a neighboring 'Dukhan' and eating 'Hachi' with garlic,

I, continuing to ponder, came to the conclusion that if I should curse beforehand all those to whom my service for the benefit of certain among them might seem disturbing, then, according to the explanation of the book I had read the night before, however much all those, as they might be called, 'who lie in the sphere of idiocy,' that is, between sleep and drowsiness, might curse me, it would have—as explained in that same book—no effect on me at all.

"And in fact, since I began to do so, I no longer feel the said instinctive uneasiness."

Well, now, patient reader, I must really conclude this opening chapter. It has now only to be signed.

He who . . .

Stop! Misunderstanding formation! With a signature there must be no joking, otherwise the same will be done to you as once before in one of the empires of Central Europe, when you were made to pay ten years' rent for a house you occupied only for three months, merely because you had set your hand to a paper undertaking to renew the contract for the house each year.

Of course after this and still other instances from life experience, I must in any case in respect of my own signature, be very, very careful.

Very well then.

He who in childhood was called "Tatakh"; in early youth "Darky"; later the "Black Greek"; in middle age, the "Tiger of Turkestan"; and now, not just anybody, but the genuine "Monsieur" or "Mister" Gurdjieff, or the nephew of "Prince Mukransky," or finally, simply a "Teacher of Dancing."

CHAPTER 2

Introduction
Why Beelzebub Was in Our Solar System

It was in the year 223 after the creation of the World, by objective time-calculation, or, as it would be said here on the "Earth," in the year 1921 after the birth of Christ.

Through the Universe flew the ship *Karnak* of the "transspace" communication.

It was flying from the spaces "Assooparatsata," that is, from the spaces of the "Milky Way," from the planet Karatas to the solar system "Pandetznokh," the sun of which is also called the "Pole Star."

On the said "transspace" ship was Beelzebub with his kinsmen and near attendants.

He was on his way to the planet Revozvradendr to a special conference in which he had consented to take part, at the request of his friends of long standing.

Only the remembrance of these old friendships had constrained him to accept this invitation, since he was no longer young, and so lengthy a journey, and the vicissitudes inseparable from it, were by no means an easy task for one of his years.

Only a little before this journey Beelzebub had returned home to the planet Karatas where he had received his arising and far from which, on account of circumstances independent of his own essence, he had passed many years of his existence in conditions not proper to his nature.

This many-yeared existence, unsuited to him, together with the perceptions unusual for his nature and the experiences not proper to his essence involved in it, had not failed to leave on his common presence a perceptible mark.

Besides, time itself had by now inevitably aged him, and the said unusual conditions of existence had brought Beelzebub, just that Beelzebub who had had such an exceptionally strong, fiery, and splendid youth, to an also exceptional old age.

Long, long before, while Beelzebub was still existing at home on the planet Karatas, he had been taken, owing to his extraordinarily resourceful intelligence, into service on the "Sun Absolute," where our LORD SOVEREIGN ENDLESSNESS has the fundamental place of HIS Dwelling; and there Beelzebub, among others like himself, had become an attendant upon HIS ENDLESSNESS.

It was just then that, owing to the as yet unformed Reason due to his youth, and owing to his callow and therefore still impetuous mentation with unequally flowing associations—that is, owing to a mentation based, as is natural to beings who have not yet become definitely responsible, on a limited understanding—Beelzebub once saw in the government of the World something which seemed to him "illogical," and having found support among his comrades, beings like himself not yet formed, interfered in what was none of his business.

Thanks to the impetuosity and force of Beelzebub's nature, his intervention together with his comrades then soon captured all minds, and the effect was to bring the central kingdom of the Megalocosmos almost to the edge of revolution.

Having learned of this, HIS ENDLESSNESS, notwithstanding his All-lovingness and All-forgiveness, was constrained to banish Beelzebub with his comrades to one of the remote corners of the Universe, namely, to the solar system "Ors" whose inhabitants call it simply the "Solar System," and to assign as the place of their existence one of the planets of that solar system, namely, Mars, with the privilege of existing on other planets also, though only of the same solar system.

Among these exiles, besides the said comrades of Beelzebub, were a number of those who merely sympathized with him, and also the attendants and subordinates both of Beelzebub and of his comrades.

All, with their households, arrived at this remote place and there in a short time on the planet Mars a whole colony was formed of three-centered beings from various planets of the central part of our Great Universe.

All this population, extraordinary for the said planet, accommodated itself little by little to its new dwelling place, and many of them even found one or another occupation for shortening the long years of their exile.

They found occupations either on this same planet Mars or upon the neighboring planets, namely, on those planets that had been almost entirely neglected on account of their remoteness from the Center and the poverty of all their formations.

As the years rolled by, many either on their own initiative or in response to needs of general character, migrated gradually from the planet Mars to other planets; but Beelzebub himself, together with his near attendants, remained on the planet Mars, where he organized his existence more or less tolerably.

One of his chief occupations was the arranging of an "observatory" on the planet Mars for the observation both of remote points of the Universe and of the conditions of existence of beings on neighboring planets; and this observatory of his, it may here be remarked, afterwards became well known and even famous everywhere in the Universe.

Although the solar system "Ors" had been neglected owing to its remoteness from the center and to many other reasons, nevertheless our LORD SOVEREIGN had sent from time to time HIS Messengers to the planets of this system, to regulate, more or less, the being-existence of the three-brained beings arising on them, for the co-ordination of the process of their existence with the general World Harmony.

And thus, to a certain planet of this solar system, namely, the planet Earth, there was once sent as such a Messenger from our ENDLESSNESS, a certain Ashiata Shiemash, and as Beelzebub had then fulfilled a certain need in connection with his mission, the said Messenger, when he returned once more to the "Sun Absolute," earnestly besought HIS ENDLESSNESS to pardon this once young and fiery but now aged Beelzebub.

In view of this request of Ashiata Shiemash, and also of the modest and cognoscent existence of Beelzebub himself, our MAKER CREATOR pardoned him and gave him permission to return to the place of his arising.

And that is why Beelzebub, after a long absence, happened now to be again in the center of the Universe.

His influence and authority had not only not declined during his exile, but, on the contrary, they had greatly increased, since all those around him were clearly aware that, thanks to his prolonged existence in the aforementioned unusual conditions, his knowledge and experience must inevitably have been broadened and deepened.

And so, when events of great importance occurred on one of the planets of the solar system "Pandetznokh," Beelzebub's old friends had decided to intrude upon him and to invite him to the conference concerning these events.

And it was as the outcome of this that Beelzebub was now making the long journey on the ship *Karnak* from the planet Karatas to the planet Revozvradendr.

On this big space-ship *Karnak,* the passengers included the kinsmen and attendants of Beelzebub and also many beings who served on the ship itself.

During the period to which this tale of ours refers, all the passengers were occupied either with their duties or simply with the actualization of what is called "active being mentation."

Among all the passengers aboard the ship, one very handsome boy was conspicuous; he was always near Beelzebub himself.

This was Hassein, the son of Beelzebub's favorite son Tooloof.

After his return home from exile, Beelzebub had seen this grandson of his, Hassein, for the first time, and, appreciating his good heart, and also owing to what is called "family attraction," he took an instant liking to him.

And as the time happened to coincide with the time when the Reason of little Hassein needed to be developed, Beelzebub, having a great deal of free time there, himself undertook the education of his grandson, and from that time on took Hassein everywhere about with him.

That is why Hassein also was accompanying Beelzebub on this long journey and was among the number around him.

And Hassein, on his side, so loved his grandfather that he would not stir a step without him, and he eagerly absorbed everything his grandfather either said or taught.

At the time of this narrative, Beelzebub with Hassein and his devoted old servant Ahoon, who always accompanied him everywhere, were seated on the highest "Kasnik," that is, on the upper deck of the ship *Karnak* under the "Kalnokranonis," somewhat resembling what we should call a large "glass bell," and were talking there among themselves while observing the boundless space.

Beelzebub was talking about the solar system where he had passed long years.

And Beelzebub was just then describing the peculiarities of the nature of the planet called Venus.

During the conversation it was reported to Beelzebub that the captain of their ship wished to speak with him and to this request Beelzebub acceded.

CHAPTER 3

The Cause of the Delay in the Falling of the Ship Karnak

The captain soon afterward entered and having performed before Beelzebub all the ceremonies appropriate to Beelzebub's rank, said:

"Your Right Reverence, allow me to ask your authoritative opinion upon an 'inevitability' that lies in the line of our course, and which will hinder our smooth falling by the shortest route.

"The point is that if we follow our intended course, then our ship, after two 'Kilprenos,'* will pass through the solar system 'Vuanik.'

"But just through where our ship must pass, there must also pass, about a 'Kilpreno' before, the great comet belonging to that solar system and named 'Sakoor' or, as it is sometimes called, the 'Madcap.'

"So if we keep to our proposed course, we must inevitably traverse the space through which this comet will have to pass.

"Your Right Reverence of course knows that this 'Madcap' comet always leaves in its track a great deal of 'Zilnotrago'† which on entering the planetary body of a being disorganizes most of its functions until all the 'Zilnotrago' is volatilized out of it.

"I thought at first," continued the captain, "of avoiding the 'Zilnotrago' by steering the ship around these spheres, but for this a long detour would be necessary which would

* The word "Kilpreno" in the language of Beelzebub means a certain period of time, equal approximately to the duration of the flow of time which we call an "hour."

† The word "Zilnotrago" is the name of a special gas similar to what we call "cyanic acid."

greatly lengthen the time of our passage. On the other hand, to wait somewhere until the 'Zilnotrago' is dispersed would take still longer.

"In view of the sharp distinction in the alternatives before us, I cannot myself decide what to do, and so I have ventured to trouble you, your Right Reverence, for your competent advice."

The captain having finished speaking, Beelzebub thought a little and then said as follows:

"Really, I do not know how to advise you, my dear Captain. Ah, yes . . . in that solar system where I existed for a long time, there is a planet called Earth. On that planet Earth arose, and still continue to arise, very strange three-centered beings. And among the beings of a continent of that planet called 'Asia,' there arose and existed a very wise three-brained being whom they called there 'Mullah Nassr Eddin.'

"For each and every peculiar situation great and small in the existence of the beings there," Beelzebub continued, "this same terrestrial sage Mullah Nassr Eddin had an apt and pithy saying.

"As all his sayings were full of the sense of truth for existence there, I also always used them there as a guide, in order to have a comfortable existence among the beings of that planet.

"And in the given case too, my dear Captain, I intend to profit by one of his wise sayings.

"In such a situation as has befallen us, he would probably say:

"'You cannot jump over your knees and it is absurd to try to kiss your own elbow.'

"I now say the same to you, and I add: there is nothing to be done; when an event is impending which arises from forces immeasurably greater than our own, one must submit.

"The only question is, which of the alternatives you mentioned should be chosen—that is, to wait somewhere or to add to our journey by a 'detour.'

"You say that to make a detour will greatly lengthen our journey but that waiting will take still longer.

"Good, my dear Captain. Suppose that by making the detour we should save a little time, what do you think: Is the wear and tear of the parts of our ship's machinery worth-while for the sake of ending our journey a little sooner?

"If the detour should involve even the most trifling damage to our ship, then in my opinion we ought to prefer your second suggestion, that is, to stop somewhere until the path is cleared of the noxious 'Zilnotrago.' By that means we should spare our ship useless damage.

"And we will try to fill the period of this unforeseen delay with something useful for us all.

"For instance, it would give me personally great pleasure to talk with you about contemporary ships in general and about our ship in particular.

"Very many new things, of which I still know nothing, have been done in this field during my absence from these parts.

"For example, in my time these big transspace ships were so complicated and cumbersome that it took almost half their power to carry the materials necessary to elaborate their possibility of locomotion.

"But in their simplicity and the freedom on them, these contemporary ships are just embodiments of 'Bliss-stokirno.'

"There is such a simplicity for beings upon them and such freedom in respect of all being-manifestations that at times you forget that you are not on one of the planets.

"So, my dear Captain, I should like very much to know how this boon was brought about and how the contemporary ships work.

"But now go and make all arrangements necessary for the required stopping. And then, when you are quite free, come to me again and we will pass the time of our unavoidable delay in conversation useful for us all."

When the captain had gone, Hassein suddenly sprang to his feet and began to dance and clap his hands and shout:

"Oh, I'm glad, I'm glad, I'm glad of this."

Beelzebub looked with affection on these joyous manifestations of his favorite, but old Ahoon could not restrain himself and, shaking his head reproachfully, called the boy—half to himself—a "growing egoist."

Hearing what Ahoon called him, Hassein stopped in front of him, and, looking at him mischievously, said:

"Don't be angry with me, old Ahoon. The reason for my joy is not egoism but only the coincidence which chances to be happy for me. You heard, didn't you? My dear grandfather did not decide only just to make a stop, but he also promised the captain to talk with him. . . .

"And you know, don't you, that the talks of my dear grandfather always bring out tales of places where he has been, and you know also how delightfully he tells them and how much new and interesting information becomes crystallized in our presences from these tales.

"Where is the egoism? Hasn't he himself, of his own free will, having weighed with his wise reason all the circumstances of this unforeseen event, decided to make a stop which evidently doesn't upset his intended plans very much?

"It seems to me that my dear grandfather has no need to hurry; everything necessary for his rest and comfort is present on the *Karnak* and here also are many who love him and whom he loves.

"Don't you remember he said recently 'we must not oppose forces higher than our own' and added that not only one must not oppose them, but even submit and receive all their results with reverence, at the same time praising and glorifying the wonderful and providential works of Our Lord Creator?

"I am not glad because of the misadventure but because an unforeseen event issuing from above has occurred, owing to which we shall be able to listen once more to the tales of my dear grandfather.

"Is it my fault that the circumstances are by chance most desirable and happy for me?

"No, dear Ahoon, not only should you not rebuke me, but you should join me in expressing gratitude to the source of all beneficent results that arise."

All this time Beelzebub listened attentively and with a smile to the chatter of his favorite, and when he had finished said:

"You are right, dear Hassein, and for being right I will tell you, even before the captain's arrival, anything you like."

Upon hearing this, the boy at once ran and sat at the feet of Beelzebub and after thinking a little said:

"My dear Grandfather, you have told me so much about the solar system where you spent so many years, that now perhaps I could continue just by logic alone to describe the details of the nature of that peculiar corner of our Universe.

"But I am curious to know whether there dwell three-brained beings on the planets of that solar system and whether higher 'being-bodies' are coated in them.

"Please tell me now about just this, dear Grandfather," concluded Hassein, looking affectionately up at Beelzebub.

"Yes," replied Beelzebub, "on almost all the planets of that solar system also, three-brained beings dwell, and in almost all of them higher being-bodies can be coated.

"Higher being-bodies, or as they are called on some

planets of that solar system, souls, arise in the three-brained beings breeding on all the planets except those before reaching which the emanations of our 'Most Holy Sun Absolute,' owing to repeated deflections, gradually lose the fullness of their strength and eventually cease entirely to contain the vivific power for coating higher being-bodies.

"Certainly, my boy, on each separate planet of that solar system also, the planetary bodies of the three-brained beings are coated and take an exterior form in conformity with the nature of the given planet, and are adapted in their details to the surrounding nature.

"For instance, on that planet on which it was ordained that all we exiles should exist, namely, the planet Mars, the three-brained beings are coated with planetary bodies having the form—how shall I tell you—a form like a 'karoona,' that is to say, they have a long broad trunk, amply provided with fat, and heads with enormous protruding and shining eyes. On the back of this enormous 'planetary body' of theirs are two large wings, and on the under side two comparatively small feet with very strong claws.

"Almost the whole strength of this enormous 'planetary body' is adapted by nature to generate energy for their eyes and for their wings.

"As a result, the three-brained beings breeding on that planet can see freely everywhere, whatever the 'Kal-da-zakh-tee,' and they can also move not only over the planet itself but also in its atmosphere and some of them occasionally even manage to travel beyond the limits of its atmosphere.

"The three-brained beings breeding on another planet, a little below the planet Mars, owing to the intense cold there are covered with thick soft wool.

"The external form of these three-centered beings is

like that of a 'Toosook,' that is, it resembles a kind of 'double sphere,' the upper sphere serving to contain the principal organs of the whole planetary body, and the other, the lower sphere, the organs for the transformation of the first and second being-foods.

"There are three apertures in the upper sphere, opening outwards; two serve for sight and the third for hearing.

"The other, the lower sphere, has only two apertures: one in front for taking in the first and second being-foods, and the other at the back for the elimination from the organism of residues.

"To the lower sphere are also attached two very strong sinewy feet, and on each of these is a growth that serves the purpose of fingers with us.

"There is still another planet, a quite small one, bearing the name Moon, in that solar system, my dear boy.

"During its motion this peculiar little planet often approached very near to our planet Mars and sometimes during whole 'Kilprenos' I took great pleasure in observing through my 'Teskooano'* in my observatory the process of existence of the three-brained beings upon it.

"Though the beings of this planet have very frail 'planetary bodies,' they have on the other hand a very 'strong spirit,' owing to which they all possess an extraordinary perseverance and capacity for work.

"In exterior form they resemble what are called large ants; and, like these, they are always bustling about, working both on and within their planet.

"The results of their ceaseless activity are now already plainly visible.

"I once happened to notice that during two of our years they 'tunnelled,' so to say, the whole of their planet.

* "Teskooano" means "telescope."

"They were compelled to undertake this task on account of the abnormal local climatic conditions, which are due to the fact that this planet arose unexpectedly, and the regulation of its climatic harmony was therefore not prearranged by the Higher Powers.

"The 'climate' of this planet is 'mad,' and in its variability it could give points to the most highly strung hysterical women existing on another of the planets of that same solar system, of which I shall also tell you.

"Sometimes there are such frosts on this 'Moon' that everything is frozen through and through and it becomes impossible for beings to breathe in the open atmosphere; and then suddenly it becomes so hot there that an egg can be cooked in its atmosphere in a jiffy.

"For only two short periods on that peculiar little planet, namely, before and after its complete revolution about its neighbor—another planet nearby—the weather is so glorious that for several rotations the whole planet is in blossom and yields the various products for their first being-food greatly in excess of their general need during their existence in that peculiar intraplanetary kingdom which they have arranged and where they are protected from all the vagaries of this 'mad' climate inharmoniously changing the state of the atmosphere.

"Nearest to that small planet is another, a larger planet, which also occasionally approaches quite close to the planet Mars and is called Earth.

"The said Moon is just a part of this Earth and the latter must now constantly maintain the Moon's existence.

"On the just mentioned planet Earth, also, three-brained beings are formed; and they also contain all the data for coating higher being-bodies in themselves.

"But in 'strength of spirit' they do not begin to compare with the beings breeding on the little planet aforementioned. The external coatings of the three-brained beings of that planet Earth closely resemble our own; only, first of all, their skin is a little slimier than ours, and then, secondly, they have no tail, and their heads are without horns. What is worst about them is their feet, namely, they have no hoofs; it is true that for protection against external influences they have invented what they call 'boots,' but this invention does not help them very much.

"Apart from the imperfection of their exterior form, their Reason also is quite 'uniquely strange.'

"Their 'being-Reason,' owing to very many causes about which also I may tell you sometime, has gradually degenerated, and at the present time, is very, very strange and exceedingly peculiar."

Beelzebub would have said still more, but the captain of the ship entering at that moment, Beelzebub, after promising the boy to tell him about the beings of the planet Earth on another occasion, began to talk with the captain.

Beelzebub asked the captain to tell him, first, who he was, how long he had been captain, and how he liked his work, and afterwards to explain some of the details of the contemporary cosmic ships.

Thereupon the captain said:

"Your Right Reverence, I was destined by my father, as soon as I reached the age of a responsible being, for this career in the service of our ENDLESS CREATOR.

"Starting with the lowest positions on the transspace ships, I ultimately merited to perform the duties of captain, and it is now eight years that I have been captain on the long-distance ships.

"This last post of mine, namely, that of captain of the ship *Karnak*, I took, strictly speaking, in succession to my father, when after his long years of blameless service to HIS ENDLESSNESS in the performance of the duties of captain from almost the very beginning of the World-creation, he had become worthy to be promoted to the post of Ruler of the solar system 'Kalman.'

"In short," continued the captain, "I began my service just when your Right Reverence was departing for the place of your exile.

"I was still only a 'sweeper' on the long-distance ships of that period.

"Yes . . . a long, long time has passed by.

"Everything has undergone change and is changed since then; only our LORD AND SOVEREIGN remains unchanged. The blessings of 'Amenzano' on HIS UNCHANGEABLENESS throughout Eternity!

"You, your Right Reverence, have condescended to remark very justly that the former ships were very inconvenient and cumbersome.

"Yes, they were then, indeed, very complicated and cumbersome. I too remember them very well. There is an enormous difference between the ships of that time and the ships now.

"In our youth all such ships both for intersystem and for interplanetary communication were still run on the cosmic substance 'Elekilpomagtistzen,' which is a totality consisting of two separate parts of the omnipresent Okidanokh.

"And it was to obtain this totality that just those numerous materials were necessary which the former ships had to carry.

"But these ships did not remain in use long after you flew from these parts, having soon thereafter been replaced by ships of the system of Saint Venoma."

CHAPTER 4

The Law of Falling

The captain continued:

"This happened in the year 185, by objective time-calculation.

"Saint Venoma had been taken for his merits from the planet 'Soort' to the holy planet 'Purgatory,' where, after he had familiarized himself with his new surroundings and new duties, he gave all his free time to his favorite work.

"And his favorite work was to seek what new phenomena could be found in various combinations of already existing, law-conformable phenomena.

"And sometime later, in the course of these occupations, this Saint Venoma first constated in cosmic laws what later became a famous discovery, and this discovery he first called the 'Law of Falling.'

"This cosmic law which he then discovered, St. Venoma himself formulated thus:

"'Everything existing in the World falls to the bottom. And the bottom for any part of the Universe is its nearest "stability," and this said "stability" is the place or the point upon which all the lines of force arriving from all directions converge.

"'The centers of all the suns and of all the planets of our Universe are just such points of "stability." They are the lowest points of those regions of space upon which forces from all directions of the given part of the Universe definitely tend and where they are concentrated. In these points there is also concentrated the equilibrium which enables suns and planets to maintain their position.'

"In this formulation of his, Saint Venoma said further that everything when dropped into space, wherever it may be, tends to fall on one or another sun or on one or another planet, according to which sun or planet the given part of space belongs to, where the object is dropped, each sun or planet being for the given sphere the 'stability' or bottom.

"Starting from this, Saint Venoma reasoned in his further researches as follows:

"'If this be so, may it not therefore be possible to employ this cosmic particularity for the locomotion we need between the spaces of the Universe?'

"And from then on, he worked in this direction.

"His further saintly labors showed that although in principle this was in general possible, yet it was impossible fully to employ for this purpose this 'Law of Falling' discovered by him. And it would be impossible owing solely to the atmospheres around most of the cosmic concentrations, which atmospheres would hinder the straight falling of the object dropped in space.

"Having constated this, Saint Venoma then devoted his whole attention to discovering some means of overcoming the said atmospheric resistance for ships constructed on the principle of Falling.

"And after three 'Looniases' Saint Venoma did find such a possibility, and later on when the building of a suitable special construction had been completed under his direction, he proceeded to practical trials.

"This special construction had the appearance of a large enclosure, all the walls of which were made of a special material something like glass.

"Then to every side of that large enclosure were fitted things like 'shutters' of a material impervious to the rays of the cosmic substance 'Elekilpomagtistzen,' and these shutters, although closely fitted to the walls of the said enclosure, could yet freely slide in every direction.

"Within the enclosure was placed a special 'battery,'

generating and giving this same substance 'Elekilpomagtistzen.'

"I myself, your Right Reverence, was present at the first trials made by Saint Venoma according to the principles he had discovered.

"The whole secret lay in this, that when the rays of 'Elekilpomagtistzen' were made to pass through this special glass, then in all the space they reached, everything usually composing the atmosphere itself of planets, such as 'air,' every kind of 'gas,' 'fog,' and so on, was destroyed. This part of space became indeed absolutely empty and had neither resistance nor pressure, so that, if even an infant-being pushed this enormous structure, it would move forward as easily as a feather.

"To the outer side of this peculiar structure there were attached appliances similar to wings, which were set in motion by means of this same substance 'Elekilpomagtistzen,' and served to give the impetus to move all this enormous construction in the required direction.

"The results of these experiments having been approved and blessed by the Commission of Inspection under the presidency of Archangel Adossia, the construction of a big ship based on these principles was begun.

"The ship was soon ready and commissioned for service. And in a short time, little by little, ships of this type came to be used exclusively, on all the lines of intersystem communication.

"Although later, your Right Reverence, the inconveniences of this system gradually became more and more apparent, nevertheless it continued to displace all the systems that had existed before.

"It cannot be gainsaid that although the ships constructed on this system were ideal in atmosphereless spaces, and moved there almost with the speed of the rays 'Etzikolnianakhnian' issuing from planets, yet when nearing some sun or planet it became real torture for the beings directing them, as a great deal of complicated maneuvering was necessary.

"The need for this maneuvering was due to the same 'Law of Falling.'

"And this was because when the ship came into the medium of the atmosphere of some sun or planet which it had to pass, it immediately began to fall towards that sun or planet, and as I have already intimated, very much care and considerable knowledge were needed to prevent the ship from falling out of its course.

"While the ships were passing near any sun or planet whatsoever, their speed of locomotion had sometimes to be reduced hundreds of times below their usual rate.

"It was particularly difficult to steer them in those spheres where there was a great aggregation of 'comets.'

"That is why great demands were then made upon the beings who had to direct these ships, and they were prepared for these duties by beings of very high Reason.

"But in spite of the said drawbacks of the system of Saint Venoma, it gradually, as I have already said, displaced all the previous systems.

"And the ships of this system of Saint Venoma had already existed for twenty-three years when it was first rumored that the Angel Hariton had invented a new type of ship for intersystem and interplanetary communication."

CHAPTER 5
The System of Archangel Hariton

"And indeed, soon after this rumor, practical experiments open to all, again under the superintendence of the Great Archangel Adossia, were made with this new and later very famous invention.

"This new system was unanimously acknowledged to be the best, and very soon it was adopted for general Universal service and thereafter gradually all previous systems were entirely superseded.

"That system of the Great Angel, now Archangel, Hariton is now in use everywhere at the present day.

"The ship on which we are now flying also belongs to this system and its construction is similar to that of all the ships built on the system of the Angel Hariton.

"This system is not very complicated.

"The whole of this great invention consists of only a single 'cylinder' shaped like an ordinary barrel.

"The secret of this cylinder lies in the disposition of the materials of which its inner side is made.

"These materials are arranged in a certain order and isolated from each other by means of 'Amber.' They have such a property that if any cosmic gaseous substance whatever enters the space which they enclose, whether it be 'atmosphere,' 'air,' 'ether,' or any other 'totality' of homogeneous cosmic elements, it immediately expands, owing to the mentioned disposition of materials within the cylinder.

"The bottom of this cylinder-barrel is hermetically sealed, but its lid, although it can be closely shut, yet is so arranged on hinges that at a pressure from within it can be opened and shut again.

"So, your Right Reverence, if this cylinder-barrel is filled with atmosphere, air, or any other such substance, then from the action of the walls of this peculiar cylinder-barrel, these substances expand to such an extent that the interior becomes too small to hold them.

"Striving to find an outlet from this, for them constricted, interior, they naturally press also against the lid of the cylinder-barrel, and thanks to the said hinges the lid opens and, having allowed these expanded substances to escape, immediately closes again. And as in general Nature abhors a vacuum, then simultaneously with the release of the expanded gaseous substances the cylinder-barrel is again filled with fresh substances from outside, with which in their turn the same proceeds as before, and so on without end.

"Thus the substances are always being changed, and the lid of the cylinder-barrel alternately opens and shuts.

"To this same lid there is fixed a very simple lever which moves with the movement of the lid and in turn sets in motion certain also very simple 'cogwheels' which again in their turn revolve the fans attached to the sides and stern of the ship itself.

"Thus, your Right Reverence, in spaces where there is no resistance, contemporary ships like ours simply fall towards the nearest 'stability'; but in spaces where there are any cosmic substances which offer resistance, these substances, whatever their density, with the aid of this cylinder enable the ship to move in any desired direction.

"It is interesting to remark that the denser the substance is in any given part of the Universe, the better and more strongly the charging and discharging of this cylinder-barrel proceed, and in consequence of course, the force of the movement of the levers is also changed.

"But nevertheless, I repeat, a sphere without atmosphere, that is, a space containing only World Etherokrilno, is for contemporary ships also the best, because in such a sphere there is no resistance at all, and the

'Law of Falling' can therefore be fully employed in it without any assistance from the work of the cylinder.

"Further than this, the contemporary ships are also good because they contain such possibilities that in atmosphereless spaces an impetus can be given to them in any direction, and they can fall just where desired without the complicated manipulations necessary in ships of the system of Saint Venoma.

"In short, your Right Reverence, the convenience and simplicity of the contemporary ships are beyond comparison with former ships, which were often both very complicated and at the same time had none of the possibilities of the ships we use now."

CHAPTER 6
Perpetual Motion

"Wait! Wait!" Beelzebub interrupted the captain. "This—what you have just told us—must surely be just that short-lived idea which the strange three-brained beings breeding on the planet Earth called 'perpetual motion' and on account of which at one period a great many of them there went quite, as they themselves say, 'mad,' and many even perished entirely.

"It once happened there on that ill-fated planet that somebody in some way or another got into his head the, as they say, 'crazy notion' that he could make a 'mechanism' that would run forever without requiring any material from outside.

"This notion so took everybody's fancy that most of the queer fellows of that peculiar planet began thinking about it and trying to realize this miracle in practice.

"How many of them paid for this short-lived idea with all the material and spiritual welfare which they had previously with great difficulty acquired!

"For one reason or another they were all quite determined to invent what in their opinion was a 'simple matter.'

"External circumstances permitting, many took up the invention of this 'perpetual motion' without any inner data for such work; some from reliance upon their 'knowledge,' others upon 'luck,' but most of them just from their already complete psychopathy.

"In short, the invention of 'perpetual motion' was, as they say, 'the rage,' and every crank felt obliged to be interested in this question.

"I was once in one of the towns there where models of every kind and innumerable 'descriptions' of proposed 'mechanisms' for this 'perpetual motion' were assembled.

"What wasn't there? What 'ingenious' and complicated machines did I not see? In any single one of these mechanisms I saw there, there must have been more ideas and 'wiseacrings' than in all the laws of World-creation and World-existence.

"I noted at the time that in these innumerable models and descriptions of proposed mechanisms, the idea of using what is called the 'force of weight' predominated. And the idea of employing the 'force of weight' they explained thus: a very complicated mechanism was to lift 'some' weight and this latter was then to fall and by its fall set the whole mechanism in motion, which motion would again lift the weight, and so on, and so on.

"The result of it all was that thousands were shut up in 'lunatic asylums,' thousands more, having made this idea their dream, either began to fail altogether to fulfill even those being-duties of theirs which had somehow or other in the course of many years been established there, or to fulfill them in such a way as 'couldn't be worse.'

"I don't know how it would all have ended if some quite demented being there, with one foot already in the grave, such a one as they themselves call an 'old dotard,' and who had previously somehow acquired a certain authority, had not proved by 'calculations' known only to himself that it was absolutely impossible to invent 'perpetual motion.'

"Now, after your explanation, I can well understand how the cylinder of the system of Archangel Hariton works. It is the very thing of which these unfortunates there dreamed.

"Indeed, of the 'cylinder' of the system of the Archangel Hariton it can safely be said that, with atmosphere alone given, it will work perpetually without needing the expenditure of any outside materials.

"And since the world without planets and hence without

atmospheres cannot exist, then it follows that as long as the world exists and, in consequence, atmospheres, the cylinder-barrels invented by the great Archangel Hariton will always work.

"Now just one question occurs to me—about the material from which this cylinder-barrel is made.

"I wish very much, my dear Captain, that you would roughly tell me what materials it is made of and how long they can last," requested Beelzebub.

To this question of Beelzebub's the captain replied as follows:

"Although the cylinder-barrel does not last forever, it can certainly last a very long time.

"Its chief part is made of 'amber' with 'platinum' hoops, and the interior panels of the walls are made of 'anthracite,' 'copper,' and 'ivory,' and a very strong 'mastic' unaffectable either by (1) 'paischakir' or by (2) 'tainolair' or by (3) 'saliakooríapa'* or even by the radiations of cosmic concentrations.

"But the other parts," the captain continued, "both the exterior 'levers' and the 'cogwheels,' must certainly be renewed from time to time, for though they are made of the strongest metal, yet long use will wear them out.

"And as for the body of the ship itself, its long existence can certainly not be guaranteed."

The captain intended to say still more, but at that moment a sound like the vibrations of a long minor chord of a far-off orchestra of wind instruments resounded through the ship.

With an apology the captain rose to leave, explaining as he did so that he must be needed on very important business, since everybody knew that he was with his Right Reverence and would not venture to trouble the ears of his Right Reverence for anything trifling.

* (1) Cold, (2) heat, and (3) water.

CHAPTER 7

Becoming Aware of Genuine Being-Duty

After the captain had gone, Beelzebub glanced at his grandson and, noticing his unusual state, asked him solicitously and with some anxiety:

"What is the matter, my dear boy? What are you thinking so deeply about?"

Looking up at his Grandfather with eyes full of sorrow, Hassein said thoughtfully:

"I don't know what is the matter with me, my dear Grandfather, but your talk with the captain of the ship has brought me to some exceedingly melancholy thoughts.

"Things of which I have never before thought are now a-thinking in me.

"Thanks to your talk, it has gradually become very clear to my consciousness that in the Universe of our ENDLESSNESS everything has not always been such as I now see and understand.

"Formerly, for instance, I should never have allowed such thoughts associatively to proceed in me, as that this ship on which we are now flying has not always been as it is at this moment.

"Only now have I come very clearly to understand that everything we have at the present time and everything we use—in a word, all the contemporary amenities and everything necessary for our comfort and welfare—have not always existed and did not make their appearance so easily.

"It seems that certain beings in the past have during very long periods labored and suffered very much for this, and endured a great deal which perhaps they even need not have endured.

"They labored and suffered only in order that we might now have all this and use it for our welfare.

"And all this they did, either consciously or unconsciously, just for us, that is to say, for beings quite unknown and entirely indifferent to them.

"And now not only do we not thank them, but we do not even know a thing about them, but take it all as in the natural order, and neither ponder nor trouble ourselves about this question at all.

"I, for instance, have already existed so many years in the Universe, yet the thought has never even entered my head that perhaps there was a time when everything I see and have did not exist, and that everything was not born with me like my nose.

"And so, my dear and kind Grandfather, now that owing to your conversation with the captain, I have gradually, with all my presence, become aware of all this, there has arisen in me, side by side with this, the need to make clear to my Reason why I personally have all the comforts which I now use, and what obligations I am under for them.

"It is just because of this that at the present moment there proceeds in me a 'process-of-remorse.' "

Having said this, Hassein drooped his head and became silent; and Beelzebub, looking at him affectionately, began to speak as follows:

"I advise you, my dear Hassein, not to put such questions to yourself yet. Do not be impatient. Only when that period of your existence arrives which is proper for your becoming aware of such essence-questions, and you actively mentate about them, will you understand what you must do in return.

"Your present age does not yet oblige you to pay for your existence.

"The time of your present age is not given you in which

to pay for your existence, but for preparing yourself for the future, for the obligations becoming to a responsible three-brained being.

"So in the meantime, exist as you exist. Only do not forget one thing, namely, at your age it is indispensably necessary that every day, at sunrise, while watching the reflection of its splendor, you bring about a contact between your consciousness and the various unconscious parts of your general presence. Try to make this state last and to convince the unconscious parts—as if they were conscious—that if they hinder your general functioning, they, in the period of your responsible age, not only cannot fulfill the good that befits them, but your general presence of which they are part will not be able to be a good servant of our COMMON ENDLESS CREATOR and by that will not even be worthy to pay for your arising and existence.

"I repeat once more, my dear boy, try in the meantime not to think about these questions, which at your age it is still early for you to think about.

"Everything in its proper time!

"Now ask me to tell you whatever you wish, and I will do so.

"As the captain has not yet returned, he must be occupied there with his duties and will not be coming back so soon."

CHAPTER 8

The Impudent Brat Hassein, Beelzebub's Grandson, Dares to Call Men "Slugs"

Hassein immediately sat down at Beelzebub's feet and coaxingly said:

"Tell me anything you wish, my dear Grandfather. Anything you tell me will be the greatest joy for me, if only because it is you who relate it."

"No," objected Beelzebub, "you yourself ask what interests you most of all. It will give me at the present moment much pleasure to tell you about just whatever you particularly wish to know."

"Dear and kind Grandfather, tell me then something about those . . . how? . . . those . . . I forget . . . yes, about those 'slugs.'"

"What? About what slugs?" asked Beelzebub, not understanding the boy's question.

"Don't you remember, Grandfather, that a little while ago, when you spoke about the three-centered beings breeding on the various planets of that solar system where you existed for such a long time, you happened to say that on one planet—I forget how you called it—that on that planet exist three-centered beings who, on the whole, are like us, but whose skin is a little slimier than ours."

"Ah!" laughed Beelzebub. "You are surely asking about those beings who breed on the planet Earth and who call themselves 'men.'

"Yes, Grandfather, yes, just that. Tell me about those 'men-beings,' a little more in detail. I should like to know more about them," concluded Hassein.

Then Beelzebub said: "About them I could tell you a great deal, for I often visited that planet and existed among them for a long time and even made friends with many of those terrestrial three-brained beings.

"Indeed, you will find it very interesting to know more about these beings, for they are very peculiar.

"There are many things among them which you would not see among any other beings of any other planet of our Universe.

"I know them very well, because their arising, their further development, and their existence during many, many centuries, by their time calculation, have occurred before my eyes.

"And not only their own arising occurred before my eyes, but even the accomplished formation of the planet itself on which they arise and exist.

"When we first arrived on that solar system and settled on the planet Mars nothing yet existed on that planet Earth, which had not yet even had time to cool off completely after its concentration.

"From the very beginning, this same planet has been the cause of many serious troubles to our ENDLESSNESS.

"If you wish I will tell you first of all about the events of general cosmic character connected with this planet, which were the cause of the said troubles of our ENDLESSNESS.

"Yes, my dear Grandfather," said Hassein, "tell me first about this. It will surely be quite as interesting as everything you relate."

CHAPTER 9

The Cause of the Genesis of the Moon

Beelzebub began his tale as follows:

"After we arrived on the planet Mars where we were directed to exist, we began slowly to settle down there.

"We were still fully absorbed in the bustle of organizing everything externally necessary for a more or less tolerable existence in the midst of that Nature absolutely foreign to us, when suddenly, on one of the very busiest days, the whole planet Mars was shaken, and a little later such an 'asphyxiating stink' arose that at first it seemed that everything in the Universe had been mixed up with something, one might say 'indescribable.'

"Only after a considerable time had passed and when the said stink had gone, did we recover and gradually make out what had happened.

"We understood that the cause of this terrible phenomenon was just that same planet Earth which from time to time approached very near to our planet Mars and which therefore we had possibilities of observing clearly, sometimes even without a 'Teskooano.'

"For reasons we could not yet comprehend, this planet, it transpired, had 'burst' and two fragments detached from it had flown off into space.

"I have already told you that this solar system was then still being formed and was not yet 'blended' completely with what is called 'The-Harmony-of-Reciprocal-Maintenance-of-All-Cosmic-Concentrations.'

"It was subsequently learned that in accordance with this said 'General-Cosmic-Harmony-of-Reciprocal-Maintenance-of-All-Cosmic-Concentrations' there had also to function in this system a comet of what is called 'vast orbit' still existing and named the comet 'Kondoor.'

"And just this very comet, although it was then already concentrated, was actualizing its 'full path' for only the first time.

"As certain competent Sacred Individuals also later confidentially explained to us, the line of the path of the said comet had to cross the line on which the path of that planet Earth also lay; but as a result of the erroneous calculations of a certain Sacred Individual concerned with the matters of World-creation and World-maintenance, the time of the passing of each of these concentrations through the point of intersection of the lines of their paths coincided, and owing to this error the planet Earth and the comet 'Kondoor' collided, and collided so violently that from this shock, as I have already told you, two large fragments were broken off from the planet Earth and flew into space.

"This shock entailed these serious consequences because on account of the recent arising of this planet, the atmosphere which might have served as a buffer in such a case had not yet had time to be completely formed upon it.

And, my boy, our ENDLESSNESS was also immediately informed of this general cosmic misfortune.

"In consequence of this report, a whole commission consisting of Angels and Archangels, specialists in the work of World-creation and World-maintenance, under the direction of the Most Great Archangel Sakaki, was immediately sent from the Most Holy Sun Absolute to that solar system 'Ors.'

"The Most High Commission came to our planet Mars since it was the nearest to the planet Earth and from this planet of ours began its investigations.

"The sacred members of this Most High Commission at once quieted us by saying that the apprehended danger of a catastrophe on a great cosmic scale had already passed.

"And the Arch-Engineer Archangel Algamatant was good enough to explain to us personally that in all probability what had happened was as follows:

"'The broken-off fragments of the planet Earth had lost the momentum they received from the shock before they had reached the limit of that part of space which is the sphere of this planet, and hence, according to the "Law of Falling," these fragments had begun to fall back towards their fundamental piece.

"'But they could no longer fall upon their fundamental piece, because in the meantime they had come under the cosmic law called "Law-of-Catching-Up" and were entirely subject to its influence, and they would therefore now make regular elliptic orbits around their fundamental piece, just as the fundamental piece, namely, the planet Earth, made and makes its orbit around its sun "Ors."

"'And so it will always continue, unless some new unforeseen catastrophe on a large scale changes it in one way or another.

"'Glory to Chance . . .' concluded His Pantemeasurability, 'the harmonious general-system movement was not destroyed by all this, and the peaceful existence of that system "Ors" was soon re-established.'

"But nevertheless, my boy, this Most High Commission, having then calculated all the facts at hand, and also all that might happen in the future, came to the conclusion that although the fragments of the planet Earth might maintain themselves for the time being in their existing positions, yet in view of certain so-called 'Tastartoonarian-displacements' conjectured by the Commission, they might in the future leave their position and bring about a large number of irreparable calamities both for this system 'Ors' and for other neighboring solar systems.

"Therefore the Most High Commission decided to take certain measures to avoid this eventuality.

"And they resolved that the best measure in the given case would be that the fundamental piece, namely, the planet Earth, should constantly send to its detached fragments, for their maintenance, the sacred vibrations 'askokin.'

"This sacred substance can be formed on planets only when both fundamental cosmic laws operating in them, the sacred 'Heptaparaparshinokh' and the sacred 'Triamazikamno,' function, as is called, 'Ilnosoparno,' that is to say, when the said sacred cosmic laws in the given cosmic concentration are deflected independently and also manifest on its surface independently—of course independently only within certain limits.

"And so, my boy, inasmuch as such a cosmic actualization was possible only with the sanction of HIS ENDLESSNESS, the Great Archangel Sakaki, accompanied by several other sacred members of that Most High Commission, set off immediately to HIS ENDLESSNESS to beseech Him to give the said sanction.

"And afterwards, when the said Sacred Individuals had obtained the sanction of HIS ENDLESSNESS for the actualization of the Ilnosoparnian process on that planet also, and when this process had been actualized under the direction of the same Great Archangel Sakaki, then from that time on, on that planet also, just as on many others, there began to arise the 'Corresponding,' owing to which the said detached fragments exist until now without constituting a menace for a catastrophe on a great scale.

"Of these two fragments, the larger was named 'Loonderperzo' and the smaller 'Anulios'; and the ordinary three-brained beings who afterwards arose and were formed on this planet also at first called them by these names; but the beings of later times called them differently at different periods, and in most recent times the larger fragment has come to be called Moon, but the name of the smaller has been gradually forgotten.

"As for the beings there now, not only have they no name at all for this smaller fragment, but they do not even suspect its existence.

"It is interesting to notice here that the beings of a continent on that planet called 'Atlantis,' which afterwards perished, still knew of this second fragment of their planet and also called it 'Anulios,' but the beings of the last period of the same continent, in whom the results of the consequences of the properties of that organ called 'Kundabuffer'—about which, it now seems, I shall have to explain to you even in great detail—had begun to be crystallized and to become part of their common presences, called it also 'Kimespai,' the meaning of which for them was 'Never-Allowing-One-to-Sleep-in-Peace.'

"Contemporary three-brained beings of this peculiar planet do not know of this former fragment of their planet, chiefly because its comparatively small size and the remoteness of the place of its movement make it quite invisible to their sight, and also because no 'grandmother' ever told them that once upon a time any such little satellite of their planet was known.

"And if any of them should by chance see it through their good, but nevertheless child's toy of theirs called a telescope, he would pay no attention to it, mistaking it simply for a big aerolite.

"The contemporary beings will probably never see it again, since it has become quite proper to their nature to see only unreality.

"Let us give them their due; during recent centuries they have really most artistically mechanized themselves to see nothing real.

"So, my boy, owing to all the aforesaid, there first arose

on this planet Earth also, as there should, what are called 'Similitudes-of-the-Whole,' or as they are also called 'Microcosmoses,' and further, there were formed from these 'Microcosmoses,' what are called 'Oduristelnian' and 'Polormedekhtic' vegetations.

"Still further, as also usually occurs, from the same 'Microcosmoses' there also began to be grouped various forms of what are called 'Tetartocosmoses' of all three brain-systems.

"And among these latter there then first arose just those biped 'Tetartocosmoses' whom you a while ago called 'slugs.'

"About how and why upon planets, during the transition of the fundamental sacred laws into 'Ilnosoparnian,' there arise 'Similitudes-of-the-Whole' and about what factors contribute to the formation of one or another of these, as they are called, 'systems of being-brains,' and also about all the laws of World-creation and World-maintenance in general, I will explain to you specially some other time.

"But meanwhile, know that these three-brained beings arising on the planet Earth, who interest you, had in them in the beginning the same possibilities for perfecting the functions for the acquisition of being-Reason as have all other forms of 'Tetartocosmoses' arising throughout the whole Universe.

"But afterwards, just in the period when they also, as it proceeds on other similar planets of our great Universe, were beginning gradually to be spiritualized by what is called 'being-instinct,' just then, unfortunately for them, there befell a misfortune which was unforeseen from Above and most grievous for them."

CHAPTER 10

Why "Men" Are Not Men

Beelzebub sighed deeply and continued to speak as follows:

"After the actualizing on this planet of the 'Ilnosoparnian' process, one year, by objective time-calculation, passed.

"During this period there had gradually been coordinated on this planet also the corresponding processes for the involution and evolution of everything arising there.

"And of course there began gradually to be crystallized in the three-brained beings there the corresponding data for the acquisition of objective Reason.

"In short, on this planet also everything had then already begun to proceed in the usual normal order.

"And therefore, my boy, if the Most High Commission under the supreme direction of the same Archangel Sakaki had not, at the end of a year, gone there again, perhaps all the subsequent misunderstandings connected with the three-brained beings arising on that ill-fated planet might not have occurred.

"This second descent of the Most High Commission to that planet was due to the fact that in spite of the measures they had taken, of which I have told you, there had not yet crystallized in the Reasons of the majority of its sacred members a complete assurance of the impossibility of any undesirable surprise in the future, and they now wished to verify on the spot the results of those measures.

"It was just during this second descent that the Most High Commission decided in any event, if only for the sake of their own reassurance, to actualize certain further special measures, among which was also that measure, the consequences of which have not only gradually turned into a stupendous terror for the three-brained beings themselves who arise on this ill-fated planet, but have even become, so to say, a malignant sore for the whole of the great Universe.

"You must know that by the time of this second descent of the Most High Commission, there had already gradually been engendered in them—as is proper to three-brained beings—what is called 'mechanical instinct.'

"The sacred members of this Most High Commission then reasoned that if the said mechanical instinct in these biped three-brained beings of that planet should develop towards the attainment of Objective Reason—as usually occurs everywhere among three-brained beings—then it might quite possibly happen that they would prematurely comprehend the real cause of their arising and existence and make a great deal of trouble; it might happen that having understood the reason for their arising, namely, that by their existence they should maintain the detached fragments of their planet, and being convinced of this their slavery to circumstances utterly foreign to them, they would be unwilling to continue their existence and would on principle destroy themselves.

"So, my boy, in view of this the Most High Commission then decided among other things provisionally to implant into the common presences of the three-brained beings there a special organ with a property such that, first, they should perceive reality topsy-turvy and, secondly, that every repeated impression from outside should crystallize in them data which would engender factors for evoking in them sensations of 'pleasure' and 'enjoyment.'

"And then, in fact, with the help of the Chief-Common-Universal-Arch-Chemist-Physicist Angel Looisos, who was also among the members of this Most High Commission, they caused to grow in the three-brained beings there, in a special way, at the base of their spinal column, at the root of their tail—which they also, at that time, still had, and which part of their common presences furthermore still had its normal exterior expressing the, so to say, 'fullness-of-its-inner-significance'—a 'something' which assisted the arising of the said properties in them.

"And this 'something' they then first called the 'organ Kundabuffer.'

"Having made this organ grow in the presences of the three-brained beings and having seen that it would work, the Most High Commission consisting of Sacred Individuals headed by the Archangel Sakaki, reassured and with good consciences, returned to the Center, while there, on the planet Earth which has taken your fancy, the action of this astonishing and exceedingly ingenious invention began from the first day to develop, and developed, as the wise Mullah Nassr Eddin would say—'like a Jericho-trumpet-in-crescendo.'

"Now, in order that you may have at least an approximate understanding of the results of the properties of the organ devised and actualized by the incomparable Angel Looisos—blessed be his name to all eternity—it is indispensable that you should know about the various manifestations of the three-brained beings of that planet, not only during the period when this organ Kundabuffer existed in their presences, but also during the later periods when, although this astonishing organ and its properties had been destroyed in them, nevertheless, owing to many causes, the consequences of its properties had begun to be crystallized in their presences.

"But this I will explain to you later.

"Meanwhile you must note that there was still a third descent of that Most High Commission to that planet, three years later according to objective time-calculations, but this time it was under the direction of the Most-Great-Arch-Seraph Sevohtartra, the Most Great Archangel Sakaki having, in the meantime, become worthy to become the divine Individual he now is, namely, one of the four Quarter-Maintainers of the whole Universe.

"And during just this third descent there, when it was made clear by the thorough investigations of the sacred members of this third Most High Commission that for the maintenance of the existence of those said detached fragments there was no longer any need to continue to actualize the deliberately taken anticipatory measures, then among the other measures there was also destroyed, with the help of the same Arch-Chemist-Physicist Angel Looisos, in the presences of the three-brained beings there, the said organ Kundabuffer with all its astonishing properties.

"But let us return to the tale I began.

"Now listen. When our confusion, caused by the recent catastrophe that had menaced that whole solar system, had passed off, we slowly, after this unexpected interruption, resumed the settlement of our new place on the planet Mars.

"Little by little we all of us made ourselves familiar with the local Nature and adapted ourselves to the existing conditions.

"As I have already said, many of us definitely settled down on the planet Mars; and others, by the ship *Occasion* which had been put at the disposal of the beings of our tribe for interplanetary communication, either went or prepared to go to exist on other planets of the same solar system.

"But I with my kinsmen and some of my near attendants remained to exist on that planet Mars.

"Yes, I must note that by the time to which my tale refers, my first Teskooano had already been set up in the observatory which I had constructed on the planet Mars and I was just then devoting myself entirely to the further organization and development of this observatory of mine, for the more detailed observation of the remote concentrations of our great Universe and of the planets of this solar system.

"Among the objects of my observations, then, was also this planet Earth.

"Time passed.

"The process of existence on this planet also began gradually to be established and it seemed, from all appearances, that the process of existence was proceeding there just as on all other planets.

"But by close observation, first, it could be clearly seen that the numbers of these three-brained beings were gradually increasing and, secondly, it was possible sometimes to observe very strange manifestations of theirs; that is, from time to time they did something which was never done by three-brained beings on other planets, namely, they would suddenly, without rhyme or reason, begin destroying one another's existence.

"Sometimes this destruction of one another's existence proceeded there not in one region alone but in several, and would last not just one 'Dionosk' but many 'Dionosks' and sometimes even for whole 'Ornakras.' (Dionosk signifies 'day'; Ornakra signifies 'month.')

It was sometimes very noticeable also that from this horrible process of theirs their numbers rapidly diminished; but on the other hand, during other periods, when there was a lull in these processes, their numbers also very noticeably increased.

"To this peculiarity of theirs we gradually got used, having explained it to ourselves that obviously, for certain higher considerations, these properties also must deliberately have been given to the organ Kundabuffer by the Most High Commission; in other words, seeing the fecundity of these biped beings, we assumed that this had been done with aforethought, in view of the necessity that they should exist in such large numbers for the needs of the maintenance of the common-cosmic Harmonious Movement.

"Had it not been for this strange peculiarity of theirs, it would never have entered anybody's head that there was anything 'queer' on that planet.

"During the period to which the aforesaid refers, I visited most of the planets of that solar system, the populated and the as yet unpopulated.

"Personally I liked best of all the three-centered beings breeding on the planet bearing the name Saturn, whose exterior is quite unlike ours, but resembles that of the being-bird raven.

"It is interesting, by the way, to remark that for some reason or other, the form of being-bird raven breeds not only on almost all the planets of this solar system, but also on most of those other planets of the whole of our great Universe upon which beings of various brain systems arise and are coated with planetary bodies of different forms.

"The verbal intercourse of these beings, ravens, of that planet Saturn is something like ours.

"But in regard to their utterance, it is in my opinion the most beautiful of any I have ever heard.

"It can be compared to the singing of our best singers when with all their Being they sing in a minor key.

"And as for their relations with others, they—I don't even know how to describe them—can be known only by existing among them and by experiencing them oneself.

"All that can be said is that these bird-beings have hearts exactly like those of the angels nearest our ENDLESS MAKER AND CREATOR.

"They exist strictly according to the ninth commandment

of our CREATOR, namely: 'Do unto another's as you would do unto your own.'

"Later, I must certainly tell you much more in detail about those three-brained beings also who arise and exist on the planet Saturn, since one of my real friends during the whole period of my exile in that solar system was a being of just that planet, who had the exterior coating of a raven and whose name was 'Harharkh.'"

CHAPTER 11

A Piquant Trait of the Peculiar Psyche of Contemporary Man

"Now let us return to those three-brained beings arising on the planet Earth, who have interested you most of all and whom you have called 'slugs.'

"I shall begin by saying how glad I am that you happen to be a long way from those three-centered beings whom you called by a word so 'insulting to their dignity' and that they are not likely ever to hear of it.

"Do you know, you poor thing, you small boy not yet aware of himself, what they would do to you, particularly the contemporary beings there, if they should hear what you called them?

"What they would have done to you if you had been there and if they had got hold of you—I am seized with horror at the very mention of it.

"At best they would have thrashed you so, that as our Mullah Nassr Eddin there says, 'you wouldn't have recovered your senses before the next crop of birches.'

"In any case, I advise you that, whenever you start anything new, you should always bless Fate and beseech her mercy, that she should always be on guard and prevent the beings of the planet Earth from ever suspecting that you, my beloved and only grandson, dared to call them 'slugs.'

"You must know that during the time of my observations of them from the planet Mars and during the periods of my existence among them, I studied the psyche of these strange three-brained beings very thoroughly, and so I already know very well what they would do to anybody who dared to give them such a nickname.

"To be sure, it was only in childish naïveté that you called them so; but the three-brained beings of that peculiar planet, especially the contemporary ones, do not discriminate such fine points.

"Who called them, why, and in what circumstances—it's all one. They have been called by a name they consider insulting—and that's quite enough.

"Discrimination in such matters is, according to the understanding of most of them, simply, as they express it, 'pouring from the empty into the void.'

"Be that as it may, you were in any case extremely rash to call the three-brained beings breeding on the planet Earth by such an offensive name; first, because you have made me anxious for you, and secondly, because you have laid up for yourself a menace for the future.

"The position is this: Though, as I have already said, you are a long way off, and they will be unable to get at you to punish you personally, yet nevertheless if they should somehow unexpectedly chance to learn even at twentieth hand how you insulted them, then you could at once be sure of their real 'anathema,' and the dimensions of this anathema would depend upon the interests with which they happened to be occupied at the given moment.

"Perhaps it is worth while describing to you how the beings of the Earth would behave if they should happen to learn that you had so insulted them. This description may serve as a very good example for the elucidation of the strangeness of the psyche of these three-brained beings who interest you.

"Provoked by such an incident as your thus insulting them, if everything was rather 'dull' with them at the given moment, owing to the absence of any other similar absurd interest, they would arrange somewhere in a previously chosen place, with previously invited people, all of course dressed in costumes specially designed for such occasions, what is called a 'solemn council.'

"First of all, for this 'solemn council' of theirs, they would select from among themselves what is called a 'president' and only then would they proceed with their 'trial.'

"To begin with, they would, as they say there, 'pick you to pieces,' and not only you, but your father, your grandfather, and perhaps even all the way back to Adam.

"If they should then decide—of course, as always, by a majority of votes—that you are guilty, they would sentence you according to the indications of a code of laws collated on the basis of former similar 'puppet plays' by beings called 'old fossils.'

"But if they should happen, by a 'majority of votes' to find nothing criminal in your action at all—though this very seldom occurs among them—then this whole 'trial' of theirs, set out on paper in detail and signed by the whole lot of them, would be dispatched—you would think into the wastepaper basket? Oh, no!—to appropriate specialists; in the given instances to what is called the 'Hierarchy' or 'Holy Synod,' where the same procedure would be repeated; only in this case you would be tried by 'important' beings there.

"Only at the very end of this true 'pouring from the empty into the void' would they come to the main point, namely, that the accused is out of reach.

"But it is just here that arises the principal danger to your person, namely, that when they are quite certain beyond all doubt that they cannot get hold of you, they will then unanimously decide nothing more nor less than, as I have already said, to 'anathematize' you.

"And do you know what that is and how it is done?

"No!

"Then listen and shudder.

"The most 'important' beings will decree to all the other beings that in all their appointed establishments, such as what are called 'churches,' 'chapels,' 'synagogues,' 'town-halls,' and so on, special officials shall on special occasions with appointed ceremonies wish for you in thought something like the following:

"That you should lose your horns, or that your hair should turn prematurely gray, or that the food in your stomach should be turned into coffin nails, or that your future wife's tongue should be three times its size, or that whenever you take a bite of your pet pie it should be turned into 'soap,' and so on and so forth in the same strain.

"Do you now understand to what dangers you exposed yourself when you called these remote three-brained freaks 'slugs'?"

Having finished thus, Beelzebub looked with a smile on his favorite.

CHAPTER 12
The First "Growl"

A little later, Beelzebub began to speak as follows:

"A story I have just recalled, connected with these 'anathemas' I have mentioned, may provide very useful material for beginning to comprehend the strangeness of the psyche of the three-brained beings of that planet which has taken your fancy; and furthermore, this story may reassure you a little and give you some hope that if these peculiar terrestrial beings should chance to learn how you had insulted them and should 'anathematize' you, then perhaps after all something 'not so very bad' might come of it for you.

"The story I am going to tell you occurred quite recently among the contemporary three-brained beings there, and it arose from the following events:

"In one of these large communities, there peaceably existed an ordinary being who was by profession what is there called a 'writer.'

"You must here know, that in long-past ages one might still occasionally run across beings of that profession who still invented and wrote something really by themselves; but in these later epochs the 'writers' among the beings there, particularly among contemporary beings, have been of those that only copy from many already existing books all kinds of ideas, and by fitting them together make a 'new book.'

"And they prefer books which have reached them from their very remote ancestors.

"It is necessary to remark that the books written by contemporary 'writers' there are, all taken together, the principal cause that the Reason of all the other three-brained beings is becoming more and more what the venerable Mullah Nassr Eddin calls 'stuff and nonsense.'

"And so, my boy:

"The contemporary writer of whom I began to speak was just a 'writer' like all the rest there, and nothing particular in himself.

"Once when he had finished some book or other, he began to think what he should write about next, and with this in view, he decided to look for some new 'idea' in the books contained in his what is called 'library,' such as every writer there is bound to have.

"As he was looking, a book called 'the Gospels' happened to fall into his hands.

"'The Gospels' is the name given there to a book once written by certain persons called Matthew, Mark, Luke, and John about Jesus Christ, a Messenger from our ENDLESSNESS to that planet.

"This book is widely circulated among those three-centered beings there who nominally exist according to the indications of this Messenger.

"This book having chanced to fall into this writer's hands, the thought suddenly entered his head: Why should not I also make a 'Gospel'?

"From investigations I had to make for quite different needs of mine, it turned out that he then further deliberated as follows:

"'Am I any worse than those ancient barbarians, Matthew, Mark, Luke, and Johnnie?

"'At least I am more "cultured" than they ever were; and I can write a much better "gospel" for my contemporaries.

"'And very decidedly it is necessary to write just a "Gospel" because the contemporary people called "English" and "American" have a great weakness for this book, and the rate of exchange of their pounds and dollars is "not half bad" just now.'

"No sooner said than done.

"And from that very day he 'wiseacred' away at his new 'Gospel.' But it was only when he had finished it, however, and had given it to the printers, that all the further events connected with this new 'Gospel' of his began.

"At any other time, nothing perhaps would have happened, and this new 'Gospel' of his would simply have slipped into its niche in the libraries of the bibliomaniacs there, among the multitudes of other books expounding similar 'truths.'

"But fortunately or unfortunately for this writer, it happened that certain 'power-possessing' beings of that great community in which he existed had just been having rotten luck at what is called 'roulette' and 'baccarat' and they therefore kept on demanding what they called 'money' from the ordinary beings of their community, whereupon, thanks to these inordinate demands for money, the ordinary beings of that community at length awoke from their usual what is called torpor and 'began-to-sit-up.'

Seeing this, the 'power-possessing' beings who remained at home became alarmed and took corresponding 'measures.'

"And among the 'measures' they took was also the immediate destruction from off the face of their planet of everything newly arising in their native land, such as could possibly keep the ordinary beings of their community from resuming their hibernation.

"And it was just at this time that the aforementioned 'Gospel' of this writer appeared.

"In the contents of this new 'Gospel' also, the 'power-possessing' beings found something which also to their understanding might keep the ordinary beings of their community from hibernating again; and they therefore decided almost immediately to 'get rid of' both the writer himself and his 'Gospel'—because they had now become quite expert in 'getting rid of' these native 'upstarts' who did not mind their own business.

"But for certain reasons they could not treat this writer in this way, and so they got excited, and hemmed and hawed about what they should do.

"Some proposed that they should simply shut him up where many 'rats' and 'lice' breed; others proposed to send him to 'Timbuktu'; and so on and so forth; but in the end they decided to anathematize this writer together with his 'Gospel,' publicly and punctiliously according to all the rules, and moreover with the very same 'anathema' with which no doubt they would have anathematized you also if they had learned how you had insulted them.

"And so, my boy, the strangeness of the psyche of the contemporary three-brained beings of this peculiar planet was revealed in the given instance in this, that when this writer and his 'Gospel' had been publicly anathematized with this 'anathema,' the result for him was, as the highly esteemed Mullah Nassr Eddin once again says: 'just roses, roses.'

"What occurred was as follows:

"The ordinary beings of the said community, seeing the fuss made about this writer by the power-possessing beings, became very greatly interested in him and avidly bought and read not only this new 'Gospel' of his but also all the books he had written before.

"Whereupon, as usually happens with the three-centered beings breeding on this peculiar planet, all the other interests of the beings of the said community gradually died down, and they talked and thought only of this writer.

"And as it also happens—whereas some praised him to the skies, others condemned him; and the result of these discussions and conversations was that the numbers interested in him grew not only among the beings of his own community but among the beings of other communities also.

"And this occurred because some of the power-possessing beings of this community, usually with pockets full of money, still continued in their turn to go to other communities where 'roulette' and 'baccarat' proceeded and, carrying on their discussion there concerning this writer, they gradually infected the beings of other communities also with this affair.

"In short, owing to the strangeness of their psyche, it has gradually come about there that even at the present time, when this writer's 'Gospel' has been long forgotten, his name is known almost everywhere as that of an 'excellent writer.'

"Anything he writes now, they all seize upon and regard as full of indisputable truth.

"Everybody today looks upon his writings with the same veneration with which the ancient Kalkians there listened to the predictions of their sacred 'Pythoness.'

"It is interesting to notice here that if at the present time you ask any being there about this writer, he would know him and of course speak of him as an extraordinary being.

"But if you were then to ask what he wrote, it would turn out that most of them, if of course they confessed the truth, had never read a single one of his books.

"All the same they would talk about him, discuss him, and of course splutteringly insist that he was a being with an 'extraordinary mind' and phenomenally well acquainted with the psyche of the beings dwelling on the planet Earth."

CHAPTER 13

Why in Man's Reason Fantasy May Be Perceived as Reality

My dear and kind Grandfather, be so kind as to explain to me, if only in a general way, why those beings there are such that they take the 'ephemeral' for the Real."

To this question of his grandson, Beelzebub replied thus:

"It was only during later periods that the three-brained beings of the planet Earth began to have this particularity in their psyche, and just this particularity arose in them only because their predominant part, which was formed in them as in all three-brained beings, gradually allowed other parts of their total presences to perceive every new impression without what is called 'being-Partkdolg-duty' but just merely as, in general, such impressions are perceived by the separate independent localizations existing under the name of being-centers present in the three-brained beings, or, as I should say in their language, they believe everything anybody says, and not solely that which they themselves have been able to recognize by their own sane deliberation.

"In general, any new understanding is crystallized in the presence of these strange beings only if Smith speaks of somebody or something in a certain way; and then if Brown says the same, the hearer is quite convinced it is just so and couldn't possibly be otherwise. Thanks merely to this particularity of their psyche and to the fact that the said writer was much spoken about in the said manner, most of the beings there at the present time are quite convinced that he is indeed a very great psychologist and has an incomparable knowledge of the psyche of the beings of his planet.

"But, as a matter of fact, when I was on that planet for the last time and, having heard of the said writer, once went myself especially to see him, on quite another matter, he was according to my understanding not only like all the other contemporary writers there, that is to say, extremely limited, and as our dear Mullah Nassr Eddin would say: 'able to see no further than his nose,' but as regards any knowledge of the real psyche of the beings of his planet in real conditions, he might safely even be called 'totally illiterate.'

"I repeat that the story of this writer is a very characteristic example showing the extent to which, in the three-brained beings who have taken your fancy, particularly in the contemporary ones, the realization of 'being-Partkdolg-duty' is absent, and how their own subjective being-convictions formed by their own logical deliberations are never, as in general it is proper to three-brained beings, crystallized in them, but only those are crystallized which depend exclusively only upon what others say about the given question.

"It was only because they failed to realize 'being-Partkdolg-duty,' which realization alone enables a being to become aware of genuine reality, that they saw in the said writer some perfection or other which was not there at all.

"This strange trait of their general psyche, namely, of being satisfied with just what Smith or Brown says, without trying to know more, became rooted in them already long ago, and now they no longer strive at all to know anything cognizable by their own active deliberations alone.

"Concerning all this it must be said that neither the organ Kundabuffer which their ancestors had is to blame, nor its consequences which, owing to a mistake on the part of certain Sacred Individuals, were crystallized in their ancestors and later began to pass by heredity from generation to generation.

"But they themselves were personally to blame for it, and just on account of the abnormal conditions of external ordinary being-existence which they themselves have gradually established and which have gradually formed in their common presence just what has now become their inner 'Evil-God,' called 'Self-Calming.'

"But all this you yourself, later on, will well understand, when I shall have given you, as I have already promised, more information about that planet which has taken your fancy.

"In any case, I strongly advise you to be very careful in the future in your references to the three-brained beings of that planet, not to offend them in any way; otherwise—as they also say there, 'With what may the Devil not joke?'—they might find out about your insulting them and, to use another of their expressions, 'lay you by the heels.'

"And in the present case there is no harm in recalling again one of the wise sentences of our dear Mullah Nassr Eddin, who says:

" ' 'Struth! What might not happen in this world. A flea might swallow an elephant.' "

Beelzebub intended to say something more, but at that moment a ship's servant entered and, approaching, handed him an "etherogram" in his name.

When Beelzebub had finished listening to the contents of the said "etherogram" and the ship's servant had gone, Hassein turned to Beelzebub again with the following words:

"Dear Grandfather, please go on talking about the three-centered beings arising and existing on that interesting planet called Earth."

Beelzebub having looked at his grandson again with a special smile, and having made a very strange gesture with his head, continued to speak as follows:

CHAPTER 14

The Beginnings of Perspectives Promising Nothing Very Cheerful

"I must tell you first that the three-brained beings on that planet also had in the beginning presences similar to those possessed in general by all what are called 'Keschapmartnian' three-centered beings arising on all the corresponding planets of the whole of our great Universe; and they also had the same, as it is called, 'duration of existence' as all the other three-brained beings.

"All the various changes in their presences began for the most part after the second misfortune occurred to this planet, during which misfortune the chief continent of that ill-fated planet, then existing under the name 'Atlantis,' entered within the planet.

"And from that time on, as little by little they created for themselves all sorts of conditions of external being-existence thanks to which the quality of their radiations went steadily from bad to worse, Great Nature was compelled gradually to transform their common presences by means of various compromises and changes, in order to regulate the quality of the vibrations which they radiated and which were required chiefly for the preservation of the well-being of the former parts of that planet.

"For the same reason, Great Nature gradually so increased the numbers of the beings there that at the present time they are now breeding on all the lands formed on that planet.

"The exterior forms of their planetary bodies are all made alike, and of course in respect of size and in their other subjective particularities, they are each coated, just as we are, in accordance with the reflection of heredity, with the conditions at the moment of conception and with the other factors that serve in general as the causes for the arising and formation of every being.

"They also differ among themselves in the color of their skin and in the conformation of their hair, and these latter particularities are determined in their presences, just as they are everywhere else, by the effects of that part of the planetary surface where the given beings arise and where they are formed until they reach the age of responsible beings, or as they say, until they become 'adult.'

"As regards their general psyche itself and its fundamental traits, no matter upon what part of the surface of their planet they arise, these traits in all of them have precisely the same particularities, among them being also that property of the three-brained beings there, thanks to which on that strange planet alone in the whole of the Universe does that horrible process occur among three-brained beings which is called the 'process of the destruction of each other's existence,' or, as it is called on that ill-fated planet, 'war.'

"Besides this chief particularity of their common psyche, there are completely crystallized in them and there unfailingly become a part of their common presences—regardless of where they may arise and exist—functions which exist under the names 'egoism,' 'self-love,' 'vanity,' 'pride,' 'self-conceit,' 'credulity,' 'suggestibility,' and many other properties quite abnormal and quite unbecoming to the essence of any three-brained beings whatsoever.

"Of these abnormal being-particularities, the particularity of their psyche the most terrible for them personally is that which is called 'suggestibility.'

"About this extremely strange and singular psychic particularity I shall specially explain to you sometime."

Having said this, Beelzebub was thoughtful, and this

time longer than usual, and then, turning again to his grandson, he said:

"I see that the three-brained beings arising and existing on the peculiar planet called Earth interest you very much, and as during our voyage on the ship *Karnak* we shall have willy-nilly to talk about many things just to pass away the time, I will tell you all I can just about these three-brained beings.

"I think it will be best for your clear understanding of the strangeness of the psyche of the three-brained beings arising on the planet Earth if I relate to you my personal descents to that planet in their order, and the events which occurred there during these descents of mine, of which I myself was a witness.

"I personally visited the surface of the planet Earth six times in all, and each of these personal visits of mine was brought about by a different set of circumstances.

"I shall begin with my first descent."

CHAPTER 15

The First Descent of Beelzebub upon the Planet Earth

"Upon that planet Earth," Beelzebub began to relate, "I descended for the first time on account of a young being of our tribe who had had the misfortune to become deeply involved with a three-brained being there, as a consequence of which he had got himself mixed up in a very stupid affair.

"There once came to my house on the planet Mars a number of beings of our tribe, also dwelling there on Mars, with the following request:

"They told me that one of their young kinsmen, 350 Martian years before, had migrated to exist on the planet Earth, and that a very disagreeable incident for all of us, his kinsmen, had recently occurred to him there.

"They told me further:

"'We, his kinsmen, both those existing there on the planet Earth and those existing here on the planet Mars, intended at first to deal with the unpleasant incident ourselves, with our own resources. But notwithstanding all our efforts and the measures we have adopted we have been unable so far to accomplish anything.

"'And being now finally convinced that we are unable to settle this unpleasant affair by ourselves independently, we venture to trouble you, your Right Reverence, and urgently beseech you to be so kind as not to withhold from us your wise advice how we may find a way out of our unhappy situation.'

"They told me further in detail in what the misfortune which had befallen them consisted.

"From all they told me I saw that the incident was disagreeable not only for this young being's kinsmen, but that it might also prove disagreeable for the beings of all our tribe.

"So I could not help deciding at once to undertake to help them to settle this difficulty of theirs.

"At first I tried to help them while remaining on the planet Mars, but when I became certain that it would be impossible to do anything effective from the planet Mars, I decided to descend to the planet Earth and there, on the spot, to find some way out. The next day after this decision of mine, I took with me everything necessary which I had at hand and flew there on the ship *Occasion.*

"I may remind you that the ship *Occasion* was the ship on which all the beings of our tribe were transported to that solar system and, as I have already told you, it was left there for the use of the beings of our tribe for the purpose of interplanetary communication.

"The permanent port of this ship was on the planet Mars; and its supreme direction had been given me from Above.

"Thus it was on this same ship *Occasion* that I made my first descent to the planet Earth.

"Our ship landed on this first visit of mine, on the shores of just that continent which during the second catastrophe to this planet, disappeared entirely from its surface.

"This continent was called 'Atlantis' and most of the three-brained beings, and likewise most of the beings of our tribe, then existed only upon it.

"Having descended, I went straight from the ship *Occasion* to the city named 'Samlios,' situated on the said continent, where that unfortunate being of our tribe, who was the cause of this descent of mine, had the place of his existence.

"The city 'Samlios' was then a very large city, and was

the capital of the largest community then on the planet Earth.

"In this same city the head of this large community existed who was called 'King Appolis.'

"And it was with just this same King Appolis that our young, inexperienced countryman had become involved.

"And it was in this city of 'Samlios' itself that I learned all the details of this affair.

"I learned, namely, that before this incident our unfortunate countryman had for some reason been on friendly terms with this King Appolis, and was often at his house.

"As it transpired, our young countryman once, in the course of conversation during a visit to the house of King Appolis, made a 'wager' which was just the cause of all that followed.

"You must first of all know that both the community of which King Appolis was the head and the city of Samlios where he existed were at that period the greatest and richest of all the communities and cities then existing on the Earth.

"For the upkeep of all this wealth and grandeur King Appolis certainly needed both a great deal of what is called 'money' and a great deal of labor from the ordinary beings of that community.

"It is necessary to premise just here that at the period of my first descent in person onto this planet, the organ Kundabuffer was no longer in the three-brained beings who interest you.

"And it was only in some of the three-brained beings there that various consequences of the properties of that for them maleficent organ had already begun to be crystallized.

"In the period to which this tale of mine refers, one of the consequences of the properties of this organ which had already become thoroughly crystallized in a number of beings there was that consequence of the property which, while the organ Kundabuffer itself was still functioning in them, had enabled them very easily and without any 'remorse-of-conscience' not to carry out voluntarily any duties taken upon themselves or given them by a superior. But every duty they fulfilled was fulfilled only from the fear and apprehension of 'threats' and 'menaces' from outside.

"It was in just this same consequence of this property already thoroughly crystallized in some beings of that period there, that the cause of this whole incident lay.

"And so, my boy, this is how it was. King Appolis, who had been extremely conscientious in respect of the duties he had taken upon himself for the maintenance of the greatness of the community entrusted to him, had spared neither his own labor nor wealth, and at the same time he demanded the same from all the beings of his community.

"But, as I have already said, the mentioned consequences of the organ Kundabuffer having by that time been thoroughly crystallized in certain of his subjects, he had to employ every possible kind of 'threat' and 'menace' in order to extract from everybody all that was required for the greatness of the community entrusted to him.

"His methods were so varied and at the same time so reasonable that even those of his 'subjects-beings' in whom the said consequences had already been crystallized could not help respecting him, although they added to his name, of course behind his back, the nickname 'Arch-cunning.'

"And so, my boy, these means by which King Appolis then obtained what was necessary from his subjects for the maintenance of the greatness of the community entrusted to him seemed to our young countryman, for some reason or other, unjust, and, as it was said, he often became very indignant and restless whenever he happened to hear of some new device of King Appolis for getting what was necessary.

"And once, while talking with the King himself, our naïve young countryman could not restrain himself, but expressed to his face his indignation and his views of this 'unconscionable' conduct of King Appolis towards his subjects.

"Not only did King Appolis not fly into a temper, as usually happens on the planet Earth when somebody pokes his nose where he has no business, nor did he pitch him out by the scruff of his neck, but he even talked it over with him and discussed the reasons for his 'severity.'

"They talked a great deal and the result of the whole of their conversation was precisely a 'wager,' that is to say they made an agreement and set it down on paper, and each of them signed it with his own blood.

"Among other things there was included in this agreement that for the obtaining from his subjects of all that was necessary King Appolis should be obliged to employ thereafter only those measures and means which should be indicated by our countryman.

"And in the event that all his subjects should fail to contribute all that which according to custom was required, then our countryman would become responsible for everything, and he pledged himself to procure for the treasury of King Appolis as much as was necessary for the maintenance and further aggrandizement of the capital and of the whole community.

"And so, my boy, King Appolis did indeed, from the very next day, fulfill very honorably the obligation which according to the agreement he had assumed; and he conducted the whole government of the country exactly according to the indications of our young countryman. The results of a government of this kind, however, very soon proved to be quite the opposite of those expected by our simpleton.

"The subjects of that community—principally, of course, those in whom the said consequences of the properties of the organ Kundabuffer had already been crystallized—not only ceased to pay into King Appolis' treasury what was required, but they even began gradually snatching back what had been put in before.

"As our countryman had undertaken to contribute what was needed and, furthermore, had signed his undertaking with his blood—and you know, don't you, what the voluntary undertaking of an obligation, especially when signed with his blood, means to one of our tribe—he had of course soon to begin making up to the treasury all that was short.

"He first put in everything he had himself, and afterwards everything he could get from his nearests, dwelling also there on the planet Earth. And when he had drained dry his nearests there, he addressed himself for assistance to his nearests dwelling on the planet Mars.

"But soon on the planet Mars also everything ran dry and still the treasury of the city of Samlios demanded more and again more; nor was the end of its needs in sight.

"It was just then that all the kinsmen of this countryman of ours became alarmed and thereupon they decided to address themselves to me with the request to help them out of their plight.

"So, my boy, when we arrived in the said city I was met by all the beings of our tribe, both old and young, who had remained on that planet.

"In the evening of the same day a general meeting was called to confer together to find some way out of the situation that had arisen.

"To this conference of ours there was also invited King Appolis himself with whom our elder countrymen had already previously had many talks on this matter with this aim in view.

"At this first general conference of ours, King Appolis, addressing himself to all, said as follows:

"'Impartial friends!

"'I personally am deeply sorry for what has occurred and what has brought about so many troubles for those assembled here; and I am distressed in all my being that it is beyond my power to extricate you from your prospective difficulties.

"'You must know, indeed,' King Appolis continued, 'that the machinery of the government of my community which has been wound up and organized during many centuries, is at the present time already radically changed; and to revert to the old order is already impossible without serious consequences, namely, without those consequences which must doubtless evoke the indignation of the majority of my subjects. The present situation is such that I alone am not able to abolish what has been created without provoking the mentioned serious consequences, and I therefore beg you all in the name of Justice to help me to deal with it.

"'Still further,' he then added, 'I bitterly reproach myself in the presence of you all, because I also am greatly to blame for all these misfortunes.

"'And I am to blame because I ought to have foreseen what has occurred, since I have existed in these conditions longer than my opponent and your kinsman, namely, he with whom I made the agreement known to you.

"'To tell the truth it was unpardonable of me to risk entering into such conditions with a being who, although he may be of much higher Reason than I, is, nevertheless, not so practiced in such affairs as I am.

"'Once more I beg all of you, and your Right Reverence in particular, to forgive me and to help me out of this sad plight, and enable me to find some issue from the situation that has been created.

"'With things as they now are, I can at present do only what you will indicate.'

"After King Appolis had left, we decided the same evening to select from among ourselves several experienced elderly beings who should weigh together, that same night, all the data and draw up a rough plan for further action.

"The rest of us then departed on the understanding that we should assemble the ensuing evening at the same place; but to this second conference of ours King Appolis was not invited.

"When we assembled the next day, one of the elder beings, elected the night before, first reported as follows:

"'We pondered and deliberated the whole night upon all the details of this lamentable event, and as a result we have unanimously come to the conclusion first of all that there is no way out but to revert to the former conditions of government.

"'Further, we all, and also unanimously, agree that to return to the former order of government must indeed inevitably provoke a revolt of the citizens of the community, and, of course, that there will certainly follow all those consequences of revolt which have already become inevitable in such circumstances during recent times on Earth.

"'And of course, as has also become usual here, many of those so-called "power-possessing" beings of this community will suffer terribly, even possibly to the degree of their complete destruction; and above all, it seemed impossible that King Appolis could escape such a fate.

"'Thereafter we deliberated in order, if possible, to devise some means of diverting the said unhappy consequences at least from King Appolis himself.

"'And we had every wish to devise such a means because at our general conference yesterday evening King Appolis himself was very frank and friendly towards us, and we should all be extremely sorry if he himself should suffer.

"'During our further prolonged deliberations we came to the conclusion that it would be possible to divert the blow from King Appolis only if during the said revolt the exhibition of the fury of the rebellious beings of this community was directed not against the King himself but against those around him, that is, those who are there called his "administration."

"'But then the question arose among us, would those near the King be willing to take upon themselves the consequences of all this?

"'And we came to the categorical conclusion that they certainly would not agree, because they would assuredly consider that the King himself had been alone to blame for it all, and that therefore he himself should pay for it.

"'Having come to all these aforesaid conclusions we finally also unanimously decided as follows:

"'In order at least to save King Appolis from what is inevitably expected, we must with the consent of the King himself replace all the beings in this community who now hold responsible posts, by beings of our tribe, and each of these latter, during the climax of this "psychosis" of the masses, must take upon himself a share of the consequences anticipated.'

"When this elected being of ours had finished his report our opinion was quickly formed, and a unanimous resolution was carried to do just as the elder beings of our tribe had advised.

"And thereupon we first sent one of our elder beings to King Appolis to put our plan before him, to which the latter agreed, once more repeating his promise, namely, that he would do everything according to our directions.

"We then decided to delay no longer and from the following day to begin to replace all the officials by our own.

"But after two days it turned out that there were not sufficient beings of our tribe dwelling on the planet Earth to replace all the officials of that community; and we therefore immediately sent the *Occasion* back to the planet Mars for our beings there.

"And meanwhile King Appolis guided by two of our elder beings, began under different pretexts replacing various officials by our beings, at first in the capital of Samlios itself.

"And when several days later our ship *Occasion* arrived from the planet Mars with beings of our tribe, similar replacements were made in the provinces also, and soon everywhere in that community what are called the responsible posts were filled by the beings of our tribe.

"And when all had been changed in this way, King Appolis, always under the guidance of these elder beings of ours, began the restoration of the former code of regulations for the administration of the community.

"Almost from the very first days of the restoration of the old code, the effects upon the general psyche of the beings of that community in whom the consequences of the mentioned property of the maleficent organ Kundabuffer had already been thoroughly crystallized began, as it was expected, to manifest themselves.

"Thus the expected discontent grew thereupon from day to day, until one day, not long after, there occurred just that which has ever since been definitely proper to be present in the presence of the three-brained beings there of all ensuing periods, and that is, to produce from time to time the process which they themselves nowadays call 'revolution.'

"And during their revolution of that time, as it has also

become proper there to these three-brained phenomena of our Great Universe, they destroyed a great deal of the property which they had accumulated during centuries, much of what is called the 'knowledge' which they had attained during centuries also was destroyed and lost forever, and the existence of those other beings similar to themselves who had already chanced upon the means of freeing themselves from the consequences of the properties of the organ Kundabuffer were also destroyed.

"It is extremely interesting to notice here one exceedingly astonishing and incomprehensible fact.

"And that is that during their later revolutions of this kind, almost all the three-brained beings there or at least the overwhelming majority who begin to fall into such a 'psychosis,' always destroy for some reason or other the existence of just such other beings like themselves, as have, for some reason or other, chanced to find themselves more or less on the track of the means of becoming free from the crystallization in themselves of the consequences of the properties of that maleficent organ Kundabuffer which unfortunately their ancestors possessed.

"So, my boy, while the process of this revolution of theirs was running its course, King Appolis himself existed in one of his suburban palaces of the city of Samlios.

"Nobody laid a finger on him, because our beings had arranged by their propaganda that the whole blame should be placed not upon King Appolis but upon those surrounding him, that is, as they are called, his administration.

"Moreover, the beings who had fallen into the said psychosis even 'suffered grief' and really pitied their king, saying that it was because their 'poor King' had been surrounded by such unconscionable and ungrateful subordinates that these undesirable revolutions had occurred.

"And when the revolutionary psychosis had quite died down, King Appolis returned to the city of Samlios and again with the help of our elder beings, gradually began replacing our countrymen either by those of his old subordinates who were still alive, or by selecting absolutely new ones from among his other subjects.

"And when the earlier policy of King Appolis towards his subjects had been re-established, then the citizens of this community resumed filling the treasury with money as usual and carrying out the directions of their King, and the affairs of the community settled again into the former already established tempo.

"As for our naïve, unfortunate countryman who was the cause of it all, it was so painful to him that he would no longer remain upon that planet that had proved so disastrous for him, but he returned with us to the planet Mars.

"And later on he became there an even excellent bailiff for all the beings of our tribe."

CHAPTER 16

The Relative Understanding of Time

After a short pause Beelzebub continued thus:

"Before telling you further about the three-brained beings who have taken your fancy and who breed on the planet Earth, it is in my opinion absolutely necessary for you, for a clear representation of the strangeness of their psyche and, in general, for a better understanding of everything concerning this peculiar planet, first of all to have an accurate representation of their time-calculation, and of how the being-sensation of what is called the 'process-of-the-flow-of-time' in the presences of the three-brained beings of that planet has gradually changed and also of how this process now flows in the presences of the contemporary three-brained beings there.

"It must be made clear to you because only then will you have the possibility clearly to represent to yourself and understand the events there which I have already related and those I shall yet relate.

"You must first know that for the definition of Time, the three-brained beings of that planet take the 'year' as the basic unit of their time-calculation, just as we do, and also, like us, they define the duration of their 'year' by the time of a certain movement of their planet in relation to another definite cosmic concentration; that is to say, they take that period in the course of which their planet, during its movement—that is, during the processes of 'Falling' and 'Catching-up'—makes what is called its 'Krentonalnian-revolution' in relation to its sun.

"It is similar to our reckoning of a 'year' for our planet Karatas, which is the period of time between the nearest approach of the sun 'Samos' to the sun 'Selos' and its next similar approach.

"A hundred of such 'years' of theirs, the beings of the Earth call a 'century.'

"And they divide this 'year' of theirs into twelve parts and each part they call a 'month.'

"For the definition of the duration of this 'month' of theirs, they take the time of that completed period during which that larger fragment—which was separated from their planet and which they now call Moon—makes, owing to the same cosmic law of 'Falling' and 'Catching-up,' its full 'Krentonalnian-revolution' in relation to their planet.

"It must be noticed that the twelve 'Krentonalnian-revolutions' of the said Moon do not correspond exactly to a single 'Krentonalnian-revolution' of their planet round its sun and therefore they have made some compromise or other when calculating these months of theirs, so that in the sum total these may correspond more or less to reality.

"Further, they divide these months of theirs into thirty 'diurnities,' or, as they usually say, 'days.'

"And a diurnity they reckon as that span of time during which their planet makes its 'completed-rotation' during the actualizing of the said cosmic laws.

"Bear in mind, by the way, that they also say 'it-is-day,' when in the atmosphere of their planet—just as in general on all the other planets on which, as I have already told you, the cosmic process called 'Ilnosoparnian' is actualized—that 'Trogoautoegocratic' process which we call 'kshtatsavacht' periodically proceeds; and they also call this cosmic phenomenon 'daylight.'

"As regards the other process, the opposite one, which we call 'kldatzacht,' they call it 'night' and refer to it as 'it-is-dark.'

"And thus the three-brained beings breeding on the planet Earth call the greatest period of the flow of time 'century,' and this 'century' of theirs consists of a hundred 'years'.

"A 'year' has twelve 'months.'

"A 'month' has an average of thirty 'days,' that is, diurnities.

"Further, they divide their diurnity into twenty-four 'hours' and an 'hour' into sixty 'minutes.'

"And a 'minute' they divide into sixty 'seconds.'

"But as in general, my boy, you do not yet know of the exceptional peculiarity of this cosmic phenomenon Time, you must first be told that genuine Objective Science formulates this cosmic phenomenon thus:

"Time in itself does not exist; there is only the totality of the results ensuing from all the cosmic phenomena present in a given place.

"Time itself, no being can either understand by reason or sense by any outer or inner being-function. It cannot even be sensed by any gradation of instinct which arises and is present in every more or less independent cosmic concentration.

"It is possible to judge Time only if one compares real cosmic phenomena which proceed in the same place and under the same conditions, where Time is being constated and considered.

"It is necessary to notice that in the Great Universe all phenomena in general, without exception wherever they arise and manifest, are simply successively law-conformable 'Fractions' of some whole phenomenon which has its prime arising on the 'Most Holy Sun Absolute.'

"And in consequence, all cosmic phenomena, wherever they proceed, have a sense of 'objectivity.'

"And these successively law-conformable 'Fractions' are actualized in every respect, and even in the sense of their involution and evolution, owing to the chief cosmic law, the sacred 'Heptaparaparshinokh.'

"Only Time alone has no sense of objectivity because it is not the result of the fractioning of any definite cosmic phenomena. And it does not issue from anything, but blends always with everything and becomes self-sufficiently independent; therefore, in the whole of the Universe, it alone can be called and extolled as the 'Ideally-Unique-Subjective-Phenomenon.'

"Thus, my boy, uniquely Time alone, or, as it is sometimes called, the 'Heropass,' has no source from which its arising should depend, but like 'Divine-Love' flows always, as I have already told you, independently by itself, and blends proportionately with all the phenomena present in the given place and in the given arisings of our Great Universe.

"Again I tell you, you will be able clearly to understand all that I have just told you only when, as I have already promised you, I shall specially explain to you sometime later all about the fundamental laws of World-creation and World-maintenance.

"Meanwhile, remember this also, that since Time has no source of its arising and cannot like all other cosmic phenomena in every cosmic sphere establish its exact presence, the already mentioned Objective Science therefore has, for its examination of Time, a standard unit, similar to that used for an exact definition of the density and quality—in the sense of the vivifyingness of their vibrations—of all cosmic substances in general present in every place and in every sphere of our Great Universe.

"And for the definition of Time this standard unit has from long ago been the moment of what is called the sacred 'Egokoolnatsnarnian-sensation' which always appears in the Most Holy Cosmic Individuals dwelling on the Most Holy Sun Absolute whenever the vision of our UNI-BEING ENDLESSNESS is directed into space and directly touches their presences.

"This standard unit has been established in Objective Science for the possibility of exactly defining and comparing the differences between the gradations of the processes of the subjective sensations of separate conscious Individuals, and also of what are called 'diverse-tempos' among various objective cosmic phenomena which are manifested in various spheres of our Great Universe and which actualize all cosmic arisings both large and small.

"The chief particularity of the process of the flow of Time in the presence of cosmic arisings of various scales consists in this, that all of them perceive it in the same way and in the same sequence.

"In order that you may meanwhile represent to yourself, if only approximately, what I have just said, let us take as an example the process of the flow of Time proceeding in any drop of the water in that decanter standing there on the table.

"Every drop of water in that decanter is in itself also a whole independent world, a world of 'Microcosmoses.'

"In that little world, as in other cosmoses, there also arise and exist relatively independent infinitesimal 'individuals' or 'beings.'

"For the beings of that infinitesimal world also, Time flows in the same sequence in which the flow of Time is sensed by all individuals in all other cosmoses. These infinitesimal beings also, like the beings of cosmoses of other 'scales,' have their experiences of a definite duration for all their perceptions and manifestations; and, also, like them, they sense the flow of Time by the comparison of the duration of the phenomena around them.

"Exactly like the beings of other cosmoses, they are born, they grow up, they unite and separate for what are called 'sex-results' and they also fall sick and suffer, and ultimately like everything existing in which Objective Reason has not become fixed, they are destroyed forever.

"For the entire process of the existence of these infinitesimal beings of this smallest world, Time of a definite proportionate duration also ensues from all the surrounding phenomena which are manifested in the given 'cosmic-scale.'

"For them also, Time of definite length is required for the processes of their arising and formation as well as for various events in the process of their existence up to their complete final destruction.

"In the whole course of the process of existence of the beings of this drop of water also, corresponding sequential definite what are called 'passages' of the flow of Time are also required.

"A definite time is required for their joys and for their sorrows, and, in short, for every other kind of indispensable being-experiencing, down to what are called 'runs-of-bad-luck,' and even to 'periods-of-thirst-for-self-perfection.'

"I repeat, among them also, the process of the flow of Time has its harmonious sequence, and this sequence ensues from the totality of all the phenomena surrounding them.

"The duration of the process of the flow of Time is generally perceived and sensed in the same way by all the aforementioned cosmic Individuals and by the already completely formed what are called 'instinctivized' units but only with that difference which ensues from the difference in the presences and states, at the given moment, of these cosmic arisings.

"It must be noticed, however, my boy, that though for separate individuals existing in any independent cosmic unit, their definition of the flow of Time is not objective in the general sense, yet nevertheless for them themselves it acquires a sense of objectivity since the flow of Time is perceived by them according to the completeness of their own presence.

"The same drop of water which we have taken as an example can serve for a clearer understanding of this thought of mine.

"Although in the sense of general Universal Objectivity, the whole period of the process of the flow of Time in that same drop of water is for the whole of it subjective, yet for the beings existing in the drop of water itself, the said given flow of Time is perceived by them as objective.

"For the clarification of this, those beings called 'hypochondriacs' can serve, who exist among the three-brained beings of the planet Earth which has taken your fancy.

"To these terrestrial hypochondriacs it very often seems that Time passes infinitely slowly and long, and, as they express themselves, 'it-drags-phenomenally-tediously.'

"And so, exactly in the same way, it might also sometimes seem to some of the infinitesimal beings existing in that drop of water—assuming, of course, that there happen to be such hypochondriacs among them—that Time drags very slowly and 'phenomenally-tediously.'

"But actually from the point of view of the sensation of the duration of Time by your favorites of the planet Earth, the whole length of the existence of the 'beings-Microcosmoses' lasts only a few of their 'minutes' and sometimes even only a few of their 'seconds.'

"Now, in order that you may still better understand Time and its peculiarities, we may as well compare your age with the corresponding age of a being existing on that planet Earth.

"And for this comparing of ours we too must take the same standard unit of Time, which, as I have already told you, Objective Science employs for such calculations.

"Bear in mind, first of all, that according to the data about which you will also learn when I shall later have specially explained to you the fundamental laws of World-creation and World-maintenance, it is also established by the same Objective Science that in general all normal three-brained beings, and amongst them certainly even the beings arising on our planet Karatas, sense the sacred 'Egokoolnatsnarnian' action for the definition of Time forty-nine times more slowly than the same sacred action is sensed by the sacred Individuals dwelling on the Most Holy Sun Absolute.

"Consequently the process of the flow of Time for the three-brained beings of our Karatas flows forty-nine times more quickly than on the Sun Absolute, and thus it should flow also for the beings breeding on the planet Earth.

"And it is also calculated that during the period of Time in which the sun 'Samos' actualizes its nearest approach to the sun 'Selos,' which period of the flow of Time is considered a 'year' for the planet Karatas, the planet Earth actualizes in relation to its Sun 'Ors' three hundred and eighty-nine of its 'Krentonalnian-revolutions.'

"From which it follows that our 'year,' according to the conventionally objective time-calculation, is three hundred and eighty-nine times longer than that period of Time which your favorites consider and call their 'year.'

"It may not be without interest for you to know that all these calculations were partly explained to me by the Great Arch-Engineer of the Universe, His Measurability, Archangel Algamatant. MAY HE BE PERFECTED UNTO THE HOLY ANKLAD. . . .

"He explained this to me when, on the occasion of the first great misfortune to this planet Earth, he came to the planet Mars as one of the sacred members of the third Most Great Commission; and the captain of the trans-space ship *Omnipresent*, with whom I had several friendly talks during that journey, also partly explained it to me during my journey home.

"Now it must be further noticed that you, as a three-brained being who arose on the planet Karatas, are at the present time still only a boy of twelve years, and in respect of Being and of Reason, you are exactly like a boy of twelve on the planet Earth who has not yet been formed and who is not yet cognizant of himself—through which being-age all the three-brained beings arising there also live during the process of their growing up to the Being of a responsible being.

"All the 'features' of the whole of your psyche—what are called your 'character,' 'temperament,' 'inclinations,' and, in short, all the particularities of your psyche which are manifested exteriorly—are exactly the same as those of a still immature and pliant three-brained being there of the age of twelve years.

"And so, it follows from all that has been said that although according to our time-calculations you are still only like a boy of twelve there on the planet Earth who is not yet formed and not yet cognizant of himself, yet according to their subjective understanding and their being-sensations of the flow of Time, you have already existed by their time-calculation. not twelve years but the whole of four thousand six hundred and sixty-eight years.

"Thanks to all I have said, you will have material for the clarification of certain of those factors which were later the cause that the average proper normal duration of their existence began gradually to diminish and that it has now already become in the objective sense almost 'nothing.'

"Strictly speaking, this gradual diminution of the average length of the existence of the three-brained beings of that ill-fated planet, which has finally brought the whole of the duration of their existence to 'nothing,' did not have one cause but many and very varied causes.

"And among these many and varied causes the first and the chief one is of course that Nature had to adapt Herself correspondingly gradually to change their presences to those they now have.

"And concerning all the rest of the causes, Justice demands that I should first of all emphasize that on that ill-fated planet these causes might never have arisen had that first cause not occurred there, from which, at least in my opinion, they all chiefly ensued, though of course very gradually.

"Concerning all this you will understand in the course of further talks of mine about these three-brained beings, and meanwhile I will tell you only of the first and chief cause, namely, why and how Great Nature Herself was compelled to take stock of their presences and to form them into such new presences.

"You must first be told that there exist in the Universe generally two 'kinds' or two 'principles' of the duration of being-existence.

"The first kind or first 'principle' of being-existence, which is called 'Fulasnitamnian,' is proper to the existence of all three-brained beings arising on any planet of our Great Universe, and the fundamental aim and sense of the existence of these beings is that there must proceed through them the transmutation of cosmic substances necessary for what is called the 'common-cosmic Trogoautoegocratic-process.'

"And it is according to the second principle of being-existence that all one-brained and two-brained beings in general exist wherever they may arise. . . .

"And the sense and aim of the existence of these beings, also, consist in this, that there are transmuted through them the cosmic substances required not for purposes of a common-cosmic character, but only for that solar system or even only for that planet alone, in which and upon which these one-brained and two-brained beings arise.

"In any case, for the further elucidation of the strangeness of the psyche of those three-brained beings who have taken your fancy, you must know this also, that in the beginning, after the organ Kundabuffer with all its properties had been removed from their presences, the duration of their existence was according to the 'Fulasnitamnian' principle, that is to say, they were obliged to exist until there was coated in them and completely perfected by reason what is called the 'body-Kesdjan,' or, as they themselves later began to name this being-part of theirs—of which, by the way, contemporary beings know only by hearsay—the 'Astral-body.'

"And so, my boy, when later, for reasons of which you will learn in the course of my further tales, they began to exist already excessively abnormally, that is to say, quite unbecomingly for three-brained beings, and when in consequence of this they had on the one hand ceased to emanate the vibrations required by Nature for the maintenance of the separated fragments of their planet, and, on the other hand, had begun, owing to the chief peculiarity of their strange psyche, to destroy beings of other forms of their planet, thereby gradually diminishing the number of sources required for this purpose, then Nature Herself was compelled gradually to actualize the presences of these three-brained beings according to the second principle, namely, the principle 'Itoklanoz,' that is, to actualize them in the same way in which She actualizes one-brained and two-brained beings in order that the equilibrium of the vibrations required according to quality and quantity should be attained.

"As regards the meaning of the principle 'Itoklanoz,' I shall also specially explain it to you sometime.

"And meanwhile remember, that although the fundamental motives for the diminution of the duration of the existence of the three-brained beings of this planet were from causes not depending on them, yet nevertheless, subsequently, the main grounds for all the sad results were—and particularly now continue to be—the abnormal conditions of external ordinary being-existence established by them themselves. Owing to these conditions the duration of their existence has, down to the present time, continued to become shorter and shorter, and now is already diminished to such a degree that, at the present time, the difference between the duration of the process of the existence of the three-brained beings of other planets in the whole of the Universe and the duration of the process of the existence of the three-brained beings of the planet Earth has become the same as the difference between the real duration of their existence and the duration of the existence of the infinitesimal beings in that drop of water we took as an example.

"You now understand, my boy, that even the Most Great Heropass of Time has also been compelled to actualize obvious absurdities in the presences of these unfortunate three-brained beings who arise and exist on this ill-fated planet Earth.

"And thanks to all I have just explained to you, you can put yourself in the position of and understand the although merciless, yet always, and in everything, just Heropass."

Having said these last words Beelzebub became silent; and when he again spoke to his grandson, he said with a heavy sigh:

"Ekh . . . my dear boy!

"Later when I shall have told you more about the three-brained beings of that ill-fated planet Earth, you yourself will understand and form your own opinion about everything.

"You yourself will very well understand that although the fundamental causes of the whole chaos that now reigns on that ill-fated planet Earth were certain 'unforeseeingnesses,' coming from Above on the part of various Sacred Individuals, yet nevertheless the chief causes for the developing of further ills are only those abnormal conditions of ordinary being-existence which they themselves gradually established and which they continue to establish down to the present time.

"In any case, my dear boy, when you learn more about these favorites of yours, not only, I repeat, will you clearly see how pitiably small the duration of the existence of these unfortunates has gradually become in comparison with that normal duration of existence which has already long ago been established as a law for every kind of three-centered being of the whole of our Universe, but you will also understand that in these unfortunates, for the same reasons, there has gradually begun to disappear and at the present time are quite absent in them, any normal being-sensations whatever concerning any cosmic phenomenon.

"Although the beings of that ill-fated planet arose, according to conventionally objective time-reckoning, many decades ago, not only have they not as yet any being-sensation of cosmic phenomena such as it is proper to all three-centered beings of the whole of our Universe to have, but there is not in the Reason of these unfortunates even an approximate representation of the genuine causes of these phenomena.

"They have not an approximately correct representation even of those cosmic phenomena that proceed on their own planet round about them."

CHAPTER 17

The Arch-absurd
According to the Assertion of Beelzebub, Our Sun Neither Lights nor Heats

"In order, my dear Hassein, that you should meanwhile have an approximate representation also of just how far that function called 'the instinctive sensing of reality,' which is proper to every three-brained being of the whole of our Great Universe, is already entirely lacking in the presences of the three-centered beings breeding on the planet Earth, and especially in those of the most recent periods, it will be enough, to begin with, I think, if I explain to you only about how they understand and explain to themselves the causes why there periodically proceed on their planet those cosmic phenomena which they call 'daylight,' 'darkness,' 'heat,' 'cold,' and so on.

"All, without exception, of the three-brained beings of that planet who have attained the age of a responsible being, and even those many and various 'wiseacrings' existing there which they call 'sciences,' are categorically certain that all the said phenomena arrive on their planet completely, so to say, ready-made, 'd-i-r-e-c-t-l-y' from their own Sun . . . and as Mullah Nassr Eddin would say in such cases, 'no more hokeypokey about it.'

"What is most peculiar, in this case, is that, except for certain beings who existed before the second Transapalnian perturbation there, absolutely no doubt whatever concerning this certainty of theirs, has ever, as yet, crept into a single one of them.

"Not only has not a single one of them—having a Reason which, though strange, has nevertheless some resemblance to sane logic—ever yet doubted the causes of the said phenomena, but not a single one of them has manifested concerning these cosmic phenomena even that strange special property of their common psyche, which also became proper to the three-brained beings of that planet alone, and which is called 'to fantasy.'"

Having said these last words, Beelzebub, after a little while, with a bitter smile, continued to talk as follows:

"You, for instance, have the normal presence of a three-brained being, and within your presence there is intentionally 'implanted' from without, 'Oskiano,' or as they say there on the Earth, 'education,' which is founded on a morality based solely on the commandments and indications of the UNI-BEING HIMSELF and the Most Holy Individuals near to Him. And yet, if you should chance to be there among them, you would be unable to prevent the process in yourself of the 'being-Nerhitrogool,' that is, the process which, again there on the Earth, is called 'irrepressible inner laughter'; that is to say, you would not be able to restrain yourself from such laughter, if in some way or another, they were suddenly clearly to sense and understand, without any doubt whatever, that not only does nothing like 'light,' 'darkness,' 'heat,' and so on, come to their planet from their Sun itself, but that their supposed 'source of heat and light' is itself almost always freezing cold like the 'hairless-dog' of our highly esteemed Mullah Nassr Eddin.

"In reality, the surface of their 'Source-of-Heat,' like that of all the ordinary suns of our Great Universe, is perhaps more covered with ice than the surface of what they call their 'North Pole.'

"Surely this 'hearth-of-heat' itself would rather borrow heat, if only a little, from some other source of 'cosmic-substance,' than send a part of its own heat to any other planet, especially to that planet which, though it belongs to its system, yet in consequence of the splitting off from it of a whole side, became a 'lopsided monstrosity' and is now already a source of 'offensive-shame' for that poor system 'Ors.'

"But do you yourself know, my boy, in general how and why in the atmosphere of certain planets during Trogoautoegocratic processes, there proceed those 'kshtatzavacht,' 'kldazacht,' 'tainolair,' 'paischakir,' and other such phenomena, which your favorites call 'daylight,' 'darkness,' 'cold,' 'heat,' and so on?" Beelzebub asked Hassein.

"If you don't clearly understand, I shall explain this also to you a little.

"Although I have promised to explain to you, only later, all the fundamental laws of World-creation and World-maintenance in detail, yet the necessity has here arisen, to touch upon, if only briefly, the questions concerning these cosmic laws, without waiting for that special talk I promised.

"And this is necessary, in order that you may be able better to take in all that we are now talking about, and also in order that what I have already told you may be transubstantiated in you in the right way.

"It is necessary to say, first of all, that everything in the Universe, both the intentionally created and the later automatically arisen, exists and is maintained exclusively on the basis of what is called the 'common-cosmic Trogoautoegocratic-process.'

"This Most Great common-cosmic Trogoautoegocratic-process was actualized by our ENDLESS UNI-BEING, when our Most Great and Most Holy Sun Absolute had already existed, on which our ALL-GRACIOUS ENDLESS CREATOR had and still has the chief place of His existence.

"This system, which maintains everything arisen and existing, was actualized by our ENDLESS CREATOR in order that what is called the 'exchange of substances' or the

'Reciprocal-feeding' of everything that exists, might proceed in the Universe and thereby that the merciless 'Heropass' might not have its maleficent effect on the Sun Absolute.

"This same Most Great common-cosmic Trogoautoegocratic-process is actualized always and in everything on the basis of the two fundamental cosmic laws, the first of which is called the 'Fundamental-First-degree-Sacred-Heptaparaparshinokh,' and the second the 'Fundamental-First-degree-Sacred-Triamazikamno.'

"Owing to these two fundamental sacred cosmic laws, there first arise from the substance called 'Etherokrilno,' under certain conditions, what are called 'crystallizations'; and from these crystallizations, but later, and also under certain conditions, there are formed various large and small, more or less independent, cosmic definite formations.

"It is just within and upon these cosmic definite formations that the processes of what are called the involution and evolution of the already formed concentrations and also of the said crystallizations take place—of course also according to the two said fundamental sacred laws—and all the results obtained from those processes in atmospheres, and further, by means of these atmospheres themselves, blend and go for the actualizing of the said 'exchange-of-matters' for the purposes of the Most Great common-cosmic Trogoautoegocrat.

"Etherokrilno is that prime-source substance with which the whole Universe is filled, and which is the basis for the arising and maintenance of everything existing.

"Not only is this Etherokrilno the basis for the arising of all cosmic concentrations without exception, both large and small, but also all cosmic phenomena in general proceed during some transformation in this same fundamental cosmic substance as well as during the processes of the involution and evolution of various crystallizations—or, as your favorites say, of those active elements—which have obtained and still continue to obtain their prime arising from this same fundamental prime-source cosmic substance.

"Bear in mind, here, that it is just because of this that the mentioned Objective Science says that 'everything without exception in the Universe is material.'

"You must also know further, that only one cosmic crystallization, existing under the name 'Omnipresent-Okidanokh,' obtains its prime arising—although it also is crystallized from Etherokrilno—from the three Holy sources of the sacred Theomertmalogos, that is, from the emanation of the Most Holy Sun Absolute.

"Everywhere in the Universe, this 'Omnipresent-Okidanokh' or 'Omnipresent-Active-Element' takes part in the formation of all both great and small arisings, and is, in general, the fundamental cause of most of the cosmic phenomena and, in particular, of the phenomena proceeding in the atmospheres.

"In order that you may be able to understand, at least approximately, concerning this Omnipresent-Okidanokh also, I must tell you, first of all, that the second fundamental cosmic law—the Sacred Triamazikamno—consists of three independent forces, that is to say, this sacred law manifests in everything, without exception, and everywhere in the Universe, in three separate independent aspects.

"And these three aspects exist in the Universe under the following denominations:

"The first, under the denomination, the 'Holy-Affirming';

"The second, the 'Holy-Denying'; and

"The third, the 'Holy-Reconciling.'

"And this is also why, concerning this sacred law and its three independent forces, the said Objective Science has, among its formulations, specially concerning this sacred law, the following: 'A law which always flows into a consequence and becomes the cause of subsequent consequences, and always functions by three independent and quite opposite characteristic manifestations, latent within it, in properties neither seen nor sensed.'

"Our sacred Theomertmalogos also, that is, the prime emanation of our Most Holy Sun Absolute, acquires just this same lawfulness at its prime arising; and, during its further actualizations, gives results in accordance with it.

"And so, my boy, the Omnipresent-Okidanokh obtains its prime arising in space outside of the Most Holy Sun Absolute itself, from the blending of these three independent forces into one, and during its further involutions it is correspondingly changed, in respect of what is called the 'Vivifyingness of Vibrations' according to its passage through what are called the 'Stopinders' or 'gravity-centers' of the fundamental 'common-cosmic sacred Heptaparaparshinokh.'

"I repeat, among the number of other already definite cosmic crystallizations, the Omnipresent-Okidanokh unfailingly always participates in both large and small cosmic formations, wherever and under whatever external surrounding conditions they may arise in the Universe.

"This 'common-cosmic Unique-Crystallization' or 'Active-Element' has several peculiarities proper to this element alone, and it is chiefly owing to these peculiarities proper to it that the majority of cosmic phenomena proceed, including, among other things, the said phenomena that take place in the atmosphere of certain planets.

"Of these peculiarities proper to the Omnipresent-Active-Element alone, there are several, but it is enough, for the theme of our talk, if we become acquainted just with two of them.

"The first peculiarity is that when a new cosmic unit

is being concentrated, then the 'Omnipresent-Active-Element' does not blend, as a whole, with such a new arising, nor is it transformed as a whole in any definite corresponding place—as happens with every other cosmic crystallization in all the said cosmic formations—but immediately on entering as a whole into any cosmic unit, there immediately occurs in it what is called 'Djartklom,' that is to say, it is dispersed into the three fundamental sources from which it obtained its prime arising, and only then do these sources, each separately, give the beginning for an independent concentration of three separate corresponding formations within the given cosmic unit. And in this way, this 'Omnipresent-Active-Element' actualizes at the outset, in every such new arising, the sources for the possible manifestation of its own sacred law of Triamazikamno.

"It must without fail be noticed also, that in every cosmic formation, the said separated sources, both for the perception and for the further utilization of this property of the 'Omnipresent-Active-Element' for the purpose of the corresponding actualizing, exist and continue to have the possibility of functioning as long as the given cosmic unit exists.

"And only after the said cosmic unit has been completely destroyed do these holy sources of the sacred Triamazikamno, localized in the 'Omnipresent-Active-Element-Okidanokh,' reblend and they are again transformed into 'Okidanokh,' but having now another quality of Vivifyingness of Vibrations.

"As regards the second peculiarity of the 'Omnipresent-Okidanokh,' equally proper to it alone, and which it is also necessary for us to elucidate just now for the given theme of our talk, you will be able to understand about that, only if you know something concerning one fundamental cosmic second-degree law, existing in the Universe, under the denomination of the 'Sacred Aieioiuoa.'

"And this cosmic law is, that there proceeds within every arising large and small, when in direct touch with the emanations either of the Sun Absolute itself or of any other sun, what is called 'Remorse,' that is, a process when every part that has arisen from the results of any one Holy Source of the Sacred Triamazikamno, as it were, 'revolts' and 'criticizes' the former unbecoming perceptions and the manifestations at the moment of another part of its whole—a part obtained from the results of another Holy Source of the same fundamental sacred Cosmic Law of Triamazikamno.

"And this sacred process 'Aieioiuoa' or 'Remorse' always proceeds with the 'Omnipresent-Active-Element-Okidanokh' also.

"The peculiarity of this latter during this sacred process is that while the direct action either of the sacred Theomertmalogos or the emanation of any ordinary sun is round about the whole of its presence, this Active-Element is dispersed into its three prime parts which then exist almost independently, and when the said direct action ceases, these parts blend again and then continue to exist as a whole.

"Here you might as well, I think, be told, by the way, about an interesting fact I noticed, which occurred in the history of their existence concerning the strangeness of the psyche of the ordinary three-brained beings of that planet which has taken your fancy, in respect of what they call their 'scientific-speculations.'

"And that is, that during the period of my many-centuried observation and study of their psyche I had occasion to constate several times that though 'science' appeared among them almost from the very beginning of their arising, and, it may be said, periodically, like everything else there, rose to a more or less high degree of perfection, and that though during these and other periods, many millions of three-brained beings called there 'scientists' must have arisen and been again destroyed, yet with the single exception of a certain Chinese man named Choon-Kil-Tez, about whom I shall tell you later in detail, not once has the thought entered the head of a single one of them there that between these two cosmic phenomena which they call 'emanation' and 'radiation' there is any difference whatever.

"Not a single one of those 'sorry-scientists' has ever thought that the difference between these two cosmic processes is just about the same as that which the highly esteemed Mullah Nassr Eddin once expressed in the following words:

"'They are as much alike as the beard of the famous English Shakespeare and the no less famous French Armagnac.'

"For the further clarification of the phenomena taking place in the atmospheres and concerning the 'Omnipresent-Active-Element' in general, you must know and remember this also, that during the periods when, owing to the sacred process 'Aieioiuoa,' 'Djartklom' proceeds in the Okidanokh, then there is temporarily released from it the proportion of the pure—that is, absolutely unblended—Etherokrilno which unfailingly enters into all cosmic formations and there serves, as it were, for connecting all the active elements of these formations; and afterwards when its three fundamental parts reblend, then the said proportion of Etherokrilno is re-established.

"Now, it is necessary to touch also, of course again only briefly, on another question, namely, what relation the 'Omnipresent-Active-Element-Okidanokh' has to the common presence of beings of every kind, and what are the cosmic results actualized owing to it.

"It is chiefly necessary to touch upon this question because you will then have still another very striking and illuminating fact for the better understanding of the difference between the various brain-systems of beings, namely, the systems called 'one-brained,' 'two-brained,' and 'three-brained.'

"Know first that, in general, every such cosmic formation called 'brain' receives its formation from those crystallizations the affirming source for whose arising, according to the sacred Triamazikamno, is one or another of the corresponding holy forces of the fundamental sacred Triamazikamno, localized in the Omnipresent-Okidanokh. And the further actualizings of the same holy forces proceed by means of the presences of the beings, just through those localizations.

"I shall sometime in the future specially explain to you about the process itself of the arising of these corresponding being-brains in the presences of beings, but meanwhile let us talk, though not in detail, about the results the Omnipresent-Okidanokh actualizes by means of these being-brains.

"The Omnipresent-Active-Element-Okidanokh enters into the presences of beings through all the three kinds of being-food.

"And this proceeds because, as I have already told you, this same Okidanokh obligatorily participates in the formation of all kinds of products which serve as all three being-foods and is always contained in the presence of these products.

"And so, my boy, the chief peculiarity of the Omnipresent-Okidanokh, in the given case, is that the process of 'Djartklom' proceeds in it within the presence of every being also but not from being in contact with the emanations of any large cosmic concentration; but the factors for this process in the presences of beings are either the results of the conscious processes of 'Partkdolg-duty' on the part of the beings themselves—about which processes I shall also explain to you in detail later—or of that process of Great Nature Herself which exists in the Universe under the name 'Kerkoolnonarnian-actualization,' which process means 'The-obtaining-of-the-required-totality-of-vibrations-by-adaptation.'

"This latter process proceeds in beings absolutely without the participation of their consciousness.

"In both cases when Okidanokh enters into the presence of a being and the process of Djartklom proceeds in it, then each of its fundamental parts blends with those perceptions which correspond with it according to what is called 'Kindred-vibrations' and which are present in the being at the moment, and further, these parts are concentrated upon the corresponding localization, that is, upon the corresponding brain.

"And these blendings are called 'being-Impulsakri.'

"It is necessary to notice further that these localizations or brains in beings serve not only as apparatuses for the transformation of corresponding cosmic substances for the purposes of the Most Great common-cosmic Trogoautoegocrat, but also as the means for beings whereby their conscious self-perfecting is possible.

"This latter aim depends upon the quality of the presence of the 'being-Impulsakri' concentrated, or, as is otherwise said, deposited, upon the said corresponding being-brains.

"Concerning the qualities of being-Impulsakri, there is among the direct commandments of our ALL-EMBRACING ENDLESSNESS even a special commandment, which is very strictly carried out by all three-brained beings of our Great Universe, and which is expressed in the following words: 'Always guard against such perceptions as may soil the purity of your brains.'

"Three-brained beings have the possibility personally to perfect themselves, because in them there are localized three centers of their common presence or three brains, upon which afterwards, when the process of Djartklom proceeds in the Omnipresent-Okidanokh, the three holy forces of the sacred Triamazikamno are deposited and acquire the possibility for their further, this time, independent actualizings.

"Just in this is the point, that the beings having this three-brained system can, by the conscious and intentional fulfilling of being-Partkdolg-duty, utilize from this process of Djartklom in the Omnipresent-Okidanokh, its three holy forces for their own presences and bring their presences to what is called the 'Sekronoolanzaknian-state'; that is to say, they can become such individuals as have their own sacred law of Triamazikamno and thereby the possibility of consciously taking in and coating in their common presence all that 'Holy' which, incidentally, also aids the actualizing of the functioning in these cosmic units of Objective or Divine Reason.

"But the great terror of it, my boy, lies just in this, that although in those three-brained beings who have interested you and who breed on the planet Earth, there arise and are present in them, up to the time of their complete destruction, these three independent localizations or three being-brains, through which separately all the three holy forces of the sacred Triamazikamno which they might also utilize for their own self-perfecting are transformed and go for further corresponding actualizations, yet, chiefly on account of the irregular conditions of ordinary being-existence established by them themselves, these possibilities beat their wings in vain.

"It is interesting to note that the said being-brains are found in the same parts of the planetary body of these three-brained beings who arise on the planet Earth as in us, namely:

"1. The brain predetermined by Great Nature for the concentration and further actualizing of the first holy force of the sacred Triamazikamno, called the Holy-Affirming, is localized and found in the head.

"2. The second brain, which transforms and crystallizes the second holy force of the sacred Triamazikamno, namely, the Holy-Denying, is placed in their common presences, also as in us, along the whole of their back in what is called the 'spinal column.'

"3. But as regards the place of concentration and source for the further manifestation of the third holy force of the sacred Triamazikamno, namely, the Holy-Reconciling—the exterior form of this being-brain in the three-brained beings there bears no resemblance whatever to ours.

"It must be remarked that in the primordial three-brained beings there, this said being-brain was localized in the same part of their planetary body as in us and had an exterior form exactly similar to our own; but for many reasons which you will be able to understand for yourself during the course of my further talks, Great Nature was compelled little by little to regenerate this brain and to give it the form which it now has in the contemporary beings.

"This being-brain in the contemporary three-brained beings there is not localized in one common mass, as is proper to the presences of all the other three-brained beings of our Great Universe, but is localized in parts, according to what is called 'Specific Functioning,' and each such part is localized in a different place of their whole planetary body.

"But although, in its exterior form, this being-center of theirs has now variously placed concentrations, nevertheless all its separate functionings are correspondingly connected with each other, so that the sum total of these scattered parts can function exactly as in general it is proper for it to function.

"They themselves call these separate localizations in their common presence 'nerve nodes.'

"It is interesting to notice that most of the separate parts of this being-brain are localized in them, just in that place of their planetary body where such a normal being-brain should be, namely, in the region of their breast, and the totality of these nerve-nodes in their breast, they call the 'Solar Plexus.'

"And so, my boy, the process of Djartklom in the Omnipresent-Okidanokh proceeds in the presence of each of these favorites of yours, and in them also, all its three holy forces are blended independently with other cosmic crystallizations, and go for the corresponding actualizations, but as, chiefly owing to the already mentioned abnormal conditions of being-existence gradually established by them themselves, they have entirely ceased to fulfill being-Partkdolg-duty, then, in consequence of this, none of those holy sources of everything existing, with the exception of the denying source alone, is transubstantiated for their own presences.

"The crystallizations arising in their presences from the first and from the third holy forces go almost entirely for the service only of the common-cosmic Trogoautoegocratic-process, while for the coating of their own presences there are only the crystallizations of the second part of the Omnipresent-Okidanokh, namely, of the 'Holy-Denying'; and hence it is that the majority of them remain with presences consisting of the planetary body alone, and thus are, for themselves, destroyed forever.

"As regards all the peculiarities proper to the omnipresent everywhere-penetrating Active-Element-Okidanokh alone, and also as regards the further results which these peculiarities actualize, you will have a complete representation of them only after I shall have explained to you in more or less detail, as I have already promised, about the fundamental laws of World-creation and World-maintenance.

"But meanwhile I shall tell you about those elucidating experiments concerning this Omnipresent cosmic crystallization at which I was personally present.

"But I must tell you that I was an eyewitness of these said elucidating experiments, not on that planet Earth which has taken your fancy—nor did your favorites make them—but on the planet Saturn where they were made by that three-brained being who during almost the whole period of my exile in that solar system was my real friend, about whom I recently promised to tell you a little more in detail."

CHAPTER 18

The Arch-preposterous

Beelzebub continued as follows:

"The cause of my first meeting with that three-centered being who subsequently became my essence-friend and by whom I saw the said experiments with the Omnipresent-Okidanokh, was as follows.

"That you may better represent to yourself the events of this tale of mine, you must first of all know that at the beginning of my exile to that solar system, certain corresponding essence-friends of mine who had not taken part in those events from which the causes of my exile had issued, performed concerning my personality that sacred process which exists in the Universe under the name of the 'Sacred Vznooshlitzval,' that is to say, concerning my personality there was implanted in the presences of those three-brained beings by means of another sacred process called 'Askalnooazar,' that which Objective Science defines by the notion, 'Trust-another-like-yourself.'

"Well, then, just after my arrival in that solar system Ors, when I began visiting its various planets and first descended upon the surface of the planet Saturn, it turned out in connection with the aforesaid, that one of the beings who had undergone the sacred action of 'Vznooshlitzval' regarding my person was what is called there the 'Harahrahroohry' of all the three-centered beings arising and existing on the planet Saturn.

"On the planet Saturn a being is called the 'Harahrahroohry' who is the sole chief over all the other beings on that planet.

"Similar beings-chiefs exist also on all the other planets upon which three-brained beings breed; they are differently named on different planets; and on your planet Earth such a chief is called a 'King.'

"The only difference is that while everywhere else, even on all the other planets of the same system, there is one such king for the whole of the given planet, on your peculiar planet Earth there is a separate king for every accidentally segregated group of these favorites of yours and sometimes even several.

"Well, then:

"When I first descended on the surface of the planet Saturn and mingled with the three-centered beings there, it chanced that I had occasion the next day to meet the Harahrahroohry himself of the planet Saturn; and during what is called our 'Exchange-of-subjective-opinions' he invited me to make his own 'Harhoory,' that is, his own palace, the chief place of my existence during the whole of my sojourn on their planet.

"And this I did.

"So, my boy, when we were once talking simply according to the flow of what is called 'being-associative-mentation,' and happened to touch on the question, among other things, of the strange results actualized in the manifestations of the particularities of the Omnipresent-Okidanokh, the venerable Harahrahroohry of the planet Saturn first mentioned that one of his learned beings-subjects, by name Harharkh, had recently devised for the elucidation of many of the previously unexplained properties of that cosmic substance, an exceedingly interesting appliance which he called a 'Rhaharahr,' the chief demonstrating part of which he called a 'Hrhaharhtzaha.'

"And further, he offered to make, if I wished, the necessary arrangements for showing me all these new inventions and for giving me every possible explanation of them.

"The result of it all was that the following day, escorted by one of that venerable Harahrahroohry's court, I went to the place of existence of that Gornahoor Harharkh where I first saw those novel elucidatory experiments with the Omnipresent-Okidanokh.

"Gornahoor Harharkh, who afterwards, as I have already told you, became my essence-friend, was then considered one of the foremost scientists among the ordinary three-brained beings of the whole Universe, and all his constatations as well as the elucidatory apparatuses he had invented were everywhere widespread, and other learned beings on the various planets were using them more and more.

"Here it will do no harm to remark that I also, thanks only to his learning, had later in my observatory on the planet Mars that Teskooano which, when it was finally established, enabled my sight to perceive, or as is said, 'approach-the-visibility' of remote cosmic concentrations, 7,000,285 times.

"Strictly speaking, it was owing to just this Teskooano that my observatory was afterwards considered one of the best constructions of its kind in the whole Universe; and, most important of all, it was by means of this Teskooano that I myself thereafter could, even while staying at home on the planet Mars, relatively easily see and observe the processes of the existence occurring on the surfaces of those parts of the other planets of that solar system which, in accordance with what is called the 'common-cosmic Harmonious-Movement,' could be perceived by being-sight at the given moment.

"When Gornahoor Harharkh was informed who we were and why we had come, he approached us and forthwith very amiably began his explanations.

"Before beginning his explanations I think it not inadvisable to warn you once and for all that all my conversations with various three-centered beings arising and existing on various planets of that system where I was obliged to exist for the 'Sins of my youth'—as for instance in the present case, the conversations with this Gornahoor Harharkh which I am now about to relate to you while we travel on the space-ship *Karnak*—all proceeded in dialects still quite unknown to you, and sometimes even, by the way, in such dialects the consonances of which were quite 'indigestible' for perception by normal being-functions assigned for this purpose.

"And so, my boy, in view of all this, I shall not repeat these conversations word for word but shall give you only their sense in our speech, continuing of course to employ those terms and 'specific-names' or rather those consonances produced by what are called 'being-vocal-chords,' which consonances are used by your favorites of the planet Earth and which have now become for you, owing to continued repetition during my tales about them, habitual and easily perceived.

"Yes . . . it must be noticed here that the word 'Gornahoor' is used by the three-brained beings on the planet Saturn in courtesy; they utter it before the name of one whom they are addressing.

"It is the same with your favorites on the planet Earth. They also have added to the name of every person the word 'Mister' or sometimes a whole meaningless phrase expressing the notion for which our honorable Mullah Nassr Eddin has the following sentence:

"And namely he says:

"'Nevertheless, there's more reality in it than in the wiseacrings of an "expert" in monkey-business.'

"Well, then, my boy . . .

"When this subsequent essence-friend of mine, Gornahoor Harharkh, was informed of what was required of him, he invited us by a sign to approach one of the special appliances which he had made and which, as it later turned out, was named by him 'Hrhaharhtzaha.'

"When we were nearer the said special and very strange construction, he pointed to it with a particular feather of his right wing and said:

"'This special appliance is the principal part of the whole of my new invention; and it is just in this that the results are revealed and shown of almost all the peculiarities of the Omnipresent-World-substance-Okidanokh.'

"And, pointing to all the other special appliances also present in the 'Khrh,' he added:

"'I succeeded in obtaining extremely important elucidations concerning the omnipresent and everywhere penetrating Okidanokh, because thanks to all these separate special appliances of my invention, it became possible, first to obtain all three fundamental parts of the Omnipresent-Okidanokh from every kind of sur- and intraplanetary process and then artificially to blend them into a whole, and secondly, also artificially to disassociate them and elucidate the specific properties of each part separately in its manifestations.'

"Having said this, he again pointed to the Hrhaharhtzaha and added that by means of the elucidating apparatus, not only can any ordinary being clearly understand the details of the properties of the three absolutely independent parts—which in their manifestations have nothing in common—of the whole 'Unique-Active-Element,' the particularities of which are the chief cause of everything existing in the Universe, but also any ordinary being can become categorically convinced that no results of any kind normally obtained from the processes occurring through this Omnipresent World-substance can ever be perceived by beings or sensed by them; certain being-functions, however, can perceive only those results of the said processes which proceed for some reason or other abnormally, on account of causes coming from without and issuing either from conscious sources or from accidental mechanical results.

"The part of Gornahoor Harharkh's new invention which he himself called the Hrhaharhtzaha and regarded as the most important was in appearance very much like the 'Tirzikiano' or, as your favorites would say, a 'huge-electric-lamp.'

"The interior of this special structure was rather like a smallish room with a door that could be hermetically closed.

"The walls of this original construction were made of a certain transparent material, the appearance of which reminded me of that which on your planet is called 'glass.'

"As I learned later, the chief particularity of this said transparent material was that, although by means of the organ of sight beings could perceive through it the visibility of every kind of cosmic concentration, yet no rays of any kind, whatever the causes they may have arisen from, could pass through it, either from within out or from without in.

"As I looked at this part of this said astonishing being-invention, I could through its transparent walls clearly distinguish inside in the center what seemed to be a table and two chairs; hanging above the table, what is called an 'electric-lamp'; and underneath it three 'things' exactly alike, each resembling the 'Momonodooar.'

"On the table and by the side of it, stood or lay several different apparatuses and instruments unknown to me.

"Later it became clear that the said objects contained in this Hrhaharhtzaha, as well as everything we had later to put on, were made of special materials invented by this Gornahoor Harharkh.

"And as regards these materials also, I shall explain a little more in detail at the proper time in the course of my further explanations concerning Gornahoor Harharkh.

"Meanwhile bear in mind that in the enormous Khrh

or workshop of Gornahoor Harharkh there were, besides the already mentioned Hrhaharhtzaha, several other large independent appliances, and among them two quite special what are called 'Lifechakans' which Gornahoor himself called 'Krhrrhihirhi.'

"It is interesting to note that your favorites also have something like this 'Lifechakan' or 'Krhrrhihirhi'; and they name such an apparatus a 'dynamo.'

"There was also there, apart, another independent large appliance, which, as it afterwards appeared, was a 'Soloohnorahoona' of special construction, or as your favorites would say, a 'pump-of-complex-construction-for-exhausting-atmosphere-to-the-point-of-absolute-vacuum.'

"While I was looking over all this with surprise, Gornahoor Harharkh himself approached the said pump of special construction and with his left wing moved one of its parts, owing to which a certain mechanism began to work in the pump. He then approached us again and, pointing with the same special feather of his right wing to the largest Lifechakan, or Krhrrhihirhi, or dynamo, further continued his explanations.

"He said, 'By means of this special appliance, there are first "sucked-in" separately from the atmosphere, or from any intra- or surplanetary formation, all the three independent parts of the Omnipresent-Active-Element-Okidanokh present in it, and only afterwards when in a certain way these separate independent parts are artificially reblended in the Krhrrhihirhi into a single whole, does the Okidanokh, now in its usual state, flow and is it concentrated there, in that "container"'—saying which, he again with the same special feather pointed to something very much like what is called a 'generator.'

"'And then from there,' he said, 'Okidanokh flows here into another Krhrrhihirhi or dynamo where it undergoes the process of Djartklom, and each of its separate parts is concentrated there in those other containers'—and this time he pointed to what resembled 'accumulators'—'and only then do I take from the secondary containers, by means of various artificial appliances, each active part of Okidanokh separately for my elucidatory experiments.

"'I shall first demonstrate to you,' he continued, 'one of the results which occur when, for some reason or other, one of the active parts of the Omnipresent-Okidanokh is absent during the process of their "striving-to-reblend" into a whole.

"'At the present moment this special construction contains a space which is indeed an absolute vacuum, obtained, it must be said, only owing firstly to the special construction of the suction pump and to the materials of special quality of which the instruments are made, which alone make experiments possible in an absolute vacuum; and secondly, to the properties and the strength of the material of which the walls of this part of my new invention are made.'

"Having said this, he pulled another lever and again continued:

"'Owing to the pulling of this lever, that process has begun in this vacuum whereby in the separate parts of the Omnipresent-Okidanokh there proceeds what is called the "striving-to-reblend-into-a-whole."

"'But since, intentionally by an "able-Reason"—in the present case myself—the participation of that third part of Okidanokh existing under the name of "Parijrahatnatioose" is artificially excluded from the said process, then this process proceeds there just now between only two of its parts, namely, between those two independent parts which science names "Anodnatious" and "Cathodnatious." And in consequence, instead of the obligatory law-conformable results of the said process, that non-law-conformable result is now actualized which exists under the denomination of "the-result-of-the-process-of-the-reciprocal-destruction-of-two-opposite-forces," or as ordinary beings express it, "the-cause-of-artificial-light."

"'The "striving-to-reblend-into-a-whole" of two active parts of the Omnipresent-Okidanokh, which is proceeding at the present moment there in this vacuum, has a force, as calculated by objective science, of 3,040,000 what are called "volts," and this force is indicated by the needle of that special appliance there.'

"Pointing to a 'something' very much like the apparatus existing also on your planet and called there 'voltmeter' he said:

"'One of the advantages of this new invention of mine for the demonstration of the given phenomenon is that in spite of the unusual power of the process of the "force-of-striving," now proceeding there, the what are called "Salnichizinooarnian-momentum-vibrations," which most beings consider also to be "rays," and which ought to be obtained and to issue from this process, do not issue out of the place of their arising, that is, out of this construction in which the particularities of the Omnipresent-Okidanokh are being elucidated.

"'And in order that the beings who are outside of this part of my invention may nevertheless also have the possibility of elucidating the force of the given process, I intentionally made the composition of the material of the wall in one place such that it has the property of permitting the passage through it of the said "Salnichizinooarnian-momentum-vibrations" or "rays."'

"Having said this, he approached nearer to the Hrahaharhtzaha and pressed a certain button. The result was that the whole of the enormous Khrh or 'workshop' was suddenly so strongly lit up that our organs of sight temporarily ceased to function, and only after a considerable time had passed could we with great difficulty raise our eyelids and look around.

"When we had recovered and Gornahoor Harharkh had pulled still another lever, which resulted in the whole surrounding space being restored to its former usual appearance, he first, with his customary angel-voice, again drew our attention to the 'voltmeter,' the needle of which constantly indicated the same figure, and then continued:

"'You see that, although the process of the clash of two opposite component parts of the Omnipresent-Okidanokh, of the same power of "force-of-striving" still continues, and that the part of the surface of this construction which has the property of admitting the passage of the said "rays" is still open, yet in spite of all this there is no longer the phenomenon which ordinary beings define by the phrase "the-causes-of-artificial-light."

"'And this phenomenon is no longer there, only because by my last pulling of a certain lever, I introduced into the process of the clash of two component parts of Okidanokh, a current of the third independent component part of Okidanokh, which began to blend proportionally with its other two parts, owing to which the result derived from this kind of blending of the three component parts of the Omnipresent-Okidanokh—unlike the process of the non-lawconformable blending of its two parts—cannot be perceived by beings with any of their being-functions.'

"After all these explanations of his, Gornahoor Harharkh then proposed that I should venture to enter with him that demonstrating part itself of his new invention, in order that I might become, there within, an eyewitness of many particular manifestations of the Omnipresent and everything-penetrating Active-Element.

"Of course, without thinking long about it, I immediately decided and gave him my consent.

"And I immediately decided, chiefly because I expected

to obtain in my being unchangeable and imperishable 'objective-essence-satisfaction.'

"When this future essence-friend of mine had my consent, he at once gave the necessary orders to one of his assistants.

"It appeared that for the actualization of what he proposed, various preparations had first to be made.

"First of all his assistants put on Gornahoor Harharkh and myself some special, very heavy suits, resembling those which your favorites call 'diving suits' but with many small heads of what are called 'bolts' projecting, and when these extremely peculiar suits had been put on us, his assistants screwed up the heads of these bolts in a certain order.

"On the inner side of these diving suits, at the ends of the bolts, there were, it appeared, special plates which pressed against parts of our planetary body in a certain way.

"It later also became quite clear to me that this was necessary, in order that there might not occur to our planetary bodies what is called 'Taranooranura,' or, as it might otherwise be said, in order that our planetary bodies should not fall to pieces as usually occurs to sur- and intraplanetary formations of every kind when they happen to come into an entirely atmosphereless space.

"In addition to these special suits, they placed on our heads a 'something' resembling what is called a 'diver's helmet,' but with very complicated, what are called 'connectors' projecting from them.

"One of these connectors, which was called the 'Harhrinhrarh,' meaning 'sustainer-of-the-pulsation,' was something long, like a rubber tube. One end of it, by means of complicated appliances on the helmet itself, was hermetically attached to the corresponding place of the helmet for the breathing organs, while the other end, after we had already entered that strange Hrhaharhtzaha, was screwed to an apparatus there, which was connected in its turn with the space, the 'presence' of which corresponded to the second being-food.

"Between Gornahoor Harharkh and myself there was also a special connector, through which we could easily communicate with each other while we were inside the Hrhaharhtzaha, from which the atmosphere was pumped out to make a vacuum.

"One end of this connector also, by means of appliances that were on the helmets, was fitted in a certain way to what are called my organs of 'hearing' and 'speech,' and the other end was fitted to the same organs of Gornahoor Harharkh.

"Thus, by means of this connector between my subsequent essence-friend and myself, there was set up, as again your favorites would say, a peculiar 'telephone.'

"Without this appliance we could not have communicated with each other in any way, chiefly because Gornahoor Harharkh was at that time still a being with a presence perfected only up to the state called the 'Sacred Inkozarno'; and a being with such a presence not only cannot manifest himself in an absolutely empty space, but he cannot even exist in it, even though the products of all the three being-foods be artificially introduced into him in such a space.

"But the most 'curious' and, as it is said, the most 'cunningly ingenious' of all the connectors there for various purposes on those strange diving suits and helmets was the connector created by that great scientist Gornahoor Harharkh to enable the 'organ-of-sight' of ordinary beings to perceive the visibility of all kinds of surrounding objects in an 'absolutely-empty-space.'

"One end of this astonishing connector was fitted in a certain way, also by means of appliances on the helmets, to our temples, while the other end was joined to what is called the 'Amskomoutator,' which in its turn was joined in a certain way by means of what are called 'wires' to all the objects within the Hrhaharhtzaha as well as to those outside, namely, to those objects whose visibility was needed during the experiments.

"It is very interesting to notice here that to each end of that appliance—a creation almost incredible for ordinary three-centered-being-Reason—two independent connectors, also of wire, were led, and through them, what are called special magnetic currents flowed from outside.

"As it was afterwards explained to me in detail, these connectors and the said special 'magnetic-currents' had, it seems, been created by that truly great scientist Gornahoor Harharkh in order that the presences of learned three-centered beings—even those not perfected to the Sacred Inkozarno—might, owing to one property of the 'magnetic current,' be 'reflected' for their own essences and that, owing to another property of this current, the presence of the mentioned objects might also be 'reflected,' so that thereby the perception of the reality of the said objects might be actualized by their imperfect organs of being-sight in a vacuum containing none of these factors or those results of various cosmic concentrations which have received such vibrations, from the actualization of which alone the functioning of any being-organ whatsoever is possible.

"Having fitted upon us the said very heavy appliances for enabling beings to exist in a sphere not corresponding for them, the assistants of this, then still great all-universal scientist Gornahoor Harharkh, with the help again of special appliances, carried us into the Hrhaharhtzaha itself; and having screwed up all the free ends of the connectors projecting from us to the corresponding apparatuses in the Hrhaharhtzaha itself, went out and hermetically closed behind them the only way by which it was still possible, if at all, to have any communication with what is called the 'Everything-representing-one-world.'

"When we were alone in the Hrhaharhtzaha itself, Gornahoor Harharkh, after turning one of what are called 'switches' there, said:

"'The work of the "pump" has already begun, and soon it will have pumped out all the results here without exception of those cosmic processes, whatever they may be, the totality of the results of which is the basis and significance, as well as the process itself, of the maintenance of the existence of everything existing in the whole of this "Everything-representing-one-world."'

"And he added in a half-sarcastic tone: 'Soon we shall be absolutely isolated from everything existing and functioning in the whole of the Universe; but, on the other hand, owing firstly to my new invention, and secondly to the knowledge we have already attained for ourselves, we have not only now the possibility of returning to the said world, to become again a particle of all that exists, but also we shall soon be worthy to become nonparticipating eyewitnesses of certain of these World-laws, which for ordinary uninitiated three-centered beings are what they call "great-inscrutable-mysteries-of-Nature" but which in reality are only natural and very simple results "automatically-flowing-one-from-the-other."'

"While he was speaking, one could feel that this pump—another also very important part of the whole of his new invention—was perfectly actualizing the work assigned to it by this being with Reason.

"To enable you to represent to yourself and understand better the perfection of this part also of the whole of this new invention of Gornahoor Harharkh, I must not fail to tell you also about the following:

"Although I personally, as a three-brained being also,

had had occasion many times before, owing to certain quite particular reasons, to be in atmosphereless spaces and had had to exist, sometimes for a long time, by means of the Sacred 'Kreemboolazoomara' alone; and although from frequent repetition, a habit had been acquired in my presence of moving from one sphere to another gradually and almost without feeling any inconvenience from the change in the presence of the 'second-being-food' occurring with the change of the presences of cosmic substances undergoing transformation and which are always around both large and small cosmic concentrations; and also, although the causes themselves of my arising and the subsequent process of my being-existence were arranged in an entirely special way, in consequence of which the various being-functions contained within my common presence had perforce gradually become also special, yet nevertheless, in spite of it all, the pumping out of the atmosphere by the said 'pump' then proceeded with such force that such sensations were impressed on the separate parts of the whole of my presence that even today I can very clearly experience the process of the flow of my state at that time and relate it to you almost in detail.

"This extremely strange state began in me shortly after Gornahoor Harharkh had spoken in a half-sarcastic tone about our imminent situation.

"In all my three 'being-centers'—namely, in the three centers localized in the presence of every three-centered being, and which exist under the names of 'Thinking,' 'Feeling,' and 'Moving' centers—there began to be perceived separately and independently in each of them in a very strange and unusual way very definite impressions that there was taking place in the separate parts of my whole planetary body an independent process of the sacred 'Rascooarno,' and that the cosmic crystallizations which composed the presences of these parts were flowing 'in vain.

"At first, what is called my 'initiative-of-constatation' proceeded in the usual way, that is, according to what is called the 'center-of-gravity-of-associative-experiencing,' but later, when this initiative-of-constatation of everything proceeding in me gradually and almost imperceptibly became the function of my essence alone, the latter not only became the unique all-embracing initiator of the constating of everything proceeding in me, but also everything, without exception, of that which newly proceeded began to be perceived by and fixed in this essence of mine.

"From the moment that my essence began to perceive impressions directly and to constate independently that, from what was proceeding, there was being entirely destroyed, as it were, in my common presence, firstly, the parts of my planetary body, and then, little by little, also the localizations of the 'second' and 'third' being-centers. At the same time, a constatation was definitely made that the functioning of these latter centers passed gradually to my 'thinking-center' and became proper to it, with the consequence that the 'thinking-center,' with the increasing intensity of its functioning, became the 'unique-powerful-perceiver' of everything actualized outside of itself and the autonomous initiator of the constating of everything proceeding in the whole of my presence as well as outside of it.

"While this strange, and to my Reason then, still incomprehensible being-experiencing was proceeding in me, Gornahoor Harharkh himself was occupied in pulling some 'levers' and 'switches,' of which there were very many at the edges of the table where we were placed.

"An incident which happened to Gornahoor Harharkh himself changed all this being-experiencing of mine, and in my common presence the usual 'inner-being-experiencing' was resumed.

"The following is what happened:

"Gornahoor Harharkh, with all those unusual heavy appliances which had been put on him as well, suddenly found himself at a certain height above the chair and began to flounder, as our dear Mullah Nassr Eddin says, 'like-a-puppy-who-has-fallen-into-a-deep-pond.'

"As it afterwards proved, my friend Gornahoor Harharkh had made a mistake while pulling the mentioned levers and switches and had made certain parts of his planetary body more tense than was necessary. In consequence, his presence together with everything on him had received a shock and also the momentum given by the shock, and, owing to the 'tempo' proceeding in his presence from taking in the 'second-being-food' and to the absence of any resistance in that absolutely empty space, he began to drift, or, as I have already said, to flounder like a 'puppy-who-has-fallen-into-a-deep-pond.' "

Having said this with a smile, Beelzebub became silent; a little later he made a very strange gesture with his left hand, and with an intonation not proper to his own voice, he continued:

"While I am gradually recalling and telling you about all this concerning the events of a period of my existence now long since past, the wish arises in me to make a sincere confession to you—just to you, one of my direct heirs who must inevitably represent the sum of all my deeds during the periods of the process of my past being-existence—and namely, I wish sincerely to confess to you that when my essence, with the participation of the parts of my presence, subject to it alone, had independently decided to take a personal part in those scientific elucidatory experiments with the demonstrating part of the new invention of Gornahoor Harharkh, and I had entered into this demonstrating part without the least compulsion from outside, yet, in spite of it all, my essence allowed to creep into my being and to be developed, side by side with the said strange experiencings, a criminally egoistic anxiety for the safety of my personal existence.

"However, my boy, in order that you may not at this moment be too distressed, it is not superfluous to add that this happened in me then for the first and also for the last time during all the periods of my being-existence.

"But perhaps it would be better for the present not to touch on questions that concern exclusively only our family.

"Let us rather return to the tale I have begun about the Omnipresent-Okidanokh and my essence-friend Gornahoor Harharkh, who was, by the way, at one time considered everywhere among ordinary three-brained beings as a 'great-scientist,' and is now, though he still continues to exist, not only considered not 'great,' but thanks to his own result, that is to say, to his own son, is what our dear Mullah Nassr Eddin would call a 'has-been' or, as he sometimes says in such cases, 'He-is-already-sitting-in-an-old-American-galosh.'

"Well, then, while floundering, Gornahoor Harharkh, with great difficulty, and only by means of a special and very complicated maneuver which he made, finally managed to get his planetary body, burdened with the various unusually heavy appliances, down onto the chair again, and this time he fixed it all with the aid of special screws which were on the chair for that purpose; and when we were both more or less arranged and communication was possible between us by means of the said artificial-connectors, he first drew my attention to those apparatuses hanging over the table which I told you were very much like the Momonodooars.

"On close inspection all these were alike in appearance

and served as three identical 'sockets,' from the ends of each of which, 'carbon-candles' projected, such as are usually to be found in the apparatuses which your favorites call 'electric-arc-lamps.'

"Having drawn my attention to these three socket-like Momonodooars, he said:

"'Each of these externally similar apparatuses has a direct connection with those secondary containers which I pointed out to you while we were still outside and in which, after the artificial Djartklom, each of the active parts of Okidanokh collects into a general mass.

"'I have adapted these three independent apparatuses in such a way that, there in this absolutely empty space, we can obtain from those secondary containers for the required experiment as much as we wish of every active part of Okidanokh in a pure state, and also we can at will change the force of the "striving-to-reblend-into-a-whole," which is acquired in them and which is proper to them according to the degree of density of the concentration of the mass.

"'And here, within this absolutely empty space, I shall first of all show you that same non-law-conformable phenomenon which we recently observed while we were outside the place where it proceeded. And namely, I shall again demonstrate to you this World-phenomenon which occurs when, after a law-conformable Djartklom, the separate parts of the whole Okidanokh meet in a space outside of a law-conformable arising and, without the participation of one part, "strive-to-reblend-into-a-whole."'

"Having said this, he first closed that part of the surface of the Hrhaharhtzaha, the composition of which had the property of allowing 'rays' to pass through it; then he pulled two switches and pressed a certain button, as a result of which the small plate lying on that table, composed of a certain special mastic, automatically moved toward the mentioned carbon-candles; and then having again drawn my attention to the Ammeter and the Voltmeter, he added:

"'I have again admitted the influx of parts of the Okidanokh, namely, the Anodnatious and the Cathodnatious of equal force of "striving-to-reblend."'

"When I looked at the Ammeter and the Voltmeter and indeed saw that their needles moved and stopped on the same figures I had noticed the first time we were still outside the Hrhaharhtzaha, I was greatly surprised, because in spite of the indications of the needles and the intimation of Gornahoor Harharkh himself, I had neither noticed nor sensed any change in the degree of my perception of the visibility of the surrounding objects.

"So, without waiting for his further explanations, I asked him:

"'But why then is there no result from this non-law-conformable "striving-to-reblend-into-a-whole," of the parts of the Okidanokh?'

"Before replying to this question, he turned off the only lamp, which worked from a special magnetic current. My astonishment increased still more, because in spite of the darkness which instantly ensued, it could clearly be seen through the walls of the Hrhaharhtzaha, that the needles of the Ammeter and Voltmeter still stood in their former places.

"Only after I had somehow got accustomed to such a surprising constatation, Gornahoor Harharkh said:

"'I have already told you that the composition of the material of which the walls of this construction in which we are at this moment are made, possesses the property of not allowing any vibrations arising from any source whatsoever to pass through it, with the exception of certain vibrations arising from nearby concentrations; and these latter vibrations can be perceived by the organs of sight of three-brained beings, and even then of course, only of normal beings.

"'Furthermore, according to the law called "Heteratogetar," the "Salnichizinooarnian-momentum-vibrations" or "rays" acquire the property of acting on the organs of perception of beings only after they have passed a limit defined by science in the following formula: "the-result-of-the-manifestation-is-proportionate-to-the-force-of-striving-received-from-the-shock."

"'And so, as the given process of the clash of the two parts of the Okidanokh has the strength of great power, the result of the clash is manifested much further than the place of its arising.

"'Now look!'

"Having said this, he pressed some other button, and suddenly the whole interior of the Hrhaharhtzaha was filled with the same blinding light which, as I have already told you, I experienced when I was outside the Hrhaharhtzaha.

"It appeared that the said light was obtained because by pressing this button, Gornahoor Harharkh had again opened that part of the wall of the Hrhaharhtzaha which had the property of permitting 'rays' to pass through it.

"As he explained further, the light was only a consequence of the result of the 'striving-to-reblend-into-a-whole' of the parts of Okidanokh proceeding in that absolutely empty space within the Hrhaharhtzaha and manifested owing to what is called 'reflection' from outside back to the place of its arising.

"After this he continued as follows:

"'I shall now demonstrate to you how and by what combinations of the processes of Djartklom and of the striving-to-reblend-into-a-whole of the active parts of Okidanokh, there arise in planets from what are called the "minerals" which compose their interior presence, definite formations of varying densities, as for instance, "mineraloids," "gases," "metalloids," "metals," and so on; how these latter are afterwards transformed owing to these same factors one into another; and how the vibrations flowing from these transformations constitute just that "totality-of-vibrations" which gives the planets themselves the possibility of stability in the process called the "Common-system-harmonious-movement."

"'For my proposed demonstrating I must obtain, as I always do, the necessary materials from outside, which my pupils will give me by means of appliances which I have prearranged.'

"It is interesting to remark that while he was speaking, he was at the same time tapping with his left foot on a certain 'something,' very much like what your favorites call the famous Morse transmission apparatus—famous be it said, of course, only on the planet Earth.

"And a little later there slowly ascended from the lower part of the Hrhaharhtzaha a small something like a box, also with transparent walls, within which, as it proved later, were certain minerals, metalloids, metals, and various gases in liquid and solid states.

"Then with the aid of various appliances which were at one side of the table, he first of all, with complicated manipulation, took out from the box some what is called 'red copper' and placed it on the mentioned plate, and then said:

"'This metal is a definite planetary crystallization and is one of the densities required for the said stability in the process called the Common-system-harmonious-movement. It is a formation from preceding processes of the action of the parts of the Omnipresent-Okidanokh; and at the present moment I wish to allow the subsequent transformation of this metal to proceed artificially and acceleratedly by means of the peculiarities of the same factors.

"'I wish to aid artificially the evolution and involution of its elements towards a greater density, or, on the contrary, towards their transformation back to a primal state.

"'To make the picture of the further elucidatory experiments clearer to you, I find I must first inform you, even if only briefly, of my first personal scientific deductions concerning the evidence of the causes and conditions owing to which there proceeds in the planets themselves the crystallizing of separate parts of the Okidanokh in these or the other said definite formations.

"'Evidently first of all from any non-law-conformable Djartklom of the Omnipresent-Okidanokh which is in the presence of every planet, its separate parts are localized in the medium of that part of the presence of the planet, that is to say, in that mineral which was at the given moment in the place where the said non-law-conformable Djartklom occurred.

"'And so if what is called the "vibration-of-the-density-of-the-elements-of-the-said-medium" has an "affinity-of-vibration" with the said active part of the Omnipresent-Okidanokh, then according to the World-law called "Symmetrical-entering," this active part blends with the presence of the said medium and becomes an inseparable part of it. And from that moment, the given parts of the Omnipresent-Okidanokh begin, together with the said elements of the said medium, to represent the corresponding densities required in planets, that is to say, various kinds of metalloids or even metals, as for instance, the metal I have placed in this sphere, and in which there will proceed artificially at this moment, at my wish, the action of striving-to-reblend-into-a-whole of the parts of the Okidanokh, and which metal, as I have already said, exists under the name of red-copper.

"'And further, having arisen in the planets in this way, the said various metalloids and metals then begin according to the common-universal-law called "Reciprocal-feeding-of-everything-existing"—as it is generally proper to arisings of every kind in which Okidanokh or any of its active parts participates—to radiate from their presences the results of their inner "Interchange-of-substances." And as is proper to radiations of every kind issuing from sur- and intraplanetary formations that have acquired in their vibrations the property of Okidanokh or of its active parts, and which are in what is called the "center-of-gravity" of every such said formation, the radiations of these metalloids and metals possess properties almost similar to the properties of Okidanokh itself or of one or another of its active parts.

"'When the said masses of different densities that have thus arisen in planets under normal surrounding conditions radiate from their common presences the vibrations required for the said World-law of Reciprocal-feeding-of-everything-existing, then, among these vibrations of various properties there is established, owing to the fundamental World-law "Troemedekhfe," a reciprocally acting contact.

"'And the result of this contact is the chief factor in the gradual change of the various densities in planets.

"'My observations over many years have almost fully convinced me that it is owing only to the said contact and its results that there is actualized the "Stability-of-harmonious-equilibrium-of-planets."

"'This metal red-copper which I have placed in the sphere of my proposed artificial actualization of the action of the active parts of Okidanokh, has at this moment what is called a "specific-density," reckoning from the unit of density of the sacred element Theomertmalogos, of 444, that is to say, the atom of this metal was 444 times more dense, and as much less vivifying, than the atom of the sacred Theomertmalogos.

"'Now see in what order its artificially accelerated transformations will proceed.'

"Having said this, he first fixed before my organ of sight the automatically moving Teskooano and then turned on and off various switches in a certain sequence; and as I looked through the Teskooano he explained to me as follows:

"'At this moment I admit the "influx" of all three parts of Okidanokh into the sphere containing this metal; and as all three parts have the same "density" and, hence, the same "force-of-striving," they reblend into a whole in this sphere without changing anything in the presence of the metal; and the Omnipresent-Okidanokh thus obtained flows in its usual state through a special connection out of the Hrhaharhtzaha and is reconcentrated in the first container which you have already seen.

"'Now look!

"'I deliberately increase the force-of-striving of only one of the active parts of the Okidanokh; for example, I increase the force called Cathodnatious. In consequence of this, you see that the elements composing the presence of that red copper begin to involve towards the quality of the substances that compose the ordinary presences of planets.'

"As he explained this, he at the same time turned on and off various switches in a certain sequence.

"Although, my boy, I then looked very attentively at everything proceeding, and everything I saw was impressed in my essence 'Pestolnootiarly,' that is, forever, yet nevertheless, not even with my best wish could I now describe to you in words a hundredth part of what then proceeded in that small fragment of a definite intraplanetary formation.

"And I will not try to put into words for you what I then saw, because I have just thought of a possibility of soon actually showing it all to you when you also can be an eyewitness of so strange and astonishing a cosmic process.

"But I will tell you meanwhile that there proceeded in that fragment of red copper something rather like those terrifying pictures which I occasionally observed among your favorites on the planet Earth through my Teskooano from Mars.

"I said 'rather-like' because what occasionally proceeded among your favorites had a visibility only possible of observation at its beginning, whereas in the fragment of red copper the visibility was continuous until the final completion of transformation.

"A rough parallel can be drawn between the occasional proceedings on your planet and the proceedings then in that small fragment of copper, if you imagine yourself high up and looking down upon a large public square, where thousands of your favorites, seized with the most intense form of their chief psychosis, are destroying each other's existence by all kinds of means invented by them themselves, and that in their places there immediately appear what are called their 'corpses,' which owing to the outrages done to them by the beings who are not yet destroyed, change color very perceptibly, as a result of which the general visibility of the surface of the said large square is gradually changed.

"Then, my boy, this subsequent essence-friend of mine, Gornahoor Harharkh, by means of switching on and off the influx of the three active parts of Okidanokh and changing their force-of-striving, also changed the density of the elements of the said metal and thereby transformed the red copper into all the other also definite intraplanetary metals of lower or higher degree of vivifyingness.

"And here, for the elucidation of the strangeness of the psyche of the three-brained beings who have taken your fancy, it is very important and interesting to note that while Gornahoor Harharkh was, with the aid of his new invention, artificially and deliberately producing the evolution and involution of the density and vivifyingness of the elements of red copper, I noticed very clearly that this metal was transformed once upon the said plate into just that same definite metal about which the sorry-savants of your planet have been wiseacring during nearly the whole of their arising and existing, in the hope of transforming other metals into this metal, and thus constantly leading astray their already sufficiently erring brethren.

"This metal is called there—'gold.'

"Gold is no other than the metal we call 'Prtzathalavr,' the specific weight of which, reckoning from the element of the sacred Theomertmalogos, is 1439; that is to say, its element is three and a fraction times less vivifying than the element of the metal red copper.

"Why I suddenly decided not to try to explain to you in detail in words all that then took place in the fragment of the said red copper, in view of my suggestion of the possibility of soon actually showing you in definite intraplanetary formations the processes of various combinations of the manifestations of the active parts of Okidanokh, was because I suddenly remembered the all-gracious promise given me by our All-Quarters-Maintainer, the Most Great Archcherub, Peshtvogner.

"And this all-gracious promise was given me, as soon as I returned from exile and had to present myself first of all to His All-Quarters-Maintainer, the Archcherub Peshtvogner, and prostrated myself to produce before him what is called the 'Essence-Sacred-Aliamizoornakalu.'

"This I had to do on account of the same sins of my youth. And I was obliged to do so, because when I was pardoned by HIS UNI-BEING ENDLESSNESS and allowed to return to my native land, certain Sacred Individuals decided to demand of me, for any eventuality, to have performed over my essence this sacred process in order that I might not manifest myself as in the days of my youth, and that the same might not thereby occur again in the Reason of most individuals dwelling here at the center of the Great Universe.

"You probably do not know yet what the Sacred-Aliamizoornakalu over an essence means? I shall later explain it to you in detail but meanwhile I shall simply use the words of our dear Mullah Nassr Eddin who explains this process as 'giving-one's-word-of-honor-not-to-poke-one's-nose-into-the-affairs-of-the-authorities.'

"In short, when I presented myself to His All-Quarters-Maintainer, he deigned to ask me, among other things, whether I had taken with me all the being-productions which had interested me and which I had collected from various planets of that solar system where I existed during my exile.

"I replied that I had taken almost everything, except those cumbersome apparatuses which my friend Gornahoor Harharkh had constructed for me on the planet Mars.

"He at once promised to give orders that everything I should indicate should be taken at the first opportunity on the next trip of the space-ship *Omnipresent*.

"That is why, my boy, I hope that everything necessary will be brought to our planet Karatas so that, when we return there, you will be able to see it all with your own eyes, and I shall be able to explain everything in detail, practically.

"And meanwhile, during our traveling here on the space-ship *Karnak*, I shall, as I have already promised you, tell you in their order about my descents there to your planet and also about the causes of what is called my 'appearances-there-in-person.' "

CHAPTER 19

Beelzebub's Tales About His Second Descent onto the Planet Earth

Beelzebub began thus:

"I descended upon your planet Earth for the second time only eleven of their centuries after my first descent there.

"Shortly after my first descent onto the surface of that planet, the second serious catastrophe occurred to it; but this catastrophe was local in character and did not threaten disaster on a large cosmic scale.

"During this second serious catastrophe to that planet, the continent Atlantis, which had been the largest continent and the chief place of the being-existence of the three-brained beings of that planet during the period of my first descent, was engulfed together with other large and small terra firmas within the planet with all the three-brained beings existing upon it, and also with almost all that they had attained and acquired during many of their preceding centuries.

"In their place there then emerged from within the planet other terra firmas which formed other continents and islands, most of which still exist.

"It was just on the said continent of Atlantis that the city of Samlios was situated, where, do you remember, I once told you that young countryman of ours existed, on whose account my first 'Descent-in-person' took place.

"During the mentioned second great disaster to that planet, many of the three-brained beings who have taken your fancy survived owing to many and various events, and their now already excessively multiplied posterity descended just from them.

"By the time of my second Descent-in-person, they had already multiplied so greatly that they were breeding again upon almost all the newly formed terra firmas.

"And as regards the question of just which causes, ensuing according to law, brought about this excessive multiplication of theirs, you will understand this also in the course of my further tales.

"You might as well, I think, notice here in connection with this terrestrial catastrophe, something about the three-brained beings of our own tribe; namely, why all the beings of our tribe existing on that planet during the mentioned catastrophe escaped the inevitable what is called 'Apocalyptic-end.'

"They escaped it for the following reasons:

"I told you once, in the course of our previous talks, that most of those beings of our tribe who had chosen this planet of yours as their place of existence, existed during my first descent chiefly on the continent of Atlantis.

"It appears that a year before the said catastrophe, our, as she is called, 'Party-Pythoness' there, when prophesying, asked us all to leave the continent of Atlantis and migrate to another small continent not very far away, where we were to exist on that definite part of its surface she indicated.

"This small continent was then called 'Grabontzi' and the part the Pythoness indicated did indeed escape the terrifying perturbation which then occurred to all the other parts of the common presence of that ill-fated planet.

"In consequence of the said perturbation, this small continent Grabontzi, which exists until now under the name of 'Africa,' became much larger, because other terra firmas which emerged from the water spaces of the planet were added to it.

"So, my boy, the Party-Pythoness there was able to warn those beings of our tribe who had been obliged to exist on that planet, and thereby to save them, as I have already told you, from the inevitable 'Apocalyptic-fate,' owing only to one special being-property which, by the way, can be acquired by beings only intentionally, by means of what is called being-Partkdolg-duty, about which I shall tell you later.

"I descended in person to the surface of that planet for the second time, for reasons that ensued from the following events.

"Once, while on the planet Mars, we received an etherogram from the Center announcing the imminent reappearance there on the planet Mars of certain Most High Sacred Individuals; and indeed, within half a Martian year, a number of Archangels, Angels, Cherubim, and Seraphim did appear there, most of whom had been members of that Most Great Commission which had already appeared on our planet Mars during the first great catastrophe to that planet of yours.

"Among these Most High Sacred Individuals there was again His Conformity, the Angel—now already an Archangel—Looisos, of whom, do you remember, I recently told you that during the first great catastrophe to the planet Earth he had been one of the chief regulators in the matter of averting the consequences of that general cosmic misfortune.

"So, my boy! The day following this second appearance of the mentioned Sacred Individuals, His Conformity, escorted by one of the Seraphim, his second assistant, made His appearance at my house.

"After Te Deums with me, and after certain inquiries of mine concerning the Great Center, His Conformity then condescended to tell me, among other things, that after the collision of the comet Kondoor with the planet Earth, he, or other responsible cosmic Individuals, superintending the affairs of 'Harmonious-World-Existence,' had frequently descended to this solar system to observe the actualizing of those measures they had taken in order to avert the consequences of that general cosmic accident.

"'And we descended,' His Conformity continued, 'because although we had then taken every possible measure and had assured everybody that everything would be quite all right, we ourselves were nevertheless not categorically convinced that no unexpectedness might occur there unforeseen.

"'Our apprehensions were justified, although, "Thanks-to-Chance," not in a serious form, that is to say, on a general cosmic scale, since this new catastrophe affected only the planet Earth itself.

"'This second catastrophe to the planet Earth,' continued His Conformity, 'occurred owing to the following:

"'When during the first disaster two considerable fragments had been separated from this planet, then for certain reasons, the what is called "center-of-gravity" of the whole of its presence had no time to shift immediately into a corresponding new place, with the result that right until the second catastrophe, this planet had existed with its "center-of-gravity" in a wrong position, owing to which its motion during that time was not "proportionately-harmonious" and there often occurred both within and upon it various commotions and considerable displacements.

"'But it was recently, when the center-of-gravity of the planet finally shifted to its true center, that the said second catastrophe occurred.

"'But now,' added His Conformity with a shade of self-satisfaction, 'the existence of this planet will be quite normal in respect of the common-cosmic harmony.

"'This second catastrophe to the planet Earth has finally quite pacified and convinced us also that a catastrophe on a great scale cannot again occur on account of this planet.

"'Not only has this planet itself now again acquired a normal movement in the general cosmic equilibrium, but its two detached fragments'—which, as I have already told you, are now called Moon and Anoolios—'have also acquired a normal movement and have become, although small, yet independent "Kofensharnian," that is, additional, planets of that solar system Ors.'

"Having thought a little, His Conformity then told me:

"'Your Reverence, I have appeared to you just for the purpose of talking over the future welfare of the large fragment of that planet, which exists at the present time under the name of Moon.

"'This fragment,' His Conformity continued, 'has not only become an independent planet, but there has now begun on it the process of the formation of an atmosphere, which is necessary for every planet and which serves for the actualization of the Most Great common-cosmic Trogoautoegocrat.

"'And now, your Reverence, the regular process of the formation of the said atmosphere on this small, unforeseenly arisen planet is being hindered by an undesirable circumstance caused by the three-brained beings arisen and existing on the planet Earth.

"'And it is just about this that I have decided to apply to you, your Reverence, and to request you to consent to undertake in the Name of the UNI-BEING CREATOR, the task of trying to spare us the necessity of resorting to some extreme sacred process, unbecoming for three-centered beings, and to remove this undesirable phenomenon in some ordinary way through the "being-Reason" they have in their presences.'

"And in his further detailed explanations, His Conformity then said, among other things, that after the second catastrophe to the Earth, the biped three-brained beings who had accidentally survived had again multiplied; that now, the whole process of their being-existence was concentrated on another, newly formed, also large continent called 'Ashhark'; that three independent large groups had just been formed on this same large continent 'Ashhark,' the first of which existed in a locality then called 'Tikliamish,' the second in a place called 'Maralpleicie,' and the third in a still existing locality then called 'Gemchania' or 'Pearl-land'; and that in the general psyche of the beings belonging to all those three independent groups, certain peculiar 'Havatvernoni' had been formed, that is, certain psychic strivings, the totality of the process of which common-cosmic strivings they themselves had named 'Religion.'

"'Although these Havatvernoni or Religions have nothing in common,' continued His Conformity, 'yet nevertheless in these peculiar religions of theirs there is very widely spread among the beings of all three groups the same custom called among them "Sacrificial-Offerings."

"'And this custom of theirs is based on the notion, which can be cognized only by their strange Reason alone, that if they destroy the existence of beings of other forms in honor of their gods and idols, then these imaginary gods and idols of theirs would find it very, very agreeable, and always and in everything unfailingly help and assist them in the actualization of all their fantastic and wild fancies.

"'This custom is at present so widespread there, and the destruction of the existence of beings of various forms for this maleficent purpose has reached such dimensions, that there is already a surplus of the "Sacred Askokin" required from the planet Earth for its former parts, that is to say, a surplus of those vibrations which arise during the sacred process of "Rascooarno" of beings of every exterior form arising and existing on that planet from which the said sacred cosmic arising is required.

"'For the normal formation of the atmosphere of the newly arisen planet Moon, the said surplus of the Sacred Askokin has already begun seriously to hinder the correct exchange of matters between the planet Moon itself and its atmosphere, and the apprehension has already arisen that its atmosphere may in consequence be formed incorrectly and later become an obstacle to the harmonious movement of the whole system Ors, and perhaps again give rise to factors menacing a catastrophe on a greater common-cosmic scale.

"'So, your Reverence, my request to you, as I have already told you, is that you should consent, since you are in the habit of often visiting various planets of that solar system, to undertake the task of specially descending on the planet Earth and of trying there on the spot to instill into the consciousness of these strange three-brained beings some idea of the senselessness of this notion of theirs.'

"Having said a few more words, His Conformity ascended and, when He was fairly high up, added in a loud voice: 'By this, your Reverence, you will be rendering a great service to our UNI-BEING ALL-EMBRACING ENDLESSNESS.'

"After these Sacred Individuals had left the planet Mars, I decided to carry out the said task at all costs and to be worthy, if only by this explicit aid to our UNIQUE-BURDEN-BEARING-ENDLESSNESS, of becoming a particle, though an independent one, of everything existing in the Great Universe.

"So, my boy, imbued with this, I flew the next day on the same ship *Occasion* for the second time to your planet Earth.

"This time our ship *Occasion* alighted on the sea which

was newly formed by the perturbation during the second great disaster to that planet of yours, and which was called there in that period of the flow of time, 'Kolhidious.'

"This sea was situated on the northwest of that newly formed large continent Ashhark, which at that period was already the chief center of the existence of the three-brained beings there.

"The other shores of this sea were composed of those newly emerged terra firmas which had become joined to the continent Ashhark, and which all together were first called 'Frianktzanarali' and a little later 'Kolhidshissi.'

"It must be remarked that this sea and also the mentioned terra firmas exist until now, but of course they now already have other names; for instance, the continent Ashhark is now called 'Asia'; the sea 'Kolhidious,' the 'Caspian Sea'; and all the Frianktzanarali together now exist under the name 'Caucasus.'

"The *Occasion* alighted on this sea Kolhidious or Caspian Sea because this sea was the most convenient for mooring our *Occasion* as well as for my further travels.

"And it was very convenient for my further travels because from the East a large river flowed into it, which watered almost the whole country of Tikliamish, and on the banks of which stood the capital of that country, the city 'Koorkalai.'

"As the greatest center of the existence of these favorites of yours was then the country Tikliamish, I decided to go there first.

"Here it might as well be remarked that although this large river then called 'Oksoseria' now still exists, yet it no longer flows into the present Caspian Sea, because after a minor planetary tremor at almost half way, it turned to the right and flowed into one of the hollows on the surface of the continent Ashhark, where it gradually formed a small sea, which still exists and is called the 'Aral Sea';

but the old bed of the former half of that large river which is now called the 'Amu Darya,' can still be seen by close observation.

"During the period of this second descent of mine in person, the country Tikliamish was considered to be and indeed was the richest and most fertile of all the terra firmas of that planet good for ordinary being-existence.

"But when a third great catastrophe occurred to the ill-fated planet, this then most fertile country of the surface of your planet, along with other more or less fertile terra firmas, was covered by 'Kashmanoon,' or, as they say, by 'Sands.'

"For long periods after this third catastrophe, this country Tikliamish was simply called 'bare desert,' and now, its parts have various names; its former principal part is called 'Karakoom,' that is, 'Black-sands.'

"During these periods the second also quite independent group of three-brained beings of your planet also dwelt on that continent Ashhark, on that part which was then called the country Maralpleicie.

"Later when this second group also began to have a center point of their existence they called it the 'city Gob' and the whole country was for a long time called 'Goblandia.'

"This locality also was afterwards covered by Kashmanoon and now the former principal part of this also once flourishing country is called simply 'The Gobi Desert.'

"And as for the third group of the three-brained beings of that time of the planet Earth, this also quite independent group had the place of its existence on the south-eastern side of the continent Ashhark, opposite to Tikliamish, quite on the other side of those abnormal projections of the continent Ashhark which also were formed during the second perturbation to this ill-fated planet.

"This region of the existence of this third group was then called, as I have already told you 'Gemchania' or 'Pearl-land.'

"Later the name of this locality also changed many times and the whole of this terra firma region of the surface of the planet Earth now exists under the name of 'Hindustan' or 'India.'

"It must without fail be remarked that at that period, that is, during this second descent of mine in person onto the surface of your planet, there was present and already thoroughly crystallized in all these three-brained beings who have taken your fancy, belonging to the three enumerated independent groups, instead of that function called 'the needful-striving-for-self-perfection,' which should be in every three-brained being, also a 'needful' but very strange 'striving' that all the other beings of their planet should call and consider their country the 'Center-of-Culture' for the whole planet.

"This strange 'needful-striving' was then present in all the three-centered beings of your planet and was for each of them, as it were, the principal sense and aim of his existence. And in consequence, among the beings of these three independent groups at that period, bitter struggles, both material and psychic, were constantly proceeding for the attainment of the mentioned aim.

"Well, then, my boy.

"We then set off from the sea Kolhidious, or as it is now called, the Caspian Sea, on 'Selchans,' that is to say, on rafts of a special kind, up the river Oksoseria, or as it is now called, the Amu Darya. We sailed for fifteen terrestrial days and finally arrived at the capital of the beings of the first Asiatic group.

"On arriving there and after arranging the place of our permanent existence there, I first began visiting the 'Kaltaani' of the city Koorkalai, that is, those establishments there which on the continent Ashhark were later called 'Chaihana,' 'Ashhana,' 'Caravanseray,' and so on, and which the contemporary beings there, especially those breeding on the continent called 'Europe,' call 'Cafés,' 'Restaurants,' 'Clubs,' 'Dance Halls,' 'Meeting Places,' and so on.

"I first began visiting these establishments of theirs because there on the planet Earth, at present just as formerly, nowhere can one observe and study the specific peculiarities of the psyche of the beings of the locality so well as in just such gathering places of theirs; and this was just what I needed to make clear to myself their real inner essence-attitude to their custom of sacrificial offerings and to enable me more readily and more easily to draw up a plan of action for the attainment of that aim for which I made this second sojourn of mine there in person.

"During my visits to the Kaltaani there, I met a number of beings, among whom was one I happened to meet rather often.

"This three-brained being there, whom I chanced to meet frequently, belonged to the profession of 'priest' and was called 'Abdil.'

"As almost all my personal activities, my boy, during that second descent of mine were connected with the external circumstances of this priest Abdil and as I happened to have during this descent of mine a great deal of trouble on his account, I shall tell you more or less in detail about this three-brained being there; and, moreover, you will at the same time understand from these tales about him the results I then attained for the purpose of uprooting from the strange psyche of your favorites the need to destroy the existence of beings of other forms in order to 'please' and 'appease' their gods and revered idols.

"Although this terrestrial being, who afterwards became

for me like one of my kinsmen, was not a priest of the highest rank, yet he was well versed in all the details of the teaching of the religion then dominant in the whole country Tikliamish; and he also knew the psyche of the followers of that religion, particularly, of course, the psyche of the beings belonging to his what is called 'congregation' for whom he was 'priest.'

"Soon after we were on 'good terms' with each other, I discovered that in the Being of this priest Abdil—owing to very many external circumstances, among which were also heredity and the conditions under which he had been prepared for a responsible being—the function called 'conscience' which ought to be present in every three-centered being, had not yet been quite atrophied in him, so that after he had cognized with his Reason certain cosmic truths I had explained to him, he immediately acquired in his presence towards the beings around him, similar to him, almost that attitude which should be in all normal three-brained beings of the whole Universe, that is to say, he became, as it is also said there, 'compassionate,' and 'sensitive' towards the beings surrounding him.

"Before telling you more about this priest Abdil, I must make clear to your Reason that there on the continent of Ashhark the mentioned terrible custom of Sacrificial-Offerings was at that time, as it is said, at its 'height,' and the destruction of various weak one-brained and two-brained beings proceeded everywhere in incalculable numbers.

"At that period, if anybody had occasion in any house to appeal to one or another of their imaginary gods or fantastic 'saints,' they invariably promised that in the event of good fortune, they would destroy in honor of their gods and saints the existence of some being or other, or of several at once; and if by chance good fortune befell them, then they carried out their promise with the utmost veneration, while, if it were otherwise, they increased their slaughter in order eventually to win the favor of their said imaginary patron.

"With the same aim, these favorites of yours of that period even divided the beings of all other forms into 'clean' and 'unclean.'

"'Unclean' they called those forms of being, the destruction of whose existence was presumably not pleasing to their gods; and 'clean,' those beings, the destruction of whose existence was, presumably, extremely agreeable to those various imaginary idols whom they revered.

"These Sacrificial-Offerings were made not only in their own houses by private beings, but were also made by whole groups, and sometimes even in public. There even then existed special places for slaughterings of this kind which were situated mostly near buildings in memory of something or somebody, chiefly of saints—of course, of the saints they themselves had elevated to 'sainthood.'

"Several such special public places, where the destruction of the beings of different exterior form was carried out, then existed in the country of Tikliamish; and among them was one most celebrated, situated on a small mountain from whence a certain thaumaturgist Aliman was supposed once upon a time to have been 'taken-alive' up to 'some-Heaven-or-other.'

"In that place, as well as in other similar places, especially at definite times of the year, they destroyed an innumerable number of beings called 'oxen,' 'sheep,' 'doves,' and so on, and even beings similar to them themselves.

"In the latter case, the strong usually brought the less strong to be sacrificed; as for instance, a father brought his son, a husband his wife, an elder brother his younger brother, and so on. But, for the most part, 'sacrifices' were offered up of 'slaves,' who then as now were usually what are called 'captives,' that is to say, beings of a conquered community, which according to the law of what is called 'Solioonensius,' had at the given period—that is, at the period when their needful tendency to reciprocal destruction was more intensely manifested in their presences—a lesser significance in respect of this chief peculiarity of theirs.

"The custom of 'pleasing-their-gods' by destroying the existence of other beings is followed there, on your planet, until now, only not on the scale on which these abominations were practiced by your favorites at that time on the continent Ashhark.

"Well, then, my boy, during the early days of my sojourn in the town Koorkalai, I often talked on various subjects with this mentioned friend of mine, the priest Abdil, but, of course, I never spoke with him about such questions as might reveal my real nature.

"Like almost all the three-brained beings of your planet whom I met during all my descents, he also took me for a being of his own planet, but considered me very learned and an authority on the psyche of beings similar to himself.

"From our earliest meetings, whenever we chanced to speak about other beings similar to himself, his responsiveness and experiencings about them always touched me deeply. And when my Reason made it quite clear to me that the function of conscience, fundamental for three-centered beings, which had been transmitted to his presence by heredity, had not yet become quite atrophied in him, then there gradually began from that moment to arise in my presence and as a result to be crystallized, a 'really-functioning-needful-striving' towards him as towards a kinsman of my own nature.

"Thereafter, he also, according to the cosmic law 'every-cause-gives-birth-to-its-corresponding-result,' of course began to have towards me 'Silnooyegordpana,' or, as your favorites would say there, 'a-feeling-of-trusting-another-like-yourself.'

"Well, then, my boy, no sooner was this clearly constated in my Reason, than the idea occurred to me to actualize through this first terrestrial friend of mine, the task for which this second descent of mine in person had been made.

"I therefore intentionally began to lead all our conversation towards the question of the custom of Sacrificial-Offerings.

"Although, my boy, considerable time has flowed since I talked with that terrestrial friend of mine, I could, perhaps, now recall word for word and repeat one of our talks we had at that time.

"I wish to recall and repeat just that talk of ours which was the last, and which served as the starting point of all the subsequent events, which though they brought the planetary existence of this terrestrial friend of mine to a painful end, brought him nevertheless to the beginning of the possibility of continuing the task of self-perfecting.

"This last talk took place in his house.

"I then explained to him frankly the utter stupidity and absurdity of this custom of Sacrificial-Offerings.

"I said to him as follows:

"'Good.

"'You have a religion, a faith in something. It is excellent to have faith in something, in whatever it might be, even if you don't exactly know in whom or in what, nor can represent to yourself the significance and the possibilities of what you have faith in. To have faith, whether consciously or even quite unconsciously, is for every being very necessary and desirable.

"'And it is desirable because owing to faith alone does there appear in a being, the intensity of being-self-consciousness necessary for every being, and also the valuation of personal Being as of a particle of Everything Existing in the Universe.

"'But what has the existence of another being, which you destroy, to do with this, and, moreover, one whose existence you destroy in the name of its CREATOR?

"'Is not that "life" just the same as yours for the CREATOR Who created you as well as this other being?

"'Thanks to your psychic strength and cunning, that is to say, to those data, proper to you, with which our same COMMON CREATOR has endowed you for the perfecting of your Reason, you profit by the psychic weakness of other beings and destroy their existence.

"'Do you understand, you unfortunate creature, what—in an objective sense—an indeed evil deed you commit by this?

"'Firstly, by destroying the existence of other beings, you reduce for yourself the number of factors of that totality of results which alone can form the requisite conditions for the power of self-perfecting of beings similar to yourself; and secondly, you thereby definitely diminish or completely destroy the hopes of our COMMON FATHER CREATOR in those possibilities which have been put into you as a three-brained being and upon whom He counts, as a help for Him later.

"'The obvious absurdity of such a terrible being-action is already clearly shown by your imagining that by destroying the existence of other beings, you do something pleasing just to that ONE who has intentionally created those beings also.

"'Can it be that the thought has never even entered your head that if our COMMON FATHER CREATOR has created that same life also, then He probably did so for some definite purpose?

"'Think,' I told him further, 'think a little, not as you have been accustomed to think during the whole of your existence, like a "Khorassanian-donkey," but think a little honestly and sincerely, as it is proper to think for a being as you call yourself, "in-the-likeness-of-God."

"'When GOD created you and these beings whose existence you destroy, could our CREATOR then have written on the foreheads of certain of His creatures that they were to be destroyed in His honor and glory?

"'If anyone, even an idiot from "Albion's Isles," were to think seriously and sincerely about it, he would understand that this could never be.

"'This was invented only by people who say they are "in-the-likeness-of-God," and not by Him, Who created people and these other beings of different form whom they destroy, as they fancy, for His pleasure and satisfaction.

"'For Him there is no difference between the life of men and the life of beings of any other form.

"'Man is life, and the beings of other exterior forms are life.

"'It is most wisely foreseen by Him that Nature should adapt the difference of exterior form of beings in accordance with those conditions and circumstances under which the process of existence of various forms of life are pre-ordained to flow.

"'Take yourself as an example; with your internal and external organs, could you go now and jump into the water and swim like a fish?

"'Of course not, because you have neither the "gills," "fins," nor "tail" a fish has, that is, a life which is preordained to exist in such a sphere as "water."

"'If it occurred to you to go and jump into the water, you would instantly choke and drop to the bottom and become hors d'oeuvre for those same fishes, who, in that sphere, proper for them, would naturally be infinitely stronger than you.

"'It is the same with the fishes themselves; could one

of them now come to us, sit with us at this table and drink in our company the "Green tea" we are now drinking?

"'Also, of course not! Because it has not the corresponding organs for manifestations of this kind.

"'It was created for the water and its internal and also external organs are adapted for the manifestations required in the water. It can manifest itself effectively and successfully and fulfill the purpose of its existence, preordained by the CREATOR, only in that sphere appropriate to it.

"'In exactly the same way, your external and all your internal organs are also created by our COMMON CREATOR in a corresponding manner. You are given legs to walk; hands to prepare and take the necessary food; your nose and the organs connected with it are so adapted that you may take in and transform in yourself those World-substances by which there are coated in the three-brained beings similar to yourself both higher-being bodies, on one of which rests the hope of our COMMON ALL-EMBRACING CREATOR for help in His needs, for the purpose of actualizations foreseen by Him for the good of Everything Existing.

"'In short, the corresponding principle is foreseen and given to Nature by our COMMON CREATOR, so that He might coat and adapt all your internal and external organs in accordance with that sphere in which the process of the existence of beings of such a brain-system as yours is preordained to flow.

"'A very good example for the clarification of this is your "own-donkey" now standing tied up in your stable.

"'Even as regards this own-donkey of yours, you abuse the possibilities given you by our COMMON CREATOR, since if this donkey is now compelled to stand unwillingly in your stable, it does so only because it is created two-brained; and this again is because such an organization of the whole of its presence is necessary for common-cosmic existence upon planets.

"'And therefore, according to law, there is absent from the presence of your donkey the possibility of logical-mentation, and consequently, according to law, he must be what you call "senseless," or "stupid."

"'Although you were created for the purpose of the common-cosmic existence on planets, and although you were created also as "a-field-of-hope" for the future expectations of our COMMON ALL-GRACIOUS CREATOR—that is to say, created with the possibilities of coating in your presence that "Higher-Sacred" for the possible arising of which the whole of our now existing World was just created—and in spite of the said possibilities given to you, that is to say, in spite of your having been created three-brained with possibilities of a logical mentation, yet you do not use this sacred property of yours for the purpose for which it was foreordained, but manifest it as "cunning" towards His other creations, as, for instance, towards your own-donkey.

"'Apart from the possibilities present in you of consciously coating in your presence the mentioned Higher-Sacred, this donkey of yours is of the same value for the common-cosmic process and consequently for our COMMON CREATOR, as you yourself, since each of you is predestined for some definite purpose, and these distinct definite purposes, in their totality, actualize the sense of Everything Existing.

"'The difference between you and your own-donkey is merely in the form and quality of functioning of the internal and external organization of your common presences.

"'For instance, you have only two legs, whereas the donkey has as many as four, any one of which, moreover, is infinitely stronger than yours.

"'Can you, for instance, carry on those two weak legs of yours as much as that donkey can?

"'Certainly not, because your legs are given you only for carrying yourself and the little that is necessary for the normal existence of a three-brained being as foreseen by Nature.

"'Such a distribution of forces and strength, which at first sight appears unjust on the part of our MOST JUST CREATOR, was made by Great Nature simply because the surplus of cosmic substances foreseeingly given you by the CREATOR and by Nature to use for the purpose of your personal self-perfecting is not given to your donkey, but in place of this, Great Nature Herself transforms the same surplus of cosmic substances in your donkey's presence for the power and strength of certain of its organs for its present existence only, but of course without the personal cognition of the donkey itself, thus enabling it to manifest the said power incomparably better than you.

"'And these variously powered manifestations of beings of diverse forms actualize in their totality just those exterior conditions in which alone it is possible for those similar to you—that is, for three-brained beings—consciously to perfect the "germ-of-Reason" placed in their presences, to the necessary gradation of Pure Objective Reason.

"'I repeat, all beings, of all brain systems, without exception, large and small, arising and existing on the Earth or within the Earth, in the air or beneath the waters, are all equally necessary for our COMMON CREATOR, for the common harmony of the existence of Everything Existing.

"'And as all the enumerated forms of beings actualize all together the form of the process required by our CREATOR for the existence of Everything Existing, the essence of all beings are to Him equally valuable and dear.

"'For our COMMON CREATOR all beings are only parts of the existence of a whole essence spiritualized by Himself.

"'But what do we see here now?

"'One form of beings created by Him, in whose presences He has placed all His hopes and expectations for the future welfare of Everything Existing, taking advantage of their superiorities, lord it over other forms and destroy their existence right and left and, what is more, they do so presumably "in His name."

"'The whole terror of it is that although such phenomenal anti-God acts take place here in every house and on every square, nevertheless it never enters the head of any of these unfortunates that these beings whose existence I or we are now destroying are equally dear to that ONE, Who has created them, and that if He created these other forms of beings as well as ourselves, it must also have been for some purpose.'

"Having said all this to my friend, the priest Abdil, I said further:

"'And what is most distressing is that every man who destroys the existence of other beings, in honor of his honored idols, does so with all his heart and is convinced beyond all doubt that he is doing a "good" deed.

"'I am quite sure that if any one of them should become aware that in destroying another's existence he is not only committing an evil deed against the true GOD and every real Saint, but is even causing them, in their essences, sorrow and grief that there should exist in the great Universe "in-the-likeness-of-God" beings-monsters who can manifest towards other creations of our COMMON CREATOR so consciencelessly and pitilessly; I repeat, if any of them should become aware of this, then certainly not one among them could with all his heart ever again destroy the existence of beings of other forms for Sacrificial-Offerings.

"'Then perhaps on the Earth also would begin to exist the eighteenth personal commandment of our COMMON CREATOR which declared: "Love everything that breathes."

"'This offering to God of sacrifices by destroying the existence of His other creations is just as if somebody from the street should now break into your house and wantonly destroy all the "goods" there, which have taken you years to collect, and cost you years of labor and suffering.

"'Think, but again think sincerely, and picture to yourself what I have just said, and then answer: Would you like it and thank the impudent thief who broke into your house?

"'Certainly not!! A million times not!!!!

"'On the contrary, your whole being would be indignant and would wish to punish this thief, and with every fibre of your psyche you would try to find a means of revenge.

"'In all probability, you would now reply that although it is indeed so . . . "I am, however, only a man. . . ."

"'That is true, you are only a man. It is good that GOD is GOD and is not so vindictive and evil as man.

"'Certainly He will not punish you nor will He revenge Himself upon you, as you would punish the mentioned robber who destroyed the property and goods it had taken you years to collect.

"'It goes without saying, GOD forgives everything—this has even become a law in the World.

"'But His creations—in this case, people—must not abuse this All-Gracious and Everywhere-Penetrating Goodness of His; they must not only care for, but even maintain all He has created.

"'But here on Earth, men have even divided beings of all other forms into the clean and the unclean.

"'Tell me what guided them when they made this division?

"'Why, for instance, is a sheep clean, and a lion unclean? Are they both not equally beings?

"'This also was invented by people. . . . And why have they invented it, and made this division? Simply because a sheep is a very weak being and moreover stupid, and they can do to it just what they like.

"'But people call the lion unclean simply because they dare not do to it what they like.

"'A lion is cleverer and, what is more, stronger than they.

"'A lion will not only not allow itself to be destroyed, but will not even permit people to approach near. If any man should venture to approach near to it, then this "Mister Lion" would give him such a crack on the noddle that our valiant's life would at once fly off to where "people from Albion's Isles" have not yet been.

"'I repeat . . . a lion is unclean simply because men are afraid of it; it is a hundred times higher and stronger than they; a sheep is clean merely because it is much weaker than they and again I repeat, much more stupid.

"'Every being, according to its nature and to the gradation of its Reason attained by its ancestors and transmitted by heredity, occupies its definite place among beings of other forms.

"'A good example for clarifying what I have just said is the difference between the already definitely crystallized presences of the psyche of your dog and of your cat.

"'If you pet your dog a little and get it used to anything you please, it will become obedient and affectionate to the point of abasement.

"'It will run after you and cut every sort of caper before you just to please you all the more.

"'You can be familiar with it, you can beat it, you can hurt it; it will never turn on you, but will always humiliate itself still more before you.

"'But try the same on your cat.

"'What do you think? Will it respond to your indignities as your dog did, and cut the same humble capers for your amusement? Of course not. . . .

"'Even if the cat is not strong enough to retaliate immediately, it will remember this attitude of yours toward it for a long time, and at some time or other will get its revenge.

"'For instance, it is said that it has often happened that a cat has bitten the throat of a man while he was asleep. I can quite believe it, knowing what may have been the cat's reasons for it.

"'No, the cat will stand up for itself, it knows its own value, it is proud, and this is merely because it is a cat and its nature is on that gradation of Reason where according to the merits of its ancestors it just should be.

"'In any case, no being, and no man, should be angry with a cat for this.

"'Is it its fault that it is a cat and that, owing to the merits of its ancestors, its presence occupies such a gradation of "consciousness-of-self"?

"'It must neither be despised for this, nor beaten, nor ill-treated; on the contrary, one must give it its due, as one occupying a higher rung on the ladder of the evolution of "consciousness-of-self." '

"By the way, my dear boy, concerning the reciprocal relations of beings, a former famous prophet from the planet 'Desagroanskrad,' the great 'Arhoonilo,' now already the assistant to the chief investigator of the whole Universe in respect of the details of Objective Morality, once said:

"'If by his Reason a being is higher than you, you must always bow down before him and try to imitate him in everything; but if he is lower than you, you must be just towards him, because you once occupied the same place according to the sacred Measure of the gradation of Reason of our CREATOR and ALL-MAINTAINER.'

"So, my dear boy, this last conversation with that Earth friend of mine produced such a strong impression on him, that for two days thereafter he did nothing but think and think.

"In short, the final outcome of it all was that this priest Abdil eventually began to cognize and sense concerning the custom of Sacrificial-Offerings almost as in reality he should have done.

"Several days after this conversation of ours, there occurred one of the two large religious festivals of the whole of Tikliamish, called 'Zadik'; and in the temple where my friend Abdil was the chief priest, instead of delivering the usual sermon after the temple ceremony, he suddenly began speaking about Sacrificial-Offerings.

"I chanced to be also in that large temple that day and was one of those who heard his speech.

"Although the theme of his speech was unusual for such an occasion and for such a place, yet it shocked nobody, because he spoke unprecedentedly well and beautifully.

"Indeed, he spoke so well and so sincerely, and cited in his beautiful speech so many persuasive and illustrative examples, that as he spoke many of the beings of Koorkalai there even began sobbing bitterly.

"What he said produced so strong an impression on all his congregation that although his speech lasted till the next day instead of the customary half-hour or hour, nevertheless even when it was over, nobody wished to leave and all stood for a long time as if spellbound.

"Thereafter, fragments from his speech began to be spread among those who had not personally heard it.

"It is interesting to notice that it was the custom then for priests to exist simply on the offerings of their parishioners, and this priest Abdil had also been in the habit of receiving from parishioners all kinds of food for his ordinary existence, as for instance roast and boiled 'corpses' of beings of various exterior forms, such as 'chickens,' 'sheep,' 'geese,' and so on. But after this famous speech of his, nobody brought him any of these customary offerings but brought or sent him only fruits, flowers, handiwork, and so on.

"The day following his speech, this Earth friend of mine at once became for all the citizens of the town Koorkalai what is called the 'fashionable-priest,' and not only was the temple where he officiated always crammed with beings of the town Koorkalai, but he was also pressed to speak in other temples.

"He delivered many such speeches concerning Sacrificial-Offerings, and each time the number of his admirers grew and grew, so that he soon became popular not only among the beings of the town Koorkalai, but also of the whole of Tikliamish.

"I do not know how it would all have ended if the whole priesthood, that is, men-beings of the same profession as my friend, had not become alarmed and anxious on account of his popularity, and had not opposed everything he preached.

"Evidently these colleagues of his were afraid that if the custom of Sacrificial-Offerings were to disappear, their own excellent incomes would disappear also, and that their authority would first totter and finally crumble.

"Day by day the number of this priest Abdil's enemies increased, and they spread new slanders and innuendoes about him in order to lower or destroy his popularity and significance.

"His colleagues began delivering addresses in their temples proving exactly the opposite of all that the priest Abdil had preached.

"At last it came to the point that the priesthood began to bribe various beings who had 'Hasnamuss' properties to plan and commit every kind of outrage upon this poor Abdil; and, indeed, these terrestrial nullities with the properties mentioned even tried on several occasions to destroy his existence by sprinkling poison on the various edible offerings brought to him.

"In spite of all this, the number of sincere admirers of his preaching daily increased.

"Finally, the whole corporation of the priesthood could stand it no longer; and on a sad day for my friend, a general ecumenical trial was held, which lasted four days.

"By the sentence of this general ecumenical council, not only was this Earth friend of mine completely excommunicated from the priesthood, but, at the same council, his colleagues also organized means for his further persecution.

"All this, of course, had little by little a strong effect on the psyche of the ordinary beings, so that even those around him who had formerly esteemed him also began gradually to avoid him and to repeat every kind of calumny about him. Even those who only a day before had sent him flowers and various other offerings and had almost worshiped him also soon became such bitter enemies of his, owing to the constant gossip, that it was as if he had not only injured them personally, but had slaughtered and butchered all their near and dear ones.

"Such is the psyche of the beings of that peculiar planet.

"In short, owing to his sincere good will to those around him, this good friend of mine endured a great deal. Even this would have been, perhaps, nothing, if the climax of unconscionableness on the part of the colleagues of my friend and the other terrestrial 'God-like' beings around him had not brought all this to an end; that is to say, they killed him.

"And this occurred in the following way:

"My friend had no relatives at all in the city Koorkalai, having been born in some distant place.

"And as for the hundreds of servants and other ordinary terrestrial nullities who had been around him owing to his former importance, they, by this time, had gradually left him, naturally because my friend was no longer important.

"Toward the end there remained with him only one very old being who had been with him quite a long time.

"To tell the truth, this old man had remained with him only on account of old age which, owing to abnormal being-existence, most of the beings there reach; that is to say, on account of his complete uselessness for anything required under the conditions of being-existence there.

"He simply had no other place to go to, and that was why he did not desert my friend, but stayed with him even when he had lost his importance and was being persecuted.

"Going into my friend's room one sad morning, this old man saw that he had been killed and that his planetary body had been hacked to pieces.

"Knowing that I was his friend, he at once ran to me to tell me about it.

"I have already told you, that I had begun to love him as one of my nearests. So when I learned about this terrible fact, there almost occurred in my whole presence a 'Skinikoonartzino,' that is to say, the connection between my separate being-centers was almost shattered.

"But during the day I feared that the same or other unconscionable beings might commit further outrages on my friend's planetary body, so I decided at least to prevent the possible actualization of what I feared.

"I therefore immediately hired several suitable beings for a great sum of money and, unbeknown to anybody else, had his planetary body removed and temporarily placed in my Selchan, that is, on my raft which was moored not far away on the river Oksoseria, and which I had not disposed of because I had intended to sail on it from there to the sea Kolhidious to our ship *Occasion*.

"This sad end of my friend's existence did not prevent his preachings and persuasions about the cessation of Sacrificial-Offerings having a strong effect on many, even on a great many.

"And indeed, the quantity of slaughterings for Sacrificial-Offerings began very perceptibly to diminish and one could see that even if the custom were not abolished completely with time, it would at least be considerably mitigated.

"And, for the time being, that was sufficient for me.

"As there was no reason for me to stay there any longer, I decided to return immediately to the sea Kolhidious and there to consider what to do further with the planetary body of my friend.

"When I arrived on our ship *Occasion* I found an etherogram for me from Mars in which I was informed of the arrival there of another party of beings from the planet Karatas, and that speedy return there was desired.

"Thanks to this etherogram a very strange idea came into my head—namely, I thought that instead of disposing of the planetary body of my friend on the planet Earth, I might take it with me and give it to the presence of the planet Mars.

"I decided to carry out this idea of mine as I was

afraid that my friend's enemies who hated him might make a search for his planetary body, and if they had chanced to learn where it had been given to the presence of that planet, or, as your favorites say, 'buried,' then doubtless they would have found it and perpetrated some atrocity on it.

"And so, from the sea Kolhidious, I soon ascended on the ship *Occasion* to the planet Mars, where our beings and several kind Martians, who had already learned of the events which had taken place on the planet Earth, paid due respect to the planetary body I had taken with me.

"They buried him with the ceremonies customary on the planet Mars, and over the spot they erected a corresponding construction.

"Anyhow, this was the first and surely will be the last what your favorites call 'grave,' for a being of the planet Earth on this so near yet so far and, for the terrestrial beings, quite inaccessible planet Mars.

"I learned afterwards that this story reached His All-Quarters-Maintainer, the Most Great Archangel 'Setrenotzinarco,' the All-Quarters-Maintainer of that part of the Universe to which that system Ors belongs, and that He manifested his pleasure by giving to whom it was proper, a command concerning the soul of this terrestrial friend of mine.

"On the planet Mars I was indeed expected by several beings of our tribe who had newly arrived from the planet Karatas. Among them, by the way, was also your grandmother who, according to the indications of the chief Zirlikners of the planet Karatas, had been assigned to me as the passive half for the continuance of my line."

CHAPTER 20

The Third Flight of Beelzebub to the Planet Earth

After a brief pause Beelzebub continued to speak further as follows:

"This time I remained at home, that is, on the planet Mars, only a short while, just long enough to see and talk with those who had newly arrived, and to give certain directions of a common tribal character.

"Having disposed of the said affairs, I descended again to your planet with the intention of continuing the pursuit of my aim, that is, the uprooting among these strange three-centered beings of their terrifying custom of doing as it were Divine work by destroying the existence of beings of other brain-systems.

"On this third descent of mine to the planet Earth our ship *Occasion* did not alight on the sea Kolhidious, which is now called there Caspian Sea, but on the sea called at that period the 'Sea of Beneficence.'

"We decided to alight on this sea because I wished this time to go to the capital of the beings of the second group of the continent Ashhark, then named the City Gob, which was situated on the southeastern shore of that sea.

"At that time, the City Gob was already a large city, and was well known over the whole planet for its production of the best 'fabrics' and the best what are called 'precious-ornaments.'

"The City Gob was situated on both banks of the mouth of a large river called the 'Keria-chi' which flowed into the Sea of Beneficence and which had its rise in the eastern heights of this country.

"Into this Sea of Beneficence, on its western side, another large river flowed called the 'Naria-chi.'

"And it was in the valleys of these two large rivers that

the beings of the second group of the continent Ashhark chiefly existed.

"If you wish, my dear boy, I shall also tell you a little of the history of the rise of this group of beings of the continent Ashhark," Beelzebub said to Hassein.

"Yes, Grandfather, yes. I shall listen to you with great interest and much gratitude," replied his grandson.

Then Beelzebub began:

"A long, long time before that period to which my present tale relates, namely, long before that second great catastrophe to that ill-fated planet, while the continent Atlantis was still existing and at the height of its splendor, one of the ordinary three-centered beings of that continent 'invented'—as my latest detailed investigations and researches cleared up—that the powdered horn of a being of that particular exterior form then called a 'Pirmaral' was very effective against what they call 'diseases' of every kind. His 'invention' was afterwards widely spread by various 'freaks' on your planet, and also there was gradually crystallized in the Reason of the ordinary beings there an illusory directing factor, from which, by the way, there is formed in the whole of the presence of each of your favorites, especially of the contemporary ones, the Reason of what is called their 'waking-existence,' which factor is the chief cause of the frequent change in convictions accumulated in them.

"Owing to just this factor, crystallized in the presences of the three-brained beings of your planet of that period, it became the rule that anyone, as they say, who 'fell ill' of some disease or other invariably had to be given this powdered horn to swallow.

"It is not without interest to remark that Pirmarals breed there at the present time also; but, since contemporary beings take them merely for one of the species of being they collectively call 'deer,' they have no special name for them.

"So, my boy, as the beings of the continent Atlantis destroyed very many beings of that form for the sake of these horns, they very soon became extinct.

"Then a number of beings of that continent, who had by this time already made a profession of hunting these beings, went hunting for them on other continents and islands.

"This hunting was very difficult, because for the capture of these Pirmarals a great many of these hunter-beings were required; so these professional hunters always took their whole families with them for assistance.

"Once several of these hunter families joined together and set off to hunt the Pirmarals on a very remote continent then called 'Iranan,' which later, after having been changed owing to the second catastrophe, was called 'the continent Ashhark.'

"This was the same continent your contemporary favorites now call 'Asia.'

"For my further tales concerning these three-brained beings who have taken your fancy, it will be very useful for you, I think, if I emphasize here that on account of various disturbances during the second terrestrial catastrophe, several parts of the continent Iranan entered within the planet, and other terra firmas emerged in their place and attached themselves to this continent, which in consequence became considerably changed and became in size almost what the continent Atlantis had been for the planet Earth before the catastrophe.

"Well, then, my boy, while this said group of hunters were once with their families pursuing a herd of these Pirmarals, they reached the shores of the water-space which was later called the Sea of Beneficence.

"Both the sea itself and its rich and fertile shores so

greatly pleased this group of hunters that they did not wish to return to the continent Atlantis, and from that time on they remained to exist there, on those shores.

"That country was at that time indeed so excellent and so 'Sooptaninalnian' for ordinary being-existence that no being who could think at all could help liking it.

"On that 'terra firma' part of the surface of your planet, not only did there exist at that period multitudes of two-brained beings of the said exterior form, namely, Pirmarals, but around this water-space were also multitudes of various kinds of 'fruit trees,' whose fruit then still served for your favorites as the principal product for their 'first being-food.'

"There were then also so many of the one-brained and two-brained beings which your favorites call 'birds' that when they flew in droves it became, as your favorites say, 'quite dark.'

"The water-space situated in the middle of that country and then named the Sea of Beneficence so abounded with fish that they could almost be caught, as they also say, with one's bare hands.

"As for the soil of the shores of the Sea of Beneficence and also of the valleys of the two large rivers flowing into it, any part of them could be adapted for growing anything you like.

"In short, both the climate of this country and everything else so delighted the hunters and their families that none of them, as I have already said, had any desire to return to the continent Atlantis, and from that time on they remained there, and soon adapting themselves to everything, multiplied and existed, as is said, 'on-a-bed-of-roses.'

"At this place in my tale I must tell you about an extraordinary coincidence which later had great consequences both for the first beings of this second group and for their descendants of most recent times.

"It seems that at the time when the said hunters from the continent Atlantis reached the Sea of Beneficence and decided to settle there, there was already existing on the shores of the same sea a being from the continent Atlantis who was at that time very important and who belonged to the sect of 'Astrosovors' and who was a member of a learned society, the like of which has never since appeared on that planet Earth and probably never will.

"This learned society then existed under the name of 'Akhaldan.'

"And this member of the Akhaldans reached the shores of the Sea of Beneficence on account of the following:

"Just before the second great catastrophe those genuine learned beings then existing on the continent Atlantis, who had organized that truly great learned society there, somehow became aware that something very serious had to happen in Nature, so they began to observe very carefully all the natural phenomena of their continent; but however hard they tried, they could in no way find out what precisely had to happen.

"A little later on and with the same aim, they sent some of their members to other continents and islands, in order, by means of these common observations, perhaps to be able to find out what was impending.

"The members sent were to observe not only Nature on the planet Earth, but also every kind of, as they then expressed themselves there, 'heavenly-phenomena.'

"One of these members, namely, the mentioned important being, had chosen the continent Iranan for his observations and, having migrated there with his servants, had settled on the shores of the said water-space later called the Sea of Beneficence.

"It was just this same learned member of the society

Akhaldan who once chanced to meet certain of the mentioned hunters on the shores of the said Sea of Beneficence, and having learned that they had also come from the continent Atlantis, was naturally very glad, and began to establish relations with them.

"And when, shortly afterwards, the continent Atlantis entered within the planet and this learned Akhaldan member had no longer any place to return to, he remained to exist with these hunters in that future Maralpleicie.

"A little later this group of hunters chose this learned being, as the cleverest, to be their chief, and still later . . . this member of the great society Akhaldan married the daughter named Rimala of one of the hunters, and afterwards shared fully in the lives of the founders of the beings of that second group of the continent Iranan, or, as it is called at the present time, 'Asia.'

"A long time passed.

"The beings of this place on the planet Earth were also born and were again destroyed; and the general level of the psyche of this kind of Earth-beings was thereby changed, of course at times for the better, at times for the worse.

"Multiplying, these beings gradually spread over this country more and more widely, although always preferring the shores of the Sea of Beneficence and the valleys of those two large rivers which flowed into it.

"Only much later the center of their common existence was formed on the southeastern shore of the sea; and this place they called the city Gob. This city became the chief place of existence for the head of this second group of beings of the continent Ashhark, whom they called 'king.'

"The duties of this king were here also hereditary and this inheritance began with the first chosen chief, who was the said learned member of the learned society Akhaldan.

"At the time to which the tale I began refers, the king

for the beings of that second group was the grandson of his great grandson, and his name was 'Konuzion.'

"My latest detailed investigations and researches showed that there had been actualized by that same King Konuzion exceedingly wise and most beneficent measures for uprooting a terrifying evil which had arisen among the beings who by the will of Fate had become his subjects. And he had actualized these said most wise and beneficent measures for the following reason:

"This same King Konuzion once constated that the beings of his community were becoming less and less capable of work, and that crimes, robberies, and violence and many other such things as had never occurred before were on the increase among them, or, if they had occurred, had seemed to be quite exceptional phenomena.

"These constatations surprised and at the same time grieved King Konuzion, who after thinking deeply about it, decided to find out the causes of this sorrowful phenomenon.

"After long observations he finally cleared up for himself that the cause of the phenomenon was a new habit of the beings of his community, namely, their habit of chewing the seed of a plant then called 'Gulgulian.' This surplanetary formation also arises on the planet Earth at the present time, and those of your favorites who consider themselves 'educated' call it 'Papaveroon,' but the ordinary beings simply call it the 'poppy.'

"Here it must without fail be noticed that the beings of Maralpleicie then only had a passion for chewing those seeds of the mentioned surplanetary formation which had without fail to be gathered at the time of what is called 'ripeness.'

"In the course of his further close observations and impartial investigations King Konuzion clearly understood that these seeds contained a 'something' that could completely change, for the time being, all the established habits of the psyche of those beings who introduced this something into themselves, with the result that they saw, understood, felt, sensed, and acted quite otherwise than they were previously accustomed to see, sense, act, and so on.

"For instance, a crow would appear to them to be a peacock; a trough of water, a sea; a harsh clatter, music; good will, enmity; insults, love; and so on and so forth.

"When King Konuzion became clearly convinced of all this, he immediately dispatched everywhere trusted and faithful subjects of his strictly to command in his name all beings of his community to cease chewing the seeds of the mentioned plant; he also arranged for the punishment and fine of those beings who should disobey this order.

"Thanks to these measures of his, the chewing of the said seeds seemed to diminish in the country of Maralpleicie; but after a very short time it was discovered that the number of those who chewed had only seemingly diminished; in reality, they were even more than before.

"Having understood this, the wise King Konuzion thereupon resolved to punish still more severely those who should continue chewing; and at the same time he strengthened the surveillance of his subjects and also the strictness of the enforcement of the punishment of the guilty.

"And he himself began going about everywhere in the city of Gob, personally examining the guilty and impressing them by various punishments, physical and moral.

"In spite of all this, however, the desired result was not obtained, as the number of those who chewed increased more and more in the city of Gob itself, and corresponding reports from other places in the territories subject to him also increased daily.

"It then became clear that the number of those who chewed had increased still more because many of the three-brained beings who had never previously chewed now began chewing merely out of what is called 'curiosity,' which is one of the peculiarities of the psyche of the three-brained beings of that planet which has taken your fancy, that is to say, curiosity to find out what effect those seeds had, the chewing of which was prohibited and punished by the king with such insistence and relentless severity.

"I must emphasize here, that though the said particularity of their psyche began to be crystallized in your favorites immediately after the loss of Atlantis, yet in none of the beings of former epochs did it function so blatantly as it does now in the contemporary three-brained beings there; they have more of it perhaps, than there are hairs on a 'Toosook.'

"So, my boy . . .

"When the wise King Konuzion finally became quite convinced that it was not possible by the described measures to extirpate the passion for chewing the seeds of Gulgulian, and saw that the only result of his measures was the death of several who were punished, he abrogated all the measures he had previously taken and again began to think seriously about a search for some other real means for destroying this evil, lamentable for his community.

"As I learned much later—owing to a very ancient surviving monument—the great King Konuzion then returned to his chamber and for eighteen days neither ate nor drank but only very seriously thought and thought.

"It must in any case be noticed here, that those latest researches of mine showed that King Konuzion was then particularly anxious to find a means of uprooting this evil, because all the affairs of his community were going from bad to worse.

"The beings who were addicted to this passion almost ceased to work; the flow of what is called money into the communal treasury entirely ceased and the ultimate ruin of the community seemed to be inevitable.

"Finally the wise king decided to deal with this evil indirectly, namely, by playing on the weaknesses in the psyche of the beings of his community. With this aim he invented a very original 'religious doctrine' corresponding to the psyche of the beings of that time; and this invention of his he spread broadcast among all his subjects by every means at his disposal.

"In this religious doctrine it was said, among other things, that far from our continent Ashhark was a larger island where existed our 'Mister God.'

"I must tell you that in those days not one of the ordinary beings knew that, besides their planet Earth, other cosmic concentrations existed.

"The beings of the planet Earth of those days were even certain that the scarcely visible 'white-points' far away in space were nothing more than the pattern on the 'veil' of the 'world,' that is to say, just of their planet; as, in their notions then, the 'whole-world' consisted, as I have said, of their planet alone.

"They were also convinced that this veil was supported like a canopy on special pillars, the ends of which rested on their planet.

"In that ingeniously original 'religious doctrine' of the wise King Konuzion it was said that Mister God had intentionally attached to our souls the organs and limbs we now have to protect us against our environment, and to enable us efficiently and profitably to serve both himself personally and the 'souls' already taken to that island of His.

"And when we die and our soul is liberated from all these specially attached organs and limbs, it becomes what it should really be, and is then immediately taken just to this island of His, where our Mister God, in accordance with how our soul with its added parts has existed here on our continent Ashhark, assigns to it an appropriate place for its further existence.

"If the soul has fulfilled its duties honestly and conscientiously, Mister God leaves it, for its further existence, on His island; but the soul that here on the continent Ashhark has idled or discharged its duties indolently and negligently, that has in short, existed only for the gratification of the desires of the parts attached to it, or finally, that has not kept His commandments—such a soul our Mister God sends for its further existence to a neighboring island of smaller size.

"Here, on the continent Ashhark, exist many 'spirits' attendant upon Him, who walk among us in 'caps-of-invisibility,' thanks to which they can constantly watch us unnoticed and either inform our Mister God of all our doings or report them to Him on the 'Day-of-Judgment.'

"We cannot in any way conceal from them, either any of our doings, or any of our thoughts.

"It was still further said that just like our continent Ashhark, all the other continents and islands of the world had been created by our Mister God and now existed as I have said, only to serve Him and the deserving 'souls' already dwelling on His island.

"The continents and islands of the world are all places, as it were, for preparation, and storehouses for everything necessary for this island of His.

"That island on which Mister God Himself and the deserving souls exist is called 'Paradise,' and existence there is just 'Roses, Roses.'

"All its rivers are of milk, their banks of honey; nobody needs to toil or work there; everything necessary for a happy, carefree, and blissful existence is there, because everything requisite is supplied there in superabundance from our own and the other continents and islands of the world.

"This island Paradise is full of young and lovely women, of all the peoples and races of the world; and each of them belongs for the asking to the 'soul' that desires her.

"In certain public squares of that superb island, mountains of various articles of adornment are always kept, from the most brilliant diamonds to the deepest turquoise; and every 'soul' can take anything he likes, also without the least hindrance.

"In other public squares of that beatific island are piled huge mountains of sweetmeats specially prepared with essence of 'poppy' and 'hemp'; and every 'soul' may take as much as he pleases at any time of the day or night.

"There are no diseases there; and of course, none of those 'lice' or 'flies' that give us all no peace here, and blight our whole existence.

"The other, smaller island, to which our Mister God sends for their further existence the 'souls' whose temporary physical parts have been idle here and have not existed according to His commandments, is called 'Hell.'

"All the rivers of this island are of burning pitch; the whole air stinks like a skunk at bay. Swarms of horrible beings blow police-whistles in every square; and all the 'furniture,' 'carpets,' 'beds,' and so on there, are made of fine needles with their points sticking out.

"One very salted cake is given once a day to every 'soul' on this island; and there is not a single drop of drinking water there. Many other things are also there of a kind that the beings of Earth not only would not like to encounter, but not even experience in thought.

"When I first came to the country of Maralpleicie, all the three-brained beings of that country were followers of a 'religion' based on the just-mentioned ingenious 'religious-doctrine,' and this 'religion' was then in full bloom.

"To the inventor himself of this ingenious 'religious-doctrine,' namely, the wise King Konuzion, the sacred 'Rascooarno' had occurred long before this time, that is to say, he had long previously 'died.'

"But of course owing once again to the strangeness of the psyche of your favorites, his invention had taken such a strong hold there that not a single being in the whole country of Maralpleicie then doubted the truth of its peculiar tenets.

"Here also in the city Gob, from the first day of my arrival, I began visiting the 'Kaltaani,' which were already called 'Chaihana.'

"It must be noticed that although the custom of Sacrificial-Offerings was also flourishing at that period in the country of Maralpleicie, it was not on the large scale on which it had flourished in the country Tikliamish.

"There in the city Gob I began deliberately looking for a corresponding being, in order to make friends with him, as I had in the city Koorkalai.

"And indeed I soon found such a friend here also, but this time he was not a 'priest' by profession.

"My friend here turned out to be the proprietor of a large Chaihana; and although I became, as it is said there, on very good terms with him, nevertheless I never had that strange 'tie' with him which arose in my essence towards the priest Abdil in the city Koorkalai.

"Although I had already existed a whole month in the city Gob, I had neither decided upon nor undertaken anything practical for my aim. I simply wandered about the city Gob, visiting first the various Chaihana, and only later the Chaihana of my new friend there.

"During this time I became familiar with many of the manners and customs of this second group and also with the fine points of their religion; and at the end of the month I decided to attain my aim here also, through their religion.

"After serious pondering I found it necessary to add something to the 'religious-doctrine' existing there, and I counted on being able, like the wise King Konuzion, to spread this addition of mine effectively among them.

"Just then I invented that those spirits in 'caps-of-invisibility' who, as it was said in that great religion, watch our deeds and thoughts in order to report them later to our Mister God, are none other than just the beings of other forms, which exist among us.

"It is just they who watch us and report everything to our Mister God.

"But we people not only fail to pay them their due honor and respect, but we even destroy their existences for our food as well as for our Sacrificial-Offerings.

"I particularly emphasized in my preaching that not only ought we not to destroy the existence of the beings of other forms in honor of Mister God, but that, on the contrary, we ought to try to win their favor and to beseech them at least not to report to Mister God those little evil acts of ours which we do involuntarily.

"And this addition of mine I began to spread by every possible means; of course, very cautiously.

"At first, I spread this invention of mine through my new friend there, the proprietor of the Chaihana.

"I must tell you that his Chaihana was almost the largest in the whole city Gob; and it was very famous for its reddish liquid, of which the beings of the planet Earth are very fond.

"So there were always a great many customers there, and it was open day and night.

"Not only did the inhabitants of the city itself go there, but also all the visitors from the whole of Maralpleicie.

"I soon became quite expert in talking with and persuading individual customers as well as all those present in the Chaihana.

"My new friend himself, the proprietor of the Chaihana, believed my invention so firmly that he didn't know what to do with himself, for repentance for his past.

"He was in constant agitation and bitterly repented his previous disrespectful attitude and his treatment of the various beings of other forms.

"Becoming day by day a more ardent preacher of my invention, he thereby not only helped to spread it in his own Chaihana, but he even began of his own accord to visit other Chaihana in the city Gob, in order to spread the truth which had so agitated him.

"He preached in the market places, and several times made special visits to the holy places, of which there were then already many in the outskirts of the city Gob, and which had been established in honor or in memory of somebody or something.

"It is very interesting to remark here that the information that serves on the planet Earth for the rise of a holy place is usually due to certain Earth beings called 'Liars.'

"This disease of 'lying' is also very widespread there.

"On the planet Earth people lie consciously and unconsciously.

"And they consciously lie there when they can obtain some personal material advantage by lying; and they unconsciously lie there when they fall ill with the disease called 'Hysteria.'

"In addition to the proprietor of the Chaihana there in the city Gob, a number of other beings very soon began unconsciously to assist me, who, like the proprietor of the Chaihana, had meanwhile become ardent supporters of my invention; and all the beings of that second group of Asiatic beings were soon eagerly spreading this invention of mine and persuading each other of it as an indubitable 'truth' that had suddenly been revealed.

"The result of it all was that there in the country of Maralpleicie, not only were Sacrificial-Offerings indeed diminished, but they even began to treat the beings of other forms with unprecedented attention.

"Such comical farces very soon began there that though I myself was the author of the invention, I nevertheless found it very difficult to refrain from laughter.

"Such comical farces occurred as, for instance, the following: a highly respectable and wealthy merchant of the city Gob would be riding in the morning on his donkey to his own shop and on the way a motley crowd of beings would drag this respectable merchant off his donkey and thoroughly maul him because he had dared to ride on it; and then the crowd, bowing low, would escort the donkey on which the merchant had been riding, wherever it chose to go.

"Or, what is called a 'woodcutter' would be hauling wood to market with his own oxen from the forest to the town.

"A mob of citizens would drag him also off his cart and after mauling him, very gently unyoke the oxen and escort them wherever they wished to go.

"And if the cart were seen in a part of the city where it might hold up the traffic, the mob of citizens would themselves drag the cart to the market and leave it there to its fate.

"Thanks to this invention of mine, various quite new customs were very soon created in the city Gob.

"As, for instance, the custom was established there of placing troughs in all the squares, public places, and at the crossroads of the town, where residents of the city Gob could in the morning throw their choicest morsels of food for dogs and other stray beings of various forms; and at sunrise, throw into the Sea of Beneficence every kind of food for the beings called 'fishes.'

"But the most peculiar of all was the custom of paying attention to the voices of beings of various forms.

"As soon as they heard the voice of a being of any form, they immediately began to praise the names of their gods and to await their blessing.

"It might be the crowing of a cock, the barking of a dog, the mewing of a cat, the squealing of an ape, or so on. . . . It would always startle them.

"Here it is interesting to notice that for some reason or other they would always on these occasions raise their heads and look upwards, even though, according to the teaching of their religion, their god and his assistants were supposed to exist on the same level as themselves, and not where they directed their eyes and prayers.

"It was extremely interesting at these moments to watch their faces."

"Pardon me, your Right Reverence," interrupted at that moment Beelzebub's old devoted servant Ahoon, who had also been listening with great interest to his tales.

"Do you remember, your Right Reverence, how many times in that same city Gob we ourselves had to flop down in the streets during the cries of beings of different forms?"

To this remark, Beelzebub said:

"Certainly I remember, dear Ahoon. How could I forget such comical impressions?

"You must know," he then continued, turning to Hassein again, "that the beings of the planet Earth are inconceivably proud and touchy. If someone does not share their views or agree to do as they do, or criticizes their manifestations, they are, oh, very indignant and offended.

"If one had the power, he would order whoever dared not to do as he did, or who criticized his conduct, to be shut up in the kind of room which is usually infested by innumerable what are called 'rats' and 'lice.'

"And at times, if the offended one had greater physical strength, and an important power-possessing being with whom he was not on very good terms was not watching him, he would simply maul the offender as the Russian Sidor once mauled his favorite goat.

"Very well knowing this aspect also of their strange psyche, I had no desire to offend them and to incur their wrath; furthermore, I was always profoundly aware that to outrage anybody's religious feeling is contrary to all morality, so, when existing among them, I always tried to do as they did, in order not to be conspicuous and attract their attention.

"Here it does no harm to notice that owing to the existing abnormal conditions of ordinary existence there among your favorites, the three-brained beings of that strange planet Earth, especially during recent centuries, only those beings who manifest themselves, not as the majority of them do, but somehow or other, more absurdly, become noticed and consequently honored by the rest; and the more absurd their manifestations and the more stupid, mean, and insolent the 'tricks' they play, the more noticed and famous they become, and the greater is the number of the beings on the given continent and even on other continents who know them personally or at least by name.

"On the other hand, no honest being who does not manifest himself absurdly will ever become famous among other beings or even be simply noticed, however good-natured and sensible he may be in himself.

"And so, my boy, what our Ahoon so mischievously reminded me about concerned just that custom, which developed there in the city Gob, of attaching significance to the voices of beings of various forms and particularly to the voice of what are called 'donkeys,' of which there were then, for some reason or other, a great many in the city Gob.

"The beings of all other forms of that planet also manifest themselves by voice, but at a definite time. For instance, the cock cries at midnight, an ape in the morning when it is hungry, and so on, but donkeys there bray whenever it enters their heads to do so, and in consequence you may hear the voice of that silly being there at any time of the day or night.

"So, my boy, it was established there in the city Gob that as soon as the sound of the voice of the donkey was heard, all who heard it had to flop down immediately and offer up prayers to their god and to their revered idols and, I must add, these donkeys usually have a very loud voice by nature and their voices carry a long way.

"Well, then, as we walked along the streets of the city Gob and saw the citizens flopping down at the braying of every donkey, we had to flop down likewise so as not to be distinguished from the others; and it was just this comical custom, I see now, that tickled our old Ahoon so much.

"You noticed, my dear Hassein, with what venomous satisfaction our old man reminded me, after so many centuries, of that comical situation of mine."

Having said this, Beelzebub, smiling, went on with the tale he had begun.

"It is needless to say," he continued, "that there also, in this second center of culture of the three-brained beings of your planet, breeding there on the continent of Ashhark, the destruction of beings of other forms for Sacrificial-Offerings entirely ceased; and, if isolated instances occurred, the beings of that group themselves settled accounts with the offenders without compunction.

"Having thus become convinced that there also, among that second group of beings of the continent Ashhark, I had succeeded so easily in uprooting, for a long time, the custom of Sacrificial-Offerings, I decided to leave; but I had it in mind, in any event, to visit also the nearest large points where the beings of the same second group were breeding; and I chose for this purpose the region of the course of the river 'Naria-Chi.'

"Soon after this decision, I sailed with Ahoon to the mouth of this river, and began to sail up against its current, having become persuaded that there had already passed from the beings of the city Gob to the beings of this group populating these large centers the same new customs and the same notions concerning Sacrificial-Offerings by the destruction of the existence of other beings.

"We finally arrived at a small town called 'Arguenia,' which in those days was considered the most remote point of the country Maralpleicie.

"Here also there existed a fair number of beings of this second Asiatic group who were engaged chiefly in obtaining from Nature what is called 'turquoise.'

"There in the small town of Arguenia I began, as usual, to visit their various Chaihana, and there also I continued my usual procedure."

CHAPTER 21

The First Visit of Beelzebub to India

Beelzebub continued to speak as follows:

"Sitting in a Chaihana in this small town of Arguenia, I once overheard a conversation among several beings seated not far from me.

"They were talking and deciding when and how they should go by caravan to Pearl-land.

"Having listened to their conversation, I gathered that they intended to go there for the purpose of exchanging their 'turquoises' for what are called 'pearls.'

"I must here, by the way, draw your attention also to the fact that your favorites of former as well as of contemporary epochs liked and still like to wear pearls and also the said turquoise, as well as many other what are called 'precious-trinkets' for the purpose, as they say, of 'adorning' their exteriors. But if you would like to know my opinion, they do so, of course instinctively, in order to offset, so to say, the 'value-of-their-inner-insignificance.'

"At that period to which my present tale refers, the said pearls were very rare among the beings of the second Asiatic group and commanded a high price among them. But in the country Pearl-land there was at the same time a great number of these pearls, and there, on the contrary, they were very cheap, because pearls at that time were exclusively obtained only from the water-spaces surrounding that country.

"The mentioned conversation of the beings who sat near me in the Chaihana in the small town Arguenia then immediately interested me, because at that time I already had the intention of going to that same Pearl-land where the three-brained beings of the continent Ashhark of the third group bred.

"And the conversation I then heard at once evoked in my mentation an association to the effect that it might be better to go to the country Pearl-land directly from here with this large caravan of these beings, rather than return the same way to the Sea of Beneficence, and from there, by means of the same ship *Occasion*, to reach this country.

"Although this journey, which in those days was almost impossible for the beings of the Earth, would take us a good deal of time, yet I thought that the journey back to the Sea of Beneficence with its unforeseeable contingencies would perhaps not take much less time.

"This association then arose in my mentation chiefly because I had long before heard a great deal about the rare peculiarities of those parts of the nature of that peculiar planet through which the proposed route of the caravan lay and, in consequence, what is called a 'being-love-of-knowledge' which was already crystallized in me, having received a shock for functioning from all that had been overheard, immediately dictated to my common presence the need to be persuaded of everything personally, directly through my own perceptive organs.

"So, my boy, owing to what I have said, I intentionally sat with the conversing beings and joined in their deliberations.

"As a result of it all, we also were then included in the company of their caravan, and two days later we set off together with them.

"I and Ahoon then passed through indeed very unusual places, unusual even for the general nature of this peculiar planet, certain parts of which, by the way, only became so because before that period this ill-fated planet had already undergone two what are called Transapalnian-perturbations, almost unprecedented in the Universe.

"From the first day we had to pass exclusively through

a region of various 'terra-firma-projections' of unusual forms, which had conglomerations of all kinds of 'intraplanetary-minerals.'

"And only after a month's travel, according to their time-calculation, did our caravan from Arguenia come to places where in the soil the possibility had not yet been quite destroyed of Nature's forming surplanetary formations and creating corresponding conditions for the arising and existing of various one-brained and two-brained beings.

"After every kind of difficulty we at last, one rainy morning, on ascending a height, suddenly saw on the horizon the outline of a large water-space bordering the edges of the continent Ashhark, which was then called Pearl-land.

"And four days later we came to the chief point of the existence of the beings of that third group, then the city 'Kaimon'.

"Having arranged there the place of our permanent existence, we did nothing during our first days there but stroll about the streets of the town, observing the specific manifestations of the beings of that third group in the process of their ordinary existence.

"It cannot be helped, my dear Hassein. Now that I have told you the history of the arising of the second group of the three-brained beings of the continent Ashhark, I must tell you also about the history of the arising of the third group."

"You must indeed tell me, my dear and beloved Grandfather," eagerly exclaimed Hassein; and, this time with great reverence, extending his hands upwards, he sincerely said:

"May my dear and kind Grandfather become worthy to be perfected to the degree of the sacred 'Anklad'!"

Without saying anything to this, Beelzebub merely smiled and continued to relate as follows:

"The history of the arising of this third group of Asiatic beings begins only a little later than that period when the families of hunters for Pirmarals first came to the shores of the Sea of Beneficence from the continent Atlantis and, having settled there, founded the second group of Asiatic beings.

"It was just in those, for your contemporary favorites, infinitely remote days, that is, not long before the second Transapalnian perturbation occurred to this ill-fated planet, that there had already begun to be crystallized in the presences of the three-centered beings then of the continent Atlantis certain consequences of the properties of the organ Kundabuffer, on account of which the need—among other needs unbecoming to three-brained beings—began to arise in them to wear, as I have already told you, various trinkets as it were for their adornment, and also a kind of famous what is called 'Talisman' which they had invented.

"One of these trinkets, then on the continent Atlantis, just as now on the other continents of the planet Earth, was and is this same pearl.

"The said pearl is formed in one-brained beings which breed in the 'Saliakooriap' of your planet Earth, that is to say, in that part of it which is called 'Hentralispana,' or, as your favorites might express it, the blood of the planet, which is present in the common presence of every planet and which serves the actualizing of the process of the Most Great common-cosmic Trogoautoegocrat; and there on your planet this part is called 'water.'

"This one-brained being in which the said pearl is formed used to breed in the 'Saliakooriapnian,' or water-areas, surrounding the continent Atlantis; but in consequence of the great demand for the said pearl and therefore of the great destruction of these one-brained 'pearl-bearing beings,' soon none were left near this continent.

Thereupon, when those beings there who made the aim and sense of their existence the destruction of these pearl-bearing beings, that is to say, who destroyed their existence only in order to procure that part of their common presence called pearl merely for the gratification of their quite absurd egoism, found no more of these said pearl-bearing beings in the water-area nearest to the continent Atlantis, they, that is, these 'professionals,' then began to look for them in other water-areas and gradually moved further and further away from their own continent.

"Once during these searches of theirs, owing to what are called 'Saliakooriapnian-displacements,' or as they say, prolonged 'storms,' their rafts came unexpectedly to a place where there proved to be a great number of these pearl-bearing beings; and the place itself was extremely convenient for their destruction.

"These water-areas where the destroyers of the pearl-bearing beings then chanced to come and where these beings bred in large numbers, were just those water-areas which surround the place then called Pearl-land and now called Hindustan or India.

"For the first days, the aforementioned terrestrial professionals of that time who had chanced to arrive there did nothing but gratify to the full their inclinations, which had already become inherent to their presences in respect of the destruction of these one-brained beings of their planet; and it was only later, after they had also by chance found out that almost everything required for ordinary existence arose in abundance on the neighboring terra firma, that they decided never to return to Atlantis but to settle there for their permanent existence.

"A few of these destroyers of pearl-bearing beings then sailed to the continent Atlantis, and having exchanged their pearls for various articles which were still lacking in the new place, they returned, bringing with them their own families as well as the families of those who had remained.

"Later several of these first settlers of this—for the beings then of that time—'new' country visited their native land from time to time for the purpose of exchanging pearls for articles required by them there; and each time they took back with them a further number of beings, either their relatives or their kinsmen or just laborers indispensable to their extensive work.

"So, my boy, from that time on, that part also of the surface of the planet Earth became known to all the three-brained beings there under the name of 'Land-of-Beneficence.'

"In this way, before the second great catastrophe to the planet Earth, many beings of the continent Atlantis already existed on this part of the continent Ashhark also, and when that second catastrophe occurred to your planet, then many of the beings who chanced to be saved from the continent Atlantis, chiefly those who already had relatives and kinsmen in that Pearl-land, also gradually collected there.

"Owing, as always, to their 'fecundity,' they gradually multiplied there and began to populate this part of the terra firma of their planet, more and more.

"At first they populated there in Pearl-land only two definite regions, namely, the regions around the mouths of the two large rivers which flowed from the interior of Pearl-land into the large water-space, just in those places near which many of the mentioned pearl-bearing beings bred.

"But when the population there greatly increased, they began to populate also the interior of that part of the continent Ashhark; but nevertheless their favorite regions continued to be the valleys of the two mentioned rivers.

"Well, then, my boy, when I first arrived in Pearl-land,

I decided to attain my aim there also by means of the 'Havatvernoni' which existed there, that is, through their Religion.

"But it turned out that amongst the beings of this third group of the continent Ashhark, there were at that time several peculiar 'Havatvernonis' or 'Religions' all based on different, quite independent what are called 'religious-teachings,' having nothing in common with each other.

"In view of this, I first began seriously studying these religious-teachings there, and having in the course of my studies constated that one of them, founded on the teaching of a genuine Messenger of our COMMON ENDLESS CREATOR, afterwards called Saint Buddha, had the most followers, I, on becoming acquainted with it, devoted most of my attention to its study.

"Before continuing to tell you about the three-brained beings breeding just on that part of the surface of the planet Earth, it is, I think, necessary to remark, even if briefly, that there existed and still exist, ever since the time when the practice of having peculiar being-Havatvernonis or Religions began to arise and exist among your favorites, two basic kinds of religious-teachings.

"One kind was invented by those three-brained beings there themselves, in whom, for some reason or other, there arises the functioning of a psyche proper to Hasnamusses; and the other kind of religious-teaching is founded there upon those detailed instructions which have been preached, as it were, by genuine Messengers from Above, who indeed are from time to time sent by certain nearest helpers of our COMMON FATHER, for the purpose of aiding the three-brained beings of your planet in destroying in their presences the crystallized consequences of the properties of the organ Kundabuffer.

"The religion which was then followed by most of the beings of the country Pearl-land and to become acquainted with which I then devoted my attention, and about which I find it necessary to tell you a little, arose there in the following way:

"As I later learned, with the multiplication of the three-brained beings of that third group, many beings among them with the properties of Hasnamusses were formed into responsible beings; and when these latter began spreading ideas more maleficent than usual among the beings of that group, there was crystallized in the presences of the majority of the three-centered beings of the third group, that special psychic property, which, in its totality, already engendered a factor which greatly hindered the normal 'exchange-of-substances' actualized by the Most Great common-cosmic Trogoautoegocrat. Well, then, as soon as this lamentable result, also issuing from this planet, was noticed by certain Most Most Sacred Individuals, it was sanctioned that a corresponding Sacred Individual should be sent there, specially to that group of beings, for the more or less tolerable regulation of their being-existence in accordance with the existence of the whole of that solar system.

"It was just then that the aforementioned Sacred Individual was sent to them who, having been coated with the planetary body of a terrestrial being, was called, as I have said, Saint Buddha.

"The coating of the said Sacred Individual with a planetary body of a terrestrial three-brained being was actualized there several centuries before my first visit to the country Pearl-land."

At this point in Beelzebub's tales, Hassein turned to him and said:

"My dear Grandfather, during your tales you have already many times used the expression Hasnamuss. I have until now understood only from the intonation of your voice and from the consonance of the word itself, that by this expression you defined those three-brained beings whom you always set apart from others as if they deserved 'Objective-Contempt.'

"Be so kind as always and explain to me the real meaning and exact sense of this word."

Whereupon Beelzebub, with a smile inherent to him, said as follows:

"Concerning the 'typicality' of the three-brained beings for whom I have adopted this verbal definition, I shall explain it to you at the proper time, but meanwhile know that this word designates every already 'definitized' common presence of a three-brained being, both those consisting only of the single planetary body as well as those whose higher being-bodies are already coated in them, and in which for some reason or other, data have not been crystallized for the Divine impulse of 'Objective-Conscience.'"

Having said only this in defining the word Hasnamuss, Beelzebub continued to speak:

"During my detailed studies of the mentioned religious teaching I also clarified that after this Sacred Individual had become finally coated with the presence of a three-brained being there and had seriously pondered how to fulfill the task that had been laid upon him from Above, he decided to attain this by means of the enlightenment of their Reason.

"Here it must without fail be noticed that by that time there had already been crystallized in the presence of Saint Buddha, as the same detailed researches of mine had made clear, a very clear understanding that in the process of its abnormal formation, the Reason of the three-centered beings of the planet Earth results in a Reason called 'instincto-terebelnian,' that is, a Reason which functions only from corresponding shocks from without; yet in spite of this, Saint Buddha decided to carry out his task by means of this peculiar Reason of theirs, that is, this Reason peculiar to the three-centered beings there; and therefore, he first of all began informing their peculiar Reason with objective truths of every kind.

"Saint Buddha first assembled many of the chiefs of that group and spoke to them as follows:

"'Beings possessing presences similar to that of the ALL-CREATOR HIMSELF!

"'By certain all-enlightened and all-justly guiding most sacred final results of the actualization of everything existing in the Universe, my essence has been sent to you to serve as a helping factor in the striving of each of you to free yourselves from the consequences of those abnormal being-properties which, in view of highly important common cosmic needs, were implanted in the presences of your ancestors and, passing by heredity from generation to generation, have reached you also!'

"Saint Buddha spoke again about this a little more in detail but only to certain beings there initiated by him.

"This second time, as it turned out, he then expressed himself in the following words:

"'Beings with presences for actualizing the hope of our COMMON FATHER!

"'Almost at the beginning of the rise of your race, there occurred in the process of the normal existence of the whole of this solar system, an unforeseen accident which threatened serious consequences for everything existing.

"'For the regulation of that common universal misfortune there was then required, among other measures, according to the explanations of certain Most High, Most Most Sacred Individuals, a certain change in the functioning of the common presences of your ancestors, namely, there was implanted into their presences a certain organ with special properties, owing to which everything external perceived by their whole presences and transformed for their own coating was afterwards manifested not in accordance with reality.

"'A little later, when the normal existence of this solar system was stabilized and the necessity for certain intentionally created abnormal actualizations had passed, our MOST ALL-GRACIOUS COMMON FATHER did not fail to give the command immediately to annul certain artificial measures, among which was the removal from the common presences of your ancestors of the now already superfluous organ Kundabuffer with all its special artificial properties; and this command was immediately executed by corresponding Sacred Individuals who superintend such cosmic actualizations.

"'After a considerable time had passed it was suddenly revealed that, although all the properties of the said organ had indeed been removed from the presences of your ancestors by the mentioned Most Sacred Individuals, yet nevertheless, a certain lawfully flowing cosmic result, existing under the name of "predisposition," and arising in every more or less independent cosmic presence owing to the repeated action in it of any function, had not been foreseen and destroyed in their presences.

"'And so it turned out that owing to this predisposition, which began to pass by heredity to the succeeding generations, the consequences of many of the properties of the organ Kundabuffer began gradually to be crystallized in their presences.

"'No sooner was this lamentable fact which proceeded in the presences of the three-brained beings breeding on this planet Earth first made clear, than by All-Gracious sanction of our COMMON FATHER, a suitable Sacred Individual was immediately sent here, so that, being coated with a presence like your own and having become perfected by Objective Reason under the conditions already established here, he might better explain and show you the way of eradicating from your presences the already crystallized consequences of the properties of the organ Kundabuffer as well as your inherited predispositions to new crystallizations.

"'During the period when the said Sacred Individual, coated with a presence like your own and who had already attained to the age of a responsible three-centered being similar to yourselves, directly guided the ordinary process of the being-existence of your ancestors, many of them did indeed completely free themselves from the consequences of the properties of the organ Kundabuffer and either thereby acquired Being personally for themselves or became normal sources for the arising of normal presences of succeeding beings similar to themselves.

"'But in consequence of the fact that before the period of the said Sacred Individual's appearance here, the duration of your existence had, owing to very many firmly fixed abnormal conditions of ordinary existence created by yourselves, already become abnormally short, and therefore the process of sacred Rascooarno had also very soon to occur to this Sacred Individual, that is to say, he also had, like you, to die prematurely, then after his death, the former conditions were gradually re-established there owing on the one hand to the established abnormal conditions of ordinary being-existence and, on the other hand, to that maleficent particularity in your psyche, called Wiseacring.

"'Owing to this said particularity in your psyche, the beings here already of the second generation after the contemporaries of the mentioned Sacred Individual who had been sent from Above began gradually to change everything he had explained and indicated, and the whole of it was finally completely destroyed.

"'Again and again the same was actualized by the Most

Most High Common Cosmic Final Results, and each time the same fruitless results were obtained.

"'In this present period of the flow of time, when the abnormal being-existence of the three-brained beings of your planet, particularly of the beings arising and existing on that part of the surface of the Earth which is called Pearl-land, is already beginning seriously to hinder the normal harmonious existence of the whole of this solar system, my essence is manifested among you from Above, in order that here on the spot, it may together with your own essences find ways and means, under the conditions already fixed here, of freeing your presences from the said consequences, now present in them, owing to the absence of foresight on the part of certain Most Saintly Final Cosmic Results.'

"After having said all this, Saint Buddha thereafter, just by means of talks with them, first cleared up for Himself and afterwards explained to them how the process of their existence must be conducted and the order in which their positive part should consciously guide the manifestations of their unconscious parts, so that the crystallized consequences of the properties of the organ Kundabuffer and also the inherited predisposition to them might gradually disappear from their common presences.

"As the same detailed researches of mine made clear to me—at that period when the inner psyche of the beings of that part of the surface of the Earth was guided by this genuine Messenger from Above, Saint Buddha—the said, for them very maleficent, consequences indeed again began gradually to disappear from the presences of many of them.

"But to the grief of every Individual with Pure Reason of any gradation whatsoever and to the misfortune of the three-brained beings of all succeeding generations who arise on that planet, the first succeeding generation of the contemporaries of this genuine Messenger from Above, Saint Buddha, also began, owing once again to that same particularity of their psyche, namely, of wiseacring—which until now is one of the chief results of the conditions of the ordinary being-existence abnormally established there—to wiseacre with all His indications and counsels, and this time to 'superwiseacre' so thoroughly that there reached the beings of the third and fourth generations nothing else but what our Honorable Mullah Nassr Eddin defines by the words:

"'Only-information-about-its-specific-smell.'

"Little by little they so changed these indications and counsels of His that if their Saintly Author Himself should chance to appear there and for some reason or other should wish to make Himself acquainted with them, He would not be able even to suspect that these indications and counsels were made by Him Himself.

"Here I cannot refrain from expressing my essence-grief at that strange practice of these favorites of yours there, which in the course of many of their centuries during the process of their ordinary existence has gradually become, as it were, conformable to law.

"And in the given case also the same established and already fixed peculiar practice there served for the modification of all the true indications and exact counsels of Saint Buddha and for the creation thereby of yet another factor for a still greater dilution of their psyche.

"This already long-established practice there consists in this, that a small, sometimes an almost trifling, cause is enough to bring about a change for the worse or even the complete destruction of any and every objectively good outer and inner previously established, what is called, 'tempo-of-ordinary-existence.'

"Because, my boy, the clarification of certain details of the arising of such a trivial cause, which was in this instance a basis for the distortion of all the true explanations and exact indications also of this genuine Messenger from Above, Saint Buddha, may provide you with excellent material for a better sensing and understanding of the strangeness of the psyche of those three-brained beings who have taken your fancy, I shall tell you about this in as great detail as possible and shall explain to you just in what sequence the said practice then arose there which led to the following sad misunderstanding which began to exist there, and which is still manifested particularly clearly.

"I must inform you first of the two following facts:

"The first is this: that I cleared up this misunderstanding much later than the period to which my present tale refers; among other things I made it clear to myself only during the period of my sixth descent there when in connection with a question concerning the Saint Ashiata Shiemash, about whom I shall soon tell you in detail, it became necessary for me to find out about the activities of that genuine Messenger from Above, Saint Buddha.

"And the second fact is this: that unfortunately the basis of the lamentable misunderstanding was certain authentic words contained in one of the explanations of Saint Buddha, Himself.

"It turned out, indeed, that Saint Buddha Himself had, in the course of His explanations to some of His closest initiates initiated by Himself, very definitely expressed Himself concerning the means of the possible destruction in their nature of the mentioned consequences of the properties of the organ Kundabuffer transmitted to them by heredity.

"He then, among other things, told them very definitely the following:

"'One of the best means of rendering ineffective the predisposition present in your nature of the crystallization of the consequences of the properties of the organ Kundabuffer is "intentional-suffering"; and the greatest intentional-suffering can be obtained in your presences if you compel yourselves to be able to endure the "displeasing-manifestations-of-others-towards-yourselves."'

"This explanation of Saint Buddha together with other definite indications of His was spread by His nearest initiates among the ordinary beings there; and after the process of the sacred Rascooarno had occurred to Him, it also began to pass from generation to generation.

"So, my boy, when, as I have already told you, those three-centered beings there among the second and third generation of the contemporaries of Saint Buddha in whose psyche, already from the time of the loss of Atlantis, that peculiarity had been fixed, called the 'organic-psychic need to wiseacre,' began—unfortunately for the ordinary three-centered beings of that period and unfortunately also for the beings of all succeeding generations and even for those of the present time—to wiseacre and superwiseacre concerning these counsels of Saint Buddha, then as a result a very definite notion became fixed and also began to pass from generation to generation, that this same 'endurance' should without fail be produced in complete solitude.

"Here that strangeness of the psyche of your favorites then manifested itself just as it now manifests itself, by their not having considered and not considering the obvious fact—obvious, that is, to every more or less sane Reason—that the Divine Teacher, Saint Buddha, in advising them to employ that kind of 'endurance,' of course had in view that they should produce this 'endurance' while existing among other beings similar to themselves, and so that by frequently producing in their presences this sacred being-actualization toward the manifestations displeasing to them of other beings similar to themselves, there might thereby be evoked in them what are called those 'Trentroodianos,' or, as they themselves would say, those 'psychic-chemical-results' which, in general, in the presence of every three-centered being, form those sacred being-data, which actualize in the common presences of the three-centered beings one of the three holy forces of the sacred being-Triamazikamno; and this holy force in beings always becomes affirming towards all the denying properties already present in them.

"So, my boy, from that time when the mentioned definite notion had begun to exist, your favorites began leaving those already established conditions of being-existence on account of which the predisposition to the crystallization of the consequences of the properties of the organ Kundabuffer had become intense in their presences, and in which conditions, as the Divine Teacher Buddha supposed, the said 'endurance' towards others' 'manifestations displeasing to oneself' could alone crystallize in their common presences that 'Partkdolg-duty' which in general is necessary for all three-centered beings.

"And so, for the purpose of this famous 'suffering' of theirs, many of the three-centered beings of that planet of yours, either singly or in groups, that is to say, with others who thought as they did, began from then on to go away from amongst beings similar to themselves.

"They even organized special colonies for this purpose, where, although existing together, they nevertheless arranged everything so as to produce this 'endurance' of theirs in solitude.

"It was just then that their famous what are called 'monasteries' came into existence, which exist down to the present time and in which, as it were, certain of your contemporary favorites as they say, 'save their souls.'

"When I first visited that Pearl-land, most of the three-brained beings there, as I have already said, were followers of that same religion which was based, as it were, on the exact counsels and indications of Saint Buddha Himself, and the faith of every one of these beings in this religion was unshakably firm.

"At the outset of my investigations into the doctrinal subtleties of that religion there, I had as yet come to no definite decision how exactly to utilize it to attain my aim; but when in the course of my investigations I clarified one very definite comprehension—proper to all the followers of that religion—which arose there again, owing to a misunderstanding, from the words that had indeed been spoken by Saint Buddha Himself, I then at once decided how just to act there through this peculiar Havatvernoni or Religion of theirs.

"It transpired that in His explanations to them about cosmic truths, Saint Buddha had, among other things, told them also that in general the three-centered beings existing on various planets of our Great Universe—and of course the three-centered beings of the Earth also—were nothing else but part of that Most Great Greatness which is the All-embracing of all that exists; and that the foundation of this Most Great Greatness is there Above, for the convenience of the embracing of the essence of everything existing.

"This Most Great Foundation of the All-embracing of everything that exists constantly emanates throughout the whole of the Universe and coats itself from its particles upon planets—in certain three-centered beings who attain in their common presences the capacity to have their own functioning of both fundamental cosmic laws of the sacred Heptaparaparshinokh and the sacred Triamazikamno—into a definite unit in which alone Objective Divine Reason acquires the possibility of becoming concentrated and fixed.

"And this has been foreseen and created in this manner by our COMMON CREATOR in order that when these certain parts of the Great All-embracing, already spiritualized by Divine Reason, return and reblend with the great Prime Source of the All-embracing, they should compose that Whole which in the hopes of our COMMON ENDLESS UNI-BEING may actualize the sense and the striving of all that exists in the whole of the Universe.

"Further, it seems Saint Buddha also told them:

"'You, three-centered beings of the planet Earth, having the possibility of acquiring in yourselves both chief fundamental, universal, sacred laws, have the full possibility also of coating yourselves with this most sacred part of the Great All-embracing of everything existing and of perfecting it by the required Divine Reason.

"'And this Great All-embracing of all that is embraced, is called "Holy Prana."'

"This quite definite explanation of Saint Buddha was well understood by his contemporaries and many of them began, as I have already said, to strive with eagerness, first to absorb and to coat in their presences the particle of this Most Great Greatness and afterwards to 'make-inherent' to it Divine Objective Reason.

"But when the second and third generations of the contemporaries of Saint Buddha began wiseacring with His explanations of cosmic truths, they just wiseacred with their peculiar Reason and fixed—for its transmission—a very definite notion to the effect that that same 'Mister Prana' already begins to be in them immediately upon their arising.

"Thanks to this misunderstanding, the beings of that period and of all subsequent generations including the contemporary, have imagined and still imagine that without any being-Partkdolg-duty they are already parts of that Most Great Greatness, which Saint Buddha Himself had personally very definitely explained.

"So, my boy, as soon as I had made this misunderstanding

clear to myself and had clearly constated that the beings of that country Pearl-land were all, without exception, convinced that they were already particles of Mister Prana himself, I then at once decided to use this misunderstanding, and there also to attain my aim through that religion of theirs.

"Before saying more about this, it must without fail be noticed that concerning these same explanations of Saint Buddha's, namely, that He had supposedly said that beings already have in themselves, at their arising, a particle of the Most Great Greatness, my personal detailed investigations quite clearly showed me that He never could possibly have said just that.

"And He could not have said it because, as the same detailed investigations of mine have cleared up to me, when Saint Buddha once happened to be among His devoted disciples in the locality 'Senkoo-ori,' He definitely said:

"'If this most sacred Prana is crystallized in you, consciously or unconsciously on the part of your "I," you must without fail bring the perfecting of the individual Reason of the totality of its most holy atoms to the required gradations; otherwise this most holy coating will, changing various exterior coatings, suffer and languish eternally.'

"Here it is interesting to notice that concerning this they were warned by still another Saint-Individual, also a genuine Messenger from Above, namely, the Saint Kirmininasha.

"And this Saint and genuine Messenger gave this warning to them in the following words:

"'Blessed is he that hath a soul; blessed also is he that hath none; but grief and sorrow are to him that hath in himself its conception.'

"So, my boy, when I made this clear to myself there

in Pearl-land, I at once decided to use this error of theirs for the accomplishment of my aim.

"There in Pearl-land also, just as in the city Gob, I first 'invented-a-detailed-addition' to the mentioned religious teaching, and afterwards by every possible means I began spreading this invention of mine.

"I began to spread there in Pearl-land that that 'Most-Sacred-Prana,' about which our Divine Teacher Saint Buddha had explained, is already present not only in people, but also in all the other beings that arise and exist on our planet Earth.

"A particle of that fundamental Most Great Great All-embracing, namely, the Most-Sacred-Prana, has already from the very beginning settled in every form of being of every scale, breeding on the surface of the planet, in the water, and also in the atmosphere.

"I regret to have to say here, my boy, that I was then constrained more than once to emphasize that these words had been uttered by the very lips of Saint Buddha Himself.

"The several beings there with whom I had meanwhile established 'friendly' relations, and whom without any discussion I first of all persuaded there of that invention, not only immediately fully believed it, but afterwards also very effectually helped me, of course unconsciously, in spreading this new invention of mine.

"Here also these friends of mine always and everywhere very zealously and passionately proved to other beings like themselves, that this was just so and could not possibly be otherwise.

"In short, there in Pearl-land, owing to this second invention of mine, the desired results were unexpectedly rapidly brought about.

"And there in Pearl-land, owing simply to my invention, your favorites so greatly changed their essence-relations towards the beings of other forms, that they not only ceased to destroy the existence of these beings for their famous Sacrificial-Offerings, but even began very sincerely with the whole of their being to regard these beings of other forms as beings like themselves.

"If only it had all continued like that, it would have been very good; but here as well, just as in the country Maralpleicie, they soon began, as is proper to them, to wiseacre and to manifest all kinds of comical aspects of their Havatvernoni.

"For instance, only a quarter of their year after the commencement of my preaching, you could see when strolling down the street of the city Kaimon, almost at every step, beings there walking on what are called 'stilts.'

"And they walked on stilts in order not to risk crushing some insect or other, a 'little being,' as they thought, just like themselves.

"Many of them were afraid to drink water that had not been freshly taken from a spring or stream, because they thought that if the water had been a long time out of the spring or stream, 'little-beings' might have got into the water, and without seeing them, they might suddenly swallow these 'poor-little-creatures-like-themselves.'

"Many of them took the precaution to wear what are called 'veils,' lest poor-little-beings-like-themselves in the air might chance to enter mouths or noses, and so on and so forth.

"From that time on, various societies began to arise there in Pearl-land in the city of Kaimon and its outskirts, whose aim was to protect 'defenseless' beings of various forms, both those existing among them and those they called 'wild.'

"Rules existed in all such societies prohibiting not only their destruction for Sacrificial-Offerings, but also the use of their planetary bodies for the 'first-being-food.'

"E-h-h-h-hkh . . . my boy.

"Owing once again merely to the strangeness of their psyche, the intentional suffering and conscious labors of this Sacred Individual, Saint Buddha, who had been specially actualized for them with a planetary presence similar to theirs, have ever since hovered and still hover in vain; nor have they yet actualized any lawfully expected real results whatsoever, but have engendered and until now continue to engender only all kinds of 'pseudo-teachings' there, like those existing there in recent times under the names of 'Occultism,' 'Theosophy,' 'Spiritualism,' 'Psychoanalysis,' and so on, which before as now, are means only for the obscuring of their already, without this, obscured psyche.

"It is needless to say that from the truths indicated by Saint Buddha Himself absolutely nothing has survived and reached the beings of the present time.

"Half of one of the words, however, managed to reach even the contemporary beings of that unparalleled planet.

"And this half of a word reached them in the following way:

"Saint Buddha among other things explained to the beings of Pearl-land how and to what part of the body of their ancestors the said famous organ Kundabuffer had been attached.

"He told them that the Archangel Looisos had by a special means made this organ grow in their ancestors at the extremity of that brain which in them, just as in you, Nature has placed along their back in what is called the 'spinal column.'

"Saint Buddha, as I also made clear, then also said that though the properties of this organ had been entirely destroyed in their ancestors, yet the material formation of this organ had remained at the lower extremities of this brain; and this material formation, being transmitted from generation to generation, had also reached them.

"'This material formation,' he said, 'now has no significance whatever in you, and it can be completely destroyed in the course of time, if your being-existence proceeds as is becoming to three-centered beings.'

"It was just when they began wiseacring and inventing various forms of that famous 'suffering' of theirs that they also played their usual 'tricks' with this word.

"Namely, first of all, as the root of the second half of this word chanced to coincide with a word in the language of that time which meant 'Reflection,' and as they had also invented a means for destroying this material formation rapidly and not merely in the course of time as Saint Buddha had told them, they also wiseacred about this word according to the following rumination of their bobtailed Reason. Of course, when this organ is in action, it ought to have in its name also the root of the word to 'reflect'; now, since we are destroying even its material basis, the name must end with a word whose root means 'former,' and because 'former' in their current language was then pronounced 'lina,' they changed the second half of this word, and instead of 'reflection,' they stuck in the mentioned 'lina,' so that instead of the word Kundabuffer, they obtained the word 'Kundalina.'

"Thus it was that a half of the word Kundabuffer survived and, being transmitted from generation to generation, finally reached your contemporary favorites also, accompanied, of course, by a thousand and one different explanations.

"Even the contemporary 'learned beings' also have a name made up of very abstruse Latin roots for that part of the spinal marrow.

"The whole of what is called 'Indian-philosophy' now existing there is based also on this famous Kundalina, and about the word itself there exist thousands of various occult, secret, and revealed 'sciences' which explain nothing.

"And as regards the way in which the contemporary terrestrial learned beings of what are called the exact sciences define the significance of this part of the spinal marrow, that, my dear boy, is a profound secret.

"And it became a secret because several centuries ago, this 'explanation' suddenly for no reason whatever entered the favorite mole of the famous 'Scheherazade,' which that incomparable Arabian fantasist chanced to have on the right side of her adorable navel.

"And there this 'learned-explanation' remains perfectly preserved down to the present day.

"When I was quite convinced that I had succeeded so easily in the destruction, perhaps for a long time, of that terrible practice among the beings of that group there in Pearl-land, I decided to stay there no longer but to return to the Sea of Beneficence to our ship *Occasion*.

"When we were quite ready to leave that Pearl-land, the intention suddenly arose in me not to return to the Sea of Beneficence by the way we had come, but by another way quite unusual in those days.

"Namely, I decided to return through the locality which was later called 'Tibet.' "

CHAPTER 22
Beelzebub for the First Time in Tibet

As the route proposed this time was most uncommon for the terrestrial three-brained beings of those days and accordingly we could not count on the possibility of joining any 'caravan' of theirs, I had, then, to organize my own caravan, and I began the same day preparing and procuring everything necessary for this purpose.

"I then procured some score of the quadruped beings called 'horses,' 'mules,' 'asses,' and 'Chami-anian' goats and so on, and hired a number of your biped favorites to look after the said beings and to do the semiconscious work required on the way for this mode of travel.

"Having procured everything necessary, I set off, accompanied by Ahoon.

"This time we passed through places still more peculiar, and through still more uncommon parts of the general Nature of that ill-fated planet; and we also encountered this time, or there came within the sphere of our vision, a much greater number of those one-brained and two-brained beings, of various forms, which are called 'wild,' and which in those days came there from very remote parts of the continent Ashhark for the purpose, as it is said there, of 'hunting.'

"The said 'wild' beings there, were at that period particularly 'dangerous' both for the three-brained beings there, and for those forms of quadruped beings which your favorites, with the 'cunning' proper to them, had already been able to make their slaves, compelling them to work exclusively for the satisfaction of their egoistic needs.

"And the said wild beings were then particularly dangerous because just at that period there was being crystallized in the presences of these wild beings that special function which arose in them, again, owing to the abnormally established conditions of the being-existence of the three-brained beings there; and about this special function I shall later explain to you in detail.

"The places through which our way went this time were then almost inaccessible to the three-brained beings of that period, chiefly on account of these wild beings.

"In those days it was possible for the three-brained beings to pass through these places only, as they say, 'by day,' that is to say, when in the atmosphere of their planet the process of 'Aieioiuoa' proceeds in the Active Element Okidanokh.

"And they could pass by day because during this time of the Krentonalnian position of their planet in relation to the rays of their sun, almost all the wild terrestrial beings are in the being-state called 'sleep,' that is to say, in a state of automatic elaboration in their presences of that energy which is necessary for their ordinary existence, which elaboration of energy proceeds in them during just this time, whereas in the three-centered beings there, on the contrary, the same is elaborated only when the said sacred property is not proceeding in the atmosphere, that is, during the period of the diurnity which they call 'night.'

"So, my boy, because of this it was possible for your favorites of those times to pass through these places only by day. At night, great vigilance and the use of various artificial shelters was required as a defense against these wild beings, both for themselves and for their 'goods.'

"During the period of the aforesaid Krentonalnian position of the planet Earth, these wild beings there are wide awake and take their first being-food; and since, by that time, they had already become accustomed to use for this purpose almost exclusively the planetary bodies of weaker beings of other forms arising on their planet, they were always trying, during that period, to get hold of such a being in order to use his planetary body for the satisfaction of that need of theirs.

"These wild beings, particularly the smallest of them, were at that time already—also, of course, owing to the abnormally established conditions of the ordinary being-existence of the three-brained beings there—perfected as regards apprehendingness and cunning up to the ideal.

"In consequence of this, all along this second route of ours, we, and especially our workmen for the semiconscious work, had to be extremely watchful and alert at night in order to guard ourselves, our quadruped beings, and our supplies.

"A whole 'gathering' of these wild beings would form round our camp at night, having come there to provide themselves with something suitable for their first food, a meeting rather like an 'assembly' of your favorites during what is called the 'quotation of stock prices' or during their 'election' of representatives to some society or other, the nominal purpose of which is the joint pursuit of a means to the happy existence of all beings like themselves without distinction of their notorious castes.

"Although we kept logs burning brightly all night, to scare these wild beings, and although our biped workers, notwithstanding that they were forbidden, destroyed with the help of the, as they are called, poisoned arrows of 'El-napara' those beings that came too near our camp, yet not a single night passed upon which what are there called 'tigers,' 'lions,' and 'hyenas' did not carry off one or more of our quadruped beings; the number of which in consequence diminished daily.

"Although, my boy, this way back to the Sea of Beneficence took us far longer than the way by which we had come here, all that we then saw and heard about the strangeness of the psyche of your favorites, during our passage through these places, fully justified the extra time spent.

"We traveled under these conditions more than a month of their time, and finally we came upon a small settlement of the three-brained beings who, as it appeared later, had only recently migrated there from Pearl-land.

"As we afterwards learned, this settlement was called 'Sincratorza'; and when this region was subsequently populated and this same place became the principal center for all the beings of that region, the whole country also came to be called by the same name.

"The name of this place was afterwards changed several times and now it is called 'Tibet.'

"As we chanced to meet the said beings just as night was coming on, we asked them for, as it is said, a 'night's lodging.'

"And when they gave us permission to pass the night under their shelter we were very glad at the prospect of a night's rest, since, indeed, we were all so exhausted by the constant warfare with these wild beings that, both for ourselves and especially for our biped workers, it was now imperative to pass at least one night in peace.

"In the course of the evening talk, it transpired that all the beings of this settlement belonged to the sect then famous in Pearl-land under the name 'The Self-tamers,' which had been formed from among the followers of just that religion which, as I have already told you, purported to be based on the direct instructions of Saint Buddha.

"There is no harm in noticing in this connection that the beings of that planet had still another peculiarity which had long before become proper to them alone, and which consists in this, that no sooner does a new common Havatvernoni, or religion, arise among them than its followers immediately begin to split up into different parties each of which very soon creates its own, as it is called, 'sect.'

"The particular strangeness of this peculiarity of theirs consists in this, that those who belong to any such sect never call themselves 'sectarians,' the name being considered offensive; they are named 'sectarians' only by those beings who do not belong to their sect.

"And the adherents of any sect are sectarian for other beings only as long as they have no 'guns' and 'ships,' but as soon as they get hold of a sufficient number of 'guns' and 'ships,' then what had been a peculiar sect at once becomes the dominant religion.

"The beings both of this settlement and of many other regions of Pearl-land became sectarians, having separated just from the religion the doctrine of which, as I have already told you, I studied there in detail and which later was called 'Buddhism.'

"These sectarians who called themselves the Self-tamers arose owing to that distorted understanding of the Buddhist religion which, as I have already told you, they called 'suffering-in-solitude.'

"And it was in order to produce upon themselves the said famous 'suffering,' without hindrance from other beings similar to themselves, that these beings with whom we passed the night had settled so far away from their own people.

"Now, my boy, because everything I learned that night and saw the next day of the followers of that sect then produced so painful an impression upon me that for very many of their centuries I could never recall it all without, as is said, 'shuddering'—not that is until very much later, when I had made perfectly clear to myself all the causes of the strangeness of the psyche of those favorites of yours—I wish to tell you in greater detail about all I then saw and learned.

"As I then made clear to myself during the night's conversation, before the migration of the followers of that sect to this isolated place they had already invented in Pearl-land a special form of 'suffering,' namely, they had decided to settle somewhere in some inaccessible place where other beings similar to themselves, not belonging to the sect and not initiated into its 'arcana,' should not prevent them from producing upon themselves this same 'suffering' of special form which they had invented.

"When after long searching they finally found this same place which we had happened to come upon—a place well suited for such a purpose as theirs—they, already solidly organized and materially secured, migrated together with their families, with great difficulties, there to that place almost inaccessible to their ordinary countrymen; and this place they then first called, as I have already told you, 'Sincratorza.'

"At first, while they were settling down in this new place, they more or less agreed among themselves; but when they began carrying out in practice the special form of 'suffering' they had invented, their families and especially their wives, having learned what this special form of suffering consisted in, rebelled, and made a great outcry about it, with the result that a schism occurred.

"The said schism among them had occurred not long before our chance meeting with them, and at the time when we came upon that Sincratorza, they were already beginning little by little to migrate to other places which they had recently found and which were even more suitable for an isolated existence.

"For a clear understanding of what follows, you must know about the fundamental cause of the schism among these sectarians.

"It turned out that the leaders of that sect, while they were still in Pearl-land, had agreed among themselves to go quite away from beings like themselves, and to stop at nothing in order to attain their deliverance from the consequences of that organ of which the divine Teacher Saint Buddha had spoken.

"In their agreement it was included that they should exist in a certain way until their final planetary destruction or, as they say, until their death, in order by this special form of existence to purify their, as they said, 'soul' of all the alien growths due to that organ Kundabuffer which, as Saint Buddha told them, their ancestors had, and, being freed from these consequences, thereby acquire the possibility, as the Divine Teacher Saint Buddha had said, of reblending with the All-embracing Holy Prana.

"But when, as I have already said, they, having settled down, set about carrying out in practice the special form of 'suffering' which they had invented, and their wives, having learned its true nature, rebelled, then many of them, having fallen under the influence of their wives, declined to carry out the obligations they had undertaken while still in Pearl-land—and as a result, they then divided into two independent parties.

"From this time on, these sectarians, formerly called the Self-tamers, now began to be called by various names; those of the Self-tamers who remained faithful to the obligations they had taken upon themselves were called 'Orthodoxhydooraki,' while the rest, who had renounced the several obligations they had undertaken in their native country, were called 'Katoshkihydooraki.'

"It transpired that at the time of our arrival in Sincratorza those of the sectarians who were named Orthodoxhydooraki had their well-organized what is called 'monastery' not far from this original settling place of theirs, and there the said special form of suffering was already proceeding.

"On resuming our journey the next day after a restful night, we passed very near the monastery of these sectarians of the Buddhist religion of the Orthodoxhydooraki doctrine.

"At that time of the day we usually made a halt to feed our quadruped workers, and so we asked the monks to allow us to make our necessary halt in the shelter of their monastery.

"Strange and unusual as it may seem, the beings there bearing the name monks did not refuse our objectively just request, but at once, and without any of the 'swaggering' that had become proper there to monks of all centuries and of all doctrines, admitted us. And we thereupon entered the very center of the sphere of the arcana of this doctrine, the kind of sphere which, from the very beginning of their arising, the beings of the planet Earth came to be very skillful in concealing from the observation even of Individuals with pure Reason. In other words, they became skillful in wiseacring something or other and in making of it, as they say, a 'mystery,' and in so thoroughly concealing this mystery of theirs from others by all sorts of means that even beings with Pure Reason cannot penetrate them.

"The monastery of the Orthodoxhydooraki sect of the Buddhist religion occupied a large square with a strongly built wall around it, which protected everything within, both from beings similar to themselves and from wild beings.

"In the middle of this enormous walled enclosure stood a large structure, also strongly built, which constituted the main part of the monastery.

"In one half of this large structure their ordinary being-existence was carried on, and in the other they practiced those special manipulations of theirs which were just the particularity of the form of belief of the followers of their sect and which to others were arcana.

"Around the outside wall, on its inner side, stood a row of small, strongly built, closely adjoining compartments, like cells.

"It was just these same 'cells' that represented the difference between this monastery and other monasteries in general on the planet Earth.

"These sentry-box structures were entirely walled in on all sides, except that near the bottom they had a small aperture through which, with great difficulty, a hand could be thrust.

"These strong sentry-box structures were for the perpetual immurement of the already 'deserving' beings of that sect—and they were to occupy themselves with their famous manipulation of what they call their 'emotions' and 'thoughts'—until the total destruction of their planetary existence.

"And so, it was when the wives of these 'self-tamer-sectarians' learned of just this that they made the said great outcry.

"In the fundamental religious teaching of this sect there was a full explanation of just what manipulations and for how long a time it is necessary to produce them upon oneself in order to merit being immured in one of the strongly built cells, there to receive every twenty-four hours a piece of bread and a small jug of water.

"At that time when we came within the walls of that terrible monastery, all these monstrous cells were already occupied; and the care of the immured, that is, giving them once in twenty-four hours, through the aforementioned tiny apertures, a piece of bread and a small jug of water, was carried out with great reverence by those sectarians who were candidates for that immurement, and who, while waiting their turn, existed in the said large building that stood in the monastery square.

"Your immured favorites did indeed exist in the said monastery sepulchres until their existence, so full of deprivations, half-starved and motionless, came quite to an end.

"When the companions of the immured learned of the cessation of the existence of any one of them, his planetary body was removed from the improvised sepulchre and immediately, in the place of the being thus self-destroyed, another similar unfortunate fanatic of that maleficent religious teaching of theirs was immured; and the ranks of these unfortunate 'fanatic monks' were being filled up by other members of that peculiar sect, constantly coming from Pearl-land.

"In Pearl-land itself all the adherents of that sect already knew of the existence of that special 'convenient' place for the actualization of the finale of their religious doctrine, purporting to have been based on the exact instructions of Saint Buddha; and in every big center they even had what are called agents who helped them to get there.

"Having rested and fed our biped and quadruped workers, we left that melancholy place of sacrifice to the same wretched organ which, in the ruminations of certain Most High Cosmic Individuals had had for some reason or other, without fail, to be implanted into the presences of the earliest three-brained beings of that ill-fated planet.

"Eh! Eh! Eh! my boy, we left there, as you can well believe, scarcely with agreeable sensations and happy reflections.

"Continuing our route in the direction of the Sea of Beneficence, we again passed through terra firmas of very many different forms, also with conglomerations of intraplanetary minerals, but which had oozed to the surface of the planet from still greater depths.

"Here I must say something about an exceedingly strange thing, which I constated, closely connected with just that part of the surface of your planet which is now called Tibet.

"At that period when I was passing through Tibet for the first time, its heights were indeed also unusually far above the surface of the Earth, but they did not differ particularly from similar elevations on other continents and on the same continent Ashhark or Asia, of which Tibet was a part.

"But when during my sixth and last personal stay on the planet Earth there, my way again took me through those, for me, extremely memorable places, I just then constated that in the interval of the few score of their centuries, the whole of that locality had projected so far from the planet that no heights on any of the other continents could even be compared with them.

"For instance, the chief range of that elevated region through which we had then passed, namely, the range of elevations which the beings there call a 'mountain-range,' had in the interval projected so far from the planet that some of its peaks are now the loftiest among all the abnormal projections of that vainly-long-suffering-planet. And if you climbed them, you could possibly with the aid of a Teskooano 'see clearly' the center of the opposite side of that peculiar planet.

"When I first constated that strange phenomenon occurring on that remarkably peculiar planet of yours, I at once thought that in all probability it contained the germ for the arising of some subsequent misfortune on a great common cosmic scale, and when I afterwards collected statistics concerning that abnormal phenomenon, this first apprehension of mine very soon more and more grew in me.

"And it grew chiefly because, in my statistics, one item concerning that phenomenon there showed an increase in every decade.

"The said item concerning those Tibetan elevations referred just to this: which of the terrestrial, as they are called 'planetary tremors,' or as this is expressed by your favorites, 'earthquakes,' occur to that planet due to these excessively lofty elevations.

"Although planetary tremors or earthquakes frequently occur to that planet of yours from other interplanetary disharmonies also that have arisen in consequence of the two already mentioned great Transapalnian perturbations, the causes of which I shall sometime explain to you, nevertheless most of the planetary tremors there, and especially during recent centuries, have occurred solely on account of those excessive elevations.

"And they occur because, in consequence of those excessive elevations, the atmosphere also of that planet has acquired and continues to acquire in its presence equally excessive elevations, that is to say, what is called the 'Blastegoklornian-circumference' of the atmosphere of the planet Earth has acquired in certain places and continues to acquire an excessively projecting materialized presence for what is called the 'reciprocal-blending-of-the-results-of-all-the-planets-of-the-given-system'; with the result that during the motion of that planet, and in the presence of what is called 'common-system-harmony,' its atmosphere at certain times 'hooks on,' as it were, to the atmosphere of other planets or comets of the same system.

"And owing to these 'hookings on' there occur in the corresponding places of the common presence of that planet of yours just those said planetary tremors or quakes.

"I must also explain to you that the region of the

common presence of the planet where such planetary tremors occur on this account, depends upon the position occupied by the planet itself in the process of the common-system-harmonious-movement, in relation to other concentrations belonging to the same system.

"Be that as it may, if this abnormal growth of the Tibetan mountains continues thus in the future, a great catastrophe on a general cosmic scale is sooner or later inevitable.

"However, when the menace I see becomes already evident, no doubt the Most High, Most Sacred Cosmic Individuals will at the proper time take the proper precautions."

"If you please, if you please, your Right Reverence," Ahoon interrupted Beelzebub, and rattled off the following:

"Allow me to report to you, your Right Reverence, some information which I happened to pick up concerning just that growth of those same Tibetan mountains about which you have deigned to speak.

"Just before our flight from the planet Karatas," continued Ahoon, "I had the pleasure of meeting the Archangel Viloyer, the Governor of our solar system, and His Splendiferousness condescended to recognize me and to speak to me.

"Perhaps you remember, your Right Reverence, that while we were existing on the planet Zernakoor, His Splendiferousness Archangel Viloyer was still an ordinary angel, and used often to drop in to see us?

"So when His Splendiferousness, during our conversation, heard the name of that solar system where we were exiled, he told me that at the last most high and most sacred reception of finally returned cosmic results, a certain Individual, Saint Lama, had had the privilege of personally presenting at the feet of our ENDLESS UNI-BEING, in the presence of all the Most High Individuals, a certain petition regarding the abnormal growth of the elevations of some planet—it seems just of that solar system—and having received this request, our ALL-GRACIOUS-ENDLESSNESS immediately ordered Archangel Looisos to be dispatched to that solar system where, as one familiar with that system, he might there on the spot clarify the causes of the manifestation of the said projections and take appropriate measures.

"That is why His Conformity Archangel Looisos is at the present time hastily winding up his current affairs in order to set off there."

"So, dear Ahoon," commented Beelzebub, and he added, "Thank you for this information. . . . Glory be to our CREATOR . . . what you have just said will probably help to destroy in my presence the anxiety which arose in me when I first constated the abnormal growth of those said Tibetan mountains, namely, my anxiety for the complete disappearance from the Universe of the precious memory of our Endlessly Revered Wisest of the Wise, Mullah Nassr Eddin."

Having said this, and giving his face its usual expression, Beelzebub continued thus:

"Through that region now called Tibet, we then continued our route, encountering hardships of every kind, and finally came to the source of the river called the Keria-chi and a few days later, sailing down to the Sea of Beneficence, we came to our ship *Occasion*.

"Although after this third descent of mine to your planet Earth, I did not go there in person for a considerable time, nevertheless, from time to time I attentively observed these favorites of yours, through my big Teskooano.

"And I had no reason for a long time to go there personally on account of the following:

"After returning to the planet Mars I soon became

interested there in a work which the three-brained beings of the planet Mars were just then carrying out on the surface of their planet.

"Clearly to understand in what work it was there that I became interested, you must know, first of all, that the planet Mars is for the system Ors, to which it belongs, what is called a 'Mdnel-outian' link in the transformation of cosmic substances, in consequence of which it has what is called a 'Keskestasantnian-firm-surface,' that is to say, one half of its surface consists of land-presence and the other of 'Saliakooriapnian' masses; or, as your favorites would say, one half of it is land or one continuous continent, and the other half is covered with water.

"So, my boy, as the three-brained beings of the planet Mars use for their first being-food exclusively only 'prosphora'—or as your favorites call it, 'bread'—they, for the purpose of obtaining it, sow on the land of half of their planet what is called 'wheat,' and as this wheat derives the moisture it needs, for what is called evolving Djartklom, only from what is called 'dew,' the result is that a grain of wheat yields only a seventh part of the accomplished process of the sacred Heptaparaparshinokh, that is to say, what is called the 'yield' of the harvest is only a seventh.

"As this amount of wheat was insufficient for their needs, while to get more of it they would have to utilize the presence of the planetary Saliakooriap, the three-centered beings there from the very beginning of our arrival there were always talking of conducting that same Saliakooriap in the requisite quantity, from the opposite side of their planet to that side on which their being-existence proceeded.

"And when several of their years later they finally decided the question and began making every preparation, they began operations just before my return from the planet Earth, that is to say, they began digging special canals for conducting the Saliakooriap.

"So, my boy, this work being extremely complicated, the beings of the planet Mars had invented and continued to invent for the work every kind of machine and appliance.

"And as there were very many peculiar and interesting ones among these machines and appliances they invented, I, being always interested in every kind of new invention, was very much taken by the said work of the beings of the planet Mars.

"By the courtesy of the kind Martians I then spent nearly all my time at these works, and that is why during that period I very seldom descended to the other planets of that solar system.

"Only sometimes I flew to the planet Saturn to rest, to Gornahoor Harharkh, who, during this time, had already become my real essence-friend, and thanks to whom I had such a marvel as that big Teskooano of mine which, as I have already told you, brought remote visibilities 7,000,285 times nearer."

CHAPTER 23

The Fourth Personal Sojourn of Beelzebub on the Planet Earth

Beelzebub continued thus:

"I descended for the fourth time to that planet Earth owing to the request of my essence-friend Gornahoor Harharkh.

"I must first of all tell you that after I had met this Gornahoor Harharkh and had become friendly with him, I always, during our 'subjective exchange of opinions,' whenever we again met, shared my impressions with him about the strange psyche of the three-centered beings of that planet of yours.

"And the result of these exchanges of opinion of ours concerning your favorites was that he finally also became so interested in them that he once even very seriously asked me to keep him always informed, even if only approximately, of my observations of them, and thereafter I sent to him, just as I did to your uncle Tooilan, copies of all my brief-notes concerning the strange particularities of their psyche.

"And how Gornahoor Harharkh came to be the cause of this descent of mine ensued from the following:

"I have already told you that after my third personal descent to your planet, I occasionally for a rest ascended to the planet Saturn to this friend of mine.

"When during these flights to him I had become convinced of his great learning, the idea once arose in me to invite him to descend on our ship *Occasion* to the planet Mars, in order there, on the spot, to help me personally with his knowledge in the details of arranging my observatory which was just then being completed.

"Here I might as well emphasize the fact that if this observatory of mine afterwards became famous and indeed the best of all the constructions of its kind in the whole of the Universe, I am chiefly indebted to the learning of this same essence-friend of mine.

"Well, then, when I spoke to Gornahoor Harharkh about this, he, without thinking long about it, agreed, and together we immediately began to deliberate how to carry out our intention.

"The problem was that our route from the planet Saturn to the planet Mars would cross such cosmic spheres as did not correspond to the presence of Gornahoor Harharkh, a being who had as yet the possibilities only for an ordinary planetary existence.

"The result of our deliberations, then, was that on the following day his chief assistant began, under his direction, to arrange a special compartment in our ship *Occasion* itself, and to furnish it with every kind of adaptation and apparatus for elaborating those substances of which the atmosphere of the planet Saturn consists, and to which Gornahoor Harharkh was adapted by Nature for existence.

"When all these preparations had been completed, we one Hrkh-hr-hoo later set out on our journey in the direction of the planet Mars and descended there at my house.

"And there, on the planet Mars, which had almost the same atmosphere as the planet Saturn, my essence-friend Gornahoor Harharkh very soon became acclimatized and began to exist almost freely.

"It was just during his stay on Mars that he devised that Teskooano, or, as your favorites call it, a 'telescope,' thanks chiefly to which, as I have already said, my observatory afterwards became particularly famous through the whole of the Universe.

"The Teskooano he constructed is indeed a marvel of being-Reason, as it increases the visibility of remote cosmic concentrations up to 7,000,285 times, during certain processes in cosmic substances proceeding in the atmospheres surrounding almost all cosmic concentrations, as well as during certain processes in the cosmic Etherokrilno of interspatial spheres.

"Thanks to this Teskooano I was sometimes fully able, while seated in my house on Mars, to observe almost everything that proceeded on those parts of the surface of other planets of this solar system which, in the process of what is called the general-system-movement, were at the given time within the sphere of vision of my observatory.

"Well then, my dear boy, while Gornahoor Harharkh was then staying with me as my guest and we were once together observing the existence of these favorites of yours, a certain fact which we happened to notice was the cause of a very serious exchange of opinions between us concerning the three-centered beings of that peculiar planet of yours.

"The result of this 'exchange of opinions' of ours was that I undertook to descend onto the surface of that planet and to bring back to the planet Saturn a certain number of the beings called there 'apes,' in order to carry out certain elucidating experiments with them concerning the fact we had noticed and which had then surprised us."

At this point of Beelzebub's tales, he was given a "Leitoochanbros," that is, a special metal plate on which is recorded the text of an etherogram received from somewhere or other, the addressee having only to hold it to his perceptive hearing organ to hear everything communicated in it.

When Beelzebub had in this way heard the contents of the Leitoochanbros handed to him, he turned to his grandson and said:

"You see, my boy, what coincidences occur in our Great Universe.

"The contents of this etherogram concern just your favorites in connection with these terrestrial beings I have just mentioned, that is, these apes.

"It has been sent to me from the planet Mars, and among other things there is communicated in it that the three-centered beings of the planet Earth have again begun to revive what is called the 'Ape question.'

"I must tell you first of all, that on account of a cause also ensuing from the abnormal being-existence there, there was long ago crystallized, and there is periodically intensified in its functioning in the presences of those strange three-brained beings arising and existing on the planet Earth, a strange factor which from time to time produces in their presences a 'crescendo impulse,' owing to which, during the periods of its action, they wish at all costs to find out whether they have descended from these apes or whether these apes have descended from them.

"Judging from the etherogram, this question is this time agitating chiefly those biped beings who breed there on the continent called America.

"Although this question always agitates them from time to time, yet every once in a while it becomes there for a long time, as they express it, 'the burning question of the day.'

"I very well remember that this 'agitation of mind' concerning the origin of these apes occurred there among them for the first time when, as they also like to express it, their 'center of culture' was Tikliamish.

"The beginning of that 'agitation of mind' there was the wiseacring of a certain 'learned being' of new formation there named Menitkel.

"This Menitkel then became a learned being, firstly

because his childless aunt was an excellent what is called matchmaker and mixed a great deal with power-possessing beings, and secondly, because when by age he was approaching the 'threshold of the being' of a responsible being, he received on his birthday a gift of a book entitled *Manual of Bon Ton and Love Letter Writing*. Being materially secure and therefore quite free, thanks to an inheritance left him by his uncle, a former pawnshop proprietor, he out of boredom compiled a massive and erudite work in which he 'spun out,' concerning the origin of these apes, an elaborate theory with every kind of 'logical proof,' but of course with such 'logical proofs' as could be perceived and crystallized only in the Reasons of those freaks who have taken your fancy.

"This Menitkel then 'proved' by his theory that these 'fellow apes' of theirs had descended neither more nor less than from what are called 'people who became wild.'

"And the other terrestrial beings of that period, as it had already become proper to them, implicitly believed this 'Auntie's darling' without any essence-criticism whatsoever, and from that time on, this question which had then agitated the strange Reason of your favorites, became a subject of discussion and fantasying, and existed right up to what is called the 'seventh-in-turn great general planetary process of reciprocal destruction.'

"Thanks to this maleficent idea, there was even fixed in the instincts of most of these unfortunates at that period still another abnormal what is called 'dictatory factor,' which began to engender in their common presences the false feeling that these ape-beings were presumably 'sacred'; and the abnormal factor engendering this sacrilegious impulse, also passing by inheritance from generation to generation, has reached the instincts of very many beings even of the present time.

"This false idea that arose and was fixed there owing

to the said 'pawnshop progeny' existed during nearly two of their centuries, and became an inseparable part of the Reason of the majority of them; and only various events proceeding from the mentioned general planetary process effaced it until it ultimately completely disappeared from their common presences.

"But when what is called their 'cultured existence' was concentrated on the continent named Europe, and when the time of the maximum intense manifestation of the peculiar illness there named 'to-wiseacre,' had again come round—which illness by the way had already long before become subject to the fundamental cosmic law of Heptaparaparshinokh, according to which it had, in respect of intensity, also to function with a certain periodicity—then, to the grief of three-brained beings of the whole of the universe, that Ape question, namely, the question who is descended from whom, again arose, and having become crystallized, again became a part of the presence of the abnormal Reason of your favorites.

"The stimulus for the revival there of this Ape question was this time also a 'learned' being, and of course also 'great,' but now a 'learned' being of quite a 'new formation' named Darwin.

"And this 'great' learned being, basing his theory on that same logic of theirs, began to 'prove' exactly the opposite of what Menitkel had said, namely, that it was they themselves who were descended from these Mister Apes.

"And as for the objective reality of the theories of both these 'great' terrestrial 'learned beings,' I am reminded of one of the wise sayings of our esteemed Mullah Nassr Eddin, namely:

"'They were both very successful, though of course not without luck, in finding the authentic godmother of the incomparable Scheherazade on an old dunghill.'

"In any case you must know and bear in mind that for many centuries just this question among similar ephemeral questions has provided material for the kind of mentation which is considered among your favorites as the 'highest manifestation of Reason.'

"These favorites of yours would in my opinion get quite a correct answer to this question which always excites them, that is, the question how the apes arose, if they were able in the given case to apply one of these sayings again of our dear Mullah Nassr Eddin, who on many occasions used to say: 'The cause of every misunderstanding must be sought only in woman.'

"If they had attempted the solution of this enigmatic question with that wisdom of his, then perhaps they would have finally discovered whence and how these countrymen of theirs had originated.

"As this question of the genealogy of these apes there is indeed exceedingly abstruse and unusual, I shall inform your Reason about this also as far as possible from every aspect.

"In fact, neither have they descended from apes nor have apes descended from them, but . . . the cause of the origin of these apes is in this case, just as in every other misunderstanding there, also—their women.

"I must tell you first of all that the species of terrestrial ape-beings now arising there under several different exterior forms, never existed at all before the second 'Transapalnian perturbation'; only afterwards did the genealogy of their species begin.

"The causes of the arising of this 'misconceived' being as well as the cause of all the other events more or less serious in an objective sense, which occur on the surface of that ill-fated planet, ensue from two sources, totally independent of each other.

"The first of them, as always, was the same lack of

foresight on the part of certain Most High, Most Very Saintly Cosmic Individuals, and the second was, in the given case, also the same abnormal conditions of ordinary being-existence established by them themselves.

"The point is that when the second Transapalnian perturbation occurred to that ill-fated planet, then, besides its chief continent Atlantis, many other large and small terra firmas entered within the planet and, in their place, new terra firmas appeared on the surface of the planet.

"These displacements of the parts of the common presence of that ill-fated planet then continued for several days, with repeated planetary tremors and with such manifestations as could not fail to evoke terror in the consciousness and feelings of beings of every kind.

"During that same period many of your three-brained favorites who chanced to survive, together with various one-brained and two-brained beings of other forms, unexpectedly struck upon other newly-formed terra firmas in entirely new places unfamiliar to them.

"It was just at this period that many of these strange Keschapmartnian three-brained beings of active and passive sex, or, as they say, 'men' and 'women,' were compelled to exist for some years there apart, that is to say, without the opposite sex.

"Before relating how this then further occurred, I must explain to you a little more in detail concerning that sacred substance which is the final result of the evolving transformations of every kind of being-food formed in the presence of every being without distinction of brain system.

"This sacred substance which arises in the presences of beings of every kind is almost everywhere called 'Exioëhary'; but your favorites on the planet Earth call it 'sperm.'

"Thanks to the all-gracious foresight and command of our COMMON FATHER AND CREATOR and according to the actualization of Great Nature, this sacred substance arises in the presences of all beings without distinction of brain system and exterior coating, chiefly in order that by its means they might, consciously or automatically, fulfill that part of their being-duty which consists in the continuation of their species; but in the presences of three-brained beings it arises also in order that it might be consciously transformed in their common presences for coating their highest being-bodies for their own Being.

"Before the second Transapalnian perturbation there, which period of their planet the contemporary three-brained beings define by the words, 'Before the loss of the continent Atlantis,' when various consequences of the properties of the organ Kundabuffer had already begun to be crystallized in their presences, a being impulse began to be formed in them which later became predominant.

"This impulse is now called 'pleasure'; and in order to satisfy it they had already begun to exist in a way unbecoming to three-centered beings, namely, most of them gradually began to remove this same sacred being-substance from themselves only for the satisfaction of the said impulse.

"Well, then, my boy. Owing to the fact that most of the three-brained beings of the planet Earth thereafter carried out the process of the removal from themselves of this sacred substance—which is constantly formed in them—not at certain periods normally established by Great Nature for beings in accordance with their organization, simply for the purpose of the continuation of their species, and also owing to the fact that most of them ceased to utilize this sacred substance consciously for coating their higher being-bodies, the result was obtained that when they do not remove it from themselves by ways which had then already become mechanical, they naturally must experience a sensation called 'Sirkliniamen,' or as your favorites there would say, the state defined by the words 'out of sorts,' which state is invariably accompanied by what is called 'mechanical suffering.'

"Remind me at some opportune moment about the said periods fixed by Nature for the normal process of the utilization of Exioëhary by beings of different brain systems for the purpose of the continuation of their species, and I shall explain it to you in detail.

"Well then, in consequence of the aforesaid, and because just like us they are also only Keschapmartnian beings, and the normal removal from their presences of this sacred substance which constantly and inevitably arises in them can proceed exclusively only with the opposite sex when they utilize it for the continuation of the species by means of the sacred process 'Elmooarno'; and also because they were not in the habit of utilizing it for the purpose of coating their higher being-bodies; these chance surviving three-brained beings there—namely, those who had already been existing as it is not becoming for three-brained beings to exist, that is to say, when during several of their years they had existed without beings of the opposite sex—began to turn to various antinatural means for the removal from themselves of the sacred substance Exioëhary formed in them.

"The beings of the male sex then turned to the antinatural means called 'Moordoorten' and 'Androperasty,' or, as the contemporary beings would say, 'onanism' and 'pederasty,' and these antinatural means fully satisfied them.

"But for the three-brained beings of the passive sex, or, as they are called, 'women,' the said antinatural methods proved to be not sufficiently satisfying, and so the poor 'women orphans' of that time, being already then more cunning and inventive than the men there, began to seek out and accustom beings of other forms of the given place to be their 'partners.'

"Well then, it was after these 'partnerships' that those kinds of beings also began to appear in our Great Universe who in themselves are, as our dear Mullah Nassr Eddin would say, 'neither one thing nor the other.'

"Concerning the possibility of this abnormal blending of two different kinds of Exioëharies for the conception and arising of a new planetary body of a being, it is necessary to explain to you also the following.

"On the planet Earth, just as on other planets of our Universe where Keschapmartnian three-brained beings breed and exist, that is to say, those three-brained beings the formation of whose Exioëhary for the purpose of creating a new being must obligatorily proceed in the presences of two distinct independent sexes, the fundamental difference between the sacred Exioëharies formed in the presences of the distinct and opposite sexes of Keschapmartnian beings, that is to say, in 'men' and 'women,' is that in the Exioëhary formed in the presences of beings of the male sex the localized sacred 'affirming' or 'positive' force of the sacred Triamazikamno participates; while for the completed formation of the Exioëhary in the presences of beings of the female sex, there participates the localized sacred 'denying' or 'negative' force of the same sacred law.

"And owing to the same all-gracious foresight and command of our FATHER of Everything Existing in the Great Universe, and according to the actualizations of Great Mother Nature, then in certain surrounding conditions and with the participation of the third separately localized holy force of the sacred Triamazikamno, namely, the holy force called 'Reconciling,' the blending of these two Exioëharies arising in two distinct independent different beings just gives, owing to the process called 'the process of the sacred Elmooarno' which proceeds between those beings of opposite sex, the beginning for the arising of a new being.

"And the possibility in the given case of such an abnormal blending of two different kinds of Exioëhary then occurred owing only to a certain cosmic law called the 'affinity of the number of the totality of vibrations,' which proceeded owing to the second Transapalnian perturbation to this ill-fated planet and which then still continued to act for its own common presence.

"Concerning this cosmic law just mentioned, it is now absolutely necessary to tell you that it arose and began to exist in the Universe after the fundamental sacred law of Triamazikamno was changed by OUR CREATOR for the purpose of rendering the Heropass harmless, and after its previously totally independent holy parts had begun to be dependent upon forces coming from outside.

"You will understand this cosmic law also in all its aspects when, as I have already promised you, I shall explain to you in detail all the fundamental laws in general of World-creation and World-existence.

"Meanwhile know, concerning this question, that in general everywhere on normally existing planets of our Great Universe the Exioëhary formed in the presence of a three-brained being who has perceptive and transformative organs for localizing the holy affirming part of the sacred Triamazikamno, that is to say, a Keschapmartnian being of the male sex, can, owing to the just-mentioned cosmic law, never be blended with the Exioëhary formed in the presence of a Keschapmartnian two-brained being of the opposite sex.

"At the same time, the Exioëhary formed in the three-brained Keschapmartnian being of the female sex can sometimes—in those cases when a special combination of the blending of cosmic forces is obtained and the mentioned law comes into effect—be completely blended under certain surrounding conditions with the Exioëhary formed in two-brained Keschapmartnian beings of the male sex, but only as the active factor in such an actualizing process of the fundamental sacred Triamazikamno.

"In short, during the said terrible years on this planet of yours, a result very rare in the Universe was obtained, that is to say, there was obtained the blending of the Exioëharies of two Keschapmartnian beings of different brain systems of opposite sexes; and as a result, there arose the ancestors of these terrestrial 'misconceived' beings now called apes, who give your favorites no peace and who from time to time agitate their strange Reason.

"But when after the mentioned terrible period there on your planet, when the relatively normal process of ordinary existence was re-established and your favorites of different sexes again began to find each other and to exist together, then the continuation of the species of the ape-beings was thereafter actualized also among beings similar to themselves.

"And this continuation of their species by these abnormally arisen ape-beings there could be further continued among themselves because the conception for the arising of the first of these abnormal beings had also proceeded owing to those same mentioned external conditions, thanks to which the presences of future Keschapmartnian beings of active or of passive sex are generally determined.

"The most interesting result of this already excessively abnormal manifestation of the three-brained beings of your planet is that there now exist a great many species of generations of ape-beings differing in exterior form, and each of these varied species bears a very definite resemblance to some form of a two-brained quadruped being still existing there.

"This came about because the blending of the Exioëhary of the Keschapmartnian three-brained beings there of the 'female sex,' which served as a beginning for the arising of the ancestors of these apes, then proceeded with the active Exioëhary of those same varied quadruped beings existing there up to the present time.

"And indeed, my boy, when during the period of my last personal stay on the planet Earth, I chanced during my travels to meet with the said various independent species of apes, and when, by a habit which has become second nature, I also observed them, I constated very definitely that the whole of the inner functioning and what are called the 'automatic posture' of each separate species of these contemporary apes there are exactly like those present in the whole of the presences of some normally arisen quadruped being there, and that even what are called their 'facial features' very definitely resemble those of the said quadrupeds; but on the other hand that what are called the 'psychic features' of all the separate species of these apes there are absolutely identical, even down to details, with those of the psyche of the three-brained beings there of the 'female sex.'"

At this point of his tales, Beelzebub made a long pause and looking at his favorite Hassein with a smile which very clearly expressed a double meaning, he, continuing to smile, said:

"In the text of the etherogram which I have just received, it is further said that in order this time finally to settle who has descended from whom—whether they from the apes or the apes from them—these freaks, your favorites, have even decided to carry out 'scientific experiments,' and furthermore that several of them have already left for the continent of Africa where many of these apes breed, with the object of bringing back from there the number required for these 'scientific investigations' of theirs.

"To judge by this etherogram, the beings of the planet

Earth who have taken your fancy are again, in their turn, up to their 'extraordinary tricks.'

"From all I have learned about them during my observations, I foresee that this 'scientific experiment' will, of course, very greatly interest other of your favorites also, and will serve for a time as material to their strange Reason for endless discussion and talks.

"And all this will be quite in the order of things there.

"Concerning the 'scientific experiment' itself, which they propose to carry out with the apes taken back from Africa, I can with certainty say beforehand, that at any rate the first part of it will without any doubt, succeed 'wonderfully well.'

"And it will succeed wonderfully well, because the apes themselves, as beings of what is called a 'Terbelnian result,' are already, owing to their nature, extremely fond of occupying themselves with 'titillation' and before the day is out, will no doubt participate in and greatly assist your favorites in this 'scientific experiment' of theirs.

"As for those beings there who are going to carry out this 'scientific experiment,' and as for any benefit from it for the other three-brained beings there, it can all be pictured to oneself if one remembers the profoundly wise saying of our same honorable Mullah Nassr Eddin, in which he says: 'Happy is that father whose son is even busy with murder and robbery, for he himself will then have no time to get accustomed to occupy himself with "titillation."'

"Yes, my boy, it seems that I have not yet told you why and by whom, since I left the solar system Ors, I am kept informed by etherograms of the most important events which proceed on various planets of that system, and, of course, also about events proceeding on your planet Earth.

"You remember I told you that my first descent in person upon the surface of that planet of yours took place on account of one of the young beings of our tribe, who then had no desire to stay there any longer but returned with us to the planet Mars, where he later became a very good chief over all the beings of our tribe existing on that planet, and who is now already the chief over all the beings in general of our tribe who for various reasons still exist on certain planets of that system Ors.

"Well then, my boy, when I left that system, I presented my famous observatory to him with everything in it, and in gratitude for this he promised to report every month, according to the time-calculation of the planet Mars, all the more important events occurring on the planets of that system.

"And now this chief keeps me very accurately informed of the most important events proceeding on all the planets on which there is a being-existence; and, knowing my great interest in the three-brained beings breeding on the planet Earth, he does his best, as I now see, to elucidate and send me information concerning all those manifestations of theirs which can give me now also the possibility of being constantly informed of the whole process of the ordinary existence of these three-brained beings, even though I find myself already inaccessibly remote even for their featherweight thoughts.

"That chief of our beings who remains there collects the various kinds of information he communicates concerning the three-brained beings of the planet Earth, either by means of his own observations of them through the great Teskooano which I left him, or from reports which, in their turn, are communicated to him by those three beings of our own tribe who chose to exist forever on the planet Earth, and all three of whom have at the present time on the continent of Europe different substantial independent undertakings indispensable for everyone existing there under the prevailing conditions.

"One of them has in one of the large cities, an 'undertaker's business'; the second, in another large city, has a bureau for what are called matchmaking and divorce; and the third is the proprietor of many offices founded by himself in various cities for what is called 'money exchange.'

"However, my boy, owing to this etherogram, I have wandered a long way from my original tale.

"Let us go back to our former theme.

"Well, then, upon this the fourth flight of mine to the planet Earth, our ship *Occasion* descended onto the sea called the 'Red Sea.'

"And we descended upon this Sea because it washed the Eastern shores of that continent where I wished to go, namely, to that continent then called Grabontzi and now called Africa, on which those ape-beings I needed then bred more than on any other of the terra firma parts of the surface of that planet of yours; and also because this sea was at that period particularly convenient for the mooring of our ship *Occasion*; but what was still more important was that on one of its sides that country was situated which was then called 'Nilia' and is now called Egypt, where those beings of our tribe then existed who wished to remain on that planet and with whose help I intended to collect the apes.

"Well, then, having descended upon the Red Sea, we sailed from the ship *Occasion* on 'Epodrenekhs' to the shore; and afterwards, on camels we came to that town where our beings existed and which was then the capital of the future Egypt.

"This capital city was then called Thebes.

"On the very first day of my arrival in the city of Thebes, one of the beings of our tribe existing there told me among other things, in the course of our conversation, that the beings of the Earth of that locality had devised a new system for observing other cosmic concentrations from their planet, and that they were then constructing what was required in order to carry it into effect; and also, as everybody there said, that the convenience and possibilities of this new system were excellent and until then unparalleled on the Earth.

"And when he had related all he had himself seen with his own eyes, I immediately became greatly interested, because from his description of certain details of this new construction there, it seemed to me that these terrestrial beings had perhaps found a means of overcoming that inconvenience about which I myself had just previously been thinking a great deal while I was completing the construction of my observatory on the planet Mars.

"And so I decided to postpone for a while my first intention of immediately going further south on that continent to collect the apes I needed, and instead, to go first where the said construction was being made, in order on the spot to become personally acquainted with it from every aspect, and to find out all about it.

"Well then, the day following our arrival in the city Thebes, accompanied by one of the beings of our tribe who already had many friends there, and also by the chief constructor of the said construction, and of course by our Ahoon also, I went this time on what is called a 'Choortetev' down the tributary of that great river now called the 'Nile.'

"Near where this river flowed into a large 'Saliakooriapnian area' those constructions were just being completed, one part of which then interested me.

"The district itself, where the work was being carried on both for this new, what they called 'observatory,' and for several other constructions for the welfare of their being existence, was then called 'Avazlin'; a few years later it came to be called there 'Caironana,' and at the present time it is simply called the 'outskirts of Cairo.'

"The mentioned constructions had been begun long before by one of what are called there 'Pharaohs,' the name by which the beings of that region called their kings; and at the time of my fourth flight to the Earth and my first visit to this place, the special constructions he had begun were already being completed by his grandson, also a Pharaoh.

"Although the observatory which interested me was not yet quite finished, nevertheless observations of the exterior visibility of cosmic concentrations could be made from it, and the results issuing from them and the reciprocal action of these results could be studied.

"Those beings who were occupied with such observations and studies were called, at that period on the Earth, 'Astrologers.'

"But when afterwards that psychic disease of theirs called wiseacring became finally fixed there, owing to which these specialists of theirs also 'shrivelled and shrank' and became specialists only in giving names to remote cosmic concentrations, they came to be called 'Astronomers.'

"Inasmuch as the difference in significance and sense, in relation to surrounding beings, between those from among the three-brained beings who have taken your fancy who at that time were such professionals, and those who have now, as it were, the same occupation, might show you, so to say, 'the obviousness of the steady deterioration of the degree of crystallization' of data engendering the 'sane logical mentation,' which ought to be present in the common presences of your favorites as three-brained beings, I therefore find it necessary to explain to you and to help you to have an approximate understanding of this difference, which is also changing for the worse.

"At that period, these terrestrial three-brained beings, already of responsible age, whom the others named 'Astrologers,' besides making the said observations and investigations of various other cosmic concentrations for the purpose of a greater, as is said, 'detailizing' of that branch of general learning of which they were representatives, fulfilled several further definite essence-obligations taken upon themselves towards surrounding beings similar to themselves.

"Among their fundamental definite obligations was that they also, like our Zirlikners, had to advise all the conjugal pairs in their what was then called 'flock,' according to the types of those pairs, about the time and form of the process of the sacred 'Elmooarno' for the purpose of a desirable and corresponding conception of their results, and when such results were actualized, or, as they themselves say, 'newly born,' they had to draw up their 'Oblekioonerish' which is the same as what your favorites call 'horoscope'; and later either they themselves or their substitutes had—during the whole period of the formation of the newly born for responsible existence and of their subsequent responsible existence—to guide them and give corresponding indications on the basis of the said Oblekioonerish and also on the basis of the cosmic laws, constantly explained by them, flowing from the actions of the results of other large cosmic concentrations in general on the process of being-existence of beings on all planets.

"These indications of theirs, and also their, so to say, 'warning counsels' consisted in the following:

"When a function became disharmonized or only began to be disharmonized in the presence of any being of their flock, then this being applied to the Astrologer of his district, who, on the basis of the said Oblekioonerish made by him, and on the basis of the changes expected, according to his calculations, in the processes proceeding in the atmosphere, flowing in their turn from the action of the other planets of their solar system, indicated just what he had to do to his planetary body, at which definite periods of the Krentonalnian movements of their planet—as for instance, in which direction to lie, how to breathe, what movements preferably to make, with which types to avoid relations, and many things of the same kind.

"In addition to all this, they assigned to the beings at the seventh year of their existence, likewise on the basis of these Oblekioonerishes, corresponding mates of the opposite sex for the purpose of fulfilling one of the chief being-duties, that is, continuation of the race, or as your favorites would say, they assigned them 'husbands' and 'wives.'

"Justice must be done to your favorites of the period when these Astrologers existed among them; they then indeed very strictly carried out the indications of these Astrologers and made their conjugal unions exclusively only according to their indications.

"Therefore, at that period, in regard to their conjugal unions, they always corresponded according to their type, just as such pairs correspond everywhere on planets on which Keschapmartnian beings also breed.

"These ancient terrestrial Astrologers made these matches successfully because even if they were very far from the knowledge of many cosmic Trogoautoegocratic truths, yet they at least already very well knew the laws of the influence of different planets of their solar system on the beings breeding on their own planet, namely, the influence of these planets on a being at the moment of his conception, for further formation, as well as for his complete acquisition of the Being of a responsible being.

"Having, thanks to the information transmitted to them from generation to generation, a many-centuried practical knowledge, they already knew which types of the passive sex can correspond to which of the active sex.

"Owing to all this, the pairs matched according to their indications almost always turned out to be corresponding, and not as it proceeds there at the present time; and that is to say they are now united in conjugal pairs who nearly always do not correspond in type; in consequence of which during the continuation of the entire existence of these couples there, about half of their, as they say, 'inner life' is spent only on what our esteemed Mullah Nassr Eddin expresses in one of his sayings by the following words:

"'What a good husband he is, or what a good wife she is, whose whole inner world is not busy with the constant "nagging of the other half."'

"In any case, my boy, if these Astrologers had continued to exist there, then surely, thanks to their further practising, the existence of the beings of this unfortunate planet would by now have gradually become such that their family relations would at least have been a little like the existence of similar beings on other planets of our Great Universe.

"But all this which was beneficently established in the process of their existence they have also sent, like all their other good attainments, without even having had time to make good use of it, 'to the gluttonous swine' of our respected Mullah Nassr Eddin.

"And these 'Astrologers' of theirs, as usually happens there, also at first began gradually to 'shrink' and then entirely, as is said, 'vanished.'

"After the total abolition among them of the duties of these Astrologers, other professionals in the same sphere appeared in their place, but this time from among the 'learned beings of new formation' who also began to observe and study, as it were, the results issuing from various large cosmic concentrations and their influence on the existence of the beings of their planet; but as the ordinary beings around these professionals soon noticed that their 'observations' and 'studies' consisted merely in inventing names for various remote suns and planets meaning nothing to them, existing in milliards in the Universe, and in measuring, as it were, by a method known to them alone, and which constituted their professional secret, the distance between the cosmic points seen from their planets through their 'child's toys' called by them 'telescopes,' they began to call them, as I have already told you, Astronomers.

"Now, my boy, that we have spoken also about these contemporary 'ultra fantasists' from among your favorites, we might as well, again imitating the form of mentation and the verbal exposition of our dear teacher Mullah Nassr Eddin, also 'illuminatingly' enlighten you about their significance, so esteemed by your favorites.

"First of all, you should know about that ordinary cosmic something actualized for these same terrestrial types, which is in general always actualized of itself for every cosmic unit and which serves for beings with Objective Reason as what is called an 'issuing source' for pondering about the explanation of the sense and meaning of any given cosmic result.

"This same something which serves as an issuing source for discovering the significance of these terrestrial contemporary types, is a wiseacring map named by them themselves—of course unconsciously—the 'map inventory of the heavenly spaces.'

"There is no need for us to draw any other logical conclusion from this issuing source specially actualized for them; it will be sufficient merely to say that the name itself of this map of theirs shows that the designations made on it cannot in any way be other than entirely relative, because with the possibilities at their disposal—though they break their esteemed heads over devising names and calculating various kinds of measurements—they can see from the surface of their planet only those suns and planets which to their good fortune do not very quickly change the course of their falling in relation to their own planet and thus give them the possibility during a long period of time—of course long as compared with the brevity of their own existence—to observe them and, as they bombastically express themselves, 'mark down their positions.'

"In any case, my boy, however worthless the results of the activities of these contemporary representatives of 'learning' among your favorites, please don't be angry with them. If they do not bring any benefit at all to your favorites, they at least do not do them any great harm.

"After all, they must be occupied with something.

"It is not for nothing that they wear spectacles of German origin and special smocks sewed in England.

"Let them! Let them be occupied with this! God bless them!

"Otherwise like most of the other freaks there who are occupied with, as they say there, 'higher matters,' they will busy themselves, out of boredom, 'leading the struggle of five against one.'

"And it is known to all that the beings who are occupied with these matters always radiate from themselves vibrations very harmful for beings around them similar to themselves.

"Well enough! Leave these contemporary 'titillators' in peace and let us continue our interrupted definite theme.

"In view of the fact, my boy, that this conscious ability expressed in the creation of such a construction unparalleled both before and after this period, of which I was then an eyewitness, was also the result of the attainments of the beings, members of the learned society Akhaldan, which was formed on the continent of Atlantis before the second great terrestrial catastrophe, I think it will be best, if, before continuing to explain to you further about the mentioned observatory and other constructions erected there for the welfare of being-existence, I should tell you, even though briefly, about the history of the arising there of such an indeed great learned society consisting of ordinary three-brained beings, as this learned society Akhaldan then was on the continent of Atlantis.

"It is imperatively necessary to inform you of this because in the course of my further explanations concerning these three-brained beings of the planet Earth who have taken your fancy I shall in all probability have to refer more than once to that society of learned beings there.

"I must also tell you about the history of the arising and existence of that society there on the continent Atlantis, so that you may also know that if the three-brained beings there on your planet—thanks to their being-Partkdolg-duty, that is to say, thanks to their conscious labors and intentional sufferings—ever attain anything, then not only do they utilize these for the good of their own Being, but also a certain part of these attainments is transmitted as with us by inheritance and becomes the property of their direct descendants.

"You can perceive such a law-conformable result there from the fact that although towards the end of the existence of the continent Atlantis abnormal conditions of ordinary being-existence had already begun to be established and that after the second great catastrophe they deteriorated at such a rate that they soon finally 'crushed' all their ableness to manifest the possibilities proper to the presences of three-brained beings, nevertheless their 'attainments of learning' passed by inheritance, at least partly, even though mechanically, to their remote direct descendants.

"I must first tell you that I learned about this history, thanks to what are called 'Teleoghinooras' which are at present in the atmosphere also of that planet Earth of yours.

"As you probably do not yet know exactly what a Teleoghinoora is, try to transubstantiate in the corresponding parts of your common presence the information concerning this cosmic actualization.

"A Teleoghinoora is a materialized idea or thought which after its arising exists almost eternally in the atmosphere of that planet on which it arises.

"Teleoghinooras can be formed from such a quality of being-contemplation as only those three-brained beings have and can actualize, who have coated their higher being bodies in their presences and who have brought the perfecting of the Reason of their higher being part up to the degree of the sacred 'Martfotai.'

"And the sequential series of being-ideas, materialized in this way, concerning any given event, are called 'Korkaptilnian thought tapes.'

"It seems that the said Korkaptilnian thought tapes concerning the history of the arising of the learned society Akhaldan were, as I found out much later, deliberately fixed by a certain 'Eternal Individual,' Asoochilon, now a saint, who became coated in the common presence of a three-brained being named Tetetos who arose on your planet on the continent of Atlantis and who had existed there four centuries before the second great 'Transapalnian perturbation.'

"These Korkaptilnian thought tapes are never destroyed as long as the given planet exists, which is in what is called the 'tempo of movement of the prime arising'; and they are subject to none of those transformations from any cosmic causes whatsoever to which all other cosmic substances and cosmic crystallizations are periodically subject.

"And however long a time may have already passed, every three-brained being in whose presence there has been acquired the ability to enter into the being-state called 'Soorptakalknian contemplation' can perceive and cognize the texts of these Korkaptilnian thought tapes.

"And so, my boy, I myself learned about the details of the arising there of the society Akhaldan partly from the text of the just-mentioned Teleoghinoora and partly from many data which I learned much later, namely, when, having become interested also in this highly important factor there, I made my usual detailed investigations.

"According to the text of the mentioned Teleoghinoora and to data which I subsequently learned, it became clear and definitely known to me that this learned society Akhaldan which arose then on the continent Atlantis and which was composed of three-brained beings of the Earth, was formed 735 years before the second 'Transapalnian perturbation' there.

"It was founded on the initiative of a being there named Belcultassi, who was then able to bring the perfecting of his higher being part to the Being of a Saint 'Eternal Individual'; and this higher part of his now already dwells on the holy planet Purgatory.

"My elucidation of all those inner and outer being-impulses and manifestations which caused this Belcultassi then to found that truly great society of ordinary three-brained beings—a society which in its time was throughout the whole Universe called 'envied for imitation'—showed that when this same later Saint Individual Belcultassi was once contemplating, according to the practice of every normal being, and his thoughts were by association concentrated on himself, that is to say, on the sense and aim of his existence, he suddenly sensed and cognized that the process of the functioning of the whole of him had until then proceeded not as it should have proceeded according to sane logic.

"This unexpected constatation shocked him so profoundly that thereafter he devoted the whole of himself exclusively to be able at any cost to unravel this and understand.

"First of all he decided to attain without delay such a 'potency' as would give him the strength and possibility to be quite sincere with himself, that is to say, to be able to conquer those impulses which had become habitual in the functioning of his common presence from the many heterogeneous associations arising and proceeding in him and which were started in him by all sorts of accidental shocks coming from outside and also engendered within him, namely, the impulses called 'self-love,' 'pride,' 'vanity,' and so on.

"And when, after incredible what are called 'organic' and 'psychic' efforts, he attained to this, he then without any mercy for these being-impulses which had become inherent in his presence, began to think and recall just when and what various being-impulses had arisen in his presence during the period preceding all this, and how he had consciously or unconsciously reacted to them.

"Analyzing himself in this manner, he began to recall just which impulses evoked which reactions in him, in his independently spiritualized parts, that is to say, in his body, in his feelings and in his thoughts, and the state of his essence when he reacted to anything more or less attentively, and how and when, in consequence of such reactions of his, he had manifested consciously with his 'I' or had acted automatically under the direction of his instinct alone.

"And it was just then that this bearer of the later Saint

Individual Belcultassi, recalling in this way all his former perceptions, experiencings, and manifestations, clearly constated in consequence, that his exterior manifestations did not at all correspond either to the perceptions or to the impulses definitely formed in him.

"Further, he then began to make similar sincere observations of the impressions coming from outside as well as those formed within himself, which were perceived by his common presence; and he made them all with the same exhaustive, conscious verifications of how these impressions were perceived by his separate spiritualized parts, how and on what occasions they were experienced by the whole of his presence and for what manifestations they became impulses.

"These exhaustive conscious observations and impartial constatations finally convinced Belcultassi that something proceeded in his own common presence not as it should have proceeded according to sane being-logic.

"As it became clear to me during my subsequent detailed investigations, although Belcultassi had become indubitably convinced of the accuracy of his observations on himself, yet he doubted the correctness of his own sensations and understandings and also the normalness of his own psychic organization; and he therefore set himself the task of elucidating, first of all, whether he was in general normal in sensing and understanding all this just in this way and not otherwise.

"To carry out this task of his, he decided to find out how the same would be sensed and cognized by others.

"With that aim he began inquiring among his friends and acquaintances to try to find out from them how they sensed it all and how they cognized their past and present perceptions and manifestations, doing this, of course, very discreetly, so as not to touch the aforementioned impulses inherent in them, namely, 'self-love,' 'pride,' and so on, which are unbecoming to three-brained beings.

"Thanks to these inquiries, Belcultassi gradually succeeded in evoking sincerity in his friends and acquaintances, and as a result it turned out that all of them sensed and saw in themselves everything just the same as he did.

"Now among these friends and acquaintances of Belcultassi, there were several earnest beings who were not yet entirely slaves to the action of the consequences of the properties of the organ Kundabuffer, and who, having penetrated to the gist of the matter also became very seriously interested in it and began to verify that which proceeded in themselves, and independently to observe those around them.

"Soon after, on the initiative of the same Belcultassi, they began to meet together from time to time, and to share their observations and new constatations.

"After prolonged verifications, observations, and impartial constatations, this entire group of terrestrial beings also became categorically convinced, just like Belcultassi himself, that they were not as they ought to be.

"Not long after, many others also having such presences joined that group of terrestrial beings.

"And later they founded that society which they named the 'Society of Akhaldans.'

"By the word Akhaldan the following conception was then expressed:

"'The striving to become aware of the sense and aim of the Being of beings.'

"From the very beginning of the foundation of this society, Belcultassi himself stood at its head, and the subsequent actions of the beings of this society proceeded under his general guidance.

"For many terrestrial years this society existed under the said name, and its member-beings were then called

'Akhaldan sovors'; but later, when the members of this society, for purposes of a general character, were divided into a number of independent groups, the members belonging to different groups came to be called by different names.

"And this division of theirs into groups occurred for the following reason:

"When they had finally become convinced that there was something very undesirable in their presences and they had begun to seek means and possibilities of achieving its removal in order to become such as, according to sane logic, they ought to have been, corresponding to the sense and aim of their existence, the elucidation of which, whatever it might cost them, they made the basis of their task, and when they proceeded to actualize in practice this task previously decided upon by their Reason, it very soon became clear that it was imperatively necessary for its fulfillment to have in their Reason more detailed information of various special branches of knowledge.

"But as it proved impossible for each and every one of them to acquire the necessary special knowledge, they divided themselves for convenience into a number of groups so that each group might separately study one of these special branches of knowledge required for their common aim.

"Here, my boy, you should notice that genuine objective science just then arose and began to exist there for the first time, and developed normally up to the time of the second great catastrophe to their planet; also that the rate of the development of some of its separate branches then progressed at an indeed unprecedented tempo.

"And in consequence many great and small cosmic, what are called 'objective truths' gradually began at that period to become evident also to those three-brained beings who have taken your fancy.

"The learned members of this first and perhaps last great terrestrial learned society were then divided into seven independent groups, or as it is otherwise said, 'sections,' and each of these groups or sections received its definite designation.

"The members of the first group of the society Akhaldan were called 'Akhaldanfokhsovors,' which meant that the beings belonging to that section studied the presence of their own planet as well as the reciprocal action of its separate parts.

"The members of the second section were called 'Akhaldanstrassovors,' and this meant that the beings belonging to that section studied what are called the radiations of all the other planets of their solar system and the reciprocal action of these radiations.

"The members of the third section were called 'Akhaldanmetrosovors,' which meant beings occupied with the study of that branch of knowledge similar to that branch of our general knowledge we call 'Silkoornano,' and which partly corresponded to what your contemporary favorites call 'mathematics.'

"The members of the fourth group were called 'Akhaldanpsychosovors,' and by this name they then defined those members of the society Akhaldan who made their observations of the perceptions, experiencings, and manifestations of beings like themselves and verified their observations by statistics.

"The members of the fifth group were called 'Akhaldanharnosovors,' which meant that they were occupied with the study of that branch of knowledge which combined those two branches of contemporary science there which your favorites call 'chemistry' and 'physics.'

"The members belonging to the sixth section were called 'Akhaldanmistessovors,' that is to say, beings who studied every kind of fact arising outside of themselves, those actualized consciously from without and also those arising spontaneously, and which of them, and in what cases, are erroneously perceived by beings.

"And as regards the members of the seventh and last group, they were called 'Akhaldangezpoodjnisovors'; these members of the society Akhaldan devoted themselves to the study of those manifestations in the presences of the three-brained beings of their planet which proceeded in them not in consequence of various functionings issuing from different kinds of qualities of impulses engendered owing to data already present in them, but from cosmic actions coming from outside and not depending on them themselves.

"The three-brained beings of your planet who became members of this society actually did a great deal in respect of approaching objective knowledge which had never been done there before and which perhaps will never be repeated.

"And here it is impossible not to express regret and to repeat that to the most great misfortune of all terrestrial three-brained beings of all later epochs, it was just then—when after incredible being-labors by members of that great society the required tempo of work had already been established with regard to discernment, conscious on their part, and also with regard to their unconscious preparation for the welfare of their descendants—that, in the heat of it all, certain of them constated, as I have already told you, that something serious was to occur to their planet in the near future.

"For the purpose of discerning the character of the anticipated serious event, they dispersed over the whole planet and shortly afterwards, as I have already told you, the aforesaid second 'Transapalnian perturbation' occurred to that ill-fated planet of yours.

"Well then, my boy, when after this catastrophe, a number of the surviving beings, members of that great learned society, gradually came together again, they, no longer having their native country, first settled together with most of the other surviving beings in the center of the continent Grabontzi, but later, when they had, on the continent Grabontzi, 'come to themselves' a little after the 'cataclysm not according to law,' which had occurred, they decided jointly to try to re-establish, and perhaps to continue to actualize in practice, all those tasks which had formed the basis of their last society.

"As the manifestations of those abnormal conditions of being-existence of most of the three-brained beings there which had already been established before the catastrophe had by this time already begun to 'boil' furiously on the said part of the surface of the continent Grabontzi, these surviving members of the society Akhaldan looked for another place on the same continent for their permanent existence more suitable for this work of theirs which demanded complete separateness.

"Such a suitable place they found in the valley of the large river flowing on the north of the said continent and there indeed they all migrated together with their families to continue in isolation the attainment of the tasks set by their society.

"This entire region, through which the said large river flowed, they first named 'Sakronakari.'

"But this name was afterwards several times changed and at the present time this region is called 'Egypt' while the said large river, then called 'Nipilhooatchi,' is now, as I have already said, called the Nile.

"Soon after certain former members of the learned society Akhaldan had settled on this part of the surface of the planet Earth, all the beings of our tribe, who then existed on the surface of that planet which has taken your fancy, migrated to the same place.

"And the relations of our tribe with that part of your planet and also with the first migration there of the chance surviving former members of the society Akhaldan were as follows:

"I told you once that just before the second 'Transapalnian perturbation' our Party-Pythoness, while prophesying, insisted that all the beings of our tribe should, without delay, migrate for the continuation of their existence on that planet, to a definite part of the surface of that same continent now called Africa.

"This definite part of the surface of the continent which the Pythoness indicated, lay just at the source of the said large river Nipilhooatchi where the beings of our tribe existed all the time the said second Transapalnian perturbation lasted, as well as later when everything had gradually resumed its relatively normal state and when most of the surviving beings had then almost forgotten what had happened and had again formed—just as if nothing had occurred to them—one of their famous 'centers of culture' in the very center of that future Africa. And it was just when the former members of the society Akhaldan were searching for a suitable place for their permanent existence, that they chanced to meet a number of the beings of our tribe who advised them to migrate to the country further down the said river.

"Our acquaintanceship and our friendly relations with many of the former members of the society Akhaldan had already begun on the continent Atlantis almost from the founding of that society.

"Do you remember I told you that when I descended to that planet for the first time and the beings of our tribe assembled in the city of Samlios with my participation in order together to find a way out of the difficult situation that had been created, those general meetings of ours were held in one of the sections of the principal cathedral of the society Akhaldan; and from that time on, good relations were established between many beings of our tribe and certain members of this society?

"And there in that future Egypt whither both had migrated in the said way, the relations of the beings of our tribe with the authentic former members themselves who chanced to be saved, and also with the descendants of other authentic members, remained uninterrupted and continued almost until the departure of our tribe from your planet.

"Although the hope of the few chance surviving members of the society Akhaldan that they would be able to resume the actualizing of the task of their society was not fulfilled, nevertheless, thanks to them alone, there still continued to be present in the presences of beings of several subsequent generations after the loss of Atlantis, the 'instinctive conviction' concerning the sense of what is called there 'completed personal Being.'

"In addition, thanks to them, something of what had been attained by the Reason of the three-brained beings there also nevertheless survived when that Reason was still normal in them; and after a while this something began mechanically to be transmitted by inheritance from generation to generation and reached the beings of quite recent periods, even to several beings of contemporary times.

"Among those results of the learned attainments of the members of the society Akhaldan which were transmitted by inheritance, were also, without question, those ingenious and solid constructions which I saw being erected during this fourth descent of mine to your planet by the beings of whom I am just going to inform you, who were breeding on that part of the surface of the continent of the present Africa.

"Although the expectations that I had formed from all that our countrymen had told me concerning the mentioned new observatory there, before I had seen it with my own eyes, were not justified, nevertheless, the observatory itself and also the other constructions of the beings then of that region proved to be exceedingly ingenious and provided data for the enrichment of my common presence by a great deal of productive information for my consciousness.

"And in order that you may clearly represent to yourself and understand how these various constructions were then erected by the three-brained beings of this region for the welfare of their being-existence, I think it will be enough if I explain to you in as great detail as possible, how the particularity of their ingenious practical invention was manifested in respect of their new observatory on account of which I had decided to visit that region.

"For this purpose I must first of all inform you of two facts connected with the change in the common presences of these three-brained beings who have taken your fancy.

"The first fact is that at the outset, while they were still existing normally, that is, as it is in general becoming to all three-brained beings to exist, and while they had what is called 'Olooestesnokhnian sight,' they could also perceive, at a distance proper to be perceived by ordinary three-brained beings, the visibility of all great as well as small cosmic concentrations existing beyond them during every process of the Omnipresent-Okidanokh which proceeded in their atmosphere.

"In addition, those of them who were consciously perfected and had thereby brought the sensibility of the perception of their organ of sight—like three-brained beings everywhere else—up to what is called the

'Olooessultratesnokhnian state,' acquired the possibility of perceiving also the visibility of all these cosmic units situated at the same distance, which arise and have their further existence dependent upon the crystallizations localized directly from the sacred Theomertmalogos, that is to say, from the emanations of our most holy Sun Absolute.

"And later, when the same constant abnormal conditions of ordinary being-existence were finally established, as a consequence of which Great Nature was compelled, for reasons of which I have already once told you, among other limitations, also to degenerate the functioning of their organ of sight into what is called 'Koritesnokhnian,' that is to say, into the sight proper to the presences of one-brained and two-brained beings, then thereafter they were able to perceive the visibility of their great as well as their small concentrations situated beyond them only when the sacred process 'Aieioiuoa' proceeded in the Omnipresent Active Element Okidanokh in the atmosphere of their planet, or, as they themselves say—according to their understanding and their own perceptions—'on dark nights.'

"And the second fact, by virtue of the same degeneration of their sight into Koritesnokhnian, is based on that law common to all beings, namely, that the results obtained from every manifestation of the Omnipresent Okidanokh are perceived by the organs of sight only when in immediate contact with those vibrations which are formed in beings and which actualize the functioning of the being-organ for perceiving, at the given moment, the visibility of cosmic concentrations situated beyond them; that is to say, only when the said results of the manifestation of the Omnipresent-Okidanokh proceed up to the limit beyond which, according to the quality of the given organ for perceiving visibility, what is called the 'momentum of the impulse' dies down, or to put it otherwise, they perceive the visibility of objects only when almost next to them.

"But if these results take place beyond the mentioned limit, then this manifestation does not at all extend to those beings in whose presences there are organs for the perception of visibility, formed only by the results of the totality of 'Itoklanoz.'

"Here it is very opportune to repeat one of the profound sayings, seldom used there, of our Mullah Nassr Eddin, which very neatly defines the given case, that is, this degree of the limitation of the perception of visibility of your contemporary favorites.

"This wise saying of his, seldom used there, consists of the following words:

"'Show me the elephant the blind man has seen, and only then will I believe that you have really seen a fly.'

"Well then, my boy, thanks to that artificial adaptation which I had then seen for the observation of other cosmic concentrations, and which was being constructed in that future Egypt on the initiative issuing from the Reasons of the remote descendants of the member beings of the learned society Akhaldan, any one of these unfortunate favorites of yours, in spite of the Koritesnokhnian sight which had long before become inherent to them, could nevertheless acquire the ability to perceive freely at any time, as they say, 'of the day and night,' the visibility of all those remote cosmic concentrations which in the process of the general 'cosmic harmonious movement' come within the sphere of the horizon of their observation.

"In order to overcome this limitation of their organ of the perception of visibility, they then invented the following:

"Their Teskooano or telescope, the construction of which, it must here be said, passed to them also from their remote ancestors, they did not fix on the surface of their planet, as was usually done there and is still done now—but they placed this Teskooano very deeply within the planet, and they carried out their observations of the cosmic concentrations found beyond the atmosphere of their planet through specially bored, pipelike hollows.

"The observatory, I then saw, had five of these hollows.

"They began, in relation to the horizon, from different places of the surface of the planet occupied by the observatory, but they all met at a small underground common hollow which was something like a cave. From there, the specialists, then called Astrologers, made their observations for the purpose of studying, as I have already told you, the visible presences and results of the reciprocal action of other cosmic concentrations belonging to their own solar system as well as to other systems of the Great Universe.

"They made these observations of theirs through any one of the mentioned hollows which looked out in different directions onto their horizon, according to the given position of their planet relative to the cosmic concentration observed in the process of the 'common cosmic harmonious movement.'

"I repeat, my boy, that although the chief peculiarity of the observatory constructed there by the three-brained beings of the future Egypt proved not to be new to me, since this principle had also been utilized in my observatory on Mars, with only this difference, that my seven long pipes were fixed not within the planet but on it, nevertheless all their innovations were so interesting in detail that, for any case that might arise, I even made, during my stay there, a detailed sketch of everything I saw, and later even used something of it for my own observatory.

"And as regards the other 'constructions' there, I shall perhaps tell you about them in detail sometime later, but meanwhile, I will only say that all these independent constructions which were then not quite finished were situated not far from the observatory itself, and were intended—as I elucidated during my inspection under the guidance of the constructor who accompanied us and who was a friend of one of our tribe—partly for the same purpose of observing other suns and planets of our Great Universe, and partly for determining and intentionally directing the course of the surrounding atmosphere in order to obtain the 'climate' desired.

"All these 'constructions' of theirs occupied a fairly large open space of that part of the said region, and were enclosed by a special lattice-work made of the plant then called there 'Zalnakatar.'

"It is extremely interesting to notice here that they erected at the chief entrance of that huge enclosure a rather large—large of course in comparison with the size of their presences—stone statue called 'Sphinx' which strongly reminded me of the statue I saw on my first descent in person to your planet in the city of Samlios, just opposite the enormous building belonging to the learned society Akhaldan and which was then called the 'chief cathedral of the society Akhaldan.'

"The statue I saw in the city of Samlios and which greatly interested me, was the emblem of this society, and was called 'Conscience.'

"It represented an allegorical being, each part of whose planetary body was composed of a part of the planetary body of some definite form of being existing there, but of the parts of those beings of other forms who, according to the crystallized notions of the three-brained beings there, had to perfection one or another being-function.

"The main mass of the planetary body of the said allegorical being was represented by the trunk of a being there of definite form, called 'Bull.'

"This Bull trunk rested on the four legs of another being existing there, also of a definite form, called 'Lion,' and to that part of the Bull trunk called its 'back' two large wings were attached similar in appearance to those of a strong bird-being breeding there, called 'Eagle.'

"And on the place where the head should be, there was fixed to the Bull trunk, by means of a piece of 'amber,' two breasts representing in themselves what are called 'Breasts of a virgin.'

"When I became interested on the continent Atlantis in this strange allegorical image, and then enquired about its meaning, one of the learned members of the Great Society of men-beings explained it to me as follows:

"'This allegorical figure is the emblem of the society Akhaldan and serves for all its members as a stimulus constantly to recall and awaken in them the corresponding impulses attributed to this allegorical figure.'

"Further he continued:

"'Each part of this allegorical figure gives to every member of our society in all the three independently associating parts of his common presence, namely, in the body, in the thoughts, and in the feelings, a shock for corresponding associations for those separate cognizances which in their totality can alone give us the possibility of gradually getting rid of those undesirable factors present in every one of us, both those transmitted to us by heredity as well as those acquired by ourselves personally, which gradually engender within us impulses undesirable for us, and as a consequence of which we are not as we might be.

"'This emblem of ours constantly reminds and indicates to us that it is possible to attain freedom from what I have mentioned only if we compel our common presence always to think, feel, and act in corresponding circumstances according to that which is expressed in this emblem of ours.

"'And this emblem of ours is understood by all of us, members of the society Akhaldan, in the following way:

"'The trunk of this allegorical being, represented by the trunk of a "Bull," means that the factors crystallized in us and which engender in our presences the impulses maleficent for us, those we have inherited, as well as those we have personally acquired, can be regenerated only by indefatigable labors, namely, by those labors for which among the beings of our planet, the Bull is particularly fitted.

"'That this trunk rests on the legs of a "Lion" means that the said labors should be performed with that cognizance and feeling of courage and faith in one's "might," the property of which "might" is possessed among all the beings of the Earth in the highest degree by the possessor of these legs—the mighty Lion.

"'The wings of the strongest and the highest soaring of all birds, the Eagle, attached to the Bull trunk, constantly remind the members of our society, that during the said labors and with the mentioned inner psychic properties of self-respect, it is necessary to meditate continually on questions not related to the direct manifestations required for ordinary being-existence.

"'And as regards the strange image of the head of our allegorical being, in the form of the "Breasts of a virgin," this expresses that Love should predominate always and in everything during the inner and the outer functionings evoked by one's consciousness, such a Love as can arise and be present only in the presences of concentrations formed in the lawful parts of every whole responsible being in whom the hopes of our COMMON FATHER are placed.

"'And that the head is fixed to the trunk of the Bull

with "amber" signifies that this Love should be strictly impartial, that is to say, completely separated from all the other functions proceeding in every whole responsible being.'

"In order, my boy, that the sense of this latter emblem put into the material called there amber, may become quite comprehensible to you, I must add that amber is one of those seven planetary formations, in the arising of which the Omnipresent Active Element Okidanokh takes part with all its three separate, independent, sacred parts, in equal proportion; and in the process of planetary actualization, these intraplanetary and surplanetary formations serve for what is called the 'impeding' of the independent flow of these three localized independent sacred parts."

At this point of his tale, Beelzebub made a short pause, as if he were thinking about something, and afterwards continued thus:

"During my narration of what I then saw on a still surviving terra firma part of the surface of your planet among the three-brained beings there, certain of whom were the direct descendants of members of the truly great learned society Akhaldan there, the result of the manifestations of my being-Reason was that, owing to various associative recollections of all kinds of impressions of the perceptions of the visibility of the exterior environment of the said region, which have become fixed in my common presence, there have been gradually revived in me all the scenes and all the associative flow of thoughts of one of these being-experiencings of mine which occurred during my last stay there on my visit just to that same contemporary Egypt, when I once sat absorbed in thought at the foot of one of these constructions, which had chanced to survive from that period, and which is now called there 'Pyramids.'

"It was just then, that in the general functioning of my Reason there was also associated among other things the following:

"Good! . . . If none of the benefits already formerly attained by the Reason of the beings of the continent Atlantis for ordinary being-existence has become the possession of the contemporary beings of this planet, then this might perhaps be logically explained simply because for cosmic reasons, not issuing at all from and not depending upon the three-brained beings there, that second great 'cataclysm not according to law' occurred, during which, not only that continent itself perished, but also everything which existed on it.

"But this Egypt!

"Was not its magnificence still quite recent?

"There is no denying it . . . owing to the third small catastrophe to that ill-fated planet, and also to the fifth, about which I shall speak later, this part also of its surface, it is true, suffered, having been covered with sands. . . . Nevertheless, the three-brained beings dwelling there did not perish, but were only scattered over various other parts of the same continent, and consequently, whatever new exterior conditions may have ensued, there should have survived in their presences, it would seem, the crystallized results of the perfected factors, transmitted to them by inheritance for normal 'being-logical-mentation.'

"And so, my boy, being desirous after this distressful 'Alstoozori' of mine, or as your favorites would say, 'sorrowful reflections,' to clear up for myself the very essence of the cause also of this lamentable fact there, I understood at the end of my minute investigations, and became aware with all my being, that this abnormality there proceeds exclusively owing only to one remarkable aspect of the chief particularity of their strange psyche, namely, that particularity which has become completely crystallized and is an inseparable part of their common presences and which serves as a factor for the periodic arising in them of what is called the 'urgent need to destroy everything outside of themselves.'

"The point is that when, during the apogee of the development of such a peculiarity—terrifying to every Reason—of the psyche of the three-brained beings, they began to manifest outside of themselves this phenomenal peculiarity of their common presences, that is to say, when they begin to carry out on some part of the surface of their planet the process of reciprocal destruction, then, at the same time, without any deliberate aim, and even without what is called 'organic need,' they also destroy everything which chances to come within the sphere of the perception of their organ of sight. During the periods of this 'phenomenal psychopathic apogee,' they destroy also all the objects in the given place and at the given time which these same beings themselves, between whom this terrifying process proceeds, have intentionally produced as well as the productions which have chanced to survive and to reach them from the beings of previous epochs.

"Well then, my boy, at the period of this fourth sojourn of mine in person on the surface of your planet, I first arrived in the country now called Egypt, and after having stayed there a few days among the remote descendants of the members of the great learned society Akhaldan, and becoming acquainted with certain surviving results of their 'being-Partkdolg-duty' for the welfare of their descendants, I afterwards, accompanied by two of our tribe, went to the southern countries of the same continent, and there, with the help of the local three-brained beings, caught the necessary number of ape-beings.

"Having accomplished this, I telepathically signalled

our ship *Occasion* which descended to us, it must be said on the first, very dark night; and when we had loaded these ape-beings into that special section of the ship *Occasion* which had been constructed for Gornahoor Harharkh under his directions, we at once reascended to the planet Mars; and three Martian days later, on the same ship and together with these apes, I ascended to the planet Saturn.

"Though we had previously decided to carry out the experiments with these apes only on the following year, when they would have become thoroughly acclimatized and orientated to existence under the new conditions, I ascended then to the planet Saturn so soon because at my last personal meeting with Gornahoor Harharkh, I had promised him to be present at his family solemnity which had soon to take place.

"And this family solemnity of Gornahoor Harharkh's was that beings like himself around him were to consecrate the first heir produced by him.

"I promised to attend this family solemnity Krikhrakhri in order to undertake, regarding his recently arisen heir, what is called the 'Alnatoorornian-being-duty.'

"Here it is interesting to remark that this kind of procedure for undertaking this being-duty, took place among the ancient three-brained beings of your planet also, and even reached your contemporary favorites, though these latter, just as in everything else, take only the external form of this serious and important procedure. The beings who undertake, as it were, these duties, are called by your contemporary favorites 'godfathers' and 'godmothers.'

"The heir of Gornahoor Harharkh was then called Rakhoorkh."

CHAPTER 24

Beelzebub's Flight to the Planet Earth for the Fifth Time

Beelzebub continued to relate as follows:

"After my fourth sojourn on the surface of the planet Earth many years again passed.

"During these years I of course, as before, sometimes attentively observed through my Teskooano the being-existence of these favorites of yours.

"During this time their number considerably increased and they had already populated almost all the large and small terra firma parts of the surface of this planet of yours; and of course there also continued to proceed among them their chief particularity, namely, from time to time they destroyed each other's existence.

"During this time, that is to say, between my fourth and fifth visits, great changes occurred to the surface of your planet; many changes also occurred there in the concentrations of the places of settlement of these favorites of yours. For example, all those centers-of-culture of theirs on the continent Ashhark where I had been in person during my previous descents upon the Earth, namely, the countries of Tikliamish and Maralpleicie, had by the time of my fifth arrival there entirely ceased to exist.

"The cause of the destruction of these centers-of-culture of theirs and of the changes on the surface of this planet in general, was again a misfortune, the third for this ill-fated planet.

"This third misfortune was entirely of a local character and occurred because during several years there had proceeded in its atmosphere unprecedented what are called 'accelerated-displacements-of-the-parts-of-the-atmosphere';

or, as your favorites there would say, 'great winds.'

"The cause of these abnormal displacements or great winds at that time was once again those two fragments which had been separated from this planet of yours during the first great calamity, and which afterwards became independent small planets of this solar system, and are now called Moon and Anoolios.

"Strictly speaking, the main cause of this terrestrial misfortune was only the larger of these separated parts, namely, the Moon; the smaller fragment, Anoolios, played no part in it whatsoever.

"The accelerated-displacements in the Earth's atmosphere resulted from the following:

"When the atmosphere on the small, accidentally arisen planet Moon had been finally formed, and the Moon, according to the already mentioned law of 'Catching-up,' continued to fall back upon its fundamental mass by the path already then established, and this newly arisen definite presence on the Moon had not yet acquired its own harmony within the common-system-harmony-of-movement, then the what is called 'Osmooalnian-friction' which was, so to say, not harmonized with the whole, evoked in the atmosphere of the Earth the mentioned accelerated-displacements or great winds.

"These unprecedented great winds then began, by the force of their currents, as it is said, to wear down the elevated 'terra-firma-parts' and to fill up the corresponding 'depressions.'

"Such depressions were also the two countries of the continent Ashhark upon which the process of existence was chiefly concentrated of the second and third groups of beings of contemporary Asia, that is to say, the main parts of the countries Tikliamish and Maralpleicie.

"At the same time sands also filled up certain parts of the country, Pearl-land, as well as that country in the middle of the continent Grabontzi, where, as I have already told you, there was formed, after the loss of Atlantis, what they called the leading 'Center-of-Culture' for all the three-brained beings there, a country which at that time was the most flourishing part of the surface of this planet of yours, and which is now the desert called 'Sahara.'

"Bear in mind also, that during the abnormal winds of that time, besides the countries mentioned, several other smallish terra firma spaces of the surface of that hapless planet were also covered by sands.

"It is interesting to note here that your contemporary favorites have also by some means or other learned about the changes that then occurred in the places of the permanent existence of the three-centered beings, and having made a label for this as well, this time the 'Great-transmigration-of-races,' they stuck it onto what they call their 'knowledge.'

"A number of the 'learned' there now puff and blow with all their might to find out why and how it all occurred, so that they can tell everybody else about it.

"Just now there are several theories about the matter there, which although they have nothing in common with each other and are each in an objective sense more absurd than the other, are nevertheless accepted there by what is called 'official-knowledge.'

"But in fact, the real cause of the transmigration of the three-centered beings there was that as soon as the said abrasion began, the beings living on the continent Ashhark, fearing to be buried by the sands, began moving to other, more or less secure places. And these migrations of the three-brained beings there proceeded in the following order:

"Most of the three-brained beings populating Tikliamish moved to the south of the same continent Ashhark, to the country which was later called 'Persia,' and the rest moved north, and settled in those regions which were afterwards called 'Kirkistcheri.'

"As for the beings populating the country Maralpleicie, one part wandered eastwards, while the rest, the major part, went towards the west.

"Having crossed the eastern heights, those who went east settled down on the shores of the large Saliakooriapnian spaces, and this country was later called 'China.'

"And that part of the beings of Maralpleicie who sought safety by moving to the west, after wandering from place to place, ultimately reached the neighboring continent, later called 'Europe,' and the three-brained beings who then still existed in the middle of the continent Grabontzi dispersed over the whole of the surface.

"And so, my boy, this fifth descent of mine in person to your planet belongs to the period of the time after this said redistribution of the groups of the communities of these favorites of yours.

"And the causes of my descent there in person were the following events:

"I must first tell you that the chief peculiarity of the psyche of your favorites, namely, the 'periodic-need-to destroy-the-existence-of-others-like-oneself,' interested me more and more with every succeeding century of theirs, and side by side with it the irresistible desire increased in me to find out the exact causes of a particularity so phenomenal for three-brained beings.

"And so, my boy, in order to have more material for elucidating this question which interested me so intensely, I, in the interval between my fourth and fifth sojourn on the planet Earth, organized my observations through the Teskooano from the planet Mars of the existence of those peculiar three-brained beings in the following way:

"I deliberately kept under observation quite a number of

their beings from among your favorites and during many of their years either I personally or somebody whom I commissioned observed them attentively, trying as much as possible not to miss anything, and to clear up from every aspect all the particularities in their manifestations during the processes of their ordinary existence.

"And I must confess, my boy, that when I happened to be quite free, I sometimes during whole 'Sinonoums' or, as your favorites there approximately define the corresponding flow of time, 'hours,' followed with great interest the movements of the said three-brained beings there under observation, and tried to explain to myself logically their what are called 'psychic-experiencings.'

"And so, during these observations of mine from the planet Mars through my Teskooano, it once flashed upon me that the length of their existence was, century by century and even year by year, becoming shorter and shorter at a very definite and equally uniform rate, and this served as the beginning of my further quite serious study of the psyche of these three-brained beings who have taken your fancy.

"Of course when I first noticed this, I at once took into account not only the chief particularity of their psyche, that is their periodic reciprocal destruction, but also the innumerable what are called 'illnesses' which exist exclusively only on that planet, the majority of which, by the way, arose and continue to arise owing to the same abnormal external conditions of the ordinary being-existence established by them, which help to make it impossible for them to exist normally up to the sacred Rascooarno.

"When I first noticed this and began to recall my previous impression about it, each of the separate independent spiritualized parts of my whole presence became filled with the conviction, and my essence perceived the mentioned 'flash,' that in truth these three-brained beings of your planet had in the beginning existed according to their time calculation for about twelve centuries, and some of them, even, for about fifteen centuries.

"To be able more or less clearly to represent to yourself the rate at which the length of their existence declined during this time, it is enough for you to know that when I left this solar system for ever, the maximum length of their existence was already from seventy to ninety of their years.

"And latterly, if anybody should exist even as long as this, all the rest of the beings of that peculiar planet would already consider that he had existed quite 'a good long time.'

"And if anybody happened to exist a little over a century he would be exhibited in their museums, and of course all the rest of the beings there would know about him because his photograph, and descriptions of the manner of his existence even to the enumeration of each of his movements, would continually be found in all their what are called 'newspapers.'

"And so, my boy, since, at the time when I suddenly constated such a fact there, I had no special business on the planet Mars and it was quite impossible to try to probe this novel peculiarity by means of the Teskooano, I therefore decided to go there myself in order perhaps to clear up for myself there on the spot the causes of this also.

"Several Martian days after my decision, I again ascended there on the ship *Occasion*.

"At the time of this fifth descent of mine in person to your planet, their 'center-for-the-incoming-and-the-outgoing-results-of-the-perfecting-of-being-rumination' or, as they themselves call it, their 'Center-of-Culture' was already the city of Babylon; so it was just there that I decided to go.

"This time our ship *Occasion* alighted on what is called the 'Persian Gulf' because we had ascertained through the Teskooano before our flight that for our further traveling, that is, to reach the town of Babylon and also for the mooring of our ship *Occasion* itself, the most convenient place would be that same Saliakooriapnian space of the surface of your planet now existing there under the name of the Persian Gulf.

"This water space was convenient for my further traveling because the large river, on the banks of which the city of Babylon stood, flowed into it, and we proposed to sail up the stream of this river to get there.

"During that period of the flow of time this 'incomparably majestic' Babylon was flourishing in every respect. It was a Center-of-Culture not only for the beings dwelling on the continent Ashhark, but also for all the beings of all those other large and small terra firmas which were adapted to the needs of ordinary being-existence on that planet.

"At the time of my first arrival there in this Center-of-Culture of theirs, they were just preparing that which was afterwards the principal cause of the acceleration of the rate of the degeneration of their 'psychic-organization,' especially in the sense of the atrophy in them of the instinctive functioning of those three fundamental factors which ought to exist in the presence of every three-brained being—namely, those factors which give rise to the being-impulses existing under the names of 'Faith,' 'Hope,' and 'Love.'

"These being-factors degenerating by heredity from generation to generation has brought it about that instead of a real being-psyche, such as should exist in the presence of every kind of three-brained being, there now already exists in the presences of your contemporary favorites, although a 'real-psyche' also, nevertheless one that can be very well defined by one of the wise sayings of our dear Mullah Nassr Eddin, which consists of the following words: 'There is everything in it except the core or even the kernel.'

"It is absolutely necessary to relate to you in as great detail as possible what occurred during that period in Babylon, as all this information may be valuable material for you for a better elucidation and transubstantiation in your Reason of all the causes which together have finally given rise to that strange psyche of the three-centered beings which your contemporary favorites already have.

"I must first of all tell you that I obtained the information concerning the events of that time which I am about to relate chiefly from those three-centered beings there whom the other beings called 'learned.'

"Before going any further, I must here dwell a little on just what kind of beings there on your planet the other beings call learned.

"The point is that, even before this fifth sojourn of mine there, that is to say before that period when Babylon, as I have told you, flourished in every respect, those beings who became learned and were regarded by others as learned were not such beings as become and are regarded as learned everywhere in the Universe, nor such as first became learned even on your planet, namely, such beings as acquire by their conscious labors and intentional sufferings the ability to contemplate the details of all that exists from the point of view of World-arising and World-existence, owing chiefly to which, they perfect their highest body to the corresponding gradation of the sacred measure of Objective Reason in order that they might later sense as much about cosmic truths as their higher being-body is perfected.

"But from the time of what is called the Tikliamishian civilization until now, those beings, especially the contemporary ones, chiefly became learned who 'learned-by-rote' as much as possible about every kind of vacuous information, such as old women love to relate about what was presumably said in olden times.

"Note, by the way, that for the definition of the importance of the learned there, our venerated Mullah Nassr Eddin also has a sentence expressed in the following words:

"'Everybody talks as if our learned know that half a hundred is fifty.'

"There on your planet, the more of such information one of your favorites mechanically learns by rote, information he himself has never verified, and which moreover, he has never sensed, the more learned he is considered to be.

"And so, my boy, we reached the city of Babylon; there were indeed a great many learned beings there gathered from almost the whole of that planet of yours.

"As the causes of the gathering of these beings in the city of Babylon at that time are extremely interesting, I will tell you also about this a little more in detail.

"The point is, that most of the learned beings of the Earth had been then assembled there under compulsion by a most peculiar Persian king, under whose dominion at that period was also the city of Babylon.

"In order to understand thoroughly which fundamental aspect ensuing from the total results of the abnormally established conditions of ordinary being-existence there gave rise to the said peculiarity of this Persian king, I must first enlighten you in respect of two facts which had become fixed long before.

"The first fact is that almost from the time of the loss of the continent Atlantis, there gradually began to be crystallized, and during later centuries became completely crystallized in the presence of every one of your favorites there, a particular 'inherency' thanks to which that being-sensation which is called 'happiness-for-one's-being'—which is experienced from time to time by every three-brained being from the satisfaction of his inner self-evaluation—appears in the presences of your favorites exclusively only when they acquire for their own possession a great deal of that popular metal there called 'gold.'

"A greater misfortune for them arising from this particular 'inherency' in their common presences is that the mentioned sensation due to the possession of the said metal is strengthened by the beings around the possessor and also by beings who learn about it only by what is called 'hearsay' and have not themselves been convinced by personal corresponding perceptions; and it is, moreover, the established custom there never to consider through which kind of being-manifestations he becomes the possessor of a great quantity of this metal, and such a being there becomes for all those around him one who evokes in their presences the functioning of that crystallized consequence of the property of the organ Kundabuffer called 'envy.'

"And the second fact is this, that when in the presences of your favorites their chief particularity functions 'crescendently' and, according to the established custom among their different communities, the process of the reciprocal destruction of each other's existence proceeds, then afterwards, when this property, only maleficent for them themselves, has run its course, and they temporarily cease these processes of theirs, then the king of that community in which a greater number of subjects survive, receiving the title of conqueror, usually takes for himself everything belonging to the beings of the conquered community.

"Such a 'king-conqueror' there usually orders his subjects to take from the conquered all their lands, all the young beings of female sex present in the conquered community, and all the what is called 'riches' accumulated by them during centuries.

"And so, my boy, when the subjects of that said peculiar Persian king conquered the beings of another community, he ordered them not to take and even not to touch any of these, but to take with them as what are called 'captives' only the learned beings of this conquered community.

"Clearly to represent and to substantiate in yourself the understanding just why such a peculiar craze arose in the individuality of that Persian king and became proper only to him, you must know that at the period of the Tikliamish civilization, in the town called 'Chiklaral' a three-brained learned being by name Harnahoom—whose essence later became crystallized into what is called an 'Eternal-Hasnamussian-individual'—invented that any old metal you like, abundant on the surface of that planet, could easily be turned into the rare metal 'gold' and all it was necessary to know for this was just one very small 'secret.'

"This maleficent fiction of his became widely spread there, and having become crystallized in the presences of the beings of that time, and being transmitted by inheritance from generation to generation, began to pass to the beings of subsequent generations as a gradually formed definite maleficent fantastic science there, under the name of 'alchemy,' under the name, that is, of that great science which had indeed existed there during those epochs long past, when in the presences of their ancestors the consequences of the properties of the organ Kundabuffer had not yet been quite crystallized, and which branch of genuine knowledge might be useful and indeed necessary for the three-brained beings there even of contemporary times.

"And as at that period to which my tale relates, this Persian king needed for some or other of his undoubtedly Hasnamussian aims, a great deal of this metal, rare on the surface of the Earth, called 'gold,' and as the notion concerning this method that had been invented by the then existing 'Hasnamussian-individual,' Harnahoom, had also reached his presence, he was eager to get gold by so easy a means.

"When this Persian king had finally decided to get gold by 'alchemy,' he then and there for the first time cognized with the whole of his being that he did not as yet know that 'little secret' without which it was absolutely impossible to fulfill this desire of his. So he then pondered how to find out that 'little secret.'

"The result of this pondering was that he became aware of the following:

"As the learned already have knowledge of every other kind of 'mystery,' then this mystery must also be known to one of them.

"Having finally arrived at such a conclusion, he, with an intensified functioning of 'being-astonishment' at why such a simple idea had never entered his head before, called several of his attendant subjects and ordered them to find out which of the learned beings of his capital knew this mystery.

"When it was reported to him the following day that not a single one of the learned beings of the capital knew this mystery, he ordered inquiries to be made also of all the learned present among the beings of the whole of his subject-community, and when after several days he again received the same negative reply, he once more began to ponder, and this time very seriously.

"His serious thinking first led his Reason to the understanding that, without any doubt, one or other of the learned beings of his community was aware of this 'secret' also, but since among beings of that clan, this strict keeping of a 'professional' mystery was very strongly developed, nobody, of course, was willing to reveal it.

"The result of his serious thinking was that he became aware that it was necessary not merely to question, but to examine the learned beings about this mystery.

"The same day, he gave appropriate instructions to his nearest corresponding assistants, and the latter already began to 'examine,' after the manner that had already long before been the way of power-possessing beings to examine ordinary beings.

"And when this peculiar Persian king became finally convinced that the learned beings of this community indeed knew nothing about this mystery, he began to look for learned beings in other communities to whom this mystery might be known.

"As the kings of the other communities were unwilling to offer their learned beings for 'examination,' he decided forcibly to compel these unconquered kings to do so. And from that time on, at the head of numerous hordes in subjection to him, he began with their help to make what are called 'military excursions.'

"This Persian king had many hordes in subjection to him because at that period, from the region of the surface of this planet of yours where that community was situated and over which he happened to be king, there had been intensified in the presences of the beings, even before this time, according to what is called the 'foreseeing-adaptation' of Great Nature, the what is called 'birth rate'; and at the given period, there was being actualized that which was demanded for the common-cosmic Trogoautoegocratic process, that is to say, from this region of the surface of your planet there had to issue more of those vibrations arising from the destruction of being-existence."

During this last explanation Hassein interrupted Beelzebub with the following words:

"Dear Grandfather, I do not understand why the issuing of the required vibrations for the purpose of the actualization of this most great cosmic process should depend on a definite region of the surface of the planet."

To this question of his grandson, Beelzebub replied as follows:

"As before long I intend to make the special question of those terrifying processes of reciprocal destruction which they call 'wars' the theme of my tales concerning the three-brained beings of the planet Earth, it is better to defer this question of yours also until this special tale, because then, I think, you will understand it well."

Having said this, Beelzebub again continued to relate about the Babylonian events.

"When the peculiar Persian king I mentioned began, thanks to the hordes in subjection to him, to conquer beings of other communities and to seize by force the learned among them, he assigned as a place for their congregation and existence the said city of Babylon, to which they were taken in order that this lord of half the then continent of Asia could thereafter freely examine them in the hope that one of them might perhaps happen to know the secret of turning cheap metal into the metal gold.

"With the same aim he even made at that time a special what is called 'campaign' into the country Egypt.

"He then made this special campaign there because the learned beings of all the continents of the planet were assembled there at that period, the opinion being widely spread there that more information for their various 'sciences' was to be obtained in this Egypt than anywhere else on their planet.

"This Persian king-conqueror then took from Egypt all the learned beings present there, both the native and those who had come from other communities; and among their number were then also several called 'Egyptian priests,' descendants of just those learned members of the society Akhaldan who had chanced to escape, and who had been the first to populate that country.

"When a little later a fresh craze arose in the presence of this peculiar Persian king, the craze for the process itself of the destruction of the existence of other beings similar to himself, and which supplanted the former craze, he forgot about the learned beings and they began to exist there freely in the city of Babylon awaiting his further directions.

"The learned beings collected in this way there in the city of Babylon from almost the whole of the planet used often to meet together and of course to discuss among themselves, as it is proper to the learned beings of the planet Earth, questions which were either immeasurably beyond their comprehension, or about which they could never elucidate anything useful whatsoever, either for themselves or for ordinary beings there.

"Well, it was just during these meetings and discussions that there arose among them, as it is in general proper to arise among learned beings there, what is called 'a-burning-question-of-the-day,' a question which in some way or other indeed interested them at that time to, as they say, 'their very marrow.'

"The question which chanced to become the-burning-question-of-the-day so vitally touched the whole being of every one of them, that they even 'climbed down' from their what are called 'pedestals' and began discussing it not only with the learned like themselves, but also here, there and everywhere with anyone they chanced to come across.

"The consequence was that an interest in this question gradually spread among all the ordinary three-brained beings then existing in Babylon, and by about the time we reached this city it had become the question-of-the-day for all the beings there.

"Not only did these learned themselves talk about and discuss this question, but similar conversations and fierce discussions proceeded like fury among the ordinary beings there also.

"It was talked about and discussed by the young and old, by men and women, and even by the Babylonian butchers. Exceedingly anxious were they, particularly the learned, to know about this question.

"Before our arrival there, many of the beings existing in Babylon had ultimately even lost their reason on account of this question, and many were already candidates for losing theirs.

"This burning-question-of-the-day was that both the 'sorry-learned' and also the ordinary beings of the city of Babylon were very anxious to know whether they had a 'soul.'

"Every possible kind of fantastic theory existed in Babylon upon this question; and more and more theories were being freshly cooked up; and every, as it is said there, 'catchy theory' had, of course, its followers.

"Although whole hosts of these various theories existed there, nevertheless they were one and all based upon only two, but two quite opposite assumptions.

"One of these was called the 'atheistic' and the other the 'idealistic' or 'dualistic.'

"All the dualistic theories maintained the existence of the soul, and of course its 'immortality,' and every possible kind of 'perturbation' to it after the death of the being 'man.'

"And all the atheistic theories maintained just the opposite.

"In short, my boy, when we arrived in the city of Babylon there was then proceeding what is called the 'Building-of-the-Tower-of-Babel.'"

Having uttered these latter words, Beelzebub became a little thoughtful and then continued as follows:

"Now I wish to explain to you about the expression I just used, namely, the 'Building-of-the-Tower-of-Babel.' This expression is very often used on your planet by the contemporary three-brained beings there also.

"I wish to touch upon this expression frequently used there and to elucidate it to you chiefly because firstly I chanced to be a witness at that time of all the events which gave rise to it, and secondly because the history of the arising of this expression and its transubstantiation in the understanding of your contemporary favorites can very clearly and instructively elucidate to you that, thanks as always to the same abnormally established conditions of ordinary being-existence, no precise information of events there which have indeed occurred to beings of former epochs ever reaches beings of later generations. And if, by chance, something like this expression does reach them, then the fantastic Reason of your favorites constructs a whole theory on the basis of just one expression such as this, with the result that those illusory 'being-ego-plastikoori,' or what they call 'psychic-picturings' increase and multiply in their presences owing to which there has arisen in the Universe the strange 'unique-psyche' of three-brained beings which every one of your favorites has.

"Well then, when we arrived in the city of Babylon, and I began mixing with various beings there and making my corresponding observations in order to elucidate the question which had interested me, then, because almost everywhere I ran across the said learned beings who had gathered and met there in great numbers, it so fell out that I began associating with them alone, and made my observations through them, and also through their individualities.

"Among the number of the learned beings whom I met for my mentioned aim, was also one named Hamolinadir who had also been brought there by compulsion from Egypt.

"Well, during these meetings of ours, almost the same relations were established between this terrestrial three-brained being Hamolinadir and myself as in general are established everywhere between three-brained beings who frequently meet.

"This Hamolinadir was one of those learned there in the common presence of whom the factors for the impulses of a three-brained being which had passed to him by heredity were not quite atrophied, and moreover it turned out that during his preparatory age the responsible beings around him had prepared him to be also more or less normally responsible.

"It is necessary to notice that many learned beings of this kind were then in the city of Babylon.

"Although this learned Hamolinadir had his arising and preparation for becoming a responsible being just there in the city of Babylon and descended from the race of beings there called 'Assyrian,' yet he became learned in Egypt where the highest school existing on Earth at that time was found, and which was called the 'School of Materializing-Thought.'

"At the age he was when I first met him he already had his 'I'—in respect of rationally directing what is called the 'automatic-psychic-functioning' of his common presence—at the maximum stability for three-centered beings of the planet Earth at that time, in consequence of which during what is called his 'waking-passive-state' he had very definitely expressed being-manifestations, as, for instance, those called 'self-consciousness,' 'impartiality,' 'sincerity,' 'sensibility of perception,' 'alertness,' and so forth.

"Soon after our arrival in Babylon, I began going with this Hamolinadir to various what are called 'meetings' of the mentioned learned beings, and listened to every kind of what they called 'reports' upon the very question which was then 'the-question-of-the-day,' and which was the cause of the 'agitation-of-the-minds-of-the-whole-of-Babylon.'

"This friend of mine, Hamolinadir, was also very much excited about the said 'burning question.'

"He was agitated and perplexed by the fact that both the already existing and the many newly appearing theories upon this question were all, in spite of their entirely contradictory proofs, equally convincing and equally plausible.

"He said that those theories in which it was proved that we have a soul were very logically and convincingly expounded; and, likewise, those theories in which quite the contrary was proved were expounded no less logically and convincingly.

"So that you may be able to put yourself in the place of that sympathetic Assyrian, I shall also explain to you that in general on your planet, then in the city of Babylon as well as at the present time, all the theories on such a question as they call it of 'the beyond,' or any other 'elucidation-of-details' of any definite 'fact,' are invented by those three-brained beings there in whom most of the consequences of the properties of the organ Kundabuffer are completely crystallized, in consequence of which there actively functions in their presence that being-property which they themselves call 'cunning.' Owing to this, they consciously—of course consciously only with the sort of reason which it has already become long ago proper for them alone to possess—and moreover, merely automatically, gradually acquire in their common presence the capacity for 'spotting' the weakness of the psyche of the surrounding beings like themselves; and this capacity gradually forms in them data which enable them at times to sense and even to understand the peculiar logic of the beings around them, and according to these data, they invent and propound one of their 'theories' concerning this or that question; and because, as I have already told you, in most of the three-brained beings there, owing to the abnormal conditions of ordinary being-existence established there by them themselves, the being-function called 'instinctively-to-sense-cosmic-truths' gradually atrophies, then, if any one of them happens to devote himself to the detailed study of any one of these 'theories,' he is bound, whether he wishes or not, to be persuaded by it with the whole of his presence.

"Well, my boy, already seven of their months after our arrival in the city of Babylon I once went with this friend of mine there, Hamolinadir, to what is called a 'general-learned-conference.'

"This 'general-learned-conference' had already been convened at that time by the learned beings previously brought there by force; and thus there were at this conference not only the learned forcibly assembled there by the mentioned Persian king who in the meantime had already got over his craze about the science of 'alchemy,' and forgotten all about it, but many other learned also from other communities who had voluntarily gathered as they then said 'for-the-sake-of-science.'

"At this 'general-learned-conference' that day, the reporters spoke by lot.

"My friend, Hamolinadir, also had to report about some topic and therefore drew a lot; and it fell to him to speak fifth.

"The reporters who preceded him either reported upon new 'theories' they had invented or they criticized theories already existing and known to everybody.

"At last came the turn of this sympathetic Assyrian.

"He ascended what is called the 'rostrum,' and as he did so some attendants hung up a notice above it indicating on which subject the given reporter would speak.

"It was the custom at that time to do so.

"The notice announced that the reporter had taken as the theme of his report the 'Instability-of-Human-Reason.'

"Thereupon, this terrestrial friend of mine first expatiated on the kind of structure which, in his opinion, the human 'head-brain' has, and in which cases and in what manner various impressions are perceived by the other brains of man, and how only after definite what is called 'agreement' between all the brains are the total results impressed on this head-brain.

"He spoke calmly at first, but the longer he spoke, the more agitated he became, until his voice rose to a shout, and shouting he began to criticize the Reason in man.

"And at the same time, he mercilessly criticized his own Reason.

"Still continuing to shout, he very logically and convincingly demonstrated the instability and fickleness of man's Reason, and showed, in detail, how easy it is to prove and convince this Reason of anything you like.

"Although in the midst of the shouting of this terrestrial friend of mine, Hamolinadir, his sobbing could be heard, nevertheless, even while sobbing, he continued to shout. Further he said:

"'To every man, and also of course to me, it's quite easy to prove anything; all that is necessary to know is which shocks and which associations to arouse in the other human brains while one or other "truth" is being proved. It is very easily possible even to prove to man that our whole World and of course the people in it, are nothing but an illusion, and that the authenticity and reality of the World are only a "corn" and moreover the corn growing on the big toe of our left foot. Besides this corn, absolutely nothing exists in the World; everything only seems, and even then only to "psychopaths-squared."'

"At this point in the speech of this sympathetic terrestrial three-brained being, an attendant offered him a bowl of water, and after he had eagerly drunk the water, he continued to speak, but now more calmly.

"He said further:

"'Take myself as an example: I am not an ordinary learned man. I am known by all Babylon and by people of many other towns as an exceedingly learned and wise man.

"'I finished the course of study higher than which has never yet existed on the Earth, and which it is almost impossible will ever exist again.

"'But what then has this highest development given to my Reason in respect of that question which, already during one or two years, is driving all Babylonians insane?

"'This Reason of mine which has received the highest development, has given me during this general dementia concerning the question of the soul nothing else but "five-Fridays-a-week."

"'During this time, I have very attentively and seriously followed all the old and new theories about the "soul" and there is not a single theory with the author of which I do not inwardly agree, since all of them are very logically and plausibly expounded, and such Reason as I have cannot but agree with their logic and plausibility.

"'During this time I have even myself written a very

lengthy work on this "question-of-the-beyond"; and many of those present here have surely become acquainted with my logical mentation and most probably there is not one of you here who does not envy this logical mentation of mine.

"'Yet at the same time I now honestly declare to you all, that concerning this "question-of-the-beyond" I myself, with the whole of the knowledge that has been accumulated in me, am neither more nor less than just an "idiot-cubed."

"'There is now proceeding among us in the city of Babylon the general public "building-of-a-tower" by means of which to ascend to "Heaven" and there to see with our own eyes what goes on there.

"'This tower is being built of bricks which outwardly all look alike, but which are made of quite different materials.

"'Among these bricks are bricks of iron and wood and also of "dough" and even of "eider down."

"'Well then, at the present time, a stupendously enormous tower is being built of such bricks right in the center of Babylon, and every more or less conscious person must bear in mind that sooner or later this tower will certainly fall and crush not only all the people of Babylon, but also everything else that is there.

"'As I personally still wish to live and have no desire to be crushed by this Babylonian tower, I shall therefore now immediately go away from here, and all of you, do as you please.'

"He uttered these last words while leaving, and ran off and since that time, I never saw that sympathetic Assyrian again.

"As I later learned, he left the city of Babylon the same day forever, and went to Nineveh and existed somewhere there to a ripe old age. I also ascertained that this Hamolinadir was never again occupied with 'sciences' and that he spent his existence only in planting 'choongary' which in contemporary language is called 'maize.'

"Well, my boy, the speech of this Hamolinadir at first made such a deep impression upon the beings there that for almost a month they went about, as it is said there, 'down-in-the-mouth.'

"And when they met each other, they could speak of nothing else but only of the various passages from this speech which they remembered and repeated.

"They repeated them so often that several of Hamolinadir's phrases spread among the ordinary beings of Babylon and became sayings for ordinary daily existence.

"Some of his phrases reached even contemporary beings of the planet Earth, and among them there is also the phrase 'The-Building-of-the-Tower-of-Babel.'

"Contemporary beings now already quite clearly picture to themselves that once upon a time a certain tower was built in this said city of Babylon to enable beings to ascend in their planetary bodies to 'God Himself.'

"And the contemporary beings of the planet Earth also say and are quite persuaded that during the building of this 'Babylonian tower' a number of tongues were confused.

"In general there reached the contemporary beings of the planet Earth a great many of such isolated expressions, uttered or fixed by various sensible beings of former epochs concerning certain details of a complete understanding from the epoch when the Center-of-Culture was Babylon as well as from the other epochs; and your favorites of recent centuries, simply on the basis of these 'scraps,' have with their already quite 'nonsensical' Reason concocted such 'cock-and-bull' stories as our Arch-cunning Lucifer himself might envy.

"Among the many teachings then current in Babylon

concerning the 'question-of-the-beyond,' two had a large number of adherents though these teachings had nothing in common.

"And it was precisely these two teachings which began to pass from generation to generation, and to confuse their 'being-sane-mentation' which had already been confused enough without them.

"Although in the course of their transmission from generation to generation the details of both these teachings underwent change, nevertheless the fundamental ideas contained in them remained unchanged and have even reached down to contemporary times.

"One of these two teachings which then had many adherents in Babylon was just the 'dualistic' and the other, the 'atheistic'; so that in one of them it was proved that in beings there is the soul, and in the other, quite the opposite, namely, that they have nothing of the kind.

"In the dualist or idealist teaching, it was said that within the coarse body of the being-man, there is a fine and invisible body, which is just the soul.

"This 'fine body' of man is immortal, that is to say, it is never destroyed.

"This fine body or soul, it was said further, must make a corresponding payment for every action of the 'physical body' whether voluntary or involuntary, and every man, already at birth, consists of these two bodies, namely, the physical body and the soul.

"Further it was said that as soon as a man is born, two invisible spirits immediately perch upon his shoulders.

"On his right shoulder sits a 'spirit-of-good' called an 'angel,' and on his left, a second spirit, a 'spirit-of-evil' called a 'devil.'

"From the very first day these spirits—the spirit-of-good and the spirit-of-evil—record in their 'notebooks' all the manifestations of the man, the spirit sitting on his right shoulder recording all those called his 'good manifestations' or 'good deeds,' and the spirit sitting on his left shoulder, the 'evil.'

"Among the duties of these two spirits is that of suggesting to and compelling a man to do more of those manifestations which are in their respective domains.

"The spirit on the right constantly strives to make the man refrain from doing those actions which are in the domain of the opposite spirit, and, perforce, more of those in his own domain.

"And the spirit on the left does the same, but vice versa.

"In this strange teaching it was further said that these two 'spirit-rivals' are always combating each other, and that each strives with might and main that the man should do more of those actions which are in his domain.

"When the man dies, these spirits leave his physical body on the Earth and take his soul to God who exists somewhere 'up-in-Heaven.'

"There up-in-Heaven this God sits surrounded by his devoted archangels and angels, and suspended in front of him is a pair of scales.

"On each side of the scales, 'spirits' stand on duty. On the right, stand the spirits who are called 'servants of Paradise' and these are the angels; and on the left stand the 'servants of Hell' and these are the devils.

"The spirits which have sat on the man's shoulder all his life bring his soul after death to God, and God then takes from their hands the notebooks in which the notes have been recorded of all the man's actions; and He places them on the 'pans of the scales.'

"On the right pan He puts the notebook of the angel; and on the left pan the notebook of the devil, and, according to the pan which falls, God commands the spirits on duty standing on the given side to take this soul into their charge.

"In the charge of the spirits standing on duty on the right is just that place called Paradise.

"It is a place of indescribable beauty and splendiferousness. In that Paradise are magnificent fruits in abundance and endless quantities of fragrant flowers, and enchanting sounds of cherubic songs and seraphic music constantly echo in the air; and many other things were also enumerated whose outer reactions according to the perceptions and cognitions abnormally inherent in the three-brained beings of that strange planet are likely to evoke in them, as they say, 'great-satisfaction,' that is to say, the satisfaction of those needs formed in their common presences, which are criminal for three-centered beings to possess, and the totality of which have driven out from their presences everything, without exception, that was put into them by our COMMON FATHER and which it is imperative for every three-brained being to possess.

"In the charge of the spirits standing on duty on the left of the scales, who, according to this Babylonian teaching, are the devils, there is what is called Hell.

"Concerning Hell it was said that it is a place without vegetation, always unimaginably hot, and without a single drop of water.

"In that Hell sounds constantly echo of fearful 'cacophony' and infuriated offensive 'abuse.'

"Everywhere there are instruments of every conceivable torture from the 'rack' and the 'wheel' to instruments for lacerating bodies and mechanically rubbing them with salt, and so on of the same kind.

"In the Babylonian idealistic teaching, it was minutely explained that in order that his soul should enter this Paradise, the man must constantly strive while on Earth to provide more material for the notebook of the spirit angel sitting on his right shoulder, otherwise there would be more material for the records of the spirit sitting on the left shoulder, in which case, such a man's soul would inevitably go to this most awful Hell."

Here Hassein could not restrain himself, and suddenly interrupted with the following words:

"And which of their manifestations do they consider good, and which bad?"

Beelzebub looked at his grandson with a very strange look and, shaking his head, said as follows:

"Concerning this, which being-manifestations are there on your planet considered good and which bad—two independent understandings, having nothing in common with each other, have existed from the most ancient times up to the present period, having passed from generation to generation.

"The first of these understandings exists there and passes from one generation to another among such three-brained beings there as were those members of the society Akhaldan on the continent Atlantis, and such as those who, although of another kind, several centuries later after the Transapalnian perturbation acquired almost the same in the foundations of their common presences and who were called 'initiates.'

"The first of these understandings exists there under the following formulation:

"Every action of man is good in the objective sense, if it is done according to his conscience, and every action is bad, if from it he later experiences 'remorse.'

"And the second understanding arose there soon after the wise 'invention' of the Great King Konuzion, which invention, passing from generation to generation through ordinary beings there, gradually spread over almost the whole planet under the name of 'morality.'

"Here it will be very interesting to notice a particularity of this morality which was grafted upon it at the very beginning of its arising and which ultimately became part and parcel of it.

"What this said particularity of terrestrial morality is, you can easily represent to yourself and understand if I tell you that, both inwardly and outwardly, it acquired exactly that 'unique property' which belongs to the being bearing the name 'chameleon.'

"And the oddity and peculiarity of this said particularity of the morality there, especially of contemporary morality, is that its functioning automatically depends entirely on the moods of the local authorities, which moods in their turn depend also automatically on the state of the four sources of action existing there under the names of 'mother-in-law,' 'digestion,' 'John Thomas,' and 'cash.'

"The second Babylonian teaching which then had many followers, and which, passing from generation to generation, also reached your contemporary favorites, was on the contrary one of the atheistic teachings of that period.

"In this teaching by the terrestrial Hasnamussian candidates of that time, it was stated that there is no God in the world, and moreover no soul in man, and hence that all those talks and discussions about the soul are nothing more than the deliriums of sick visionaries.

"It was further maintained that there exists in the World only one special law of mechanics, according to which everything that exists passes from one form into another; that is to say, the results which arise from certain preceding causes are gradually transformed and become causes for subsequent results.

"Man also is therefore only a consequence of some preceding cause and in his turn must, as a result, be a cause of certain consequences.

"Further, it was said that even what are called 'supernatural phenomena' really perceptible to most people, are all nothing but these same results ensuing from the mentioned special law of mechanics.

"The full comprehension of this law by the pure Reason depends on the gradual impartial, all-round acquaintance with its numerous details which can be revealed to a pure Reason in proportion to its development.

"But as regards the Reason of man, this is only the sum of all the impressions perceived by him, from which there gradually arise in him data for comparisons, deductions, and conclusions.

"As a result of all this, he obtains more information concerning all kinds of similarly repeated facts around him, which in the general organization of man are in their turn material for the formation of definite convictions in him. Thus, from all this there is formed in man—Reason, that is to say, his own subjective psyche.

"Whatever may have been said in these two teachings about the soul, and whatever maleficent means had been prepared by those learned beings assembled there from almost the whole planet for the gradual transformation of the Reason of their descendants into a veritable mill of nonsense, it would not have been, in the objective sense, totally calamitous; but the whole objective terror is concealed in the fact that there later resulted from these teachings a great evil, not only for their descendants alone, but maybe even for everything existing.

"The point is, that during the mentioned 'agitation-of-minds' of that time in the city of Babylon, these learned beings, owing to their collective wiseacrings acquired in their presences, in addition to all they already had, a further mass of new data for Hasnamussian manifestations, and when they dispersed and went home to their own countries, they began everywhere, of course unconsciously, to propagate like contagious bacilli all these notions which all together, ultimately, totally destroyed the last remnants and even the traces of all the results of the holy labors of the Very Saintly Ashiata Shiemash.

"The remnants, that is to say, of those holy 'consciously-suffering-labors' which he intentionally actualized for the purpose of creating, just for three-centered beings, such special external conditions of ordinary being-existence in which alone the maleficent consequences of the properties of the organ Kundabuffer could gradually disappear from their presences, so that in their place there could be gradually acquired those properties proper to the presence of every kind of three-brained being, whose whole presence is an exact similitude of everything in the Universe.

"Another result of the diverse wiseacrings by those learned beings of the Earth then in the city of Babylon concerning the question of the soul, was that soon after my fifth appearance in person on the surface of that planet of yours this, in its turn, Center-of-Culture of theirs, the incomparable and indeed magnificent Babylon, was also, as it is said there, swept away from the face of the Earth to its very foundations.

"Not only was the city of Babylon itself destroyed but everything also that had been acquired and accomplished by the beings who had, during many of their centuries, formerly existed there.

"In the name of Justice, I must now say that the prime initiative for the destruction of the holy labors of Ashiata Shiemash did not spring, however, from these learned of the Earth who were then assembled in the city of Babylon, but from the invention of a learned being very well known there, who also existed there on the continent Asia several centuries before these Babylonian events, namely, from the invention of a being named 'Lentrohamsanin' who, having coated his higher-being-part into a definite unit, and having perfected himself by Reason up to the required gradation of Objective Reason, also became one of those three hundred and thirteen Hasnamussian-Eternal-individuals who now exist on the small planet bearing the name of Retribution.

"About this Lentrohamsanin I shall also tell you, since the information concerning him will serve to elucidate for your understanding the strange psyche of those three-brained beings who exist on that peculiar remote planet.

"But I shall tell you about this Lentrohamsanin only when I have finished speaking about the Very Saintly Ashiata Shiemash, as the information relating to this now already Most Very Saintly Individual Ashiata Shiemash and his activities in connection with this planet of yours is most important and of the utmost value for your understanding of the peculiarities of the psyche of these three-brained beings who have taken your fancy and who breed on the planet Earth."

CHAPTER 25

The Very Saintly Ashiata Shiemash, Sent from Above to the Earth

"And so, my boy!

"Now listen very attentively to the information concerning the Most Very Saintly, now already Common Cosmic Individual, Ashiata Shiemash and his activities connected with the existence of the three-brained beings arising and existing on that planet Earth which has taken your fancy.

"I have already more than once told you, that by the All Most Gracious Command of Our OMNI-LOVING COMMON FATHER ENDLESSNESS, our Cosmic Highest Most Very Saintly Individuals sometimes actualize within the presence of some terrestrial three-brained being, a 'definitized' conception of a sacred Individual in order that he, having become a terrestrial being with such a presence, may there on the spot 'orientate himself' and give to the process of their ordinary being-existence such a corresponding new direction, thanks to which the already crystallized consequences of the properties of the organ Kundabuffer, as well as the predispositions to such new crystallizations, might perhaps be removed from their presences.

"It was seven centuries before the Babylonian events I have spoken of, that there was actualized in the planetary body of a three-brained being there a 'definitized' conception of a sacred Individual named Ashiata Shiemash, who became there in his turn a Messenger from Above, and who is now already one of the Highest Most Very Saintly common-cosmic Sacred Individuals.

"Ashiata Shiemash had his conception in the planetary body of a boy of a poor family descended from what is called the 'Sumerian Race,' in a small place then called 'Pispascana' situated not far from Babylon.

"He grew up and became a responsible being partly in this small place and partly in Babylon itself, which was at that time, although not yet magnificent, already a famous city.

"The Very Saintly Ashiata Shiemash was the only Messenger sent from Above to your planet who succeeded by His holy labors in creating on that planet conditions in which the existence of its unfortunate beings somewhat resembled for a certain time the existence of the three-brained beings of the other planets of our great Universe on which beings exist with the same possibilities; and He was also the first on that planet Earth, who for the mission preassigned to Him refused to employ for the three-brained beings of that planet the ordinary methods which had been established during centuries by all the other Messengers from Above.

"The Very Saintly Ashiata Shiemash taught nothing whatever to the ordinary three-brained beings of the Earth, nor did He preach anything to them, as was done before and after Him by all the Messengers sent there from Above with the same aim.

"And in consequence chiefly of this, none of His teachings passed in any form from His contemporaries even to the third generation of ordinary beings there, not to mention the contemporary ordinary beings there.

"Definite information relating to His Very Saintly Activities passed from generation to generation from the contemporaries of the Very Saintly Ashiata Shiemash to the beings of the following generations through those called there 'initiates,' by means of a certain what is called 'Legominism' of His deliberations under the title of 'The Terror-of-the-Situation.'

"In addition to this, there has survived from the period

of His Very Saintly Activities and there still exists even till now, one of several what are called 'marble tablets' on which were engraved His 'counsels' and 'commandments' and 'sayings' to the beings contemporary with Him.

"And at the present time this surviving tablet is the chief sacred relic of a small group of initiated beings there, called the 'Brotherhood-Olbogmek,' whose place of existence is situated in the middle of the continent Asia.

"The name Olbogmek means, 'There are not different religions, there is only one God.'

"When I was personally on the surface of your planet for the last time, I happened by chance to become acquainted with the Legominism which transmits to the initiated men-beings of the planet Earth of remote generations these deliberations of the Saintly Ashiata Shiemash under the title of 'The Terror-of-the-Situation.'

"The Legominism was of great assistance to me in elucidating certain strange aspects of the psyche of these peculiar beings—just those strange aspects of their psyche which, with all my careful observations of them during tens of centuries, I had previously been unable to understand in any way whatsoever."

"My dear and beloved Grandfather, tell me, please, what does the word Legominism mean?" Hassein asked.

"This word Legominism," replied Beelzebub, "is given to one of the means existing there of transmitting from generation to generation information about certain events of long-past ages, through just those three-brained beings who are thought worthy to be and who are called initiates.

"This means of transmitting information from generation to generation had been devised by the beings of the continent Atlantis. For your better understanding of the said means of transmitting information to beings of succeeding generations by means of a Legominism, I must here explain to you a little also about those beings there whom other beings called and call initiates.

"In former times there on the planet Earth, this word was always used in one sense only; and the three-brained beings there who were called initiates were those who had acquired in their presences almost equal objective data which could be sensed by other beings.

"But during the last two centuries this word has come to be used there now in two senses:

"In one sense it is used for the same purpose as before, that is to say, those beings there are so named who became initiates thanks to their personal conscious labors and intentional sufferings; and thereby, as I have already told you, they acquire in themselves objective merits which can be sensed by other beings irrespective of brain-system, and which also evoke in others trust and respect.

"In the other sense, those beings call each other by this name who belong to those what are called there 'criminal gangs' which in the said period have greatly multiplied there and whose members have as their chief aim to 'steal' from those around them only 'essence-values.'

"Under the pretence of following 'supernatural' or 'mystic' sciences, these criminal gangs there are really occupied, and very successfully, with this kind of plunder.

"And so, any and every genuine member of such a gang there is called an initiate.

"There are even 'great-initiates' among these terrestrial initiates, and these great-initiates especially at the present time, are made out of those ordinary initiates of new formation who in their 'virtuoso-affairs' pass, as is said there, through 'fire-water-copper-pipes-and-even-through all-the-roulette-halls-of-Monte-Carlo.'

"Well then, my boy, Legominism is the name given to the successive transmission of information about long-past events which have occurred on the planet Earth from initiates to initiates of the first kind, that is, from really meritorious beings who have themselves received their information from similar meritorious beings.

"For having invented this means of transmitting information, we must give the beings of the continent Atlantis their due; this means was indeed very wise and did indeed attain their aim.

"This is the sole means by which information about certain events that proceeded in times long past has accurately reached the beings of remote later generations.

"As for the information which passed from generation to generation through the ordinary mass of beings of that planet, it has either completely disappeared, having been soon forgotten, or there remains of it, as our dear Mullah Nassr Eddin expresses it, only the 'tail-and-mane-and-food-for-Scheherazade.'

"Hence it is that when a few scraps of information about some event or other do happen to reach the beings of remote later generations, and the learned beings of new formation there concoct their 'hotchpotch' out of these scraps, there then occurs a most peculiar and most instructive 'phenomenon'; namely, when the cockroaches there chance to hear what is in this hotchpotch, 'the-evil-spirit-of-Saint-Vitus' existing there immediately enters their common presences and begins to rage quite merrily.

"How the contemporary learned beings of the planet Earth concoct their hotchpotch from scraps of information which reach them is very well defined in one of the wise sentences of our dear Mullah Nassr Eddin, which consists of the following words: 'A flea exists in the World just for one thing—that when it sneezes, that deluge should occur with the description of which our learned beings love so much to busy themselves.'

"I must tell you that when I used to exist among your favorites it was always difficult for me to refrain, as your favorites say, from 'laughter,' when one or another of the learned beings there delivered a 'lecture' or related to me personally about some past events, of which I had myself been an eyewitness.

"These lectures or 'stories' there are crammed with fictions so absurd that even if our Arch-cunning Lucifer or his assistants tried to invent them, they could not succeed."

CHAPTER 26

The Legominism Concerning the Deliberations of the Very Saintly Ashiata Shiemash Under the Title of "The Terror-of-the-Situation"

"The 'Legominism,'" Beelzebub continued to speak, "through which the deliberations of the Very Saintly Ashiata Shiemash were transmitted, had the following contents:

"It began with the prayer:

"'In the name of the causes of my arising, I shall always strive to be just towards every already spiritualized origination, and towards all the originations of the future spiritualized manifestations of OUR COMMON CREATOR, ALMIGHTY AUTOCRAT ENDLESSNESS, Amen.

"'To me, a trifling particle of the whole of the GREAT WHOLE, it was commanded from Above to be coated with the planetary body of a three-centered being of this planet and to assist all other such beings arising and existing upon it to free themselves from the consequences of the properties of that organ which, for great and important reasons, was actualized in the presences of their ancestors.

"'All the sacred Individuals here before me, specially and intentionally actualized from Above, have always endeavored while striving for the same aim to accomplish the task laid upon them through one or other of those three sacred ways for self-perfecting, foreordained by OUR ENDLESS CREATOR HIMSELF, namely, through the sacred ways based on the being-impulses called "Faith," "Hope," and "Love."

"'When I completed my seventeenth year, I began as commanded from Above, to prepare my planetary body in order, during my responsible existence, "to be able to be" impartial.

"'At this period of my "self-preparation," I had the intention upon reaching responsible age, of carrying out the task laid upon me, through one or other of the said three sacred being-impulses also.

"'But when during this period of my "self-preparation" I chanced to meet many beings of almost all "types" formed and existing here in the city of Babylon, and when during my impartial observations, I constated many traits of their being-manifestations, there crept into me and progressively increased an "essence-doubt" as to the possibilities of saving the three-centered beings of this planet by means of these three sacred ways.

"'The different manifestations of the beings I then encountered, which increased my doubts, gradually convinced me that these consequences of the properties of the organ Kundabuffer, having passed by heredity through a series of generations over a very long period of time, had ultimately so crystallized in their presences, that they now reached contemporary beings already as a lawful part of their essence, and hence these crystallized consequences of the properties of the organ Kundabuffer are now, as it were, a "second nature" of their common presences.

"'So, when I finally became a responsible being, I decided that before making my choice among the mentioned sacred ways, I would bring my planetary body into the state of the sacred "Ksherknara," that is, into the state of "all-brained-balanced-being-perceptiveness," and only when already in that state, to choose the way for my further activities.

"'With this aim, I then ascended the mountain "Veziniama," where for forty days and nights I knelt on my knees and devoted myself to concentration.

"'A second forty days and nights I neither ate nor

drank, but recalled and analyzed all the impressions present in me of all the perceptions I had acquired during my existence here, during the period of my "self-preparation."

"'A third forty days and nights I knelt on my knees and also neither ate nor drank, and every half-hour I plucked two hairs from my breast.

"'And only when, thereafter, I had finally attained complete freedom from all the bodily and spiritual associations of the impressions of ordinary life, I began to meditate how to BE.

"'These meditations of my purified Reason then made it categorically clear to me, that to save the contemporary beings by any of the sacred ways was already too late.

"'These meditations of mine made it categorically clear to me that all the genuine functions proper to man, as they are proper to all the three-centered beings of our Great Universe, had already degenerated in their remote ancestors into other functions, namely, into functions included among the properties of the organ Kundabuffer which were very similar to the genuine sacred being-functions of Faith, Love, and Hope.

"'And this degeneration occurred in all probability in consequence of the fact that when the organ Kundabuffer had been destroyed in these ancestors, and they had also acquired in themselves factors for the genuine sacred being-impulses, then, as the taste of many of the properties of the organ Kundabuffer still remained in them, these properties of the organ Kundabuffer which resembled these three sacred impulses became gradually mixed with the latter, with the result that there were crystallized in their psyche the factors for the impulses Faith, Love, and Hope, which although similar to the genuine, were nevertheless somehow or other quite distinct.

"'The contemporary three-centered beings here do at times believe, love, and hope with their Reason as well as with their feelings; but how they believe, how they love, and how they hope—ah, it is exactly in this that all the peculiarity of these three being-properties lies!

"'They also believe, but this sacred impulse in them does not function independently, as it does in general in all the three-centered beings existing on the various other planets of our Great Universe upon which beings with the same possibilities breed; but it arises dependent upon some or other factors, which have been formed in their common presences, owing as always to the same consequences of the properties of the organ Kundabuffer—as or instance, the particular properties arising in them which they call "vanity," "self-love," "pride," "self-conceit," and so forth.

"'In consequence of this, the three-brained beings here are for the most part subject just to the perceptions and fixations in their presences of all sorts of "Sinkrpoosarams" or, as it is expressed here, they "believe-any-old-tale."

"'It is perfectly easy to convince beings of this planet of anything you like, provided only during their perceptions of these "fictions," there is evoked in them and there proceeds, either consciously from without, or automatically by itself, the functioning of one or another corresponding consequence of the properties of the organ Kundabuffer crystallized in them from among those that form what is called the "subjectivity" of the given being, as for instance: "self-love," "vanity," "pride," "swagger," "imagination," "bragging," "arrogance," and so on.

"'From the influence of such actions upon their degenerated Reason and on the degenerated factors in their localizations, which factors actualize their being-sensations, not only is there crystallized a false conviction concerning the mentioned fictions, but thereafter in all sincerity and faith, they will even vehemently prove to those around them that it is just so and can in no way be otherwise.

"'In an equally abnormal form were data moulded in them for evoking the sacred impulse of love.

"'In the presences of the beings of contemporary times, there also arises and is present in them as much as you please of that strange impulse which they call love; but this love of theirs is firstly also the result of certain crystallized consequences of the properties of the same Kundabuffer; and secondly this impulse of theirs arises and manifests itself in the process of every one of them entirely subjectively; so subjectively and so differently that if ten of them were asked to explain how they sensed this inner impulse of theirs, then all ten of them—if, of course, they for once replied sincerely, and frankly confessed their genuine sensations and not those they had read about somewhere or had obtained from somebody else—all ten would reply differently and describe ten different sensations.

"'One would explain this sensation in the sexual sense; another in the sense of pity; a third in the sense of desire for submission; a fourth, in a common craze for outer things, and so on and so forth; but not one of the ten could describe even remotely, the sensation of genuine Love.

"'And none of them would, because in none of the ordinary beings-men here has there ever been, for a long time, any sensation of the sacred being-impulse of genuine Love. And without this "taste" they cannot even vaguely describe that most beatific sacred being-impulse in the presence of every three-centered being of the whole Universe, which, in accordance with the divine foresight of Great Nature, forms those data in us, from the result of the experiencing of which we can blissfully rest from the meritorious labors actualized by us for the purpose of self-perfection.

"'Here, in these times, if one of those three-brained

beings "loves" somebody or other, then he loves him either because the latter always encourages and undeservingly flatters him; or because his nose is much like the nose of that female or male, with whom thanks to the cosmic law of "polarity" or "type" a relation has been established which has not yet been broken; or finally, he loves him only because the latter's uncle is in a big way of business and may one day give him a boost, and so on and so forth.

"'But never do beings-men here love with genuine, impartial and nonegoistic love.

"'Thanks to this kind of love in the contemporary beings here, their hereditary predispositions to the crystallizations of the consequences of the properties of the organ Kundabuffer are crystallized at the present time without hindrance, and finally become fixed in their nature as a lawful part of them.

"'And as regards the third sacred being-impulse, namely, "essence-hope," its plight in the presences of the three-centered beings here is even worse than with the first two.

"'Such a being-impulse has not only finally adapted itself in them to the whole of their presences in a distorted form, but this maleficent strange "hope" newly formed in them, which has taken the place of the being-impulse of Sacred Hope, is now already the principal reason why factors can no longer be acquired in them for the functioning of the genuine being-impulses of Faith, Love, and Hope.

"'In consequence of this newly-formed-abnormal hope of theirs, they always hope in something; and thereby all those possibilities are constantly being paralyzed in them, which arise in them either intentionally from without or accidentally by themselves, which possibilities could perhaps still destroy in their presences their hereditary predispositions to the crystallizations of the consequences of the properties of the organ Kundabuffer.

"'When I returned from the mountain Veziniama to the city of Babylon, I continued my observations in order to make it clear whether it was not possible somehow or other to help these unfortunates in some other way.

"'During the period of my year of special observations on all of their manifestations and perceptions, I made it categorically clear to myself that although the factors for engendering in their presences the sacred being-impulses of Faith, Hope, and Love are already quite degenerated in the beings of this planet, nevertheless, the factor which ought to engender that being-impulse on which the whole psyche of beings of a three-brained system is in general based, and which impulse exists under the name of Objective-Conscience, is not yet atrophied in them, but remains in their presences almost in its primordial state.

"'Thanks to the abnormally established conditions of external ordinary being-existence existing here, this factor has gradually penetrated and become embedded in that consciousness which is here called "subconsciousness," in consequence of which it takes no part whatever in the functioning of their ordinary consciousness.

"'Well, then, it was just then that I indubitably understood with all the separate ruminating parts representing the whole of my "I," that if the functioning of that being-factor still surviving in their common presences were to participate in the general functioning of that consciousness of theirs in which they pass their daily, as they here say, "waking-existence," only then would it still be possible to save the contemporary three-brained beings here from the consequences of the properties of that organ which was intentionally implanted into their first ancestors.

"'My further meditations then confirmed for me that

it would be possible to attain this only if their general being-existence were to flow for a long time under foreseeingly-corresponding conditions.

"'When all the above-mentioned was completely transubstantiated in me, I decided to consecrate the whole of myself from that time on to the creation here of such conditions that the functioning of the "sacred-conscience" still surviving in their subconsciousness might gradually pass into the functioning of their ordinary consciousness.

"'May the blessing of OUR ALMIGHTY OMNI-LOVING COMMON FATHER UNI-BEING CREATOR ENDLESSNESS be upon my decision, Amen.'

"Thus ended the Legominism concerning the deliberations of the Very Saintly Incomparable Ashiata Shiemash, under the title of 'The Terror-of-the-Situation.'

"So, my boy, when, as I have already told you, early in my last descent in person onto the surface of your planet, I first became acquainted in detail with this Legominism which I have just repeated, and had at once become interested in the deductions of this later Most High Very Saintly Common Cosmic Individual Ashiata Shiemash, there existed neither any other Legominisms nor any other sources of information concerning His further Very Saintly Activities among those favorites of yours, so I then decided to investigate in detail and without fail to make clear to myself which were the measures He took and how He subsequently actualized them, in order to help these unfortunates to deliver themselves from the consequences of the properties of the organ Kundabuffer which had passed to them by heredity and were so maleficent for them.

"And so, as one of my chief tasks during this last sojourn of mine in person there, on the surface of your planet, I made a detailed investigation and elucidation of the whole of the further Very Saintly Activities there among your favorites of that Great Essence-loving now

Most High Very Saintly Common Cosmic Individual Ashiata Shiemash.

"And as regards that 'marble tablet' which has by chance survived since the time of the Very Saintly Activities of the Great Ashiata Shiemash, and is now there the principal sacred relic of the brotherhood of the initiated beings called the Brotherhood-Olbogmek, I happened to see and read the contents engraved on it during this last sojourn of mine there.

"During my subsequent elucidations it turned out that later on, when this Very Saintly Ashiata Shiemash had established there the particular conditions of ordinary being-existence which He had planned, several of these tablets were, on His advice and initiative, set up in corresponding places of many of the large towns, and there were engraved upon them all kinds of sayings and counsels for corresponding existence.

"But when their big wars later on again began, all these tablets were also destroyed by these strange beings themselves, and only one of them, namely, that one now with these brethren, somehow survived, as I have already told you, and is now the property of this Brotherhood.

"On this still surviving marble were inscriptions concerning the sacred being-impulses called Faith, Love, and Hope, namely:

"'Faith,' 'Love,' and 'Hope'

Faith of consciousness is freedom
Faith of feeling is weakness
Faith of body is stupidity.

Love of consciousness evokes the same in response
Love of feeling evokes the opposite
Love of body depends only on type and polarity.

Hope of consciousness is strength
Hope of feeling is slavery
Hope of body is disease.

"Before continuing to tell you more about the activities of the Very Saintly Ashiata Shiemash for the welfare of your favorites, I must, I think, elucidate to you, a little more in detail, that inner impulse which is called there by your favorites Hope, and concerning which the Very Saintly Ashiata Shiemash constated that the case is worse than with the other two.

"And the personal observations and investigations I later specially made, regarding this said strange impulse present in them, clearly showed me that in truth the factors for engendering this abnormal impulse in their presences are most maleficent for them themselves.

"Thanks to this abnormal hope of theirs a very singular and most strange disease, with a property of evolving, arose and exists among them there even until now—a disease called there 'tomorrow.'

"This strange disease 'tomorrow' brought with it terrifying consequences, and particularly for those unfortunate three-brained beings there who chance to learn and to become categorically convinced with the whole of their presence that they possess some very undesirable consequences for the deliverance from which they must make certain efforts, and which efforts moreover they even know just how to make, but owing to this maleficent disease 'tomorrow' they never succeed in making these required efforts.

"And this is just the maleficent part of all that great terrifying evil, which, owing to various causes great and small, is concentrated in the process of the ordinary being-existence of these pitiable three-brained beings; and by putting off from 'tomorrow' till 'tomorrow,' those unfortunate beings there who do by chance learn all about what I have mentioned are also deprived of the possibility of ever attaining anything real.

"This strange and for your favorites maleficent disease

'tomorrow' has already become a hindrance for the beings of contemporary times, not only because they have been totally deprived of all possibilities of removing from their presences the crystallized consequences of the properties of the organ Kundabuffer, but it had also become a hindrance to most of them in honestly discharging at least those being-obligations of theirs which have become quite indispensable in the already established conditions of ordinary being-existence.

"Thanks to the disease 'tomorrow,' the three-brained beings there, particularly the contemporary ones, almost always put off till 'later' everything that needs to be done at the moment, being convinced that 'later' they will do better and more.

"Owing to the said maleficent disease 'tomorrow' most of those unfortunate beings there who accidentally or owing to a conscious influence from without, become aware through their Reason in them of their complete nullity and begin to sense it with all their separate spiritualized parts, and who also chance to learn which and in what way, being-efforts must be made in order to become such as it is proper for three-brained beings to be, also, by putting off from 'tomorrow' till 'tomorrow,' almost all arrive at the point that on one sorrowful day for themselves, there arise in them and begin to be manifest those forerunners of old age called 'feebleness' and 'infirmity,' which are the inevitable lot of all cosmic formations great and small toward the end of their completed existence.

"Here I must without fail tell you also about that strange phenomenon which I constated there during my observations and studies of the almost entirely degenerated presences of those favorites of yours; namely, I definitely constated that in many of them, toward the end of their planetary existence, most of the consequences of the properties of that same organ which had become crystallized in their common presences begin to atrophy of their own accord and some of them even entirely disappear, in consequence of which these beings begin to see and sense reality a little better.

"In such cases a strong desire appears in the common presences of such favorites of yours, to work upon themselves, to work as they say, for the 'salvation-of-their-soul.'

"But needless to say, nothing can result from such desires of theirs just because it is already too late for them, the time given them for this purpose by Great Nature having already passed; and although they see and feel the necessity of actualizing the required being-efforts, yet for the fulfillment of such desires of theirs, they have now only ineffectual yearnings and the 'lawful-infirmities-of-old-age.'

"And so, my boy, my researches and investigations concerning the further activities of the Very Saintly Ashiata Shiemash for the welfare of the three-brained beings arising and existing on this planet of yours eventually made the following clear to me.

"When this great and, by His Reason, almost incomparable Sacred Individual became fully convinced that the ordinary sacred ways which exist for the purpose of self-perfection for all the three-brained beings of the Universe, were no longer suitable for the beings of this planet, He then, after His year of special observation and studies of their psyche, again ascended to that same mountain Veziniama, and during several terrestrial months contemplatively pondered in which way He could actualize His decision, that is, to save the beings of this planet from those hereditary predispositions to the crystallizations of the consequences of the properties of the organ Kundabuffer, by means of those data which survived in their subconsciousness for the fundamental sacred being-impulse, Conscience.

"These ponderings of His then first of all fully convinced Him that though it were indeed possible to save them by means of the data which survived in their common presences for engendering this sacred being-impulse, nevertheless, it would only be possible if the manifestations of these data which survived in their subconsciousness were to participate without fail in the functioning of that consciousness of theirs, under the direction of which their daily-waking existence flows, and furthermore if this being-impulse were to be manifested over a long period through every aspect of this consciousness of theirs."

CHAPTER 27

The Organization for Man's Existence Created by the Very Saintly Ashiata Shiemash

Beelzebub continued to relate further as follows:

"My further researches and investigations also cleared up for me that after the Very Saintly Ashiata Shiemash had pondered on the mountain Veziniama and had formulated in his mind a definite plan for his further Most Saintly Activities, he did not again return to the city of Babylon but went straight to the capital city Djoolfapal of the country then called Kurlandtech, which was situated in the middle of the continent Asia.

"There he first of all established relations with the 'brethren' of the then existing brotherhood 'Tchaftantouri'—a name signifying 'To-be-or-not-to-be-at-all'—which had its quarters not far from that city.

"This said brotherhood was founded five of their years before the arrival there of the Very Saintly Ashiata Shiemash on the initiative of two genuine terrestrial initiates, who had become initiates according to the principles existing, as it was then said there, before the Ashiatian epoch.

"The name of one of these two terrestrial three-brained beings of that time, who had become genuine initiates there, was 'Poundolero' and of the other 'Sensimiriniko.'

"I must remark by the way, that both of these two terrestrial genuine initiates of that time had already by then 'coated' in their common presences their higher being-parts to the gradation called 'completion' and hence they had time during their further existence to perfect these higher parts of theirs to the required gradation of Sacred Objective Reason, and now their perfected higher being-parts have even 'become worthy' to have and already now have the place of their further existence on the holy planet Purgatory.

"According to my latest investigations, when, in all the separate spiritualized parts of the common presences of these two three-brained beings of that period, Poundolero and Sensimiriniko, there arose and was continuously sensed the suspicion, which later became a conviction, that, owing to some obviously nonlawful causes, 'something-very-undesirable' for them personally had been acquired and had begun to function in their general organization and that at the same time it was possible for this something-very-undesirable to be removed from themselves by means of their own data within themselves, they then sought several other beings like themselves who were striving for this same aim, in order together to try to achieve the removal from themselves of this said something-very-undesirable.

"And when they soon found beings responding to this aim amongst what are called the 'monks' of places called 'monasteries' of which there were already many of that period in the environs of the town Djoolfapal, they together with these monks chosen by them, founded the said 'brotherhood.'

"And so, after arriving in the town Djoolfapal, the Very Saintly Ashiata Shiemash established corresponding relations with these brethren of the mentioned brotherhood who were working upon that abnormally proceeding functioning of their psyche which they themselves had constated, and he began enlightening their Reason by means of objectively true information, and guiding their being-impulses in such a way that they could sense these truths without the participation either of the abnormally crystallized factors already within their presences, or of the factors which might newly arise from the results of the external perceptions they obtained from the abnormally established form of ordinary being-existence.

"While enlightening the brethren of the said brotherhood in the mentioned way and discussing his suppositions and intentions with them, the Very Saintly Ashiata Shiemash occupied himself at the same time in drawing up what are called the 'rules,' or, as it is also said there, 'statutes,' for this brotherhood, which he, in association with these brethren he initiated of the former brotherhood Tchaftantouri, founded in the town Djoolfapal and which later was called the brotherhood 'Heechtvori,' which signified 'Only-he-will-be-called-and-will-become-the-Son-of-God-who-acquires-in-himself-Conscience.'

"Later, when, with the participation of these brethren of the former brotherhood Tchaftantouri, everything had been worked out and organized, the Very Saintly Ashiata Shiemash sent these same brethren to various places and commissioned them under his general guidance to spread the information that in the subconsciousness of people there are crystallized and are always present the data manifested from Above for engendering in them the Divine impulse of genuine conscience, and that only he who acquires the 'ableness' that the actions of these data participate in the functioning of that consciousness of theirs in which they pass their everyday existence, has in the objective sense the honest right to be called and really to be a genuine son of our COMMON FATHER CREATOR of all that exists.

"These brethren then preached this objective truth at first chiefly among the monks of the mentioned monasteries—many of which, as I have already said, existed in the environs of the town itself.

"The result of these preachings of theirs was that they first of all selected thirty-five serious and well-prepared what are called 'novices' of this first brotherhood Heechtvori, which they founded in the city Djoolfapal.

"Thereafter, the Very Saintly Ashiata Shiemash, while continuing to enlighten the minds of the former brethren of the brotherhood Tchaftantouri, then began with the help of these brethren to enlighten the Reason of those thirty-five novices also.

"So it continued during the whole of one of their years; and only after this did some of them from among the brethren of the former brotherhood Tchaftantouri, and from among the thirty-five said novices, gradually prove worthy to become what are called 'All-the-rights-possessing' brethren of this first brotherhood Heechtvori.

"According to the statutes drawn up by the Very Saintly Ashiata Shiemash, any brother could become an All-the-rights-possessing brother of the brotherhood Heechtvori, only when in addition to the other also foreseen definite objective attainments, he could bring himself—in the sense of 'ableness-of-conscious-direction-of-the-functioning-of-his-own-psyche'—to be able to know how to convince to perfection a hundred other beings and to prove to them that the impulse of being-objective-conscience exists in man, and secondly how it must be manifested in order that a man may respond to the real sense and aim of his existence, and moreover so to convince them that each of these others, in their turn, should acquire in themselves what is called the 'Required-intensity-of-ableness,' to be able to convince and persuade not less than a hundred others also.

"It was those who became worthy to become such an All-the-rights-possessing brother of the brotherhood Heechtvori who were first called by the name of 'priest.'

"For your complete elucidation concerning the Very Saintly Activities of Ashiata Shiemash, you must also know that afterwards, when all the results of the Very

Saintly Labors of the Very Saintly Ashiata Shiemash were destroyed, both this word priest there and also the word initiate about which I have already told you, were used and still continue to be used by your favorites down to the present time in two quite different senses. In one sense this word priest was since then and now still is commonly used, but only in certain places and for unimportant separate groups of those professionals existing there whom everybody now calls there 'confessors' or 'clergymen.'

"And in the other sense, those beings were called and are still called by this word priest who by their pious existence and by the merits of their acts performed for the good of those around them, stand out so much from the rank and file of the ordinary three-brained beings there, that whenever these ordinary beings there have occasion to remember them, there arises and proceeds in their presences the process called 'gratitude.'

"Already during that same period while the Very Saintly Ashiata Shiemash was enlightening the Reason of the brethren of the former brotherhood Tchaftantouri as well as of the newly collected thirty-five novices, there began to spread, among ordinary beings of the city Djoolfapal and its environs, the true idea that in the common presences of men-beings all the data exist for the manifestation of the Divine impulse conscience, but that this Divine impulse does not take part in their general consciousness; and that it takes no part because, although their manifestations bring them, certain what are called 'quite-late-repaying-satisfactions' and considerable material advantage, nevertheless they thereby gradually atrophy the data put into their presences by Nature for evoking in other beings around them, without distinction of brain system, the objective impulse of Divine-Love.

"This true information began to spread, thanks chiefly

to the superlatively wise provision of the Very Saintly Ashiata Shiemash which obliged everyone striving to become an All-the-rights-possessing brother of the brotherhood Heechtvori to attain, as I have already told you, in addition to all kinds of definite self-merits, the 'ableness' to know how to convince all the three separate spiritualized and associating parts of a further hundred three-brained beings there, concerning the Divine impulse conscience.

"When the organization of the first brotherhood Heechtvori in the city Djoolfapal had been more or less regulated and was so established that the further work could already be continued independently, by means only of the directions issuing from the Reason then present in the brotherhood, then the Very Saintly Ashiata Shiemash himself selected from among those who had become All-the-rights-possessing brothers of the brotherhood, those who had already sensed the said Divine impulse, consciously by their Reason and unconsciously by the feelings in their subconsciousness, and who had full confidence that by certain self-efforts this Divine being-impulse might become and forever remain an inseparable part of their ordinary consciousness. And those who had sensed and become aware of this Divine conscience, and who were called 'first-degree-initiates,' he set apart, and he began to enlighten their Reason separately concerning these 'objective truths,' which before that time were still quite unknown to the three-brained beings.

"It was just these outstanding 'first-degree-initiated-beings' who were then called 'Great Initiates.'

"Here it must be remarked that those principles of being of the initiated beings there, which were later on called there 'Ashiata's renewals,' were then renewed by the Very Saintly Ashiata Shiemash.

"Well, then, it was to those same Great Initiates who were first set apart that the Very Saintly Ashiata Shiemash, now already the Most Very Saintly, then among other things also elucidated in detail what this being-impulse 'objective conscience' is, and how factors arise for its manifestation in the presences of the three-brained beings.

"And concerning this he once said as follows:

"'The factors for the being-impulse conscience arise in the presences of the three-brained beings from the localization of the particles of the "emanations-of-the-sorrow" of our OMNI-LOVING AND LONG-SUFFERING-ENDLESS-CREATOR; that is why the source of the manifestation of genuine conscience in three-centered beings is sometimes called the REPRESENTATIVE OF THE CREATOR.

"'And this sorrow is formed in our ALL-MAINTAINING COMMON FATHER from the struggle constantly proceeding in the Universe between joy and sorrow.'

"And he then also further said:

"'In all three-brained beings of the whole of our Universe without exception, among whom are also we men, owing to the data crystallized in our common presences for engendering in us the Divine impulse of conscience, "the-whole-of-us" and the whole of our essence, are, and must be, already in our foundation, only suffering.

"'And they must be suffering, because the completed actualizing of the manifestation of such a being-impulse in us can proceed only from the constant struggle of two quite opposite what are called "complexes-of-the-functioning" of those two sources which are of quite opposite origin, namely, between the processes of the functioning of our planetary body itself and the parallel functionings arising progressively from the coating and perfecting of our higher being-bodies within this planetary body of ours, which functionings in their totality actualize every kind of Reason in the three-centered beings.

"'In consequence of this, every three-centered being of our Great Universe, and also we men existing on the

Earth, must, owing to the presence in us also of the factors for engendering the Divine impulse of "Objective Conscience," always inevitably struggle with the arising and the proceeding within our common presences of two quite opposite functionings giving results always sensed by us either as "desires" or as "nondesires."

"'And so, only he, who consciously assists the process of this inner struggle and consciously assists the "nondesires" to predominate over the desires, behaves just in accordance with the essence of our COMMON FATHER CREATOR HIMSELF; whereas he who with his consciousness assists the contrary, only increases HIS sorrow.'

"Owing to all I have just said, my boy, at that period scarcely three years had passed when, on the one hand, all the ordinary beings of the town Djoolfapal and its environs and also of many other countries of the continent Asia, not only already knew that this Divine being-impulse of 'genuine conscience' was in them, and that it could take part in the functioning of their ordinary 'waking consciousness,' and that in all the brotherhoods of the great prophet Ashiata Shiemash all the initiates and priests elucidated and indicated how and what had to be done in order that such a Divine impulse should take part in the functioning of the mentioned ordinary waking consciousness, but furthermore, nearly everybody even began to strive and to exert himself to become priests of the brotherhood Heechtvori of which many brotherhoods were already founded during that period and functioned almost independently in many other countries of the continent Asia.

"And these almost independent brotherhoods arose there in the following order:

"When the common work of the brotherhood founded in the town Djoolfapal was finally established, the Very Saintly Ashiata Shiemash began sending the said great initiates with corresponding directions to other countries and towns of the continent Asia, in order to organize similar brotherhoods there also, while he himself remained in the town Djoolfapal from where he guided the activities of these helpers of his.

"However it might have been, my boy, it then so turned out that almost all of your favorites—those strange three-brained beings—also wished and began to strive with all their spiritualized being-parts to have in their ordinary waking-consciousness the Divine genuine objective conscience, and in consequence, most of the beings of Asia at that time began to work upon themselves under the guidance of initiates and priests of the brotherhood Heechtvori, in order to transfer into their ordinary consciousness the results of the data present in their subconsciousness for engendering the impulse of genuine Divine conscience, and in order to have the possibility, by this means, on the one hand of completely removing from themselves, perhaps forever, the maleficent consequences of the properties of the organ Kundabuffer, both those personally acquired and those passed to them by heredity and, on the other hand, of consciously taking part in diminishing the sorrow of OUR COMMON ENDLESS FATHER.

"Owing to all this, the question of conscience already began to predominate at that period during the ordinary process of being-existence both in the waking-consciousness state and in the 'passive-instinctive' state among your favorites, particularly among those who existed on the continent Asia.

"Even those three-brained beings of that time in whose presences the taste of this Divine impulse had not yet been transubstantiated, but who had in their strange peculiar consciousness, proper to them alone, only empty information concerning this being-impulse which could be present in them as well, also exerted themselves to manifest in everything in accordance with this information.

"The total result, however, of everything I have mentioned, was that within ten terrestrial years there had disappeared of their own accord those two chief forms of ordinary being-existence abnormally established there, from which there chiefly flow and still continue to flow, most of the maleficent causes the totality of which engenders all kinds of trifling factors which prevent the establishment of conditions there for at least a normal outer being-existence for these unfortunate favorites of yours.

"And namely, firstly their division into numerous communities with various forms of organization for external and even internal existence, or as they themselves express it, 'state-organizations,' ceased to exist, and secondly in these said numerous communities there also disappeared equally, of their own accord, those various what are called 'castes' or 'classes' which had long before been established there.

"And in my opinion, as you also will surely understand eventually, it was precisely this second of the two mentioned chief abnormally established forms of ordinary being-existence, namely, the assigning of each other to different classes or castes that had specially become there the basis for the gradual crystallization in the common presences of these unfortunate favorites of yours, of that particular psychic property which, in the whole of the Universe, is inherent exclusively only in the presences of those three-brained beings.

"This exclusively particular property was formed in them soon after the second Transapalnian perturbation there, and, gradually undergoing development and becoming strengthened in them, was passed from generation to generation by heredity, until it has now already passed to the contemporary beings as a certain lawful and inseparable part of their general psyche, and this particular property of their psyche is called by themselves 'egoism.'

"Some time later, in its appropriate place, during my further tales concerning the three-brained beings existing on the planet Earth, I shall also explain to you in detail how thanks to those conditions of external being-existence which were established there, your favorites first began assigning each other to various castes, and how, thanks to subsequent similar abnormalities, this same maleficent form of mutual relationship then established there has continued even until now. But meanwhile, concerning this exceptionally particular property of their general psyche, namely, egoism, it is necessary for you to know that the cause of the possibility of the arising in their common presences of this particular property was that, owing always to the same abnormal conditions established from the very beginning after the said second Transapalnian-perturbation there, their general psyche had become dual.

"This became fully evident to me when, during the period of my last sojourn on the surface of this planet of yours, I became deeply interested in the mentioned Legominism concerning the deliberations of the Very Saintly Ashiata Shiemash entitled 'The Terror-of-the-Situation.' I began in the course of my further detailed researches and investigations relating to his subsequent Very Saintly Activities and their results, to investigate the causes in which way and why the crystallization of the mentioned factors obtained from the particles of the emanation of the Sorrow of OUR COMMON FATHER CREATOR for the actualizing of the Divine being-impulse of objective conscience, proceeded in their presences, that is to say, just in their said subconsciousness, and thus avoided that final degeneration to which are subject all the data placed in them for engendering in their presences the being-impulses Faith, Love, and Hope, and I was convinced that this strange anomaly there fully justifies one of the numerous wise sentences of our highly esteemed, irreplaceable, and honorable Mullah Nassr Eddin which states:

"'Every - real - happiness - for - man - can - arise - exclusively - only - from - some - unhappiness - also - real - which - he - has - already - experienced.'

"The mentioned duality of their general psyche proceeded because on the one hand various what are called 'individual-initiatives' began to issue from that localization arising in their presences, which is always predominant during their waking existence, and which localization is nothing else but only the result of the accidental perceptions of impressions coming from without, and engendered by their abnormal environment, which perceptions in totality are called by them their 'consciousness'; and on the other hand, similar individual-initiatives also began to issue in them, as it is proper to them, from that normal localization existing in the presences of every kind of being and which they call their subconsciousness.

"And because the mentioned individual-initiatives issue from such different localizations during their waking-existence, each of them, during the process of his daily existence is, as it were, divided into two independent personalities.

"Here it must be remarked that just this said duality was also the cause that there was gradually lost from their presences that impulse necessary to three-brained beings, which is called 'Sincerity.'

"Later, the practice of deliberately destroying the just mentioned being-impulse called Sincerity even took root among them, and now, from the day of their arising, or, as they say, from the day of their 'birth,' the three-brained beings there are accustomed by their producers—or, as they say, 'parents'—to an entirely contrary impulse, namely, 'deceit.'

"To teach and to suggest to their children how to be insincere with others and deceitful in everything, has become so ingrained in the beings of the planet Earth of the present time, that it has even become their conception of their duty towards their children; and this kind of conduct towards their children they call by the famous word 'education.'

"They 'educate' their children never to be able and never to dare to do as the 'conscience' present in them instinctively directs, but only that which is prescribed in the manuals of 'bon ton' usually drawn up there just by various candidates for 'Hasnamusses.'

"And of course when these children grow up and become responsible beings, they already automatically produce their manifestations and their acts; just as during their formation they were 'taught,' just as they were 'suggested to,' and just as they were 'wound up'; in a word, just as they were 'educated.'

"Thanks to all this, the conscience which might be in the consciousness of the beings of that planet is, from their earliest infancy, gradually 'driven-back-within,' so that by the time they are grown up the said conscience is already found only in what they call their subconsciousness.

"In consequence, the functioning of the mentioned data for engendering in their presences this said Divine impulse conscience, gradually ceased long ago to participate in that consciousness of theirs by means of which their waking-existence flows.

"That is why, my boy, the crystallization in their common presences of the Divine manifestation issuing from Above for the data of the arising of this sacred being-impulse in them, proceeds only in their subconsciousness—which has ceased to participate in the process of their ordinary, daily existence—and that is why these data have escaped that 'degeneration' to which all the other sacred being-impulses were subject, and which they also ought to have in their presences, namely, the impulses Faith, Love, and Hope.

"Furthermore, if, for some reason or other, the actions of the Divine data, crystallized in their presences for the said being-impulse, should now begin to manifest themselves in them from their subconsciousness and should strive to participate in the functioning of their abnormally formed ordinary 'consciousness,' then no sooner are they aware of it than they at once take measures to avoid it, because it has already become impossible in the conditions already existing there for anyone to exist with the functioning in their presences of this Divine impulse of genuine objective conscience.

"From the time when the said egoism had become completely 'inoculated' in the presences of your favorites, this particular being-property became, in its turn, the fundamental contributory factor in the gradual crystallization in their general psyche of the data for the arising of still several other quite exclusively-particular being-impulses now existing there under the names of 'cunning,' 'envy,' 'hate,' 'hypocrisy,' 'contempt,' 'haughtiness,' 'servility,' 'slyness,' 'ambition,' 'double-facedness,' and so on and so forth.

"These exclusively particular properties of their psyche which I have just named, utterly unbecoming to three-brained beings, were already fully crystallized in the presences of most of your favorites and were the inevitable attributes of the psyche of every one of them even before the period of the Very Saintly Ashiata Shiemash; but when there began to be fixed and to flow automatically in the process of their being-existence the new form of existence intentionally implanted in them by Ashiata Shiemash himself, then these strange properties, previously present in their psyche, entirely disappeared from the presences of most of the three-brained beings there. Later, however, when they themselves destroyed all the results of the Very Saintly Labors of this Essence-Loving Ashiata Shiemash, these same psychic properties maleficent for themselves gradually again arose anew in all of them, and, for them the contemporary three-brained beings there, they are already the foundation of the whole of their essence.

"Well, then, my boy, when the data arose in the common presences of your favorites for engendering this 'Unique-particular' being-impulse egoism and when gradually evolving and giving rise to factors ensuing from it for other also particular but now secondary strange being-impulses, this said 'Unique-property' egoism usurped the place of the 'Unique-All-Autocratic-Ruler' in their general organization; then, not only every manifestation but even what is called the 'desire-for-the-arising' of such a Divine being-impulse became a hindrance to the actions of this 'All-Autocratic-Ruler.' And in consequence of this, when eventually your favorites had already, by force of necessity, both consciously and unconsciously, always and in everything, prevented it partaking in the functioning of that consciousness of theirs through the control of which it had become proper for them to actualize their waking-existence, the actions of those Divine data were gradually, as it were, removed from the functioning of their ordinary 'consciousness' and participated only in the functioning of their said subconsciousness.

"And it was only after my detailed researches and investigations had made all the foregoing clear to me, that I understood why there arose and why there still exists that division of themselves there into various classes or castes which is particularly maleficent for them.

"My later detailed researches and investigations very definitely and clearly showed me that, in that consciousness of theirs, which they call their subconsciousness, even in the beings of the present time, the said data for the acquisition in their presences of this fundamental Divine impulse conscience does indeed still continue to be crystallized and, hence, to be present during the whole of their existence.

"And, that these data of this Divine being-impulse are still crystallized and their manifestations still continue to participate in the process of their being-existence, was, apart from the said investigations, further confirmed by the fact that I frequently had a good deal of difficulty on account of it, during the periods of my observation of them from the planet Mars.

"The point is, that, through my Teskooano from the planet Mars, I could freely observe without any difficulty whatsoever, the existence proceeding on the surfaces of the other planets of that solar system, but making my observations of the process of the existence proceeding on the surface of your planet was, owing to the special coloration of its atmosphere, a real misery.

"And this special coloration occurred, as I later ascertained, because there appeared from time to time, in the presence of this atmosphere, large quantities of those crystallizations which were frequently radiated from the presences of these favorites of yours, owing to that particular inner impulse which they themselves call 'Remorse-of-Conscience.'

"And this proceeded because in those of them who chance to receive and experience some kind of what is called 'shock-to-organic-shame,' the associations proceeding from their previous impressions almost always become changed, calmed, and sometimes even for a time entirely cease in them, which associations as I have already told you, consist mostly of various kinds of what is called 'rubbish.'

"In consequence, there is then automatically obtained, in these three-brained beings there, such a combination of functioning in their common presences as temporarily frees the data present in their subconsciousness for the manifestation of the Divine impulse conscience and for its participation in the functioning of their ordinary consciousness, with the result that this said Remorse-of-Conscience proceeds in them.

"And as this Remorse-of-Conscience gives rise to the mentioned particular crystallizations which issue from them with their other radiations, the result is that the totality of all these radiations occasionally gives the atmosphere of this planet of yours that particular coloration which hinders the being-organ of sight from penetrating freely through it.

"Here it is necessary to say, that these favorites of yours, particularly the contemporary ones, become ideally expert in not allowing this inner impulse of theirs, called Remorse-of-Conscience, to linger long in their common presences.

"No sooner do they begin to sense the beginning, or even only, so to say, the 'prick' of the arising of the functioning in them of such a being-impulse, than they immediately, as it is said 'squash' it, whereupon this impulse, not yet quite formed in them, at once calms down.

"For this 'squashing' of the beginning of any Remorse-of-Conscience in themselves, they have even invented some very efficient special means, which now exist there under the names of 'alcoholism,' 'cocainism,' 'morphinism,' 'nicotinism,' 'onanism,' 'monkism,' 'Athenianism,' and others with names also ending in 'ism.'

"I repeat, my boy, at a suitable occasion I shall explain

to you in detail also about those results issuing from the abnormally established conditions of ordinary existence there, which became factors for the arising and the permanent existence there of this for them maleficent assignment of themselves to various castes.

"I shall without fail explain this to you, because the information elucidating this abnormality there, may serve as very good data for your further logical comparisons for the purpose of better understanding the strangeness of the psyche of these three-brained beings who have taken your fancy.

"Meanwhile transubstantiate in yourself the following: when the mentioned particular psychic property of 'egoism' had been completely formed in the common presences of these favorites of yours, and, later, there had also been formed in them various other secondary impulses already mentioned by me which ensued and now still continue to ensue from it—and furthermore, in consequence of the total absence of the participation of the impulse of sacred conscience in their waking-consciousness—then these three-brained beings arising and existing on the planet Earth, both before the period of the Very Saintly Activities of Ashiata Shiemash and also since have always striven and still continue to strive to arrange their welfare during the process of their ordinary existence, exclusively for them themselves.

"And as in general, on none of the planets of our great Universe does there or can there exist enough of everything required for everybody's equal external welfare, irrespective of what are called 'objective-merits,' the result there is that the prosperity of one is always built on the adversity of many.

"It is just this exclusive regard for their own personal welfare that has gradually crystallized in them the already quite particularly unprecedented and peculiar properties of their psyche which I cited, as for instance 'cunning,' 'contempt,' 'hate,' 'servility,' 'lying,' 'flattery,' and so on, which in their turn, on the one hand are factors for an outer manifestation unbecoming to three-brained beings, and on the other hand are the cause of the gradual destruction of all those inner possibilities of theirs, placed in them by Great Nature, of becoming particles of the whole of the 'Reasonable Whole.'

"Well then, my boy, at the time when the results of the Very Saintly Labors of the Essence-loving Ashiata Shiemash had already begun to blend with the processes of what is called their 'inner' and 'outer' being-existence, and when thanks to this, data for the Divine impulse conscience, surviving in their subconsciousness, gradually began to share in the functioning of their 'waking-consciousness,' then the being-existence both personal and reciprocal began to proceed on this planet also, almost as it does on the other planets of our great Universe on which three-brained beings exist.

"These favorites of yours also then began to have relations towards each other only as towards the manifestations varying in degree of a UNIQUE COMMON CREATOR and to pay respect to each other only according to the merits personally attained by means of 'being-Partkdolg-duty,' that is, by means of personal conscious labors and intentional sufferings.

"That is why, during that period, there ceased to exist there the said two chief maleficent forms of their ordinary existence, namely, their separate independent communities and the division of themselves in these communities into various castes or classes.

"At that time, also, there upon your planet, all the three-brained beings began to consider themselves and those like themselves merely as beings bearing in themselves particles of the emanation of the Sorrow of our COMMON FATHER CREATOR.

"And all this then so happened because when the actions of the data of the Divine being-impulse began to participate in the functioning of their ordinary waking-consciousness, and the three-brained beings began manifesting themselves towards each other, solely in accordance with conscience, the consequence was that masters ceased to deprive their slaves of freedom, and various power-possessing beings of their own accord surrendered their unmerited rights, having become aware by conscience and sensing that they possessed and occupied these rights and positions not for the common welfare but only for the satisfaction of their various personal weaknesses, such for instance as 'vanity,' 'self-love,' 'self-calming,' and so on.

"Of course, at that period also, there continued to be all kinds of chiefs, directors and 'adviser-specialists,' who became such chiefly from difference of age and from what is called 'essence-power,' just as there are everywhere on all planets of the Universe on which there breed three-brained beings of varying degrees of self-perfecting, and they then became such, neither by hereditary right nor by election, as was the case before this blissful Ashiatian epoch and as again afterwards became and even till now continues to be the case.

"All these chiefs, directors and advisers then became such in accordance with the objective merits they personally acquired, and which could be really sensed by all the beings around them.

"And it proceeded in the following way:

"All the beings of this planet then began to work in order to have in their consciousness this Divine function of genuine conscience, and for this purpose, as everywhere in the Universe, they transubstantiated in themselves what are called the 'being-obligolnian-strivings' which consist of the following five, namely:

"The first striving: to have in their ordinary being-existence everything satisfying and really necessary for their planetary body.

"The second striving: to have a constant and unflagging instinctive need for self-perfection in the sense of being.

"The third: the conscious striving to know ever more and more concerning the laws of World-creation and World-maintenance.

"The fourth: the striving from the beginning of their existence to pay for their arising and their individuality as quickly as possible, in order afterwards to be free to lighten as much as possible the Sorrow of our COMMON FATHER.

"And the fifth: the striving always to assist the most rapid perfecting of other beings, both those similar to oneself and those of other forms, up to the degree of the sacred 'Martfotai,' that is, up to the degree of self-individuality.

"At this period when every terrestrial three-centered being existed and worked consciously upon himself in accordance with these five strivings, many of them thanks to this quickly arrived at results of objective attainments perceptible to others.

"Of course, these objective attainments then, as it is said, 'attracted-the-attention' of all around them, who thereupon made those who had attained stand out from their midst and paid them every kind of respect; they also strove with joy to merit the attention of these outstanding beings and to have for themselves their counsel and advice how they themselves could attain the same perfecting.

"And these outstanding beings of that period began in their turn to make the most attained among themselves stand out and this outstanding being thereby automatically became, without either hereditary or other right, the chief of them all, and recognizing him as chief, his directings were spread correspondingly, and this recognition included not only the separate neighboring parts of the surface of your planet, but also even the neighboring continents and islands.

"At that period the counsel and guidance and in general every word of these chiefs became law for all the three-brained beings there and were fulfilled by them with devotion and joy; not as it had proceeded there before the results obtained by the Very Saintly Labors of Ashiata Shiemash, nor as it again proceeded and still continues to proceed since they themselves destroyed the fruits of his Very Saintly Labors.

"That is to say, these strange three-brained beings, your favorites, now carry out the various commands and orders of their 'chiefs' and, as they are called 'kings,' only from fear of what are called 'bayonets' and 'lousy cells,' of which there are a great many at the disposition of these chiefs and kings.

"The results of the Very Saintly Labors of Ashiata Shiemash were then also very definitely reflected in respect of that terrible peculiarity of the manifestation of the psyche of your favorites, namely, in their 'irresistible-urge-for-the-periodic-destruction-of-each-other's-existence.'

"The process of reciprocal destruction established there and ensuing from that terrible particularity of their psyche entirely ceased on the continent Asia, and only proceeded occasionally on those large and small parts of the surface of that planet of yours, which were far from the continent Asia. And this continued there only because owing to their distance the influence of the initiates and priests could not reach and be transubstantiated in the presence of the beings breeding on these parts of the surface of your planet.

"But the most astonishing and significant result of the Very Saintly Labors of Ashiata Shiemash was that at that period not only did the duration of the existence of these unfortunates become a little more normal, that is to say, it began to increase, but also what they call the 'death rate' also diminished, and at the same time the number of their results manifested for the prolongation of their generation, that is, as they say, their 'birth rate,' diminished to at least a fifth.

"Thereby there was even practically demonstrated one of the cosmic laws, namely, what is called 'the-law-of-the-equilibration-of-vibrations,' that is, of vibrations arising from the evolutions and involutions of the cosmic substances required for the Most Great Omnicosmic Trogoautoegocrat.

"The said decline in both their death rate and their birth rate proceeded because, as they approximated to an existence normal for the three-centered beings, they also began to radiate from themselves vibrations responding more closely to the requirements of Great Nature, thanks to which Nature needed less of those vibrations which are in general obtained from the destruction of the existence of beings.

"You will also understand well about this cosmic law 'equilibration-of-vibrations' when at the proper time I shall explain to you in detail, as I have already many times promised you, concerning all the general fundamental cosmic laws.

"It was just in this way, my boy, and in such a sequence that there in that period, thanks to the conscious labors of the Very Saintly Ashiata Shiemash, the said welfare unprecedented for your favorites was gradually created; but to the infinite sorrow of all more or less consciously thinking individuals of all gradations of Reason, shortly after the departure from this planet of the Very Saintly Ashiata

Shiemash, these unfortunates themselves, after the manner that had become in general proper to them before, in respect of every good attainment of their ancestors, totally destroyed it all; and thus it was they destroyed and thus it was they swept away from the surface of their planet all that welfare, so that even the rumor has failed to reach contemporary beings there that once upon a time such bliss existed.

"In certain inscriptions which have survived from ancient times and have reached the contemporary beings of that planet, there is, however, some information that there once existed on their planet, what is called a special kind of 'state-organization' and that at the head of every such state were beings of the highest attainments.

"And on the basis of this information, the contemporary beings have invented just a mere name for this state-organization; they call it a 'priest-organization' and that is all.

"But what constituted this priest-organization, how and why it was? . . . is it not all the same to the contemporary beings of the planet Earth what ancient savages did!!! . . ."

CHAPTER 28

The Chief Culprit in the Destruction of All the Very Saintly Labors of Ashiata Shiemash

"You remember that I have already told you that the basis of the initiative for the arising there of the factors which became the causes of the final destruction of the still surviving remains of the beneficent results of the conscious labors of the Very Saintly Ashiata Shiemash for the subsequent generations of your favorites did not issue from the learned beings who were then assembled from almost the whole of the surface of the Earth in the city of Babylon, but that these latter—as it had long before become proper to most of the terrestrial learned beings of new formation—were only like 'contagious bacilli,' the unconscious disseminators of every kind of then existing evil for their own and for subsequent generations.

"The basis for all the further great and small maleficent activities and unconscious maleficent manifestations of the learned beings of that time concerning the destruction of even the last remnants of the results, beneficent for the three-brained beings there, obtained from the very saintly conscious labors of the Essence-loving Ashiata Shiemash, were—as my later detailed researches concerning these further very saintly activities made clear to me—the 'invention' of a learned being, well known there in his time, also belonging to the number of learned beings of new formation and named Lentrohamsanin.

"As a result of his inner what is called 'double-gravity-centered' existence, the 'highest being-part' of the presence of this terrestrial three-brained being was coated and perfected up to the required gradation of Objective Reason, and later this 'highest being-part' became, as I have once already told you, one of those three hundred and thirteen 'highest being-bodies' who are called 'Eternal-Hasnamuss-individuals' and who have the place of their further existence in the Universe on a small planet existing under the name of 'Eternal-Retribution.'

"Now, strictly speaking, about this terrestrial three-brained being Lentrohamsanin, I would have to fulfill my promise and to explain to you in detail about the expression Hasnamuss, but I prefer to do so a little later in the proper place of the sequence in this tale.

"The mentioned maleficent 'invention,' or as they themselves, that is, the contemporary terrestrial learned beings, name such an invention of a learned being there of 'new formation,' a 'composition,' or even a 'creation,' was actualized, as I have already told you, two or more centuries before the time when, during my fifth sojourn there, I first reached the city of Babylon, where partly by coercion and partly voluntarily, learned beings had been assembled from the surface of almost the whole of the planet.

"The maleficent composition of that learned being of former centuries reached the learned beings of the said Babylonian epoch by means of what is called a 'Kashireitleer,' on which this invention was engrossed by the said learned Lentrohamsanin himself.

"I find it very necessary to inform you a little more in detail about the history of the arising of this Lentrohamsanin and also how, owing to which accidental circumstances of his environment, he later became there a great learned being and authority for his contemporary beings of almost the whole surface of your planet.

"In addition to this history itself being very characteristic, it can also serve as a good elucidatory example of that practice which has long ago become firmly established in the process of the existence of these three-brained beings who have taken your fancy, the result of which is that several of them at first become so to say authorities for other learned beings of new formation and thereby later for all the unfortunate ordinary beings there.

"The details concerning the conditions of the arising and subsequent formation of this Lentrohamsanin into a responsible being chanced to become clear to me, by the way, during my investigations of which aspects of the strange psyche of your favorites were the basis for the gradual change and ultimately also for the total destruction of all those beneficent special forms and customs in the process of their being-existence, which had been introduced and firmly fixed in this process by the ideally foreseeing Reason of our now Omnicosmic Most Very Saintly Ashiata Shiemash during the period of his self-preparation to be that which he now is for the whole of the Universe.

"It was then that I learned that this Lentrohamsanin arose, or, as it is said there, 'was born,' on the continent Asia, in the capital of Nievia, the town Kronbookhon.

"The conception of his arising resulted from the blending of two heterogeneous Exioëharies formed in two already elderly three-brained Keschapmartnian beings there.

"His 'producers' or, as it is said there, his 'parents,' having chosen as the place for their permanent existence the capital of Nievia, moved there three terrestrial years before the arising of that later Universal Hasnamuss.

"For his elderly and very rich parents he was what is called a 'first-born,' for although the blending of their Exioëharies had been many times actualized between them before him, yet, as I found out, they, being deeply engaged in the business of acquiring riches and not wishing to have any hindrance for this, had recourse at each actualizing of this sacred blending to what is called 'Toosy,' or, as your contemporary favorites express themselves, 'abortion.'

"Towards the end of his activities in acquiring riches, 'the-source-of-the-active-principle-of-his-origin,' or, as it is said there, his father, had several of his own what are called 'caravans' and he also owned special 'caravansaries' for the exchange of goods in various cities of this same Nievia.

"And 'the-source-of-the-passive-principle-of-his-origin,' that is, his mother, was at first of the profession of what is called 'Toosidji,' but later, on a small mountain, she organized what is called a 'Holy-place' and published broadcast among other beings information concerning its supposed special significance, namely, that beings of the female sex, without children would, on visiting this place, acquire the possibility of having them.

"When this couple, in what is called 'the-decline-of-their-years,' had already become very rich, they moved to the capital city Kronbookhon in order to exist there, but only for their own pleasure.

"But soon they felt that without a real 'result' or as they say there 'in-childlessness,' there cannot be full pleasure, and from that time on, without sparing what is called 'money,' they took every kind of measure to obtain such a result.

"With this end in view, they visited various Holy-places existing there for that purpose, of course with the exception of their own 'Holy-mountain,' and resorted to every kind of what are called 'medical means' which purported to assist the blending of heterogeneous Exioëharies; and when eventually by chance such a blending was actualized, then there indeed arose, after a certain time, just that long-awaited result of theirs, later called Lentrohamsanin.

"From the very first day of his arising, the parents were, as it is said, completely wrapped up in what they described as their 'God-sent-result' or son; and they spent vast sums on his pleasures and on what was called his 'education.'

"To give their son the very best 'upbringing' and 'education' the Earth could provide, became for them, as it is said there, their 'Ideal.'

"With this aim, they hired for him various what are called 'tutors' and 'teachers,' both from among those existing in the country Nievia and from various distant lands.

"These latter, that is, these foreign 'tutors' and 'teachers,' they then invited chiefly from the country which at the present time is called 'Egypt.'

"Already by the time this terrestrial what is called 'Papa's-and-Mama's-darling' was approaching the age of a responsible being, he was, as it is said there, very well 'instructed' and 'educated,' that is, he had in his presence a great deal of data for all kinds of being 'egoplastikoori,' consisting, as it is usual there according to the abnormally established conditions of their existence, of various fantastic and dubious information; and later, when he became a responsible being he manifested himself automatically through all kinds of corresponding accidental shocks.

"When this later great learned being there reached the age of a responsible being, and although he had indeed a great deal of information or, as it is called there, 'knowledge,' nevertheless, he had absolutely no Being in regard to this information or knowledge which he had acquired.

"Well, when the said Mama's-and-Papa's-darling became a learned being there of new formation, then because on the one hand there was no Being whatsoever in his presence, and on the other hand because there had already by this time been thoroughly crystallized in him those consequences of the properties of the organ Kundabuffer which exist there under the names of 'vanity,' 'self-love,' 'swagger,' and so forth, the ambition arose in him to become a famous learned being not only among the beings of Nievia, but also over the whole of the surface of their planet.

"So, with all his presence he dreamed and ruminated how he could attain this.

"For many days he then thought seriously, and finally he decided first of all to invent a theory upon a topic which nobody before him had ever touched upon; and secondly, to inscribe this 'invention' of his upon such a Kashireitleer as nobody had ever before inscribed or would ever be able to in the future either.

"And from that day, he made preparations for the actualizing of that decision of his.

"With the help of his many slaves he first prepared a Kashireitleer such as had never before existed.

"At that period of the flow of time on the planet Earth, the Kashireitleers were generally made from one or another part of the hide of a quadruped being called there 'buffalo,' but Lentrohamsanin made his Kashireitleer from a hundred buffalo hides joined together.

"These Kashireitleers were replaced there later by what is called 'parchment.'

"Well, when this unprecedented Kashireitleer was ready, the subsequently great Lentrohamsanin inscribed upon it his invention concerning a topic which, indeed, it had occurred to nobody to discuss before, and for which, in truth, there was no reason why it should have been.

"Namely, in those wiseacrings of his, he then criticized in every way the existing order of collective existence.

"This Kashireitleer began thus:

"'Man's greatest happiness consists in not being dependent on any other personality whatsoever, and in being free from the influence of any other person, whoever he may be!'

"Some other time, I will explain to you how your favorites,

the strange three-brained beings there on the planet Earth, in general understand freedom.

"This subsequently Universal Hasnamuss inscribed further as follows:

"'Undeniably, life under the present state-organization is now far better for us than it used to be before; but where then is that real freedom of ours upon which our happiness must depend?

"'Don't we work and labor as much now as during all other former state-organizations?

"'Haven't we to labor and sweat to get the barley indispensable to us to live and not to starve to death like chained dogs?

"'Our chiefs, guides, and counselors are always telling us about some other sort of world, supposedly so much better than here among us on the Earth, and where life is in every respect beatific for the souls of those men who have lived worthily here on the Earth.

"'Don't we live here now "worthily"?

"'Don't we always labor and sweat for our daily bread?

"'If all that our chiefs and counselors tell us is true and their own way of living here on the Earth really corresponds to what is required of their souls for the other world, then of course God ought, and even must, in this world also, give more possibilities to them than to us ordinary mortals.

"'If all that our chiefs and counselors tell and try to make us believe is really true, let them prove it to us, ordinary mortals, by facts.

"'Let them prove it to us, for instance, that they can at least change a pinch of the common sand, in which, thanks to our sweat, our daily bread arises, into bread.

"'If our present chiefs and counselors do this, then I

myself will be the first to run and kneel and kiss their feet.

"'But meanwhile, as this is not so, we ourselves must struggle and we ourselves must strive hard for our real happiness and for our real freedom and also to free ourselves from the need of having to sweat.

"'It is true that for eight months of the year we now have no trouble in obtaining our daily bread; but then, how we must labor those four summer months and exhaust ourselves getting the barley we need!

"'Only he who sows and mows that barley knows the hard labor required.

"'True, for eight months we are free, but only from physical labors, and for this, our consciousness, namely, our dearest and highest part, must remain day and night in slavery to these illusory ideas which are always being dinned into us by our chiefs and counselors.

"'No, enough! We ourselves, without our present chiefs and counselors who have become such without our onsent, must strive for our real freedom and our real happiness.

"'And we can only obtain real freedom and real happiness if we all act as one, that is to say, all for one and one for all. But for this, we must first destroy all that is old.

"'And we must do so to make room for the new life we shall ourselves create that will give us real freedom and real happiness.

"'Down with dependence on others!

"'We ourselves will be masters of our own circumstances and no longer they, who rule our lives and do so without our knowledge and without our consent.

"'Our lives must be governed and guided by those whom we ourselves shall elect from our midst, that is by men only from amongst those who themselves struggle for our daily barley.

"'And we must elect these governors and counselors on the basis of equal rights, without distinction of sex or age, by universal, direct, equal, and open ballot.'

"Thus ended the said famous Kashireitleer.

"When this subsequent Universal Hasnamuss, Lentrohamsanin, had finished inscribing this Kashireitleer, indeed unprecedented there, he arranged an enormous and costly banquet to which he invited all the learned beings from all Nievia, taking upon himself all their traveling expenses; and at the end of this banquet, he showed them his Kashireitleer.

"When the learned beings then gathered at that free feast from almost the whole of Nievia saw that indeed unprecedented Kashireitleer, they were at first so astounded that they became, as it is said there, as if 'petrified' and only after a considerable time did they gradually begin looking at each other with dumbfounded glances, and exchanging opinions in whispers.

"Chiefly they asked one another how was it possible that not a single learned being nor a single ordinary being had known or guessed that there in their own country such a learned being with such knowledge existed.

"Suddenly one of them, namely, the oldest among them who enjoyed the greatest reputation, jumped up on the table like a boy, and in a loud voice and with the intonation which had already long before become proper to the learned beings there of new formation, and which has also reached the contemporary learned beings, uttered the following:

"'Listen, and all of you be aware that we, the representatives of terrestrial beings assembled here who have thanks to our great learning already attained independent individuality, have the happiness to be the first to behold with our own eyes the creation of a Messiah of Divine consciousness sent from Above to reveal World-truths to us.'

"Thereupon began that usual maleficent what is called 'mutual inflation,' which had already long been practiced among the learned beings of new formation and chiefly on account of which no true knowledge which has chanced to reach them ever evolves there as it does everywhere else in the Universe, even merely from the passage of time itself; but, on the contrary, even the knowledge once already attained there is destroyed, and its possessors always become shallower and shallower.

"And the rest of the learned beings then began shouting and pushing each other in order to get near Lentrohamsanin; and addressing him as their 'long-awaited-Messiah' they conveyed to him by their admiring glances what is called their 'high-titillation.'

"The most interesting thing about it all is that the reason why all the other learned beings were so greatly amazed and so freely gave vent to what are called their 'learned snivellings' lay in a certain extremely strange conviction which had been formed in the psyche of your favorites, thanks as always to the same abnormally established conditions of ordinary existence, that if anybody becomes a follower of an already well-known and important being, he thereby seems to be to all other beings almost as well known and important himself.

"So it was on the strength of his being very rich, and what is more important, already very famous, that all the other learned beings of that time, of the country Nievia, immediately manifested themselves approvingly towards this Lentrohamsanin.

"Well then, my dear boy, when after the said banquet, the learned beings of Nievia returned home, they immediately began firstly to speak among their neighbors and later more and more widely, here, there and everywhere, about that unprecedented Kashireitleer itself, and, secondly, already foaming at the mouth, to persuade and convince everybody of the truth of those 'revelations' which that great Lentrohamsanin had inscribed on this Kashireitleer.

"The result of it all was that the ordinary beings of the town Kronbookhon as well as of other parts of the country Nievia talked among themselves of nothing but these 'revelations.'

"And gradually, as it also usually happens there, almost everywhere beings became divided into two mutually opposing parties, one of which favored the 'invention' of the subsequent Universal Hasnamuss, and the other, the already existing and well-fixed forms of being-existence.

"Thus it continued during almost a whole terrestrial year, during which time the ranks of the contending parties increased everywhere and towards each other there grew one of their particular properties called 'hate'; the result of which was that one sorrowful day in the town of Kronbookhon itself, there suddenly began among the beings, who had become followers of one or the other of the two said mutually opposite currents, their process of what is called 'civil war.'

"'Civil war' is the same as 'war'; the difference is only that in ordinary war, beings of one community destroy the beings of another community, while in a civil war the process of reciprocal destruction proceeds among beings of one and the same community, as, for example, brother annihilates brother; father, son; uncle, nephew, and so on.

"At the outset, during the four days that the horrible process was at its height in Kronbookhon, and the attention of the other beings of the whole country of Nievia was concentrated on it, everything was still relatively quiet in the other towns, but here and there, small, what are called 'skirmishes' occasionally took place. When at the end of the fourth day, those who were for the 'invention' of Lentrohamsanin, that is for the learned beings, were victorious in Kronbookhon, then, from that time on, the same process also began at all the large and small points of the whole surface of Nievia.

"That widespread terrifying process continued until there appeared 'hordes' of learned beings who, as it is said, 'feeling-firm-ground-beneath-their-feet' compelled all the surviving beings to accept the ideas of Lentrohamsanin and immediately destroyed everything, and from then on, all the three-brained beings of Nievia became followers of the 'invention' of Lentrohamsanin and soon after, in that community, there was established a special what is called 'Republic.'

"A little later, the community Nievia, being at that period great and what is called 'powerful,' began, as it also usually happens there, 'making war' on the neighboring communities for the purpose of imposing upon them also her new form of state-organization.

"From that time on, my boy, on the largest continent of your planet, the processes of reciprocal destruction among these strange three-brained beings began to proceed as before; and at the same time, there were gradually changed and finally destroyed those various beneficent forms of their ordinary existence which had already been fixed thanks to the ideally foreseeing Reason of our now Most Very Saintly Ashiata Shiemash.

"Thereupon there again began to be formed on the surface of your planet—only to be destroyed anew and to give place to others—numerous separate distinct communities with every kind of 'form-of-inner-state-organization.'

"Although the direct effect of that maleficent invention of the now Universal Hasnamuss Lentrohamsanin was that among your favorites the practice was revived of existing in separate distinct communities and they again resumed their periodic reciprocal destruction, yet within many of these newly arisen independent communities on the continent Asia, beings still continued to conform in their ordinary existence to many of the unprecedently wisely foreseen usages of the Very Saintly Ashiata Shiemash for their ordinary being-existence, which usages had already been inseparably fused into their automatically flowing process of daily existence.

"And those to blame for the final destruction of these said usages and customs that still remained in certain communities, were those learned beings who were then assembled in the city of Babylon.

"And they were then to blame in this respect owing to the following:

"When owing to that famous question of the Beyond, they organized the 'general-planetary-conference' of all the learned beings there, there happened to be also among the learned beings who went to Babylon on their own accord, the great-grandson of Lentrohamsanin himself, who had also become a learned being.

"And he took with him, there to the city of Babylon, an exact copy of the mentioned Kashireitleer, but made on papyrus, the original of which had been inscribed by his great-grandfather and which he had obtained by inheritance, and at the very height of the 'frenzy' concerning the 'question-of-the-soul' during one of the last big general meetings of the learned beings, he read aloud the contents of that maleficent 'invention' of his great-grandfather's; whereupon, it occurred—as it had also become proper to the 'sorry-learned-beings' of this planet, thanks to their strange Reason—that from one question which interested them, they at once passed to quite another, namely, from the question 'of-the-soul' to the question of what is called 'politics.'

"Thereupon in the city of Babylon, meetings and

discussions again began everywhere concerning the various kinds of already existing state-organizations and those which in their opinion ought to be formed.

"As the basis of all their discussions they took, of course, the 'truths' indicated in the invention of Lentrohamsanin, this time expounded on what is called a papyrus that had been taken there by his great-grandson, and a copy of which almost every learned being who was then in Babylon carried in his pocket.

"For several months they discussed and argued, and as a result, they this time 'split' into parties; that is to say all the learned beings then in the city of Babylon split into two independent what are called 'sections,' under the following names:

"The first: 'Section of Neomothists.'

"The second: 'Section of Paleomothists.'

"Each of these sections of learned beings soon had its adherents from among the ordinary beings in the city of Babylon; and once again things would certainly have ended also with a civil war if the Persian king, hearing of it all, had not immediately 'cracked' them on their 'learned noddles.'

"A number of these learned beings were executed by him, others were imprisoned with lice, and still others were dispatched to places, where even now, as Mullah Nassr Eddin would say, 'French champagne' could not be taken. Only a few of those who were clearly shown to have been occupied with all this, only because, as it is said there, they were 'mad,' were permitted to return to their own countries, and those among them who had taken no part whatever in 'political-questions' were not only also given full liberty to return to their native land, but by the order of the mentioned Persian king, their return to their native land was even accompanied with every kind of honor.

"Well then, my boy, those Babylonian learned beings who, owing to various reasons, survived and were scattered everywhere over the surface of almost the whole of the planet, continued by momentum their wiseacring, the basis of which, they made—of course, not consciously but simply mechanically—those two leading questions which had arisen and which had been the 'questions-of-the-day' during the said Babylonian events, namely, the famous questions concerning the 'soul' of men and the 'inner-communal-organization.'

"The result of these wiseacrings of theirs was that over the whole continent of Asia civil wars again broke out in various communities, and the processes of mass reciprocal-destruction between different communities.

"The destruction which thus proceeded of the remnants of the results of the conscious labors of the Very Saintly Ashiata Shiemash, continued on the continent of Asia for about a century and a half; yet, in spite of this, in some places there were preserved and even by momentum were still carried out certain forms that had been created by Ashiata Shiemash for their beneficent being-existence.

"But when the three-brained beings there who arose and existed on the neighboring continent, now called Europe, then began taking part in the Asiatic wars, and when 'hordes' with the arch-vainglorious Greek called 'Alexander-of-Macedonia' at their head, were dispatched thence and passed almost everywhere over the continent of Asia, they made, as it is said, a 'clean sweep' from the surface of that ill-fated planet of everything that had been established and had still been preserved and carried out; so clean a sweep, that it left not even the trace of the memory that there could once have existed on the surface of their planet such a 'bliss,' specially and intentionally created for their existence by such a Reason, whose possessor is now one of our seven MOST VERY SAINTLY OMNICOSMIC INDIVIDUALS, without whose participation even our UNI-BEING COMMON FATHER does not allow himself to actualize anything.

"And now, my boy, after my tale about this Lentrohamsanin—thanks to which you obtained to a certain degree a conspective account of the consequences for subsequent generations ensuing from the activities of such a typical representative of Eternal-Hasnamuss-individuals from among the three-brained beings of the planet Earth—it will now be quite opportune to explain to you, as I promised, a little more in detail about the significance of the word Hasnamuss.

"In general, those independent individuals are called and defined by the word Hasnamuss in whom, among what are called 'Individual-impulses,' a certain 'something' arises, which participates in what is called the 'completed formation' of independent individualities in the common presences of three-brained beings both of the highest possible coating as well as of those who consist only of the planetary body alone.

"This 'something' in these separate cosmic individuals arises and blends in the process of the transformation of substances in them with the crystallizations resulting from the action of the entire 'spectrum' of certain what are called 'Naloo-osnian-impulses.'

"This 'Naloo-osnian-spectrum-of-impulses' consists, on the basis of that chief cosmic law, the sacred Heptaparaparshinokh, according to the source of its essence in respect of the 'perception-of-engenderings' and the 'resulting-manifestations,' of seven heterogeneous aspects.

"If these separate aspects of the entire 'spectrum' of Naloo-osnian-impulses are described according to the notions of your favorites and expressed in their language, they might then be defined as follows:

(1) Every kind of depravity, conscious as well as unconscious
(2) The feeling of self-satisfaction from leading others astray
(3) The irresistible inclination to destroy the existence of other breathing creatures
(4) The urge to become free from the necessity of actualizing the being-efforts demanded by Nature
(5) The attempt by every kind of artificiality to conceal from others what in their opinion are one's physical defects
(6) The calm self-contentment in the use of what is not personally deserved
(7) The striving to be not what one is.

"This certain 'something' which arises in the presences of definite individuals owing to the enumerated Naloo-osnian-impulses, besides being the cause of what are called 'serious-retributive-suffering-consequences' for these individuals themselves, also has the particularity, that as soon as the action of what is called 'intense-effort' ceases in one of these individuals, the radiations proper to one or other of the aspects of the manifestations of this 'something' have a greater effect on those around him and become a factor for engendering the same in them.

"In the common presence of every kind of three-brained being, there can arise during the process of his planetary existence, four kinds of independent Hasnamuss-individuals.

"The first kind of Hasnamuss-individual is a three-brained being who, while acquiring in his common presence that something, still consists only of his planetary body and who, during the process of his sacred Rascooarno, is subject to the corresponding consequences of the presence in him of the properties of this something and is thus destroyed forever such as he is.

"The second kind of Hasnamuss-individual is that Kesdjan body of a three-brained being which is coated in his common presence with the participation of that same something and which, acquiring—as is proper to such a cosmic arising—the property of 'Toorinoorino,' that is, nondecomposition in any sphere of that planet on which he arose, has to exist, by being formed again and again in a certain way, such as he is, until this certain something will have been eliminated from him.

"The third kind of Hasnamuss-individual is the highest being-body or soul, during the coating of which in the common presence of a three-brained being this something arises and participates; and he also acquires the property of Toorinoorino, but this time proper to this highest being-body; that is to say, this arising is no longer subject to decomposition not only in the spheres of that planet on which he had his arising, but also in all other spheres of the Great Universe.

"The fourth kind of Hasnamuss-individual is similar to the third, but with this difference, that the Hasnamuss of the third kind has the possibility of at some time succeeding in becoming so to say 'cleansed' from this something, whereas for this fourth kind such a possibility is lost forever.

"That is why this fourth kind of Hasnamuss is called an 'Eternal-Hasnamuss-individual.'

"For these four kinds of Hasnamuss-individuals, owing to their having in their presences this something, the mentioned retributive-suffering-consequences are various and correspond both to the nature of each kind as well as to what is called 'objective-responsibilities' ensuing from the primordial providence and hopes and expectations of our COMMON FATHER concerning these cosmic actualizations.

"For the Hasnamuss of the first kind, namely, when this something is acquired by a being still consisting only of just a planetary body alone, the decomposition of this planetary body of his does not proceed according to the general rule, that is to say, the cessation of the functioning in his organism of every kind of sensed-impulse does not proceed simultaneously with the approach of the 'sacred Rascooarno,' that is, death.

"But the process of the sacred Rascooarno begins in him still during his planetary existence and proceeds in parts, that is, one by one there gradually cease to participate in his common presence, the functioning of one or other of his separate independent spiritualized 'localizations'—or, as your favorites would say there, in such a being, first of all, one of his brains with all its appertaining functions dies; later on, the second one dies, and only then does the final death of the being approach.

"In addition to this, after the final death, the 'disintegration-of-all-the-active-elements' of which the given planetary body was formed, proceeds firstly much more slowly than usual, and secondly, with the inextinguishable action—only lessened in proportion to the volatilization of the active elements—of the mentioned 'sensed-impulses' he had during life.

"For the second kind of Hasnamuss-individual, that is, when the Kesdjan-body of a three-brained being becomes such, the corresponding consequences are that such an indeed unfortunate arising, freed from the planetary body of a three-brained being, on the one hand not having the possibility of perfecting himself independently of and without a planetary coating, does not succeed in eliminating from his presence this maleficent something even not always acquired by his own fault, which something is always and with everything in the Universe an obstacle for the correct flowing of the common cosmic Trogoautoegocratic process; on the other hand, owing to the property in him of Toorinoorino, that is, not being subject to decomposition in any sphere of that solar system in which he is formed, he must inevitably be again coated in a planetary body and in most cases with the exterior form of a being of one- or two-brained system; and in view of the brevity in general of the duration of beings of these planetary forms and also not having time to adapt himself to a single exterior form, he must constantly begin all over again in the form of another being of the planet with the full uncertainty as to the result of this coating.

"And as regards the third kind of Hasnamuss-individual, namely, when the highest being-body of a three-brained being becomes such, and when this certain something participates in his coating in such a quality that he never loses the possibility of freeing himself from it, the matter is still more terrible, chiefly because he—as a higher cosmic arising, who according to the foreseeing FIRST-SOURCED-PRINCIPLE-OF-EVERYTHING-EXISTING was predetermined to serve the aim of helping the government of the whole increasing World, and on whom from the moment of the completion of his formation, even when he was not yet perfected in Reason, was placed the responsibility for every subjective voluntary as well as involuntary manifestation—has the possibility to succeed in eliminating from his presence this something, exclusively only by the action of the results of intentionally actualized Partkdolg-duty, that is to say, of 'conscious-labors-and-intentional-sufferings.'

"Hence such a higher being-body must inevitably always suffer correspondingly, having already acquired the gradation of what is called the 'degree-of-cognition-of-one's-own-individuality,' until this certain something is entirely eradicated from his common presence.

"As a place for the suffering existence of such a high order of Hasnamuss-individuals, the HIGHER-SACRED-INDIVIDUALS have intentionally allotted, from the totality of the large cosmic concentrations, four planets, disharmonized in their subjective functioning, situated in various most remote corners of our Great Universe.

"One of these four disharmonized planets called 'Eternal-Retribution' is specially prepared for the 'Eternal-Hasnamuss-individuals' and the other three for those 'Higher being-bodies' of Hasnamusses in whose common presences there is still the possibility of 'at some time or other' eliminating from themselves the mentioned maleficent something.

"The three small planets exist under the names of:

(1) 'Remorse-of-conscience'
(2) 'Repentance'
(3) 'Self-Reproach.'

"Here it is interesting to notice that from among all the 'highest being-bodies' which have been coated and perfected in every kind of exterior form of three-brained being there have, so far, reached the planet 'Retribution' from the whole Universe, only three hundred and thirteen, two of whom had their arising on your planet and one of these is the 'highest being-body' of this Lentrohamsanin.

"On that planet Retribution, these Eternal-Hasnamuss-individuals must constantly endure those incredible sufferings called 'Inkiranoodel' which are like the sufferings called Remorse-of-Conscience but only much more painful.

"The chief torture of the state of these 'highest being-bodies' is that they must always experience these terrifying sufferings fully conscious of the utter hopelessness of their cessation."

SECOND BOOK

CHAPTER 29

The Fruits of Former Civilizations and the Blossoms of the Contemporary

According to the associative flow of my tales concerning the three-brained beings breeding on the planet Earth who have taken your fancy, I must now, my boy, without fail explain to you a little more about those two powerful communities there named 'Greeks' and 'Romans,' who made a 'clean sweep' from the surface of that ill-fated planet of even the memory of the results obtained from the Most Saintly Labors of the Essence-loving Ashiata Shiemash.

"I must tell you first of all that at that period when on the surface of your planet, on the continent of Asia, there was actualized from Above within the presence of a three-brained being the already definitized sacred conception of our now Omnicosmic Very Saintly Ashiata Shiemash, and later also, during the periods of His Very Saintly Activities and the subsequent gradual destruction by your favorites of all the results obtained from them, there also existed on the neighboring continent, then already called Europe, great numbers of those strange three-brained beings who have taken your fancy, and who had already long before grouped themselves into various independent communities.

"Among the number of those independent communities, there were during those periods, owing to those cosmic laws which I have once mentioned to you, those two large and, as they say there, 'most-powerful' communities, that is to say, well organized and possessing more means for the processes of reciprocal destruction, the Greeks and Romans.

"And about these, from the point of view of your contemporary favorites, 'very-ancient' communities, I must furthermore not fail to explain to you and possibly in detail, because not only did they then, as I have already said, make a clean sweep from the face of that unfortunate planet of the last results beneficial for all the three-brained beings of all subsequent epochs, and even of all traces of the memory of the Very Saintly Labors of the Essence-loving Ashiata Shiemash, but they were also the cause that real 'nonsense' already proceeds in the Reasons of the contemporary favorites of yours, and that there is completely atrophied in them that 'fundamental-being-impulse' which is the main lever of objective morality, and which is called 'organic shame.'

"A closer acquaintance with these big groupings of your favorites and with various forms of 'bliss' prepared by them and which have passed to the beings of later epochs, will give you a good idea and enable you to understand exactly how separate independent communities are formed there, and also how a given community, having become powerful quite independently of the beings themselves, takes advantage of the fact and sets about destroying everything already attained by the other 'less powerful' communities, and forces upon them their own 'new inventions,' in most cases sincerely imagining that they truly are just what the others need.

"I must warn you, my boy, that my story of the history of their arising and of everything later connected with those ancient communities called Greeks and Romans is not based on the results of my personal investigations; no, I shall only give you the information about them which I got from one of those beings of our tribe who wished to remain to exist forever on that planet of yours.

"The circumstances were these: in descending to the planet Earth for the sixth and last time, I proposed to attain, at any cost, the final elucidation to myself of all the genuine causes why the psyche of those three-brained beings, which should be like the psyche of the rest of the three-brained beings of our Great Universe, had on that planet become so exceptionally strange.

"And having during my investigations repeatedly constated that a fundamental cause of the various abnormalities of the general psyche of the contemporary beings was what is called 'civilization' sown by those two large groups of beings called Greeks and Romans, I was obliged to inquire into certain details about them also.

"But as I was fully occupied at that time with my researches concerning the activities of the Very Saintly Ashiata Shiemash, I commissioned the elucidation of the history of the arising of these two independent groupings of your favorites—in respect of what is called, their 'subjective-being-Being'—to that same being of our tribe who as I have already told you, still carries on an 'undertaker's business' in a large city on the continent of Europe down to the present time.

"From the investigations of this countryman of ours, it seems that long ago before the period to which my tale about the majestic city of Babylon referred, namely, at the time when the process of the existence of those strange beings was proceeding mainly on the continent Asia alone, and when their chief center of culture was Tikliamish, there were on that said continent of Europe, which is now the chief place of existence of your favorites, as yet no definitely organized communities.

"There then chiefly existed on that continent two-brained and one-brained beings called 'wild quadrupeds' and 'reptiles,' but of your favorites, the biped beings, there were then on that continent only a number of small groups, almost as 'wild' as the 'quadrupeds' themselves.

"The occupation of these small groups of biped beings

was merely the destruction of the 'quadruped' and 'reptile' beings, and occasionally also of each other.

"And the numbers of your favorites on that continent Europe only increased when emigrants from Maralpleicie, wandering from one place to another, finally arrived and settled there.

"Towards the close of that period there migrated from Tikliamish to that continent Europe a number of beings of the first Asiatic group who followed two quite distinct occupations: namely, some of them were engaged in various marine occupations, and others in what are called there 'cattle raising' and 'sheep farming.'

"The cattle-raising families populated chiefly the southern shores of the continent, because those parts were at that time very convenient for the maintenance and grazing of such quadruped beings.

"And that group of terrestrial beings was then called 'Latinaki,' a word that signified 'shepherds.'

"At first these shepherds existed with their families and flocks scattered in different places; but later on their numbers gradually increased, partly from the immigration of beings from the continent Asia having the same occupation as themselves, and partly because they were becoming more and more prolific, owing to the fact that the Nature of the planet Earth was beginning to adapt Herself to the deteriorating quality of the vibrations She demanded that had to be formed from their radiations, by substituting those vibrations which are now obtained only from the process of their sacred Rascooarno, or as they say 'from-their-death.'

"And thus when, thanks to all this, their numbers had considerably increased and external conditions demanded frequent relations between separate families, they formed their first common place, and this common place they called 'Rimk.'

"It was from that group of Asiatic shepherds that the later famous Romans originated; their name having been taken from the name of their first common place Rimk.

"Those Asiatic beings who were engaged in 'marine occupations,' namely, in fishing and in gathering sponges, coral, and seaweed, emigrated with their families for the convenience of their profession and settled either on the western shores of their own continent Ashhark, on the southeastern shores of the continent Europe, or on the islands of the straits which still divide the continents Asia and Europe.

"The beings of those newly formed groups of three-brained terrestrial beings were then called 'Hellenaki,' a word that meant 'fishermen.'

"The number of the beings, of that group also, gradually increased owing to the same causes already mentioned respecting the group of shepherds.

"The name of the beings of this second group changed many times and finally they came to be called 'Greeks.'

"And so, my dear boy, the beings of these two groups were one of the chief causes that the Reasons of the contemporary favorites of yours have become mechanical, and that the data for engendering the impulse of being-shame have become completely atrophied in them.

"The Greeks were the cause why the Reasons of the three-brained beings there began gradually to degenerate and ultimately became so degenerate that among contemporary beings it is already as our dear Mullah Nassr Eddin says, 'a-real-mill-for-nonsense.'

"And the Romans were the cause why, as a result of successive changes, those factors are never crystallized in the presences of the contemporary three-brained beings there, which in other three-brained beings engender the impulse called 'instinctive shame'; that is to say, the being impulse that maintains what are called 'morals' and 'objective morality.'

"Thus it was that those two communities arose there, which afterwards, as it often happens there, became very solid and powerful for a definite period. And the history of their further maleficent 'prepared inheritance' for the beings of subsequent generations is as follows:

"According to the investigations of our mentioned countryman, it seems that the earliest ancestors of the beings of the community, which was later called 'Greece,' were often obliged, on account of the frequent storms at sea which hindered them in their marine occupations, to seek refuge during the rains and winds, in sheltered places, where out of boredom, they played various 'games' which they invented for their distraction.

"As it later became clear, these ancient fishermen amused themselves at first with such games as children now play there—but children, it must be remarked, who have not yet started contemporary schooling—because the children there who do go to school have so much homework to do, consisting chiefly of learning by rote the 'poetry' which various candidate Hasnamusses have composed there, that the poor children never have time to play any games.

"Briefly, these poor bored fishermen played at first the ordinary children's games already established there long before; but afterwards when one of them invented a new game called 'pouring-from-the-empty-into-the-void,' they were all so pleased with it that thereafter they amused themselves with that alone.

"This game consisted in formulating some question always about some 'fiddle-faddle' or other, that is to say, a question about some deliberate piece of absurdity, and the one to whom the question was addressed had to give as plausible an answer as possible.

"Well, it was just this same game that became the cause of all that happened later.

"It turned out that among those ancient bored fishermen, there were several so 'bright' and 'ingenious' that they became expert in inventing, according to the principle of that peculiar 'game,' very long explanations.

"And when one of them discovered how to make what was afterwards called 'parchment' from the skin of the fish called 'shark,' then some of these skillful fellows, just to 'swagger' before their companions, even began inscribing these long explanations of theirs on these fishskins, employing those conventional signs which had been invented earlier, for another game called 'mousetrap.'

"Still a little later, when these bored fishermen had already given place to their descendants, both these inscribed fishskins and the craze for the said peculiar 'game' passed on to the latter by inheritance; and these various new inventions, both their own and their ancestors', they called first by the very high-sounding name 'science.'

"And from then on, as the craze for 'cooking up' these sciences passed from generation to generation, the beings of that group, whose ancestors had been simple Asiatic fishermen, became 'specialists' in inventing all kinds of sciences such as these.

"These sciences, moreover, also passed from generation to generation and a number of them have reached the contemporary beings of that planet almost unchanged.

"And hence it is that almost a half of what are called the 'egoplastikoori' arising in the Reason of the contemporary beings of that ill-fated planet, from which what is called a 'being-world-outlook' is in general formed in beings, are crystallized just from the 'truths' invented there by those bored fishermen and their subsequent generations.

"Concerning the ancient shepherds who later formed

the great powerful community called 'Rome,' their ancestors also were often forced, on account of bad weather, to put their flocks into sheltered places, and to pass the time together somehow or other.

"Being together, they had 'various talks.' But when everything had been talked out and they felt bored, then one of them suggested that as a relief they should take up the pastime which they called for the first time 'cinque-contra-uno' (five-against-one), an occupation which has been preserved down to the present time, under the same name, among their descendants who continue to arise and exist there.

"So long as only the beings of the male sex then engaged in that occupation, everything went 'quietly and peacefully,' but when a little later their 'passive halves,' that is to say their women, also joined in, who, immediately appreciating it, soon became addicted to it, they then gradually attained in these 'occupations' such 'finesses,' that even if our All-universal Arch-cunning Lucifer should rack his honorable brains, he could not even invent a tithe of the 'turns' these erstwhile shepherds then invented and 'prepared' for the beings of the succeeding generations of that ill-fated planet.

"And so, my boy, when both these independent groupings of terrestrial three-brained beings multiplied and began acquiring every variety of those effective 'means,' namely, the means of reciprocal destruction, whose acquisition is the usual aim of all communities there during all periods of their existence, they then began carrying out these 'processes' with other independent communities there—for the most part, of course, with the less powerful communities, and occasionally among themselves.

"Here it is extremely interesting to notice that when periods of peace occurred between these two communities there—communities of almost equal strength in respect of the possession of efficient means for the processes of reciprocal-destruction—the beings of both groups whose places of existence were adjacent often came into contact and had friendly relations with each other, with the result that little by little they picked up from each other those specialties which had first been invented by their ancestors and which had become proper to them. In other words, the result of the frequent contact of the beings of those two communities was that the Greek beings, borrowing from the Roman beings all the finesses of sexual 'turns,' began arranging their what are called 'Athenian nights,' while the Roman beings, having learned from the Greek beings how to cook up 'sciences,' composed their later very famous what is called 'Roman law.'

"A great deal of time has passed since then. The inventors of both those kinds of being-manifestation have already long been destroyed, and their descendants who chanced to become 'powerful' have been destroyed also. And now . . . the contemporary three-brained beings of that planet spend, even with emotion, more than half their existence and being-energy, acquired somehow or other, in absorbing and actualizing unconsciously and sometimes even consciously those two ideals, the initiators of whose arising were the said bored Asiatic fishermen and shepherds.

"Well then, my boy, later on, it seems, when both these groupings of your favorites acquired many of the said efficient means for the successful destruction of the existence of beings like themselves, and when they had become quite expert in persuading, or by the potency of their means compelling beings of other countries to exchange their inner convictions for those ideals invented by their ancestors, then, as I have said, they first conquered the neighboring communities situated on the continent Europe, and afterwards, for the same purpose, with the help of the hordes they collected during that period, turned towards the continent Asia.

"And there already on the continent Asia, they began spreading that maleficent influence of theirs, first among beings populating the western shores of that continent—in whom, as I have already said, being-impulses for a more or less normal being-existence had been implanted during centuries—and afterwards, they gradually began advancing into the interior.

"This advance of theirs into the interior of the continent Asia proceeded very successfully, and their ranks were constantly being increased, chiefly because the learned beings who had been in Babylon then continued everywhere on the continent Asia to infect the Reasons of beings with their Hasnamussian political ideas.

"And they were also helped very much by the fact that there were still preserved in the instincts of the Asiatic beings the results of the influences of the initiates and priests, disciples of the Very Saintly Ashiata Shiemash, who in their preachings had inculcated, among other things, one of the chief commandments of Ashiata Shiemash which declared:

"'Do not kill another even when your own life is in danger.'

"Profiting by all this, these former fishermen and shepherds were very easily able to advance, destroying on the way all those who declined to worship the 'gods' they themselves had finally acquired, that is to say, their fantastic 'science' and their phenomenal depravity.

"At first these 'sowers-of-evil' for all the three-brained beings there of all the succeeding generations, arising on the continent Europe, and especially the Greeks, moving into the interior of the continent Asia, acted if slowly nevertheless effectively.

"But when some time later there appeared and stood

at the head of what is called an 'army' that completely formed Arch-Vainglorious Greek, the future Hasnamuss, Alexander of Macedonia, then from that time on, there began to proceed that clean sweep of the last remnants of the results of the very saintly intentional labors of our now Common Cosmic Most Very Saintly Ashiata Shiemash, and again there was resumed, as it is said, the 'old-old-story.'

"Although every time the place of the center of culture of your favorites, those strange three-brained beings, has been changed, and what is called a new 'civilization' has arisen, and each new civilization has brought for the beings of succeeding epochs something both new and maleficent, nevertheless, not one of these numerous civilizations has ever prepared so much evil for the beings of later epochs, including of course the contemporary epoch, as that famous 'Greco-Roman civilization.'

"Without mentioning the large number of other minor psychic features, unbecoming to be possessed by three-brained beings and now existing in the presences of your favorites, that civilization is mainly to blame for the complete disappearance from the presences of the three-brained beings of succeeding generations, and especially of the contemporary beings, of the possibility for crystallizing the data for 'sane-logical-mentation' and for engendering the impulse of 'being-self-shame.'

"Namely, the 'ancient-Greek-fantastic-sciences' caused complete atrophy of the former, and the 'ancient-Roman-depravity,' of the latter.

"In the early period of that Greco-Roman civilization, the said maleficent impulses, which have now become being-impulses, namely, the 'passion-for-inventing-fantastic-sciences' and the 'passion-for-depravity,' were inherent in the Greek and Roman beings alone; and later, when, as I have already said, the beings of both these communities chanced to acquire the said strength and began coming into contact with and influencing the beings of other communities, the beings of many other communities of your unfortunate favorites gradually began to be infected by these peculiar and unnatural being-impulses.

"This took place, on the one hand, as I have already said, owing to the constant influence of both these communities, and, on the other hand, owing to that peculiarity of their psyche—common to all the three-brained beings of that planet, and already well fixed in it before this—which is called there 'imitation.'

"And thus, little by little, these 'inventions' of those two ancient communities have brought it about that already, at the present time, the psyche of your favorites—shaky enough already before then—has now become so unhinged in all of them, without exception, that both their 'world outlook' and the whole ordering of their daily existence rest and proceed exclusively on the basis of those two said inventions of the beings of that Greco-Roman civilization, namely, on the basis of fantasying, and of 'striving-for-sexual-gratification.'

"Here it is very interesting to notice that although, as I have already told you, thanks to the inheritance from the ancient Romans, 'organic-self-shame'—proper to the three-brained beings—has gradually and entirely disappeared from the presences of your favorites, nevertheless there has arisen in them in its place something rather like it. In the presences of your contemporary favorites there is as much as you like of this pseudo being-impulse which they also call 'shame,' but the data for engendering it, just as of all others, are quite singular.

"This being-impulse arises in their presences only when they do something which under their abnormally established conditions of ordinary being-existence is not acceptable to be done before others.

"But if nobody sees what they do, then nothing they do—even if in their own consciousness and their own feelings it should be undesirable—engenders any such impulse in them.

"The 'bliss' prepared there by the ancient Romans has in recent times already so penetrated the nature of your favorites breeding on all the continents of that ill-fated planet, that it is even difficult to say which beings of which contemporary communities have inherited most from these 'obliging' Romans.

"But as regards the inheritance passed down from the ancient Greeks, namely, the passion for inventing various fantastic sciences, this has not become inherent to all the three-brained beings of contemporary times equally, but it has passed down only to certain beings arising among the beings of all the contemporary large and small communities breeding on all the terra firma parts of the surface of that peculiar planet.

"Proportionately, this passion, namely, 'to-invent-fantastic-sciences,' has passed down from the ancient Greeks mainly to the beings of the contemporary community existing there under the name of 'Germany.'

"The beings of that contemporary Germany can be boldly called the 'direct-heirs-of-the-ancient-Greek-civilization'; and they can be so called, because at the present time it is just they who chiefly bring every kind of new science and invention into contemporary civilization.

"Unfortunately, my boy, the beings of that contemporary community Germany have in many respects, as it is said, surpassed the beings of ancient Greece.

"Thanks to the sciences invented by the ancient Greeks, only the being-mentation of other beings was spoiled and still continues to be spoiled.

"But in addition to this, the contemporary beings of that community Germany have become very skillful also in inventing those sciences, thanks to which the said specific disease there of wiseacring has been very widely spread among other of your favorites; and during the process of this disease in them, many of them semi-consciously or even quite automatically chance to notice some small detail of the common cosmic process which actualizes Everything Existing, and afterwards, informing others of it, they together use it for some of their, as they are called, new inventions, thereby adding to the number of those 'new means,' of which during the last two of their centuries so many have accumulated there, that their total effect has now already become, what is called, the 'resultant-decomposing-force,' in contradistinction to what is called the 'resultant-creative-force' of Nature.

"And indeed, my boy, owing merely to the sciences invented by the beings of the contemporary Germany, other three-brained beings of your planet belonging both to that same community and to other communities have now acquired the possibility of inventing, and now they almost every day invent here and there, some such new invention or new means and, employing them in the process of their existence, have now already brought it about that poor Nature there—already enfeebled without this through no fault of her own—is scarcely able to actualize what are called her 'evolutionary' and 'involutionary' processes.

"For your clear representation and better understanding how these contemporary direct heirs have surpassed their 'legators,' I must now explain to you also about certain widely used means existing there at the present time, which owe their existence exclusively to these 'Nature-helping' direct heirs of ancient Greece.

"I will explain to you certain of these means there, now existing and in use everywhere, which have been invented by the beings of that contemporary community Germany.

"I should like first to emphasize, by the way, one very odd phenomenon, namely, that these contemporary 'substitutes' for the ancient Greeks give names to their said maleficent inventions, names which for some reason or other all end in 'ine.'

"As examples of the very many particularly maleficent inventions of those German beings, let us take just those five what are called 'chemical substances,' now existing there under the names of (1) satkaine, (2) aniline, (3) cocaine, (4) atropine and (5) alisarine, which chemical substances are used there at the present time by the beings of all the continents and islands as our dear Mullah Nassr Eddin says: 'Even-without-any-economizing.'

"The first of the enumerated means, specially invented by the German beings, namely, 'satkaine,' is nothing else but 'Samookoorooazar,' that is to say, one of those seven what are called 'neutralizing gases' which arise and are always present in the common presence of each planet and which take part in the 'completed crystallization' of every definite surplanetary and intraplanetary formation, and which in separate states are always and everywhere what are called 'indiscriminate-destroyers-of-the-already-arisen.'

"About this German invention, I once also learned there among other things, that when one of the beings of that community, for reasons I recently described, happened to obtain this gas from some 'surplanetary' and 'intraplanetary' definite formations, and noticed in the said way its particularity, and told several others about it, then, owing to the fact that there was then proceeding in the presences of the beings of their community, consequently in them themselves, what is called 'the-most-intense-experiencing' of the chief particularity of the psyche of the three-brained beings of your planet, namely, 'the-urgent-need-to-destroy-the-existence-of-others-like-themselves'—and indeed, the beings of that community were then fully absorbed in their process of reciprocal destruction with the beings of neighboring communities—these others thereupon at once 'enthusiastically' decided to devote themselves entirely to finding means to employ the special property of that gas for the speedy mass destruction of the existence of the beings of other communities.

"Having begun their practical researches with this aim in view, one of them soon discovered that if this gas is concentrated in a pure state in such a way that it could be freely liberated in any given space at any given time it could easily be employed for the mentioned aim.

"That was sufficient, and from then on, this gas, artificially isolated from the general harmony of the actualization of Everything Existing, began to be liberated in a certain way into space by all the other ordinary beings of that community during the processes of reciprocal destruction, just when and just where the greatest number of beings of other, as they are called 'hostile' communities were grouped.

"When this isolated, particularly poisonous cosmic-substance is intentionally liberated into the atmosphere under the said conditions, and when striving to reblend with other corresponding cosmic substances it happens to enter the planetary bodies of three-brained beings nearby, it instantly and completely destroys their existence, or, at best, permanently injures the functioning of one or other part of their common presence.

"The second of the chemical substances I enumerated, namely, 'aniline,' is that chemical coloring substance, by means of which most of those surplanetary formations can be dyed from which the three-brained beings there make all kinds of objects they need in the process of their ordinary being-existence.

"Although thanks to that invention your favorites can now dye any object any color, yet, what the lastingness of the existence of these objects becomes—ah, just there lies their famous Bismarck's 'pet cat.'

"Before that maleficent aniline existed, the objects produced by your favorites for their ordinary existence, such, for instance, as what are called 'carpets,' 'pictures,' and various articles of wool, wood, and skin, were dyed with simple vegetable dyes, which they had learned during centuries how to obtain, and these just-enumerated objects would formerly last from five to ten or even fifteen of their centuries.

"But now, thanks merely to the aniline, or to dyes of other names into which this same aniline enters as the basis, there remains of the objects dyed with new colors at most, after about thirty years, only perhaps the memory of them.

"I must also say that the beings of the contemporary community Germany have been the cause not only that thanks to this maleficent aniline the productions of all the contemporary beings of this planet are quickly destroyed, but also that productions from ancient times have almost ceased to exist on that ill-fated planet.

"This latter occurred because for various Hasnamussian purposes and for their famous, as they call them, 'scientific aims,' they collected the surviving ancient productions from all countries and, not knowing how to preserve ancient objects, they only hastened their speedy destruction.

"But they used and still use those 'antiques' they collected as 'models' for 'cheap goods' which are everywhere known on that ill-fated planet by the name of 'Ersatz.'

"As for the third of the enumerated chemical substances

they invented, namely, 'cocaine,' that chemical substance is not only also of great assistance to Nature in more rapidly decomposing the planetary formations—in this instance, their own planetary bodies—but this chemical means has an effect on the psyche of the contemporary beings of the planet Earth surprisingly similar to that which the famous organ Kundabuffer had on the psyche of their ancestors.

"When their ancestors had that invention in themselves of the Great Angel Looisos, then, thanks to this organ, they were always exactly in the same state as the contemporary beings are when they introduce into themselves this German invention called cocaine.

"I must warn you, my boy, that even if the action of that German invention is similar to the action of the famous organ Kundabuffer, it happened without any conscious intention on the part of the contemporary beings of the community Germany; they became colleagues of the Great Angel Looisos only by chance.

"At the present time almost all the beings who become genuine representatives of contemporary civilization very meticulously and with the greatest delight and tenderness introduce into themselves this 'blessing' of contemporary civilization, of course, always to the glory, as our dear Mullah Nassr Eddin says, of the 'cloven-hoofed.'

"The fourth of the enumerated chemical substances, namely, 'atropine,' is also everywhere there in great demand at the present time for a great variety of purposes; but its most common use is for a certain exceedingly strange purpose.

"It seems that thanks to the same abnormally established conditions there of ordinary being-existence, their organ of sight has acquired the property of regarding the faces of others as good and pleasing only when they have dark eyes.

"And when this chemical substance, called atropine, is in a certain way introduced into the eyes of beings the pupils become dilated and darker; and, because of this, most of them introduce this atropine into their eyes, in order that their faces may appear good and pleasing to others.

"And truly, my dear boy, those terrestrial beings who introduce this 'German blessing' into their eyes do have very 'dark eyes' until they are forty-five.

"I said until forty-five, because so far there has never been a case there when a being using this means could see and still continue its use after the age of forty-five.

"'Alisarine,' the fifth and last of the enumerated inventions, is also widespread everywhere.

"And that 'blessing' of contemporary civilization is used there chiefly by what are called 'confectioners' and other specialists who prepare for the other beings of that planet most 'tasty' articles for their first food.

"The confectioners and other professionals there who prepare the said tasty articles for the first food of the rest of your favorites use this same German 'sure-fire' composition, alisarine, of course unconsciously, for that purpose which has there already finally become the ideal for the whole of the contemporary civilization, which purpose is expressed in the language of our honored Mullah Nassr Eddin in the following words: 'As-long-as-everything-looks-fine-and-dandy-to-me-what-does-it-matter-if-the-grass-doesn't-grow.'

"Anyhow, my boy, those contemporary substitutes for the beings of ancient Greece are already now a great help to poor Nature—though only in the process of decomposition—with all their practical attainments based on the 'sciences' they have themselves invented. It is not for nothing that our dear Mullah Nassr Eddin has the following wise expression: 'Better-pull-ten-hairs-a-day-out-of-your-mother's-head-than-not-help-Nature.'

"Strictly speaking, the capacity to cook up 'fantastic sciences' and to devise new methods for ordinary being-existence there, did not pass from the ancient Greeks to the beings of that contemporary Germany alone; the same capacity was perhaps no less also inherited by the beings of another contemporary community, also an independent one, and also in her turn enjoying dominion.

"That other contemporary community of your favorites is called 'England.'

"There has even passed from ancient Greece to the beings of that second contemporary community England, and directly to them alone, one of their most maleficent inventions which the beings of that contemporary community have most thoroughly adopted and now actualize in practice.

"This particularly maleficent invention of theirs the ancient Greeks called 'Diapharon,' and the contemporary beings call 'sport.'

"About this contemporary sport there I shall explain to you in as much detail as possible at the end of my tale; but you must meanwhile know, that though the beings of that community England also now invent large quantities of the various new objects required by your favorites in the process of their ordinary being-existence, nevertheless they do not invent chemical substances like the beings of the contemporary community Germany, no . . . they invent chiefly what are called 'metalwares.'

"Especially in recent times, they have become expert in inventing and in distributing to the beings existing over the whole of the surface of your planet, vast quantities of every kind of metalwares called there locks, razors, mousetraps, revolvers, scythes, machine guns, saucepans, hinges, guns, penknives, cartridges, pens, mines, needles, and many other things of the same kind.

"And ever since the beings of this contemporary community started inventing these practical objects, the ordinary existence of the three-brained beings of your planet has been, just as our dear Mullah Nassr Eddin says, 'not-life-but-free-jam.'

"The beings of that contemporary community have been the benefactors of the other contemporary beings of your planet, offering them, as they say there, 'philanthropic aid,' especially as regards their first being-duty, namely, the duty of carrying out from time to time the process of 'reciprocal destruction.'

"Thanks to them, the discharge of that being-duty of theirs has gradually become for your contemporary favorites, the 'merest trifle.'

"In the absence of those inventions it used to be exceedingly arduous for these poor favorites of yours to fulfill that being-duty, because they were formerly forced to spend a good deal of sweat for it.

"But thanks to the adaptations of every kind invented by those contemporary beings, it is now as again our esteemed Mullah Nassr Eddin says, 'just roses, roses.'

"The contemporary beings now scarcely need to make any effort whatsoever in order to destroy completely the existence of beings like themselves.

"Sometimes sitting quietly in what they call their 'smoking rooms' they can destroy, just as a pastime, as it were, tens and sometimes even hundreds of others like themselves.

"I might as well now, I think, tell you a little also about the still existing direct descendants of the beings of the mentioned Greek-Roman civilizations.

"The descendants of the beings of the once 'great' and 'powerful' community Greece there, still continue to exist and also to have their own independent community, but for the other independent communities there, they have at the present time scarcely any significance whatever.

"They already no longer do as their ancestors did there, who were supreme specialists in cooking up all kinds of 'fantastic sciences'; for if a contemporary Greek cooked up a new science, the beings of the other communities of the present time would not pay it the smallest attention.

"And they would pay no attention to it, chiefly because that community has not at the present time enough of what are called 'guns' and 'ships' to be for the other contemporary beings there what is called an 'authority.'

"But though the descendants of the former great Greeks, namely, the Greeks of the present time, have lost the trick of being what is called an 'imagined-authority' for other three-brained beings there, they have now perfectly adapted themselves there on almost all the continents and islands to keeping what are called 'shops,' where without any haste, slowly and gently, they trade in what are called 'sponges,' 'halva,' 'Rahat-Lokoum,' 'Turkish delight,' etc., and sometimes 'Persian-dried-fruit,' never forgetting the dried fish called 'Kefal.'

"And as for the descendants of the famous Romans, although they too continue to arise and exist, they no longer even bear the name of their ancestors, though they still call the chief place of their community by the name 'Rome.'

"The contemporary beings of the community formed by the descendants of those former shepherds, afterwards the great Romans, are called by the other beings there 'Italians.'

"Except for that specific being-impulse which the ancient Roman beings were the first on that planet to crystallize in their presences, and which subsequently spread gradually to all the other three-brained beings of that planet, scarcely anything else has passed by inheritance from their ancestors to these beings called Italians.

"The beings of that contemporary community Italy exist at the present time very quietly and peacefully, doing nothing more than unostentatiously inventing ever new forms of their harmless and very innocent what is called 'macaroni.'

"Nevertheless, there had passed to certain beings of that contemporary Italy, by heredity from their ancestors, one special and very peculiar 'property' called 'giving-pleasure-to-others.'

"Only they manifest this inherited need, that is to say this 'giving-pleasure,' not towards beings there like themselves, but to beings of other forms.

"It must in fairness be stated that the said special property passed to beings of various parts of contemporary Italy not from the great Romans alone; this inherited property became more 'naturalized' by their ancestors of considerably later epochs, namely, at the time when they began spreading, among other beings both of their own community and of the neighboring weaker communities, the doctrines, already changed for their egoistic purposes, of a certain genuine 'sacred-Messenger-from-Above.'

"At the present time the beings of various parts of contemporary Italy actualize this property of giving-pleasure-to-others in the following way:

"The existence of the quadruped beings called 'sheep' and 'goats,' whose planetary bodies they also use for their first food, they do not destroy all at once; but in order to give this 'pleasure' they do it 'slowly' and 'gently' over a period of many days; that is to say, one day they take off one leg, then a few days later, a second leg, and so on, for as long as the sheep or goat still breathes. And sheep and goats can breathe without the said parts of their common presence for a very long time because, in the main functions of the taking in of cosmic substances for the possibility of existing, these parts do not participate, though they do participate in the functions which actualize those impulses giving self-sensations.

"After what I have already said, there seems no need to say any more about the descendants of those Romans who were once so 'menacing' and so 'great' for the other communities there.

"Now let us talk about that particularly maleficent invention of the ancient Greeks, which is being actualized in practice at the present time by the beings of the contemporary community there, called England, and which invention they call 'sport.'

"Not only have the beings of the contemporary community, England, namely, those beings who chiefly actualize during the process of their ordinary existence this particularly maleficent invention of the ancient Greeks, added, thanks to its maleficent consequences, one more sure-fire factor for shortening the duration of their existence—already trifling enough without that—but also, experiencing in their turn at the present time the greatness of their community, they are in consequence authorities for the other three-brained beings there; and, furthermore, because they have made the actualizing of the invention in practice their ideal and its spreading their aim, they, at the present time, by every possible means, strongly infect the beings of all other large and small communities of that ill-fated planet with that invention of theirs.

"The basis for that very serious misconception there was the disappearance from the common presences of those favorites of yours of the possibility of the crystallization in them of those factors which actualize 'logical mentation' in three-brained beings.

"And in consequence of the absence in them of this 'logical mentation,' all of them, almost without exception, merely because certain candidates for Hasnamuss there have asserted that they could obtain something 'good' for themselves by means of this sport—an assertion they believe with all their presence—have now, in the hope of attaining this same something, given themselves up entirely to that sport.

"None of these unfortunates know and probably never will reflect that not only is nothing good obtained by them from this maleficent sport of theirs, but they, as I have already told you, solely owing to this sport alone, still further shorten the duration of their existence which is already sufficiently trifling without this.

"So that you may better represent to yourself and understand why the duration of their existence is being still further diminished on account of this sport, it is now opportune to explain to you a little more in detail about what I have already promised you to explain, namely, the difference between the duration of being-existence according to the 'Fulasnitamnian' principle and according to the 'Itoklanoz' principle.

"You remember that when I explained to you how these favorites of yours define the 'flow-of-time' I said that when the organ Kundabuffer with all its properties was removed from their presences, and they began to have the same duration of existence as all normal three-brained beings arising everywhere in our Universe, that is, according to what is called the Fulasnitamnian principle, they also should then have existed without fail until their 'second-being-body-Kesdjan' had been completely coated in them and finally perfected by Reason up to the sacred 'Ishmetch.'

"But later, when they began existing in a manner more and more unbecoming for three-brained beings and entirely ceased actualizing in their presences their being-Partkdolg-duty, foreseen by Great Nature, by means of which alone it is possible for three-brained beings to acquire in their presences the data for coating their said higher-parts—and when, in consequence of all this, the quality of their radiations failed to respond to the demands of the Most Great common-cosmic Trogoautoegocratic process—then Great Nature was compelled, for the purpose of 'equalizing-vibrations,' gradually to actualize the duration of their existence according to the principle called Itoklanoz, that is the principle upon which in general is actualized the duration of existence of one-brained and two-brained beings who have not the same possibilities as the three-brained beings, and who are therefore unable to actualize in their presences, the said—foreseen by Nature—'Partkdolg-duty.'

"According to this principle, the duration of being-existence and also the whole of the contents of their common presences are in general acquired from the results arising from the following seven actualizations surrounding them, namely, from:

(1) Heredity in general
(2) Conditions and environment at the moment of conception
(3) The combination of the radiations of all the planets of their solar system during their formation in the womb of their productress
(4) The degree of being-manifestation of their producers during the period they are attaining the age of responsible being
(5) The quality of being-existence of beings similar to themselves around them
(6) The quality of what are called the 'Teleokrimalnichnian' thought-waves formed in the atmosphere surrounding them also during their period of attaining the age of majority—that is, the sincerely manifested good wishes and actions on the part of what are called the 'beings-of-the-same-blood,' and finally,

(7) The quality of what are called the being-egoplastikoori of the given being himself, that is his being-efforts for the transubstantiation in himself of all the data for obtaining objective Reason.

"The chief particularity of existence according to this principle Itoklanoz is that in the presences of beings existing according to it, dependent upon the enumerated seven exterior actualizations, there are crystallized in their 'being-localizations' which represent in beings the central places of the sources of actualization of all the separate independent parts of their common presence—or, as your favorites say, in their brains—what are called 'Bobbin-kandelnosts,' that is to say, something that gives in the given localizations or brains a definite quantity of possible associations or experiencings.

"And so, my boy, because these contemporary favorites of yours, these three-brained beings of the planet Earth, already arise only according to the principle Itoklanoz, therefore from the moment of conception up to the age of responsible being there are crystallized in their brains these Bobbin-kandelnosts with very definite possibilities of actualizing the processes of association.

"For the greater elucidation of this question and for your better understanding, and also not to waste time on explanations concerning the essence itself and also the forms of functioning of such definite cosmic realizations as these just-mentioned Bobbin-kandelnosts, which are lawfully crystallized in the localizations or brains of those beings who exist only on the basis of Itoklanoz, I intend to take as an elucidating example just those 'Djamtesternokhi' such as your favorites also have and which they call 'mechanical watches.'

"As you already well know, although such Djamtesternokhi or mechanical watches are of different what are called 'systems,' yet they are all constructed on the same principle of 'tension-or-pressure-of-the-unwinding-spring.'

"One system of Djamtesternokhi or mechanical watch contains a spring exactly calculated and arranged so that the length of the duration of its tension from unwinding may be sufficient for twenty-four hours; another system has a spring for a week, a third for a month, and so on.

"The Bobbin-kandelnost in the brains of beings existing only according to the principle Itoklanoz corresponds to the spring in mechanical watches of various systems.

"Just as the duration of the movement of mechanical watches depends upon the spring they contain, so the duration of the existence of beings depends exclusively on the Bobbin-kandelnosts formed in their brains during their arising and during the process of their further formation.

"Just as the spring of a watch has a winding of a definite duration, so these beings also can associate and experience only as much as the possibilities for experiencing put into them by Nature during the crystallization of those same Bobbin-kandelnosts in their brains.

"They can associate and consequently exist just so much, and not a whit more nor less.

"As mechanical watches can act as long as the spring has what is called 'the-tension-of-winding,' so the beings in whose brains the said Bobbin-kandelnosts are crystallized can experience and consequently exist until these Bobbin-kandelnosts formed in their brains—owing to the mentioned seven external conditions—are used up.

"And so, my boy, as the results of Partkdolg-duty were no longer thereafter obtained in the presences of your favorites, and the duration of their existence began to depend exclusively on the results of the seven accidentally arranged external conditions I have just enumerated, then thanks to all this, the length of their existence, especially among the contemporary beings, has become very varied.

"At the present time, the duration of their existence may

be from one of their minutes up to seventy or ninety of their years.

"And so, owing to all I have just said, however your favorites may exist, whatever measures they may adopt and even if, as they say, they should 'put-themselves-in-a-glass-case,' as soon as the contents of the Bobbin-kandelnosts crystallized in their brains are used up, one or another of their brains immediately ceases to function.

"The difference between mechanical watches and your contemporary favorites is only that in mechanical watches there is one spring, while your favorites have three of these independent Bobbin-kandelnosts.

"And these independent Bobbin-kandelnosts in all the three independent 'localizations' in three-brained beings have the following names:

"The first: the Bobbin-kandelnost of the 'thinking-center.'

"The second: the Bobbin-kandelnost of the 'feeling-center.'

"The third: the Bobbin-kandelnost of the 'moving-center.'

"Even that fact, which I have recently often repeated, namely, that the process of the sacred Rascooarno is actualized for these favorites of yours in thirds—or, as they themselves would say, they begin to 'die-in-parts'—proceeds also from the fact that, arising and being formed only according to the principle Itoklanoz and existing nonharmoniously, they disproportionately use up the contents, namely, their Bobbin-kandelnosts of these three separate independent brains, and hence it is that such a horrible 'dying' as is not proper to three-brained beings frequently occurs to them.

"During my stay there among them, I personally very often constated their 'dying-by-thirds.'

"This was possible because, although, in the presences

of your favorites, especially the contemporary ones, the Bobbin-kandelnost of one of their brains may be entirely used up, nevertheless the beings themselves would sometimes continue to exist for quite a long time.

"For instance, it often happens there, that, owing to their specifically abnormal existence, the contents of one of the Bobbin-kandelnosts may be used up in one of them, and if it is of the moving-center, or as they themselves call it, the 'spinal-brain,' then although such a contemporary three-brained being there continues to 'think' and to 'feel,' yet he has already lost the possibility of intentionally directing the parts of his planetary body.

"Here it is interesting to notice that when one of your contemporary favorites already partially dies for good in this way, then their contemporary Zirlikners, or as they are called 'physicians,' look upon such a death as most certainly a disease, and with every kind of wiseacring that has become proper to them, start treating it; and they give these supposed diseases every sort of name consonant with an ancient language utterly unknown to them, called 'Latin.'

"The very widely spread diseases there have such names as the following: 'hemiplegia,' 'paraplegia,' 'paralysis progressiva essentialis,' 'tabes dorsalis,' 'paralysis agitans,' 'sclerosis disseminata,' and so on and so forth.

"Such deaths by thirds, there on the planet Earth which has taken your fancy, have occurred particularly frequently during the last two centuries, and they occur to those of your favorites who, thanks either to their profession, or to one of their what are called 'passions,' arising and acquired by the beings belonging to all large and small communities there, on account of the same abnormally arranged conditions of their ordinary being-existence, have during their being-existence lived through in a greater or smaller degree the contents of the Bobbin-kandelnost of one or another of their being-brains.

"For instance, a one-third death on account of the Bobbin-kandelnost of the moving-center or 'spinal-brain' often occurs there among those terrestrial beings who give themselves up to that occupation which the beings belonging to the contemporary community England now practice, thanks to the maleficent invention of the ancient Greeks, and which maleficent occupation they now call sport.

"The character of the pernicious consequences of that maleficent occupation there you will well understand when I tell you that during my stay among those favorites of yours I once prepared a special section of my statistics for elucidating to myself how long these three-brained beings there can exist, who become what are called 'wrestlers' by profession, and never once in those statistics of mine, did I notice that any of them had existed longer than forty-nine of their years.

"And a one-third death through the premature using up of the Bobbin-kandelnost of the feeling-center occurs for the most part among those terrestrial beings who become by profession what are called 'representatives-of-Art.'

"Most of these terrestrial professionals, especially the contemporary ones, first fall ill with one or another form of what is called 'psychopathy,' and thanks to this, they later in their psychopathy intentionally learn, as they say, to 'feel'; and thereafter repeatedly feeling these abnormal being-impulses, they gradually use up the contents of the Bobbin-kandelnost of their feeling-center, and thus disharmonizing the tempo of their own common presences bring themselves to that peculiar end which is not often met with even among them there.

"Here, by the way, it is very interesting also to notice that the one-third death through the feeling-center occurs among your favorites also thanks to one very peculiar form of 'psychopathy,' called there 'altruism.'

"And concerning premature partial death through the Bobbin-kandelnost of the thinking-center—the deaths of this kind among your favorites occur in recent times more and more frequently.

"This kind of death through the thinking-center occurs there chiefly among those favorites of yours who try to become or have already become scientists of new formation, and also among those who during the period of their existence fall ill with the craze for reading what are called 'books' and 'newspapers.'

"The result among those three-brained beings there of reading superfluously and associating only by thoughts, is that the contents of the Bobbin-kandelnost of their thinking-center are exhausted before the contents of the Bobbin-kandelnosts of their other being-centers.

"And so, my boy, all these misfortunes, namely, the shortening of the duration of their existence and also many other consequences, maleficent for them themselves, occur to your favorites exclusively only because they have even until now not yet learned of the existence of the cosmic law called 'Equalization-of-many-sourced-vibrations.'

"If only such an idea occurred to them and they were merely to perform their usual wiseacrings with it, perhaps then they would get to understand one very simple, as they call it, 'secret.'

"I admit that somebody would be certain to understand this 'secret' because, in the first place it is simple and obvious, and secondly because they discovered it long ago and they even often employed it in what they call 'practical use.'

"They even use this simple secret, to which I referred, for those mechanical-watches which we took for comparison as an elucidating example concerning the duration of their existence.

"In all the mechanical watches of various systems they use this said simple secret for regulating what is called the 'tension' of the said spring or the corresponding part of the general mechanism of the watch; and it is called, it seems, the 'regulator.'

"By means of this regulator it is possible to make the mechanism of a watch, wound for instance for twenty-four hours, go a whole month, and on the contrary, thanks to this regulator, it is possible to make the same winding for twenty-four hours finish in five minutes.

"In the common presence of every being existing merely on the basis of Itoklanoz, 'something' similar to the regulator in a mechanical watch is present and is called 'Iransamkeep'; this 'something' means: 'not-to-give-oneself-up-to-those-of-one's-associations-resulting-from-the-functioning-of-only-one-or-another-of-one's-brains.'

"But even if they should understand such a simple secret it will be all just the same; they still would not make the necessary being-effort, quite accessible even to the contemporary beings and thanks to which, by the foresight of Nature, beings in general acquire the possibility of what is called 'harmonious association,' by virtue of which alone energy is created for active being-existence in the presence of every three-brained being and consequently in them themselves. But at the present time, this energy can be elaborated in the presences of your favorites only during their quite unconscious state, that is to say during what they call 'sleep.'

"But in your favorites, specially in your contemporary favorites, who exist constantly passively under the direction of only one of the separate spiritualized parts of their common presence and thereby constantly manifest themselves entirely by their factors for negative properties also lawfully arisen in them, and hence, by negative manifestations, there proceeds in them that same disproportionate expenditure of the contents of their various Bobbin-kandelnosts, that is to say, the possibilities, placed in them by Nature according to law, of action by only one or only two of their brains, are always experienced, in consequence of which the contents of one or two of their Bobbin-kandelnosts are prematurely exhausted; whereupon, just like those mechanical watches in which the winding is run down or the force of their regulators is weakened, they cease to act.

"Sometime later, I shall explain to you in detail not only why, when beings, existing only according to the principle Itoklanoz, exist by the direction of only one or two of their spiritualized sources, and not harmoniously, that is to say, with all three combined, and in agreement, that particular brain of theirs in which there were superfluous associations is prematurely used up in them and consequently dies during the period of its existence, but also why, owing to this, the other Bobbin-kandelnosts also are used up, even without their own action.

"But here you must also know that even on your planet, one still occasionally finds one of your favorites whose duration of planetary existence extends to five of their centuries.

"You will then understand very well, that in the case of certain of your favorites even of recent times, who, by some means or other, find out and correctly transubstantiate in their Reason concerning certain details of the law of association proceeding in the separate brains of beings, and also concerning the reciprocal action of these independent associations, and who exist more or less according to what I have said, the Bobbin-kandelnosts formed in their separate being-brains are not used up, as they are among the other beings there, but their common presence acquires the possibility of existing much longer than the other three-brained beings there.

"During my stay there for the last time, I myself personally met several of these terrestrial contemporary three-brained beings who were already two, three, and even about four of their centuries old. I met them mostly among a small 'brotherhood' of the three-brained beings there, composed of beings from almost all of their what are called 'religions,' and whose permanent place of existence was in the middle of the continent Asia.

"The beings of that brotherhood, it seems, partly elucidated for themselves the mentioned laws of association in being-brains, and in part such information reached them from ancient times through genuine initiates there.

"As for that same contemporary community, whose beings have become the chief victims of that particularly maleficent invention of the beings of the said ancient civilization, they not only now use it in the process of their own existence but they try to infect strongly the beings of all the other communities with the same evil. Moreover, owing to that maleficent sport of theirs, these unfortunates not only still further diminish the duration of their own existence—already trifling without this—but thanks to that action of theirs, they will, in my opinion, eventually entail for their community what quite recently occurred to a large community there named 'Russia.'

"I thought about it during my stay there before my final departure from that planet.

"And I first began thinking about it when I learned that the power-possessing beings also of that no less great contemporary community were already utilizing that maleficent means of theirs, sport, for their own Hasnamussian aims, exactly as the power-possessing beings of the community

Russia had, for their similar aims, utilized what is called 'the-question-of-Russian-vodka.'

"Just as the power-possessing beings of the community Russia then tried, by every kind of artifice, to instill into the weak wills of the ordinary beings the necessity of the intensive use of the said 'Russian vodka,' so also the power-possessing beings of that community England are now already also maneuvering to intrigue the ordinary beings of their community with this same sport and to urge them to it by every means.

"The apprehensions which then arose in me are already, it seems, being justified.

"And I conclude this from the etherogram I recently received from the planet Mars, in which among other things it was said that though there are more than two and a half millions of what are called 'unemployed-beings' in that community England, yet the power-possessing beings there take no measures concerning this, but endeavor to spread still more widely among them that same famous sport of theirs.

"Just as in the large community Russia the contents of all what are called 'newspapers' and 'magazines' used to be always devoted to the question of Russian vodka, so now in that community England, more than half of the text of all their 'evil-sowers' is devoted to that famous sport."

CHAPTER 30
Art

AT THIS place of his tales, Beelzebub became silent and turning suddenly to his old servant Ahoon, who was also sitting there listening to him with the same attention as his grandson Hassein, he said:

"And you, old man, are you also listening to me with the same interest as our Hassein? Weren't you yourself personally with me everywhere on that planet Earth and didn't you see with your own eyes and sense for yourself everything about what I am relating to Hassein?

"Instead of just sitting there openmouthed at my tales, you also tell our favorite something. . . . There is no getting out of it. We have got to tell him all we can about those strange three-brained beings, seeing that they have so intensely interested him.

"Surely you must have been interested in one aspect or another of these queer ducks; well, tell us something just about that aspect."

When Beelzebub had finished speaking, Ahoon, having thought a while, replied:

"After your subtly psychological tales about all these 'unintelligibles,' how can I intrude with my tales?"

And then, with an unusual seriousness and preserving the style and even entire expressions of Beelzebub himself, he continued:

"It is, of course. . . . How shall I put it? My essence even was often thrown out of balance by those strange three-brained beings, who with their 'virtuoso-caperings' nearly always used to supply an impetus for evoking the being-impulse of amazement in one or in another of my spiritualized parts."

And then addressing Hassein, he said:

"All right, dear Hassein!

"I will not, like His Right Reverence, relate to you in detail about any particular oddity of the psyche of those three-brained beings of our Great Universe who have taken your fancy. No, I will only remind His Right Reverence of one factor, the cause of which arose during our fifth stay on the surface of that planet, and which, when we were there for the sixth and last time, had become the chief cause why, in every one of those favorites of yours, from the very first day of their arising until their formation as responsible beings, their ableness of normal being-mentation is step by step distorted and finally transformed almost into a 'Kaltusara.'"

Thereupon, addressing Beelzebub himself, he, with a timid look and in a hesitant tone, continued to speak:

"Don't blame me, your Right Reverence, for venturing to express to you the opinion which has just arisen in me, and which is the outcome of my reflexions on data already perhaps worn too thin for mind-conclusions.

"While relating to our dear Hassein about all the various reasons that have brought it about that the psyche of the contemporary three-brained beings of the planet Earth who have taken his fancy has become transformed, as you once deigned to express yourself, into a mill for grinding out nonsense, you scarcely even mentioned one factor, perhaps more important than the others, which, during recent centuries, has served as the basis for it.

"I intend to speak about that factor which has already become definitely maleficent for the contemporary beings and at the arising of the cause of which, you yourself were present, as I very well remember during our stay then in Babylon; I mean the factor they themselves call 'art.'

"If you should consent in your wisdom to take up that question in detail, then, according to my understanding, our dear Hassein will have perhaps the choicest material for his better elucidation of all the abnormal strange-nesses of the psyche of the three-brained beings, who in most recent times arise on that planet Earth which has interested him."

Having said this and having with the tip of his tail wiped off the drops of sweat which had formed on his forehead, Ahoon became silent and adopted his usual attentive posture.

With an affectionate glance, Beelzebub looked at him and said:

"Thank you, old man, for reminding me of this. It is true that I have scarcely even mentioned that indeed harmful factor—created also by them themselves—for the final atrophy even of those data for their being-mentation which by chance have still survived.

"All the same, old man, though it's true that I have not so far once referred to it, that does not mean that I have not considered it at all. Having still a good deal of time before us during the period of our traveling, I should in all probability, in the course of my subsequent tales to our common favorite Hassein, have remembered in its time about that of which you have reminded me.

"However, perhaps it will be very opportune to speak just now about this contemporary terrestrial art because, as you said, during our fifth stay there in person, I was really a witness of the events which gave rise to the causes of this contemporary evil there and which arose, thanks, as always, to the same learned beings there who assembled in the city of Babylon from almost the whole of the surface of that ill-fated planet."

Having said this, Beelzebub then turned to Hassein and spoke as follows:

"This same already definite idea there, now existing there under the denomination art is, at the present time for those unhappy favorites of yours, one of those automatically acting data the totality of which of itself gradually, and though almost imperceptibly yet very surely, converts them—that is, beings having in their presences every possibility for becoming particles of a part of Divinity—merely into what is called 'living flesh.'

"For an all-round enlightenment of the question about the famous contemporary terrestrial art, and for your clear understanding of how it all came about, you must first know about two facts that occurred in that same city Babylon during our fifth flight in person onto the surface of that planet of yours.

"The first is, how and why I then came to be a witness of the events which were the basis of the reasons for the existence among the contemporary three-brained beings of the planet Earth of that now definitely maleficent notion called art; and the second is which were the antecedent events that in their turn then served as the origin of the arisings of these reasons.

"Concerning the first, I must say that during our stay then in the city of Babylon, after the events I have already related which occurred among always the same learned terrestrial three-brained beings assembled there from almost the whole planet, that is to say, after they had split into several independent groups and were, as I have already told you, already absorbed in a question of what is called 'politics,' and as I intended at that time to leave Babylon and to continue my observations among the beings of the then already powerful community called Hellas, I decided without delay to learn their speech. From then on I chose to visit those places in the city of Babylon and meet those beings there, which would be of most use in my practical study of their speech.

"Once when I was walking in a certain street of the city of Babylon not far from our house, I saw on a large building which I had already many times passed, what is called an 'Ookazemotra,' or, as it is now called, on the Earth, a 'signboard' which had been just put up and which announced that a club for foreign learned beings, the 'Adherents-of-Legominism,' had been newly opened in that building. Over the door hung a notice to the effect that the enrollment of members of the club was still going on, and that all reports and scientific discussions would be conducted only in the local and Hellenic languages.

"This interested me very much, and I thought at once whether it would not be possible for me to make use of this newly opened club for my practice in the Hellenic speech.

"I then inquired of certain beings who were going in or coming out of that building, about the details concerning the club; and, when, thanks to the explanation of one learned being, with whom, as I chanced to find out, I was already acquainted, I had made it all more or less clear to myself, I then and there decided to become also a member of that club.

"Without thinking long about it, I entered the building and passing myself off as a foreign learned being, I requested, as an adherent of Legominism, to be enrolled as a member of the club; I managed to do this very easily, owing to that old acquaintance whom I had met by chance and who, like the others, took me for a learned being like himself.

"Well then, my boy, having thus become what is called a 'full member' of that club, I used afterwards to go there regularly and to talk there chiefly with those learned members who were familiar with the Hellenic speech which I needed.

"As regards the second fact, this proceeded from the following Babylonian events.

"It must be remarked that among the learned beings

of the planet Earth who were then in Babylon and who were gathered there partly by coercion from almost the whole of the planet by the mentioned Persian king, and partly voluntarily on account of the already mentioned famous question of the 'soul,' there were several among the beings brought there by coercion who were not, like the majority, learned beings of 'new formation,' but who, with a sincerity proceeding from their separate spiritualized parts, strove for High Knowledge only with the aim of self-perfection.

"Owing to their genuine and sincere striving, to the corresponding manner of their existence and to their being-acts, these several terrestrial beings had already, even before their arrival in Babylon, been considered initiates of the first degree by those terrestrial three-brained beings worthy to become what are called 'All-the-Rights-Possessing-Initiates-according-to-the-renewed-rules-of-the-Most-Saintly-Ashiata-Shiemash.'

"And thus, my boy, when I began going to the said club, it became quite clear to me, both from the conversations with them and from other data, that these several terrestrial learned beings who sincerely strove to perfect their Reason had from the beginning kept to themselves in the city of Babylon, and never mixed in any of those affairs with which the general mass of these Babylonian learned beings there of that time very soon became involved.

"These several learned beings kept themselves apart there, not only in the beginning when all the other learned beings who were then in the city of Babylon first opened a central place for their meetings in the very heart of the city, and when for their better mutual support both materially and morally, they founded there a central club for all the learned beings of the Earth; but also later on, when the whole body of learned beings was divided into three separate 'sections' and each section had its independent club in one or another part of the city of Babylon, they identified themselves with none of the said three sections.

"They existed in the suburbs of the city of Babylon and scarcely met any of the learned beings from the general mass; and it was only several days before my admittance among them as a member of this club, that they for the first time united for the purpose of organizing the club of the 'Adherents-of-Legominism.'

"These learned beings about whom I am speaking had all without exception been taken to the city of Babylon by coercion and they were for the most part those learned beings who had been taken there by the Persian king from Egypt.

"As I later learned, this uniting of theirs had been brought about by two learned beings who were initiates of the first degree.

"One of these two initiated learned beings of the Earth who had his arising among, as they are called, the Moors, was named Kanil-El-Norkel. The other learned initiated being was named Pythagoras, and he arose from among, as they are called, the Hellenes, those Hellenes who were afterwards called Greeks.

"As it later became clear to me, these two learned beings happened to meet in the city of Babylon and during what is called their 'Ooissapagaoomnian-exchange-of-opinions,' that is to say during those conversations the theme of which was, which forms of being-existence of the beings can serve for the welfare of the beings of the future, they clearly constated that in the course of the change of generations of beings on the Earth a very undesirable and distressing phenomenon occurs, namely, that, during the processes of reciprocal destruction, that is during what are called 'wars' and 'popular risings,' a great number of initiated beings of all degrees are for some reason or other invariably destroyed, and, together with them, there are also destroyed forever very many Legominisms through which alone various information about former real events on the Earth is transmitted and continues to be transmitted from generation to generation.

"When the two mentioned sincere and honest learned beings of the Earth constated what they then called such a 'distressing phenomenon,' they deliberated a long time about it with the result that they decided to take advantage of the exceptional circumstance that so many learned beings were together in one city to confer collectively for the purpose of finding some means for averting at least this distressing phenomenon, which proceeded on the Earth owing to the abnormal conditions of the life of man.

"And it was just for this purpose that they organized that said club and called it the 'Club-of-Adherents-of-Legominism.'

"So many like-thinking beings at once responded to their appeal, that two days after my own admission as a member of this club, the enrollment of new members already ceased.

"And on the day when new members ceased to be admitted, the number of those enrolled amounted to a hundred and thirty-nine learned beings; and it was with this number of members that the club existed until the said Persian king abandoned his former caprice connected with those terrestrial learned beings.

"As I learned after my enrollment as a member of that club, all the learned beings had arranged on the very first day of its opening a general meeting at which it was unanimously resolved to hold daily general meetings, when reports and discussions on the two following questions were to be made: namely, the measures to be taken by the members of the club on their return home for the collection of all the Legominisms existing in their native lands, and for placing them at the disposal of the learned members of this club which they had founded; and secondly, what was to be done in order that the Legominisms might be transmitted to remote generations by some other means than only through initiates.

"Before my enrollment as a member of the club, a great variety of reports and discussions concerning these two mentioned questions had already proceeded at that general meeting of theirs; and on the day of my entry a great deal was said on the question how to obtain the participation in the main task of the club of initiated beings, of the followers of those so-called 'Ways' then called 'Onandjiki,' 'Shamanists,' 'Buddhists,' and so on.

"Well then, on the third day after my enrollment as a member of this club, there was uttered for the first time that word which has chanced to reach contemporary beings there and which has become one of the potent factors for the total atrophy of all the still surviving data for more or less normal logical being-mentation, namely, the word 'art' which was then used in a different sense and whose definition referred to quite a different idea and had quite another meaning.

"This word was uttered in the following circumstances:

"On the day when the word 'art' was used for the first time and its real idea and exact meaning were established among the other reporters, there stepped forward a Chaldean learned being, very well known in those times, named Aksharpanziar, who was then also a member of the club for Legominists.

"As the report of that already very aged Chaldean learned being, the great Aksharpanziar, was then the origin for all the further events connected with this same contemporary art there, I will try to recall his speech and repeat it to you as nearly as possible word for word.

"He then said as follows:

"'The past and especially the last two centuries have shown us that during those inevitable psychoses of the masses, from which wars between states and various popular revolts within states always arise, many of the innocent victims of the popular bestiality are invariably those who, owing to their piety and conscious sacrifices, are worthy to be initiates and through whom various Legominisms containing information about all kinds of real events which have taken place in the past are transmitted to the conscious beings of succeeding generations.

"'Just such pious men as these always become such innocent victims of the popular bestiality only because, in my opinion, being already free within and never wholly identifying themselves as all the rest do, with all the ordinary interests of those around them, they cannot, for that reason, participate either in the attractions, pleasures, and sentiments, or in the similarly clearly sincere manifestations of those around them.

"'And in spite of the fact that in ordinary times they exist normally and in their relations with those around them are always well-wishing in both their inner and outer manifestations and thus acquire in normal periods of everyday life the respect and esteem of those around them, yet when the mass of ordinary people fall into the said psychosis and split into their usual two opposing camps, then these latter, in their state of bestialized reason during their fighting, begin to entertain morbid suspicions of just those who in normal times have always been unassuming and serious; and then, if it should happen that the attention of those under this psychosis should rest a little longer on these exceptional men, they no longer have any doubt whatever that these serious and outwardly always quiet men have undoubtedly also in normal times been nothing more nor less than the "spies" of their present enemies and foes.

"'With their diseased Reasons these bestialized men categorically conclude that the previous seriousness and quietness of such men were nothing else but simply what are called "secrecy" and "duplicity."

"'And the result of the psychopathic conclusions of these bestialized men of one or the other hostile party is that without any remorse of conscience whatever they put these serious and quiet men to death.

"'In my opinion what I have just said has most frequently been the cause why the Legominisms about events which really took place on the Earth have, in the course of their passage from generation to generation, also totally disappeared from the face of the Earth.

"'Well then, my highly esteemed colleagues, if you wish to know my personal opinion, then I shall sincerely tell you with all my being that in spite of all I have told you about the transmission of true knowledge to distant generations through corresponding initiates by means of Legominisms, there is now nothing whatever to be done through these means.

"'Let this means be continued as before, as it has been on the Earth from the dawn of centuries and as this form of transmission by initiates through their "ableness-to-be" was renewed by the great prophet Ashiata Shiemash.

"'If we contemporary men desire at the present time to do something beneficent for men of future times, all we must do is just to add to this already existing means of transmission some new means or other, ensuing from the ways of our contemporary life on the Earth as well as from the many-centuried experience of former generations, in accordance with the information that has come down to us.

"'I personally suggest that this transmission to future generations be made through the human what are called "Afalkalna," that is through various productions of man's hands which have entered into use in the daily life of the people, and also through the human "Soldjinoha," that is through various procedures and ceremonies which have already been established for centuries in the social and family life of people and which automatically pass from generation to generation.

"'Either these human Afalkalna themselves, and in particular those which are made of lasting materials, will survive and for various reasons will be handed down to men of distant generations, or copies of them will pass from generation to generation, thanks to the property which is rooted in the essence of man of giving out as one's own, after having changed some minor detail, one or another of the productions of man which have reached them from long past epochs.

"'In regard to the human Soldjinoha, as for instance various "mysteries," "religious ceremonies," "family-and-social-customs," "religious-and-popular-dances," and so on, then although they often change in their external form with the flow of time, yet the impulses engendered in man through them and the manifestations of man derived from them always remain the same; and thus by placing the various useful information and true knowledge we have already attained within the inner factors which engender these impulses and these useful manifestations, we can fully count on their reaching our very remote descendants, some of whom will decipher them and thereby enable all the rest to utilize them for their good.

"'The question now is only this, by what means can such a transmission through the various human Afalkalna and Soldjinoha as I have described be actualized?

"'I personally suggest that this be done through the Universal Law called the "Law of Sevenfoldness."

"'The Law of Sevenfoldness exists on the Earth and will exist forever and in everything.

"'For instance, in accordance with this Law, there are in the white ray seven independent colors; in every definite sound there are seven different independent tones; in every state of man, seven different independent sensations; further, every definite form can be made up of only seven different dimensions; every weight remains at rest on the Earth only thanks to seven "reciprocal thrusts," and so on.

"'Well then, of the knowledge now existing which we have personally attained or which has reached us from times past, just that knowledge which we shall agree is useful for our remote descendants must be indicated in some way or other in the said human Afalkalna and Soldjinoha, so that in the future it may be perceived by the pure Reason of man by means of this great Universal Law.

"'I repeat that the Law of Sevenfoldness will exist on the Earth as long as the Universe exists, and it will be seen and understood by men in all times as long as human thought exists on the Earth, and it can therefore boldly be said that the knowledge indicated in this manner in the mentioned productions will exist also forever on the Earth.

"'And as regards the method itself, that is to say, the mode of transmission through this Law, in my opinion, it can be actualized in the following way:

"'In all the productions which we shall intentionally create on the basis of this Law for the purpose of transmitting to remote generations, we shall intentionally introduce certain also lawful inexactitudes, and in these lawful inexactitudes we shall place, by means available to us, the contents of some true knowledge or other which is already in the possession of men of the present time.

"'In any case, for the interpretation itself, or, as may be said, for the "key" to those inexactitudes in that great Law, we shall further make in our productions something like a Legominism, and we shall secure its transmission from generation to generation through initiates of a special kind, whom we shall call initiates of art.

"'And we shall call them so because the whole process of such a transmission of knowledge to remote generations through the Law of Sevenfoldness will not be natural but artificial.

"'And so, my highly accomplished and impartial colleagues. . . .

"'It must now be clear to you that if for some reason or another the information useful for our descendants concerning knowledge already attained by men about past events on the Earth fails to reach them through genuine initiates, then, thanks to these new means of transmission which I have suggested, men of future generations will always be able to reflect upon and make clear to themselves, if not everything now already existing, then at least those particular fragments of the common knowledge already existing on the Earth, which chance to reach them through these said productions of the hands of contemporary man as well as through those various existing ceremonies in which, by means of this great Law of Sevenfoldness and with the help of these artificial indications of ours, we shall now put what we wish.'

"With these words the great Aksharpanziar then concluded his report.

"Considerable excitement and noisy discussion followed his speech among all the members of the club of the Adherents of Legominism, and the outcome of it was that they then and there unanimously decided to do as the great Aksharpanziar had suggested.

"A brief interval was then allowed for eating, after which they all assembled again, and the second general meeting of that day continued throughout the night.

"Well, the unanimous decision was then carried, to begin the following day making what are called 'minia-images'—or, as the contemporary three-brained beings call them, 'models'—of various productions; to try to work out the possible and most suitable means of indication, on the principles laid down by the great Aksharpanziar; and thereafter to bring these minia-images or models of theirs to the club for exhibition and exposition to the other members.

"Within the following two days many of them already began bringing the minia-images they had made and showing them with the appropriate explanations; and they also began demonstrating every variety of those acts which beings of that planet had before occasionally performed in the process of their ordinary existence and which they still manifest up till now.

"Among the number of the models they brought and the various being-manifestations they demonstrated were combinations of different colors, forms of various constructions and buildings, the playing on various musical instruments, the singing of every kind of melody, and also the exact representation of various experiencings foreign to them, and so on and so forth.

"Shortly after, for the sake of convenience, the members of the club divided themselves into a number of groups, and each seventh part—which they called a 'day'—of that definite period of time which they called a 'week' they devoted to the demonstration and exposition of their productions in one particular branch of knowledge.

"Here it is interesting to notice that this definite period

of the flow of time, namely, a week, has always been divided on your planet into seven days; and this division was even made by the beings of the continent Atlantis, who expressed in it that same Law of Sevenfoldness with which they were quite familiar.

"The days of the week were then on the continent Atlantis called as follows:

(1) Adashsikra
(2) Evosikra
(3) Cevorksikra
(4) Midosikra
(5) Maikosikra
(6) Lookosikra
(7) Soniasikra.

"These names were changed there many times and at present the beings there name the days of the week thus:

(1) Monday
(2) Tuesday
(3) Wednesday
(4) Thursday
(5) Friday
(6) Saturday
(7) Sunday.

"Well then, as I have already told you, they then devoted each day of the week to the production of one or another specialty, either of their hands or of some other form of consciously designed being-manifestation.

"Namely, Mondays they devoted to the first group, and this day was called the 'day-of-religious-and-civil-ceremonies.'

"Tuesdays were given over to the second group and was called the 'day-of-architecture.'

"Wednesday was called the 'day-of-painting.'

"Thursday, the 'day-of-religious-and-popular-dances.'

"Friday, the 'day-of-sculpture.'

"Saturday, the 'day-of-the-mysteries,' or, as it was also called, the 'day-of-the-theater.'

"Sunday, the 'day-of-music-and-song.'

"On Mondays, namely, on the 'day-of-religious-and-civil-ceremonies,' the learned beings of the first group demonstrated various ceremonies in which the 'fragments-of-knowledge' that had been previously selected for transmission, were indicated by means of inexactitudes in the Law of Sevenfoldness, chiefly in the inexactitudes of the lawful movements of the participants in the given ceremonies.

"For instance, let us suppose that the leader of the given ceremony, the priest, or according to contemporaries, the clergyman, has to raise his arms towards Heaven.

"This posture of his infallibly demands, in accordance with the Law of Sevenfoldness, that his feet should normally be placed in a certain position; but these Babylonian learned beings intentionally put the feet of the said leader of the ceremony not as they should be placed in accordance with this Law, but otherwise.

"And in general it was just in all these 'otherwises' that the learned beings of that group indicated in the movements of the participants in the given religious ceremony, by a conventional what is called 'alphabet,' those ideas which they intended should be transmitted through these ceremonies to the men-beings of their remote descendants.

"On Tuesdays, namely, on the 'day-of-architecture,' the learned beings belonging to the second group brought various models for such proposed buildings and constructions as could endure a very long time.

"And in this case, they set up these buildings not exactly in accordance with the stability ensuing from the Law of Sevenfoldness, or as the beings there were mechanically already accustomed to do, but otherwise.

"For instance, the cupola of a certain construction had,

according to all the data, to rest on four columns of a certain thickness and definite strength.

"But they placed this said cupola on only three columns; and the reciprocal thrust, or, as it is also expressed, the 'reciprocal resistance,' ensuing from the Law of Sevenfoldness for supporting the surplanetary weight, they took not from the columns alone, but also from other unusual combinations ensuing from the same Law of Sevenfoldness with which the mass of the ordinary beings of that time were also already acquainted; that is to say, they took the required degree of resistance of the columns chiefly from the force of the weight of the cupola itself.

"Or still another example; a certain stone, according to all the data established there both mechanically from long-centuried practice and also thanks to the fully conscious calculations of certain beings with Reason there, ought infallibly to have its definite strength corresponding to a certain power of resistance; but they infallibly made and placed this cornerstone so that it did not correspond at all to the mentioned data; but the strength and power of resistance for the support of the superimposed weight required on the basis of the Law of Sevenfoldness they took from the setting of the lower stones, which in their turn they did not lay according to the established custom, but again they based their calculations on the manner of laying the still lower stones, and so on.

"And it was just in these unusual combinations of the laying of stones, ensuing from the Law of Sevenfoldness, that they indicated, also by means of a conventional 'alphabet,' the contents of some or other useful information.

"This group of learned members of the club of the Adherents-of-Legominism further indicated what they wished in their minia-images or models of proposed constructions, by utilizing the law called 'Daivibrizkar,' that is, the law of the action of the vibrations arising in the atmosphere of enclosed spaces.

"This law, which has utterly failed to reach the contemporary three-brained beings of that planet, was then quite familiar to the beings there, that is to say, they were already quite aware that the size and form of enclosed spaces and also the volume of air enclosed in them influence beings in particular ways.

"Utilizing this law, they indicated their various ideas in the following way:

"Let us suppose that according to the character and purpose of some building or other it is required that from the interiors of the given building, in accordance with the Law of Sevenfoldness and with the mechanical practice of centuries, definite sensations must be evoked in a certain lawful sequence.

"Then utilizing the law of Daivibrizkar they combined the interiors of this proposed building in such a way that the required sensations were evoked in the beings who entered them, not in the anticipated familiar lawful sequence but in some other order.

"And it was just in these deviations from the lawful sequence of sensations that they placed whatever they wished in a certain way.

"Wednesdays—the day-of-painting—were devoted to the combining of different colors.

"On those days the learned beings of the given group brought for demonstration every kind of object necessary for domestic use made of such colored materials as could last a very long time; namely, they brought 'carpets,' 'fabrics,' 'chinkrooaries,' that is, drawings made in various colors on specially tanned leather capable of lasting many centuries, and things of similar kind.

"By means of variegated colors of threads, various representations of the nature of their planet and various forms of beings also breeding there were drawn or embroidered on these productions.

"Before continuing to speak about in which way those terrestrial learned beings then indicated various fragments of knowledge in their combinations of various colors, one fact concerning what I am just relating must be noticed—a fact definitely distressing for those favorites of yours and which was also obtained in their presences on account of the same abnormal forms of their daily existence established by them themselves.

"First I wish to explain to you also about the gradual change for the worse in the quality of the formation in them of those 'organs-of-perception' which should be formed in the presence of every kind of being, and about the organ which in this case particularly interests us, the organ for the perception and distinguishing of what is called the 'blending-of-gravity-center-vibrations,' which reach their planet from the spaces of the Universe.

"I am speaking about what is called the 'common-integral vibration of all sources of actualizing,' namely, about that which the learned being Aksharpanziar, of whom I spoke, called the 'white ray' and about the perceptions of impressions from separate 'blendings of gravity center vibrations' which are distinguished by beings as separate what are called 'tonalities-of-color.'

"You must know that at the very beginning of the arising and existence of the three-brained beings of the planet Earth, before the period when the organ Kundabuffer was introjected into them and later when this organ was totally removed from their presences and even after the second Transapalnian catastrophe there, almost up to the time of our third flight in person to the surface of that planet, the said organ was actualized in them with what is called a 'sensibility-of-perception' similar to that which is actualized in the common presences of all ordinary three-brained beings of the whole of our Great Universe.

"Formerly, at the periods mentioned, in all the three-brained beings arising on this planet, this organ was formed with the sensibility of perceiving the mentioned blendings of separate 'gravity-center-vibrations-of-the-white-ray' and of distinguishing one third of the quantity of the 'tonalities-of-color' of all the 'tonalities' obtained in the presences of the planets as well as in all other greater and smaller cosmic concentrations.

"Objective science has already accurately established that the number of separate interblendings of 'gravity-center-vibrations-from-the-common-integral-vibration,' namely, the 'tonalities-of-color,' is exactly equal to one 'Hooltanpanas,' that is to say, according to the calculations of the terrestrial three-brained beings, of five million, seven hundred and sixty-four thousand eight hundred and one tonalities.

"Only a third of this total number of the blendings or tonalities, with the exception of the one tonality which is accessible only to the perception of our ALL-MAINTAINING ENDLESSNESS, that is to say, one million, nine hundred and twenty-one thousand and six hundred tonalities, perceived by the beings as 'differences-of-color,' can be perceived by all the ordinary beings on whatever planet of our Great Universe they arise.

"But if the three-brained beings complete the perfecting of their highest part, their perceiving organ of visibility thereby acquires the sensibility of what is called 'Olooestesnokhnian sight,' then they can already distinguish two-thirds of the total number of tonalities existing in the Universe, which number, according to terrestrial calculation, amounts to three million, eight hundred and forty-three thousand and two hundred differences of tonality of color.

"And only those three-brained beings who perfect their

highest being-part to the state of what is called 'Ishmetch' become able to perceive and distinguish all the mentioned number of blendings and tonalities, with the exception of that one tonality which, as I have already told you, is accessible to the perception only of our ALL-MAINTAINING CREATOR.

"Although I intend to explain to you in detail in the future how and why in the presences of the 'Insapalnian-cosmic-concentrations' every kind of definite formation acquires the property, from evolving and involving processes, of producing various effects upon the mentioned organ of the beings, nevertheless I do not consider it superfluous to touch upon this question also now.

"It is necessary to say, first of all, that according to the completed result of the fundamental cosmic law of the holy Heptaparaparshinokh, that is, that cosmic law which was called by the three-brained beings of the planet Earth of the mentioned Babylonian period the Law of Sevenfoldness, the 'common-integral-vibration' like all the already 'definitized' cosmic formations is formed and consists of seven what are called 'complexes-of-results' or, as it is also sometimes said, of 'seven-classes-of-vibrations' of those cosmic sources, the arising and further action of each of which also arise and depend on seven others, which in their turn arise and depend on seven further ones, and so on right up to the first most holy 'unique-seven-propertied-vibration' issuing from the Most Holy Prime Source; and all together they compose the common-integral-vibration of all the sources of the actualizing of everything existing in the whole of the Universe, and thanks to the transformations of these latter they afterwards actualize in the presences of the cosmic 'Insapalnian-concentrations' the said number of the various 'tonalities-of-color.'

"And as regards the details of the most holy 'unique-seven-propertied-vibrations,' you will understand them only when, as I have already many times promised you, I shall have explained to you in detail in its proper time all about the most great fundamental laws of World-creation and World-maintenance.

"And meanwhile concerning the given case you ought to know that when this said common-integral-vibration, that is, what the terrestrial three-brained beings call the 'white ray,' enters with its presence proper to it into the 'spheres-of-the-possibilities' for its transformation in the presence of an Insapalnian planet, then there proceeds also in it, just as in the case of every already 'definitized' cosmic arising possessing the possibility of still further actualization, that cosmic process called Djartklom, that is, it itself remains as a presence, but its essence, as it were, disintegrates and produces processes for evolution and involution by the separate 'gravity-center-vibrations' of its arising and these processes are actualized thus: one of the gravity-center-vibrations is derived from the others and is transformed into a third, and so on.

"During such transformations, this said 'common-integral-vibration,' that is the white ray, acts with its gravity-center-vibrations upon other ordinary processes proceeding nearby in intraplanetary and surplanetary arisings and decompositions, and, owing to 'kindred-vibrations,' its gravity-center-vibrations dependently upon and in accordance with the surrounding conditions blend and become a part of the whole common presence of these definite intraplanetary or surplanetary formations, in which the said processes proceed.

"Well then, my boy, during the periods of my descent in person to the planet Earth, I, at first without any conscious intention on the part of my Reason, and later already quite intentionally, noticed and finally definitely constated the progressive deterioration in all of them of this 'being-organ' also.

"Deteriorating century by century, the 'sensibility-of-perception' of that organ also—namely, the organ by means of which there chiefly proceeds for the presences of the three-brained beings what is called the 'automatic-satiation-of-externals' which is the basis for the possibility of natural self-perfecting—had reached such a point that at the time of our fifth stay there during the period called by the contemporary beings there the period of the 'Greatness-of-Babylon,' that organ of theirs could perceive and distinguish the blending of the gravity-center-vibrations of the white ray at most up to the third degree only of what are called its 'sevenfold-strata,' that is up to only 343 different 'tonalities-of-color.'

"Here it is interesting to note that quite a number of the three-brained beings of the Babylonian epoch themselves already suspected the gradual deterioration of the sensibility of that organ of theirs, and certain of them even founded a new society in Babylon that started a peculiar 'movement' among the painters of that time.

"This peculiar movement of the painters of that time had the following program: 'To-find-out-and-elucidate-the-Truth-only-through-the-tonalities-existing-between-white-and-black.'

"And they executed all their productions exclusively utilizing only the tonalities ensuing from black up to white.

"When I got to know of that particular movement of painting there in Babylon, its followers were already using for their productions about fifteen hundred very definite shades of what is called the 'color gray.'

"This new movement in painting there, among the beings who were also striving to learn the truth at least in something, made what is called a 'great stir'; and it was even the basis for the arising of another and still more peculiar 'movement,' this time among what are called the Babylonian 'Nooxhomists,' among just those beings of that time who studied and produced what are called new 'combinations-of-concentrations-of-vibrations' which act in a definite way on the sense of smell of the beings and which produce definite effects in their general psyche, that is to say, among those beings there who made it their aim to find the truth by means of smells.

"Certain beings who were then enthused by this founded, in imitation of the followers of the said branch of painters, a similar society and the motto of their new movement was: 'To-search-the-truth-in-the-shades-of-smells-obtained-between-the-moment-of-the-action-of-cold-at-freezing-and-the-moment-of-the-action-of-warmth-at-decomposition.'

"Like the painters, they also then found between these said two definite smells about seven hundred very definite shades, which they employed in their elucidating experiments.

"I do not know to what these two peculiar 'movements' then in Babylon would have led and where they would have ceased, if a newly appointed chief of the city, during the time we were there, had not begun prosecuting the followers of that second new 'movement' because with their already sufficiently keen sense of smell they had begun to notice and unwittingly to expose certain of his what are called 'shady dealings,' with the result that he used every possible means to suppress everything connected not only with that second new movement, but with the first as well.

"As regards that organ of theirs about which we began to speak, namely, the organ for the perception of the visibility of other cosmic arisings which were beyond them, the deterioration of its sensibility, continuing also after the Babylonian period, reached the point that during our last stay on the surface of this planet your favorites already had the possibility of perceiving and distinguishing, instead of the one million nine hundred and twenty-one thousand and six hundred 'tonalities-of-color' which they ought to have perceived and distinguished, only the result of the penultimate what is called 'sevenfold-crystallization-of-the-white-ray,' that is forty-nine tonalities, and even then only some of your favorites had that capacity, while the rest, perhaps the majority, were deprived of even this possibility.

"But what is most interesting in respect of this progressive deterioration of that most important part of their common presence is the sorry farce that results, namely, that those contemporary three-brained beings there who can still manage to distinguish the mentioned miserable fraction of the total number of tonalities—namely, merely forty-nine—look down with superior self-conceit and with an admixture of the impulse of pride upon those other beings who have lost the capacity to distinguish even this miserable number, as upon beings with abnormal deficiency in that said organ of theirs; and they call them diseased, afflicted by what is called 'Daltonism.'

"The last seven blendings of the 'gravity-center-vibrations-of-the-white-ray,' then in Babylon just as now among the contemporary beings there, had the following names:

(1) Red
(2) Orange
(3) Yellow
(4) Green
(5) Blue
(6) Indigo
(7) Violet

"Now hear in just which way the learned beings then in Babylon belonging to the group of painters indicated various useful information and fragments of the knowledge they had attained, in the lawful inexactitudes of the great cosmic law then called the Law of Sevenfoldness, by means of the combinations of the mentioned seven independent definite colors and other secondary tonalities ensuing from them.

"In accordance with that definite property of the 'common-integral-vibration,' that is, of the white ray, during the process of its transformations about which I have just spoken and which was already then familiar to the Babylonian learned painters, one of its 'gravity-center-vibrations' or one of the separate colors of the white ray always ensues from another and is transformed into a third, as, for example, the orange color is obtained from the red, and further itself passes in its turn into yellow, and so on and so forth.

"So, whenever the Babylonian learned painters wove or embroidered with colored threads or colored their productions, they inserted the distinctions of the tonalities of the colors in the crosslines as well as in the horizontal lines and even in the intersecting lines of color, not in the lawful sequence in which this process really proceeds, in accordance with the Law of Sevenfoldness, but otherwise; and in these also lawful 'otherwises,' they placed the contents of some or other information or knowledge.

"On Thursdays, namely, the days which the learned beings of this group assigned for 'sacred' and 'popular' dances, there were demonstrated with the necessary explanations every possible form of religious and popular dances, either those already existing which they only modified, or quite new ones which they created.

"And in order that you should have a better idea and well understand in which way they indicated what they wished in these dances, you must know that the learned beings of this time had already long been aware that every posture and movement of every being in general, in accordance with the same Law of Sevenfoldness, always consists of seven what are called 'mutually-balanced-tensions' arising in seven independent parts of their whole, and that each of these seven parts in their turn consists of seven different what are called 'lines-of-movement,' and each line has seven what are called 'points-of-dynamic-concentration'; and all this that I have just described, being repeated in the same way and in the same sequence but always on a diminishing scale, is actualized in the minutest sizes of the total bodies called 'atoms.'

"And so, during their dances, in the movements lawful in their accordance with each other, these learned dancers inserted intentional inexactitudes, also lawful, and in a certain way indicated in them the information and knowledge which they wished to transmit.

"On Fridays, days devoted to sculpture, the learned beings belonging to this group brought and demonstrated what were then called minia-images or models, and which were made from the material there called 'clay.'

"Those minia-images or models which they brought for exhibition and familiarization represented, as a rule, individual beings or various groups of beings either similar to them or of other beings of all kinds of exterior form breeding on their planet.

"Among these productions were also various what are called 'allegorical beings' which were represented with the head of one form of a being there, with the body of another, and with the limbs of a third, and so on.

"The learned beings belonging to this group indicated all that was requisite in the lawful inexactitudes allowed by them in connection with what was then called the 'Law of Dimensions.'

"You must know that to all the three-brained beings of the Earth and also of course to the sculptors of that period, it was already known that, in accordance always with the same great Law of Sevenfoldness, the dimensions of any definite part of any whole being ensue from the seven dimensions of other of his secondary parts, which in their turn ensue from seven tertiary parts, and so on and so forth.

"According to this, each large or small part of the whole totality of the planetary body of a being has exactly proportionately increasing or diminishing dimensions in relation to his other parts.

"For a clear understanding of what I have just said, the face of any three-brained being can serve as a good example.

"The facial dimensions of every three-centered being in general, and also the facial dimensions of the three-centered beings of the planet Earth who have taken your fancy, are the result of the dimensions of seven different fundamental parts of the whole of his body, and the dimension of each separate part of the face is the result of seven different dimensions of the whole face. For instance, the dimensions of the nose of any being are derived from the dimensions of the other parts of the face, and on this nose in its turn there are actualized seven definite what are called 'surfaces' and these surfaces also have seven lawful dimensions down to the said atom itself of this face of theirs, which as I have said is one of the seven independent dimensions composing the dimensions of the whole planetary body.

"In the deviations from these lawful dimensions, the learned sculptors among the members of the Adherents-of-Legominism then in the city of Babylon indicated all kinds of useful information and fragments of knowledge already known to them which they intended to transmit to the beings of remote generations.

"On Saturdays—the day-of-mysteries, or the day-of-the-theater—the demonstrations produced by learned members of this group were the most interesting, and, as it is said, the most 'popular.'

"I personally preferred these Saturdays to all the other days of the week and tried not to miss one of them; and I preferred them because the demonstrations arranged on those days by the learned beings of that group frequently provoked such spontaneous and sincere laughter among all the other terrestrial three-centered beings who were in the given section of the club, that I sometimes forgot among which three-centered beings I was, and that being-impulse manifested itself in me which is proper to arise only in one-natured beings like myself.

"At the outset the learned beings of that group demonstrated before the other members of the club various forms of being-experiencings and being-manifestations. Then, later, they collectively selected from all that was demonstrated what corresponded to the various details of one or another already existing mystery, or of one newly created by themselves; and only after all this did they indicate in those being-experiencings and manifestations reproduced by them what they wished, by means of intentionally allowed deviations from the principles of the Law of Sevenfoldness.

"Here it is necessary to notice that although in former epochs mysteries occasionally containing many instructive notions chanced to reach some of their generations mechanically and sometimes passed from generation to generation to beings of very remote generations, yet those mysteries in the contents of which the learned members of the club of the Adherents-of-Legominism then intentionally placed varied knowledge, calculating that it would reach beings of very remote generations, have during recent times almost totally ceased to exist.

"These mysteries there incorporated in the process of their ordinary existence centuries earlier already began gradually to disappear soon after the Babylonian period. At first their place was taken by what are called their 'Kesbaadji,' or, as they are now called there on the continent Europe, 'puppet shows' (Petrushka); but, afterwards they were finally ousted by their still existing 'theatrical-shows' or 'spectacles' which are there now one of the forms of that said contemporary art of theirs which acts particularly perniciously in the process of the progressive 'shrinking' of their psyche.

"These 'theatrical spectacles' replaced the mysteries after the beings at the beginning of the contemporary civilization—to whom only 'a-fifth-to-a-tenth' was passed down of the information about how and what these said Babylonian learned mysterists had done—began to think of imitating them in this also and set about doing, as it were, the same.

"From that time on, the other beings there called these imitators of the mysterists, 'players,' 'comedians,' 'actors,' and, at the present time, they already call them 'artists,' of whom I may say very many have sprung up during recent times.

"And these learned beings of that time belonging to the group of the mysterists indicated various useful information and the knowledge already attained by them, by means of what are called 'currents-of-associative-movements' of the participants in these mysteries.

"Although the three-brained beings of your planet then already well knew about the laws of the 'currents-of-associative-movements,' yet absolutely no information whatsoever concerning these laws has passed to the contemporary three-brained beings.

"As this said 'currents-of-associative-movements' does not proceed in the presences of the three-brained beings who have taken your fancy, as it generally proceeds in the presences of other three-brained beings, and as there were quite special reasons there for this, proper to them alone, I must therefore first of all explain it to you in rather more detail.

"The process is the same as that which also proceeds in us, but it proceeds in us when we are intentionally resting to allow the whole functioning of our common presence freely to transform, without hindrance by our will, all the varieties of being-energy required for our all-round active existence, whereas in them these said various being-energies can now arise only during their total inactivity, that is during what they call their 'sleep,' and then of course only 'after-a-fashion.'

"Owing to the fact that they, like every other three-brained being of the whole of our Great Universe, have three separate independent spiritualized parts, each of which has, as a central place for the concentration of all its functioning, a localization of its own which they themselves call a 'brain,' all the impressions in their common presences whether coming from without or arising from within are also perceived independently by each of these 'brains' of theirs, in accordance with the nature of these impressions; and afterwards, as it is also proper to proceed in the presences of every kind of being without distinction of brain-system, these impressions together with previous impressions compose the total and thanks to occasional shocks evoke in each of these separate 'brains' an independent association.

"So, my boy, from the time when these favorites of yours completely ceased consciously to actualize in their common presences the 'being-Partkdolg-duty,' thanks only to the results of which what is called sane 'comparative mentation' as well as the possibility of conscious active manifestation can arise in beings from various associations, and from the time when their separate 'brains,' associating now quite independently, begin engendering in one and the same common presence three differently sourced being-impulses, they then, thanks to this, gradually, as it were, acquire in themselves three personalities, having nothing in common with each other, in respect of needs and interests.

"Rather more than half of all the anomalies arising in the general psyche of your favorites, particularly those of recent times, are due in the first place to their having in their entire presence a process of three different kinds of independent associations evoking in them the being-impulses of three localizations of different kinds and of different properties; and secondly, because there is a connection between these three separate localizations in them as there is also in general in the presences of every kind of three-brained being predetermined by Great Nature for other what are called 'common-presence-functionings'; and thirdly, because from everything perceived and sensed, that is from every kind of shock, associations of three different kinds of impressions proceed in the three said localizations in consequence of which three totally different kinds of being-impulses are evoked in one and the same whole presence; then, on account of all this, a number of experiencings are nearly always proceeding in them at one and the same time, and each of these experiencings by itself evokes in the whole of their being an inclination for a corresponding manifestation, and in accordance with the definite parts of their total presence a corresponding movement is thus actualized.

"Just these said differently sourced associative experiencings proceed in their common presences and ensue one from the other also in accordance with the same Law of Sevenfoldness.

"The learned members of the club of the Adherents-of-Legominism belonging to this group then in Babylon, indicated what they wished in the movements and in the actions of the participants in the mysteries in the following way:

"For instance, suppose that in order to fulfill his role in the given mystery, according to lawful associations, a participant evoked in one or another of his 'brains' some new impression or other, he was bound to react by some or other definite manifestation or movement; but he would intentionally produce this manifestation or movement not as he ought to have produced it, according to the Law of Sevenfoldness, but otherwise, and in these 'otherwises' they inserted in a certain way whatever they considered necessary for transmission to distant generations.

"In order, my boy, that you should have a concrete representation of these Saturday demonstrations, at which I was always glad to be present in order to rest from my intense activities at that time, I will give you an illustrative example of how these learned mysterists demonstrated before the other learned members of the club of the Adherents-of-Legominism various being-experiencings and manifestations according to the flow of associations, from among the number of which fragments for future mysteries were selected.

"For these demonstrations, they constructed in one of the large halls of the club a specially raised place which they then called the 'reflector-of-reality,' but beings of subsequent epochs to whom the information concerning these Babylonian learned mysterists chanced to be transmitted and who began imitating them and doing as it were the same, called and still call their constructions of a similar kind 'stages.'

"Well, then, two of the participants would always come upon these 'reflectors-of-reality' or stages, first; and then usually one of them stood for a while and, as it were, listened to his own what is called 'Darthelhlustnian' state, or, as it is sometimes otherwise said, to the state of his own inner 'associative-general-psychic-experiencings.'

"Listening in this way, he would make it clear to his Reason, for instance, that the sum total of his associating experiencings emerged in the form of an urgent inclination to hit another being in the face, the sight of whom had always served as the cause for the beginning of the association of those series of impressions present in him which had always evoked in his general psyche disagreeable experiencings offensive to his own self-consciousness.

"Let us suppose that these disagreeable experiencings always proceeded in him when he saw someone who was then called 'Irodohahoon,' which professional there contemporary beings now call a 'policeman'!

"Having then made this Darthelhlustnian psychic state and inclination of his clear to his Reason, but at the same time being on the one hand well aware that in the existing conditions of external social existence it was impossible for him to gratify his inclination to the full, and, on the other hand, being already perfected by Reason and being well aware of his dependence on the automatic functioning of the other parts of his common presence, he clearly understands that on the gratification of this inclination of his depends the fulfillment of some imminent and important being-duty of his, of great importance to those around him; and having thought over everything in this way, he decides to gratify this urgent inclination of his as best he can by at least doing a 'moral injury' to that Irodohahoon by evoking in him associations that would lead to unpleasant experiencings.

"With this object in view, he turns to the other learned

being who has come onto the stage with him, and treating him now as an Irodohahoon or policeman, he would say:

"'Hi! you! Don't-you-know-your-duty? Don't-you-see-that-there . . . ?' pointing with his hand at that moment in the direction of another small room of the club where were the other participants of the demonstrations of that day, 'Two-citizens-a-"soldier"-and-a-"cobbler"-are-fighting-in-the-street-and-disturbing-the-public-peace-and-here-you-are-leisurely-strolling-about-imagining-yourself-God-knows-who-and-leering-at-the-passing-wives-of-honest-and-respectable-citizens! Just-you-wait-you-scamp! Through-my-chief-the-city's-chief-physician-I-shall-report-to-your-chief-your-negligence-and-breach-of-duty!'

"From that moment, the learned being who had spoken would become a physician, because he had chanced to call his chief the head physician of the city, while the second learned being whom the former had called a policeman would assume the role of a policeman. Two other participating learned beings were then immediately called from the other room by the one who assumed the role of policeman, and they assumed the roles of cobbler and soldier respectively.

"And these two latter learned beings assumed and had to manifest themselves in just those roles, namely, one in the role of a soldier and the other in the role of a cobbler, only because the first learned being, having himself in accordance with his Darthelhlustnian state assumed the role of a physician, had called them soldier and cobbler respectively.

"Well then, these three learned beings who were thus cast impromptu by the fourth learned being for fulfilling every kind of perception and manifestation, which had to flow by law, of types foreign to them, or, as your favorites say, of 'strange roles,' namely, of the roles of cobbler, soldier, and policeman, further produced their experiencings, and, from them, their reflex manifestations, thanks to the being-property in them called 'Ikriltazkakra'—a property also well known to the learned beings of the planet Earth of that period, who were already able to perfect their presences up to the ableness of actualizing this property.

"Three-centered beings can acquire this said being-property called Ikriltazkakra only if there is already personally acquired in their presences what is called 'Essoaieritoorassnian-will,' which in its turn can be obtained thanks to always the same being-Partkdolg-duty, that is, to conscious labors and intentional sufferings.

"So it was in this way that the learned members of the group of the mysterists then in Babylon became players of strange roles and demonstrated before the other learned members of the club the experiencings and the actions ensuing from them, which were produced in accordance with the directing of their well-informed Reason.

"And thereafter, as I have already said, they, together with the other learned members of the club of the Adherents-of-Legominism who were present, selected the corresponding for their aim from among the being-impulses demonstrated in such a way, which according to the law of the flowing of different-sourced associations, had to be experienced and manifested in the definite actions of the beings, and only then did they include those selected in the details of some mystery or other.

"Here it is very important to emphasize that then in Babylon the three-brained learned beings who belonged to the group of the mysterists did indeed reproduce in action amazingly well and accurately the subjective particularities of the perceptions and manifestations of various types foreign to them.

"They reproduced them well and accurately not only because as I have already explained they possessed the being-property Ikriltazkakra, but also because the learned beings of the planet Earth of that time were very well aware of what is called the 'law-of-typicality,' and that the three-brained beings of their planet are ultimately formed into twenty-seven different definite types, and also in which cases what had to be perceived and how it had to be perceived, and how they had to manifest themselves.

"Concerning the said being-property I have just called Ikriltazkakra, I must add further that just this property alone gives beings the possibility of restraining themselves within the limits of all these impulses and promptings which are evoked at any given moment in their common presences by the associations flowing in that brain in which they themselves have consciously given the start for the associations of one or another series of impressions already present in them; and it is only thanks to this property that beings have the possibility of perceiving every kind of detail of the psyche of the type they have already previously well studied and of manifesting themselves similarly to it and fully impersonating it.

"In my opinion, it is on account of the absence of just that property that the majority of all these anomalies have arisen which have resulted in the three-brained beings of the planet Earth, who have taken your fancy, becoming possessed of such a strange psyche.

"You must know that in the presences of the three-brained beings of the present time, as well as in the presences of every kind of three-brained being in general, every new impression is accumulated in all their three separate 'brains' in the order of what is called 'kindredness,' and afterwards they take part with the impressions already previously registered in the associations evoked in all these three separate brains by every new perception in accordance with and in dependence upon what are called the 'gravity-center-impulses,' present at the given moment in their whole presence.

"So, my boy, in view of the fact that there continue to flow in the presences also of your contemporary favorites three kinds of independent associations which also continue to evoke different kinds of being-impulses, and at the same time that they have already entirely ceased the conscious actualization in their presences of all those cosmic results by means of which alone the mentioned being-property can be acquired in three-brained beings, then, in consequence, the common presence of each of your contemporary favorites during the process of his existence consists, as I have already told you, as it were, of three quite separate personalities—three personalities which have and can have nothing in common with each other, either in respect of the nature of their arising or in respect of their manifestations.

"Hence it is that there just proceeds in them that particularity of their common presence which is that with one part of their essence they always intend to wish one thing; at the same time with another part they definitely wish something else; and thanks to the third part, they already do something quite the contrary.

"In short, what happens in their psyche is just what our dear teacher Mullah Nassr Eddin defines by the word a 'mix-up.'

"Concerning the demonstration of the Babylonian learned beings of that time belonging to the group of the mysterists, I must add that in the course of the action the number of participants was gradually increased by their other colleagues, as required by various voluntary associative happenings.

"And besides all this, every participant thus engaged in the fulfillment of the perceptions and accurate automatic manifestations that happened to be connected with him and were proper to a personality of a type quite foreign to him had, at the same time that he was fulfilling that role, to give himself time, under some plausible pretext, to change into a corresponding costume.

"And they changed their costume in order to manifest themselves more clearly and more strikingly in the fulfillment of the roles they assumed, so that the other learned members present of the club of the Adherents-of-Legominism who checked and selected the fragments of the future mysteries could more easily and better follow them and make the best selection of everything they saw.

"On Sundays, namely, on the days consecrated to music and singing, the learned beings belonging to this group first produced on various sound-producing instruments, and also with their voices, every kind of what is called 'melody' and then explained to all the other learned beings how they indicated in these works of theirs whatever they wished.

"They also had it in view to implant these works of theirs in the customs of various peoples, calculating that these 'melodies' they created, passing from generation to generation, would reach men of remote generations who, having deciphered them, would discover the knowledge put into them and that had already been attained on the Earth, and would also use it for the benefit of their ordinary existence.

"For your understanding of how the learned beings there of that group made their indications in the 'musical' and 'vocal' productions of theirs, I must first explain to you about certain special particularities of the perceptive organ of hearing in the common presences of every kind of being.

"Among the number of these special particularities is the property called 'Vibroechonitanko.'

"You must know that those parts of the brains of beings

which objective science calls 'Hlodistomaticules,' and certain of which on your planet the terrestrial 'learned physicians' call 'nerve-brain-ganglia,' are formed of what are called 'Nirioonossian-crystallized-vibrations,' which in general arise in the completed formation of every being as a result of the process of all kinds of perceptions of their organ of hearing; and later on, these Hlodistomaticules, functioning from the reaction upon them of similar but not yet crystallized vibrations, evoke in the corresponding region which is subject to the given brain, the said Vibroechonitanko or, as it is sometimes called, 'remorse.'

"In accordance with the foresight of Great Nature these said Hlodistomaticules serve in the presences of beings as real factors for assisting the arising of the processes of association at those moments, when either the promptings arisen within are absent or the shocks coming from without do not reach their brains.

"And the as yet noncrystallized 'Nirioonossian-vibrations' in general arise and later enter into the common presence of the beings, either by means of what are called the 'vocal cords' of every kind of being or by means of certain artificial 'sound-producing-instruments' which the beings have invented.

"When these vibrations, arisen from the said sources, enter the presences of the beings they touch the Hlodistomaticules of one or another brain, then, according to the general functioning of the whole being, they produce the said process of 'Vibroechonitanko.'

"The second particularity of the functioning of the perceptive organ of hearing is that in general, by the action of vibrations obtained from the sequence of sounds of every kind of melody, the association is usually evoked in the presences of the beings in one or another of the three brains, just in that brain in which at the given moment what is called 'the-momentum-of-what-was-experienced' is increasing more intensively, and the sequence of the impulses evoked for experiencing usually proceeds in an automatic order.

"The learned musicians and singers then in the city of Babylon combined their melodies in such ways that the sequence of the vibrations of the sounds should evoke in the beings a sequence of associations, and therefore also impulses for experiencings, not in the usual automatic order, that is to say, so that the sequence of vibrations, on entering into the common presence of the beings, should evoke the Vibroechonitanko in the Hlodistomaticules, not of just one brain, as it usually proceeds according to which brain at the given moment the associations predominate, but should evoke it now in one brain, now in another, and now in the third; thus they also provided for the quality or, as they themselves would say, the numbers of the vibrations of the sounds which would affect one or another brain.

"This latter, namely, from which vibrations, in which brain of the beings, which data are formed and for which new perceptions these data might be what are called 'determinants-of-new-resultants,' they were also already quite familiar with.

"Owing to these sequences of sounds which they combined simultaneously in the presences of beings, different kinds of impulses arose, which evoked various quite opposite sensations, and these sensations in their turn produced unusual experiencings in them and reflex movements not proper to them.

"And truly, my boy, the sequence of sounds they combined did indeed affect all the beings into whose presence they entered, exceedingly strangely.

"Even in me, a being cast, as they would say, in another mold, various being-impulses were engendered and were alternated with an unusual sequence.

"It happened in this way because as the sounds of their melodies which they had combined in a definite sequence entered into my common presence, Djartklom proceeded in them, or as it is otherwise said, the sounds were 'sorted out' and acted equally upon all the three variously caused Hlodistomaticules, with the consequence that the associations proceeding in me in the three independent brains—though simultaneously and with an equal intensity of similar associations but differently natured series of impressions—engendered in my presence three quite different promptings.

"For instance, the localization of my consciousness, or as your favorites would say my 'thinking-center,' engendered in my common presence, let us suppose, the impulse of joy; the second localization in me, or my 'feeling-center,' engendered the impulse called 'sorrow'; and the localization of the body itself, or as once again your favorites would call it, my 'moving-center,' engendered the impulse of 'religiousness.'

"And it was just in these unusual impulses engendered in the beings by their musical and vocal melodies, that they indicated what they wished.

"And so, my boy, after all I have already related about this terrestrial contemporary famous art, I imagine you have enough to understand why and how, during the period of my fifth stay in person on your planet, I happened to be a witness of the events of the causes of its arising and in what connection and with what meaning it was pronounced for the first time just then at that period which your contemporary favorites call the 'Babylonian civilization.'

"So I will now already speak about those facts there, after learning which, you will be able clearly to represent to yourself and approximately to understand how greatly the 'logical mentation' in all these three-brained beings who have taken your fancy must have deteriorated in so short a time that without any what is called 'constancy-of-self-individuality' they have submitted to be made 'slaves' of those few from among their midst who are called 'wastrels,' and who, in consequence of the total loss of the divine impulse 'conscience' could for their egoistic aims create from this 'empty word' art which chanced to reach them, also such a 'sure-fire-factor' in all of them for the final atrophy of all the data that still survived in them for 'conscious-Being.'

"When during the period of my sixth and last stay there in person, I heard everywhere about this contemporary art of theirs and came in contact with its results, and when I made clear to myself just what it was all about, then having recalled my Babylonian friends of that time and about their good intentions toward their remote descendants, I made clear to myself more in detail as opportunities occurred just which results were obtained from all that of which I happened then to be a witness, and about which I have just been telling you.

"Initiating you now into the impressions, hidden from strangers and which became fixed in my common presence, and which were the result of my conscious perceptions during my last stay there in person on the surface of your planet concerning this contemporary art of theirs, my 'I' with an arisen and profound being-impulse of regret must now emphatically state that of all the fragments of knowledge already attained by the beings of the Babylonian civilization—which fragments, it must be allowed, also contained a great deal—absolutely nothing has reached the beings of contemporary civilization for the benefit of their ordinary being-existence, apart from a few 'empty words' without any inner content.

"Not only absolutely nothing whatever reached them of all the various fragments of general knowledge already then known on the Earth, which the learned beings the Adherents-of-Legominism indicated in lawful divergences from the sacred law of Heptaparaparshinokh, or, as they called it the Law of Sevenfoldness, but in the interval of time between these two civilizations of theirs their being-rumination has so deteriorated that they now already do not know nor even suspect the existence of such an all-universal law on their planet.

"And as regards this word art itself, upon which, thanks to the strangeness of their Reason, there has been 'piled up' during this time, as they themselves would say, 'devil-knows-what,' I must tell you that my special investigations regarding this word made it clear to me that when this word among the other words and separate expressions used by the learned beings of that time also began automatically to pass from generation to generation and chanced to get into the vocabulary of certain three-brained beings there, in whose presences, owing to various surrounding circumstances, the crystallizations of the consequences of the properties of the organ Kundabuffer proceeded in that sequence and 'reciprocal-action,' as a result of which they predisposed the arising in their common presences of data for the Being of Hasnamuss-individuals; then this said word for some reason or other happening to please just this kind of three-brained being there, they began using it for their egoistic aims, and gradually made from it that very something which, although it continues to consist of, as it is said, 'complete vacuity,' yet has gradually collected about itself a fairylike exterior, which now 'blinds' every one of these favorites of yours who keeps his attention on it only a little longer than usual.

"Besides this word art, from among the number of other definite words used in their discussions by the learned beings there in Babylon who were members of the club of the Adherents-of-Legominism there also passed automatically from generation to generation quite a number of other words and even several what are called 'foggy notions' çoncerning certain definite understandings of that time.

"Among the latter, both in respect of its name and caricature-like imitations, are their contemporary theaters now existing there.

"You remember, I have already told you that both the hall and the demonstrations themselves of the learned beings belonging to the group of mysterists then at Babylon were designated by the word 'theater.'

"If I now explain to you a little more in detail concerning this contemporary theater of theirs, then perhaps you will have enough material for the elucidation, first of all, concerning what came of all the good intentions and efforts of the learned beings of the Babylonian period; and secondly, what had passed from all that had already been attained in respect of true knowledge, from the times of that 'Babylonian culture' to the beings of this contemporary 'European culture,' in which the said art has become mainly covered with the mentioned fairylike exterior; and thirdly, you will sense certain aspects of the maleficence of that contemporary famous art of theirs.

"A certain amount of information concerning the activity of the group of the mysterists, the learned members of the club of the Adherents-of-Legominism, also reached, as I have just told you, the beings of the contemporary epoch, who, wishing to imitate them also in this, began building for this purpose special halls which they also called 'theaters.'

"The three-brained beings of the contemporary civilization quite frequently assemble in considerable numbers in these theaters of theirs in order to observe and presumably to study the various prepared manifestations of their 'actors,' as they have quite recently begun to call them, just as the other learned members of the club of the Adherents-of-Legominism studied then in Babylon the reproductions of the learned beings of the group of the mysterists.

"These theaters of theirs came to have a significance of the greatest importance in the ordinary process of existence of your favorites, and on account of this they built particularly large buildings for this purpose which rank in most of their contemporary cities as the most remarkable constructions.

"It will do no harm, I think, to comment here upon the misunderstanding connected with the word 'artist.'

"I am bound to comment upon this, because this word was also transmitted to your contemporary favorites from the Babylonian epoch, but it was transmitted not like other words, that is, merely as empty words without sense, but just as one single particle of the consonance of a word then used.

"You must know that the learned beings then in Babylon, the members of the club of the Adherents-of-Legominism, were called by the other learned beings of that time who were well disposed towards them, as they also called themselves, by the name which your contemporary favorites would write as 'Orpheist.'

"This word is composed from two definite roots of words then in use, which in contemporary times would signify 'right' and 'essence.' If someone was called thus, it meant that he 'rightly sensed the essence.'

"After the Babylonian period, this expression also automatically passed from generation to generation with almost the same meaning, but nearly two centuries ago, when the beings of that time began wiseacring with the mentioned data, particularly in connection with that 'empty' word art, and when various what are called 'schools-of-art' arose and everybody considered himself a follower of one or another of those schools, well just then, never having understood its genuine sense and chiefly because among the number of the said schools of art there was also a school of a certain, as the contemporary beings already called him, 'Orpheus,' a figure invented by the ancient Greeks, they then decided to invent a new word defining their 'vocation' more exactly.

"So instead of the said expression Orpheist they just invented the word artist, which had to mean 'he-who-is-occupied-with-art.'

"In order better to represent to yourself all the causes subsequently arising also from that misunderstanding there, you must first of all know that before the second terrestrial Transapalnian catastrophe, when these favorites of yours still arose and prepared themselves normally for responsible existence, they, by means of intentionally producing from themselves corresponding consonants for their what is called 'speech,' that is for mutual intercourse, had and could pronounce—also like all the three-brained beings of all the Great Universe—consonants up to three hundred and fifty-one definite what are called 'letters.'

"But later on, when thanks as always to the same conditions of ordinary being-existence abnormally established by themselves, every kind of property proper to the presences of three-brained beings gradually deteriorated, this 'being-ableness' also deteriorated in them and at such a tempo that whereas the beings of the Babylonian period could use for conversation among themselves only seventy-seven definite consonants, the deterioration continued at such a tempo after the Babylonian period, that five centuries later, the beings there could use at most only thirty-six definite 'letters,' and the beings of certain communities could not reproduce even this number of separate articulate sounds.

"So, my boy, as the information concerning the Babylonian

period passed from generation to generation to the succeeding generations not only by means of what is called 'verbal transmission,' but still also by means of marks on durable materials, that is, as it would be expressed there, by means of 'inscriptions' consisting of conventional signs which then stood for definite 'being-articulate-sounds' or letters—then, when at the beginning of the contemporary civilization certain beings there began to decipher them 'from-a-bit-here-and-a-bit-there' and realized that they could not sound or pronounce many of these definite letters, they then invented what is called a 'written compromise.'

"This mentioned written compromise was that instead of the signs or letters which they could not pronounce, although they understood the sense of this pronunciation, they decided to employ a slightly similar letter of their alphabet at the time, and in order that everybody should understand that it was not that letter but quite another, they always wrote by its side a letter of the ancient Romans, now existing but already meaningless, called in English 'h' and among the contemporary French 'ahsh.'

"From then on, all the other of your favorites began doing the same; they added to each of these suspicious letters this Roman 'inheritance.'

"When this written compromise was invented, they had about twenty-five of these suspicious 'letters,' but in the course of time, as their ableness to pronounce deteriorated with the increase of their wiseacring, the number of the letters they specially invented for such a 'being-ableness' diminished, and by the time the word artist was invented they had already only eight of these letters; and in front of this notorious 'h,' they wrote letters, partly ancient Greek and partly ancient Latin, which they indicated in the following way: 'th,' 'ph,' 'gh,' 'ch,' 'sch,' 'kh,' 'dh,' and 'oh.'

"The basis they had for the arising of such a misunderstanding there was the compromising sign 'ph.'

"And it was the basis because it appeared in the word by which the learned mysterists were designated and also in the word which stood for a personality invented by the ancient Greeks, with whose name, as I have already said, one of the schools-of-art then existing had been connected; and the result of this was that the mentioned representatives of this terrestrial art of that time, with their already now quite bobtailed reason, thought that it was nothing more than the word indicating 'the-followers-of-this-historical-personality-Orpheus,' and as many of them did not regard themselves as his followers, then instead of the mentioned word they just invented the word artist.

"As we have seen, not every inheritance of the ancient Romans turned out to be maleficent for the beings of subsequent generations, but in the given case this little letter 'h' of theirs has been even an inspiring factor for engendering that 'being-ableness' in the presences of such beings of subsequent generations to whom it became already definitely proper to have no initiative or 'ableness' of their own, and they wished and succeeded in substituting for the already long-existing definite expression 'Orpheist' the new word artist.

"Here it is important to inform you concerning a great strangeness there in respect of the mentioned gradual atrophy in the presences of the three-brained beings of this planet of such a 'being-ableness' as the capacity to reproduce the 'consonants' required for verbal intercourse.

"The point is that the tempo of the deterioration of this being-capacity does not proceed in the common presences of beings in the psychic and organic functioning of their planetary bodies in everyone in every generation uniformly; but it alternates, as it were, at different times and on different parts of the surface of this planet, affecting at one time more the psychic and at another time the organic part of the functioning of the planetary body.

"A very good elucidating example of what I have just said is afforded by the sensations of the taste and the capacity to pronounce those two definite consonants or those letters known there at the present time and used among almost all the contemporary beings who breed on all parts of the surface of your planet, and which passed to them through the ancient Greeks from times long past.

"The said two letters were called by the ancient Greeks 'theta' and 'delta.'

"Here it is interesting to notice that your favorites of very ancient times specially used just these two letters for giving distinct names to two quite opposite meanings.

"Namely, they used the letter 'theta' in words which expressed ideas relating to the notion of 'good' and the second letter 'delta' they used in words relating to the notion of 'evil'; as for example, 'theos,' that is 'god,' and 'daimonion,' that is 'demon.'

"The notion and 'taste' of the consonance of both these letters passed to all the beings of the contemporary civilization, but both these different letters, having entirely different essences, they for some reason or other indicated by means of one and the same sign, namely, the sign 'th.'

"For instance, the beings of the contemporary community called Russia, however hard they try, cannot pronounce these said two letters at all, yet, nevertheless, they very definitely sense their difference, and whenever they have to use these letters in words with definite notions, then although the letters they pronounce do not correspond at all, yet they correctly sense their difference and do not use one letter for the other.

"On the other hand, the beings of the contemporary community called England still pronounce each separate letter almost as the ancient Greeks pronounced it; but while doing so sense no difference in them, and without the least embarrassment employ, for words of entirely opposite meanings, one and the same conventional sign in the form of their famous 'th.'

"For instance, when beings of the contemporary England utter their favorite and frequently used expression 'thank you,' you can clearly hear the ancient letter 'theta'; and when they pronounce the word they like no less, and also frequently use—the word 'there'—you hear quite distinctly and definitely the ancient letter 'delta'; but, all the same, for both these letters they use without any what is called remorse the same 'universally paradoxical' 'th.'

"However, I think I've talked enough about terrestrial philology.

"We had better continue to clear up first the causes why it has been customary among your contemporary favorites to have such theaters everywhere, and afterwards what their contemporary actors do in these theaters, and how they manifest themselves there.

"As regards the question why it became the custom among them to assemble, often in considerable groups, in these theaters of theirs, it was in my opinion because these contemporary theaters of theirs and all that goes on in them happen to correspond very well to the abnormally formed common presences of most of these contemporary three-brained beings, in whom there had been already finally lost the need, proper to three-brained beings, to actualize their own initiative in everything, and who exist only according to chance shocks from outside or to the promptings of the consequences crystallized in them of one or other of the properties of the organ Kundabuffer.

"From the very beginning of the arising of those theaters of theirs, they assembled and now assemble in them for the purpose of watching and studying the reproductions of their contemporary 'actors'; no . . . they assemble only for the satisfaction of one of the consequences of the properties of the organ Kundabuffer, a consequence which had been readily crystallized in the common presences of the majority of them, and called 'Oornel,' which the contemporary beings now call 'swaggering.'

"You must know that thanks to the mentioned consequences of the properties of the organ Kundabuffer most of the contemporary beings acquire in their presence a very strange need to evoke the expression in others of the being-impulse called 'astonishment' regarding themselves, or even simply to notice it on the faces of those around.

"The strangeness of this need of theirs is that they get satisfaction from the manifestation of astonishment on the part of others regarding their appearance, which exactly conforms with the demands of what are called 'fashions,' that is to say with just that maleficent custom of theirs, which began there since the Tikliamishian civilization and which has now become one of those being-factors which automatically gives them neither the time nor the possibility to see or sense reality.

"This maleficent custom for them is that they periodically change the external form of what is called 'the-covering-of-their-nullity.'

"Here, by the way, it is interesting to note that it has gradually become the rule in the general process of the ordinary existence of these three-brained beings who have taken your fancy that the changes of the appearance of the mentioned covering are governed by such beings there of both sexes as have already 'become worthy' to become candidates for Hasnamuss-individuals.

"In this respect, the contemporary theaters turned out to be corresponding for your favorites, because it is very convenient and easy for them to show off, as they like to say, their 'chic coiffures' or the 'specially-tied-knot-of-their-cravat,' or the daringly bared, what is called 'Kupaitarian-part-of-their-body,' and so on and so forth, while at the same time they can look at the new manifestations of the 'fashions' already actualized according to the up-to-date indications of those same candidates for 'Hasnamuss-individuals.'

"To get a clear picture of what these contemporary 'actors' do during their 'swaggerings' in these theaters, you must first be told about yet another exceedingly strange 'illness' existing there under the name of 'dramatizacring'; the predisposition to which illness arises in the presences of certain of them thanks only to the carelessness of what are called their 'midwives.'

"This criminal carelessness on the part of their midwives is that in most instances, before doing her job, she calls on the way at the houses of her other clients and drinks there rather more than usual of the 'wine' offered her, so that while she is doing her job she unconsciously makes exclamations, fixed in the process of the ordinary existence of your favorites, like the 'exorcism' of what are called their 'magicians,' and at the moment of, as they say, 'its-appearance-in-God's-world,' the new unfortunate being first imbibes the words of this maleficent exorcism:

"And this exorcism consists of the following words: 'Eh, you, what a mess you've made!'

"Well, my boy, thanks to that criminal carelessness on the part of the midwife, the unfortunate newly appeared being acquires in his presence just that predisposition to the mentioned strange illness.

"If such a three-brained being there who has acquired at his first appearance the said predisposition to the illness of dramatizacring should by the time he reaches the age of a responsible being, know how to write and should wish to write something, then he suddenly gets this strange illness and begins wiseacring on paper, or, as it is said there, 'composing' various what are called 'dramas.'

"The contents for these works of theirs are usually various events which are supposed to have occurred or which might occur in the future, or finally, events of their own contemporary 'unreality.'

"In addition to this, among the symptoms of this peculiar illness there appear in the common presence of the sick being seven other very specific particularities.

"The first is that when this strange illness arises and is already functioning in the presence of a being, particular vibrations are spread around him which act on his environment—as they say—just like the 'smell of an old goat.'

"The second is that from the change of the inner functioning in such a being, the exterior form of his planetary body undergoes the following changes: his nose is held aloft; his arms, as it is said, akimbo; his speech is punctuated by a special cough, and so on.

"The third, that such a being always becomes afraid of certain perfectly harmless, natural, or artificial formations, as for instance, what are called 'mice,' 'hands-clenched-in-a-fist,' 'the-wife-of-the-chief-stage-manager-of-the-theater,' 'the-pimple-on-his-nose,' 'the-left-slipper-of-his-own-wife,' and many other formations outside of himself.

"The fourth particularity makes him lose entirely all capacity for understanding the psyche of the surrounding beings similar to himself.

"The fifth, that inwardly and also in his manifestations he criticizes everybody and everything not connected with him himself.

"The sixth, that the data for the perception of anything objective are more atrophied in him than in all other terrestrial three-brained beings.

"And the seventh and last peculiarity is that there

arise in him what are called 'hemorrhoids,' which, by the way, is the sole thing that he carries with modesty.

"It usually then further happens there that if the sick being has an uncle who is a member of one or other of their 'parliaments,' or if he himself gets acquainted with the widow of a 'former-business-man,' or if the period of his preparation for becoming a responsible being has for some reason or other been spent in such an environment or under such conditions that he has automatically acquired the property called 'slipping-in-without-soap,' then what is called the 'producer,' or, as he is also called, the 'owner-of-lambs,' takes this work of his and orders the mentioned contemporary actors to 'reproduce' it exactly as it was wiseacred by this being who has fallen ill with this strange illness of dramatizacring.

"And these contemporary actors there first reproduce this work themselves alone, without strangers, and they reproduce it until it is exactly as the sick being himself has indicated and as the producer has ordered, and when finally their reproduction proceeds without the participation of their own consciousness and feelings and these contemporary actors themselves are completely transformed into what are called 'living automatons,' then and then only, with the help of those among them who have not yet become entirely living automatons—for which reason they later acquire the name of 'stage managers'—they do the same thing under their direction, but already now in the presence of other ordinary beings assembled in these contemporary theaters.

"Thus you can now, from all I have just said, easily conclude that, besides many definitely maleficent consequences which I shall soon touch upon more in detail, these theaters cannot of course provide anything for that lofty aim which the Babylonian learned beings then had in view when they created for the first time such a form of conscious reproduction of perceptions and of the associative reactions to them of other beings similar to themselves.

"All the same, it must be admitted that from their theaters and from these contemporary actors of theirs they obtained, of course accidentally, for the processes of their ordinary being-existence one 'not-bad-result.'

"To understand in what this 'not-bad-result' consists, I have first to explain another particularity which becomes proper to the common presence of beings who arise according to the principle Itoklanoz.

"In accordance with this principle, the forming in the presence of such beings of energy necessary for what is called their 'waking state' depends on the quality of the associations which proceed in their common presence during their 'complete passivity' or as those favorites of yours say, 'during sleep'; and vice versa, that energy necessary for the 'productiveness' of this said 'sleep,' is formed in its turn also from the associative process proceeding in them during this waking state, which is dependent on the quality or intensity of their activity.

"And this began to apply also to these terrestrial three-brained beings from the time when, as I have already once told you, Great Nature was compelled to substitute for the 'Fulasnitamnian' principle until then proper to their presences, the principle Itoklanoz. Thereupon there was acquired and there is up till now in the process of their existence such a particularity, that if, as it is said among them, they 'sleep well,' then they will also be awake well and, vice versa, if they are awake badly then they will also sleep badly.

"So, my boy, as during recent times they have existed very abnormally, then in consequence that established automatic tempo has even become changed which had previously more or less helped the proper associations to proceed in them, and as a result they now sleep badly and when awake are even worse than before.

"And why these contemporary theaters of theirs with their contemporary actors have become useful for improving the quality of their sleep was due to the following circumstances.

"After the need to actualize being-Partkdolg-duty in themselves had entirely disappeared from the presences of most of them, and every kind of association of unavoidably perceived shocks began to proceed in the process of their waking state only from several already automatized what are called 'series-of-former-imprints' consisting of endlessly repeated what are called 'impressions-experienced-long-ago,' there then began to disappear in them and still continues to disappear even the instinctive need to perceive every kind of new shock vital for three-brained beings, and which issue either from their inner separate spiritualized being-parts or from corresponding perceptions coming from without for conscious associations, for just those being-associations upon which depends the intensity in the presences of beings of the transformation of every kind of 'being-energy.'

"During the latter three centuries the process itself of their existence has become such that in the presences of most of them during their daily existence those 'being-confrontative-associations' almost no longer arise, which usually proceed in three-brained beings thanks to every kind of new perception, and from which alone can data be crystallized in the common presences of three-brained beings for their own individuality.

"Well then, when your favorites, existing in such a manner in their 'daily life,' go to these contemporary theaters and follow the senseless manipulations of these contemporary actors, and receive 'shocks' one after the other from every kind of reminiscence, already previously perceived, of not less senseless and absurd notions, then during this waking state of theirs, they willy-nilly obtain more or less tolerable being-associations, so that when they go home and go to bed they sleep much better than usual.

"Although indeed these contemporary theaters with all that proceeds in them happen to be in this way—but of course only 'for today'—an excellent means for the better sleep of your favorites, nevertheless the objectively evil consequences of these theaters for beings, and particularly for the rising generation, are incalculable.

"The chief harm for them from these theaters is that they are an additional factor for the complete destruction in them of all possibilities of ever possessing the need, proper to the three-brained beings, called the 'need-for-real-perceptions.'

"They have become such a maleficent factor chiefly owing to the following:

"When they go to their theaters and, sitting quietly, look on at every kind of varied many-sided, even though senseless, 'manipulations' and manifestations of their contemporary actors, then although they are in their usual waking state, yet every kind of association, both 'thinking' and 'feeling,' proceeds in them exactly as they proceed during their complete passivity or sleep.

"Namely, when they receive a large number of accidentally corresponding shocks for stimulating the shocks already fixed, and previously perceived and automatized in a series of impressions, and when they reflex these with the functioning of what are called 'organs-of-digestion-and-sex,' then, in consequence, obstacles arise in their presences for the proceeding even of those pitiable conscious being-associations which have already somehow become automatized to produce in them a more or less correct tempo for the transformation of the substances required for that passive existence of theirs, during which there must be transformed substances required for their active existence.

"In other words, when they happen to be in these theaters, they are not entirely in that passive state in which the proceeding of the transformation of substances required for their usual waking state has somehow become automatized in them also, with the result that these contemporary theaters of theirs have come to be for them only an additional maleficent factor for the destruction, as I said, of the 'need-for-real-perceptions.'

"Among many other aspects of the maleficence of this contemporary art of theirs, one of the most obviously ignored, but for all the three-brained beings there one of the very harmful in respect of the possibility of the acquisition of conscious what is called 'individual-being,' is the radiations of the representatives of contemporary art themselves.

"Although these maleficent radiations gradually become there the lot or specific attribute of the representatives of all the branches of their art, yet my detailed 'physio-chemical-investigation' definitely showed me that they are always most maleficent in those mentioned contemporary artists or actors who mime in these contemporary theaters of theirs.

"The maleficence for all the other of your favorites of the totality of the radiations issuing from them has become distinctly noticeable, particularly in recent times of their present civilization.

"Although certain of the ordinary beings there long ago used to become such professionals, yet in former times, on the one hand, every kind of data for Hasnamussian properties did not become completely crystallized in the presences of all these professionals, and on the other hand, other of your favorites obviously instinctively felt the maleficent influence issuing from these professionals and hence were on their guard and behaved towards them in a corresponding manner and very carefully.

"Namely, in former centuries such artists or actors were everywhere relegated by other beings to the lowest caste and were regarded with contempt. And even at the present time there, in many communities, for instance on the continent Asia, it is not proper to shake hands with them, as one almost always does when meeting beings similar to oneself.

"Even up till now in these said communities, it is also considered defiling to sit with such actors at the same table and to eat together with them.

"But the contemporary beings of that continent, which at the present time is the chief place of what is called their 'cultured existence,' not only put these contemporary actors on a level with themselves in their inner relations, but even largely imitate their appearance, and at the present time do so pretty thoroughly.

"The custom of shaving the beard and mustache, now followed by all your favorites, is a very good example for confirming what I have just said.

"I must tell you that in past epochs these terrestrial professional actors had always to go with shaved mustaches and beards during the ordinary process of their existence.

"They had to shave these 'expressers' of masculinity and activity, first of all because, always playing the roles of other beings, they had often to change their appearance and for this they not only had to put on their face a corresponding what is called 'paint' but also to wear wigs and false mustaches and beards, which they could not possibly do if they had their own beards and mustaches; and secondly, because the ordinary beings of all former communities there, considering such actors dirty and a harmful influence and fearing to fail to recognize them if they chanced to meet them in ordinary conditions of existence and of somehow touching them, then promulgated everywhere a severe law, that the beings of the profession of artists or actors have always to shave their mustaches and beards in order to be unmistakable for other beings.

"While explaining just now to you the cause of the arising of the custom of shaving mustaches and beards among actors there, I recall a very sensible what is called 'measure-of-justice' of the three-brained beings of the epoch of the 'Tikliamishian civilization' connected also with the shaving of the hair, but in this case with the hair growing on the heads of the beings there.

"A law was then established and strictly enforced that those petty criminals among them who, after trial and sentence by seven elderly beings of the given district, had been assigned to one of the four already previously established categories of 'immorality' and 'crime'—with which beings all of what are called their 'prisons' are now usually crowded—should for a definite term go about always and everywhere with one of the four corresponding sides of their heads shaved; and, furthermore, any such convicted being was obliged to uncover his head whenever he met or spoke with others.

"It is interesting to note that there then also existed a law of the same kind about shaving the head in regard to the immoral behavior of women.

"And namely, in regard to women, a sentence existed and was also very strictly enforced in this instance by seven elderly local women who had earned respect by their previous conduct.

"And the penal measures for women corresponded to the four manifestations which were then considered there, for women, as the greatest laxity and immorality.

"Namely, if all her neighbors noticed, and all the seven mentioned elderly women confirmed it, that the given woman had behaved without due regard to and negligently towards her family duties, then according to the law she had for a definite term to appear everywhere with painted lips.

"But if various women noticed that she had begun to manifest toward her children with a weakening of her maternal impulses, then under the same conditions those around her condemned her to go about everywhere, also for a definite term, with the left half of her face made up and painted white and red.

"And a woman who attempted to violate her chief what is called 'wifely duty,' that is who deceived or who only tried to deceive her legal husband or who attempted to destroy a new being conceived in her, was obliged by the same procedure to be always and everywhere, also for a definite term, made up and painted white and red, this time over the whole of her face."

At this point of the tales, Beelzebub was interrupted by Ahoon with the following words:

"Your Right Reverence: all your explanations concerning terrestrial art and those three-brained beings there who now practice it and are so to say its representatives, and particularly your elucidations concerning the contemporary 'comedians' there or actors, have suggested to me to use all the impressions fixed in my common presence which I took in during my last stay on the surface of this planet Earth, which has taken our dear Hassein's fancy, and to give him a good piece of very practical advice."

Having said this, Ahoon intended to look expectantly at the face of Beelzebub with his usual glance, that is without blinking for a long time, but as soon as he had noticed his usual, though always sorrowful yet kind and indulgent smile, he, without waiting for the requested permission, and as if confused, at once turned this time to Hassein and spoke as follows:

"Who knows? Maybe, our dear Hassein, you will indeed

have to be on that planet Earth and to exist among those peculiar three-brained beings who have taken your fancy."

And this time, again keeping the style and intonations of Beelzebub himself, he continued:

"It is just for this reason, that I now wish to initiate you for any eventuality into the results of the various impressions which I involuntarily perceived concerning the resulting types as well as concerning the particularities of their manifestations of those said contemporary representatives of art there.

"You must know that those beings who are assumed to be the adepts of this contemporary art which is adorned with a false halo are not only put on their own level by the other three-brained beings there of the contemporary civilization, particularly during the several latter decades, and imitated by them in their exterior manifestations, but they are always and everywhere undeservingly encouraged and exalted by them; and in these contemporary representatives of art themselves, who really in point of their genuine essence are almost nonentities, there is formed of itself without any of their being-consciousness a false assurance that they are not like all the rest but, as they entitle themselves, of a 'higher order,' with the result that in the common presences of these types the crystallization of the consequences of the properties of the organ Kundabuffer proceeds more intensively than in the presences of all the other three-brained beings there.

"Just in regard to such unfortunate three-brained beings the surrounding abnormal conditions of ordinary being-existence are already so established that there are bound to be crystallized in their common presences and to become an inseparable part of their general psyche those of the consequences of the organ Kundabuffer which they now themselves call 'swagger,' 'pride,' 'self-love,' 'vanity,' 'self-conceit,' 'self-enamoredness,' 'envy,' 'hate,' 'offensiveness,' and so on and so forth.

"These enumerated consequences are particularly conspicuously and strongly crystallized in just those contemporary 'representatives-of-art' who are the 'manipulators' of the contemporary theaters there, and they are particularly strongly crystallized in them because, always performing the roles of beings similar to themselves, whose Being and significance in the process of their existence are ordinarily far superior to their own, and also, as I have already said, being themselves really almost nonentities, they with their already wholly automatized Reason, gradually acquire false notions about themselves.

"With such an already quite automatized 'consciousness,' and completely 'nonsensical feelings,' they feel themselves to be immeasurably superior to what they really are.

"I must confess, dear Hassein, that though during our earlier visits to the surface of that planet of yours and also at the beginning of this last sojourn there, I went about everywhere and had various relations with those three-brained beings who have taken your fancy, I scarcely ever felt in my common presence a genuine impulse of being-pity for the infinitely unhappy Fate of these favorites of yours due to circumstances hardly depending on themselves at all.

"But when, towards the end of that sixth sojourn there, certain of them were formed with the kind of inner presence which is now possessed by all the representatives of almost all the branches of that art of theirs, and when these newly arisen types taking part in the process of ordinary being-existence on the basis of equal rights with the other three-brained beings there happened to get into the field of the reception of my sight with their already exaggerated, inner, abnormal, what is called 'being-self-appreciation,' then they served as a shock for the beginning of the arising in me of the impulse of pity, not only for them themselves, but also for all these unfortunate favorites of yours in general.

"Try now to give your attention not to all the three-brained beings in general, nor to the other representatives of their contemporary art, but just to those who have become and have acquired the title of artists or actors.

"Every one of them really being in respect of genuine essence almost what is called a nonentity, that is, something utterly empty but enveloped in a certain visibility, they have gradually acquired such an opinion of themselves, by means of favorite exclamations always and everywhere repeated by them themselves like 'genius,' 'talent,' 'gift,' and still a number of other words empty also like themselves, that it is as if, among similar beings around them, only they have 'divine origin,' only *they* are almost 'God.'

"Now listen and try to transubstantiate for use, at the proper time in the corresponding parts of your common presence, my really very practical advice.

"This practical advice of mine is that, if for some reason or other you should have to exist, particularly in the near future, among the three-brained beings of that planet Earth which has taken your fancy—I say in the near future, because the presences of these three-brained beings who have taken your fancy and all the already fixed exterior conditions of their ordinary being-existence frequently degenerate—and if you should have some work or other there, proper to every conscious three-brained being, which has as its basis the aim of attaining welfare for surrounding beings, and the fulfillment of which depends partly on them themselves, then in whatever community of the contemporary civilization this may proceed, if you should have to meet in the interests of your work these contemporary terrestrial types in what are called their 'circles,' you must never fail to be very, very careful and take every kind of requisite measures to keep on good terms with them.

"Why you must be so careful towards just them, and in

order that you may in general better represent to yourself and understand from every aspect these terrestrial contemporarily arisen types, I must without fail mention two further facts which became quite clear there.

"The first is that, owing as always to the same conditions of ordinary being-existence abnormally established there, and also to the existing 'illusorily inflated' maleficent idea of their famous art, these representatives of art gradually become crowned, as I have already said, with an imaginary halo in the preconceived picturings and notions of other three-brained beings there, and thereby automatically acquire an undeserved authority, in consequence of which all the rest of your favorites always and in everything assume that any opinion they express is authoritative and beyond dispute.

"And the second fact is that these contemporary types who have recently arisen there, acquire, as they are formed, a corresponding inner presence that permits them to become, quite unconsciously on their part, just as easily somebody's slave, as, thanks merely to chance exterior conditions, they can become his worst enemy.

"That is just why I advise you to be very, very careful not to make enemies among them, so as not to make a lot of trouble for yourself in the actualizing of your affairs.

"Well then, dear Hassein, the very 'Tzimus' of my advice to you is that if you should indeed have to exist among the beings of that planet Earth and have dealings with these representatives of contemporary art, then you must first of all know that you must never tell the truth to their face.

"Let Fate spare you this!

"Any kind of truth makes them extremely indignant, and their animosity towards others almost always begins from such indignation.

"To such terrestrial types you must always say to their

face only such things as may 'tickle' those consequences of the properties of the organ Kundabuffer unfailingly crystallized in them and which I have already enumerated, namely, 'envy,' 'pride,' 'self-love,' 'vanity,' 'lying,' and so on.

"And the means of tickling which infallibly act on the psyche of these unfortunate favorites of yours are, as I noticed during my stay there, the following:

"Suppose that the face of one of these representatives of art resembles the face of a crocodile, then be sure to tell him that he is the image of a bird of paradise.

"If one of them is as stupid as a cork, say that he has the mind of Pythagoras.

"If his conduct in some business is obviously 'super-idiotic' tell him that even the great cunning Lucifer could not have thought out anything better.

"Suppose that on his features you see signs that he has several terrestrial diseases from which he is progressively rotting day by day, then with an expression of astonishment on your face ask him:

"'Do, please, tell me, what is your secret for always looking so fresh, like "peaches-and-cream,"' and so on. Only remember one thing . . . never tell the truth.

"Although you have to behave in this manner toward all the beings in general of that planet, it is particularly necessary to do so toward the representatives of all the branches of contemporary art."

Having said this, Ahoon, with the affectation of a Moscow suburban matchmaker at the marriage of her clients, or of the proprietress of a Parisian fashion workroom in what is called a 'high-life-café,' began rearranging the folds of his tail.

And Hassein, looking at him with his usual sincerely grateful smile, said:

"Very many thanks to you, dear Ahoon, both for your advice and, in general, for your elucidation of certain details of the strangeness of the psyche of the three-brained beings of that in all respects ill-treated planet of our Great Universe."

And then he turned to Beelzebub himself with the following words:

"Please tell me, kind Grandfather. Is it really possible that nothing has resulted from the intentions and efforts of those Babylonian learned beings and that indeed, nothing whatsoever has passed of those fragments of knowledge which were already then known on the Earth to the contemporary three-brained beings of that strange planet?"

At this question of his grandson, Beelzebub said as follows:

"To the great sorrow of everything existing in the Universe, scarcely anything has survived, my boy, from the results of their labors, and hence nothing has become the property of your contemporary favorites.

"The information they indicated in the said manner passed from generation to generation, only, in all, for a few of their succeeding centuries.

"Thanks to their chief particularity, namely, to the 'periodic-process-of-reciprocal-destruction,' there almost wholly disappeared from amongst the ordinary beings there, soon after the period of the 'Babylonian-magnificence,' not only the Legominism concerning the keys to the lawful inexactitudes in the Law of Sevenfoldness contained in each of the branches of the 'being-Afalkalna' and 'Soldjinoha,' but, as I have already told you, there gradually also disappeared even the very notion of the Universal Law of the holy Heptaparaparshinokh, which in Babylon they then called the Law of Sevenfoldness.

"Every kind of conscious production of the beings of the Babylonian period was gradually destroyed, partly owing to decay from time and partly owing to the processes of 'reciprocal destruction,' that is to say, to that degree of that psychosis of theirs called the 'destruction-of-everything-existing-within-the-sphere-of-the-perception-of-visibility.'

"Thanks chiefly to these two causes, almost all the consciously actualized results of the learned beings of the Babylonian epoch gradually disappeared from the surface of that ill-fated planet and at such a tempo that after three of their centuries scarcely any of them were left.

"It must also be noticed that, thanks to the second mentioned cause, there also gradually diminished and finally almost entirely ceased the employment of that new form—which had been established since Babylonian times—for the transmission of information and various fragments of knowledge to subsequent generations, through the beings they called 'Initiates-of-Art.'

"About the disappearance there of just that practice of certain beings becoming Initiates-of-Art I know very well, because just before my departure forever from that planet I had to elucidate this very carefully for another aim of mine.

"And for the purpose of making this clear, I even specially prepared a very good 'Tiklunia' from among the beings there of the female sex and made these elucidations of mine through her.

"Tiklunias were formerly called there 'pythonesses' but contemporary ones are now called 'mediums.'

"So then, I made it clear that there in most recent times only four of such beings, Initiates-of-Art, still remained by means of whose what is called 'immediate-line-of-inheritance' the keys to the understanding of the ancient art still continue to be transmitted, and this transmission by inheritance now proceeds there under very complex and arcane conditions.

"Of these four contemporary initiated beings, one comes from amongst those who are called 'redskins' who dwell on the continent America; another, from among the beings dwelling on what are called the Philippine Islands;

the third, from the beings of the continent Asia, from the country called 'The-Source-of-the-River-Pianje'; and the fourth and last, from amongst those who are called 'Eskimos.'

"Now listen why I used the expression 'almost,' when I said that at the end of three of their centuries after the Babylonian period there 'almost' entirely ceased to exist every kind of conscious and automatic reproduction of the being-Afalkalna and Soldjinoha.

"The point is that two branches of the conscious hand-productions of the beings of the Babylonian period chanced upon favorable conditions and some of them passed from generation to generation partly consciously and partly automatically on the part of the transmitting beings.

"One of the said two branches recently ceased to exist; but the other has even reached certain beings of contemporary times almost unchanged.

"This branch which reached beings of contemporary times is called there 'sacred dances.'

"And thanks to this branch alone, which survived from the period of the Babylonian learned beings, a very limited number of three-brained beings there now have the possibility, by means of certain conscious labors, to decipher and learn the information hidden in it and useful for their own Being.

"And the second mentioned branch which recently ceased to exist was that branch of the knowledge of the Babylonian learned beings which they called the 'combination-of-different-tonalities-of-color' and which the contemporary beings now call 'painting.'

"The passing of this branch from generation to generation proceeded almost everywhere but, though gradually disappearing also everywhere with the flow of time, it yet proceeded in quite recent times at a still quite regular tempo both consciously and automatically only among the beings of the community called 'Persia.'

"And it was only just before my last departure from that planet of yours, when the influence of beings of a similar profession from the contemporary 'European culture' began to become noticeable also there in Persia, and when the beings of that profession in the community Persia began to wiseacre, that such a transmission entirely ceased.

"It must also be noticed that in spite of all this, not a few of the still surviving productions of the Babylonian times reached the beings of the contemporary civilization, chiefly the beings breeding on the continent Europe. But these productions which reached the beings of this contemporary civilization—and not originals but only half-decayed copies made by their recent ancestors who had not become entirely what are called 'plagiarists'—they simply, without suspecting the 'well-of-wisdom' concealed in them and without taking corresponding practicable measures, stuffed into what are called 'museums' where these old copies are gradually either totally destroyed or partially mutilated by frequent copyings from them, made by means of various eroding and oxidizing compositions as, for instance, 'alabaster,' 'fish glue' and so on, only so that the copyists might swagger before their friends or cheat their teachers, or achieve some other Hasnamussian aim.

"It must in fairness be remarked that now and again certain beings also of the contemporary civilization have suspected that something was concealed in the productions which chanced to reach them in the original, specially created then in Babylon by the members of the club of the Adherents-of-Legominism, or in those copies which were made during their transmission from generation to generation by various conscientious professionals, that is by such professionals to whom, as I have already said, it was still not quite proper to plagiarize, and who therefore did not resort to the detailed remaking of others' productions in order to give them out as their own, and thereafter while searching very seriously for this something, certain of those inquiring beings of that European civilization even found in them a certain definite 'something-or-other.'

"For instance, at the beginning of the contemporary European civilization one of these beings, a certain monk named Ignatius, who had formerly been an architect, attained even to the possibility of deciphering the hidden knowledge and useful information in the productions of almost all the branches of what was already called 'ancient' art, which had reached him from the Babylonian epoch.

"But when this monk Ignatius was about to share what is called this said 'discovery' of his with other beings there like himself, namely, with two of his what are called comrades, monks—together with whom he as a specialist had been sent by his Abbot for the purpose of directing the laying of what are called the 'foundations' of a temple, which later became famous—then, for some trifling reason ensuing from the consequences of one of the properties of the organ Kundabuffer crystallized in them called 'envy,' he was murdered while asleep and his planetary body was thrown into the water-space surrounding that small island on which it was proposed to erect the said temple.

"The said monk Ignatius arose and was formed for the Being of a responsible being, on the continent Europe; but when he reached the age of a responsible being, then with the aim of enriching himself with information concerning the profession which he had made the aim of his existence, namely, the profession there called 'architecture,' he left for the continent of Africa. And just he it was who entered as a monk into the 'brotherhood' which existed on that continent Africa, under the name of the 'Truth Seekers'; and afterwards, when this brotherhood migrated to the continent Europe and increased, and when its brethren began to be called 'Benedictines,' he himself was already an 'All-the-Rights-Possessing-Brother' of this said brotherhood.

"The temple I referred to exists there even up till now and is called, it seems, 'Mont-Saint-Michel.'

"In this Europe still several other inquiring beings noticed from time to time lawful inexactitudes in the works of various branches of art which had reached them from ancient times; but no sooner did they find the key to the understanding of these inexactitudes than their existence came to an end.

"Still one other, that is, another being from that continent Europe, also noticed them, and continuing to interest himself further and laboring perseveringly, he began fully to decipher the productions of almost all the branches of art.

"And this wise terrestrial three-brained being was named 'Leonardo da Vinci.'

"At the conclusion of my present tale about the terrestrial contemporary art, I might as well, I think, remark about yet one other of the many specific particularities of just those beings of the contemporary civilization who are occupied with this famous art.

"This specific particularity of theirs is that whenever one or other of the mentioned beings, namely, of the beings who notice in various productions which have reached them from ancient times some very 'lawful illogicality' and begin to produce the given branch in quite a new manner, perhaps in order to make the said lawful illogicality practically clear to himself, then most of the beings around him belonging to the profession of the same branch at once become his followers and begin doing supposedly the same thing but of course without either aim or sense.

"And it is just because of this said 'specific' psyche of the beings there, representatives of contemporary art, that on the one hand new what are called 'movements' of art are always arising there among your favorites, and, on the other hand, that those which are somehow arranged rightly by the preceding generations even though only 'after-a-fashion' are constantly dwindling.

"Although this proceeds among the representatives of all the branches of contemporary art, yet for some reason or other it is the beings who are occupied in the branch they call 'painting' who are most susceptible to it.

"Hence it is that at the present time there exists among these contemporary professions a great many 'new movements' of painting which have arisen in this way and which have nothing in common among themselves. These new movements of painting are known there by the names of 'cubism,' 'futurism,' 'synthesism,' 'imagism,' 'impressionism,' 'colorism,' 'formalism,' 'surrealism,' and many other similar movements, whose names also end in 'ism.'"

At this place in Beelzebub's tale the hoofs of all the passengers of the transspace ship *Karnak* suddenly, as it were, radiated from themselves "something phosphorescent."

This meant that the ship *Karnak* was nearing the place of her destination, that is the planet Revozvradendr. Hence, a bustling movement began among the passengers preparing to descend from the ship.

Beelzebub, Hassein, and Ahoon ended their conversation and hurriedly began to prepare themselves also.

The phosphorescent gleaming of the hoofs was obtained because, concentrated in a particular proportion, there were directed from the engine room to that part of the ship the holy parts of the sacred Omnipresent Okidanokh.

CHAPTER 31

The Sixth and Last Sojourn of Beelzebub on the Planet Earth

When after two "Ornakres*" the cosmic intersystem ship *Karnak* had left the spheres of the atmosphere of the planet Revozvradendr and began to fall back in the direction of the solar system 'Pandetznokh' onto the planet Karatas, Hassein, having sat down in his usual place, addressed Beelzebub with the following words:

"My dear and beloved Grandfather . . . be kind as always and tell me something more about the three-centered beings breeding on that planet which is called Earth."

In reply to this, Beelzebub related about his sixth and last visit on the planet Earth.

He began thus: "I was on that planet for the sixth time just before I received my full pardon and permission to leave that most remote solar system situated even almost beyond the reach of the immediate emanations of the Omni Most Holy Sun Absolute, that is, just before my return here to the center of the Universe to the place of my arising, to the immediate bosom of our COMMON UNI-BEING-ENDLESSNESS.

"This time, circumstances unexpectedly so came about that I had to exist there among these peculiar beings a fairly long time, namely, a little less than a year of our time, or, by the time calculation there, more than three hundred years.

"As initial cause of this last visit of mine to the surface

* An "Ornakre" is approximately equal to that period of the flow of time which on Earth we would define as a "month."

of that planet which has pleased you, the following circumstances served:

"You must know that after my fifth visit to the surface of that planet of yours, I continued likewise, as before, to observe from time to time the existence of those three-brained beings who please you.

"I observed them particularly attentively at those periods when there proceeded among them their chief particularity, namely, their processes of 'reciprocal destruction.'

"And I observed so attentively at these periods because I wished to make unquestionably clear to myself the causes of the periodic manifestations of such an exceptionally terrible need of their strange psyche—strange to the point of the phenomenal.

"When I happened to be a little freer I would at times follow for almost a whole Martian day or night every kind of their manifestations during these processes.

"Well, thanks to these special observations of mine, both from the planet Mars and during my former personal sojourns there among them, I had a more or less definite understanding concerning all the ways and means used by them for a more effective destruction of each other's existence.

"Well, my boy, once while watching as usual this process of theirs from the planet Mars through my big Teskooano I suddenly noticed that which served as the initial cause impelling me to undertake my sixth descent; namely, I saw this time that, without moving from their place, they did with a certain thing something which resulted in a tiny puff of smoke, whereupon a being from the opposite side immediately fell down either totally destroyed or with one or other part of his planetary body mutilated or destroyed forever.

"Such a means of reciprocal destruction I had never

seen before; and there had not yet been crystallized in my presence any data for a confrontative logical explanation of the possibility on their part of using such a means for destroying the existence of other beings similar to themselves.

"Concerning each and every of their ways and means, the purpose of which was the destruction of each other's existence, I had already had before this a definite logical confrontation which explained to me just what are the accidentally arisen surrounding factors that bring forth in them impulses and stimuli as the result of which their essence is gradually brought to such a phenomenal beingableness to destroy, for no rhyme or reason, the existence of other beings similar to themselves.

"But for this new means, which I now saw for the first time, for destroying each other's existence, my former logical and psychological explanations could not indeed in any way be applied.

"I had formerly explained to myself that such an exclusively abnormal inherency in their psyche is not selfacquired by the beings of the given epoch, but I understood that this terrifying periodic being-need was acquired and gradually assimilated by them during the course of very many of their centuries, also, of course, thanks to the abnormal conditions of existence established by the beings of past generations, and that this being-need had already become finally inherent in the contemporary threebrained beings, owing to external circumstances not depending upon them, and that it had become inevitably proper to them to occupy themselves with this.

"And indeed, my boy, during these processes, they usually instinctively at first refrain from such an unnatural manifestation, but later when every one of them already in the environment of the process itself willy-nilly sees and becomes convinced that the destruction of the existence of those similar to themselves proceeds so simply, and that the number of the destroyed always grows and grows—well then, each of them involuntarily begins instinctively to feel and automatically to value his own existence. And having become persuaded by his own eyes that the possibility of losing his own existence depends, at the given moment, absolutely only on the number of beings of the enemy side not destroyed, then in consequence of the strengthened functioning in his imagination of the presence of the impulse called 'cowardice,' and on account of the impossibility at each moment of reasonable deliberation by his being-mentation, weakened already without this, he begins from a natural feeling of self-preservation to strive with all his Being to destroy as many as possible of the existences of the beings of the enemy side in order to have the greater chance of saving his own existence. And gradually progressing in this feeling of self-preservation of theirs, they then reach the state, as they themselves say, of 'bestiality.'

"But as regards that means of the destruction of the existence of other beings similar to themselves which I then saw, it was now impossible to apply to it this logical confrontation at which I had just arrived, simply because I then clearly saw that the enemy sides stood fairly far apart, that all warring beings were among their own, and that in these semifavorable conditions, they quietly and absolutely cold-bloodedly, out of boredom as it were, did something with the help of a 'something' and thereby destroyed the existence of other beings similar to themselves.

"Well, this same new means of theirs for the destruction of each other's existence just strengthened in my essence the need to make indubitably clear and to understand all the genuine causes of this phenomenally strange psyche which had become proper to the presences exclusively of those peculiar three-brained beings.

"As I had nothing particular to do at this time on the planet Mars, I decided to wind up without delay my current affairs and personally to descend to your planet, and there, on the spot, at any cost, to elucidate this question which had always troubled me, in order that having solved it I might no longer think about these phenomena of our Great Universe.

"Several Martian days later I just flew there, as always on the same ship *Occasion.*

"We decided to descend this time onto the continent Asia near the locality called 'Afghanistan,' since before we had flown off, we had made it clear through our Teskooano that the 'turn-of-the-process-of-reciprocal-destruction' was proceeding at that time in just the said country.

"Having descended onto the locality near this Afghanistan, we decided to send our ship *Occasion* for mooring somewhere further from those places where your favorites had recently been breeding.

"You must know that to find a suitable mooring place for our ship *Occasion* on the surface of your planet has already in recent times become anything but easy, since your favorites have furnished themselves with very many kinds of contrivances for what is called 'marine locomotion,' which contrivances they also call ships, and these ships of theirs are constantly flitting about in all directions, mostly around the continents.

"We had, it is true, the possibility of making our ship *Occasion* invisible to their organs of perception of visibility, but we could not annihilate its presence, and without this it could not remain stationary on the water because of the constant danger that their ships might bump into it.

"Well, for this reason we this time decided to send our

ship for mooring to what is called the 'North Pole,' where their ships have as yet no possibility of going.

"While we were descending onto the surface of this planet of yours, the process of reciprocal destruction which had been proceeding in Afghanistan finished; but all the same, I remained to exist near this Afghanistan, as it was just on that part of the continent Asia that at that period these processes of theirs most frequently proceeded.

"Since I had in view, on this last personal flight of mine onto the surface of your planet, to obtain without fail a 'completed awareness' of the causes of the questions which were constantly troubling my essence, namely, to make clear to myself the causes in all their aspects why the psyche of those three-brained beings who please you has become such an 'anomaly'; I did not, as I have already told you, soon return home to the planet Mars, as I did on previous occasions, but I remained to exist among your favorites about three hundred of their years.

"As I now commence the narration of the information elucidating the state of the results already obtained from every cause in the common presences of the three-brained beings of the planet Earth, which pleases you, my essence prompts me and animates my 'I' and all the separately spiritualized parts of my common presence to emphasize, first of all, that during this last personal sojourn of mine on the surface of your planet I had to study very seriously and even to elucidate experimentally the details not only of the psyche of single individuals of your favorites taken separately, but likewise the perceptions and manifestations of the psyche of these single individuals taken in a general mass—dependently upon the combinations of surrounding conditions and the results brought forth by them and also upon their mutual reactions.

"For the purpose of these elucidating experiments of

mine I was even obliged this time to have recourse to the help of those branches of general knowledge which we call 'Samonoltooriko,' 'Gasometronoltooriko,' and 'Sakookinoltooriko,' that is, to those branches the similarities to which are found among your favorites also, these specialties being named 'medicine,' 'physiology,' and 'hypnotism.'

"Just at the beginning of this sixth personal sojourn of mine I soon categorically made clear, thanks to my experimental investigations, that most of the causes of the strangeness of their psyche are found not in that usual consciousness of theirs, in which alone they have already automatized themselves to exist in what is called their waking state, but in that consciousness of theirs which, thanks to their abnormal ordinary being-existence, was gradually driven within their common presence and which although it should have been their real consciousness, yet remains in them in its primitive state and is called their 'subconsciousness.'

"This subconsciousness is, however, just that part of their general psyche about which . . . do you remember? I have told you already that it was first noticed by the Very Saintly Ashiata Shiemash, who constated that in that part of their psyche there are not yet atrophied the data for the fourth sacred impulse which is named 'Objective-Conscience.'

"When I had chosen as the place of my fundamental existence the locality in the center of the continent Asia called 'Turkestan,' I not only went from there to the places where the processes which interested me proceeded, but during the pauses or lulls in these processes I also traveled a great deal, visiting almost all the continents, and during these travels I encountered beings of most, as they say, 'peoples.'

"During these travels of mine I remained nowhere for

long excepting in certain independent countries on the continent Asia called 'China,' 'India,' 'Tibet,' and of course also that lately largest half-Asiatic half-European community called 'Russia.'

"In the beginning I devoted all the time I had free from observations and investigations concerning the chief aim which I had set myself for this time, to the study of languages there, in order to have greater possibilities of better establishing everywhere corresponding relations with the beings of all 'types,' belonging to every kind of their 'peoples' there.

"Maybe, my boy, you do not yet know that it is also on this ill-fated planet only that there exists the excessive absurdity which consists in this: that there for mutual 'spoken relations' among themselves, again thanks to the abnormal external conditions of their ordinary existence, there are as many diverse languages or 'dialects' that have nothing in common with each other as there are separate independent groups into which they have gradually become split; whereas on all other planets of our Great Universe where three-brained beings breed, there is everywhere one common what is called 'sound-manifesting-mutual intercourse.'

"Yes . . . and this 'polyglotism' is also one of the characteristics and exclusive particularities of these strange three-brained beings who please you.

"And there for every scrap of terra firma, or even for each insignificant independent group accidentally separated from each other upon such a scrap, there was formed by these strange beings, and there still continues to be formed, for 'spoken relations' a quite separate speech.

"Thanks to this, it now happens there on the planet Earth that if one of the inhabitants of any locality of this planet by chance finds himself in another place of the same planet, he has no possibility whatever of intercourse with the beings there similar to himself, unless he learns their language.

"Even I, who had then learned perfectly eighteen of their different languages, found myself during my travels under conditions at times where I had not even the possibility of getting fodder for my horse, in spite of the fact that my pockets were full of what is called there 'money,' for which in general they will give you with the greatest joy there anything you please.

"It may happen there that if one of these unfortunate beings existing in some town or other, knowing all the languages used in that town, finds it for some reason or other necessary on another occasion to be in some other place at a distance of fifty or so of what are called there 'miles'—which distance corresponds approximately to one of our 'Klintrana'—then this ill-fated three-brained being, happening to be even at this insignificant distance from the place of his somehow or other established existence—owing to the abnormality there, referred to, and also of course because in the common presences of these unfortunate beings the data in general for instinctive perception were long ago atrophied—becomes absolutely helpless and can neither ask for what he really needs, nor understand a word of what is said to him.

"These numerous languages of theirs not only have nothing in common with each other, but one of them will sometimes be so built up that it has absolutely no correspondence with the possibilities of those organs of the common presence of the being which are specially adapted by Nature for this purpose and which are called 'vocal cords'; and even I, who have a much greater possibility in this respect, was entirely unable to utter certain words.

"The beings of the planet Earth themselves, however, realized this 'absurdity' of theirs, and recently while I was still there, a number of 'representatives' of their different 'solid' communities met somewhere together jointly to find a means for a way out of this difficulty.

"The fundamental purpose of these representatives of the contemporary 'important' communities who assembled together was to select one of the languages already existing there and to make it common for the whole planet.

"However, as usual, nothing resulted either from this really sensible intention of theirs, owing as ever, of course, to those same usual dissensions of theirs, thanks to which all their promising beginnings always fall through.

"In my opinion you will find it useful if I tell you a little more in detail why, in the given case, these said 'dissensions' of theirs occurred, as this will be a very characteristic example of all the 'dissensions' in general arising among them.

"At the outset, these said representatives of the contemporary solid communities, why I don't know, fixed their choice of a common planetary language on one of the three following languages existing at present, called: 'Ancient Greek,' 'Latin,' and . . . the language newly composed by the contemporary beings, 'Esperanto.'

"The first of the said three languages was the one which was worked up and which served for the 'spoken relations' of the beings of that ancient community there, which, as I have already told you, arose from a small group of Asiatic fishermen and which group later became a solid community, the beings of which were during a long period specialists there in the 'invention of sciences.'

"From the beings of this community, that is from these said ancient Greeks, not only many different sciences but likewise their language reached contemporary beings.

"But the second language which they proposed to make a common planetary language, namely, 'Latin,' was the language spoken by the beings of that ancient solid community formed, as I have also told you, from a small group of Asiatic shepherds, whose descendants were later the cause of the fact that in the presences of all the beings there of subsequent generations there was gradually formed and ultimately in the contemporary beings became already definitely fixed and obligatorily inherent in them, that perverted function thanks to which all impulses arising in them, in the sense of striving for evolution, are already automatically paralyzed at their very roots, and which they themselves call 'sexuality.'

"Well, when these representatives of various contemporary 'powerful' communities met in order collectively to choose one or another of the mentioned three languages, they could not settle upon any one of the three languages owing to the following considerations:

"Latin they found poor in the sense of the number of words.

"And indeed, my boy, the shepherds with their limited needs could not create a many-worded language; and although Latin became later on the language of a large community, yet beyond the special words required for orgies, they did not introduce into it anything that could suit the contemporary beings of your planet.

"And as regards the Greek language, then although by the wealth of its vocabulary it might indeed serve as a universal language for their whole planet, because these former fishermen, in 'inventing' every possible kind of fantastic 'science,' happened also to devise very many corresponding words which remained in that language, yet these representatives of the contemporary powerful communities could not fix their choice upon it owing to a peculiar particularity which also flows from this same strange psyche of theirs.

"The point is that all the beings assembled to select a common planetary language were representatives of communities which had become at the period of their contemporary civilization powerful or, as they also say, 'great.'

"But this ancient Greek language continues at the present time to be spoken by the beings of a contemporary small community called 'Greece,' who, though they are descendants of the former 'great Greeks,' have not now at their disposal as many of what are called 'guns' and 'ships' as those 'important communities' whose representatives were just then assembled in order unanimously to select one common language for the whole planet.

"Therefore, in all probability each of these representatives deliberated somewhat as follows:

"'Heavens above! can anybody use a language which is spoken by the beings of such a trifling community? It hasn't even guns to entitle its representatives to equal participation in our "international five-o'clocks."'

"And indeed such contemporary beings there, namely, such as become representatives of important communities, know nothing of course of the true reasons why, that is, on their planet, beings similar to them, dwelling on one or another part of the surface of their planet or who make up this or the other community, become at times temporarily 'important' or 'great.'

"They do not even begin to suspect that this proceeds not because of any particular qualities in the beings themselves of the given communities, but depends exclusively only from what part of the surface of their planet, in correlation with the harmonious movement of the whole of their solar system, there is required at the given period for the purposes of the most great Omni-Universal-Trogoautoegocratic process more of those vibrations arising either from their radiations or from the process of the sacred Rascooarno proceeding with them.

"And in regard to the third language which these assembled representatives also proposed making the common planetary language, namely, that language which they call Esperanto—over it there did not indeed then arise among them even their usual squabbles which they characterize with the words 'foaming-at-the-mouth'—they themselves, with all the bobtailedness of their reason, immediately reflected that this language could not now in any way be useful for their purpose.

"The inventors of this language must have imagined that a language is like one of their contemporary sciences which can be cooked up at home in one's study; indeed, it never entered into their heads that every more or less 'practical' language can be formed only in the course of many centuries and even then only during the process of more or less normal being-existence.

"This new invention there, this language Esperanto, might however do for our highly esteemed Mullah Nassr Eddin for composing the amusing anecdotes he tells his hens . . . !

"In short, this promising beginning of theirs, in this business of establishing one common planetary language, changed nothing there in their 'height of absurdity' and everything remained as before down till now, that is, this comparatively petty planet, with a petty 'half-dead terra firma,' continues to remain, as again our dear teacher Mullah Nassr Eddin says, 'a thousand-tongued hydra.'

"Well, my boy . . . when I commenced my investigations, in regard this time to the fundamental aim I had set myself, in order to become assuredly aware of all the causes which produced such a peculiar psyche in the presences of the three-brained beings of the planet pleasing to you, and when therefore it soon became necessary for me to make clear certain of what are called 'hidden details' in the common presence of this psyche of theirs, there unexpectedly arose for me just at the beginning of this last personal stay of mine among them a very serious difficulty consisting in this: that the bringing to light of these properties hidden within them, namely, the properties found in their subconsciousness, turned out to be possible exclusively only with the intentional help on the part of them themselves, that is, with the help of that consciousness of theirs, which with the flow of time had become proper to be possessed by them during their waking state. Furthermore, I made clear to myself that it was necessary that this said voluntary help should come from the three-brained beings there of all the types of which in general during recent times they had begun to be completely formed.

"But meanwhile, by this time, as it proved, there had already been almost atrophied in them every kind of data for the arising in their presences of the being-impulse called 'sincerity.' And it was atrophied to such a degree that they no longer had the possibility, even if they wished, to be sincere, and not only with other beings but even with their own selves, that is, they already could not with one of their spiritualized parts criticize and judge another part of themselves impartially.

"It must be said here that my subsequent special researches revealed to me that the causes of the atrophying of the data, which should be in them also, for the possibility of being sincere with themselves, had one basis; while the causes of the atrophying of the possibilities of being sincere with others, had another.

"The basis for the atrophying of the first of the mentioned data is derived from the fact of the disturbance of the co-ordination of their common psyche.

"The point is that, then, at the beginning of this sixth existence of mine among them, on the one hand, in their general presences data yet continued always to be crystallized for the arising in them, as in all the three-brained beings in general, of the being-impulse called 'self-remorse,' and which they themselves call 'Remorse of Conscience';

while on the other hand every kind of their inner and outer manifestations in the ordinary process of their being-existence began to become always less and less becoming to three-brained beings.

"Consequently, in their presences there arise more and more frequently the causes for the manifestation of the said being-impulse of Remorse of Conscience. And as the sensations thereby induced, which are similar to those which arise from 'being-Partkdolg-duty,' infallibly lead to the suppression and the enslaving of the 'denying-principle' inherent in the common presences of the three-brained beings, called 'self-calming'; then in them, during every kind of inner and outer manifestation of their common presences, which flow from the natural stimuli of one or another separately independently spiritualized localizations proper to be present in the three-centered beings, each time with the arising of this sensation of self-remorse, disagreeable to them, at first intentionally on the part of their ruminating parts, and later, thanks already to the habit which they had created, there began to be stifled and gradually to cease, 'self-criticism.' And so, by reason of this 'impotency' arising and always increasing in their organization, which involved, by constant repetition, the whole disharmony of all the functioning of their psyche, there gradually almost disappeared from their common presences such data also infallibly inherent in every three-brained being of all our Great Universe for manifesting sincerity even towards themselves.

"As basis for the disappearance from their common presences of data for 'ableness-to-be' sincere with other beings similar to themselves, there served just that abnormal form of their mutual relationship long before established there, which, as I have already told you, was based on their mutual division into different what are called 'castes' or 'classes.'

"When there began among them and soon became inevitable the habit of allocating one another to these various maleficent castes of theirs, then from that time, in the common presence of each one of them, there were gradually crystallized two particular quite opposite what are called 'organic properties,' the manifestation of which, little by little, even ceased to depend on either their ordinary consciousness or on their 'subconsciousness.'

"These two properties consist in this, that they always behave towards each other either, so to say, 'haughtily' or 'servilely.'

"During the manifestation of both these properties there are paralyzed in them all relations on what are called 'equal terms' with anybody whomsoever, thanks to which not only the inner sincere but also even the outer ordinary habitual relations have become established among them in such a way that already it has become quite usual, particularly in recent times, that if someone belongs to a caste considered higher than the caste of another, then in everything and always in relation to this other there arise in him impulses called there either 'haughtiness' or 'contempt' or 'patronage' or 'condescension,' and so on. And if somebody considers his own caste lower than that of another, then there will infallibly arise in him impulses which they call 'self-abasement,' 'false humility,' 'sycophancy,' 'bootlicking,' 'cringing,' and many other such specific impulses, the totality of which constantly corrodes in their presences what is called 'awareness-of-one's-own-individuality,' which ought to be present in them also.

"The said property which already became inherent in their common presences gradually led to this, that they lost the habit and automatically ceased to be able to be sincere with other beings similar to themselves, even with those belonging to their own caste.

"It was for this reason, my boy, that I decided while existing among these favorites of yours this time, to choose, from among the professions existing there, that one which gives the possibility at times of automatically establishing among them those relations by which they can be sincere up to a certain degree, and this in order that the possibility might be open to me to make the investigations which were indispensable to me, and by this means to obtain materials for my elucidations.

"That is why I then became just such a professional there as is called at the present time a 'physician.'

"This profession there corresponds somewhat to that profession which those whom we call our 'Zirlikners' have.

"Besides this said profession, there is, by the way, there yet another profession, with the representatives of which some of your favorites automatically become more sincere perhaps than with others, particularly concerning those, as they express themselves, 'inner-experiencings' of theirs which I needed most of all for my elucidation.

"However, although that profession might yield more material for my investigations, I did not wish to choose this profession for myself, to which what are called 'confessors' most often devote themselves, for the sole reason that this profession constantly constrains one to play outwardly a role and never allows one to consider one's inner real impulses.

"Before telling you further, I must, I think, enlighten you a little also about what the contemporary physicians there represent in themselves, who ought to correspond to our Zirlikners.

"You probably already well know that Zirlikners among us on the planet Karatas, as also in general beings similar to them on other planets of our Great Universe upon which breed already-formed three-brained beings, and from the number of whom are several, who, called differently on different planets, take upon themselves essential obligations in relation to the environment of beings similar to themselves—well, these Zirlikners are those responsible individuals who voluntarily devote the whole of their existence to helping any being of that region to fulfill his being-obligations, if this being for some reason or other, or simply thanks to a temporary irregular functioning of his planetary body, ceases to be able to fulfill his inner or outer being-duty by himself.

"It must without fail be noticed that in former times also on your planet such professionals as are now called there physicians were almost the same and did almost the same as our Zirlikners among us; but gradually with the flow of time, the responsible beings there who devoted themselves to such a profession, namely, to the fulfillment of such a high voluntary being-duty taken upon themselves, degenerated like everything on that strange planet and became also absolutely peculiar.

"And at the present time there, when the functioning of his planetary body in one or other of your contemporary favorites becomes deranged in this or that respect, and when this being ceases to be able to fulfill his being-obligations, these contemporary physicians of theirs are also called in for help; and, no question about it, these physicians do also indeed come; but how they help and how they discharge by their inner essence the obligations taken upon themselves, it is precisely here, as our highly esteemed Mullah Nassr Eddin says, that 'the dead camel of the merchant Vermassan-Zeroonan-Alaram is buried.'

"Know first of all that at the present time there those contemporary three-brained beings become those professionals who for the most part, during the period of their preparation to be responsible beings, succeed, as is said there, in 'learning by rote' much miscellaneous information concerning those means for getting rid of every possible kind of what are called their 'illnesses,' means which old women in their dotage, during all previous times on their planet, employed upon or advised for three-brained beings there to this end.

"Among the number of such means for getting rid of the said illnesses, there are chiefly various remedies existing under the name of 'medicines.'

"Well, when one of the contemporary beings becomes a responsible professional, and when other beings needing his help apply to him for this help, he uses or prescribes just these mentioned remedies.

"Here it will be very useful for the development of your reason, if to your common presence is added a 'logicnestarian-implantation' from information concerning one particular very peculiar property which is acquired in the psyche of these contemporary professionals of the planet Earth.

"This peculiar psychic property is acquired by those terrestrial professionals as soon as they receive the title of 'qualified physician,' and it functions constantly in them during their wish to help other beings who need their aid.

"The point is that, in their common presences, both the intensity of the desire to help and the quality itself of the help given always depend exclusively on the smell there is in the house to which he is called.

"Namely, if the house to which such a contemporary professional is called for help smells of what are called 'English pounds,' then in it, thanks to this smell, not only does his inner 'being-wish' to help the suffering being increase to the point of what is called 'ne plus ultra,' but even in outer manifestations his planetary body at once assumes the form of a 'Dzedzatzshoon,' i.e., a 'beaten dog.'

"In the case of most contemporary physicians there even appears on their faces from this smell what are called 'bootlicking' expressions, and their 'bobtail' becomes pressed tight, almost glued, 'between their legs.'

"But if the house to which such a terrestrial 'Zirlikner' is called for help to a needy being smells of what are called 'cancelled-German-marks,' then his inner being-wish to help the person in need also increases, but only in this respect, that he may write out as quickly as possible what is called a 'prescription,' invented by the Germans, and the more quickly leave the house.

"Here also, I must tell you that when in this second case the contemporary terrestrial beings who have the profession of physician leave the house of the person who needed their help and walk along the street, then all their exteriors, even the muscles of their faces, invariably express something as follows: 'Eh, you curs, look out! otherwise I shall crush you like cockroaches; don't you see that here comes not just anybody, but a genuine representative of science who has fully assimilated the knowledge given by the highest contemporary seat of learning!!'

"It will be most opportune now to tell you a little also concerning those 'medicinal means' I mentioned, which exist there in great numbers under every kind of name and which on the advice of these contemporary physicians are introduced into themselves by other ordinary beings, ostensibly as an aid in their various illnesses.

"And it is also infallibly necessary to tell you about it . . . for . . . who knows . . . you too may suddenly have to exist at some time or other on that peculiar planet among these queer folk, and you would not know how to deal with these numerous medicinal means and what significance to give them.

"First of all, know and remember this, that the young three-brained beings there, particularly of the most recent times, who prepare themselves to take, when they arrive at the age of responsible existence, the profession of a physician only learn by rote as many names as possible from among the many thousands of these said medicinal means now known there.

"And later, when they have already become responsible beings having this profession and receive the official title of physician and when they are called upon to help the beings who need it, then their whole help consists in this that they make a being-effort of a certain intensity just to remember the names of several of these medical means and to write them later on a scrap of paper called by them 'prescription,' with the intention of prescribing that mixture which should be introduced into the planetary body of, as they say, the 'invalid.' The intensity, however, of their effort depends first of all on the 'social status' of the being needing their help, and secondly on the number of eyes fixed upon them by the beings surrounding the given sick being.

"Well, further, this said prescription thus written by them is taken by the near relatives of the person needing the help of the contemporary Zirlikner there to one of their contemporary what are called 'pharmacies,' where their 'pharmacists' prepare the required 'mixtures.'

"And how in general such mixtures are prepared in these pharmacies and exactly of what they are composed, well, just this you will well understand if I relate to you one only of the numerous informations I learned concerning it, and which I was told by one of the beings there having just this profession of a pharmacist.

"This, my present tale, refers to that period when I had already often begun to frequent that large community which was called Russia.

"Well, in one of the two chief places of existence of this said large community, namely, in the one which was called 'Moscow,' friendly relations happened to be established between myself and such a professional, that is, a pharmacist.

"According to the notions there, this pharmacist was already an old being and his character was very kind, and even, so to say, obliging.

"He belonged to what is called there the 'Jewish faith.'

"It is necessary to tell you here, that there, on almost all the continents at the present time, these pharmacists are, why I don't know, mostly beings belonging to the Jewish faith.

"And so . . . when I used to go to that second chief place of Russia, where that acquaintance of mine, the pharmacist, existed, I would always call on him and there in the back room of his pharmacy, which as a rule they call a 'laboratory,' I used to chat with him about every kind of 'fiddle-faddle.'

"Once when I went as usual into this said laboratory of his, I saw that he was pounding something in a mortar, and, as is usually done there on these occasions, I inquired what he was doing.

"To this he replied to me thus:

"'I am pounding burnt sugar for this prescription,' and here he handed me a scrap of paper on which the usual prescription was written of a widely spread medicinal means existing there under the name of 'Dover's powder.'

"This powder is called there 'Dover's,' because it was invented by a certain Englishman whose name was Dover, and it is used there chiefly for coughs.

"I read the prescription he gave me and I saw that sugar was no part of it, and much less burnt. . . . Whereupon I expressed to him my amazed perplexity.

"Whereat, with a good-natured smile, he answered me, 'Of course sugar has no part in this prescription, but instead it does contain a certain percentage of "opium."'

"And he further explained as follows:

"'This Dover's powder is, I don't know why, a very popular remedy among us in Russia, and it is used by almost all the peoples of our enormous empire.

"'Many hundreds of thousands of packets of powder are used here daily all over the country and the opium this powder ought to contain is, as you know, no cheap thing and if real opium were put into this powder, the opium alone would cost us pharmacists six or eight kopecks a packet, and we have to sell this powder for three to five kopecks. Besides, even if all the opium from the whole of the globe were collected the position would be the same, there would not be enough for our Russia alone.

"'So instead of the prescription of Doctor Dover we pharmacists have invented another prescription consisting of such substances as are easily obtainable and which are accessible and profitable for everybody.

"'That is why we pharmacists make this powder of soda, burnt sugar, and a small quantity of quinine; all of these substances are cheap . . . well, quinine is, it is true, a little expensive . . . but then, you see, not much of it is required. Of the total 100 per cent of the composition of these powders, there will only be about 2 per cent of quinine.'

"Here I could not help interrupting him: 'You don't mean it? . . . But it's not possible! . . . Has no one ever discovered that instead of Dover's powder you give them this particular mess?'

"'Of course not,' laughingly replied this good acquaintance of mine. 'These things can be detected only by sight and taste; and this Dover's powder which we make, however you turn it and under whatever microscope you examine it, is in color the same as it should be according to the genuine prescription of this Doctor Dover. And as to taste, it is absolutely impossible thanks chiefly to the proportion of quinine which we put into it, to distinguish it from the genuine powder made with the real opium.'

"'But the analysis?' I asked him.

"'What analysis?' he replied sarcastically, though also with a kind smile. 'A thorough analysis of a single powder would cost so much that, with this money, you could buy not only half a hundredweight of this powder, but possibly even open a whole pharmacy with it; so it is understandable that, for three or five kopecks, nobody is likely to be such a fool.

"'Strictly speaking, nowhere is the analysis about which you are thinking ever done.

"'Each town, it goes without saying, has its "analytic-chemists," and even every municipality has such "specialists" in its service.

"'But what do they amount to and what do they know, these specialist "analytic-chemists"?

"'Perhaps you do not know how these specialists who occupy such responsible posts study, and what they understand? . . . No? . . .

"'Then I shall also tell you about this.

"'For instance, some mama's darling, a young man, inevitably with a pimpled face—and he is pimpled because his mama considered herself a high-brow and thought it was "indecent" to speak of and to point out certain things to her son, whereupon this son of hers, not yet having formed his own consciousness, did that which was "done" in him, and the results of these "doings" of his, as with all such young people, appeared on his face as pimples, which are very well known even to contemporary medicine . . .

"'Well, my honorable doctor . . .' it was thus that the pharmacist continued.

"Before, however, continuing, my boy, to tell you further what the kind pharmacist said, I must tell you that when I became a professional physician there, your favorites everywhere called me 'doctor.'

"I will some time without fail explain to you about that

title of theirs, because owing to that hateful word doctor, a very sad and tragic misunderstanding occurred there once to our dear Ahoon.

"And now listen to what that kind pharmacist there said to me further.

"He said, 'This young man, this mama's darling, with the pimpled face, studies at a certain university to become a specialist analytic-chemist, but there at the university he is bound to study those special books usually fabricated in Germany by "learned beings" there.'

". . . And really, my boy, among these contemporary Germans, especially during recent times, the invention of 'scientific' books in all branches has also increased.

"Since analysis is also a branch of their science, so in this branch also a great mass of books has already been accumulated among these German scientific beings, and almost all the peoples of Europe as well as other countries use these scientific books.

"Well, that kind pharmacist said further: 'It is this young man who has finished his University course and consequently drawn his knowledge concerning what is called the "complex of substances" from the books fabricated by the German scientific beings, who must make the analysis of our Dover's powder.

"'In those German books from which he gathered his knowledge of the complex of substances it is of course also stated of which elements these and the other substances consist, and the formulas of these elements are also certain to be quoted.

"'It is also explained in these books what appearance these substances have in which are present all the elements which should be in them, and how their external appearance changes if these elements are not in them. Several homemade means for recognizing the substances are also given in these German books, as for instance, by sight, by taste, by burning, and by certain means that ancient grandmothers of olden times had heard tell of, and so on and so forth.

"'After finishing the course, this young man then receives the title of analytic-chemist. Sometimes it happens that before receiving a responsible post, the young man happens to get "practice" consisting usually in this, that he serves for a certain time at a "slaughterhouse," where he helps the local chemist, also a former mama's darling, to ascertain with the aid of a microscope, in a certain way only known to themselves, whether the pork contains trichinae; and only later, when a place is vacant somewhere, is he appointed to the official post of analytic-chemist.

"'Well, dear Doctor, such an official analytic-chemist receives our Dover's powder for analysis. On receiving it he recognizes it as Dover's powder either by looking at it or by tasting it as ordinary mortals do, or because the sender writes to him that it is precisely Dover's powder.

"'For this analysis he takes up from his table what they call his "pharmaceutical guide," also composed by Germans, which every official analytic-chemist is bound to have; and there in that guide he hunts up the place where are written the formulas of powders of all kinds.

"'As Dover's powder is known everywhere, it is of course also included in that book.

"'Thereafter our highly respected analytic-chemist takes from his table a form on which official title is indicated and writes:

"'"The powder sent to us for analysis proves to be, according to all the data, Dover's powder. The analysis showed it to contain . . ." And he copies a formula from his German pharmaceutical guide, deliberately increasing or diminishing some of the figures, but increasing or diminishing them of course only very slightly so that they may not slap you in the eye.

"'And he does this first of all so that everyone should

know that he has written the results of his analysis not any old way but that he has really investigated the matter; and secondly, because, whatever you may say, he as town pharmacist being also an official person will little wish, I think, to make enemies for himself in the town where he lives.

"'The form thus written is dispatched to him who sent the Dover's powder, and the famous analytic-chemist himself is quite at peace as no one knows that he has made no analysis at all, nor could anyone check him, first because he is the only official analytic-chemist in the town, and secondly, because even if one of these powders of ours should be taken to any other phenomenal chemist in another town, nothing alarming could happen . . . are there no other Dover's powders in the world? The packet of powder he analyzed no longer exists, because naturally in making the analysis he had to destroy it.

"'Besides, no one is to be found who, for the sake of three kopecks' worth of Dover's powder, would kick up such a fuss.

"'At all events, venerated Doctor, for thirty years now I have been making these powders according to the prescription of "ours," and I certainly sell them; and up to today I have never had any misunderstanding on account of these Dover's powders of ours. And no misunderstanding can occur; because Dover's powder is already generally known everywhere and everybody is convinced that it is excellent for a cough.

"'And all that is required of any remedy is that it should be known to be a good one.

"'As regards how the remedy is made and what it contains, what does it matter?

"'Personally, in my handling of these remedies for many years, a definite opinion has been formed in me that none of the remedies known to contemporary medicine can be of any use at all without faith in it.

"'And faith in a person concerning any remedy arises only when the given remedy is known and when many people say that it is very good for a certain illness.

"'It is just the same with this powder of ours; once it is called Dover's powder, that is enough, because everybody already knows it and many people often say of it that it is excellent for coughs.

"'And besides, speaking candidly, our new composition of Dover's powder is much better than the real one made from the prescription of Dover himself, if only because it contains no substance injurious to the organism.

"'For instance, according to the prescription of Doctor Dover himself opium must enter into the composition of his powder.

"'And you know the properties of opium? If a man takes it often enough even in small doses, his organism soon gets so accustomed to it that later, if he ceases dosing himself, he suffers intensely.

"'But from the powder made from our prescription this would never happen, since it contains none of that opium or any other substance harmful to the organism.

"'In short, my esteemed Doctor, every one ought, when walking in the streets, to shout from the bottom of his heart: "Long live the new prescription for Dover's powder!"'

"He was going to say something more, but just then a boy brought him from the pharmacy itself a whole stock of various prescriptions, upon seeing which he rose and said to me:

"'Excuse me, Doctor. I am compelled to stop our friendly chat and to get busy on the preparation of these innumerable orders.

"'By bad luck both of my assistants are absent today, one of them because his esteemed other half must bring into "God's world" today one more mouth to feed, and the other has to attend the courts because a chauffeur is being accused of kidnapping his daughter.'

"Well, enough of that. . . .

"If you should really have to exist among these favorites of yours, you will at least know from this last talk of mine that although the physicians there write a dozen wiseacring names in their prescriptions, yet in these official establishments of theirs which are called pharmacies their remedies are prepared almost always after the fashion of that Dover's powder.

"It even happens there that occasionally these kind pharmacists prepare early in the morning a whole barrel of some liquid and a whole box of some powder, and during the entire day they satisfy everyone bringing prescriptions, either by pouring from that common barrel or by taking powder from that common box.

"In order that this mixture prepared betimes should not always have the same appearance, these kind professionals put in something for coloring with various colors and for changing the taste and smell.

"In spite of all that I have said, however, I advise you very strongly to be extremely careful with one kind of their remedies, because it does sometimes happen there that these kind pharmacists put into these mixtures something poisonous for the planetary body—of course, by mistake.

"Moreover, for the beings with normal reason the custom has been established there, of course accidentally, always to depict on the labels of mixtures of that kind what is called a 'skull and crossbones,' so that it may be possible always to distinguish that kind of poisonous remedy from the ordinary medicinal means.

"However, in any case, do remember that from among the number of many thousands of known 'medical means' applied by the contemporary physicians there, only three, and even then only sometimes, produce some or other real results for the planetary bodies of your contemporary ordinary three-brained beings.

"One of these three medical means which does sometimes nevertheless produce a useful reaction is that substance, or, more strictly speaking, those active elements entering into it, which the beings of Maralpleicie learned how to obtain from the plant poppy and which they were the first to call opium.

"The second substance is that which is called there 'castor oil'; this substance was already used long ago by the beings of Egypt for embalming their mummies, and it was they who also noticed that this substance has, among other things, that action for which it is now used.

"But the knowledge about this castor oil passed also to these beings of Egypt from the beings of the continent Atlantis, who belonged to the learned society Akhaldan.

"And the third substance is that which has been obtained there by beings from the dawn of centuries from what is called the 'Cinchona tree.'

"Now listen, my boy, to the information about the newly invented name of those terrestrial contemporary physicians articulated as 'doctor.'

"It would seem that this invention is that also of the beings of the 'important' community of Germany there, and they invented this articulation for the purpose of defining some merit or other of some among them, but this same invention of theirs, which was widely spread on the whole of their planet, became, for some reason or other, the ordinary nominal name for all the contemporary physicians there.

"It must be even emphasized that, thanks to this invention of theirs, there was added there yet one more to the number of factors, the totality of which constantly leads them into error and by which their being-mentation, already weakened without this, becomes year by year more 'makhokhitchne.'

"On account of this new word of theirs, even our Ahoon, in spite of his having an incomparably more normal presence, and being clothed with a being-reason of higher quality, had while we were there a very disagreeable, even an almost idiotic misunderstanding.

"As for the rest, it will in my opinion be much better if he tells you about it himself."

Having said this, Beelzebub addressed himself to Ahoon in the following words:

"Tell us, old man, how this then happened and what made you for several days the whole time 'Skoohiatchiny' and 'Tsirikooakhtz,' or as the three-brained beings of the planet Earth would say, made you just 'grumble' and be 'irritable' like your friend there, Dame Bess."

To this Ahoon, again imitating the style of Beelzebub and this time even his very intonation, began to relate as follows:

"This misunderstanding happened to me owing to the following cause:

"During this sixth visit of ours to the planet Earth, just towards the very end, we had to exist, by the way, for a little while also in the capital of those same German beings who, as His Reverence condescended to say, invented just this word, accursed for me, 'doctor.'

"In the hotel where we had the place of our existence, next to my room, or as is said there in the 'number' next to mine, there existed a very sympathetic pair of beings who had only recently completed the sacrament of the Union of the Active with the Passive for the purpose of serving the Great All-Universal Trogoautoegocratic process for the prolongation of their generation, or, as they themselves would say, had 'been married,' and they were still considered 'newlywed.'

"Well, with this young couple I accidentally became acquainted in the house of some friends of mine, after which this couple often began to invite me to their room for what is called there a 'cup-of-tea'; at other times I even myself, without their invitation, used to drop in on them in order to shorten the wearisome 'German' evenings.

"She was, as is said there, 'in an interesting condition' and, according also to their expression, was expecting her first-born.

"They, as well as I, were in that capital for an indefinite period, and on the business for the profession of the Active half of this young couple, and they were therefore existing in that hotel in which we were just staying.

"There once resounded from them a very nervous rapping on the wall of my room.

"I instantly ran to them and it turned out there, that 'himself' was not at home, for on that very day he had had to go off somewhere; and during this time she had felt faint and, almost without consciousness, had instinctively rapped on my wall.

"When I entered she already felt somewhat better, but imploringly asked me to hurry for a 'doctor.'

"I instantly of course rushed out into the street. But once there I thought: But where am I to go now?

"Suddenly I remembered that not far from our hotel a being lived whom everybody called 'doctor'; it was even marked on a metal plate in front of his name on the door that he was a 'doctor'; and it was to this 'doctor' that I ran.

"But it turned out that he was dining, and therefore his servant asked me to wait a little in the drawing-room, having explained to me that the 'doctor' would have finished dinner immediately with his guests and would soon be coming out.

"I, of course, sat down in the drawing room awaiting this 'doctor,' but it could scarcely be said that I sat very quietly.

"I was sitting there as if, as beings say there, 'on live coals' because I was most anxious about the condition of my neighbor.

"But the 'honorable doctor,' however, never came. Almost twenty minutes passed. I could not bear it any longer and rang the bell.

"When the servant entered I asked her to remind the 'doctor' about me and to say that I was in a very great hurry and could not wait any longer for him.

"She went away.

"Another five minutes passed.

"At last the 'doctor' himself appeared.

"Hurriedly, I shortly explained to him what I wanted from him; but to my astonishment he began to laugh irrepressibly at my request.

"I thought: Obviously during dinner with his friends this 'doctor' has drunk more than one glass too much of 'German beer.'

"And only when he had calmed down a little from his hysterical laughter could he tell me that to his great regret he was not a 'doctor of medicine' but only a 'doctor of philosophy.'

"At that moment I experienced such a state, as if, as it were, I were for the second time hearing our ENDLESSNESS'S 'sentence' of exile passed upon His Reverence and those nearest him, and in consequence upon me.

"Well, our dear Hassein!

"I left the drawing room of that 'doctor' and was once more out in the street in the same position as before.

"Just then, a taxi happened to pass.

"I got into it and began to reflect: Where, now?

"I then remembered that in that café where I sometimes went, a being also almost always went whom everybody called 'doctor.'

"I ordered the chauffeur to hurry to this café.

"There a waiter known to me told me that this same 'doctor' had indeed been there, but had just left with some of his acquaintances; and that he, the waiter, had accidentally overheard from their conversation that they were going to such and such a restaurant, and gave me the name of this restaurant.

"Although this restaurant was some way away, yet nevertheless I ordered the chauffeur to go there, as I knew of no other 'doctor.'

"At length, in half an hour, we came to this restaurant and there I very soon found this 'doctor.'

"Once again, this time, he turned out not to be a 'physician' but . . . 'a doctor of jurisprudence.'

"I was completely, as is said there, 'in the soup.'

"At last it entered my head that I might address myself to the headwaiter of the restaurant and explain to him in detail what I required.

"This headwaiter turned out to be a very kind being. He not only explained to me what had to be done, but even went with me to a certain physician, this time called a 'doctor-accoucheur.'

"We found him by chance at home and he was kind enough to agree to go with me at once. But while we were on the way, my poor neighbor had already brought forth a boy, her first-born, and having somehow swaddled the baby without anyone's help, was already sound asleep after the terrible torments she had borne in solitude.

"And so, from that day I have with my whole being hated the sound of the word 'doctor,' and to each of the beings of the planet Earth I would advise him to use this word only when he is very angry.

"That you may the better understand the significance of the contemporary physicians on your planet, it is also necessary to tell you of the saying of our highly esteemed Mullah Nassr Eddin concerning these same contemporary physicians.

"He speaks of them thus: 'For our sins, God has sent us two kinds of physicians, one kind to help us die, and the other to prevent us living.'"

CHAPTER 32

Hypnotism

"And so," Beelzebub continued, "at this sixth sojourn of mine in person on the surface of that planet Earth of yours, I decided to settle there for a long stay and to become a professional physician there. I did indeed become one, only not such a physician as most of them are there, but I chose for myself the profession of what is called there 'physician-hypnotist.'

"I became such a professional there firstly because during recent centuries only such physician-professionals there obtain an entrée to all their 'classes' or 'castes' of which I spoke, and, since they enjoy great confidence and authority, ordinary beings are disposed to a sincerity towards them that permits them to penetrate, as is said there, their 'inner world.'

"Secondly, I decided to become such a professional, in order, also parallel with the attainments of my personal aims, to have the possibility at the same time of giving genuine medical assistance to certain of those unfortunates.

"Indeed, my boy, on all the continents there and among all the beings, to whatever class they may belong, there has been during recent times and there still is a great need for just such physicians.

"I may say that I already had a very wide experience in this specialty, having during my previous elucidation of certain subtle points of the psyche of individual favorites of yours many times had recourse to methods used there by such a kind of physician.

"I must tell you that formerly your favorites, like all the other three-brained beings of the whole Universe, were without that particular psychic property which permits them to be brought into what is called a 'hypnotic state.' To get into that state became proper to your favorites, thanks to a certain combination obtained in their psyche and derived from the disharmony of the functioning of their common presence.

"This strange psychic property had its rise soon after the destruction of Atlantis and began to become finally fixed in the presence of every one of them from the time when their 'Zoostat,' that is the functioning of their 'being-consciousness,' began to be divided in two and when two entirely different consciousnesses having nothing in common with each other were gradually formed in them, namely, those two different consciousnesses, the first of which was called by them simply 'consciousness' and the second—when they finally noticed it in themselves—was called and still continues to be called 'subconsciousness.'

"If you try clearly to represent to yourself and to transubstantiate in the corresponding parts of your common presence all I am about to explain to you, you will perhaps then thoroughly understand nearly half of all the causes why the psyche of these three-brained beings who have taken your fancy and who breed on the planet Earth has finally become such a unique phenomenon.

"This psychic particularity, namely, of falling into a 'hypnotic state,' is, as I have already said, inherent to the three-brained beings only of this planet of yours, and one can therefore say that if they did not exist, then in all our Great Universe there would not exist in general even a being-notion of 'hypnotism.'

"Before explaining to you further about all this, it is here appropriate to emphasize that although during the last twenty centuries almost the entire process of the ordinary waking existence of most of the three-brained beings who have taken your fancy, particularly of the beings of contemporary times, flows under the influence of this inherency of theirs, nevertheless they themselves give the name hypnotic state only to that state of theirs during which the processes of this particular property flow in them acceleratedly and the results of which are obtained concentratedly. And they fail to notice, or, as they would say, they are not struck by irregular results of this inherency which has recently become fixed in the ordinary process of their existences, because, on the one hand, in the absence in them in general of normal self-perfecting, they have not what is called a 'wide horizon,' and on the other hand, arising and existing according to the principle Itoklanoz, it has already become inherent in them 'quickly-to-forget' what they perceive. But when the said results of this inherency of theirs are obtained 'acceleratedly-concentratedly,' then every kind of irregular manifestation, their own and those of others, become real to such a degree that they become acutely obvious even to their bobtailed reason and therefore unavoidably perceptible.

"But even if certain of them should by chance notice something illogical in their manifestations or in the manifestations of others, then, thanks to the absence in them of the knowledge of the law of 'typicality,' they at best ascribe it to the particularities of the character of the given beings.

"This 'abnormal' particular property of their psyche was first constated by the learned beings of the city Gob of the country Maralpleicie; and even then they made it a serious and detailed branch of science which spread over the whole of the planet under the name of 'non-responsible-manifestations-of-personality.'

"But later, when the turn of their 'regular-process-of-reciprocal-destruction' came round again, this detailed branch of their science, which was then still comparatively normal, began like all their good attainments to be gradually forgotten and finally also entirely disappeared.

"And only many centuries later did this branch of their science again show signs of reviving.

"But . . . thanks to the fact that at this period most of the learned beings there had already become learned beings of 'new formation,' they sat upon this new revival so firmly that before the poor thing had time to develop, it soon found its way into their common what is called 'rubbish heap.'

"And this happened in the following way:

"A humble learned being there, unlike his contemporaries, Mesmer by name, and by birth from what is called 'Austria-Hungary,' once happened to notice clearly during certain of his experiments the real duality of consciousness in beings like himself.

"He was greatly impressed by this and devoted himself entirely to this question which interested him.

"Continuing to observe and to study, he almost succeeded in understanding the reason. But when later he began making practical experiments for the elucidation of certain details, well it was just then that there began to be manifested toward him that particularity proper to the learned beings of 'new formation' there.

"This particularity of the learned beings of the Earth of new formation is called 'pecking to death.'

"As this honest Austro-Hungarian learned being then began making his elucidating experiments not as all the learned beings of the Earth of new formation had in general become mechanized to do, he was, according to the custom there, very meticulously 'pecked to death.'

"And this process of the pecking to death of this poor Mesmer was then so effective that it has already passed by its own momentum to the learned beings of the Earth from generation to generation.

"For instance, all the books now existing there on the question of this hypnotism—and of such books there are thousands there—always begin by saying that this Mesmer was nothing more nor less than a rogue with an itching palm and a charlatan of the first water, but that our 'honest' and 'great' learned beings very soon saw through him and prevented his doing any kind of mischief.

"The more the learned beings of recent times of this peculiar planet are themselves personally, in the sense of 'idiotism,' 'squared,' the more they criticize Mesmer and say or write concerning him every possible kind of absurdity to bring him into contempt.

"And in doing this, they criticize exactly that humble and honest learned being of their planet, who, if he had not been pecked to death would have revived that science, which alone is absolutely necessary to them and by means of which alone, perhaps, they might be saved from the consequences of the properties of the organ Kundabuffer.

"There is no harm in remarking here that just when I was leaving that planet forever, precisely the same was being repeated there as had occurred to this Mesmer. Namely, on this occasion, an honest and humble learned being there from among the beings of the community France, after persistent and conscientious labors came across the possibility of curing that terrible disease, the spreading of which also had in recent times assumed a general planetary character.

"This terrible disease is called there 'cancer.'

"As this Frenchman also made practical experiments, not in the usual fashion there, for the elucidation of the details of his discovery, other contemporary learned beings thereupon also manifested toward him that same particularity of theirs—'to peck him to death.'

"Possibly now, in your presence also there already begin to be crystallized the data for the engendering always in corresponding cases of the being-impulse of an 'indubitable conviction' concerning this fact that thanks only to the learned beings of new formation there, in whom there has already been implanted the mentioned particularity, namely, of not failing to peck to death every colleague of theirs who does not do the same as has already been fixed by the abnormally established conditions of ordinary being-existence established there, there will never proceed in the presences of the three-brained beings of this ill-fated planet Earth of yours what is called the sacred 'Antkooano,' upon which, among other things, the Very Saintly Ashiata Shiemash also counted.

"About this 'essence-loving-hope' of his, I chanced to learn during my investigations concerning His Very Saintly Activities there.

"You, my boy, perhaps still do not know in what, namely, the cosmic process of the sacred Antkooano consists?

"The sacred Antkooano is the name of that process of perfecting the Objective-Reason in the three-centered beings, which process proceeds by itself simply from the 'flow of time.'

"As a rule, everywhere on those planets of our Great Universe upon which three-brained beings breed, the perfecting of Objective-Reason can proceed in them only from personal conscious labors and intentional sufferings.

"This sacred Antkooano can proceed only in those planets upon which in general all cosmic truths have become known to all the beings.

"And all cosmic truths usually become known to all on these planets, thanks to the fact that the beings of the given planet who by their conscious labors learn some truth or other share it with other beings of their planet, and in this way all the cosmic truths gradually become known by all the beings of the given planet without any distinction.

"Thanks to this sacred process, intentionally actualized by our ALL-FORESEEING COMMON ENDLESS FATHER, it is foreseen that in the three-brained beings of the given planet, during the process in their presences of the fundamental cosmic holy law of Triamazikamno, the superfluity of its third holy force thereby obtained, namely, the force of the 'sacred reconciling,' should by itself crystallize data in them for engendering that something which is what is called 'being-Egoaitoorassian-will.'

"Well, then . . . the mentioned particular property recently newly fixed in the common presences of your favorites is that the functioning of their mentioned Zoostat, or as they themselves would say, of their 'spiritual part,' passes into that functioning of their common whole which properly proceeds during their completely passive state, that is, during their 'sleep,' and during this sleep of theirs the entire functioning of their planetary body continues to remain such as it became proper to it to be during their waking state.

"In order that you should better represent to yourself and understand the results flowing from such an astonishing 'psychic property,' you must first of all know about two facts actualized in the common presences of these favorites of yours.

"One of these facts is produced in their common presence thanks to the existing cosmic law of 'self-adaption-of-Nature'; and the other fact flows from the abnormal conditions of ordinary being-existence established by them themselves about which I have repeatedly spoken.

"The first fact is, that from the time when owing to their abnormal existence there began to be formed in them what is called the 'two-system-Zoostat,' that is, two independent consciousnesses, then Great Nature began gradually to adapt Herself and finally adapted Herself to this, that after they arrive at a certain age, there begin to proceed in them two 'Inkliazanikshanas' of different what are called 'tempos,' that is, as they themselves would say, two 'blood circulations' of different kind.

"From this certain age mentioned, each one of these 'Inkliazanikshanas' of different tempo, that is to say each 'blood circulation,' begins to evoke in them the functioning of one of their mentioned consciousnesses; and vice versa, the intensive functioning of either consciousness begins to evoke in them the kind of blood circulation corresponding to it.

"The difference between these two independent kinds of blood circulation in their common presences is actualized by means of what is called 'tempo-Davlaksherian-circulation,' or, according to the expression there of what is called contemporary medicine, the 'difference-of-the-filling-of-the-blood-vessels'; that is to say, in the condition of the waking state, the 'center-of-gravity-of-the-blood-pressure' in their common presences obtains in one part of the general system of blood vessels, and in the condition of the passive state, in another part of the vessels.

"And the second fact—the fact ensuing from the abnormal conditions of the being-existence of your favorites—is that when, from the very beginning of the arising of their offspring, they intentionally try by every kind of means, for the purpose of making them respond to these abnormal conditions round them, to fix in their 'logicnestarian-localizations' as many impressions as possible obtained exclusively only from such artificial perceptions as are again due to the results of their abnormal existence—which maleficent action of theirs towards their offspring they call 'education'—then the totality of all such artificial perceptions gradually segregates itself in their common presences and acquires its own independent functioning, connected only as much with the functioning of their planetary body as is necessary merely for its automatic manifestation, and the totality of these artificial perceptions is then perceived by them, owing to their naïveté, as their real 'consciousness.' But as for the sacred data for genuine being-consciousness put into them by Great Nature—which consciousness ought to be possessed by them from the very beginning of their preparation for responsible existence together with the properties inherent in them which engender in them the genuine sacred being-impulses of 'faith,' 'hope,' 'love,' and 'conscience'—these data, becoming gradually also isolated and being left to themselves, evolve independently of the intentions of the responsible beings, and of course also independently of the bearers of them themselves, and come to be regarded as what is called the 'subconsciousness.'

"Thanks only to such a, in the objective sense,

maleficence, but according to their naïve subjective understanding 'benevolence' towards their offspring, all the sacred data put in by Great Nature Herself for forming in them their real being-consciousness become isolated and remain during the entire period of their existence in their almost primitive state, and every kind of impression unavoidably perceived by means of the six 'being-Skernalitsionniks,' or, in their terminology, 'sense-organs,' present in their presences for the specific perception of externals—by the way, they count them as five—come to be localized and, acquiring their isolated functioning, gradually become predominant for the whole of their common presence.

"Although such a 'localization' of accidentally perceived 'impressions' is found in them and although they are aware of its action, yet, in respect of any functioning inherent in their planetary body as well as in respect of the acquisition in their common presence of Objective-Reason, it plays no part.

"All these impressions, intentionally or accidentally perceived, from which the said localizations are formed ought to be in them only as material for confrontative logic for that real being-consciousness which they should have in themselves, and the accidental results of the perception of which, in their naïveté, they sometimes now confidently regard merely as reflexes of their, in their opinion, insignificant what is called 'animal instinct.'

"Only thanks to the single fact that your favorites, especially the contemporary ones, do not know at all and even do not suspect the necessity of at least adapting their famous education to the said subconsciousness of their offspring, but that they always and in everything intentionally assist every one of the rising generation to perceive impressions only from the abnormally artificial, then thanks only to this, when every one of them reaches the age of a responsible being all his being-judgments and all his deductions from them are always purely peculiarly-subjective in him and have no connection not only with the genuine being-impulses arising also in him, but also neither with those general cosmic lawful phenomena, to sense which by Reason is proper to every three-brained being, and by means of which there is established that connection between all the three-brained beings of all our Great Universe for the collective fulfillment of the common universal functioning, for which purpose everything existing in the Universe just exists.

"For your wider understanding of this particular 'psychic state' it is necessary to tell you further that even up to now they arise with every kind of data for acquiring genuine being-Reason, and at their arising there are not yet in their presences any 'logicnestarian-growths' from which there is later localized and from which there is acquired the isolated functioning in them of the said 'false consciousness.' But only later, during their development and their preparation to become responsible beings, either by themselves or by the intentional directing of their as they call them 'parents' or 'teachers'—that is to say, responsible beings who undertake the responsibility of the preparation of the given beings for responsible existence—they begin, as I said, to help intentionally in taking in and fixing only those impressions which later are data for the impulses corresponding to surrounding abnormally established conditions; and only then, being gradually formed, there just begins to be predominant in their common presence this said artificially formed 'consciousness' of theirs.

"And the totality of these localized data, existing in their presences and spiritualized in them for the genuine being-consciousness which they call subconsciousness, not having and not acquiring any 'logicnestarian-growths' for confrontation and criticism, but having from the very beginning only possibilities of engendering the sacred being-impulses called 'faith,' 'love,' 'hope,' and 'conscience,' always believes, always loves, and always hopes in everything newly perceived.

"And so, when thanks to a change of tempo of their blood circulation there is obtained a temporary suspension of the action of the localization of that false consciousness which has already become the 'autocratic ruler' of their common presences, thereby giving the sacred data of their genuine consciousness the possibility of unhindered blending with the total functioning of the planetary body during the period of their waking state, then indeed my boy, if the crystallization of data for engendering in that localization an idea of something opposite to that which has already arisen in them and somehow become fixed, is assisted in a corresponding manner, and if moreover the actions evoked by this idea are directed upon a disharmonized part of the planetary body, an accelerated change in it possible.

"When, during the period of the Tikliamishian civilization, the learned beings of the locality Maralpleicie first constated in their common psyche the special possibility of such 'combinations,' and began to search for ways of intentionally bringing one another into this special state, they soon understood and found the possibility of actualizing this by means of what is called 'being-Hanbledzoin,' namely, that cosmic substance, the essence of which the three-brained beings of the contemporary civilization came close to understanding, and which they called 'animal magnetism.'

"Since for the explanation of the given case and also perhaps for my following explanations, you must know more in detail concerning being-Hanbledzoin, I find it necessary before speaking further to inform you just now about this cosmic substance.

"Hanbledzoin is nothing else than the 'blood' of the Kesdjan body of the being; just as the cosmic substances called in totality blood serve for nourishing and renewing the planetary body of the being, so also Hanbledzoin serves in the same way for nourishing and perfecting the body Kesdjan.

"It is necessary to tell you that in general the quality of the composition of the blood in three-brained beings and also in the common presences of your favorites depends on the number of the being-bodies already 'completely formed.'

"Blood in the presences of three-brained beings may be composed of substances arising through the transformation of three separate independent what are called 'general-cosmic-sources-of-actualizing.'

"The substances of that part of the being-blood which is designed by Nature for serving the planetary body of the being arise by means of the transformation of substances of that planet on which the given beings are formed and exist.

"But the substances which are designed for serving the Kesdjan body of the being, the totality of which is called Hanbledzoin, are obtained from the transformation of elements of other planets and of the sun itself of that system, where the given three-brained being has the place of his arising and existence.

"Finally, that part of the being-blood which almost everywhere is called the sacred being-Hanbledzoin, and only on certain planets is called the 'sacred Aiësakhaldan,' and which part serves the highest part of the being called the soul, is formed from the direct emanations of our Most Holy Sun Absolute.

"Substances required for the blood of the planetary body of the being enter into them through their 'first-being-food,' or, as your favorites say, 'through food.'

"But the substances needed both for coating and for perfecting the higher-being-body-Kesdjan enter into their common presences through their, as they say, 'breathing,' and through certain what are called 'pores' of their skin.

"And the sacred cosmic substances required for the coating of the highest being-body, which sacred being-part of theirs, as I have already told you, they call soul, can be assimilated and correspondingly transformed and coated in them, just as in us, exclusively only from the process of what is called 'Aiëssirittoorassnian-contemplation' actualized in the common presence by the cognized intention on the part of all their spiritualized independent parts.

"Although you will be able thoroughly to understand about all those cosmic substances with which the three independent being-bodies are coated and perfected in the common presences of your favorites only when, as I have already promised, I shall relate to you in general about the chief cosmic fundamental laws of World-creation and World-existence, nevertheless for a fuller elucidation of our present theme it is now necessary to explain a little about the changed form of the actualization in the common presences of your favorites of the 'second-being-food' automatically taken in by them.

"At the beginning, after the destruction of the organ Kundabuffer, when they, like all the other three-brained beings of our Great Universe also began to have a 'Fulasnitamnian-existence,' this second-being-food was normally transformed and all the fundamental elements proper to it, those which arise from the transformation of their own planet and those which flow into their atmosphere from the transformation in other concentrations of their solar system, were assimilated by their common presence according to the definite data already present in them, and the superfluity of certain of its component elements not used by individual beings automatically passed, as in us, into the possession of the surrounding meritorious beings similar to them.

"But later when, as I have already said, most of them began to exist in a way unbecoming to three-brained beings, Great Nature was constrained to change their Fulasnitamnian-existence into an existence according to the principle of Itoklanoz, and when gradually in the presences of most of them those definite crystallizations foreseen by Great Nature—which crystallizations are the most important part of the composition of the second-being-food, and which when assimilated by beings are transformed into substances for the coating and for the further perfecting of their higher-body-Kesdjan—ceased, owing to their abnormal being-existence, to be assimilated either consciously or automatically for the purpose indicated, then in consequence of this and also because the afflux of these substances, transformed in other concentrations and getting into the atmospheres of the planets, continued all the time to flow into the atmosphere of your planet, the result was that on this ill-fated planet, among your unfortunate favorites, there arose still another definite 'disease' which has already become quite definite in its harmful action upon them.

"The point is that not being used up for their predetermined purpose, the said definite cosmic crystallizations become, during certain displacements of their atmosphere, concentrated in certain of their atmospheric strata, and entering into them from time to time—dependently on various external surrounding conditions and also on the inner state of the common presences of your favorites, which by the way arises in them chiefly from the form of their mutual relationship—just into them as into apparatuses foreseen by Nature in general for the transformation of cosmic substances needed for serving the aims of the Most Great general-cosmic-Trogoautoegocrat, and not meeting there 'substrata' corresponding to the requirements of the lawful process of Djartklom, they, that is these cosmic crystallizations, during their subsequent free completed evolutions or involutions for passing into other crystallizations proper to this planet and before completing their transformations, produce upon planetary bodies, thanks already to other accidental factors, that action by which such a mentioned specific disease newly arisen there is characterized.

"Here it is opportune to notice that such a disease there

having such a specific cause was named differently by your favorites at different times on different parts of the surface of their planet; and the contemporary beings likewise name it differently and also 'wiseacre' differently regarding the explanations of its cause.

"From among the great number of names of this disease of theirs the most widely spread there at the present time are 'grippe,' 'influenza,' 'Spanish influenza,' 'dengue,' and others.

"As regards the introduction into themselves of the second kind of being-food, which continues among beings even still up to now, then, since they lost the possibility of existing according to the Fulasnitamnian principle, certain of the ingredients of the substances of the second-being-food continue to serve only for assisting the transformation of the first-being-food and for removing from the planetary body certain elements already used by them.

"Now let us speak further about a particular psychic property of your favorites and about my activities at that time among them in the capacity of a 'physician-specialist' when I acted upon them by means of this particular psychic property of theirs.

"Though this 'hypnotism,' or as they prefer to say this branch of their 'science,' arose and became official only recently, yet it had already had time to become for them another of the very serious factors which brought about a still greater 'confusion' of their psyche, already muddled enough without this in the majority of them, and which still further deranged the functioning of their planetary body.

"After I had become a professional, namely, a 'physician-hypnotist,' I grew a little interested also in this official science of theirs, so that when I later made my usual researches concerning various serious questions, as for instance the investigations concerning the results of the activities of the Very Saintly Ashiata Shiemash, and chanced to come across something bearing upon questions of this branch of their science, I elucidated to my Reason also this 'misunderstanding-question' there.

"As the automatic impelling causes—which have become there usual for contemporary beings—for the revival also of such a branch of their contemporary science were exceedingly peculiar and even as they themselves would say 'piquant facts,' it will in my opinion be very interesting to tell you a little more in detail also about this said 'revival.'

"Although contemporary learned beings there affirm that the beginning of this branch of their science was made by a certain English professor named Brade and that it was developed by the French professor Charcot, yet in reality, this was not so at all.

"From my detailed investigations of this said question, by the way, it became also clear that the former, Brade, had unmistakable signs of the properties of a Hasnamuss, and the latter, Charcot, had the typical properties of a mama's darling.

"And terrestrial types of this kind, particularly the contemporary ones, can never discover anything quite new.

"And indeed, it appeared that this matter proceeded there in the following way:

"A certain Italian abbot, Pedrini by name, was in his town what is called a 'confessor' for a convent.

"To this abbot confessor there often came for confession a nun named Ephrosinia.

"From the stories told about her, it seems that she frequently fell into a certain particular state, and while in this state she displayed manifestations unusual for her environment.

"During confession she complained to the abbot Pedrini that at times she was unmistakably under the influence of 'diabolical suggestions.'

"Everything she herself said and the stories circulated about her interested the abbot Pedrini and he became very desirous of convincing himself personally about them.

"Once during confession he tried by all possible means to evoke frankness in this nun, and he got to know among other things that this 'nun-novice' had had a 'lover,' who had once given her his portrait framed in a very beautiful frame, and that she permitted herself during periods of 'resting' from her prayers to admire this picture of her 'sweetheart' and that, as it seemed to her, the diabolical suggestion proceeded in her, just at these said periods of her 'resting.'

"All this told frankly by the nun still further excited the interest of the abbot Pedrini and he decided at all costs to find out the cause of it, and with this aim in view he first of all asked the nun Ephrosinia to be sure to bring with her to the next confession the portrait of her sweetheart together with the frame.

"At the next confession the nun took with her this said portrait.

"There was nothing very special about it but the frame indeed was unusual, it being all encrusted with mother-of-pearl and various colored stones.

"While the abbot and the nun were together examining the portrait in the frame, the abbot suddenly noticed that something particular began to proceed with the nun.

"First she became pale and for a certain time she became, as it were, petrified, and then there began with her on the spot precisely in all details, the same manifestations which proceed there among the newly married at what is called the 'first night.'

"After all this, the abbot Pedrini desired still more to make clear to himself all the causes of such an unusual manifestation.

"But as regards the nun, she recovered two hours after the beginning of this particular state of hers, and it was discovered that she knew and remembered nothing of what had happened to her.

"As the abbot Pedrini himself alone could not unravel

this phenomenon, he turned for help to his acquaintance, a certain 'Doctor Bambini.'

"Well, when the abbot Pedrini told everything in detail to the doctor Bambini, the latter also became very much interested, and from then on they both began to occupy themselves with the elucidation of it all.

"They first made various elucidating experiments upon the nun Ephrosinia herself, and after several what are there called 'seances' they noticed that this nun invariably fell into such a peculiar state of hers only when her gaze rested rather a long time on one of the brilliant colored stones, on what is called a 'Persian turquoise,' which was among the adornments of the frame of this portrait.

"But later when with this same Persian turquoise they continued to make their elucidating experiments upon others, they then soon became categorically convinced, firstly, that in almost any one of the three-brained beings without distinction of sex who gazes for a long time at shining and brilliant objects of a certain kind, there begins to proceed a state similar to the one which proceeded with the first subject of their experiments; and secondly, they noticed further that the form of manifestation of the subject during the state varies and is found to be dependent on the former being-experiences which chanced to be predominant and on the shining objects with which a connection was accidentally established during such experiences of theirs.

"Well, my boy . . .

"When the information concerning such observations, deductions and experiments of these two beings belonging to the community Italy were spread among the contemporary learned beings of 'new formation' and many of these latter also began wiseacring about it, and finally when by chance, as it usually happens among them, they learned that it is possible in beings similar to them when in this state, to change in an accelerated way the impressions formerly fixed in them to new ones, then certain of them began to use this particular psychic property inherent in them for the purpose of curing.

"And from then on, such a means of curing was called by them 'hypnotic cure,' and those beings who were occupied with this means of curing, 'physician-hypnotists.'

"The question as to what this state of theirs is and why it obtains in them remains an open one for them even up till now, and reply to it they cannot.

"From that time on there began to appear and there exist till now hundreds of every possible kind of theory and thousands of thick books devoted to this question, thanks to which the minds of the ordinary three-brained beings of this ill-fated planet, already sufficiently muddled without this, become still more muddled.

"This branch of their science has perhaps come to be for them more maleficent than the fantastic inventions of the ancient Hellenic fishermen and of the contemporary beings of the community Germany.

"Thanks merely to this branch of their science, there was acquired in the psyche of the ordinary beings of this ill-fated planet several still new forms of what are called 'being-Kalkali,' that is, 'essential strivings' which became cast into forms of definite 'teachings' existing there under the names of 'Anoklinism,' 'Darwinism,' 'anthroposophism,' 'theosophism,' and many others under names also ending with 'ism,' thanks to which even those two data of their presences, which still helped them to be at least a little as it is becoming to three-centered beings to be, finally disappeared in them.

"And these essential data which have until recently been in them engendered in them the being-impulses they called 'patriarchality' and 'religiousness.'

"This branch of their contemporary science was the cause not only of the acquiring by their common presences of several further new maleficent Kalkali, but it was also the cause of the derangement in many of them of the, without this, abnormal functioning of their psyche, which to their great misfortune was already long before this disharmonized up to the degree of what is called 'Alnokhoorian cacophony.'

"You will understand this well, if I tell you that during that curing practice of mine there, when I later again became a physician-hypnotist there and existed mostly on the continent called Europe and on other countries situated near to it, almost half of my patients consisted of those who were ill only because of this said maleficent science of theirs which had become widely spread there.

"And this was obtained because when these 'learned-beings-of-new-formation' began writing various books about these questions, with every kind of fantastic theory, many ordinary beings there began to read them and became crazy with their fantasies and themselves began trying to evoke this hypnotic state in each other and as a result they brought themselves to the point of becoming my patients.

"Among such patients of mine were the wives of husbands who, having chanced to read these works, wished to suggest to their wives their egoistic wishes; for similar reasons children of unreasonable parents became my patients; various men who were found to be under the orders, or as it is said there, 'under the thumb' of their mistresses, and so on and so forth.

"And all this only thanks to the fact that these 'sorry-learned-beings-of-new-formation' cooked up their Hasnamussian theories concerning this distressing state of theirs.

"None of the theories now current among them concerning this question of hypnotism even approximate in the least to reality.

"Most recently, by the way, when I was on this ill-fated planet a new maleficent means began to flourish there for doing the same with the psyche of the beings there, as there did and still does this branch of their science hypnotism.

"And this new maleficent means they call 'psycho-analysis.'

"You must without fail also know that when beings of the period of the Tikliamishian civilization constated for the first time about this particular psychic property of theirs, and soon made it clear that by its means they could destroy in each other certain properties particularly unbecoming to be in them, then the process itself of bringing someone into this state began to be regarded by them as a sacred process and was performed only in their temples before the congregation.

"But in the presences of your contemporary favorites not only does there absolutely not arise any being-impulse of 'contrition' about this essential property of theirs, and not only do they not consider its concentrated manifestation, intentionally yet unavoidably evoked by them, as 'sacred'; but they have already adapted it, the process itself and the accidentally obtained results, for serving them as a means for 'tickling' certain consequences of the properties of the organ Kundabuffer firmly fixed in them.

"For instance, even when they meet together for one or another established 'patriarchal ritual' like a 'wedding,' 'baptism,' 'saint's day,' and so on, one of the great diversions is trying to bring one another into the said state.

"It is lucky that they still do not know—and it must be hoped that they never will know—other methods besides the one first discovered by the beings of the community Italy, the abbot Pedrini and the doctor Bambini, namely, the gazing at a shining brilliant object, by means of which method, as I have already told you, certain of them can indeed be brought into such a mentioned 'concentrated state.'"

CHAPTER 33

Beelzebub as Professional Hypnotist

Beelzebub continued to relate further as follows:

"When I existed among your favorites as a professional hypnotist I made my elucidating experiments upon their psyche chiefly by means of that said particular state of theirs, which the contemporary beings there call the 'hypnotic state.'

"For bringing them into this state, I had at first recourse to the same means by which the beings of the period of the Tikliamishian civilization brought each other into this state, namely, by acting upon them with my own Hanbledzoin.

"But when later there often began to arise in my common presence the being-impulse called 'love-of-kind,' and, apart from my personal aims, I had to produce this said state in very many three-brained beings there for their personal benefit, and as this means proved very harmful for my being-existence, I invented another means, thanks to which I obtained the same effect without the expenditure of my own Hanbledzoin.

"I then invented and very soon became expert in quickly changing the mentioned 'difference-of-the-filling-of-the-blood-vessels' by means of a certain hindering of the movement of the blood in certain blood vessels.

"By means of this hindering I obtained the result that although the already mechanized tempo of the blood circulation of their waking state remained in beings, yet at the same time their real consciousness, that is, the one which they themselves call subconsciousness, began also to function.

"This new means of mine proved of course incomparably better than that which is used even up till now by beings of your planet, who make the person they hypnotize gaze at a shining or brilliant object.

"It cannot be denied that, as I have already told you, it is possible to bring them into such a psychic state by making them fix their gaze on a brilliant or bright object, but not all beings there, not by a long way, the reason being that although from their fixed gaze on a shining object there may proceed in their general blood circulation the change of the 'filling-of-the-blood-vessels,' nevertheless the chief factor for this must be the, on their part, intentional or automatic concentration of thought and feeling.

"And this latter can be obtained in them either from an intense expectation, or from that process proceeding in them which they express by the word 'faith,' or from the arising emotion of the sensation of fear of something about to happen, or finally from the functions already contained within the presence of the given being which they call 'passions,' as for instance 'hate,' 'love,' 'sensuality,' 'curiosity,' and so on and so forth.

"That is why in beings called there 'hysterical,' in whom there is lost temporarily or forever the possibility of concentration of 'thought' and 'feeling,' it is impossible by means of fixing their gaze upon a shining object to obtain in their blood circulation the change of the difference of the 'filling-of-blood-vessels,' and hence it is also impossible to obtain in them this said hypnotic state.

"But by the means I invented, namely, a definite action upon the 'blood-vessels' themselves, it was possible to bring into this state not only anyone you please of these three-brained beings who have taken your fancy, but even also many one-brained and two-brained beings breeding there, as for instance, various what they call 'quadrupeds,' 'fishes,' 'birds,' and so on and so forth.

"But as regards the said impulse, love-of-kind, which led me to seek for a new means of bringing your favorites into such a state which had already become proper to them—this arose in me and gradually became dominant in me for a while chiefly because, during these therapeutic activities of mine, ordinary three-brained beings there belonging to all castes, here, there, and everywhere, soon began to love and esteem me and to consider me almost as one sent to them from Above to help them to deliver themselves from their pernicious habits; in short, they began to manifest toward me their most sincere, almost genuine being-impulse of 'Oskolnikoo' or as they themselves say 'thankfulness' and 'gratitude.'

"This being-Oskolnikoo or gratitude was manifested towards me not only by those I saved and by those nearest to them, but by almost everybody who had been in this or another way in contact with me or who had heard of me, but only with the exception of those professionals among them who were their physicians.

"These latter on the contrary hated me in the extreme and would strain every nerve to impair somehow the good feelings which arose in ordinary beings towards me; and they hated me simply because I very soon became their serious rival.

"Strictly speaking, they had indeed cause to hate me, because already after only a few days of my therapeutic activities hundreds of patients used to attend my daily consultations and hundreds of others tried to become clients of mine, while my poor rivals had to sit for long periods in their famous offices and impatiently wait for any odd patient who might stray in like a 'lost sheep.'

"They waited for these lost sheep with great impatience, because certain of these latter were transformed into what are called 'milch cows' from which they milk, as was already customary there, that something which they defined by the word 'oof' or 'dough.'

"All the same, justice demands this to be said for them that during recent times it was indeed quite impossible to exist there without this 'oof' and particularly for those three-brained beings who are there the contemporary famous physicians.

"And so, my boy, I began my activities in the capacity of a physician-hypnotist, as I have already told you, in the center of the continent Asia, in various towns of Turkestan.

"I was first in the town of that part of Turkestan which later came to be called 'Chinese Turkestan' in contradistinction to that part of it which, from the time of its conquest by beings belonging to the large community Russia, has been called 'Russian Turkestan.'

"There was a very great need in the towns of Chinese Turkestan for such a physician as I then became, because among the three-brained beings breeding on this part of the surface of this planet of yours there was developed at that period more strongly than usual two forms of their most pernicious what are called 'organic habits,' which also had become proper to be acquired in the presences of the beings of that ill-fated planet.

"One of these pernicious organic habits was what is called there the 'smoking of opium,' and the other was the 'chewing of anasha,' or, as it is otherwise named, 'hashish.'

"They obtain this opium as you already know from the plant poppy, and hashish from a surplanetary formation there called 'Chakla' or 'hemp.'

"As I have just said, at this period of my activities, my existence passed at first chiefly in various towns of Chinese Turkestan, but circumstances so fell out that later I preferred to be in the towns of Russian Turkestan.

"Here among the beings of Russian Turkestan, one of the said 'pernicious habits' or as they themselves call them 'vices,' namely, the smoking of opium, was very rare, and the chewing of anasha was even rarer, but on the other hand, the use of what is called 'Russian vodka' flourished luxuriantly there.

"This maleficent means is obtained there chiefly from the surplanetary formation called the 'potato.'

"From the use of the said vodka, not only does the psyche of the ill-fated three-brained beings there become, just as from 'opium' and 'anasha' also, utterly 'nonsensical' but in addition certain important parts of their planetary body also gradually completely degenerate.

"Here I may say, my boy, that it was just then, at the beginning of these activities of mine among your favorites, that I instituted for the purpose of better conducting my investigations in the domain of their psyche, those 'statistics' of mine which later on gradually interested certain most Very Saintly Cosmic Individuals of a higher gradation of Reason.

"Well then, while I existed as a physician there among the beings breeding in the towns of Turkestan, I had to work so hard, especially towards the end, that certain functions of my planetary body began to get out of order, and I began to consider therefore how to manage to have the possibility at least for a certain time of doing nothing but only rest.

"I could of course return to my home on the planet Mars for this purpose, but then there arose before me my personal-individual 'being-Dimtzoneero,' that is, my being-duty towards what is called the 'essence-word' I had given to myself.

"And this essence-word I had given myself, when beginning my sixth descent, was to exist there among your favorites until such time as I should finally have made clear to my mind all the facts which were the causes of the gradual formation of the mentioned exclusively strange being-psyche of their common presence.

"Well then, as by that time I had still not fulfilled this essence-word which I had given myself, that is to say, I had not yet had time to learn all the details needed for a full elucidation of the problem, I considered a return to the planet Mars premature.

"But to remain in this Turkestan and to organize my existence there in such a way as to have the full possibility of giving my planetary body the required rest I could not, in any way, because in almost all the beings there on that part of the surface of your planet, breeding in both Chinese and Russian Turkestan, there had already been crystallized, either through personal perceptions or from the descriptions of others, data for recognizing my appearance; at the same time, each of the ordinary beings of this country wished to speak with me concerning either himself personally or his nearest on account of one of the vices in the deliverance from which I had chanced to become there such an unparalleled specialist.

"What I then devised and carried out to escape from this situation was the reason why Turkestan—concerning which place there are and will be preserved in my common presence the data then fixed for pleasant memories—ceased to be for me the place of my permanent existence on your planet at the period of this last stay of mine; and thereafter the cities of the 'famous' Europe with their cafés with the 'black liquid'—made of nobody knows what—replaced the towns of Turkestan with their 'Tchai-kanas' and their delicious fragrant teas.

"I decided to go to the country which is a part of the continent Africa and is there called Egypt.

"I chose this country because Egypt was indeed at that period the best place for resting, and many three-brained beings there possessing what is called 'material wealth' went there for that purpose from all the other continents.

"Having arrived there, I settled down in the city called 'Cairo' and very soon organized the external form of my ordinary existence in such a way as to have that rest for my planetary body after the said intense and strenuous labors.

"Do you remember, I already told you that I was in this Egypt for the first time during my fourth appearance on the surface of that planet of yours, where I descended for the purpose of collecting with the help of several beings of our tribe existing there, a certain number of the chance-arisen 'freaks' called 'apes'; and I furthermore then told you that I inspected in that country many interesting artificial constructions, among which was also that particular observatory, which had then interested me, for the observation of cosmic concentrations.

"At my sixth descent, of all the numerous interesting constructions that had previously existed there scarcely anything existed any longer.

"They had all been destroyed, partly by the beings there themselves, thanks to what are called their 'wars' and 'revolutions,' and partly they came to be covered by sands.

"These sands were a consequence partly of those great winds I have already mentioned, and partly also of that planetary tremor which was afterwards called by the beings of this Egypt the 'Alnepoosian earthquake.'

"During this planetary tremor, an island then called 'Siapora' situated on the north side of a still existing island called 'Cyprus,' gradually in a very peculiar way entered into the planet during five terrestrial years, and while this process lasted, there proceeded in the surrounding great Saliakooriapnian space extraordinary what are called 'low' and 'high tides,' as a result of which a great deal of sand from beneath the Saliakooriap rose to the surface of this terra firma and mingled with sands of the already mentioned origin.

"Now do you know, my boy, what has gradually arisen in me while I have been telling you all this about Egypt and of what all my being has now already become finally aware—namely, an unpardonable error I made in my tales concerning the three-brained beings breeding on the planet Earth.

"Do you remember that at one time I told you that not one of the achievements of the beings of past generations had ever reached beings of subsequent generations?

"Well it has become aware in me that I have made a mistake about this.

"Not once during my preceding tales concerning these beings who have taken your fancy has there ever been recalled in my being-association an event which took place there just one day before my flight forever from the surface of that planet, and which event proves that something after all did reach even your contemporary favorites from among the achievements of the beings of the remote past.

"The emanations of joy which then arose in me from my pardon by our ALL-JUST CREATOR OMNIPOTENT ENDLESSNESS and from His gracious permission to me to return to the bosom of my first arising must have prevented me from absorbing those impressions sufficiently intensely for there to be in the corresponding part of my general whole such 'completedly-crystallized' data as should engender in beings, during being-associations arising from the result of one-sourced manifestations, the repetitions of what has already been sensed.

"But now, as I was speaking of this contemporary Egypt and there was revived before my 'being-sight' pictures of certain localities of that part of the terra firma surface of the planet which had once pleased me, the faint impressions I had previously of this said event there became gradually coated in me into a definite awareness and to be clearly recollected in me.

"Before telling you about this event there, which cannot be described otherwise than as sadly tragic, I must for your more or less clear representations about it once more tell you something about the three-brained beings there of the continent Atlantis who then constituted the learned society under the name of Akhaldan.

"Certain members of this society who already had some notion of the sacred Omnipresent Okidanokh discovered, by their persistent labors, how to obtain from their own atmosphere and also from certain surplanetary formations each of its sacred parts separately, and by keeping these sacred cosmic 'force-bearing' substances in a concentrated state, how to perform, with their help, their definite scientific elucidatory experiments.

"The learned members of the said great learned society then also discovered among other things, that they could, by means of the separately localized third part of the Omnipresent Okidanokh, namely, by means of its sacred 'neutralizing-force' or 'force-of-reconciling,' bring every kind of planetary what are called 'organic' formations into such a state that they remained forever with all those active elements contained in them at the given moment, that is to say, they could stop and absolutely arrest their future inevitable what is called 'decay.'

"The knowledge of the ableness of such an actualization passed by inheritance to certain beings of this Egypt, namely, to those initiated beings who were the direct descendants of the learned members of the Akhaldans.

"Well, many centuries after the loss of Atlantis, beings of this Egypt, on the basis of the knowledge which had reached them, also discovered how, by means of that same sacred neutralizing-force of the sacred Okidanokh, to preserve the planetary bodies of certain of them forever in a nondecaying and nondecomposing state after the sacred Rascooarno, or as they say, after death had proceeded in them.

"And indeed, by the time of my sixth visit to that planet all the beings and everything which had been in this Egypt during my former visit, had entirely ceased to exist and not even any notion of it all was preserved.

"But those planetary bodies upon which they employed the mentioned means remained intact and exist there even to the present time.

"And these surviving planetary bodies are called by the contemporary beings 'mummies.'

"The transformation of the planetary bodies into mummies was effected by the beings of Egypt by a very simple means; namely, they kept the planetary body assigned for this purpose about half a month in what is there called castor oil, and later they introduced into it the sacred 'substance-force' dissolved in a corresponding way.

"Well, my boy, according to the researches and investigations of one of our countrymen who exists there even up till now, about which I was informed by an etherogram after my final departure from the surface of your planet, it turned out that once, when their process of 'reciprocal-destruction' began between the community of beings breeding on this Egypt and the beings of a neighboring community, and when at the same time one of their, as they are called, 'Pharaohs' came to the end of his existence, the beings whose business it was to preserve the bodies of meritorious beings everlastingly were unable, owing to the approach of beings hostile to them, to keep the planetary body of this Pharaoh in castor oil as long as was necessary, that is to say, half a month; but nevertheless, they put this body into castor oil, placed it in a hermetically closed room and, having dissolved in a certain way the said sacred substance-force they introduced it into the said room so as to obtain in this way what they wished.

"This definite sacred something would have remained for untold centuries in its pristine state among these three-brained beings who long ago ceased to have any reverence in their essence; but as in the presences of these contemporary, as it is possible to call them, 'unconscious sacrilegists,' a criminal passion has arisen that evokes in them a need to despoil even the sanctuaries of beings of past generations, they dug down even into this chamber which ought to have been for them a profoundly revered sanctuary, and they committed that blasphemous deed whose result is now the cause of my becoming aware with all my being of my mistake—of just that mistake I made when I so confidently assured you that nothing whatever had reached the beings of the contemporary civilization from the beings of epochs long past; whereas this said contemporary Egyptian event is a consequence of one result which reached them of the attainments of these ancient ancestors of theirs who used to exist on the continent Atlantis.

"Such a result of the scientific attainments of beings of long, long past epochs reached the contemporary beings and became their possession for the following reason.

"Perhaps, my dear Hassein, you already know, like all the responsible beings of our Great Universe, and even those still only at the period of the second half of their preparation to become such, even without regard to the degree of their being-rumination, that the common presence of the planetary body of every being and in general of any other 'relatively independent' great or small cosmic unit must consist of all the three localized sacred substance-forces of the holy Triamazikamno, namely, of the substance-forces of the Holy-Affirming, Holy-Denying, and Holy-Reconciling, and that it must be sustained by them all the time in a corresponding and balanced state; and if for some reason or other, there enters into any presence a superfluity of the vibrations of any one of these three sacred forces, then infallibly and unconditionally, the sacred Rascooarno must occur to it, that is the total destruction of its ordinary existence as such. Well, my boy, because there had arisen in the presences of your contemporary favorites, as I have already told you, their further criminal need to despoil the sanctuaries of their ancestors, and certain of them with the purpose of satisfying their criminal needs even forced open in the mentioned way the hermetically closed rooms, then the sacred substance-force of the Holy-Reconciling existing in these rooms localized in a separate state, having had not sufficient time to blend with the space, entered into their presences and actualized its property proper to it according to Law.

"I shall say nothing now concerning just how and in what form the psyche of the three-brained beings breeding there on this part of the terra firma surface of your planet came to be molded.

"Some time later perhaps, in its proper place, I shall explain this to you also; and meanwhile, let us return to our interrupted theme.

"The program of my external existence in this said Egypt included among other things, the practice of taking a walk every morning in the direction of what are called the 'Pyramids' and 'Sphinx.'

"These Pyramids and Sphinx were the sole, chance, poor surviving remains of those magnificent constructions which were erected by the generations of the most great Akhaldans and by the Great Ancestors of the beings of this said Egypt, and of which I was a witness at my fourth sojourn on this planet of yours.

"I failed to have a thorough rest in this Egypt because of circumstances which soon led me to depart from there; and the circumstances that led to my premature departure from Egypt were, strictly speaking, the reason why the towns of dear Turkestan with their pleasant 'Tchai-kanas' were replaced as I have already told you by the cities of their famous contemporary cultured continent Europe with the not less famous 'cafe-restaurants,' in which, as I have already told you, instead of fragrant teas they offer you a black liquid consisting of nobody knows what."

CHAPTER 34
Russia

"All the further events, during this last sojourn of mine on the surface of the planet Earth, connected with the abnormal form of the usual being-existence of those three-brained beings who please you, and, at the same time, many trifling incidents of all kinds which elucidated the characteristic details of their peculiar psyche, began from the following:

"Once, walking one morning by the said Pyramids, a certain elderly being, a stranger, and in exterior appearance not a native, approached me, and greeting me in the manner customary there, addressed me with the following words:

"'Doctor! You will perhaps do me the kindness to allow me to be your companion on your morning walks? I have noticed that you always walk in this neighborhood alone. I am also very fond of walking here of a morning and as I, too, am quite alone here in Egypt, I venture to propose to you that I should accompany you on these walks of yours.'

"Since the vibrations of his radiations in relation to mine appeared not acutely 'Otkalooparnian,' or, as your favorites in such a case would say, 'since he appeared to be sympathetic,' and furthermore because I myself had already thought of establishing here also corresponding mutual relations with someone, in order as a rest from active mentation to converse sometimes by following only the course of freely flowing associations, I at once agreed to his proposition and from that day forth began to spend the time of my morning strolls with him.

"During our further acquaintanceship, it transpired that this foreigner was a subject of that large community called

'Russia,' and that among his compatriots he was an important power-possessing being.

"During these walks of ours together it so happened that we began, why I don't know, to talk chiefly about the weak will of the three-brained beings and about those weaknesses unworthy of them, which they themselves call 'vices' and to which they, particularly the contemporary beings, accustom themselves very quickly, and which finally become for them a basis, in the sense of the aim of their existence, as well as in the sense of the quality of their being-manifestations.

"Once during one of these conversations of ours he, addressing me suddenly, said:

"'My dear Doctor! In my native land during recent times the passion for alcohol is strongly developed and widely spread among people of all classes, which passion as you know always, sooner or later, leads in general to those forms of mutual relationship which usually bring about the destruction of the century-old pillars and attainments of Society.

"'This is just why several farsighted compatriots of mine, having at last understood all the seriousness of such a situation as had arisen in our country, collected together, in order perhaps to devise conjointly some means or other for the prevention of any catastrophic consequence. For the realization of this task of theirs, they there and then decided to found a society under the name of "The Trusteeship of People's Temperance," and they chose me to be the head of this enterprise.

"'At the present time, the activities of the "Trusteeship," as regards the organization of measures for the struggle against the said state evil, are in full swing.

"'We have already done much and we have in view to do much more.'

"Having said this, he became a little thoughtful and continued thus:

"'If now, my dear Doctor, you were to ask my personal opinion as to the results expected from this Trusteeship of ours, sincerely speaking, I should, although I am at the head of it, find it very difficult to say anything good about it.

"'As regards the general position of affairs of this Trusteeship of ours, I meanwhile personally place my hope only in a "chance."

"'In my opinion, the whole evil consists in this, that this Trusteeship is under the protection of several groups, upon whom any realization of its task just depends, but as these groups each follow their own particular aims and wishes concerning each separate question, then, over the solution of each separate question concerning the basic aim of the Trusteeship, controversy always reigns. And thanks to this, day by day, instead of improving the conditions for a speedy possibility of a realization, indeed, of the aim which has been set as a basis of this very important actualization for my dear Fatherland, there only increases among the separate members of our Trusteeship all kinds of misunderstandings, personal considerations, gossip, intrigue, plots, and so on and so forth.

"'As regards myself, personally, I have during recent times so much thought, rethought, and consulted with various people who have more or less "life-experience," in order to find some way or other out of the situation which has turned out so sorrowfully, that I reached such a state that I nearly fell ill and was compelled by the insistence of those near to me to undertake this journey here to Egypt with the sole object of resting. But alas! Now here in Egypt even, I have met with no success, because always those same black thoughts of mine give me no peace.

"'Now, my dear Doctor, that you already know approximately the gist of that affair, which was the cause for my present spiritual unbalance, I will frankly confess to you my inner thoughts and hopes which have arisen in connection with my acquaintanceship with you.

"'The point is,' he continued, 'that during our frequent and lengthy talks on the subject of the evil vices of people and about the possible measures for getting rid of them, I reached a full conviction of your thorough competency in questions of the subtle understanding of people's psyche, as well as in the creating of conditions for the struggle against their weaknesses. And that is why I regard you as the only man who might be the source of every kind of initiative for the organization, as well as for the carrying out in life of the activities of the Trusteeship founded there at home for the struggle against alcoholism.

"'Yesterday morning an idea came into my head, over which I thought the whole day and evening, and it is about this that I finally decided to ask you.

"'Would you consent to go to my country, to Russia, and, after you have seen everything on the spot that is going on there, help us to organize this Trusteeship of ours, in such a way that it may indeed become of that use to my country for which it was founded?'

"He further added: 'Your just humaneness gives me courage to address this request to you, as well as the assurance that you will not, of course, refuse to take part in the work of saving perhaps millions of people.'

"When this sympathetic elderly Russian finished speaking, I, having thought a little, replied that I might very possibly consent to his proposal to go to Russia, since that country might perhaps be very suitable also for my chief aim.

"Further I said to him: 'At the present time I have but one aim, namely, specifically to clear up for myself all the details of the manifestations of the human psyche of individuals existing separately as well as in groups. Well now, for the elucidation of the state and manifestations of the psyche of large groups, Russia would perhaps be very suitable for me since, as I have understood during our talks, the disease of the "passion for alcohol" is spread there in your country among almost the entire population, thanks to which I shall the more often have the possibility of carrying out my experiments on various types, each separately as well as in a mass.'

"After this talk with the important Russian being, I soon got ready, and several days after left Egypt together with him. Two weeks later we were already in the chief place of existence of this large community, in the town at that time still called 'Saint Petersburg.'

"After we arrived there, my new acquaintance immediately gave himself up to his own affairs which had very greatly accumulated during his long absence.

"By that time, among other things, there had already been finished there the construction of that large building which was destined by the Trusteeship to this aim of struggling against alcoholism, and my new acquaintance immediately began to apply himself to the organization and preparation of all that was necessary for what they call there the 'inauguration' of that building and the starting of the activities connected with it.

"I began, however, during that time, to go about everywhere as is usual for me, and to frequent the beings of this city, belonging to various what are called there 'classes,' in order to become acquainted with the characteristic particularities of their manners and customs.

"Well, it was then that I constated, among other things, that in the presences of the beings belonging to just this contemporary community, their, as it is called, 'Ego-Individuality' began during the recent centuries to form itself particularly sharply dual.

"After I had constated this and began specially to investigate this question there, I finally elucidated that this dual individuality obtained in their common presences, chiefly owing to a noncorrespondence between what is called the 'tempo-of-the-place-of-their-arising-and-existence' and the 'form-of-their-being-mentation.'

"In my opinion, my boy, you will very well understand this particularly sharp 'duality-of-the-beings' of this large community, if I repeat to you word for word the opinion about them of our esteemed Mullah Nassr Eddin which he gave me personally.

"It is necessary for me to tell you that during the second half of this last sojourn of mine among your favorites, I happened more than once to meet that terrestrial uniquely wise Mullah Nassr Eddin and to have personal 'exchange of opinion' with him on various, as it is said there, 'life questions.'

"This personal meeting of mine with him, in the course of which he, with a wise saying of his, defined the real essence of the beings of that large community there, took place on one of the parts of the surface of your planet called 'Persia' in a locality named 'Ispahan,' where I happened to be for my investigations concerning the Most Saintly Activities of Ashiata Shiemash, and also for clearing up on the spot that question I needed of just how there arose for the first time the form of their so-called 'politeness,' now everywhere existing there and also maleficent for them.

"Even before my arrival in Ispahan, I already knew that the esteemed Mullah Nassr Eddin had left for the town 'Talaialtnikoom' to stay with the stepson of the eldest daughter of his godfather.

"After I had arrived in this latter town, I immediately

sought him out and the whole time I was there often visited him and, sitting on the roof, as was the custom in this country, we would chat together about every kind of what are called there 'subtle-philosophic-questions.'

"Once, on the second or third day apparently, after my arrival there, on going to him in the morning, my eye was struck by an unusual movement in the streets: everywhere there were being cleaned, swept, and hung out what are called 'carpets,' 'shawls,' 'flags,' and so on.

"I thought: 'Evidently one of the two celebrated annual festivals of the beings of this community is beginning.'

"On ascending to the roof, and having exchanged the usual greetings with our dear, most eminent and wise Mullah Nassr Eddin, I asked, pointing with my hand to what was happening in the street, what it was all about.

"Over his face spread his customary benevolent and as always enchanting grimace, which nevertheless had a slight shade of contempt, and he intended to say something, but at that moment there resounded in the street below the shouts of the 'town criers' and the clattering of many horses.

"Then our wise Mullah, without uttering a word, got up heavily and having taken me by the sleeve led me to the edge of the roof and then winking cunningly at me with his left eye, he turned my attention to a big 'cavalcade' which was rapidly galloping past and which consisted, as I later found out, chiefly of beings who are called 'cossacks' belonging to that same large community there, 'Russia.'

"In the center of this large 'cavalcade' there rolled by what is called a 'Russian phaeton,' harnessed with four horses driven by an unusually fat and 'imposing-looking' coachman. This imposing exterior, also quite Russian in manner, was due to the pads put in corresponding parts under his clothes. In this phaeton sat two beings, one of the type of that country Persia, and the other, a typical what is called 'Russian general.'

"When the said cavalcade had moved off a long way, Mullah first of all uttering his favorite saying: 'So-and-so-and-so-must-be; do-not-do-what-must-not-be,' and having also uttered his favorite exclamation, somewhat resembling 'Zrrt!!,' he returned to his place and suggested to me that I should do the same, then, having arranged the still smoldering charcoal on his 'Kalyan,' he sighed deeply and pronounced the following tirade, which, as always, was not immediately understandable.

"'Just now, in the company of a large number of "well-bred-turkeys," a "crow" of this country passed by, who although one of the chiefs and of high rank, was yet nevertheless rumpled and badly molting.

"'During recent times, I don't know why, "high-rank-crows" of this country no longer in general take a single step without these "well-bred-turkeys"; they evidently do this in the hope that maybe, perhaps, the pitiable remains of the feathers would, owing to their being constantly within the powerful radiations of these turkeys, become a little stronger and cease to fall out.'

"Although I understood positively nothing about what he had just said, yet already well knowing his habit of expressing himself first of all allegorically, I was not at all surprised and did not question him, but patiently awaited his further explanations.

"And indeed, when after he had pronounced the tirade and had thoroughly finished 'hubble-bubbling' the water in his 'Kalyan,' he—while giving in his subsequent speech with the 'subtle venom' which is proper to him, a definition of the whole presence and general essence of the beings of the contemporary community 'Persia'—explained to me that he compared the beings of this same community 'Persia' to the birds, crows, while the beings of the large community 'Russia' who formed just that cortege which had galloped along the street, he compared to the birds, turkeys.

"He developed this thought of his in a long dissertation thus: 'If we analyze impartially and sum up statistically this understanding and picturing which obtain among people of the contemporary civilization concerning the races which populate Europe, in contradistinction to other continents, and make an analogy between these races and birds, then the people who represent the very "Tzimus" of contemporary European civilization, namely, those who arise and dwell on the continent Europe, must infallibly be called peacocks, that is, the birds who have the most beautiful and most gorgeous exterior, while the people who dwell on other continents must be called crows, that is, the most good-for-nothing and dirty of all birds.

"'But for those contemporary people who obtain the basis and the required conditions for their arising on the continent of Europe and who are formed on it, but whose subsequent life, and consequently further "stuffing," proceeds for some reason or other on other continents, and also for those contemporary people who, on the contrary, appear on "God's Earth" on any continent and obtain their further "stuffing" under the conditions arising and reigning on the continent Europe, no better "comparison" can be found than the bird turkey.

"'This latter bird, more than all other birds, expresses a something which is neither fish, flesh, fowl, nor good red herring, but which represents in itself, as is said, "a-half-with-a-quarter-plus-three-quarters."

"'The best representatives of these "turkeys" are the contemporary people of Russia and it was by these turkeys, namely, that one of the chief crows of this country was surrounded who not long ago rapidly passed by us.

"'These Russians moreover correspond ideally to this peculiar bird turkey, as the following considerations of mine show:

"'Arising and being formed on the continent Asia, but chiefly owing to a clean heredity, organic as well as psychic, forged in the course of many centuries in conditions of existence obtained on the said continent, they become, in all respects, the possessors of the nature of Asiatic people, and consequently they should also at the present time be crows. But in view of the fact that in recent times they have all been striving hard to become Europeans and have with intent been thoroughly stuffing themselves accordingly, they, thereby, little by little, are ceasing to be crows; and as, according to several undoubtedly lawful data, they cannot turn into real peacocks, they, leaving the 'crows' behind and not yet reaching to the 'peacocks,' are in themselves as I have said, ideally turkeys.

"'Although the turkey is a very useful bird for the household, because its meat—if of course the turkey is killed in that special way which people of old nations have there learned thanks to long centuries of practice—is better and more tasty than that of all other birds, yet, in its living state, the turkey is a very strange bird and has a certain very special psyche, to understand which, even though only approximately, is, especially for our people with their half passive minds, quite impossible.

"'One of the many specific features of the psyche of this strange bird is that the turkey, why I don't know, considers it always necessary to swagger, and thus will often for no reason whatever puff himself out.

"'Even when nobody is looking at him he swaggers and puffs himself out, though he does so in this case exclusively because of his own imagination and silly dreams.'

"Having said this, Mullah Nassr Eddin got up slowly

and heavily, and again pronouncing his favorite saying: 'So-and-so-this-must-be-it' but this time with the ending 'don't-sit-long-where-you-shouldn't-sit,' took me by the arm and together we descended from the roof.

"Here, my boy, while giving the subtlety of the psychological analysis of our most wise Mullah Nassr Eddin its due, justice demands that it should be said that if these Russians have become such exemplary turkeys, we have, in this case, to blame it only once more on those beings of the community Germany.

"The beings of Germany were in this case guilty owing to the fact that when they invented their famous aniline dyes, they overlooked one of the specific peculiarities of these dyes.

"The point is that with the help of these dyes it is possible to dye all natural colors, except one only, namely, genuine natural black, any other color.

"And it is thanks to this lack of foresight in these German beings that the scandalous misfortune for the poor Russians came about—that is to say, it is owing to the fact that the feathers of the crows are dyed by nature, as it 'unsuspectingly-and-unexpectedly' turned out, just a genuine black, which, even with these aniline dyes invented by themselves, cannot possibly be dyed any other color owing to the said vile imperfection of these dyes—that these poor Russian 'crows' cannot therefore possibly become peacocks. And what is worst of all, having ceased to be crows and not yet having become peacocks, they willy-nilly turn into the bird turkey, which expresses ideally, as has been formulated by our dear teacher, 'Half-with-a-quarter-plus-three-quarters.'

"Well, thanks to the wise definition of the esteemed Mullah Nassr Eddin which he told me himself, I clearly understood for the first time why all the beings of that large community there, when they reach responsible age become possessors of so sharply dual an individuality.

"But enough about this. Listen further now to the events in which I happened to take part after my arrival in the chief place of existence of the community Russia, then called Saint Petersburg.

"As I have already said, while my acquaintance, the said important Russian, settled up his affairs which had become disorganized during his absence, I began to go about everywhere and meet beings there, of different, as is said, 'class' and 'position,' in order to study the characteristic particularities of their manners and customs, and to make clear for myself the cause of their so-called 'organic need' for alcohol, and the manifest consequences also of the result of its effects on their common presences.

"It is interesting to remark that during these meetings of mine with the various three-brained beings belonging to various 'castes' and 'positions,' I had already by then constated several times, and it had, after more attentive observation, become quite evident to me, that the majority of them carried in themselves the germ of that 'particular-functioning-of-their-common-presences' which had already long before been habitually arising in your favorites owing to a certain combination of two independent causes coming from outside.

"The first of these causes is a common cosmic law which exists under the name of 'Solioonensius,' and the second is a sharp deterioration of the conditions of the usual being-existence of the beings on some part or other of the surface of this planet of yours.

"I speak about that germ of the 'particular-functioning-of-their-common-presences,' which after several of their years became molded in the presences of all beings of this community in such a usual form as had already during certain definite periods become in general inherent in them, and as had become what is called a 'stimulating factor' for their specific manifestations, which also became proper only to three-brained beings of the planet Earth; and the totality of these manifestations among the beings of the large community was this time called there 'Bolshevism.'

"I will explain to you later about this same 'particular-functioning-of-their-common-presences.'

"I touched upon this question in this place only to give you a representation of the already particularly abnormal conditions of being-existence among which my activities among the beings of this large community flowed at this period during this sojourn of mine in their chief place of existence, St. Petersburg.

"Even before my arrival in this city, I had had in view to actualize one of my intentions, for the fulfillment of which everything that was necessary had been already prepared by me.

"The point is that already long before this I had intended to set up in one or other of their great inhabited spots a 'something,' of the kind of what they call there a 'chemical laboratory,' in which I intended, by means decided on beforehand to proceed with special experiments on several deeply concealed aspects of their ever the same strange psyche.

"And so, my boy, when I had stayed in this city and when I discovered that almost half my time there might be free, I decided to make use of the chance of being temporarily 'half-occupied,' and set about the actualization of this intention of mine.

"From the information I obtained, I learned that in order to set up such a laboratory there, it was obligatorily required first of all to have a permit from the local power-possessing beings, and that is why I quickly began to take steps to get this permit.

"The first steps I took showed me that on account of the laws which had been so long before fixed in the process of existence of this community, a permit to have the right to have one's own chemical laboratory had to be issued there by a certain what is called 'department' of one of their what are called 'ministries.'

"That is why I betook myself to that same department; but it turned out that although the staff of this department acknowledged that it was their obligation to issue that kind of permit, yet they themselves did not know how it had to be done.

"And they did not know this, as I later understood, simply because no one had ever applied to them for this permit, and on this account these unfortunate beings had not acquired the customary for them what is called 'automatic-habit' for the manifestation of such a 'being-duty' as theirs of this kind.

"Here it must in general be noticed that there during the last centuries almost every 'being-manifestation' for the fulfillment of their being-duty in the presences of those beings who become power-possessing is already actualized, thanks exclusively only to the functioning of the data which are formed in them from manifold automatic repetitions of the same thing.

"As regards the power-possessing beings of this community, the crystallization of these peculiar automatic 'being-data' at this period of the flow of time, proceeded in them much more intensely than anywhere else, and was expressed so sharply that sometimes it even seemed as if there were completely absent in them in general all data whatsoever for the immediate bringing forth of being-impulses proper in general to beings.

"This crystallization proceeded in them, as I later elucidated, in consequence of the action of the cosmic law

Solioonensius, which cosmic law I some time ago mentioned to you.

"But as to what I said, namely, that nobody applied for a permit to the staff of the mentioned department, this by no means happened because none of the inhabitants of this chief place of existence needed a chemical laboratory; no, on the contrary, never had there been in that town so many similar chemical laboratories as at this very period of the flow of time, and doubtless all the owners of the necessary permits had procured them from somewhere or other in some or other way.

"They could not help having them. It was just for this that there existed in this chief place of their existence, as in general there exists in all large and small communities in times of peace, a particular as they say 'administrative body,' which comprises the 'basic-hope-of-a-complete-bliss-for-power-possessors,' which they themselves call the 'gendarmerie' and 'police,' one of the chief obligations of the representatives of which is to see that everyone, for every kind of enterprise there, should have a corresponding permit, and indeed, it must not be supposed that the what are called 'lynx-eyed' beings, representatives of the said 'basic-hope-of-a-complete-bliss-for-power-possessors,' would 'let anything slip by' and allow anywhere any laboratory whatever without the corresponding permit from the power-possessors.

"A basic reason for this seeming contradiction was something quite different.

"It is necessary to tell you that there already in this community the attitude towards the laws and regulations fixed in the past by the beings for 'normal'—according to their understanding—mutual relationship and in general for ordinary existence, began to become such that only those of the ordinary beings could obtain and profit by everything to which they had objective right who knew how to act to the contrary, i.e., against laws and regulations existing there.

"Of these private laboratories, such as I wished to set up, not one but thousands could there be had; it was merely necessary to know first of all what abnormal 'goings' and 'comings' were the practice for procuring the permits for these laboratories, and then to act in accordance with these abnormalities.

"I, however, on account of the short time I had stayed there, had not yet had time to make clear for myself all the subtleties of the ordinary being-existence which had begun in this community, as I said, to become particularly abnormal.

"That is why, when I set out to take steps to get the permit I required, there began for me those endless vexations, or, as they themselves say in such cases, the 'idiotic dilly-dallyings' which were also fixed not long before in the process of their being-existence, and in addition all this turned out in the end to be quite without result and unnecessary.

"It began with this: when I had reached the aforesaid department and addressed myself to the staff there, they all began to eye each other perplexedly and to whisper together, and several of them rummaged through fat tomes in the hope obviously of finding some written rule about the issuing of these permits. Finally the oldest of them came toward me and importantly required from me that I should first of all bring him from a certain other department certain information concerning my personal, as they express it, 'loyalty.'

"It was from just this that my further endless perambulations began, from one department to another, from, as they say, one administration to another, from one official specialist to another . . . and so on without end.

"Thus the business continued until from the so-called

'district-officer' I had to go to the so-called 'parish priest' and so on, all but to the official city midwife.

"Besides this, one of these departments, why I don't know, required that a certificate issued by another department should be stamped by a third.

"In one department I had to sign a certain paper; in another to answer questions having nothing to do with chemistry; while in a third it was explained to me and I was advised how I must manage with the equipment of the laboratory so as not to be poisoned, and so on and so forth.

"It turned out as I later elucidated, that I had been, without at all suspecting it at the time, with an official among whose obligations was that of dissuading from this 'abominable' intention those who wished to set up chemical laboratories.

"But the most amusing of all was that, for obtaining this permit it was necessary in turn to apply to those official servants who had not even the remotest notion of what in general a laboratory was.

"I do not know how all this would have finished, if, having wasted almost two months, I had not myself in the end thrown up all these foolish hustlings around.

"I threw them all up for a reason which was not without its humor.

"According to the rules of all these senseless dillydallyings, I had to get among others a 'paper' from a doctor, official also, certifying that no danger would menace my personal health from my occupation in this laboratory.

"I went to this official doctor; but when he first of all desired to sound me thoroughly and for this requested me to undress entirely so that he might tap me all over with his little hammer, I could not of course in any way consent. And I could not consent to this, because, if I had bared myself, I should inevitably have betrayed my tail which there on your planet I skillfully hid under the folds of my dress.

"And you of course well understand that if any one of them were to have seen it, then everyone would very soon have known that I was not a being of their planet, after which it would have become already entirely impossible to remain among them and to continue the experiments interesting to me for the elucidation of the strangeness of their psyche.

"That is why I went from this doctor without the 'paper' necessary for me, and from that time I threw up everything and no longer tried to obtain a permit to set up my own laboratory.

"In spite of the fact that I went about there everywhere pursuing my special aim, hustling at the same time for the said permit, I nevertheless often met that important Russian, my first acquaintance, who, although he was, as I said, very busy with his own affairs, nevertheless found time to visit me or to receive me at his house.

"At these meetings we almost always talked only about the alcoholism in his fatherland, and about the measures for struggling with this evil.

"From such an exchange of opinion, there each time accumulated in me more and more material, as my impartial observations and studies of all the aspects of the psyche of the local beings were crystallizing in me always newer and newer data concerning them.

"This important Russian laid very great weight on my considerations and remarks on what had already been done by the Trusteeship of People's Temperance and also concerning the projects of future undertakings, and was always sincerely delighted by the justice of my observations.

"And in the beginning, all my suggestions which he reported at the general meetings of the Trusteeship were always accepted for actualization.

"But when several participants of this Trusteeship accidentally learned that the initiative for many useful measures had issued from me—some foreign doctor or other, not even a European—then every kind of habitual, as it is called 'intrigue' and 'protest' arose against the proposals coming from me, and also against the head of the Trusteeship himself.

"Those guilty of all the misunderstandings which led up to this sorrowful end to such an important institution as the Trusteeship, created for the welfare of all the three-brained beings of this many-millioned community, were always and in everything the learned beings of 'new format.'

"The point is that, owing to the insistence of certain hereditary power-possessing beings, there were among the number of the permanent chief participants of this new institution several what are called 'learned physicians.'

"They happened to be among the leaders of this Trusteeship, in consequence of the fact that in the presences of the hereditary power-possessing beings of that period there had again already become finally fixed and had become the inviolable part of their essence always the same 'inner overlord' of theirs, maleficent for the terrestrial three-brained beings, named by them 'self-calming,' which by itself became for those unfortunates the sense and aim of their existence. And therefore in order not to make any being-effort at all, they insisted that these learned physicians should also unfailingly take part in this important institution of great social significance.

"In recent times there, why I don't know, the beings

there of this profession most often became learned beings of 'new format.'

"It is further also necessary to tell you here that when from among these learned beings of 'new format' some become power-possessing and happen to take up important responsible posts in the process of ordinary existence, they then often serve much more as the sources of every kind of subsequent misunderstanding than the hereditary power-possessing beings.

"And they serve as these sources of misunderstandings obviously in consequence of this, that in the common presences of these beings there are acquired and in a particular way are interwoven the characteristic inherencies which had already become proper to your favorites of three quite different contemporary types, namely, power-possessing beings, learned beings of 'new format,' and the contemporary 'professional physicians.'

"And so, my boy, on the initiative and insistence of several hereditary power-possessing beings of that community, especially on that of those who, although they outwardly still continue to be power-possessing yet in inner significance are only as they are called 'emptied sand boxes' (deflated gasbags), there were called to power for the business of actualizing such a serious task as the 'relative saving' of many millions of beings similar to themselves, those genuine 'stuffed turkeys,' or, as they would be called there, 'upstarts.'

"While at first these same upstarts who had by chance received power carried on among themselves alone every kind of petty 'intrigue' proper to them, it was still for the general undertaking there only 'half-a-calamity,' but when, thanks to every kind of what is called 'subterfuge' also proceeding from them, there also began these intrigues between all the participants of this Trusteeship, and they all split up into different notorious 'parties,' which pernicious custom there for a successful actualization of every promising beginning is very widely spread, then also such a good beginning as this Trusteeship for the general welfare of contemporary three-brained beings began, as they say, to 'crack at the seams.'

"Those petty 'intrigues' of theirs proceeded in full between the separate parties as well as between the separate members of that absolutely indispensable state organization, just at the time I arrived with my first Russian acquaintance in the chief place of existence of the said community.

"When those 'upstarts' who had accidentally received power learned that many of the 'counsels' and 'indications' on the business of improving the organization proceeded from me, that is, just from a professional like themselves, but who was not included in their so-called corporation, well, just then, understanding well that none of their intrigues and subterfuges could have any significance at all for me, they directed them against the head of the Trusteeship chosen by themselves.

"It is, apropos, very interesting lightly to remark here that, although every kind of data for bringing forth various being-impulses which they should have are in general feebly crystallized in the presence of these contemporary professionals there, then the data which brings forth the impulse called 'corporate feeling' for some reason or other is crystallized and functions in them very strongly.

"And so, my boy, as long as I did not yet know that to be occupied with 'intrigues' and dodges, or, as sometimes they themselves still express it, 'mutually-to-get-rid-of-each-other,' is already unavoidably inherent in power-possessing beings of this community, I still hoped for and patiently awaited that time when eventually the corresponding conditions would give me the possibility of actualizing my fundamental aim, namely, the possibility of proceeding with the 'elucidatory experiments' on the psyche of the terrestrial beings *en masse*. But when it became definitely clear to me that here in this community under the existing conditions of reciprocal relationships it would be impossible for me to succeed in this, and I also became convinced that it was impossible to get one's own chemical laboratory there honestly, i.e., strictly according to the laws fixed in this community, I decided to remain there no longer, but to depart, in order to seek suitable conditions for my said aim, to some other European community.

"When my first acquaintance, the important Russian, learned about this decision of mine, he was greatly grieved; greatly grieved also were yet several other Russian beings who indeed wished more or less good for their fatherland, and who, during this period, had had time to become clearly convinced that my knowledge and my experience might be very useful for their fundamental aim.

"On the day of my suggested departure, this Trusteeship was preparing to open the big building which, as I have already told you, was just designed for the aim of the struggle against alcoholism and which the beings there on the day of its opening called by the name of their czar, 'The People's Building of the Emperor Nicholas II.'

"On the eve of my departure my first acquaintance, the important Russian, came to me unexpectedly and, having sincerely expressed his regret at my departure, begged me very earnestly to postpone it for several days so that after the consecration and opening of the said building he might travel with me and incidentally rest a little from the recent bustle, intrigues, and subterfuges.

"As I had no special reason to hurry, I agreed and postponed my departure for an indefinite time.

"Two days later the opening of this building took place and, having the previous evening received what is called 'an official invitation,' I betook myself to that ceremony.

"Well, at this general state solemnity of the contemporary many-millioned community, to which came even he himself, as they call him, 'His Majesty the Emperor,' there began there, in respect of my person, what is called 'Ooretstaknilkaroolni,' which generally speaking always flows from the totality of the surrounding abnormalities and, being formed automatically in the psyche of every one of the three-brained beings of this ill-starred planet, holds them so to say in an 'exitless magic circle.'

"And the further events proceeded in the following order:

"On the day of the said state solemnity while the ceremony was still proceeding, my first acquaintance the Russian suddenly ran towards me shoving his way through the beings who appeared there in all the blaze of various what are called 'orders' and 'regimentals,' and in a joyous voice told me that I was to have the 'happiness' of being presented to His Majesty the Czar; having said this and speaking rapidly, he hurried away.

"It turned out that at this solemnity there he had had some conversation with the Emperor about me, as a result of which it had been decided that I should be presented to him.

"Such a presentation to the Emperor, Czar, or King is considered there as a very very great piece of luck, and that is why my acquaintance having received such a permission rejoiced beyond words on my behalf.

"Evidently he wished by this presentation to give me great 'pleasure' and by this to calm his own conscience, as he considered himself to blame for my unsuccessful stay in this capital.

"After this event, two days passed.

"On the third morning, looking by chance out of the

window of my lodging into the street I saw there quite an unusual commotion; everyone was cleaning, everywhere there was sweeping, many of what are called the 'gendarmerie' and 'police' were walking up and down.

"To my question as to what caused all this, our Ahoon explained to me that on that day, in our street, the arrival of a very important general of that community was expected.

"On this same day, in the afternoon, while I was sitting at home and talking with one of my new acquaintances, the concierge of the house came running in to me, agitated and bewildered, and stammering exclaimed: 'Hi . . . s, his . . . Ex . . . Exce . . . ce . . . ce . . . lency!' But he did not have time to finish before His Excellency himself entered. As soon as the unfortunate concierge saw him appear, he appeared as if struck dumb by lightning, and then, having pulled himself together, he hurriedly, as it is said there, 'backed' out of the room.

"But His Noble Excellency himself, with a very friendly smile, although with a shade of what is called 'hauteur' characteristic of all the power-possessing beings of that community at that time, came towards me, at the same time examining with great curiosity the 'antiques' which were in my room, and, shaking me in a special way by the wrist, sat down in my favorite armchair.

"Afterward, continuing to examine the antiques, he said:

"'You will in a day or two be presented to our "Great Autocrat," and since it is I who attend to these affairs I have come to you just to explain to you how and what you must do on such a great and important occasion of your life.'

"Having said this, he suddenly stood up and approaching what is called a china figure of old Chinese workmanship which stood in a corner of my room, he exclaimed with impulsive rapture which thrilled his whole presence: 'How charming! . . . Where did you get this marvel of ancient wisdom . . . ?'

"And not ceasing to look at the said figure and giving himself up to the feeling of his rapture, or, more strictly speaking, with all his feelings coursing together through him, he further continued:

"'I myself am very much interested in all ancient art, but chiefly in Chinese, and that is why, of the five rooms given up to my collection, three are filled with productions of ancient Chinese work alone.'

"Continuing to speak in this strain about his adoration for the production of ancient Chinese masters, he without ceremony again sat down in my armchair and began to enlarge upon antiques in general, their value and where they are to be found.

"During this conversation he suddenly and hastily took his watch from his pocket, automatically looked at it, stood up quickly and, once on his feet, said:

"'How vexing! I am obliged to interrupt our chat, interesting to the highest degree, as I must hurry home where doubtless the great friend of my youth and his charming wife are already waiting for me.

"'He is here for a short while, passing through on his way abroad from the provinces, and I have not seen him since we served in the same regiment and received different appointments, I to the Court, and he to a civil post.'

"He afterward further added: 'And as regards the instructions I am required to give you, about which I had come to you, I will send my adjutant this very day, and he will explain everything to you, and no worse than I perhaps would.'

"After this, with fussy self-importance, he left me.

"And indeed, on the evening of the very same day, as

His Noble Excellency had promised me, one of his adjutants came to my house who was still, as is said there, a 'young man,' that is a being who had only quite recently attained to responsible age. This adjutant of his who came had the very marked specific type of a terrestrial three-brained being whom in recent times among your favorites one has often come across, and who is very well defined by the words mama's and papa's darling.

"This former mama's darling, when he arrived and began to speak to me, manifested himself at first towards me quite automatically according to the data fixed in his common presence by the rules enforcedly inculcated into him of what are called bon ton; and when a little later it became clear to his being-rumination that I belonged neither to his own caste nor to a higher one, but appeared to be one of those beings who according to the abnormal understanding of the beings of that community are considered little higher than what are called 'savages,' he immediately changed his tone and again quite automatically began to manifest himself towards me according to the data for 'commanding' and 'ordering about,' data also already fixed in the common presences of the beings of that community of that period who belonged to that caste, and he began to point out how I must 'enter,' 'leave,' and 'move,' and when and what words must be spoken.

"Besides the fact that in the course of two hours he had shown me by his own example how, namely, one had to manifest, he declared to me that he would return on the morrow and he ordered me to practice, so that, as he expressed himself, no misunderstanding at all might arise which might lead to where even 'Makar did not drive his goats.'

"When on the day of my, as they call it, 'supreme presentation' I arrived there where the chief of this large community had the place of his residence, I was met at the railway station itself by 'His High Excellency' in person, who had arrived there accompanied by five or six of his adjutants, and from that moment he himself began—of course quite without the participation of, as it is called, his 'personal-subjective-initiative,' but guided only by automatic habit acquired by him, thanks to the doing of always one and the same thing—to subjugate all my separate spiritualized parts and all the self-manifestations of my common presence, taking it as it were under the directive of his own 'I.'

"From this moment, I had, in the sense of my 'outer manifestations,' as our esteemed Mullah Nassr Eddin would say, to 'dance in everything to his tune.'

"As soon as we had left the station and were seated in the carriage, he immediately began to show me and to prompt me as to what and how I had to act and speak and what I had not to do or say.

"And when later, in that hall where the celebrated presentation took place, he further showed and directed my presence . . . about this we can neither speak now in the language of a Scheherazade, nor describe it with the pen of a Mr. Canineson.

"In the hall every movement, every step I made, even to the blinking of my eyelids, were seen in advance, and prompted to me by this important general.

"However, in spite of all the absurdity of this procedure, if one takes into account that the perfection of a being depends on the quality and quantity of his inner experiencings, then objective justice demands that due must be given for this to your favorites, that on that day they compelled me, of course, unconsciously, to undergo and to feel perhaps more than I had undergone and felt during all the centuries of my personal sojourn there among them.

"However that may be, I must yet say that having

agreed to this 'famous presentation' for the purpose of observation and investigation of the peculiar and such a 'contorted' psyche of your favorites, and after all the 'great agitation' which I had lived through on that day, I finally breathed freely only in the carriage of the train after my tormentors, particularly that important general, had left me alone by myself.

"In the course of the whole of that day, I was so occupied with the fulfillment of all the innumerable foolish manipulations required from me and which fatigued me in view of my declining years, that I did not even notice what the unfortunate Emperor there looked like or how he manifested himself in this comedy.

"Now, my boy, if you will strive to assimilate well the information about the subsequent events which happened to me and which were the results of this famous presentation of mine to His Majesty the Emperor, then you will probably acquire the possibility of clearly picturing to yourself and well understand how, there among your favorites, particularly in this large community Russia at that period, their what is called 'individual significance,' particularly in recent centuries, began to be appraised and be built up for the majority of these unfortunates always exclusively on the basis of the outer ephemeral as they are called 'Vietro-yretznel,' as, in the given case, it similarly took place in relation to me.

"This gradual acquiring of the habit of judging the merits of beings according to the outer ephemeral appearance in all other beings, developed and continued to develop their imagination, which became strengthened about this, that just in this consists the acquisition of 'being-individuality,' and all began subjectively to strive only for this.

"That is why at the present time, all of them from the very beginning of their arising gradually lose from their common presences even the 'taste' and 'desire' for what is called 'objective-being-Being.'

"The manifestations of the mentioned 'Vietro-yretznel' personally in relation to my person began to have their action already from the very morning of the following day, in this sense that every data for 'being-notion' about my personality which had been before this already soundly fixed in the presences of all the beings there who knew me suddenly sharply changed, thanks only to this 'objectively maleficent' official presentation of me to their highest power-possessing beings.

"My personal significance and their notions about all my qualities and merits also changed for their individuality; I suddenly became for all 'important' and 'wise,' 'extraordinary' and 'interesting,' and so on and so forth; that is, the possessor of all kinds of abnormal being-qualities thought out by themselves.

"As a very characteristic example which will well make clear to you what I have just said, the following illustration may serve:

"The proprietor of that shop where, before going to my business, I bought the provisions for my kitchen, wished on the first morning after this, as is sometimes said there, 'royal audience' of mine, to bring, happen what may, my purchases home to me himself. All the police standing at the street corners in that district in which I temporarily dwelt, and who already knew me well as a newcomer physician, began at the sight of me, while still standing some way off, to salute just as they saluted that important general of theirs.

"The same evening the chief of that department to which I had first of all applied, himself personally brought me to my house that unfortunate permit, giving me the right to have my own laboratory, and to receive which I had languished for three months waiting on the doorsteps of every kind of 'official' and 'unofficial' establishment. And on the second day I received yet four other permits for this from various departments of other ministries into whose province it did not at all enter to issue such permits, but to whom on account of this same dilly-dallying of theirs I had had to apply during my senseless hustlings.

"The owners of the houses, shopkeepers, children, and in general all who dwelt in the same street as I did, became as amiable with me as if I intended to leave each of them a large 'American legacy,' and so on and so forth.

"After this 'Emptykralnian' happening to me, I, by the way, further learned that this unfortunate czar of theirs also always prepares himself for such official meetings with beings strange to him.

"Of these official meetings like this he has very many, almost every day and even several times a day: here, a parade of the troops; there, an 'audience' with the ambassador of some other emperor; in the morning, a 'delegation'; at noon, a 'presentation' such as mine; later a 'reception' of different what are called 'representatives-of-the-people'; and with each of these it is necessary for him to talk, or even to make them an entire speech.

"As each word of every such terrestrial 'czar' can have and often does have serious consequences not only for the beings of that community of whom he is czar, but also for the beings of other communities, therefore each word must be thought out from every side.

"Well, for this, around these emperors or czars who become such by hereditary rights or by election, there are many specialists from among the ordinary three-brained beings there, in order that they may prompt them as to what they must do and say in every circumstance; and these promptings and directions must be carried out in such a way that the strangers may not notice that their emperor or czar manifests not from his own but from others' initiative.

"And in order to remember all this, these czars must of course also practice.

"And what it means to practice, you can probably already picture to yourself after what I have just told you. I understood this with all my Being, when I prepared myself for my illustrious presentation.

"During my existence on that planet, such a preparation by the way was necessary for me personally only once. Were such preparations necessary every day and for every separate occasion, then may one be spared from experiencing such a merciless fate.

"I personally at least would not under any conditions be in the skin of such a terrestrial emperor or czar, and would neither wish it for my very worst enemy nor for the enemy of my nearest.

"After this unforgettable 'supreme presentation' of mine, I very soon left St. Petersburg for other parts of the continent of Europe and began to have as the chief places of my existence various cities of the countries which were situated both on that same continent Europe as well as on other continents. I was again later, many times, but for other affairs, in the same community Russia, where during that period of the flow of time their great process there of reciprocal-destruction took place and the destruction of everything already attained by them, which this time, as I have already told you, was called by them 'Bolshevism.'

"You remember I promised to relate to you about the fundamental real causes of this archphenomenal process.

"Well, it is necessary to tell you that this grievous phenomenon arises there thanks to two independent factors, the first of which is the cosmic law Solioonensius, and the second is always the same abnormal conditions of ordinary being-existence established by them themselves.

"In order that you should the better understand about both these factors, I will explain to you about each of them separately, and will begin by the cosmic law Solioonensius.

"First of all you must be told that all the three-brained beings, on whatever planet they may arise, and whatever exterior coating they may receive, always await the manifestations of the action of this law with impatience and with joy, somewhat how your favorites await what are called their feasts of 'Easter,' 'Bairam,' 'Zadik,' 'Ramadan,' 'Kaialana,' and so on.

"The only difference is in this, that your favorites await these feasts of theirs with impatience because on these 'holydays' it has become customary among them to allow themselves to be more 'jolly' and to 'booze' freely; while the beings of the other planets await the action of Solioonensius with impatience because, thanks to it, the need for evolving, in the sense of the acquiring of Objective-Reason by them, increases in them by itself.

"As regards the causes which bring forth this same action of this cosmic law, they are for each planet different and always flow from and depend upon what is called the 'common cosmic Harmonious-Movement'; moreover, frequently for your planet Earth, what is called the 'center-of-gravity-of-causes' is the 'periodic tension' of the sun of its system, which tension proceeds in its turn thanks to the influence upon this sun of a neighboring solar system, which exists under the name of 'Baleaooto.'

"In this latter system however, such a center-of-gravity-of-causes arises because among the number of its 'concentrations' there is a great comet Solni, which, according to certain known combinations of the common-cosmic Harmonious-Movement at times approaches on its falling very near to its sun Baleaooto, which is forced by this to make a 'strong tension' in order to maintain the path of its own falling. This tension provokes the tension of the suns of the neighboring systems, among the number of which is the system Ors; and when the sun Ors strains itself not to change its path of falling inherent to it, this sun Ors in its turn provokes the same tension in all the concentrations of its own system, among which is also the planet Earth.

"The tension in all the planets acts also on the common presences of all beings arising and breeding on them, always engendering in the beings, besides desires and intentions of which they are not aware, the feeling called 'sacred Iabolioonosar,' or as your favorites would say, the feeling of religiousness, namely, that 'being-feeling' which at times appears in the desire and striving for, as I have already said, speedier self-perfecting in the sense of Objective-Reason.

"It is interesting that when this sacred feeling, or another similar to it, which was also engendered by a certain common cosmic actualization, proceeds in the common presences of your favorites, then they accept it as a symptom of certain of their numerous diseases, and in the given case, for example, they call this feeling 'nerves.'

"It is necessary to remark that such an impulse inherent in the presence of all three-brained beings of our Great Universe formerly arose and became actualized almost normally in the majority of terrestrial beings of that time, namely, from the time of the removal of the organ Kundabuffer from the common presences of the three-brained beings of the planet Earth right up to the second Transapalnian-perturbation.

"But later, among the number of chief evils which flow from the conditions of ordinary being-existence established by them themselves, specially when in the presences of every terrestrial three-brained being, there began to become predominant the 'evil-inner-God' of theirs I mentioned, named there self-calming, then it occurred that in them under the influence of the action of Solioonensius, instead of the desire and striving for a speedier self-perfection a something began to arise such as they themselves characterize by the words 'need of freedom,' which chiefly serves the cause of the arising there of these same grievous processes of theirs similar to this last 'Bolshevism.'

"I will explain to you somewhat later how they represent to themselves this famous freedom of theirs, and now I will only tell you that that feeling which arises from the action of Solioonensius strengthens in them the need for some or other general change in the conditions of their ordinary external being-existence which until then were more or less stable.

"After the second Transapalnian perturbation to this ill-starred planet of yours, that is, 'after-the-loss-of-Atlantis,' the action of the cosmic law Solioonensius in the general presences of these favorites of yours was actualized at least forty times and almost from the very beginning, each time, thanks already to this strange 'need of freedom' which has since been fixed in the majority of them, almost the same proceeded as in recent years still proceeds on that part of the surface of your planet on which the totality of the existing groups is called 'Russia.'

"Here it is extremely important also to notice that the existence itself of these terrifying processes could not in any way take place there among the three-brained beings of the planet Earth if those data which had remained intact in their subconsciousness for the engendering of the being-impulse conscience, to which data the Most Saintly Ashiata Shiemash was the first to turn his attention and upon which he relied for the fulfillment of his mission, had taken part in the functioning of that consciousness of theirs which has become habitual for them during their waking state.

"Only in consequence of the fact that the data for the sacred impulse of being-conscience do not take part in the function of this consciousness of theirs, the actions of the law Solioonensius, just as well as of other inevitable cosmic laws, are molded into such abnormal and for themselves pitiable forms.

"Although the whole totality of causes serves as the sources for the arising of the second factor, yet in my opinion the basic cause also in the given case is nevertheless this fact, that their famous 'subdivision-into-castes' becomes established among them regarding their mutual relationship among themselves, which subdivision has constantly existed there with the exception only of that period when there was definitely rooted among them the results of the Most Saintly Labors of Ashiata Shiemash.

"The difference is only in this, that in former centuries the division into different castes proceeded from the consciousness and intention of several separate individuals there, while now this proceeds quite automatically without the participation of anyone's will or anyone's consciousness.

"Now, my boy, I find it opportune to explain to you a little about this, namely, in what way and in what gradations these favorites of yours became automatically sorted out from their different celebrated castes, and how they later already began to subdivide themselves into these castes.

"When, according to various chance circumstances, and wherever significant groups of them became concentrated and they exist together, then several of them—in whom firstly for some reason or other the consequences of the properties of the organ Kundabuffer had been previously well crystallized, the totality of which crystallizations in general gives to their common presences the impulses for what is called 'cunning,' and secondly, in whose hands at the given time there appear for some reason or other many different, what are called 'terrifying means,' or what they themselves call 'weapons'—quickly set themselves apart from other beings and putting themselves at their head, constitute the beginnings of what are called the 'ruling class.'

"And further, since in all the three-brained beings of the planet Earth, and particularly of recent periods, the sacred being-impulse called conscience does not take part in the functioning of their general consciousness, in consequence of which in them there is absent even the very need for making any conscious being-effort at all—then they, that is, the beings who had set themselves apart and who had assigned themselves to the ruling class, profiting by the said terrifying means, compel other beings of the given groupings to produce for them even those efforts which every being should inevitably actualize in ordinary being-existence.

"And other beings of these groupings, also not wishing for the same reasons personally to produce these 'being-efforts,' no, not even for others, and at the same time being afraid of the mentioned terrifying means of the beings of the ruling class, begin to have recourse to all kinds of cunning in order, as is said there, to 'load-on-one-another's-backs' such being-efforts as are inevitably required for the beings of the ruling class.

"And as a result the beings of every such grouping usually sort themselves out gradually and fall into diverse categories according to the degree of skill of their artfulness. And so from the division of the beings into categories of this kind, there just begins in the following generations a subdivision and an assigning of each other into these famous castes of theirs.

"From this assigning of each other into castes of diverse kinds, there is already by itself infallibly crystallized in the common presence of each of them in relation to the beings who belong to all other castes that being-data which is called 'hate,' just that data which was never in any other beings in the whole of our Great Universe, and which in its turn engenders in the common presence of everyone those impulses 'shameful' for the three-brained beings, which they themselves call 'envy,' 'jealousy,' 'adultery,' and many other similar impulses.

"And so, my boy, these terrifying processes of reciprocal-destruction and of the destruction of everything already attained by them there, proceed partly from this, that in those periods when in their common presences the action of the cosmic law Solioonensius becomes evident, besides the already mentioned need for freedom, in them, on the one hand, the intensity of the action of the data for engendering constantly the impulse of 'timidity' before power-possessors automatically diminishes, which data has already become inherent in their common presences, and on the other hand the intensity of the action of that said strange being-data increases, which data provokes 'hate' in the given case in relation to the beings who belong to other castes.

"That is why I said that this subdivision of theirs into castes which bring about the totality of the results of these 'unique-strange-being-data' which always increase in their functionings and which flow, as you may have already, from all that I have told you, doubtless been convinced, also from the conditions of their abnormal ordinary being-existence, just serves chiefly as the second factor for the arising of these terrifying processes.

"These terrible processes usually arise and flow in the following sequence:

"It always begins with this, that several beings from one or another grouping, namely, those in whom for some reason or other there were previously crystallized data stronger than in other beings—which data engender the mentioned strange impulses in relation to the beings who belong to other castes, particularly to the beings who belong to the caste of the 'ruling-class'—seeing and feeling reality more than others under the influence of the action of Solioonensius they begin as is said there to 'clamor,' and these 'clamoring orators' become in relation to those around them such as are at the present time there usually called 'leaders.'

"And further, thanks on the one hand to this clamor and, on the other hand, thanks to the action of always the same cosmic law Solioonensius, which action is always combined abnormally in the presences of all of them, others also begin to clamor. When these 'clamorers' among the ordinary beings begin already, excessively cacophonically, to act upon what are called 'the-effeminate-nerves-of-the-left-half' of several of the power-possessing beings of the given community, and these latter order those whose job it is to grease with what is called 'Scottish cream' the navels of several particularly loud-voiced clamorers, then there begin these excesses of theirs which, progressively increasing, reach their zenith, yet to their misfortune ultimately always lead to nothing.

"These processes of theirs, if they had even but a little improved the existence of beings of subsequent generations, then perhaps, from the point of view of a strictly impartial observer, they might even not have appeared to be so terrifying, yet to the misfortune of all three-brained beings of our Great Universe, the calamity is just in this that as soon as the 'blissful action' of this cosmic lawful manifestation ceases, and these terrifying processes come to an end, then there again begins the old story and their ordinary being-existence becomes 'more bitter' than before, and, parallel with this, there also deteriorates what is called their 'sane-awareness-of-the-sense-and-aim-of-their-existence.'

"This latter deteriorates in my opinion chiefly because, after these processes, the leading beings of the former ruling class are usually replaced by beings who proceed from other different castes, and who before this last process did not have in the persons of their representatives, either of the present or past generations, anything in common either consciously or unconsciously with that being-manifestation in which is included the ability to lead the outer and now and then even the inner process of the being-existence of surrounding beings, who although 'similar to them,' yet in the sense of Reason had not yet attained to their degree.

"Justice demands it to be admitted that although in the common presences of the three-brained beings there of the old ruling class the data present in their subconsciousness for the engendering of real being-conscience also did not take part in the functioning of their what is called waking-consciousness, yet, at least, they usually have the habit of ruling, acquired by heredity and improving automatically from generation to generation.

"In the presences of the beings who had newly attained to power not only is real being-conscience absent, as it was also absent in the beings of the former ruling class, but further, in them in addition, those 'charms' begin particularly stormily to manifest and give extraordinary and terrifying results, which 'charms' are crystallized in general in the presences of terrestrial three-brained beings especially of recent times in consequence of the properties of the organ Kundabuffer, such as 'vanity,' 'pride,' 'self-conceit,' 'self-love,' and others, which, as they had as yet hardly ever been satisfied to a sufficient degree, are in them in their functionings, particularly new.

"To these terrestrial beings who become impromptu power-possessing and who have not any hereditary data at all in themselves even for the automatic ability to rule, one of the sayings of our dear Teacher can well be applied, which he expresses in the following words:

"'I never yet met that idiot who, accustomed to shuffle in a pair of old shoes, would feel comfortable in smart new ones.'

"And really, my boy, when, each time on the planet Earth, the action of Solioonensius ceases, and their 'relatively normal' existence, already somehow established, again begins among your favorites, then the 'newly-baked-power-possessing' beings usually cut those capers thanks to which the birth rate of what are called 'slugs,' 'snails,' 'lice,' 'mole crickets,' and many other similar parasites who destroy everything good, each time always increases more and more on that planet.

"As I have begun to speak about Bolshevism, then I will relate to you here on this subject, in order yet once again to give you an example of one peculiarity of the being-existence of your favorites which had already become fully proper to them, about one of their naïve arguments which is not without its humor.

"This naïveté of theirs, which may arise through an already excessively wretched logical-confrontative being-rumination, consists in this, that although all events there without exception, in the sense of mutual relationships among themselves, proceeded during the last two centuries exclusively already by themselves without any participation of the consciousness or intention of whomever it may be of the contemporary beings, they nevertheless always ascribe with certainty and even with jealousy all the results, good as well as bad, flowing from these events to one or another among them similar to themselves.

"And such an abnormality which had become fixed in the totality of their spiritualized parts resulted from the following causes.

"First of all, from their common presences there gradually

totally disappeared all those being-data, the totality of which in general is capable of engendering in the presences of beings a property called 'presentiment of the future,' in consequence of which they are entirely deprived of the possibility, in any degree whatever of foreseeing imminent events; secondly, having a narrow what is called 'horizon' and a 'short memory,' they not only know nothing about long-past events on their planet, but even do not remember about that which proceeded quite recently—almost even yesterday; and thirdly, these cosmic laws are unknown to them, thanks to which there chiefly arise those sorrowful events which proceed among them. Owing to all this, these same contemporary favorites of yours are sure in all their presences that this terrifying process, which they call Bolshevism, proceeded for the first time on their planet and that nothing like this already 'darling' civilization of theirs had ever existed previous to them; and they are even sure that this has happened thanks only to the evolution of the gradually progressing reason of the beings similar to themselves of their planet.

"Their confrontative argument on the subject of similar processes which had taken place many times in the past on their planet may serve as a very good example for the illustration and characterization of the phenomenal dullness and bluntness of that being-rumination which they have.

"According to the common-sense of every three-brained being, similar processes had to proceed, and since I became interested in the strange psyche of these favorites of yours and occupied myself with every aspect of the observation of them, I myself have been a witness as I have said, no less than forty times, of exactly similar processes which I would call the process of the 'destruction-of-everything-within-sight.'

"It is interesting to notice that almost half of all these

terrifying processes proceeded not very far from that place where their, as they themselves call it, 'cultured existence' is now concentrated; they proceeded on that part of the surface of their planet which they name Egypt.

"These terrifying processes proceeded on this same Egypt so often, in consequence of the fact that this part of the surface of your planet, during the course of long periods of time, found itself in relation to the common-cosmic Harmonious-Movement in the position of what is called the 'center-of-gravity-radiations,' and that is why the influence of the cosmic law Solioonensius often acted on the presence of the three-brained beings breeding there, and often brought forth in them such an abnormality.

"A parallel comparison of the real data concerning the events which took place on the same Egypt and those data about them which became fixed in the being-representation and understanding of almost every responsible being of famous contemporary 'culture,' and which are known to them, as it were, thanks to their already 'perfected reason' might serve as an obvious illustrative example of from what general data their 'logical mentation' at the period of their responsible existence is built up and consists, and likewise gives me the possibility yet once again to notice and emphasize to you all the maleficence in an objective sense of their usage, which was finally fixed in the process of their ordinary existence, and which they themselves call by the high-sounding words, 'education' and 'schooling' of the growing generation.

"The point is that, among the number of all possible kinds of ephemeral fantastic informations from the totality of which, as a result, their strange Reason proper to them alone is formed there, there is likewise the history of this same Egypt.

"This fantastic history evidently thought out by some

or other candidate for Hasnamuss individuals among them, was even made for them what is called an 'obligatory subject' in all educational establishments, in which this 'history,' among other similar 'stupidities,' is strongly 'hammered' into their separate concentrations for the functioning of spiritual perceptions and manifestations, that is into what they themselves would call the 'brains' of these unfortunate future responsible beings; and further, when they become such, these 'fantastic-informations-learned-by-them-parrotlike' by compulsion serve them as material for being-associations and for 'logical-confrontative-mentation.'

"That is why, my boy, at the present time there on that ill-fated planet, every being who has already reached responsible age, instead of the real knowledge which every normal three-brained being should have concerning the events which took place on their planet in the past, knows about everything in the same way in which, as in the present case, he ruminates with his being-Reason and 'unconsciously' becomes aware with all his being about this same Egypt.

"There's no gainsaying it, each one of the already, according to them, responsible three-brained beings of this strange planet, already knows thanks to their system of education and schooling, the history of the beings who existed in the past on this Egypt.

"Yet how, thanks to the said means of perception of informations which they themselves call 'learning-parrotlike,' he knows this, and what totality of the being-representation about this 'results' from all three of his spiritualized being-parts, you may picture to yourself with your own eyes, and clearly understand from the following illustration of mine.

"Almost every one of them 'knows' that among ancient Egyptians there were twenty-four dynasties. But if any one of them is asked, 'Why are there so many dynasties among them?' it would then appear that he had never even thought about it.

"Further if one continues to insist on an answer, then this same being who up to now knew and was sure with all his being that there were twenty-four dynasties among the ancient Egyptians, he at best—of course on the condition if one helps him to be able to be sincere and to express aloud associations flowing in his mentation—reveals his logical mentation in some such way:

"'Among the Egyptians there were twenty-four dynasties. . . .

"'Well . . .

"'This proves that among the Egyptians there existed a monarchical state organization and that the position of the "king" passed by inheritance from father to son, and as it was customary that the kings of one generation should have the same family name, and that all the kings who had this name composed one dynasty, then therefore they had as many different dynasties of kings as there were family names' . . . very 'understandable,' and as 'clear' as the 'patch on the baggy trousers' of the honorable Mullah Nassr Eddin.

"And if any of the beings of contemporary 'culture' infallibly desires and will continue to 'pant' in order to explain well to his Reason why among these ancient Egyptians the family name of their kings changed so often, then again, at very best, his being-mentation will associate approximately in the following sequence. He will say:

"'Evidently in olden times in this Egypt it often happened that the kings, or as they are named there Pharaohs, grew tired of reigning and abdicated their power—and this abdication in all probability proceeded in the following way and approximately under the following circumstances.

"'Let us suppose that some Pharaoh or other named "John Geoffrey" lived peacefully and with full satisfaction, and ruled over all the Egyptians.

"'Well, once this same king or Pharaoh John Geoffrey felt a very great "weariness" from this reigning of his, and one sleepless night, having pondered over his "kingly position" first of all constated and realized with all his being that, wish it or not, one grows tired of reigning, and that this occupation, in general, is an extremely trying "job" and could not be said to be, for his personal felicity, either useful or safe.

"'The Pharaoh John Geoffrey became impressed with this realization and, profiting by the experience of his existence in the past, decided to try and find out how to "prevail upon" somebody or other, so that this "other" might deliver him from the said, for him, undesirable weariness.

"'To this end, he probably invited some or other still ordinary John Geoffrey to come to him, and in a very polite way spoke to him, roughly as follows:

"' "My highly honorable and incomparably kind John Geoffrey, I frankly confess to you, as to my only friend and subject worthy of my trust, that this kingdom over which I rule has already grown too wearisome for me and this has happened perhaps because I am already extremely tired.

"' "As regards my dear son and heir, to whom I might now hand over the kingdom, he, speaking between ourselves, is, in spite of his very strong and healthy appearance, in fact neither one nor the other.

"' "You as a father known for his love for his posterity will surely understand if I tell you that I very much love my son and heir, and that I would not like him to reign and get tired as I have; wherefore, I have just decided to propose to you, as a faithful subject and personal friend, to deliver me and my son from reigning and to take this high obligation upon yourself."

"'And since evidently this still ordinary John Geoffrey was firstly, as is said there, a "good sport," and secondly being a "rascal" who had much "vanity," he with tears in his eyes shrugged his shoulders—"If I must be lost, then let me be lost"—consented, and from the very next day began to reign.

"'As the family name of this second John Geoffrey was different, therefore on the very next day the number of Egyptian dynasties was increased by yet one more.

"'And so, as many Pharaohs of this Egypt often grew tired and, loving their sons, did not desire the same for them, they renounced their kingdoms in this way to others, and hence so many dynasties "piled up" there.'

"In reality, however, the change of dynasty in this Egypt did not proceed so simply, and in the intervals between two dynasties there proceeded such perturbations in comparison with which this contemporary Bolshevism is 'merely child's play.'

"In the heat of this contemporary Bolshevism, I happened several times to be an eyewitness of the sincere indignation of several of those who, for some reasons, of course personally independent of them, did not happen to take part in this same process, and who could therefore half-consciously observe from the outside and with all their presences grow sincerely indignant at the actions of the individual beings similar to themselves who were active persons in this terrifying process, namely, at the action of those individuals similar to them, whom on this occasion they called, and still up to now call 'Bolsheviks.'

"In my opinion, it will do no harm here, apropos, to tell you that that being-experiencing of theirs which is excellently characterized by the words, 'vainly-to-grow-sincerely-indignant,' also appears to be one of the unfortunate particularities of the psyche of these ill-fated three-brained beings who please you, especially of the contemporary ones.

"Thanks only to this psychic abnormality, there gradually become more deranged in their common presences many functionings, both of their planetary body, already deranged without this, and of their 'body-Kesdjan'—if of course this second being-body is already coated in them and has attained to the required, what is called, 'individuality.'

"And such an abnormality of their psyche, namely, 'vainly-to-grow-indignant,' or as they themselves say 'vainly-to-grow-agitated,' also flows from this, that from their common presences there has already long since disappeared the 'being-horizon' proper to be present in the three-brained beings, as well as the 'instinctive-sensing-of-reality-in-its-real-light.'

"On account of the absence in their psyche of these two particularities, they could not even approximately suspect that individuals similar to themselves were in no way the cause of these terrifying processes there, and that these processes of their ill-fated planet proceed from two inevitable great causes. The first of these causes is just the cosmic law Solioonensius, entirely independent of them; and the second cause, partly dependent on them, consists in this that, thanks to the totality of all the results of the abnormal conditions of ordinary being-existence established by themselves, which still continue to be crystallized in their common presences, the data for bringing forth the sacred impulse 'conscience' do not in general take part in any of them in the functioning of their ordinary waking state, in consequence of which the action of the first cause takes just this terrible form.

"They, as I have already said, could not even approximately consider and understand that, during these common planetary terrifying processes, individual persons are in no way the cause, and only by chance happen to be in those posts, the occupation of which, on account of the conditions of mutual existence which had already been established, compels them to manifest themselves in one or other role, the results of which roles, according to lawconformity entirely independent of them themselves, are cast into these or other forms.

"In the heat of this last process of theirs, namely, during this Russian Bolshevism, the contemporary beings of other communities grew very sincerely agitated when the beings, who by chance had become as it were 'active' in this distressing process, gave orders to other ordinary beings, as it is said, to 'shoot' any Tom, Dick, or Harry.

"For the clarity of my further explanation concerning these terrifying processes of your unfortunate favorites, you must be further told about this, that this last process proceeded and until today continues to proceed on a large area of the surface of this ill-fated planet, and that during recent times these favorites of yours have very greatly increased in quantity. If therefore we compare the quantity of the contemporary three-brained beings who have been destroyed during this last process, with those destroyed in the previous process, then this last process will indeed seem 'child's play.'

"In order that you may better understand this and compare those former processes with this contemporary Bolshevism, I will now give you a couple of little scenes from former history, from, let us say, the Egypt I have already mentioned.

"When, in one of the intervals between the dynasties of these Egyptian Pharaohs or kings, there proceeded in Egypt a process such as this contemporary Bolshevism, the chief committee of the 'revolutionaries' announced to all the population of that country among other things, that 'elections' would soon begin for the chiefs of the large and small points of theirs, or as they say 'towns' and 'villages,' and that these elections would proceed on the following principles:

"Those were to be elected as chiefs for the towns and villages who would put in their 'sacred' vessels more of what are called 'kroahns' than others; a kroahn was the name given then in Egypt to sacrificial offerings.

"The point is that, according to what is called the 'religion' of the beings of this country, it was the custom among others during 'religious ceremonies' which proceeded in special places to put before each ordinary being who went to these ceremonies special 'clay vessels,' so that each ordinary being there had to put into these sacred vessels each time after the utterances of certain prayers, vegetables or fruit specially designated for the given day.

"Well, these 'worthy' things for offering as sacrifices were then called kroahns. In all probability this 'manipulation' was devised by the 'theocrats' of that time as a profitable item for the welfare of their, as they are called, 'sycophants.'

"In that decree about which I have just told you, it was stated that on that occasion kroahns had to consist of the eyes of 'outcasts,' by which word the ordinary three-brained beings there called those beings behind their backs who belonged to the caste of the ruling class, by which name then all the beings of this caste 'wholesale' were called without excluding the beings of the 'passive half,' children or old folk.

"Further in this announcement it was stated that he who would have on the day of the elections the most kroahns in his sacred vessel would be appointed as chief of the whole of Egypt, and in the remaining towns and villages those would be appointed as chiefs who in their sacred vessels had the correspondingly greatest number of kroahns.

"You may picture to yourself, my boy, what on that day began to be accomplished everywhere in that Egypt, in order to have in their sacred vessels the greatest number of eyes of the beings who belonged in that period of the flow of time to the caste of the ruling class.

"On another occasion also there in Egypt, I became a witness of a not less terrifying scene.

"For a clear representation about this also terrifying scene, it is first of all necessary to tell you that there, that is in this Egypt, there was formerly in every one of their large points or 'towns' a large square on which proceeded all kinds of public, as they are called, 'religious' and 'military' ceremonies, where during these ceremonies were gathered masses of the beings from the whole of Egypt.

"These beings, and specially the masses of beings who belonged at the given moment to the weak castes, impeded the ceremonies, and therefore a certain Pharaoh ordered ropes to be stretched around these squares so that the beings who belonged to the 'simple' castes should not disturb the progress of the ceremony.

"But when the said ropes were stretched, it soon became evident that they would not withstand the pressure of the crowd and might often break. Then the Pharaoh ordered what are called 'metal ropes' to be made, whereupon those who are called 'priests' there, consecrated them and gave them the name of 'sacred cables.'

"These sacred cables around the squares for the public ceremonies, particularly in the large towns of Egypt, had at that time a colossal length, sometimes reaching to one 'centrotino,' or, as the contemporary beings of your planet would say, ten miles long.

"Well, I was a witness of how a crowd of ordinary

Egyptian beings began to string onto one of these sacred cables—just like an Asiatic shashlik—the beings, without distinction of sex or age, who up till then had belonged to the ruling class.

"And the very same night, with the help of forty pairs of buffalo, this original 'skewer' was dragged and thrown into the river Nile.

"I saw such punishment meted out in this spirit, both during my stay personally on the surface of this planet of yours, as well as through the large Teskooano from the planet Mars.

"And these contemporary favorites of yours, naïve already to the *nth* degree, grew sincerely indignant that these contemporary 'Bolsheviks' of theirs shot a certain Tom Brown.

"If we compare the actions of the former three-brained beings there, who were subject to this 'psychic state,' with the actions of these contemporary Bolsheviks, then they, i.e., the contemporary Bolsheviks, ought even to be given praise and thanks that in spite of the fact that the various consequences of the properties of the organ Kundabuffer are infallibly completely crystallized in their common presences—as in general in the presences of contemporary three-brained beings—they, in the very heat of that period when they were entirely 'puppets' under the influence of the inevitable cosmic law Solioonensius, manifested themselves with these consequences in such a way that the dead body of the person shot by them could at least be recognized as whose it was, namely, 'Tom Brown's and nobody else's.' "

In this place of his tale, Beelzebub deeply sighed, and gazing at one spot, became concentratedly thoughtful.

Hassein and Ahoon, with a shade of surprise, but also with some sadness on their faces, began to stare expectantly at him with, as it were, a stark fixed gaze.

A little later Hassein, having first made quite an unintelligible grimace, and then with a voice expressing pained tenderness, turned to Beelzebub who was still continuing to think.

"Grandfather! Dear Grandfather! Manifest please aloud those informations which you have in your common presence particularly dear to me, and which you have learned during your long existence and which may serve me as material for the elucidation of that question which has just arisen in my essence, and even for the approximate representation of which I have as yet positively no data for a logical confrontation in any of the spiritualized parts of my common presence.

"This question arising in my essence, the answer to which has already become necessary to the whole of my presence, consists in this: To inquire about the reasons why, namely, if these unfortunate three-brained beings who breed on the planet Earth do not have the possibility, owing to reasons not depending on themselves, of acquiring and having in the period of their responsible existence Divine Objective Reason, why since they arose so long ago and their species has continued to exist such a long time, could not those customs have been gradually formed by now, only thanks to the flow of time, in the process of their ordinary existence even under those abnormal conditions, and those proper 'instinctive-automatic-habits' have been acquired in the presences of every being in general, thanks to which their ordinary existence, both 'egoistically personal' as well as 'collectively general,' might flow more or less tolerably in the sense of objective reality?"

Having said this, our poor Hassein began questioningly to gaze at the Cause of the Cause of his arising.

At the question of his favorite grandson, Beelzebub began to relate the following:

"Why of course . . . my dear boy. In the course of long centuries of their existence, and among them as everywhere on planets where beings arise who spend likewise part of the time of their existence simply in the ordinary process, many customs and also what are called 'moral habits,' at times very good and useful for their ordinary existence, were also gradually formed, and even at the present time are sometimes formed among several of their groupings; but herein lies the evil, that such a being-welfare as becomes fixed in the process of ordinary existence from the flow of time alone, and which improves thanks to transmission from generation to generation, also soon either entirely disappears or is changed to such a direction that these happy achievements of theirs are transformed of their own accord into 'unhappy' ones and increase the number of those small factors maleficent for them, the totality of which year by year 'dilutes,' more and more, both their psyche as well as their very essence.

"If they were even to possess and were to use at least those 'trifles' worthy of the three-brained beings, then this would already be to the good for them, or as they themselves would say, 'would-in-any-case-be-better-than-nothing.'

"Of course, if at least any of these good customs, fixed by them in the process of their existence, and already automatized 'moral habits' could have survived and been transformed by inheritance into the mode of existence of their subsequent generations, then thanks at least to this, their, in the objective sense, 'desolate' existence would have seemed to be, to an outside impartial observer, at least a little reconcilable.

"The causes of the complete destruction and change of even this being-welfare for their tolerable existence achieved by time, both of good customs as well as 'moral usages,' are of course also engendered by these abnormal conditions for the ordinary being-existence around them established by them themselves.

"As a concentrated result flowing from these abnormal conditions around them and which became the basic cause for this evil of theirs, there is a special property which arose not long ago in their psyche which they themselves call 'suggestibility.'

"Thanks to this strange property which had only recently become fixed in their psyche, all the functionings in their common presences began gradually to change, and as a result, each of them, particularly the beings who arose and became responsible during the last centuries of theirs, already began to represent in themselves such a peculiar cosmic formation as has in itself the possibility of acting exclusively only if it were to find itself constantly under the influence of another formation similar to itself.

"And indeed, my boy, at the present time, these three-brained beings who please you, must already as separate persons as well as entire large and small groupings, infallibly 'influence' or find themselves under the 'influence' of others.

"For your better representation and all-round understanding in what way customs and automatic habits useful for their ordinary existence acquired by them during centuries also disappear without a trace, or change for the worst on account of the mentioned property of their strange psyche, we will take as an example just these same terrestrial three-brained beings with their customs whom all other beings of your planet call 'Russians' and who represent the majority of that community named Russia.

"In consequence of the fact that the existence of beings which had been put as a basis of the formation of this large contemporary community there and of their subsequent generations, proceeded in the course of many centuries in the neighborhood of beings who belonged to those Asiatic communities, who, thanks to various events, existed so relatively long a period in consequence of which in the process of their ordinary existence—as this in general happens from a long existence—very many good customs and 'moral habits' were gradually formed by themselves and became fixed in the process of their ordinary existence, then these Russians, after meeting with the beings of these, for terrestrial beings, ancient communities and even at times having friendly mutual relationships with them, gradually adopted and began to use in the process of their ordinary existence, many of the useful customs and 'moral habits.'

"And so, my boy, thanks to the mentioned strange property of the three-brained beings of this planet of yours, which property, as I have already told you, arose and gradually became, soon after the Tikliamishian civilization, fixed in their general psyche—the intensity of the fixing proceeded chiefly in consequence of all the more deteriorating conditions around them of ordinary being-existence established by themselves—and which special psychic property already from the very beginning became obligatorily inherent in the common presences of beings composing this later largest community there, then on account of all this, they all in former centuries found themselves under the influence of beings of one or other of the Asiatic communities, and all the, as it is called, 'external-mode' and 'psychic-associative-form' of their ordinary existence proceeded also under their influence.

"And so, again in consequence of the fact that in the common presences of the three-brained beings of this planet Earth of yours who dwell on that part of the continent

Asia which was called, and until now is called Russia, 'being-Partkdolg-duty' also finally ceased to be actualized, on account of which this, for them, most maleficent property of their psyche, namely, 'suggestibility,' began gradually to increase; and in consequence of the fact that they, thanks to changed circumstances which flowed from always the same terrifying process of periodic reciprocal destruction, existing only on that ill-starred planet, were deprived of the former influence and were compelled, not having the possibility of independent existence, to fall under new influences, they this time fell under the influence of beings of European communities, chiefly of the community which exists there under the name 'France.'

"Since the beings of this community France began automatically to influence the psyche of the beings of the community Russia, and these latter began even to strive to imitate the beings of this community France in everything, thus all the good customs among them which were already present in the process of their existence and those moral habits which had become inherent in them, either half-consciously or automatically taken by them from the beings of ancient Asiatic communities, were gradually forgotten, and new ones—French—acquired.

"Among the customs and automatic moral habits useful for the beings of the community Russia, transmitted to them from the beings of old Asiatic communities, there were thousands of indeed very good ones.

"From these thousands of good customs and useful habits, let us take for example at least two: the custom, after using the first being-food, of chewing what is called 'keva'; and the usage of periodically washing oneself in what are called 'hammams.'

"Keva is a certain mastic prepared from various roots which is chewed after eating and which however long it is chewed hardly ever decomposes, but on the contrary becomes still more elastic.

"This mastic was also invented by a certain being with good Reason who belonged to one of the old Asiatic communities.

"The use of chewing this keva consists in this, that by chewing it, much what is called there on Earth 'saliva' and also other substances are formed in beings, which are worked out by their planetary bodies so that their first being-food may be the better and more easily transformed in them, or as they themselves say, so that this food may be the better and more easily 'digested and assimilated.'

"Thanks to this keva their teeth are also strengthened and the cavities in their mouths too are cleaned from the remains of the first food; the use of keva is very necessary for your favorites, particularly for this second purpose, as these remains, not decomposing owing to the chewing of keva, do not give off that disagreeable 'odor' from their mouths which has already become proper particularly to the contemporary three-brained beings there.

"And the second custom, namely, the washing at times in special rooms of theirs called the 'hammam' was also invented by a certain ancient Asiatic being.

"In order clearly to understand the necessity for this second custom in the process of the existence of terrestrial beings, the following must be first explained to you.

"The functioning of the planetary body of beings of all forms of external coatings is adapted by Nature in general in such a way that the process of their nourishment with the second being-food, which your favorites call 'breathing of air,' proceeds in them, and this nourishment is taken in not only through the organs of breathing, but also through what are called the 'pores' present in their skin.

"Through the 'pores' of the skin of the beings, not only

the new second being-food enters, but also through several of these pores, after the transformation of this second being-food, those parts of this food are given off from the skin which are either no longer necessary for the planetary body of the beings or which are already the result of its transmutation.

"These unnecessary parts should be given off from the said 'pores' of the skin of beings by evaporating gradually by themselves, thanks to those factors which obtain from the process proceeding in that sphere itself where the given beings exist, as for instance, from the movement of the atmosphere, from accidental contacts and so on.

"Now, when your favorites invented the covering of themselves with what are called 'clothes,' then, since these clothes of theirs began to hinder the normal elimination or evaporation of those parts of the second being-food unnecessary for the planetary body, these unnecessary substances having no possibility of evaporating into space and at the same time always continuing to accumulate, they, condensing, begin to form in these various pores of their skin the accumulation of a certain 'oily-something.'

"From that time on, among a number of other factors, this also began to aid in the formation on this ill-fated planet of innumerable and various illnesses which taken altogether are the chief cause of the gradual shortening of the length of the existence of these unfortunates.

"Well, my boy, when still in, as your contemporary favorites say, the 'dim ancient past,' a wise and learned being by name 'Amambakhlootr,' also from the continent Asia there, once clearly constated during his conscious observations of various facts proceeding around him, that this 'oily-something' which collects in the pores of the skin, has also a maleficent influence on the general functioning of the whole planetary body, he began to elucidate and seek for means for wiping out at least this evil.

"As a result of the investigations and long deliberations of this Amambakhlootr, and of several other also learned beings who then became his followers and began to help him, they arrived at the conclusion and became convinced of the impossibility of obtaining that beings similar to themselves should not wear clothes, and that it was necessary to seek a method for artificially eliminating from the pores of the skin these remains of the 'second-food' by means of implanting in the psyche of the beings around them some or other being-usage, which in the course of time would become indispensably necessary to them and in this way enter into their habits and customs.

"And that these Asiatic learned beings with this great Amambakhlootr at their head then experimentally elucidated and actualized this in practice, well, this served as a beginning of those hammams which exist there in places even till now.

"At that time, they during the learned experiments elucidated among other things, that by ordinary washing, even with hot water, it was impossible to obtain the elimination of these deposits from the pores of the skin, as these excretions of the planetary body are found not on the surface of the skin but in the depths of the pores.

"Their further elucidatory experiments showed them that the cleansing of the 'pores' of the skin from these deposits was possible only by means of slow warming, thanks to which, this deposited 'oily-something' acquires the possibility of gradually dissolving and of being eliminated from the pores of the skins of beings.

"Well, for this same purpose, they then invented and actualized in practice special rooms which later came to be called hammams, the sense and significance of which they knew how to spread among the beings of the whole continent in such a way that in the psyche of all the

Asiatic beings, the need was implanted in the process of their existence for the use of these rooms for the given procedure.

"Well, it is this need of going periodically to such hammams which had already become inherent in the beings of the continent Asia, and which later passed also to the beings of this community Russia.

"As regards this 'oily-something' which collects in certain pores of the skin of your favorites, it is necessary further to tell the following:

"As this substance, i.e., the 'oily-something,' like everything in general that exists in our Great Universe, cannot remain in one and the same state, therefore there inevitably proceed with these substances in these pores the processes of what are called evolution and involution required by Great Nature. And in consequence of the fact that during these processes, from all cosmic, what are called 'temporary' or 'transitory' arisings, there are given off what are called 'secondary' active elements, that is, those which are temporarily crystallized by the momentum of vibrations, and which, as is known to all, have the property, when adjacent to the organ of smell of beings, of being perceived very 'cacophonically,' therefore there on the planet Earth, there is always given off from your favorites who do not use the said hammams, a particular 'Rastropoonilo' or as they themselves say 'odor,' which even they consider 'not altogether pleasant.'

"And indeed, my boy, there on certain continents, particularly on the continent Europe, where the custom of going to the hammam does not obtain, it was very difficult for me as a being with a very acute sense of smell to exist among those three-brained beings on account of this specific 'Rastropoonilo' or as they sometimes call it, odor, which issues from them.

"This unpleasant odor which issues from those, the

pores of whose skin are never specially cleaned, was so strong that I could without any difficulty detect to which community the given being belonged, and even by those odors I could distinguish one being from another.

"Now the variety of these specific odors depends upon how long the decomposition of these 'oily-excretions' found in the pores of the skin has proceeded.

"These unpleasant odors fortunately for them do not affect them so 'tormentingly.'

"And they do not affect them because their sense of smell is very slightly developed and besides this, existing always among these odors, they gradually become accustomed to them.

"And so, my boy, just this custom, namely, of washing themselves periodically in special hammams, was taken by the Russians from the Asiatic beings; but when they fell under the influence of the European beings and for the most part, as I have already told you, of the beings of the community France, then in view of the fact that these French beings have not the custom of going to the hammam, they also gradually ceased to use hammams and thus this good custom established for centuries among them began little by little to disappear.

"Formerly, almost every Russian family had its own hammam, but recently when I was in their chief place of existence, the former St. Petersburg, for the last time, and where at that time more than two millions of these Russian beings existed, there were only seven or eight of such hammams there—and even then, only those beings went to these hammams who were called there 'house porters' and 'workmen,' that is, beings who happened to come there to the capital from distant villages where the custom of going to the hammam or, as they sometimes call it, the 'bath' had not yet been quite wiped out.

"Now, as regards the main population of this capital

who consisted chiefly of the beings of what are called the ruling class, they, these beings, in recent times did not go to the hammam at all, and if any 'queer fellow' were still sometimes from old habit to go, he would then try in every way that no one else in his caste should know about it.

"'May crooked luck save him,' otherwise such 'gossip' would fly around about this bold fellow as would inevitably 'ruin' the whole of his future career.

"To go to the hammam is now considered among beings belonging to the ruling class as very 'indecent' and 'unintelligent.' But indecent and unintelligent only because the contemporary 'most intelligent' beings of their planet, who according to their understanding are the French, do not go to the hammam.

"These unfortunates do not know of course that these same French, thanks always to the same reasons, namely, thanks to the abnormally established conditions of ordinary being-existence still but a few decades ago, not only did not go to the hammam, but these French, particularly, as they are called, the 'intelligentsia,' did not even wash themselves in the morning in order not to spoil their, at that time, fashionable artificial appearance which was difficult to rearrange.

"Now as regards the second of the good customs taken as an example by us, the fulfilling of which two centuries ago was still organically needed by every being of this community Russia, namely, the custom of chewing keva after the use of the first being-food, this custom already no longer exists there at all now among contemporary Russians.

"It must be remarked that at the present time the custom of chewing keva without meanwhile understanding its purport, began to implant itself while I was still there among the beings dwelling on the continent called

'America,' where the use of such keva, or as they have already called it, by another name, 'chewing gum,' is very widely spread and even takes on the dimensions of a great manufacturing branch of commerce there. Meanwhile it is interesting to notice that the fundamental part of this American chewing gum is exported just from Russia, namely, from the locality called 'Caucasia.' The beings dwelling in this locality do not even know why these 'mad' Americans import this unnecessary root good for nothing and for nobody.

"Of course to no one of them does the thought even enter his head that these Americans importing this 'good-for-nothing' root are indeed, though in a subjective sense, 'mad,' yet in an objective sense they are merely, as they themselves express it, 'daylight robbers' of the beings of this Russia.

"Well, my boy; in the same way a mass of other good customs as well as moral habits, adopted in the course of centuries by these Russian beings and already well fixed in the process of their ordinary existence during the last two centuries when these Russians became the object of influence of the European beings, began gradually to disappear, and instead of them new customs and new moral habits were formed among them, which they have at the present time, such as the usage of 'kissing a lady's hand,' 'being polite only with young ladies,' 'looking at a wife before her husband with the left eye,' and so on and so forth.

"It is necessary to emphasize with an impulse of regret, that at the present time the same continues to proceed in the processes of the ordinary existence of the beings of all communities there, on whatever continent it may be.

"I hope, my boy, that by now you may approximately picture to yourself and be satisfied about the question arising in your being, why, namely, in spite of the fact that there among those unfortunate favorites of yours, their species has arisen and existed so long a time, could not those automatic being-usages and 'instinctive habits' have, by now, been formed, by which their existence although even with the absence of objective consciousness, might flow more or less tolerably.

"I repeat: thanks to the said property which only recently became fixed in their general psyche, it has already become natural at the present time, and as it were according to law, always either to influence another or to find oneself under the influence of others.

"In both cases the results of the action of this peculiar property are obtained without any consciousness on their part, and even without their desire.

"From all that I have told you about this, that these contemporary Russians always follow the example of someone and imitate somebody, it can be clearly understood how much of the functioning of the data for being-confrontative-logical-mentation is already deteriorated in the presences of terrestrial three-brained beings.

"In general, to follow the example of others or set an example to others is considered and cognized as fully reasonable and inevitably necessary everywhere in the Universe among all three-brained beings, and that the three-brained beings of this large community Russia follow the example of the beings of the community France, this on their part is even very sensible. Why not take example from what is good?

"But these unfortunates, on account of the said particular property of their psyche, and of still several other specific features of their strange character which have finally become fixed in them, thanks to the total disappearance from their common presences of the usage of sometimes actualizing being-Partkdolg-duty, became what is called 'adopters-by-compulsion,' and began to follow the example also of what is bad and even to reject their own good customs only because they do not exist elsewhere.

"They could not for instance consider even this, that conditions of ordinary existence among these French beings are perhaps being built up all the time abnormally and therefore they had not yet had time to become aware of the necessity of sometimes, as in the given case, washing themselves in hammams and chewing keva after using the first being-food.

"But to throw away good customs already acquired, for the sole reason that they do not exist among the beings of this France from whom they take example—this is already indeed genuine 'turkeyness.'

"Although this strange peculiarity which I have just called 'turkeyness,' has already become inherent in almost all the three-brained beings who breed on this planet of yours, yet the 'manifestation' and the results of it are noticed to a great extent among the three-brained beings who breed on the continent Europe.

"This I constated and understood later when I departed from St. Petersburg to travel in various countries of this continent Europe, on which this time I remained for a long while and not for a short time as had happened on my former travels, and I had therefore time for observation and investigation of the finer details of the psyche, not only of separate beings, but also of many together in all kinds of surrounding conditions.

"The form of external existence of all communities existing on this continent Europe is little distinguished from the external form of existence of the beings of that large community Russia.

"The form, however, of existence of the beings of the various groupings of this continent differs among themselves only in so much as, thanks to the accidental longer or shorter continuity of the existence of the given community, there had been time for certain good customs and 'instinctive habits' to be automatically acquired and which became proper to the beings only of just this said community.

"Here, by the way, it is necessary to remark that the duration there of the existence of any community plays indeed a great role in the sense of the acquisition by beings of its good customs and instinctive habits.

"But unfortunately for all the three-brained beings of the whole Universe of every degree of Reason, the existence of every grouping of theirs, already more or less organized, is in general short-lived, thanks of course to that ever same chief particularity of theirs, namely, 'periodic reciprocal destruction.'

"As soon as good being-usages for automatic existence begin to be established in the general process of any of their groupings, this terrifying process suddenly begins to proceed, and thus either these good customs and 'automatic habits' acquired during centuries are totally destroyed, or the beings of the given grouping, thanks already to the mentioned property, fall under the influence of beings of another grouping who have nothing in common with those under whose influence they were before this, and therefore very soon all these customs and moral habits acquired during centuries are replaced by other 'new ones,' which in most cases are premature and which in most cases are good for only, as is said, 'a day.'"

CHAPTER 35

A Change in the Appointed Course of the Falling of the Transspace Ship Karnak

At this point of Beelzebub's conversation with his kinsmen, he was told that the captain of the ship sought permission to speak with him personally.

Soon after Beelzebub had given his consent, the captain entered and with a respectful salute addressed Beelzebub and said:

"Your Reverence, at the beginning of our journey you condescended to let fall a word which hinted that on the return journey you would perhaps decide to stop on the way at the holy planet Purgatory to see the family of your son Tooilan. If this is indeed your intention, then it will be better if you give me the order to do so now, because we shall soon be passing through the solar system Khalmian, and if having passed this system we do not direct the falling of our ship immediately more to the left, we shall greatly lengthen the path of its falling."

"Yes, please, my dear Captain," Beelzebub replied. "There is nothing against stopping on the way at this holy planet. No one knows whether there will be another such happy occasion for me to go there and visit the family of my dear son Tooilan."

When the captain saluted and was on the point of going out, Beelzebub suddenly, as if remembering, stopped him and addressed him in the following words:

"Wait, my dear Captain, I want to ask you to accede to yet another of my requests." And when the captain, drawing nearer, had sat down in his appointed place, Beelzebub continued thus:

"My request to you is that you consent after the visit

to the holy planet Purgatory, to give our ship *Karnak* such a course of falling that on the way we may reach the surface of the planet Deskaldino.

"The point is that, in the present period of the flow of time on that planet, the Great Saroonoorishan, my first educator, so to say the fundamental cause of all the spiritualized parts of my genuine common presence, has the place of his permanent existence.

"I should like, as at that first time, before going to the sphere on which I arose, to profit by this occasion and fall once more at the feet of the prime creator of my genuine being, the more so, since just now, returning from my perhaps last conference, the entire satisfactoriness of the present functioning of all the separate spiritualized parts of my common presence was revealed not only to me myself, but also to most of the individuals I met, and in consequence, the being-impulse of gratitude towards that Great Saroonoorishan arose in me and is still inextinguishably maintained.

"I very well know, my dear Captain, that I am giving you no easy task, because I have already been a witness of the difficulties in carrying out this same request of mine, when, returning for the first time after my gracious pardon to the place of my arising on the planet Karatas, I desired before descending onto it, to visit the surface of the planet Deskaldino. On that occasion, when the captain of the intersystem ship *Omnipresent* had agreed to this and directed the falling of the *Omnipresent* in the direction of the atmosphere of that planet and was indeed able to carry out my request, I was able, before my return to my native land, to reach the surface of the planet Deskaldino and I had the happiness of greeting the Great Saroonoorishan, the creator of my genuine being-existence, and to receive from him his 'creator-benediction,' most dear and most precious to me."

To this request of Beelzebub's, the captain of the ship *Karnak* answered:

"Very good, your Reverence, I will think out how it may be possible to carry out your desire. I do not know just what obstacles there were then for the captain of the ship *Omnipresent*, but in the present case, on the direct route between the holy planet Purgatory and the planet Deskaldino, there lies the solar system called Salzmanino, in which there are many of those cosmic concentrations which, for purposes of the general cosmic Trogoautoegocratic process, are predetermined for the transformation and radiation of the substances Zilnotrago; and therefore the direct falling of our ship *Karnak*, unhindered, through this system, will scarcely be possible. In any case, I will try in one way or another to satisfy the desire expressed by your Reverence."

Having said this the captain rose and, respectfully saluting Beelzebub, went out.

When the captain of the ship had left the place where Beelzebub was sitting with his kinsmen, Hassein ran to his grandfather and again sitting down as usual at his feet, coaxingly asked Beelzebub to continue to relate what had happened to him after his departure from the capital of that large community of the beings of the planet Earth which was called St. Petersburg.

CHAPTER 36

Just a Wee Bit More About the Germans

Beelzebub began thus:

"From St. Petersburg I first of all went to what are called the Scandinavian countries, and after traveling through these countries, I settled in the chief point of the beings of the contemporary grouping called 'Germany.'"

Having said this and having patted the curly head of Hassein, Beelzebub with a good-natured smile but with an admixture of what is called slyness, continued thus:

"Now, my boy, wishing to give you a certain understanding of the peculiar psyche of the three-brained beings of this contemporary European grouping also, I will this time change my practice, namely, of initiating you into various details for elucidating information, but will set you such a problem that from the solving of it you will in the first place exhaustively make clear to yourself the specificness of the psyche of the beings of just this European grouping, and in the second place, it will serve as ideal practice for your mentation.

"This original problem which I have devised for you is that while actively meditating, you are to deduce those logical data, the totality of which should make clear to you the very essence of the reason why just among the beings of this contemporary European grouping, in whatever part of what they call their 'Fatherland' they happen to be, one innocent custom obtains, according to which, whenever they gather in any place for some feast or other, or simply for what is called a 'spree,' they unfailingly and invariably sing one and the same song, composed by themselves and in the highest degree original, consisting of the following words:

Blödsinn, Blödsinn,
Du mein Vergnügen,
Stumpfsinn, Stumpfsinn,
Du meine Lust.

"And so, my boy, if you succeed in making anything out of this fact, then for your common presence there will be actualized in full the wise saying of our dear teacher, Mullah Nassr Eddin, which he expressed in the following words: 'The-very-greatest-happiness-consists-in-obtaining-the-pleasurable-with-the-profitable.'

"For you it will be pleasurable because you will have ideal practice for your active mentation, and profitable, because you will thoroughly understand the specificness of the psyche of the three-brained beings who interest you, who breed on the planet Earth, and who belong to this contemporary European grouping.

"In view of the fact, as I have once already told you, that the beings of this contemporary grouping are the direct substitutes of the ancient Greeks in respect of 'inventing' every possible kind of 'science,' and in view of the fact that your deductions from the problem I have set you might be diametrically opposite to confrontative-logical possibilities, I find it necessary to help you a little and to inform you further concerning two facts.

"The first fact is that certain words of this song have no corresponding words in any other language, in spite of the fact that this planet of yours is called, in respect of the existence there of an innumerable number of languages, a 'thousand-tongued-hydra'; and the second fact is that when it finally became inherent to the beings of this grouping, just as to the ancient Greeks, to invent every maleficent means for 'disintegrating' what is called 'logical-being-mentation,' already sufficiently disintegrated without this, they also invented among other things for their language, a certain so-called 'grammatical-rule,' according to which they always during any kind of 'exchange of opinions,' even to the present day, place the particle of negation after the affirmative, as for instance, they always, instead of saying 'I-do-not-want-this,' say 'I-want-this-not.'

"Thanks to this grammatical rule of theirs, either listener during an exchange of opinions, first of all receives a suggestion as if it were subject to actualization and thus there must proceed in him a certain 'being-Diardookin,' or as they themselves would say, a certain 'experiencing,' and only later, at the end, when speaking according to their grammatical rule, do they pronounce their famous 'nicht'; so that each time, as a result, there is accumulated in their common presences that which in totality actualizes, though slowly yet surely, this mentioned 'specificness' in their common psyche, and from this fact, you should be able to elucidate this original problem I have set you."

CHAPTER 37
France

Further, Beelzebub continued to speak thus:

"After Germany, I had for a short time the place of my existence again there on the continent Europe among the beings of the community called 'Italy'; and after Italy, among the beings of that community, who became for the beings of the community Russia what are called the 'sources' for the satisfaction of that 'vice' which long before had become fixed in the abnormal process of the ordinary being-existence of terrestrial three-brained beings of recent centuries, and which is called 'suggestibility'; that is, I settled among the beings of the community France.

"Now, my boy, I wish to inform you about the specific aspects of the psyche of those French three-brained beings in such a way that you may, at the same time, make clear to yourself how much in general among those three-brained beings of the planet Earth who please you, the normal possibility for the crystallization of all being-data, in the sense of the capacity to ruminate impartially and personally, has already deteriorated and how at the present time subjective essence-opinion about every reality is formed in them at times entirely opposite to that which should be obtained by the perception of that reality, directly received by them personally through impressions.

"In my opinion, it will be well if we take these same French beings as an example for making clear what I have just told you.

"The point is that at the present time among beings of all groupings breeding on that continent Europe on which, as they express it, their 'cultured existence' is now concentrated, as well as on all other continents, there became infallibly crystallized already from the very beginning of their formation into responsible beings, data for their representation about the individuality of these same French beings, which data brings forth in them such a definite understanding that these French, of all beings similar to them of their planet, are, as they express it, the most 'depraved' and 'immodest.'

"Before this, namely, before my choice of the community France as the place of my permanent existence, data was formed in my common presence for just such a representation about them, because, going about everywhere and existing among the beings there of all kinds of groupings which exist at the present time on almost all terra firma parts of the surface of your planet, I frequently heard during all conversations such an opinion concerning the French beings.

"Although earlier, as I have already told you, I had sometimes been in just that community France, I had, nevertheless, on my preceding visits, paid no special attention to the particulars of the psyche of those beings and to that opinion which beings of nearly all the other communities there had about them.

"This time, however, when I settled in one of the provincial towns there, and my presence, of course, instinctively expected to perceive impressions from 'immoral' and 'depraved' manifestations of the local three-brained beings, I, to my great and ever-increasing surprise, ascertained first of all that I would not perceive anything of the kind.

"A little later, when I began to go about among them, and even to make friends with some of them and with their families, the data for this as it is called 'automatic opinion' about them not only began to become decrystallized in me, but there began to become crystallized in me the 'required-being-data' for finding out just what was the cause that data could become crystallized in the common presences of other communities for such an opinion about them which did not correspond to reality.

"All this interested me more and more each day, because, existing among them, it gradually became clear to me that the beings of that community were not only not the most depraved and immoral, but on the contrary they seemed to be the most 'patriarchal' and 'modest' beings of all the three-brained beings who were grouped on the continent Europe.

"So I then began specially to observe and to acquire corresponding information, in order to elucidate for myself just that contemporary terrestrial question.

"While I was there in that provincial town, I was unable to elucidate anything for myself, but later, when I happened to go to the capital of those French beings, then there, from the very first day, the basic causes of that misunderstanding also began to be gradually elucidated in my Reason.

"For the elucidation of these causes, the following facts then served there, and also my impartial observations and considerations.

"When I went this time to that capital named 'Paris'—which, by the way, had now in the logicnesterian-crystallization of the contemporary three-brained beings of your planet, breeding on all the continents, already completely become also such a center of their imagined culture as the cities Samlios, Koorkalai, Babylon and so on, were for the beings of former periods in their time—I went straight from the railway station to the hotel which had been recommended to me while still in the city of Berlin by an acquaintance of mine.

"The first thing that I happened to notice was that all the servants of that hotel then consisted of foreigners who mostly spoke the English language, whereas, not so long ago, as it seems, all the servants of this same hotel spoke only the Russian language.

"The day after my arrival in that contemporary Samlios, I inquired for a certain being belonging to a community called Persia to whom I had an introduction from one of my good friends existing in the capital of that community.

"This new acquaintance of mine, the Persian being, suggested in the evening of that day that I should go with him to what is called the 'Boulevard des Capucines' and sit for a while in the then famous 'Grand Café.'

"When we arrived at this Grand Café we sat down at one of the many tables which took up, as is usual there in Paris, half the pavement.

"As I have already told you, a Café serves the same purpose for the beings on the continent Europe as their Tchai-kanas do for the beings dwelling on the continent Asia. The only difference is this: on the continent 'Asia' in a Tchai-kana they give you a certain reddish liquid to drink, squeezed from a certain well-known flower there, while here on the continent Europe, although in these establishments they also give a liquid to drink, yet that liquid is not only firstly completely black, but secondly, from what it is squeezed—no one knows except the proprietor of that establishment.

"We began to drink the black liquid served to us, called 'coffee.'

"I noticed here also that all the staff of this Grand Café, or, as they say here, the 'waiters,' were beings from other groupings, mostly from the European community called 'Italy.'

"You must know that in general in this part of the city Paris, or in this 'foreign Paris,' each business is a specialty of the beings of one or other of the contemporary communities of the continent Europe or other continents.

"And thus, having sat down at a table in that famous Grand Café or rather in the street in front of the Grand Café, we began to watch the passing people just strolling by, passing and strolling on the other half of the pavement of this Grand Café.

"Among the strolling crowd were beings of almost all the separate groupings both of this continent Europe as well as of the other continents, mostly of course from those communities whose turn it was at that period to be rich; there predominated, however, in that crowd, beings of the continent America.

"The beings of the continent America had already there in Paris finally taken the place in recent times of the beings of the great community Russia after the 'death' of this latter.

"There strolled by there, beings chiefly belonging to the caste of the ruling class, who often come there, as they say, to the 'capital of the world' to 'have a good time.'

"There were many businessmen also among them, who had come there to Paris for what are called the 'fashion-goods,' chiefly for perfumery and women's clothes.

"Among the varied crowd walking on the Boulevard des Capucines, many young people could also be noticed who had come there to learn how to dance 'fashionable dances' and make 'fashionable hats.'

"As we, while talking, were examining that mixed crowd, whose faces expressed their satisfaction at the fulfillment of a long-awaited dream, my new acquaintance, the young Persian, suddenly turned to me in surprise and pointing with his finger at a passing couple, exclaimed:

"'Look! Look! There go genuine French people!'

"I looked and saw that indeed this couple greatly resembled those beings whom I had seen in the provincial towns of that community France.

"After they had disappeared from sight in the crowd, we began to discuss in order to understand the reason why that genuine French couple came to be in this part of their 'capital.'

"After various surmises, we unanimously agreed that that couple probably lived in some outlying part of genuine French Paris and had gone, for some family feast or other at their relatives, to another part of this French Paris which lay just on the opposite side.

"Evidently at that family feast they had drunk rather excessively and returning home after the feast, they did not want to make a detour, and decided to take the direct route. And this direct route evidently passed just by the Grand Café.

"Probably for this reason alone, did these genuine French people appear in this part of Paris.

"Talking, we continued to look at the strolling crowd decked out in the latest fashions.

"Although the majority of them were decked out in these latest fashions, yet from everything, it was obvious that these clothes of theirs had only just been bought—today or yesterday—and from close observation and comparison of their faces with their clothes, one could, without doubt, be convinced that in the ordinary process of their existence at home they rarely had the possibility of being so richly dressed and of feeling so free from care.

"When, among these 'visiting foreign princes,' as some of the 'natives' call them, all sorts of also foreign 'professionals-of-both-sexes,' already 'well-acclimatized' to that part of Paris, were walking 'in mass,' my new acquaintance, the young Persian, suggested to me that he should become my 'Paris cicerone' and that we should go to what are called the 'disreputable places of Paris' and look at French 'depravity.'

"I agreed, and we went from that Grand Café, first of all to what is called a 'brothel' situated near by.

"There, in the first place, I learned that the owner of this 'noble establishment' was a certain Spaniard.

"In the rooms of this house was a crowd of women: 'Poles,' 'Viennese,' and 'Italians,' and even two 'Negresses' were there.

"I had wanted to see how genuine Frenchwomen appeared in this setting, but from my inquiries it became clear that there was not even one Frenchwoman in this establishment.

"After this brothel we again went on to the Boulevards, and began to walk and observe the strolling, varied crowd.

"And there also everywhere we met large numbers of the beings of the feminine sex with the obvious signs on them of the aim of their 'nocturnal quests' on these Boulevards.

"All these women belonged to the already enumerated nationalities, as well as to others, namely, there were also 'Swedes,' 'English,' 'Russian,' 'Spaniards,' 'Moldavians,' and so on there, but scarcely one genuine Frenchwoman.

"Soon some dubious-looking beings of the male sex began to accost us and proposed to us that we do with them a certain 'Grand Duke.'

"At first I did not understand what 'Grand Duke' meant, but on various inquiries it became clear that these strange words had acquired there a definite meaning quite recently, namely, from the time when the now dead 'monarchic Russia' flourished there.

"It turned out that the beings there of that time, belonging to the caste of the ruling class of that dead Russia were very fond of the 'capital of the world' and often went there; and almost every one of them, out of 'swank,' gave himself out as a titled individual, such as 'Count,' 'Baron,' or 'Prince,' but most frequently of all, as a 'Grand Duke.' And, since all of them obligatorily paid 'visits' to dubious places of 'foreign Paris,' the professional guides now call such a 'tour' the *tournée du Grand Duc* (which in English means 'the Grand Duke's tour').

"Having taken one of these guides, we also went to see the nocturnal 'sights' of that contemporary Koorkalai.

"We visited various of these 'haunts'; we were in the café of the 'homosexuals,' and in the club of the 'Lesbians,' and in many of those 'evil hearths' where every 'abnormality' proceeds, which are repeated from time to time in all the chief 'centers-of-culture' of these unfortunates.

"Visiting these disreputable places, we eventually reached the streets of the famous, as it is called 'Montmartre,' not strictly on Montmartre itself, but on the lower slope of the district of that name, which abounds in every kind of nocturnal maleficent 'disreputable establishment,' destined however not for the beings of that community France, but exclusively for the beings only who come there from other separately independent groupings, or, as they themselves say, for 'foreigners.'

"Besides many of these dubious establishments, there likewise exist there a great many night restaurants, for foreign visitors also, which are open the whole night long.

"All this district in general only becomes animated at night; by day it is almost, as they express it there, 'dead,' and of foreign visitors not one ever goes there.

"In all these restaurants there are what are called 'open stages' on which they show various 'amazing things,' which proceed, as it were, among those beings similar to themselves who belong to other communities existing on other parts of the surface of their planet.

"They show that 'stomach dance' of the African beings, the Caucasians with their 'dagger dances' and the 'mulattos' with their snakes—in a word, whatever is considered at that season to be a 'fashionable novelty'!

"But all that they show there in the 'Montmartre theaters,' as if it proceeded among the beings similar to them breeding on other continents of their planet, has in no case anything in common with what I, who had existed everywhere and who had been greatly interested to see and study all specific manifestations of the beings of each given locality, had in fact seen there on the spot.

"In recent times in this Montmartre, very many what are called 'special Russian restaurants' had been opened, and both in these special Russian restaurants, as well as other restaurants, the so-called 'artists' and 'actors' are beings of just the great community Russia, mostly from the beings of the former ruling class there.

"It will be as well to notice and to draw your attention to the fact that the fathers and grandfathers of these 'artists' or 'actors' of the contemporary 'Montmartre theater restaurants' still only quite recently in these various establishments there in Montmartre—thanks of course to what is called the 'sweat of peasants'—laughed at and insulted the individual dignity of the beings of other communities, but now their children and grandchildren themselves are humbled and serve as objects for the satisfaction of the 'Hasnamussian caprices' of what are called the 'much-moneyed beings' of other communities.

"As regards such a condition of affairs, our wise Mullah Nassr Eddin has also a very wise saying; he, namely, says:

"'If a father likes to ride though it be but a child's sled, his son must obligatorily be prepared to drag the great village sleigh up the mountainside.'

"While I sat in one of those restaurants with my said new friend, the Persian, he was called away by some other acquaintances, Persians, and I remained alone at the table with the champagne, the ordering of which in these restaurants at night in Montmartre is in general obligatory."

At this point in his tale Beelzebub sighed deeply, and then continued thus:

"Just now, while telling you about that evening spent in the restaurant in Montmartre among the contemporary three-brained beings breeding on that planet Earth which pleases you, there involuntarily revived in me the 'being-Sarpitimnian-experiencing,' which I experienced at that time, and now at this moment the memory of all that I experienced is so intensely and repeatedly associated in all the three spiritualized parts of my common presence, that I am compelled to digress from the theme begun, in order that I may share with you these sad and distressing reflections which were induced in me in those dreadful surroundings in Montmartre by my solitude after the said young Persian, who became my cicerone in Paris, had left me.

"Then, namely, for the second time in the whole of my existence, there proceeded in my Being the process of this same being-Sarpitimnian-experiencing, which had engendered in my common presence a revolt on account of various unforeseeingnesses on the part of our Most High, Most Saintly Cosmic Individuals, and of all the objective misfortunes flowing from them, which have already obtained and, maybe, will still continue to obtain on this planet Earth as well as in all our Great Universe.

"How was it possible not to foresee in their calculations of the harmonious movement of cosmic concentrations that the comet Kondoor would collide with this ill-fated planet Earth?

"If those who should have done so had foreseen this, then all subsequent unfortunate consequences issuing one from the other would not have happened and there would not have been the need to implant in the first three-brained beings of that ill-fated planet that, for them, maleficent organ Kundabuffer which was the cause of all subsequent distressing and terrifying results.

"It is true that later when it was no longer necessary and this for them maleficent organ was destroyed, they yet again did not foresee that by the destruction of the organ itself the possibility was not destroyed that in the future the given consequences of its properties would, owing to a certain manner of existence of the beings, become crystallized in the presences of their descendants.

"In other words, they did not foresee for the second time also that even if it were possible to destroy that organ, yet the fundamental Cosmic Law Heptaparaparshinokh with its 'Mdnel-Ins' nevertheless remains, in the sense of the evolutionary process for the three-brained beings of the planet Earth just as for everything existing in the whole Universe.

"It was thanks particularly to the second almost criminal 'unforeseeingness' that this situation, terrifying for the three-brained beings, obtains there, namely, that on the one hand there are in their common presences as in the presences of all the three-brained beings of our Great Universe, all the possibilities for coating the 'higher-being-bodies,' and at the same time, thanks to the crystallization which has become inherent in them of the various consequences of the organ Kundabuffer, it is almost impossible for them to carry the higher sacred parts coated in them up to the required degree of perfecting. And since, according to the fundamental common cosmic laws, such a formation as their 'higher-being-part,' coated in the common presences of three-brained beings, is not subject to decomposition on planets, and since the planetary body of the beings cannot endlessly exist on planets and the process of the sacred Rascooarno must inevitably proceed with them at the proper time, therefore, their unfortunate higher bodies arising in the terrestrial three-brained beings must inevitably languish also forever in all kinds of exterior planetary forms.

"Sitting then in solitude in the restaurant in Montmartre and watching the contemporary favorites of yours gathered there, I continued to ponder:

"How many centuries have passed since that time when I began to observe the existence of the three-brained beings of this ill-fated planet!

"During these long centuries many sacred Individuals have been sent down to them here from Above with the special aim of helping them to deliver themselves from the consequences of the properties of the organ Kundabuffer, yet nevertheless nothing has changed here and the whole process of ordinary being-existence has remained as before.

"During this time, no difference whatsoever has arisen between those three-brained beings of this planet, who existed nearly a hundred of their centuries ago, and the contemporary ones.

"Are not the beings sitting here the same, and do they not behave as unbecomingly as the beings of the city Samlios on the continent Atlantis, which was considered by all the three-brained beings of that time as the 'source-and-place-of-concentration-of-the-results-of-attainments-in-the-sense-of-the-perfecting-of-their-Reason'—or as the contemporary beings here would say, 'the-chief-center-of-culture'—and where I also sat among the beings there in their, as they then called similar restaurants, 'Sakroopiaks'?

"And after Atlantis had perished, and many, many centuries had passed, when I was on the continent Asia in the city of Koorkalai, their new center-of-culture of that ancient community there called Tikliamish, and sat at times among them in their Kaltaani which were similar also to contemporary restaurants, was I not witness of similar 'scenes'?

"There in front of me, that stout contemporary gentleman with the enormous foreign growth on his neck is sitting with two young street girls . . . dress him in the costume of a 'Kafirian,' will he not be exactly like that very type I saw then sitting in a Kaltaan of the city Koorkalai?

"Or over there, on the left, at another table a contemporary young man is sitting, who in a squeaky voice convincingly holds forth to his bottle-companion about the causes of disorders which proceed in some community . . . dress his head in a 'chambardakh' and would he not be exactly like a real, as they were then called, 'Klian-of-the-mountains'?

"And that tall man pretending to be an important gentleman, sitting alone in the corner, making eyes at a lady who sits with her husband among the neighboring company . . . is he not a real 'Veroonk'?

"And these waiters, exactly like dogs with their tails between their legs, who serve the people sitting there . . . are they not 'Asklay-slaves'?

"And in their majestic city Babylon, where I also happened to be, many of their centuries later . . . was it not the same there? Were not the three-brained beings of the city Babylon those same Asklays, Kafirians, Veroonks, Klians, and so on? . . .

"Only their dress and the names of their nationalities have changed.

"During Babylonian times they were called 'Assyrians,' 'Persians,' 'Sikitians,' 'Aravians,' and by other different names ending in 'ian.'

"Yes . . . and now again, after so many centuries, I am again here, in their contemporary center-of-culture, the city Paris.

"And again it is the same . . . shoutings, uproar,

laughter, scoldings . . . the same as in the city Babylon, as in the city Koorkalai, or even in Samlios, their first center-of-culture. . . .

"Do not these three-centered beings of today gather together to pass the time in a way unbecoming to three-centered beings, in as unbecoming a way as three-centered beings used to pass the time in all former periods of existence on that unfortunate planet?

"And during the time in which I have observed these unfortunates, not only whole peoples of many of their centers of culture have disappeared without trace, but also the terra firma on which they existed has either completely changed or disappeared from the face of that planet, as happened for instance to the continent Atlantis.

"After Samlios, their second center became the continent 'Grabontzi.' Have not the peoples inhabiting it also disappeared from the continent Africa in the same way? And if the continent itself has not disappeared, yet at least that place where its center lay is now so covered with sand that, besides what is called the 'Sahara desert,' nothing exists.

"Again many centuries passed; their center was formed in Tikliamish. What remains of it, but deserts now called 'Red sand'?

"If some nation formerly famous has perhaps survived in its thousandth generation, then it is now vegetating in complete nothingness somewhere not far from that place where that nation dwelt.

"Then again many centuries passed.

"I saw their center Babylon; what has remained of this truly great Babylon? A few stones of the city itself and a few remnants of peoples formerly great, who, although they continue still to exist, are yet regarded by contemporary beings as quite insignificant.

"And what will become of this contemporary center-of-culture of theirs, of the city Paris, and of the peoples powerful today who surround it: French, Germans, English, Dutch, Italians, Americans, and so forth? . . . future centuries will show.

"But meanwhile, only one thing is certain: these unfortunate germs of 'higher-being-bodies,' which arose and still continue to arise in some of the three-brained beings here, are compelled, as I have already told you, to 'languish' in the presences of all kinds of abnormal forms, to actualize which, owing to the nonlawful consequences arising from the lack of foresight of some of our Most-High-Most-Most-Sacred-Common-Cosmic-Individuals, has become proper to this maleficent planet Earth.

"I was still absorbed in such thoughts, so sad personally for my essence, when my new friend, the young Persian, returned.

"Having sat a little longer in that restaurant where it had already become extremely noisy and stifling, we decided to go on to another restaurant which was also there in Montmartre.

"But when we got up and were about to leave, a company of beings who were sitting beside us at another table, having overheard our conversation about the new place to which we intended going, spoke to us and asked us to sit a little at their table, and then go on together to where we had proposed going. They asked us to wait until a friend of theirs would arrive.

"These new acquaintances of ours turned out to be beings from the continent America.

"Although it grew more and more unpleasant in that restaurant and the noise of the drunken voices increased, yet we at first agreed to wait for their friend; but when in a far corner of the room of that restaurant a row suddenly started, we left without waiting for those American beings.

"And the row in the far corner of the room started, as it transpired, because one being who was in the company of others struck one of them on the head with a champagne bottle, only because this latter would not agree to drink to the health of a certain prime minister of some government there, but wished to drink without fail to the health of the 'Toogoortski-Sultan.'

"One of the Americans who did not want to wait any longer for his friend went with us to the other restaurant.

"On closer acquaintance with this American three-brained being, he turned out to be merry, observant, and loquacious.

"All the way, and then there at the new place we went to, he talked all the time and made us laugh, chiefly because he very skillfully and aptly noticed the comic aspects of the people we met and of the people sitting in the new restaurant.

"Later, from inquiries, it became clear that this American was the owner of a big school of fashionable dancing there in Paris.

"From all he told us about his business, I understood that the pupils of his school consisted entirely of American beings who learned chiefly one favorite American dance, the 'fox trot.'

"I also understood that this dance, the fox trot, was purely American in origin and that it is popular and danced in full swing chiefly there in America.

"And that was why, when we together had all chosen a new brand of champagne, and this merry American stopped his chatter a little, I asked him:

"'Tell me, please, respected sir, if this is so, why do you not have your school over there at home in America instead of here, in the city Paris, so far from your own country and from the place of the "arising" of this "beneficent" fox trot?'

"'What! What! . . .' he exclaimed in a sincerely surprised tone. 'But I have a large family!

"'If I had my school in my native country, not only

would my family die of hunger, but I should not even be able to rent a damp room in New York to shelter us during bad weather from the freezing North winds there.

"'But here in the city Paris, thank the Lord, there are plenty who wish to learn that fox trot, and who will pay well for it.'

"'I do not understand,' I interrupted. 'You tell me that your pupils are entirely of your countrymen who come here, and at the same time you say that nobody over there would attend your school. How am I to understand this?'

"'That is just the point,' answered the honorable American.

"'The cause of this is a very little psychological kink from the number of those many other specific kinks which all together make up the stupidity of my compatriots.

"'The point is that my school is in Paris, or, as "clever" men say at home in America, in the "contemporary Babylon."

"'And this contemporary Babylon is very popular among all our Americans, and all of them consider it an obligation to visit this world capital.

"'Every one of our Americans who has saved up, if only a little, must without fail come here.

"'And, by the way, you must know it is not so easy for us to save up in America. It is only here in Europe that they think that, in America, dollars almost roll about the streets. But in reality those American dollars, I repeat, are not at all easily acquired by those who live there. Every cent must be earned by one's own physical labor.

"'They do not at all pay at home in America as they do here in certain European countries for various ephemeral values, such as fame, renown, talent, and so forth.

"'For example, here in Europe, if some, let us say, painter, happens to paint at some time or other a good picture, and he becomes famous, then ever afterwards, no matter what trash he may produce, the public will always pay a great deal of money for that trash, simply because it is said to be the work of that "famous" painter.

"'At home in America, however, things are very different in this respect. Everything is done there for cash, and every work is judged by its measure and weight. Name, talent, genius, and that kind of merchandise, is cheap with us and therefore dollars are acquired in America with great difficulty.

"'But fortunately for me, our Americans have many other weaknesses and among them is the passion "to see Europe."

"'Owing to that same passion, every American, even depriving himself at times of essential necessities, tries hard and with great difficulty to economize little by little the dollars he has earned, only to have the possibility of visiting Europe and of course the "capital of the world" . . . Paris.

"'That is why there are always enough of my compatriots here, as is said, "to sink a ship"—this is the first reason. And the second reason is that, as our Americans have still another exaggerated weakness, namely, vanity, their imagination is flattered that people will say that they have learned the fox trot not in some Philadelphia or Boston, but in Paris itself, where fashionable novelties for all the Earth originate, and as the fox trot is a fashionable novelty, the "Paris fox trot" is then for them, so to say, the result of the last word in civilization.

"'And so, thanks to these two ferments in our Americans, I, a poor dancing teacher, always have a sufficient number of Americans here who pay me well.

"'It is true, they pay me in francs and not in dollars, but the money-changers must also earn something—they too have families.'

"After this explanation of his, I asked him further:

"'Tell me also, please, my dear sir, is it possible that

your compatriots come here to the city Paris and stay here so long only to study this fox trot of yours?'

"'Why only the fox trot?' he replied.

"'During this time they also visit Paris itself and its outskirts, and sometimes they even travel quite far. In short, they also "study" Europe during this time.

"'They "visit" and "study" Europe in order, as they say there at home, "to complete their education and schooling"; but between ourselves, it is only said as one of the parrotlike phrases of those among us who pretend to be real English, whereas in reality my compatriots see Paris as well as Europe, only to satisfy their weakness of vanity.

"'They see it, not to be more learned or to become more informed, but only to be able to boast afterwards there at home in conversation with their acquaintances, that they have, so to say, been in Europe and seen there this, that, or the other.

"'Here in Europe in every convenient place, there is even for this purpose a branch of an establishment under the name of "Book and Son" which suits this particular need very well, and of course there is also one of these branches here in Paris.

"'Well, these dear compatriots of mine collect together like a flock of sheep, in groups of several scores, and that whole party of "tourists" sits in an enormous what is called "Book's bus" and go where they are taken.

"'On that Book's bus, besides the "chauffeur" there is another person, called a "Book's sleepy-type."

"'During the trip of that famous Book's bus, this same "sleepy-type" in a weak voice calls out from time to time the names of the places and the various historical and nonhistorical "sights" of Paris and its environs, learned parrotlike according to the "itinerary" mapped out by Book himself. In a word, this is the way my dear compatriots "study" Europe.

"'These "sleepy-types" have very weak voices and look half-consumptive because they are usually very tired and don't get enough sleep; and this is probably explained by the fact that many of these types work hard somewhere at night, besides working for "Book and Son," in order to get, together with the tiny earnings from "Book and Son," enough for their families to live on, as it is no easy task to support a family, especially in Paris.

"'And the fact that my dear compatriots hear little of what these "sleepy-types" with weak voices say has no great significance. Is it not the same to them what that sleepy-type mutters, or in what voice? For it is quite unnecessary for them to know any of the details of what they are seeing. Is it not all the same to them what they see and what it all means? All they need is but the "fact" that they were in that place itself and in a general way saw everything.

"'They are fully satisfied with this, for afterwards in conversation they can freely say with a "clear conscience" that they were here, there, and everywhere, and all the other Americans will think that the speaker is not just the tail of a donkey, but that he also has been in Europe and has visited everything there and seen every "sight" that every contemporary "educated" person must see.

"'Ekh! . . . my good Sir. Do you think that it is I alone who live by the "stupidities" of my compatriots?

"'What am I? . . . I am a little man, only a dancing teacher.

"'But did you notice that fat man sitting with me in the first restaurant? Well . . . that is a real "shark." Many of them, incidentally, have "sprung up" at home in America, especially in recent times.

"'That fat man, an Americanized English Jew, is the principal partner of a well-known, very solid American firm.

"'This firm has its branches in many cities in America

as well as in Europe, and the fat man who sat with me in the first restaurant is the one who fulfills the duties of director of the Paris branch of the firm.

"'That firm not only fills its pockets through the stupidities of its compatriots, but into the bargain it unfortunately adds much of its own "meanness."

"'And they concoct this "mélange" in the following way: the branch of the firm here, advertising itself well by American methods, is already widely known to my compatriots, and therefore, many of them, owing to always their same "vanity" and to other weaknesses, proper by the way to those beings of whom my compatriots mostly consist, always order their so-called fashionable dresses from this branch here, and the branch here sends to them "from the capital of the world" "real French models."

"'All this is done "quite honorably," according to all contemporary commercial rules on the basis of "triple-entry bookkeeping" and "Shachermacher-accounting."

"'As regards, so to say, the "intimate side of the business" of this American "solid firm" of ours, founded by various American "sharks," it is just here that these "sharks" skin everyone, and this only for the benefit of their own bottomless pockets.

"'Well, when this Paris branch receives a mail order direct from its American clients, this same mail order is then sent d.i.r.e.c.t.l.y. to the German branch, and there, in Germany, where materials and labor are much cheaper than here in Paris, the branch there s.l.o.w.l.y. and l.e.i.s.u.r.e.l.y. carries out this American "mail order" according to all the codes of "Paris fashions," whereupon it very calmly sticks onto its production a "Paris label" and, again, d.i.r.e.c.t.l.y . . . forwards it by steamer via Hamburg to its New York branch, from which the client receives her order, happy and proud that tomorrow she will wear "not just anything" but a real "Paris dress," sewed in Paris itself, after the "latest Paris fashions."

"'What is most interesting of all is that nobody is offended at this "commission business" of this "solid firm," but on the contrary it is "convenient" and "easy" and "profitable" for everyone. From this "commerce" of theirs, even the French, the hosts of the "capital of the world," "gain," but . . . it is true, they only gain in so far as they make profit out of the postage stamps which it is necessary to stick on the letters during correspondence between the customers and the Paris Branch.

"'As you see, everyone is satisfied and everyone is pleased, and even benefited; and the chief thing is that the axiom of political economy, now accepted by everybody, is justified, namely, that without international exchange of goods, countries cannot possibly exist.

"'But what am I? . . . I am only a poor dancing teacher! . . .'

"That jolly American was going to say something else, but at that moment a great hubbub arose in the next room of the restaurant and desperate voices of men and women who sat there were heard. We got up and only when we went out into the street did we find out that a being of the female sex from the community called 'Spain' had flung 'vitriol' into the face of another being, also of the female sex, from the community called 'Belgium,' because the latter had given a cigar case as a present, engraved with the inscription, 'Always ready at your service,' to a being of the male sex from the community called 'Georgia,' whose Paris existence had been supported till this day by the first woman.

"When we got into the street it was very late; it was already dawn, and having parted from that amusing American, we went to our hotels.

"While pondering, on my way home from that famous Montmartre, over everything I had seen and heard, it was then that I well understood why and how such an opinion not corresponding to reality about the beings of that community France which they always have, had been formed in the beings belonging to other communities.

"Thanks to everything I had seen and heard in that part of the city Paris, it had become clear to me that those beings of other communities who come here to France, come first of all to this part of Paris and to other such places where everything without exception is organized and adapted especially for them by foreigners like themselves, but who had come there long before and consequently had learned to speak the local language much better than they.

"And in view of the fact that generally the capacity for being-rumination in contemporary beings becomes atrophied and what is called a 'wide-being-horizon' is absent, they take everything and regard everything as 'French' and afterwards, when they return to their community again, they always relate to other beings of their community about everything they have seen, heard, and experienced in that part of Paris as if it were entirely of French origin and that French beings did it all.

"In this way, such an opinion about the French is gradually formed in other beings, not at all corresponding to reality.

"Moreover, there is also another and deeper cause for this opinion which had been formed about the beings of the community France in the peculiar consciousnesses of the beings of other communities, and in the given case it is also based on one of the peculiarities of their general psyche. This peculiarity is acquired in them, once again thanks to that maleficent usage invented by themselves which they call 'education.'

"The point is that there, in children, from the very first day, as they express it, of 'their appearance on God's earth,' when Nature herself is still continuing to form the given prime conception of the future three-brained responsible being, they begin, by this same maleficent 'education' of theirs, to hinder Nature from herself producing the necessary formation.

"This is not all: Thanks to their maleficent usage 'to-educate,' they fill and drive into what are called the 'Spetsi-tooalitivian-concentrations,' or as they themselves would say, the 'brains' of these newly born beings, all kinds of their ephemerally fantastic ideas, which brains are localized in general in beings for the perception and accumulation of all kinds of impressions, as well as of the results of conscious being-awareness, and which among the newly born are still quite pure and of maximum perceptivity.

"The greatest misfortune for them is that this maleficent process continues to proceed for the majority of them almost up to the age when they should already be responsible beings.

"As a result of all this, that mentioned peculiarity of their general psyche just obtains which is derived from the following: firstly, the general functioning, present in their whole being, of the sum of almost all their functions for active being-manifestations, little by little adapts itself to respond only to the sum of these false and fantastic ideas; and, secondly, the whole presence of each one of them gradually accustoms itself to perceive all subsequent new external impressions without any participation at all of those being-factors which in general are put in the beings for new perceptions, that is to say, to perceive them also only according to these previously introduced false and fantastic ideas present in them.

"In their new perceptions, the contemporary three-brained beings there ultimately lose even the need itself for embracing as a whole everything newly seen or newly heard, and the newly seen and newly heard only serve them as shocks, so that in them associations proceed of the information previously installed in them and corresponding to this newly seen and newly heard.

"This is why, when these contemporary favorites of yours already become responsible beings, everything newly seen and newly heard is perceived by them of its own accord automatically without the participation of any effort whatsoever on the part of their essence-functions, and without at all evoking in them, as I have already said, the being-need itself of sensing and understanding everything proceeding within them as well as without.

"In a word, they are satisfied with that alone, which someone once consciously or unconsciously put into them.

"I hope, my dear boy, that after all I have now told you, it will by itself become clear to you, why, just among the three-brained beings of other groupings on your planet, data as regards the beings of the separate grouping which exists there under the name of France, have been crystallized for such an opinion not corresponding to reality.

"However this may be, yet for the ordinary beings of this France, it was a great misfortune that the contemporary three-brained beings there of other separate groupings selected, for their what are called 'cultured manifestations,' the capital of that community.

"At any rate, I personally pity with all my essence the ordinary beings of this community, that their capital, even though only one definite part of it, has begun to be considered the contemporary 'center-of-culture' for that whole planet.

"One must simply even be astonished, that the majority of beings of the community France could, although without the participation of their consciousness, nevertheless preserve in their presences those data for the two being-impulses on which objective being-morality is chiefly based, and which are called 'patriarchality,' that is, love of family, and 'organic-shame,' in spite of the fact that they exist in the sphere of conditions of ordinary being-existence there which have now become quite abnormal, thanks to the fact that their capital, as I have already told you, has to their misfortune begun to be considered, and really is, the contemporary 'chief-center-of-culture' for the whole of that ill-fated planet.

"Owing to all this, in this contemporary center of the whole planet, as it had for a long time been the practice, those beings rush and flock from the whole planet, who have completely given themselves up to the 'evil-God' reigning there already without limit inside each of them, namely, to that 'evil-God' who became their Ideal, and the conception of whom is very well expressed in the words: 'to-attain-to-a-complete-absence-of-the-need-for-being-effort-and-for-every-essence-anxiety-of-whatever-kind-it-may-be'; and coming here to France, they must of course have, consciously or unconsciously, a corresponding harmful influence on the beings of the whole community.

"How great a misfortune it is for the ordinary beings of that France that the contemporary 'center-of-culture' should lie within their community, you will well understand, my boy, if I tell you about one of the consequences of this. I learned about it thanks to that information which was communicated to me in one of the latest etherograms concerning the three-centered beings of that planet of yours.

"It is necessary to tell you that it had already become in general customary that when beings from the whole of the planet, who have already completely given themselves up to their, as I said, inner 'evil-God,' flock to this chief center of culture, then these beings, among other of their maleficent actions, further do this: they occupy themselves out of idleness, in order to satisfy their whims, with devising 'new-forms-of-manifestations-of-their-Hasnamussianing,' or as is said there, with 'new fashions,' and spread them from there over the whole of the planet.

"This Hasnamussian usage, that of devising 'new fashions,'

existed in former civilizations also; during the Tikliamishian civilization it existed under the name of 'Adiat,' and at the time of Babylon, under the name of 'Haidia.'

"'Adiat,' 'Haidia,' or 'fashions,' consist in this: the beings devise various new means of being-manifestation in ordinary existence, and means for changing and disguising the reality of one's appearance.

"Adiat, Haidia, or fashions, are like our customs for daily being-existence which are established for the daily use of the three-brained beings for the alleviation of inevitable exterior conditions independent of beings, and which usually gradually enter everywhere into the daily use of beings as a necessary need, essential for them. These said contemporary customs or fashions of theirs are, firstly, only temporary and thus serve for the satisfaction only of the personal insignificant aims of these present and future Hasnamusses, which become phenomenally abnormal and trivially egoistic; and secondly, they are neither more nor less than the results of automatic Reason based on that relative understanding, which generally flows from the abnormally established conditions there of ordinary being-existence.

"Thus, in this same city Paris, about one and a half of their centuries ago, several of these Hasnamussian candidates 'invented' that the beings of the female sex there should go about with their hair cut, and this maleficent invention of theirs began to spread like wildfire by ways and means already established there.

"But as at that period, in the beings of the female sex of that same community France, the feelings of morality and patriarchality were still very strong, they did not adopt that maleficent invention; but the beings of the female sex of the communities called England and America did adopt it, and began to cut their hair.

"Moreover as the beings of the female sex of both these

communities there began voluntarily to deprive themselves of that part of themselves which is adapted also by Great Nature for certain exchanges of cosmic substances, Nature did not fail to react and began to produce corresponding results, which will certainly take the forms, as had already occurred twice on this planet: the first time, in the country 'Uneano,' now 'Kafiristan,' where there appeared what are called 'Amazons,' and the second time in ancient Greece, where there was created the 'religion of the poetess Sappho.'

"And while in these two contemporary communities, namely, in the community England and in the community America, the cutting of women's hair has already produced, in the first case 'suffragettes,' and in the second what are called 'Christian Scientists' and 'theosophists,' and moreover when this Hasnamussian fashion of cutting the hair of beings of the female sex became universally spread, as you will learn from the continuation of my tale, a proportionate increase was everywhere noticed—as I was informed by the etherogram I received—in the number of the illnesses of these unfortunate beings of the female sex, which they call women's diseases, namely, various sorts of venereal inflammations of the sexual organs, such as 'vaginitis,' 'uteritis,' 'ovaritis,' and what they call 'cancer.'

"And so, my boy, although this same fashion, the cutting of the hair of the beings of the female sex, invented in this Paris itself by beings with Hasnamussian properties, was not then in the beginning implanted in this same community France, yet owing to their capital being the collecting place for the beings with Hasnamussian properties from other countries who continue to persist in this maleficent invention, these latter have ultimately succeeded in implanting it; and the beings of the female sex, there in France also, likewise have begun to cut their hair, and at the present time this cutting of their hair is in full swing for nearly all of them. At the hairdressers even, chiefly of course there in their capital Paris, they have to take their turn as I was informed in this etherogram, exactly as people had to take their turn not long ago in the community Russia for receiving 'American flour.' And from this contagious rush of women to the hairdressers to get their hair cut, court proceedings are already arising between these hairdressers and the fathers, husbands, and brothers of these 'shorn lambs,' and many what are called 'divorces' are also obtained.

"It is interesting that the judges there, as it was also communicated in that etherogram, in each case acquitted the hairdressers on the grounds that the beings of the female sex who went to them were already over sixteen years of age, and had therefore, owing to the laws there, reached their majority and were free to do as they pleased.

"But, of course, had these French judges, and in general the judges of the whole planet, known that there exists in the Universe a definite law concerning all the formations without exception, which serve the Great Trogoautoegocrat in the transformation of cosmic substances, then they would without any doubt completely change their opinion concerning that understanding which they express by the word 'majority.'

"The point is that, according to that definite cosmic law, all those separate individuals, among whom are numbered also all Keshapmartnian beings of the female sex, are for the transformation of cosmic substances the sources of all those active elements which in further cosmic formations must serve in the process of the Great Holy Law Triamazikamno for fusion as its second holy force, that is, they always are, as is said, the 'negative' or 'passive principle.'

"And so, owing to this definite cosmic law, which I have just mentioned, these sources which transform the active elements which serve as the passive principle can never be free to have any independent manifestations. Only those sources can have this independence which transform the active elements which must serve for the Holy Triamazikamno as the 'affirming' or 'active principle.'

"That is just why these sources which serve as the passive principle cannot be responsible for their manifestations, that is, they cannot be, as they say, 'major.'

"While telling you about this separate grouping of the three-brained beings, that is about France, I must also tell you for the fullness of its characterization that in France there are also beings of the ruling class, who also invented very 'good means' for the calming of the minds of the ordinary beings of their community, just as the power-possessing beings of the big community Russia employ such a means for the encouragement of the use of the famous Russian vodka, and the power-possessing beings of the community England at the present time attain the same by their not less famous 'sport.'

"However, it must be admitted that although the power-possessing beings of the community France also adopt these 'good means' and successfully attain their egoistic aims, yet these means, though, be it said, to no credit of the power-possessing beings of the communities of England and Russia, bring scarcely any harm to the planetary bodies themselves of the ordinary beings.

"This is not all: by these means they unconsciously brought and bring to the ordinary beings of their community a certain benefit, diverting them and giving them temporary relief from the ill effects of their fascination by 'fashions,' invented by present and future Hasnamusses gathered in this capital from various countries, and under the slavery of which fashions the ordinary beings of this same France have now fallen even more than all other beings of other communities.

"These 'good means' are called there 'fairs,' and at the present time such fairs are held in the principal squares of all their towns and villages in turn, and moreover, just in those squares in which, about two centuries ago, the three-brained beings there usually held discussions on what they call 'religious-moral subjects.'

"In justice it must be said, my boy, that these French fairs are very very gay places.

"I confess that even I myself liked to visit them and pass there an hour or two, thinking about nothing.

"At these French fairs everything can be had 'cheap' and 'fine.'

"For instance, every being there, for a trifling fifty centimes, can 'whirl' to complete 'stupor' on various what are called 'pigs,' 'chameleons,' 'whales,' and so forth, and on various American and non-American new inventions designed just to produce 'stupor.'

"If a being recovers too quickly from all these ways of getting 'stupefied,' he can then have there, also for a few more centimes, something very tasty, most often prepared right on the spot.

"It is true that from these tasty things the beings, as far as their stomachs are concerned, often become . . . h'm . . . h'm . . . but what is this in comparison with the pleasure they have had in eating them.

"And in case any of the ordinary beings there wishes as they say to 'try his luck' again for a few centimes, he can satisfy this desire there also on the spot; he may try his luck in every way, for at those famous French fairs there is every means of gambling that exists there on the planet Earth, for speculation as well as for fun, and almost all their games of chance are seen there.

"In a word, all the games, beginning with the 'roulette of Monte Carlo' and ending with the game of 'Snipsnapsnorum.'"

CHAPTER 38

Religion

Beezlebub continued further:

"Now I shall explain to you also a little about that 'obstruction' which served as one of the chief causes for the gradual dilution of the psyche of these unfortunate favorites of yours, and, namely, concerning their peculiar 'Havatvernoni' which they always have, the totality of the functioning and the effect of which, in the common presences of the beings, they themselves call 'religiousness.'

"Such an, in the objective sense, indeed, 'archmaleficent' factor for the gradual automatic 'dwindling' of their psyche arose there, on this ill-starred planet, also since various consequences of the properties of always the same for them accursed organ Kundabuffer began to be crystallized in them, and changing its outer form, began to be transmitted from generation to generation.

"And so, when, on the one hand, thanks to these crystallizations, there began to be acquired in the common presences of certain terrestrial three-brained beings, the first germs of what are called Hasnamussian properties, in consequence of which such beings began, as is proper to them for their egoistic aims, to invent for the 'confusion' of surrounding beings similar to themselves, various fictions, among which were also every kind of fantastic, what are called 'religious teachings'; and when, on the other hand, other of your favorites began to have faith in these fantastic religious teachings, and gradually lost their 'sane mentation' thanks to these same crystallizations, then from that time on there began to arise in the process of the ordinary existence of these strange three-brained beings a large number of 'Havatvernoni' or 'religions' having nothing in common with each other.

"Although all these many, varied Havatvernoni or religions of theirs have decidedly nothing in common with each other, yet nevertheless all are built up on the religious teachings, which in their turn, are built up exclusively on that, in the objective sense, 'maleficent idea,' which they themselves called 'Good and Evil,' and which 'idea,' strictly speaking, was the chief factor for the gradual 'dilution' of their general psyche and which still quite recently served as the cause of great events among the 'blissful' 'higher-being-bodies' or, as they are called there, 'souls' who dwell on that holy planet in the direction of which we are at the present moment falling.

"The history of all that which recently happened on this holy planet Purgatory ought, in my opinion, to be told you without fail, first of all because these events have a common-cosmic character and are connected with the general individuality of every relatively separately formed responsible Individual, and secondly, because certain members of your 'genealogical tree' involuntarily served as the cause of the arising of these events.

"But I shall relate about it only at the end of my present tale, as I have a very worthy reason for this concerning the development of your 'being-mentation.' About this worthy reason and also about what considerations I have concerning such an intention of mine, I shall most likely also explain to you in its proper time.

"Meanwhile know that there, among these terrestrial three-brained beings who please you, there existed and exists a great quantity of all kinds of 'religious doctrines,' on which these numerous 'religions' of theirs are just built up, and that they usually arise in the following way:

"I already told you that when it became clear that thanks to the unforeseeingness of certain Most-High-Sacred-Cosmic-Individuals, the results of the consequences of the organ Kundabuffer, invented and later removed by these sacred Individuals, began to become crystallized in the common presences of these unfortunate three-brained beings, thanks to which it became almost impossible for them correctly to become perfected to the Being, which three-brained beings ought to have, then our ABUNDANTLY LOVING COMMON FATHER condescended to actualize sometimes in the common presences of certain of them wherever they may arise the germ of a sacred Individual, so that these latter being completedly formed up to responsible age and acquiring Reason in the conditions which had already become fixed in the general process of the existence of the three-brained beings of this planet, should become aware of reality and indicate to the surrounding beings similar to themselves, how they ought, with the Reason present in them, to guide the process of the functioning of their separate spiritualized parts, in order in this way to decrystallize the already crystallized consequences of the properties of the organ Kundabuffer, and also to succeed in destroying in themselves the predisposition to new crystallizations.

"And so, my boy, after the sacred Rascooarno proceeds to these terrestrial three-brained beings—or, as they themselves express it, when they die—in the presences of whom are actualized the germs of Sacred Individuals, their contemporaries usually in order to remember and also in order to transmit to the beings of subsequent generations all that these Sacred Individuals had indicated and explained according to their attainments of responsible age, collect it all into one whole, and all this 'collected-into-one-whole' usually just serves as the beginning of all kinds of religious teachings there.

"The strangeness of the psyche of your favorites in respect of the religious teachings which arise in this way among them, manifests itself in this, that they already from the very beginning understand 'literally' all that has been said and explained by these genuine Sacred Individuals actualized from Above and they never take into account in which environment and for which case this or that was said and explained.

"And further, already during the transmission from generation to generation of these religious teachings, the sense of which had already from the very beginning been distorted, they begin to adopt in regard to them the following two factors, which had already become fixed in the general existence of these strange three-brained beings. The first of these consists in this, that those beings, who in the given period of the 'flow-of-time' belong to the caste called the ruling class, immediately hook on to these religious teachings just that, for them, most maleficent 'question' which exists on this ill-starred planet under the name of 'Religion-for-the-State-or-the-State-for-Religion,' and corresponding to this, they gradually begin with every kind of artfulness to juggle with the previously fixed facts for the justification of their own egoistic aims; and the second consists in this, that certain ordinary beings there, owing to the fault of their producers, acquired in their common presences, during their arising as well as during their formation into responsible beings, the inherency of what is called 'psychopathy' and 'parasitism'—in consequence of which they do not have and cannot have in themselves any data at all for the manifestation of any being-duty whatever it might be—and become, as it were, authorities for all the trifling details of the new religious teachings which have already arisen in the mentioned way, and begin, as it is said, 'to-peck-like-crows-at-a-jackal's-carcass' that totality, already 'pecked' from the very beginning without this, of what had been spoken and indicated by the genuine Sacred Individuals, intentionally actualized from Above.

"Speaking briefly, the result of the mentioned two factors

among the three-brained beings of this strange planet, which had been fixed in the process of ordinary existence, and, namely, the inherency in the beings belonging to the caste of the ruling class, and the psychopathy of certain of their ordinary beings, is that they always get divided on questions of religion—soon after its foundation, on whatever religious doctrines these religions may have been built up—into their famous 'sects,' and these sects in their turn get divided into other sects, and thanks to this, just the same occurs there in all epochs on this comparatively not large planet in the sense of religions, as with the large number of the spoken languages there, referring to which our highly esteemed Mullah Nassr Eddin called it 'a thousand-tongued hydra,' and in the present case he would say 'varied-titillating-titillations.'

"During my observations on the process of the existence of these peculiar three-brained beings, there had been many times actualized from Above, in the common presences of certain of them, the germs of these Sacred Individuals and almost on each occasion—with the exception only of the Most Most Sacred Ashiata Shiemash, and all connected with Him which flowed from His own Most Great Labors—after their completed formation and their fulfillment of the mission imposed on them from Above, when the process of the sacred Rascooarno was completed with them, such religious teachings always began in the mentioned way to arise among these peculiar beings there, i.e., they, at first, as I said, collected into one whole all that was indicated and explained in detail by these Sacred Individuals intentionally actualized from Above, for the purpose of remembering it all themselves and also for the purpose of transmission to subsequent generations, yet, of course, into one whole which they collected from the very beginning, as it is said there, 'from-bits-here-and-there,' and later, as all of this which was collected together fell into the hands of just those two mentioned types there, well, just then they began, as I already expressed it, 'to peck at' all this, and further dividing themselves up into their famous what are called sects, already compose new fantastic religious teachings thought out by themselves, as a result of which there always obtains on this planet of yours, firstly, a large number of religions as numerous as the colors in the 'rainbow,' and secondly, as it is said, 'the-same-old-story.'

"During recent centuries your favorites had many hundreds of these peculiar independent religious teachings in the common-planetary-process of their being-existence and the basis for all of them was the totality of the indications and explanations which had still survived and which had arisen in the mentioned way, given to them by the Sacred Individuals intentionally actualized among them from Above.

"On these survived totalities, by which, during recent times, they were in a strange manner inspired and from which with their bobtailed reason they borrowed ideas for the inventions of their still newer and newer religious teachings, there were based five religions which still exist today, namely, those religions called:

(1) The Buddhistic
(2) The Hebrew
(3) The Christian
(4) The Mohammedan
(5) The Lamaist.

"Concerning the first of them, and, namely, the Buddhistic religion, I have already once told you.

"The second, namely, the Hebrew, is founded, as it were, precisely on the teaching of the Saint Moses, by which name one of the genuine Sacred Individuals was called, who in His turn was intentionally actualized from Above.

"The actualization of this Sacred Individual proceeded there in the planetary body of a boy, who arose in the country now called Egypt, a little after my fourth personal sojourn on the surface of this planet of yours.

"This Sacred Individual, whom your favorites at the present time call 'Saint Moses,' accomplished a great deal for them and left them many of those exact and corresponding indications for ordinary existence, so that if they would adopt and actualize them normally, then, indeed, all the consequences of the properties of the absolutely maleficent for them organ Kundabuffer might become gradually decrystallized, and even the predisposition for new crystallizations might be destroyed.

"But to the common misfortune of all beings, with just a little Reason, of all our Great Universe, they began gradually to mix into all the counsels and indications of this 'normality-loving' Saint Moses, as it was already proper to them to do, such a mass of what are called 'spices,' that the saintly author himself could not with all his wish recognize anything of his own in this, as it were, totality collected by them of all he had explained and indicated.

"Your favorites of already the first generation of the contemporaries of Saint Moses, evidently found it profitable for their special aims to insert in these religious teachings almost the entire fantastic teaching which I already told you when I related that among the ancient three-brained beings of the second grouping on the continent Ashhark or contemporary Asia, there was a king named Konuzion, a subsequent Saint, who, for the purpose of saving his subjects from the pernicious habit of chewing the seed of the poppy first invented his fantastic 'religious doctrine.'

"After Saint Moses, that Sacred Individual was actualized there who laid the beginnings of that religion which your contemporary favorites call Christianity.

"This Sacred Individual, called by your favorites 'Jesus Christ,' was actualized in the planetary body of a boy of that race of terrestrial three-brained beings whom Saint Moses, on the command from Above, chose from among the beings of the country Egypt and led to what is called the 'Land of Canaan.'

"After this Jesus, there were actualized, also on the continent Asia, two other Sacred Individuals, on whose teachings the beings there founded two of the enumerated religions existing there until today.

"And, namely, one of these two Sacred Individuals was Saint Mohammed, who appeared among the, as they are called, Arabs, and the other—Saint Lama—appeared among the beings dwelling in the country named Tibet.

"At the present time, the first of the five religious teachings I mentioned, and, namely, the Buddhistic, is spread chiefly among the beings dwelling in the country India, the former 'Gemchania,' and in the countries called China and Japan.

"The followers of the second religious teaching, and, namely, the Hebrew, are now scattered over the whole planet.

"In this place of my tales it will do no harm also to remark the cause itself, owing to which the followers of the teaching of this Moses are scattered over the whole planet, as, from this explanation, you will well understand about one peculiar property of the organ Kundabuffer and, namely, about the property which evokes the feeling called 'envy,' and you will also understand in what way each property of this organ, however small it may be, may be the cause of very great consequences.

"The point is that the beings who chiefly professed the

teaching of this Moses, then very well organized themselves in their community and therefore in the psyche of the beings of all other communities of that period, this same property called envy began to be crystallized in relation to the beings of this community.

"And so strongly was this property crystallized in them that even after the flow of many of their centuries when the Hebrew community already ceased to be organized and powerful, and this former powerful community came to an end—as occurs there according to law to all powerful communities—then not only was this relation towards the beings of the descendants of this community on the part of the beings of other communities not destroyed, but even in the majority of them, the feeling of envy towards them has already become organic.

"The third religion, founded on the teaching of Jesus Christ, very soon became in its primordial form so widely spread that almost one third of all the three-centered beings of this planet were its followers.

"But thereafter they began gradually to 'strip' also this religious teaching based on 'resplendent Love,' and transformed it into something also 'resplendent,' but already, as our dear Mullah Nassr Eddin says, into a 'resplendent-Terasakhaboora' from the fairy tale 'Kasoaadjy.'

"In the case of this great religious teaching, indeed, it also happened among them, that its followers divided themselves, on account of exterior details of small importance, into various sects, and came to be called not just 'Christians' as all the first followers of this teaching called themselves—but 'Orthodox,' 'Sevrodox,' 'Ypsylodox,' 'Hamilodox,' and various other cognomens also ending in 'dox.'

"And into this teaching of truth and verity, they began also to mix for various egoistic and political reasons, fragments taken from other religious teachings already existing there, but fragments such as had not only nothing in common with the teaching of Jesus, but which sometimes even flatly contradicted the truths this Divine Teacher taught.

"They mixed in it a great deal from the teaching of Saint Moses which by that time had already been thoroughly distorted: and much later, namely, during the period which contemporary beings there called the 'Middle Ages,' the so-called 'elders of the church' inserted into this Christian religion nearly the whole of that fantastic doctrine invented by those 'learned' beings in the city of Babylon, who belonged to the school of the dualists, about which I have already told you.

"The 'elders of the church' in the Middle Ages probably inserted this last doctrine for the convenience of their own 'shops' and for the 'shops' of their assistants, because of the famous 'paradise' and 'hell' contained in it.

"And therefore at the present time, in place of the teaching of the Divine Teacher Jesus Christ, in which among other things was revealed the power of the All-lovingness and All-forgivingness of our CREATOR, suffering for beings—it is now already taught there that our CREATOR mocks the souls of those who follow this teaching."

"Dear and kind Grandfather mine, explain to me, please, what is meant by 'elders of the church'?" asked Hassein.

"They call 'elders of the church' there, those beings who become professional dignitaries of the highest rank of any religious teaching."

Having merely replied thus laconically, Beelzebub continued further:

"By the way, I may tell you here that among a rather small group of terrestrial beings the teaching of Jesus Christ was preserved unchanged, and, passing from generation to generation, has even reached the present time in its original form.

"This smallish group of terrestrial beings is designated

'the Brotherhood of the Essenes.' The beings of this brotherhood succeeded at first in introducing the teaching of this Divine Teacher into their own being-existence, and subsequently in transmitting it from generation to generation to later generations, as a very good means for freeing themselves from the consequences of the properties of the organ Kundabuffer.

"Now as regards the fourth great religion existing there now, which arose several centuries after the Christian religion, and was founded on the teaching of the full-of-hope Saint Mohammed, this religion at first spread there widely: and it might perhaps have become eventually a 'hearth of hope and reconciliation' for them all if these strange beings had not stirred this also into a hotchpotch.

"On the one hand its followers also mixed into it something from the fantastic theory of the Babylonian dualists, but, on the other hand, the 'elders of the church' of this religion, called in this case 'Sheiks-Islamists,' themselves invented and added to it many things about the blessings of the notorious 'paradise,' which as it were, existed 'in the other world,' such blessings as perhaps could never even have entered the head of the chief Governor of Purgatory, His All-Quarters-Maintainer the Archcherub Helkgematios, even if he were deliberately to try to imagine them.

"Although the followers of this religion also, from the very first, split into many different 'groups' and 'subgroups'—which, by the way, continue there even up till now—nevertheless they all subscribe to one or another of its two independent, as they are called, 'schools,' which were formed at the very beginning of its arising.

"These two schools of the Mohammedan religion are called there the 'Sunnite' and the 'Shiite.'

"It is very interesting to note that the psychic hatred of each other formed in the psyche of the beings who belong to these two independent schools of one and the same religion has, on account of their frequent clashes, now been transformed completely into an organic hate.

"Beings of certain European communities have during recent centuries greatly contributed by their incitement to the rise of this peculiar transformation of that strange being-function.

"And they have employed and continue to employ this incitement in order that the animosity between the beings who follow these two independent schools of one and the same religion, should increase and that they should never unite, since if this were to happen, there might soon be an end there for those European communities.

"The point is that nearly half of the ordinary three-brained beings there are followers of this Mohammedan teaching, and only as long as this mutual hatred exists among them will they mean nothing terrifying in the sense of 'reciprocal destruction' to European communities.

"And hence it is that accidentally arisen 'newly baked' communities always rub their hands and rejoice when sparks fly between these Sunnites and Shiites, because they then count on a long and secure existence for themselves.

"Now, as regards the fifth teaching, namely, the teaching of Saint Lama, also a genuine messenger from our ENDLESSNESS, the teaching of this Sacred Individual was spread among those three-brained beings there, who, on account of the geographical conditions, scarcely ever happened to come into contact with other beings of this ill-starred planet, and in consequence have scarcely been affected by the abnormally established conditions of ordinary being-existence there.

"One part of this teaching also its followers also soon changed and destroyed, but its other part already more or less entered into the existence of this little group of beings, and began to produce the expected results, thanks to which the hope grew even among the highest Sacred Individuals that this teaching, created by the saintly labors of Saint Lama, might sometime actualize what had already become a necessity in the Megalocosmos for everything that exists.

"But your favorites did not allow even this to happen, but by their 'military expedition' or 'Anglo-Tibetan' war, without so much as a thought, knocked this possibility soundly on the head.

"About this 'military expedition' I will tell you a little later.

"And I shall tell you about it chiefly because I myself happened by chance to be an eyewitness of all those lamentable events there.

"I must first tell you how there on your planet, it is now desired—of course with the help of the 'Swivel-eyed General'—finally to 'dispatch' even the remnants of those two named religions still existing there, which, although they are already changed even beyond recognition, yet nevertheless have during the last centuries made the ordinary existence of the three-brained beings there, though very remotely yet all the same a tiny bit, like the ordinary existence of the three-brained beings breeding on the other corresponding planets of our Great Universe, and for certain of them their phenomenally haphazard existence somewhat tolerable objectively.

"Namely, I shall here tell you how there is just now proceeding the process of the final 'dispatch' of two of the great religions of the five mentioned, now existing, which were founded, though 'from-bits-here-and-there,' nevertheless on the teachings of genuine messengers of our ENDLESSNESS Himself: one, on the teaching of Saint Jesus, and the other, on the teaching of Saint Mohammed.

"I repeat that both these great religions there were

founded 'from-bits-taken-here-and-there' from the teachings of two genuine messengers of HIS ENDLESSNESS, and though the three-brained beings there of former centuries 'stripped' both these teachings much as the Russian Sidor 'stripped' his goats, yet nevertheless some even down to the present time believed in something and hoped for something owing to these teachings, and thereby made their desolate existence a little more bearable.

"But these contemporary and now archstrange three-brained beings there have taken upon themselves to sweep this also entirely from off the face of their planet.

"Although the process of the strangeness of their peculiar psyche, namely, the process of the final destruction of these two great religions, began after my departure from their solar system, yet thanks to the contents of an etherogram about the beings of that strange planet which I received just before our flight from the planet Karatas I understand how things were, and can now already say with complete conviction that they will no longer stop at stripping them, but without further ado entirely destroy even their very traces.

"In the said etherogram, by the way, it was conveyed to me that there on your planet, first of all in the city of Jerusalem a University specially for Jewish youths was being opened, and secondly that in the community Turkey an order was promulgated closing all what are called 'dervish monasteries' and prohibiting men from wearing the 'fez' and women the 'yashmak.'

"The first half of the message, namely, that a University for Jewish youths was opening in the city of Jerusalem, made it clear to me that this Christian religion also had already come to an end.

"But to understand this, you must first know that not so long ago all the communities existing there on the continent Europe, the beings of which are for the most part followers of this religion, together produced, on account of this same city Jerusalem, their great wars against those beings, followers of other religions, and these great wars of theirs they called 'Crusades.'

"They produced these 'wars' or 'crusades' only in order that this city of Jerusalem—in which this Divine Teacher Jesus Christ had existed, suffered, and died—should become exclusively Christian; and during these Crusades of theirs nearly half the beings of male sex of that continent were completely destroyed.

"And now in this same city of Jerusalem, they have opened their contemporary university for Jewish youths and almost certainly, too, with the common consent of all those same European Christian communities.

"Just that nationality is called 'Jewish' in which the Divine Jesus appeared and existed, and the beings of which tortured and crucified Him on a cross.

"Although the present generation of 'Jews' are not direct enemies of Jesus Christ, yet they each also now have the conviction that this Jesus who appeared among their ancestors and came to be regarded as a Sacred Personality by all the followers of the Christian religion, was, quite simply, a fervent and sick 'visionary.'

"Among contemporary beings of the planet Earth a 'university' is just that 'hearth' on which everything acquired during decades and centuries by preceding beings is burned, and upon this 'hearth' one-and-a-half-day tasty lentil soup is quickly cooked to take the place of everything attained by the centuried conscious and unconscious efforts and labors of their unfortunate ancestors.

"This is quite enough to show me and to convince me with my whole Being what will eventually become of this Jerusalem, now that they have opened there their own famous university, and, moreover, for Jewish youths.

"I already see in my mind's eye that before many of

their years have passed, there will be on the spot where the planetary body of the Divine Jesus was buried, a place for parking contemporary cars, that is, a parking place for those machines which for contemporary beings were just the marvel needed to drive them crazy.

"Furthermore, not only have these sacrilegious beings gradually distorted for their egoistic and political aims the teachings of this Divine Teacher, but they have now begun to destroy even the memory of it.

"But there! That also has long been in the style of your favorites.

"In this connection I may say that the whole of what is called contemporary civilization there tends only to increase the speed of this machine invented by them and maleficent just for themselves.

"And indeed, in the last etherogram I received about the three-brained beings of that ill-fated planet, I was informed among other things that a 'record' speed of this machine had already been established there of 325 miles an hour.

"Of course, such a 'record' will only lead to this, that the already sufficiently trifling size of their ill-fated planet will become, even in their bobtailed being-picturings of reality, completely trifling.

"Well, the LORD CREATOR be with them, my boy!

"Whatever speed they may attain with this 'machine' of theirs, all the same, if they remain as they are, not only they themselves but even their thought will never go any further than their atmosphere.

"Now as regards the second great religion which was founded, as I have already told you, upon 'bits-here-and-bits-there' from the teaching of the full-of-hope Saint Mohammed, this religion from the very beginning of its arising began to be particularly applied and used for their egoistic and political aims by beings there with Hasnamussian properties, and hence it is the most 'stripped' of all.

"The power-possessing beings of certain communities there gradually mixed into this divine teaching, for their said Hasnamussian aims, such 'spices' of their own invention that a 'Sherakhoorian-combination' resulted, the secret of which would be the envy of all the contemporary famous European as they are called 'pastry cooks' and 'chefs.'

"And so . . .

"Judging by the latter half of the contents of this etherogram, the process of the entire destruction of this second great religion is bound to proceed or had already proceeded there, on account of that order mentioned in the etherogram promulgated by the power-possessing beings of the community Turkey.

"The point is, that this same community of Turkey is one of the largest of all the communities there whose beings profess this religion.

"I must first tell you that from the beginning of the rise of this Mohammedan religion, certain beings of this same community took in the teaching of this religion in its primary form very well, and began gradually to incorporate it into their daily existence.

"And therefore, although the teaching of this religion was gradually changed under the influence of the power-possessing beings there, nevertheless, among these same certain beings there, this teaching of Mohammed passed from generation to generation in an unchanged form.

"Until now, therefore, there has at least been a faint hope that if sometime these strange beings should suddenly settle down, this teaching would infallibly regenerate and actualize those aims for which it was created by the full-of-hope Saint Mohammed.

"So, my boy! . . . These same certain beings there

were called 'dervishes' and it was concerning the closing of just their monasteries that the order was indeed given in that contemporary community Turkey.

"Of course, by the destruction in Turkey of this 'dervishism' those last dying sparks will also be entirely extinguished there which, preserved as it were in the ashes, might sometime rekindle the hearth of those possibilities upon which Saint Mohammed counted and for which he had hoped.

"And as regards the other order communicated to me in that etherogram and promulgated in that same community Turkey, namely, the prohibition upon beings of the 'male sex' to wear the formerly famous fez and upon the beings of the 'female sex,' the yashmak, the consequences of these innovations are very clearly depicted in my being-picturings about the future.

"Thanks to these innovations, there is no doubt but that exactly the same will be repeated with the beings of this Turkey as occurred to the beings of the large community Russia after they had also begun to imitate everything European.

"It may be noted, for example, that, indeed, in all the beings of that large community Russia, only one or two centuries ago, before they had yet begun to imitate everything European, these two being-functions still obtained which are called 'Martaadamlik' and 'Nammuslik,' or—as these being-feelings are still called—the 'feeling-of-religiousness' and the 'feeling-of-patriarchality.'

"And it was just those same being-feelings which a couple of centuries ago made the beings of that large community famous among other beings of the whole of this planet in respect of their morality and the patriarchality of their family foundations.

"But when afterwards they began imitating everything European, both these being-feelings still remaining in them began gradually to atrophy in them, and now at the present time almost all the beings of that community have become, in the sense of religiousness and patriarchality, such . . . the notion of which our wise teacher Mullah Nassr Eddin expresses by the mere exclamation:

"'Eh! . . . get along with you. . . .'

"In Russia, moreover, none of this began with the yashmak or the fez.

"No. These headdresses were not worn there.

"But it was begun there with the 'beard' of the beings of the male sex. For the three-brained beings of the male sex there, the 'beard' is the same as our tail is for us, which, as you already know, adds, to the beings of male sex among us, masculinity and activity.

"It is now the turn of these unfortunate Turks.

"Once they have proposed to change their fezzes for European 'bowlers' the rest will follow of itself.

"Of course, the psyche of these Turkish beings will also soon degenerate as it degenerated in the beings of the community of Russia.

"The difference between the Russians beings and the Turks is only in this, that for the Russians one being only, namely, their czar, was the cause for this transformation of their psyche, whereas for the beings of the community Turkey, several beings were its cause.

"And there were several, because these Turks recently changed their old many-centuried established state-organization for a new one, a certain special 'republican' form, and in place of one ruler, as had obtained among them during their former state-organization, there were several.

"If even this former state-organization of theirs was bad, yet to counterbalance this there was a single ruler who introduced innovations solely for his community, and, furthermore, all of them old patriarchal.

"And now in this community Turkey: of the chief

leaders there are several, and each of them is a wiseacre who forces upon the unfortunate ordinary beings of the whole of this community his callowness, not responding at all either to the already long ago crystallized needs of the psyche of the beings of this community or to their established pillars of their being-morality.

"It is very interesting to notice further that just as formerly the Russian czar was supplied by his nearest old patriarchal functionaries with a great quantity of what is called 'money,' obtained by the sweat of the peasants, and was sent to the continent of Europe to study in the various communities there a great number of methods of government, in order that when he returned he might the better orientate himself in the ruling of his community; so likewise these present callow Turkish rulers were also provided by their own 'patriarchal' fathers with much 'money,' this time however obtained by the sweat of the 'Khaivansanansaks,' and also sent to the continent Europe to receive there what they call a 'good education' for the future welfare of their fatherland.

"And so, my boy, in both of these cases, because their future rulers of the two large many-millioned communities went to the continent of Europe quite young and had not yet at all become aware of their responsibility, but chiefly thanks to this that they were provided with money from the said source, the existence of the beings there on the continent of Europe was absorbed and permanently crystallized in them as so 'splendiferous and beneficial' that when afterwards, on account of the abnormally established conditions of existence in their country, they became leaders of these many-millioned communities, they, like the Russian Czar, could not help aiming to make the existence of their compatriots, to their bobtailed notions, happy as well.

"Much good, by the way, the present chief rulers of this community Turkey saw and absorbed in the community Germany to which they were sent for the purpose of studying what is called 'militarism,' that is, the special finesses for directing the processes of reciprocal destruction.

"That is why these present chief rulers of the community of Turkey existed a long time in that community Germany and were for a considerable time there what are called 'Junkers.'

"Specially much good, indeed, they saw and absorbed in that Germany in its capital Berlin on the street called 'Unter den Linden.'

"I do not yet know what future benefactions these new Turkish rulers will create for their compatriots, but meanwhile they have already done their fatherland one very very good 'patriotic' deed.

"Thoroughly to understand the essence of this patriotic deed, you must first know that in the capital of this community Turkey, in the streets and alleys of those quarters called 'Galata' and 'Pera' all the female beings of a 'special designation' used to belong to foreign communities, though these same women earned and spent 'genuine Turkish lire.'

"But thanks to the recent innovations, they have now come to the full and certain hope that very soon these genuine 'patriotic Turkish lire' of theirs will no longer be at the disposal or use of the female beings of any foreign community alien to them, but will be used only by their own 'dear she-compatriots.'

"It is not for nothing that our highly esteemed Hadji Nassr Eddin says: 'What is most important is to have plenty of money, and then even our *Nammus* may creak.'

"Or sometimes, in such cases, he also says in Turkish itself: '*Dooniyninishi, pakmazli pishi, geyann purnundah pussar eshahi dishi'* (which saying in English means: 'World deeds are like honey-cakes, from which the eater must grow an ass's tooth').

"Now let us talk about what I promised to tell you a little more in detail, namely, about the teachings of the last Sacred Individual who appeared among the beings of Tibet, Saint Lama, and about the causes of the complete destruction of that teaching also.

"The teaching and preachings of this Saint were not so widely spread there, because of the geographical conditions of that locality where he appeared, and where he taught those unfortunate three-centered beings also what they must do to free themselves from the consequences of the properties of the organ Kundabuffer.

"On account of its geographical conditions, beings of this country were little in touch, as I have already told you, with the abnormal conditions of ordinary being-existence of the beings of other communities, and in consequence certain of them were more receptive of the teaching of this last Sacred Individual, and this teaching therefore just entered into their essence and began gradually to be actualized already in practice also.

"So, my boy, during many years there circumstances gradually so arranged themselves in that country called Tibet, that the local beings became grouped according to the degree of their inner transubstantiation of the teaching of this Saint Lama, and according to the degree of their need to work upon themselves; and having correspondingly organized their ordinary existence, they, thanks to their isolated environment due to this inaccessibility of their country for beings of other communities, had the possibility of working, without hindrance according to the instructions of Saint Lama, upon their liberation from the consequences of the properties of that organ which their first, earliest ancestors, to their common misfortune, were forced to have.

"Certain beings among their number had already attained such a deliverance, many others were already on the path of this attainment, while many of them were hopeful of one day also reaching the way of this achievement.

"But just when the conditions and environment for productive work in this direction had at last taken a definitive turn in the right direction in this Tibet—well, it was just then that that happened thanks to which the possibility for the beings of this country also of one day freeing themselves from the misfortune oppressing them, had to perish completely, or, at any rate, be again delayed for many years.

"But before telling you about just what happened there, you must still know the following:

"Only a few centuries ago, the chief particularity of the three-brained beings who please you, namely, the process of their periodic reciprocal destruction, used to proceed there on your planet between beings of different communities of one and the same continent, namely, the continent on which they bred, and if occasionally by exception this process arose between beings of different continents, then it occurred only between beings dwelling on the neighboring borders of two adjacent continents. And this was because locomotion by water was still very difficult for terrestrial beings some centuries ago.

"But after a contemporary being there had by chance discovered the possibility of using the power of artificially rarefied water for such locomotion, or as they say, the 'power of steam,' and had devised suitable vessels for that purpose, these terrestrial beings thereafter just began going for such processes to other borderlands of the neighboring continents or even to other continents.

"During the last century one of these favorite places on another continent for the beings of this peculiar planet, was the country of ancient Gemchania or as contemporary beings say there 'India.'

"Do you remember that I once told you that to that self-same Gemchania of the continent Ashhark, now Asia, beings of the continent Atlantis used to sail in the beginning for pearls, and how, later, that it was also they who first populated that country?

"So, my boy, this same unfortunate former Gemchania, now 'India,' has become during recent centuries the favorite place also of the contemporary beings of the continent Europe, but this time for their processes of reciprocal destruction.

"They began to sail there and there to produce their processes of reciprocal destruction both among themselves and with the beings breeding there; that is to say, either beings of one European community strove to destroy the existence of the beings belonging to another also European community, or similar processes proceeded between local beings with the European beings helping one side or the other side.

"The processes of reciprocal destruction of local character there in that unfortunate Gemchania were very frequent especially during the last eighteen or fifteen centuries.

"And this was so, firstly because, in consequence of a similar great process, the beings there, who had earlier belonged to only two different communities, split into a great number of independent small communities, and secondly because there also then occurred such a combination in the general psyche of beings of that locality, that the 'fits' of this property, and, namely, the striving for reciprocal destruction occurred in the beings of that part of the surface of the planet Earth everywhere not simultaneously, but at different times.

"And this further new combination of their general psyche occurred also thanks to a slight unforeseen misunderstanding connected with the common Harmonic-Movement of the whole of that solar system.

"I will some time explain to you also about the details of that misunderstanding.

"And meanwhile let us return to our tale we have begun. And thus . . .

"That part of the surface of the planet Earth occupied by India has remained, in respect of natural wealth, the same in recent centuries as formerly.

"And therefore, when in the peculiar psyche of the European beings who had gone to that country for the process of reciprocal destruction the need to carry on this terror had passed, those beings stayed on there, and either prepared themselves for subsequent similar processes, or, as they say, 'earned' enough to send the required goods for the ordinary existence of their families who had remained on the continent Europe.

"And all kinds of goods they 'earned' there by means of their trades consisting for the most part of manufacturing what are called 'copper buttons,' 'hand mirrors,' 'beads,' 'earrings,' 'bracelets,' and various other such gew-gaws for which it appeared the beings of that country also had a weakness.

"Quite from the beginning of this period, the beings of the continent Europe began in various ways to take from the local beings there in Gemchania their lands also, on which they began to exist, just as on the continent Europe, in separate groups according to the community from which they had emigrated.

"These beings from different communities of Europe continued also to manifest there toward each other the kind of strange being-relationships which beings of one European community manifested then and still continue to manifest towards beings belonging to other communities of the same continent; namely, thanks also to the consequences of the properties of the organ Kundabuffer, they cultivate feelings which had been crystallized in them, into the forms of particular functions existing there under the names of, 'envy,' 'jealousy,' 'sandoor' (i.e., wishing the death or weakness of others), and so on.

"And there in Gemchania too, beings of one community began to pipe with full blast against beings of another community that 'Hasnamussian music' they call 'policy,' that is, they began to 'criticize' each other, to 'lower each other's standing,' to 'down each other,' and so on, their aim being to create what is called 'prestige' among the local beings in relation to their own community.

"In the course of such a 'policy' one of the heads of a certain European community in some way or other learned the 'secret' how to influence the psyche of beings of other communities to acknowledge the authority of and give supremacy to the beings of his own community.

"Afterwards when the beings who had learned this secret—the principle of the action of which was called 'Ksvaznell' or 'inciting one against the other'—initiated the other heads of his community into it, and they all made it the basis of their 'policy'; then, indeed the beings of this community began everywhere and in everything to obtain predominance.

"Although both the former heads of the beings of this community and also that being himself who had hit upon the secret Ksvaznell, already long ago perished, yet subsequent generations—continuing now of course automatically to employ this 'secret'—gradually not only took into their own hands almost the whole of this Gemchania, but also subordinated to their influence the very essence of all the beings breeding on that part of the planet Earth.

"In spite of the fact that two centuries had passed, yet at that period to which my further tale refers concerning the destruction by contemporary beings of the labors of Saint Lama, it all continued in the same way.

"Having become proud of their success, the recent heads of that mentioned European community who had the luck, thanks to this same secret Ksvaznell alone, gradually to subordinate all to their influence and to grasp everything into their hands, wished to lay their 'paws' even on that which had until then been considered unattainable.

"Namely, they decided to take possession of also that neighboring country called Tibet which was then considered to be inaccessible; and therefore, one day—for them, fine, but for all the rest of the beings of that planet a sorry day—they assembled many beings of their community and still more from among the number of small local communities already conquered by them, and with the help of every possible new invention of their contemporary 'European civilization' for the process of reciprocal destruction, they began very quietly to move towards this country hitherto considered inaccessible.

"In spite of the help of these European 'new inventions' of every kind, this movement of theirs up country was very difficult, and cost them very dearly, not only in, what they call there, 'pounds,' but also in what they call 'casualties.'

"While this crowd of every possible kind of terrestrial three-brained being still quietly but against great difficulties moved up, the beings themselves who dwelled above in Tibet as yet suspected nothing whatever of what these European beings called their 'military expedition' against their country.

"And they learned about it only when that mob was already up.

"When the beings of this high country learned of this unusual event, they immediately became alarmed and agitated, because they had grown accustomed to the notion during many centuries that the place of their existence was inaccessible to everybody and that beings of other communities, no matter what might be their means for the process of reciprocal destruction, would be unable to penetrate to them in any way.

"So certain were they of this that they had not even once cast a glance downwards to see what was being done during this time in respect of the aim of penetrating into their inaccessible country, and hence they did not take any corresponding measures in advance.

"It was from this that the sorrowful events subsequently came which were finally to destroy all the results created by that full-of-faith Sacred Individual, Saint Lama.

"First of all it is necessary to tell you that this high country was a place of existence also of that small group, consisting of seven beings there, who, according to the rules established from the very beginning, were guardians of the most secret instructions and last counsels of Saint Lama.

"This group consisted of these seven beings who, following the indications of Saint Lama for freeing themselves from the consequences of the properties of the organ Kundabuffer, had brought their self-perfecting up to the final degree.

"When this 'group of beings of Seven' learned of this event, it dispatched the chief among them to join the agitated chiefs of the whole country, in a conference which took place in the capital just on the day of the arrival of these uninvited guests from below.

"The assembled heads of the Tibetan beings unanimously

decided at this first conference of theirs very peaceably and courteously to request these uninvited visitors to return whole and hearty to from where they had come, and to leave in peace both themselves and their peaceful country that did no harm to anybody.

"When, after several days, it became clear that these uninvited guests would not consent to return, but as a consequence of this request even hastened to move forward more deeply into the country, the members of the first council became even more alarmed, arranged a second council and began to deliberate what to do to prevent these beings from entering, as it is said, 'a-stranger's-house-without-invitation.'

"A quantity of every sort of means were proposed for removing from their country these beings who had broken, like ravens, into a stranger's nest; but one in particular found support: to destroy utterly to the last man all these uninvited 'swaggerers.'

"And this, my boy, could have indeed been easily done, because such is the country that without any additional means, merely by stones thrown down from the mountains, a single being could destroy thousands of enemy beings passing along the valleys, and especially was this possible because every one of them knew the lie of his native country like the palm of his hand.

"By the close of the conference, all the heads of the country Tibet had become so excited that they would almost certainly have decided to carry out the proposal supported by the majority, if the head of that small 'group of Seven,' who as I have already told you had been sent to this council by the other members, had not intervened in this stormy council.

"This head 'of Seven,' later a Saint, while persuading the other participants in this conference that what they had proposed must not be done, said among other things:

"'The existence of every being is equally precious and dear to our COMMON CREATOR GOD; therefore the destruction of these beings, so great a number of them too, would give no small grief to THAT ONE, WHO, even without this, is overburdened with the care and sorrow of all that exists among us on Earth.'

"All that this future Saint then said in the assembly of Tibetan chiefs was so generally persuasive that they decided not only to take no measures against the strangers, but even to take every kind of precaution that no one should hinder the march of current events.

"Thereupon the beings appearing from below as uninvited guests, meeting with no opposition anywhere, moved forward there into the heart of that unique country, which hitherto had been isolated from all the conditions of ordinary being-existence growing always worse on your planet.

"Well then, there just proceeded that which resulted in a great calamity not only for all present and future beings of this unlucky country, but perhaps even for all, in general, present and future three-brained beings of the whole of that unfortunate planet.

"The point is, that at the final conference of the heads of the whole of Tibet, a resolution was carried, by the way, that certain members of the council, chosen by lot, should go to those districts through which these foreign beings would pass, in order to warn in advance the local population of the considered decision of their leaders, and persuade them to permit nobody, under any circumstances, to hinder the passing of these foreigners.

"Among the number of those sent to the districts through which the foreign armed beings would pass the choice fell upon the chief also of this small 'group of Seven.'

"And when this future Saint arrived for the purpose mentioned at one large point, near which the armed crowd of foreign beings had camped for a needed rest, a stray bullet fired—intentionally or accidentally—in the street of this large point by one of these newcomers from below, 'killed-on-the-spot' this future Saint.

"In this way ended the existence of the chief of the small group of nearly perfected brothers, and overcome by the terror of such an event, nothing more remained for them but only to take all the necessary steps to bring home the planetary body of their former chief.

"In order that you may clearly represent to yourself the real terror of the situation experienced by these six brothers who were left without their chief, and also well understand all the resulting calamitous consequences, I must first of all explain to you, even though briefly, the history of the rise and existence in this country named Tibet, of this small group, which had always consisted of seven three-brained beings of your planet.

"This group was formed and existed long before the appearance on the planet Earth of the last Sacred Individual, Saint Lama.

"From very early times it was composed of seven beings, directly initiated by Saint Krishnatkharna, also a messenger of our ENDLESSNESS specially sent to the three-centered beings of the planet Earth breeding in the country Gemchania.

"When Saint Buddha afterwards appeared there in Gemchania, and made clear that many instructions of Saint Krishnatkharna were not yet obsolete for the psyche of the beings of that same country, and that these instructions, when absorbed by any of the beings there, contribute to the destruction of those consequences of the properties of the organ Kundabuffer, to help them in freeing themselves from which he had himself also been sent to them, and when He decided to put these instructions of Saint Krishnatkharna as a whole into the basis of his own teaching also, then these seven beings there, initiated directly by Saint Krishnatkharna—after Buddha had taught them the aim and necessity of their existence, and they had clearly sensed this and were convinced that the instructions of Saint Buddha not only at heart did not contradict the instructions of Saint Krishnatkharna, but even corresponded more perfectly to the psyche of the beings of that given period—became followers of Saint Buddha.

"And still later, when Saint Lama appeared specially for the beings of the country Tibet, and he also in his turn found that many instructions of Saint Buddha would still correspond very well with the psyche of the beings of that country—if only certain changes of detail were admitted into them corresponding to the change in external conditions of existence which had been brought about under the influence of time—he therefore also put into the basis of his teaching many instructions from the verities pointed out already by Saint Krishnatkharna before him and renewed by Saint Buddha; then this small group of initiated beings as well as other groups already followers of Buddha, having also clearly sensed that the additions and changes brought to his teaching by Saint Lama corresponded better to the contemporary psyche, became followers of Saint Lama.

"Among the beings of this small group there existed a rule, which, by the way, they kept very strictly, in accordance with which certain secret instructions of Saint Lama concerning the beings of their group were transmitted from generation to generation through their chief alone, and he could initiate into these secrets the other six, only after certain attainments on their part.

"That is just why all the six members of this small organization, all of whom had already merited and were ready to be accepted for initiation in the near future, were so horrified, as I have said, when they learned about the destruction of their chief. With the destruction of this, at that time, sole initiate, there was lost to them forever the possibility of becoming initiated into these secret instructions of Saint Lama.

"Owing to the fact that the destruction of their chief proceeded so unexpectedly, that sole remaining possibility became even doubtful for them 'of receiving these instructions' by communicating with the Reason of the destroyed chief by means of the process, the 'sacred Almznoshinoo,' for the existence of which they not only knew the possibilities, but they also had in themselves all the data required for such an actualization.

"You, probably, my dear boy, know nothing yet about this sacred process?

"That process is called the sacred Almznoshinoo by means of which three-centered beings who have themselves already had time to coat and to bring their own body Kesdjan up to completed functioning and to a definite degree of Reason, intentionally produce the coating or, as it is otherwise said, the 'materialization' of the body Kesdjan of any being already entirely destroyed, to such a density that this body acquires again for a certain time the possibility of manifesting in certain of its functions proper to its former planetary body.

"This sacred process can be produced upon the body Kesdjan of that being who also during his existence had brought his higher being-body up to the completed functioning, and in whom, in addition, the Reason of this body had been brought up to the degree called the sacred 'being-Mirozinoo.'

"In our Great Universe, besides the process of the intentional coating of the being-body Kesdjan of an already destroyed being, another process exists called the most sacred 'Djerymetly.'

"And this most sacred process consists in this, that when there is intentionally first produced the coating of the highest being-body, namely, the 'body of the soul,' only afterwards, as in the first case, is the sacred Almznoshinoo produced.

"It is possible of course to produce both these processes only in that case, if such higher-being bodies are still in those spheres contactable by the sphere of that planet on which these 'sacred sacraments' are produced.

"And in addition, these formations evoked intentionally and consciously by definite beings can exist and maintain connection and communication with them only as long as the beings who produce these formations, consciously feed the body Kesdjan with their own sacred 'Aiësakhaldan.'

"Thus, those six remaining members of the small 'group-of-Seven' might have had recourse to this same sacred process Almznoshinoo for communication with the Reason of their destroyed chief, if they, having foreseen the possibility of this sudden decease of their chief, had made beforehand while he still existed a certain preparation, necessary for completing this process.

"In order that you may understand about the essence of this preparation for the sacred process, the sacrament Almznoshinoo, it is necessary for you to know about two particular properties of the 'being-Hanbledzoin,' i.e., the 'blood' of the being-body Kesdjan.

"The first of these properties of the being-Hanbledzoin consists in this, that, if any part of it be separated and removed, then wherever and however far it may be taken, a 'threadlike connection' is formed between this part and the fundamental concentration of all this cosmic substance, in such a way that this connection is formed of this same substance, and its density and thickness increase and diminish proportionately with the distance between the fundamental concentration of this substance and its separated part.

"And the second particular property of this Hanbledzoin consists in this, that when it is introduced into the fundamental concentration of this substance and has mixed with this primordial concentration, it is distributed in it everywhere in uniform densities and in uniform quantities, wherever the given concentration may be and in whatever quantity this same Hanbledzoin may accidentally or intentionally be introduced.

"And so, in consequence of the fact that the body Kesdjan of the being is coated with those substances which in their totality make this cosmic formation much lighter than that mass of cosmic substances which surrounds the planets and is called the planetary atmosphere, then as soon as the body Kesdjan of the being is separated from the planetary body of the being, it at once rises according to the cosmic law called 'Tenikdoa,' or as it is sometimes called the 'law of gravity,' to that sphere in which it finds the weight proper to it equally balanced and which is therefore the corresponding place of such cosmic arisings; then, in consequence of all this, the preliminary preparation consists in this, that beforehand, still during the planetary existence of that being, on the body Kesdjan of whom it is intended after his decease to produce the sacrament of the sacred Almznoshinoo, a particle of his Hanbledzoin must be taken and this particle must be either kept in some corresponding surplanetary formation, or be introduced into those beings themselves who produce this 'ritual,' and intentionally blend with the Hanbledzoin of their own body Kesdjan.

"In this way, when the three-brained perfected being foredesigned for this sacrament Almznoshinoo ceases his planetary existence, and his body Kesdjan is separated from his planetary body, then thanks to the first particular property of this being-Hanbledzoin that connection begins to be established about which I have just told you, between the given body Kesdjan and that place where the particle of his Hanbledzoin was preserved beforehand or those beings who intentionally coated this particle in their own bodies Kesdjan.

"In order to be clear in our subsequent talks upon this question, you must now be told just here that the said connection—one end of which is kept in the body Kesdjan which has risen to its corresponding sphere and the other end of which stays either within those surplanetary formations in which the particle from the general mass of the Hanbledzoin of the given body Kesdjan was fixed, or in those beings who intentionally blended the Hanbledzoin of the given body Kesdjan with the Hanbledzoin of their own body Kesdjan—can exist in space only for a limited period, namely, only until the completion of the appointed movement of that planet, on which the given being had arisen, around its sun.

"And at the beginning of such a new completing movement the said threads completely disappear.

"And they disappear because, in the atmosphere surrounding all planets, the evolution and the involution of cosmic substances required for the great cosmic Trogoautoegocrat in accordance with the fundamental sacred cosmic law Heptaparaparshinokh, again commence flowing only for the Trogoautoegocratic process of local character, i.e., within the limits of the given solar system's what is called 'own activity' and in consequence of which all, without exception, of the cosmic substances which happen to be in the given atmosphere during the period of this movement, and among them the said connections also, are immediately transformed into those cosmic substances which must be present in these atmospheres.

"So, my boy! Until these completed movements have come to an end, those beings existing on planets who either have in themselves a particle of the Hanbledzoin of any body Kesdjan or have at their disposal the surplanetary formation in which that part of the Hanbledzoin was fixed, can—assuming, of course, that they have all the corresponding data for carrying it out—at any time attract such a body back to the sphere of the solid part of the planet, and saturating it to the condensation corresponding to their own Hanbledzoin, in this way establish relations with the Reason of that already completedly formed independent cosmic unit.

"And this attraction or as it is sometimes said 'materialization' is produced, as I have already told you, by means of what is called 'Vallikrin,' that is by the conscious injection in a certain way of one's own Hanbledzoin into the ends of these connections.

"Several times, even before this Tibetan case, this sacred process Almznoshinoo had already been produced on your planet by the three-centered beings of different periods, and about the information concerning these sacred processes of former times, several Legominisms existed.

"It was through these Legominisms also that this small group of Tibetan beings already knew all the details of the procedure relating to this sacred process, and of course they also knew about the need of the special preliminary preparation for it.

"But having now no other possibility of learning all the secret sacraments, except only by attempting to enter into relations with the Reason of their deceased chief, they decided to try to carry out this sacred sacrament upon the body Kesdjan of their former chief, even without the said preliminary preparation.

"And so, owing to this risk of theirs, that proceeded there which served as the cause of the mentioned great misfortune.

"As my further investigations showed me, this great misfortune occurred in the following way:

"When these six 'great initiates' still existing with their planetary existence began by twos in turns uninterruptedly for three days and three nights to produce upon the planetary body of their former chief the process Vallikrin, that is, the inpouring of their own Hanbledzoin into this body, then, because of the absence of the said preliminary preparation of the connection with his body Kesdjan, their Hanbledzoin did not go to the actualization where it should have gone, but only accumulated chaotically over this planetary body of their former chief; and since, unfortunately for them, during these same days, a reinforced blending of the sacred active element Okidanokh was proceeding in the atmosphere above that locality, or as the beings say there, there were 'great thunderstorms,' then, between these two cosmic 'results,' still only in the process of transition from one definite cosmic phenomenon to another, a what is called 'Sobrionolian contact' resulted.

"And it was thanks to that contact there, on that small area of that ill-starred planet, that that accelerated cosmic phenomenon resulted called 'Noughtounichtono,' that is to say, the sudden and instantaneous evolution of all cosmic formed crystallizations, and, namely, all the neighboring surplanetary formations, were immediately transformed into the prime-source substance Etherokrilno.

"This Sobrionolian contact, or as it would be said on your planet Earth this 'explosion,' was so powerful that during this Noughtounichtono there, everything without any exception was transformed into Etherokrilno, both the planetary body of the chief of this small group of beings as well as all the six other brethren there who had completed this sacred sacrament, and likewise in general all the spiritualized or only concentrated surplanetary formations which were in the given region within an area of one 'Shmana,' or as your favorites would say 'one square kilometer.'

"Among these destroyed formations, reproduced both naturally as well as artificially by the beings, there were also all the what are called 'books' which belonged to these seven terrestrial genuine great initiated beings, and other things which had served as means for keeping in memory everything concerning all the three genuine Sacred Individuals intentionally actualized from Above, and, namely, Saint Krishnatkharna, Saint Buddha, and Saint Lama.

"Now, my boy, I think the sense of those words of mine will appear clear to you, by which I defined the significance of this charming military expedition, and, namely, when I said, that this was a great misfortune not only for the beings of the given country, yet, perhaps, also for all the three-brained beings of the whole of the planet.

"And so, my boy, it has now become clear to you how there on your planet all the five religions I named, still remaining there at the present time and which were founded on the teachings of five different genuine saints sent to the three-brained beings from Above for helping them to free themselves from the consequences of the properties of the organ Kundabuffer, how, although all these five religions have gradually become changed, thanks as always to the same conditions of ordinary being-existence abnormally established just by them, until they were eventually turned for any sane mentation into children's fairy tales, yet nevertheless these five religions still served for some of them as a support for these inner moral motives, owing to which during certain previous periods, their mutual existence became more or less becoming to three-centered beings.

"But now, after the final destruction of even the last remnants of these religions, it is difficult even to foresee how it will all end.

"The last of these five religions, namely, that founded on the teaching of the genuine messenger Saint Lama, has been finally and even 'with a crash' destroyed by that charming military expedition of theirs.

"The last but one, namely, that founded on the teachings of Saint Mohammed, they are now destroying by means of the abolition of the former famous fezzes and yashmaks with the 'gracious' assistance of the 'German Junkers.'

"And as regards the final destruction of the still earlier arisen religion, namely, that founded on the teaching of Jesus Christ, that is, the religion and teaching upon which the highest Individuals placed great hopes—the contemporary three-brained beings there, who have already become archstrange, are completely destroying it by organizing in that city of Jerusalem their university for the contemporary Jewish youth.

"The religion founded on the teaching of Saint Moses, although it existed for a long time and is still maintained after a fashion by its followers, yet, owing to the organic hatred formed in the beings of other communities toward the beings who follow this religion, due only to that 'maleficent' idea existing there called 'policy,' infallibly sooner or later they will doubtlessly 'croak it' as well and also 'with a crash.'

"And finally, as regards that religion there which was, so to say, founded on the teaching of Saint Buddha, I have already told you that, thanks to their notorious suffering, based on a misunderstood idea, they have from the very beginning turned this teaching into a means for their own, as they themselves say, 'mental perversity.'

"By the way, it must be noted that in the beginning the 'Tanguori' and after them 'Brahmanists,' 'Shuenists,' and so on, occupied themselves with this mental perversity there, and now at the present time those called theosophists and other 'pseudolearned' occupy themselves with the same thing."

Having thus spoken, Beelzebub became silent for a short while, during which it was seen that he concentratedly pondered over something, and afterwards he said:

"At this moment I am considering that it will be very, very useful for your Reason if I tell you more about a certain event connected also with the sacrament of the sacred Almznoshinoo which concerns that Sacred Individual the conception of whom was actualized among your favorites and who, having become formed, was named 'Jesus Christ.'

"I will tell you about this important event, connected with the actualization among them of this Sacred Individual, the notion about which the contemporary favorites of yours define by the words 'The Death and Resurrection of Jesus Christ.'

"Your acquaintance with this fact will be another example for you for enlightening you about the sense and essential significance of the sacred sacrament Almznoshinoo, and in addition you will also have a clear example of what I have already told, how—thanks only to the strange inherency in their general psyche, called wiseacring—the sense of even those crumbs 'collected-from-bits-here-and-there-into-one-whole' spoken and indicated to them by the genuine Sacred Individuals intentionally actualized among them from Above, were already so distorted by the first generation of the contemporaries of the given Sacred Individuals, that from all what they call religious teachings information reached the beings of subsequent generations suitable perhaps only for the inventing of what are called 'children's fairy tales.'

"The point is, that when this Sacred Individual Jesus Christ was actualized in the planetary body of a terrestrial three-brained being, and when afterwards He had to be separated from his exterior planetary coating, then just this same sacred process 'Almznoshinoo' was also produced on his body Kesdjan by certain terrestrial three-brained beings in order to have the possibility—in view of the violent interruption of his planetary existence—of continuing to communicate with his Divine Reason and of obtaining in this way the information about certain cosmic Truths and certain instructions for the future which he did not finish giving them.

"The information concerning this great event was accurately noted by certain participants in the performance of this sacred process and was intentionally related, for a definite purpose, to the ordinary beings around them.

"And so, my boy, in consequence of the fact that that period of time coincided with that 'particularly sharp functioning' which I already once mentioned, of the strange reason of these three-brained beings pleasing to you—in the sense of the periodic 'Ekbarzerbazia' which had long been an inherent need for them 'to-lead-into-error-beings-around-them-similar-to-themselves'—at which period, many of them strove to be called 'learned,' of course, of 'new format,' and also on account of the fact that at that time there were many such beings among the mentioned ordinary beings around them, then they 'inserted' for transmission to subsequent generations, in most of the notes and expressions of those stories of the witnesses about this sacred process, such 'absurdities' that in addition to this indubitable information, that Jesus Christ was crucified on a cross, and that after the crucifixion

He was buried, they also proved just as convincingly that after His crucifixion and burial, Jesus Christ was resurrected and continued to exist among them and to teach this and that, and only afterwards did He raise Himself with His planetary body to Heaven.

"The result of this kind of, in the objective sense, 'criminal wiseacring' of theirs, was that in the beings of subsequent generations, genuine faith in all this Divine and uniquely accomplished teaching of salvation of the All-Loving Jesus Christ was totally destroyed.

"These absurdities which were written down began gradually to engender in the presences of certain of the beings of subsequent generations the impulse of doubt, not only concerning what I have just said, but also doubt relating in general to all the real information and accurate instructions and explanations of this Sacred Individual intentionally actualized among them from Above.

"The data, however, for the doubt of these mentioned certain terrestrial three-brained beings of subsequent generations began to be crystallized and became an inalienable part of their common presences, chiefly because even in them in spite of the process, inherent in them, of almost automatic existence, yet nevertheless during a long period of time—many of their centuries—they gradually acquired from this automatic crystallizing, data for a more or less correct instinctive sensing of certain cosmic truths, as for instance, concerning the indubitable truth, that if the process of the sacred Rascooarno occurs to any being, or as they say 'if someone dies' and is moreover buried, then this being will never exist again, nor furthermore will he ever speak or teach again.

"And so, those of these unfortunates, in whom in short there still continued to proceed, very slightly, the functioning of being-mentation according to the law of sane logic, and who had not at all accepted such illogical and unusual incoherencies, ultimately lost all faith in any Truth whatsoever, really given and explained by this Sacred Individual Jesus Christ.

"And as regards the remaining terrestrial three-brained beings, who by the way in general represent in themselves the majority, then they, becoming usually transformed at the corresponding age—owing to many causes, but chiefly because already from the earliest years of their existence it became proper to them to occupy themselves with what is called 'Moordoorten'—into what are called 'psychopaths,' accept blindly, literally, and word for word, entirely without any being-logical mentation, all these 'fantastic absurdities' which reached them; and a kind of special peculiar 'faith' in all this religious teaching becomes automatically formed in them as if it represented in itself the totality of all the 'truths' connected with and related to just this Sacred Individual Jesus Christ who was indeed intentionally actualized among them from Above.

"The information about what is called 'the Lord's Supper' given in the 'noted totality,' still existing today among your contemporary favorites, representing as it were the real accurate history of this Sacred Individual, and which is called by them the 'Holy Writ,' was nothing else but a preparation for the great sacrament Almznoshinoo on the body Kesdjan of Saint Jesus Christ.

"It is interesting to notice that even in this totality noted 'from-bits-here-and-there,' which your favorites call the Holy Writ, there are many precise words and even whole phrases, uttered at that 'Lord's Supper' by the Saint Jesus Christ Himself, as well as by those directly initiated by Him who in this same Holy Script are called 'disciples' or 'apostles,' and which words and phrases your favorites, particularly the contemporary ones, also understand, as always and everything, only 'literally,' without any awareness of the inner meaning put into them.

"And such a nonsensical 'literal' understanding proceeds in them, of course, always owing to the fact that they have entirely ceased to produce in their common presences Partkdolg-duty, which should be actualized by being-efforts, which in their turn alone crystallize in the three-brained beings data for the capacity of genuine being-pondering.

"That is why, my boy, in the given case also they could not ponder at least only about the fact that, when this Sacred Individual Jesus Christ was actualized among them and when this same existing Holy Writ of theirs was compiled, so many definite words were not used by beings similar to these compilers as are used at the present time.

"They do not consider that at that period 'being-mentation' among the beings of this planet was still nearer to that normal mentation, which in general is proper to be present among three-brained beings, and that at that time the transmission of ideas and thoughts was in consequence still what is called 'Podobnisirnian,' or, as it is still otherwise said 'allegorical.'

"In other words, in order to explain to themselves, or to any others, some act or other, the three-brained beings of the planet Earth then referred to the understanding of similar acts which had already formerly occurred among them.

"But, meanwhile, this also now proceeds in them according to the principle called 'Chainonizironness.'

"And this first proceeded there because, thanks as always to the same abnormally established conditions of ordinary existence, their being-mentation began to proceed without any participation of the functioning of their what are called 'localizations of feeling,' or according to their terminology 'feeling center,' chiefly in consequence of which this mentation of theirs finally became automatized.

"And hence, during all this time, in order to have the possibility of even approximately making clear to themselves or explaining anything to anyone, they were themselves automatically compelled and continue to be compelled to invent very many almost nonsignificant names for things and also words for ideas, great and small; and therefore the process of their mentation began little by little to proceed, as I have already said, according to the principle 'Chainonizironness.'

"And it is just with this mentation of theirs that your contemporary favorites try to decipher and to understand a text written still in the 'Similnisirnian' manner for the mentation of beings, contemporary with the Divine Jesus Christ.

"And so, my boy, it is necessary to explain to you about a certain fact, in the highest degree absurd and in the objective sense blasphemous, for a greater clarification of the real nothingness of this Holy Writ, still existing today among your favorites, which, apropos, became particularly widely spread after their last process of reciprocal destruction, and in which as you already surmise, there is everything you please, excepting reality and truth.

"I will inform you, namely, concerning what is said in this contemporary Holy Writ, which has as it were reached them in an unchanged form, about the chief, most reasonable and most devoted of all the beings, directly initiated by this Sacred Individual or, as they would say, about one of his Apostles.

"This devoted and favorite Apostle initiated by Jesus Christ Himself was called 'Judas.'

"According to the present version of this Holy Writ everyone who wishes to draw on the true knowledge will acquire such a conviction, which will also be fixed in his essence, that this same Judas was the basest of beings conceivable, and that he was a conscienceless, double-faced, treacherous traitor.

"But in fact, this Judas was not only the most faithful and devoted of all the near followers of Jesus Christ, but also, only thanks to his Reason and presence of mind all the acts of this Sacred Individual could form that result, which if it did not serve as the basis for the total destruction of the consequences of the properties of the organ Ḳundabuffer in these unfortunate three-brained beings, yet it was nevertheless, during twenty centuries the source of nourishment and inspiration for the majority of them in their desolate existence and made it at least a little endurable.

"In order that you may better represent and make clear to yourself the genuine individuality of this Judas, and the significance of his manifestation for the future, I must first still inform you that when this Sacred Individual Jesus Christ, intentionally actualized from Above in a planetary body of a terrestrial being, completely formed Himself for a corresponding existence, He decided to actualize the mission imposed on Him from Above, through the way of enlightening the reason of these three-brained terrestrial beings, by means of twelve different types of beings, chosen from among them and who were specially enlightened and prepared by him personally.

"And so, in the very heat of His Divine Activities, surrounding circumstances independent of Him were so arranged, that not having carried out His intention, i.e., not having had time to explain certain cosmic truths and to give the required instructions for the future, He was compelled to allow the premature cessation of his planetary existence to be accomplished.

"He then decided, together with these twelve terrestrial

beings intentionally initiated by Him, to have recourse to the sacred sacrament Almznoshinoo—the process of the actualization of which sacred sacrament was already well known to all of them, as they had already acquired in their presences all the data for its fulfillment—so that He should have the possibility, while He still remained in such a cosmic individual state, to finish the preparation begun by Him for the fulfillment of the plan designed for actualization of the mission imposed on Him from Above.

"And so, my boy, when having decided on this and being ready to begin the preliminary preparation required for this sacred sacrament, it then became clear that it was utterly impossible to do this, as it was too late; they were all already surrounded by beings, called 'guards,' and their arrest and everything that would follow from it was expected at any moment. And it was just here that this Judas, now a Saint and formerly the inseparable and devoted helper of Jesus Christ and who is 'hated' and 'cursed' owing to the naïve nonreasonableness of the peculiar three-brained beings of your planet, manifested himself and rendered his great objective service for which terrestrial three-brained beings of all subsequent generations should be grateful.

"This wise, onerous, and disinterestedly devoted manifestation taken upon himself consisted in this, that while in a state of desperation on ascertaining that it was impossible to fulfill the required preliminary procedure for the actualization of the sacred Almznoshinoo, this Judas, now a Saint, leaped from his place and hurriedly said:

"'I shall go and do everything in such a way that you should have the possibility of fulfilling this sacred preparation without hindrance, and meanwhile set to work at once.'

"Having said this, he approached Jesus Christ and

having confidentially spoken with Him a little and received His blessing, hurriedly left.

"The others, indeed without hindrance, finished everything necessary for the possibility of accomplishing this sacred process Almznoshinoo.

"After what I have just said, you should now without any doubt understand how the three-brained beings, of the two types indicated by me of the planet Earth which has taken your fancy, have distorted for their various egoistic aims all the truths to such an extent, that about this Judas, now a Saint—thanks to whom alone such a blessed hearth of tranquillity from their desolate existence had arisen and existed for them for twenty centuries—there has been crystallized in the presences of the beings of all subsequent generations such an unprecedented unjust representation.

"I personally even think that if this Judas was presented in their Holy Writ as a type of this kind, then it may have been for this reason, that it was necessary for someone or other, also belonging to the mentioned types, to belittle in this way, for a certain purpose, the significance of Jesus Christ Himself.

"And, namely, He appeared to be so naïve, so unable to feel and see beforehand, in a word, so unperfected that in spite of knowing and existing together with this Judas so long, He failed to sense and be aware that this immediate disciple of His was such a perfidious traitor and that he would sell Him for thirty worthless pieces of silver."

At this point in Beelzebub's tales, he and all the passengers of the inter-solar-system ship *Karnak* suddenly sensed in their organ of taste a special sour-bitterish taste.

This signified that their ship was approaching that place of their destination, in the given case the holy planet Purgatory.

They sensed the sour-bitterish taste because a special

magnetic current was released from the steering compartment of the ship to inform all the passengers of the approach to the place of destination.

Beelzebub therefore interrupted his tale and glancing affectionately at his grandson, said:

"Now we shall have, willy-nilly, to stop our talk about this Sacred Individual Jesus Christ, but nevertheless, my boy, when we arrive home and exist on our dear Karatas, remind me sometime when I am free, to finish telling you about the whole of this history in detail.

"All the history of the actualization of this Sacred Individual in a planetary body among your favorites, both concerning His existence among the beings of various groupings of this planet of yours, and also concerning His violent end, is very, very interesting just for you who wish to explain to your reason all the details of the strange psyche of these peculiar three-brained beings—and it will be very instructive and interesting to know that part of the history of this Saint Jesus Christ, which relates to the period of His existence there from the ages of twelve to twenty-eight, according to their time-calculation."

CHAPTER 39
The Holy Planet "Purgatory"

After several Dionosks the cosmic ship *Karnak* left the holy planet, and again began to fall further in the direction of the place of its final destination, and, namely, in the direction of that planet on which Beelzebub had had the place of his arising and whither he was returning to finish his long existence; to finish that long existence of his, which, on account of certain definite circumstances, he had to fulfill on various cosmic concentrations of our Great Universe and always under conditions very unfavorable for him personally, yet which he nevertheless objectively fulfilled quite meritoriously.

And so, when the usual tempo of the falling of the ship *Karnak* had been re-established, Hassein, the grandson of Beelzebub, again sat down at his feet and turning to him, said:

"Grandfather, oh, dear grandfather! Explain to me, please, why, as my uncle Tooilan told me, does our COMMON ALL-EMBRACING UNI-BEING AUTOCRAT ENDLESSNESS appear so often on this holy planet on which we have just been?"

At this question of his grandson, Beelzebub this time became thoughtful a little longer than usual and then, also with greater concentration than was usual for him, slowly said:

"Yes . . . I do not know, my dear boy, with what to begin this time in order to answer this question of yours in such a form as would satisfy me also, since among many other tasks I have set myself in respect of you, as regards your 'Oskiano,' there is also this, that you, at your age, should have an exhaustive knowledge and understanding about this holy planet.

"In any case, you must first of all be told that this same holy planet, which is called Purgatory, is for the whole of our Great Universe, as it were, the heart and place of concentration of all the completing results of the pulsation of everything that functions and exists in the Universe.

"Our COMMON-FATHER-CREATOR-ENDLESSNESS appears there so often only because this holy planet is the place of the existence of the, in the highest degree, unfortunate 'higher-being-bodies,' who obtained their coating on various planets of the whole of our Great Universe.

"The 'higher-being-bodies' who have already merited to dwell on this holy planet suffer, maybe, as much as anybody in the whole of our Great Universe.

"In view of this, our ALL-LOVING, ENDLESSLY-MERCIFUL AND ABSOLUTELY-JUST CREATOR-ENDLESSNESS, having no other possibility of helping these unfortunate 'higher-being-bodies' with anything, often appears there so that by these appearances of HIS HE may soothe them, if only a little, in their terrible inevitable state of inexpressible anguish.

"This planet began to actualize that aim for which it now exists much later than that period of the flow of time when the completing process of the 'creation' of the now existing 'World' was finished.

"In the beginning all these 'higher-being-bodies' who at the present time have the place of their existence on this holy planet went directly on to our Most Most Holy Sun Absolute, but later when that all-universal calamity, which we call the 'Choot-God-litanical period' occurred in our Great Universe, then after this terrifying common-cosmic calamity, similar 'higher-being-bodies' who now dwell on this holy planet ceased to have the possibility of blending directly with our Most Most Holy Sun Absolute.

"Only after this 'Choot-God-litanical period' did the necessity appear for such a kind of general-universal functioning which this holy planet 'Purgatory' actualizes at the present time.

"It was just from this time that the whole surface of this holy planet was correspondingly organized and adapted in such a way that these 'higher-being-bodies' might have the place of their already unavoidable existence on it."

Having said this, Beelzebub became a little thoughtful and with a slight smile continued to tell the following:

"This holy planet is not only the center of the concentrations of the results of the functioning of all that exists, but it is also now the best, richest, and most beautiful of all the planets of our Universe.

"When we were there, you probably noticed that we always saw and sensed that from there all the space of our Great Universe or, as your favorites would say, all the 'skies' reflected, as it were, the radiance which recalls the radiance of the famous and incomparable 'Almacornian turquoise.' Its atmosphere is always pure like the 'phenomenal-Sakrooalnian-crystal.'

"Everywhere there, every individual with all his presence senses 'everything external,' 'Iskoloonizinernly,' or as your favorites would say 'blissfully-delightfully.'

"On that holy planet, as the informed say, of springs alone, both mineral and fresh, which for purity and naturalness are unequalled on any other planet of our Universe, there are about ten thousand.

"There, from the whole of our Universe are gathered the most beautiful and best songbirds, of which as the informed also say, there are about twelve thousand species.

"And as for the surplanetary formations, such as 'flowers,' 'fruits,' 'berries,' and all others of the same kind, words are inadequate. It can be said that there are collected and acclimatized there almost the whole 'flora,' 'fauna,' and 'foscalia' from all the planets of our Great Universe.

"Everywhere on that holy planet, in corresponding gorges, are convenient caves of all kinds of 'interior form'—made partly by Nature Herself and partly artificially—with striking views from their entrances, and in these caves there is everything that can be required for a blissful and tranquil existence, with the complete absence of any essence-anxiety whatever in any part of the presence of any cosmic independent Individual, such as 'higher-being-bodies' can also become.

"It is just in these caves that those 'higher-being-bodies' exist by their own choice, who, owing to their merits, come to this holy planet from the whole of our Great Universe for their further existence.

"Besides all I have mentioned, there are also there the very best, in regard to convenience as well as to speed, what are called 'Egolionopties,' or, as they are still sometimes called, 'Omnipresent-platforms.'

"These Egolionopties freely move in all directions in the atmosphere of the holy planet, at any desired speed, even at that speed in which the second degree suns of our Universe fall.

"The system of this kind of 'Egolionopty' was, it seems, invented specially for this holy planet by the famous angel, now already Archangel Herkission."

Having uttered these last words, Beelzebub suddenly became silent and again deeply thoughtful, and Hassein and Ahoon looked at him with surprise and interrogation.

After a fairly long time had passed, Beelzebub, shaking his head in a special manner, again turned to Hassein and said:

"I am just now thinking that it would be very reasonable on my part, if to this question of yours—'why our ENDLESSNESS so often rejoices this holy planet with HIS appearance'—I would answer in such a way, so that I could, apropos, explain to you also what I have already several times promised you to explain.

"That is to say, about the fundamental cosmic laws by which our present World is maintained and on the basis of which it exists; and this moreover should be done, because if both of these questions are taken together, only then will you have all-round material for a complete representation and exhaustive understanding about this holy planet Purgatory, and at the same time learn something more about the three-brained beings who have interested you and who arise on the planet Earth.

"I wish to give you also now as many clear and detailed explanations as possible concerning this holy planet, as, sooner or later, you will have to know about this, because every responsible three-brained being of our Universe, irrespective of the nature of the causes and place of his arising and also of the form of his exterior coating, will ultimately have to learn about everything concerning this holy planet.

"And he must know all this in order to strive to exist in that direction which corresponds just to the aim and sense of existence, which striving is the objective lot of every three-brained being, in whom, whatever the causes might be, the germ arises for the coating of a 'higher-being-body.'

"And so . . . my boy, first of all I must once more and in greater detail repeat that our ENDLESSNESS was forced to create the whole World which now exists at the present time.

"In the beginning, when nothing yet existed and when the whole of our Universe was empty endless space with the presence of only the prime-source cosmic substance 'Etherokrilno,' our present Most Great and Most Most Holy Sun Absolute existed alone in all this empty space, and it was on this then sole cosmic concentration that our UNI-BEING CREATOR with HIS cherubim and seraphim had the place of HIS most glorious Being.

"It was just during this same period of the flow of time that there came to our CREATOR ALL-MAINTAINER the forced need to create our present existing 'Megalocosmos,' i.e., our World.

"From the third most sacred canticle of our cherubim and seraphim, we were worthy of learning that our CREATOR OMNIPOTENT once ascertained that this same Sun Absolute, on which HE dwelt with HIS cherubim and seraphim was, although almost imperceptibly yet nevertheless gradually, diminishing in volume.

"As the fact ascertained by HIM appeared to HIM very serious, HE then decided immediately to review all the laws which maintained the existence of that, then still sole, cosmic concentration.

"During this review our OMNIPOTENT CREATOR for the first time made it clear that the cause of this gradual diminishing of the volume of the Sun Absolute was merely the Heropass, that is, the flow of Time itself.

"Thereupon our ENDLESSNESS became thoughtful, for in HIS Divine deliberations HE became clearly aware that if this Heropass should so continue to diminish the volume of the Sun Absolute, then sooner or later, it would ultimately bring about the complete destruction of this sole place of HIS Being.

"And so, my boy, in view of this, our ENDLESSNESS was then just compelled to take certain corresponding measures, so that from this Heropass the destruction of our Most Most Holy Sun Absolute could not eventually occur.

"Further, again from the sacred canticle of our cherubim and seraphim, but this time the fifth sacred canticle, we were worthy of learning that after this Divine ascertainment of HIS, our ENDLESSNESS devoted HIMSELF entirely to finding a possibility of averting such an inevitable end, which had to occur according to the lawful commands of the merciless Heropass, and that after HIS long Divine deliberations, HE decided to create our present existing 'Megalocosmos.'

"In order that you may more clearly understand how our ENDLESSNESS decided to attain immunity from the maleficent action of the merciless Heropass and of course how HE ultimately actualized it all, you must first of all know that before this, the Most Most Holy Sun Absolute was maintained and existed on the basis of the system called 'Autoegocrat,' i.e., on that principle according to which the inner forces which maintained the existence of this cosmic concentration had an independent functioning, not depending on any forces proceeding from outside, and which were based also on those two fundamental cosmic sacred laws by which at the present time also, the whole of our present Megalocosmos is maintained and on the basis of which it exists, and, namely, on the basis of those two fundamental primordial sacred cosmic laws, called the sacred Heptaparaparshinokh and the sacred Triamazikamno.

"About both of these fundamental cosmic primordial sacred laws, I have already once told you a little; now however I shall try to explain to you about them in rather more detail.

"The first of these fundamental primordial cosmic sacred laws, namely, the law of Heptaparaparshinokh, present-day objective cosmic science, by the way, formulates in the following words:

"'The-line-of-the-flow-of-forces-constantly-deflecting-according-to-law-and-uniting-again-at-its-ends.'

"This sacred primordial cosmic law has seven deflections or, as it is still otherwise said, seven 'centers of gravity' and the distance between each two of these deflections or 'centers of gravity' is called a 'Stopinder-of-the-sacred-Heptaparaparshinokh.'

"This law, passing through everything newly arising and everything existing, always makes its completing processes with its seven Stopinders.

"And in regard to the second primordial fundamental cosmic law, and, namely, the Sacred-Triamazikamno, common-cosmic objective science also formulates with the words:

"'A new arising from the previously arisen through the "Harnel-miaznel," the process of which is actualized thus: the higher blends with the lower in order to actualize the middle and thus becomes either higher for the preceding lower, or lower for the succeeding higher; and as I already told you, this Sacred-Triamazikamno consists of three independent forces, which are called:

the first, 'Surp-Otheos';
the second, 'Surp-Skiros';
the third, 'Surp-Athanotos';

which three holy forces of the sacred Triamazikamno the said science calls as follows:

the first, the 'Affirming-force' or the 'Pushing-force' or simply the 'Force-plus';

the second, the 'Denying-force' or the 'Resisting-force' or simply the 'Force-minus';

and the third, the 'Reconciling-force' or the 'Equilibrating-force' or the 'Neutralizing-force.'

"At this place of my explanations concerning chiefly the fundamental laws of 'World-creation' and 'World-maintenance,' it is interesting to notice by the way, that the three-brained beings of this planet which has taken your fancy, already began, at that period when the consequences of the properties of the organ Kundabuffer were not yet crystallized in their common presences, to be aware of these three holy forces of the Sacred-Triamazikamno and then named them:

> the first, 'God-the-Father';
> the second, 'God-the-Son'; and
> the third, 'God-the-Holy-Ghost';

and in various cases expressed the hidden meaning of them and also their longing to have a beneficent effect from them for their own individuality, by the following prayers:

> 'Sources of Divine
> Rejoicings, revolts and sufferings,
> Direct your actions upon us.'
>
> . . .

or 'Holy-Affirming,
Holy-Denying,
Holy-Reconciling,
Transubstantiate in me
For my Being.'

. . .

or 'Holy God,
Holy Firm,
Holy Immortal,
Have mercy on us.'

. . .

"Now, my boy, listen further very attentively.

"And so, in the beginning as I have already told you, our Most Most Holy Sun Absolute was maintained by the help of these two primordial sacred laws; but then these primordial laws functioned independently, without the help of any forces whatsoever coming from outside, and this system was still called only the 'Autoegocrat.'

"And so, our ALL-MAINTAINING ENDLESSNESS decided to

change the principle of the system of the functionings of both of these fundamental sacred laws, and, namely, HE decided to make their independent functioning dependent on forces coming from outside.

"And so, in consequence of the fact that for this new system of functioning of the forces which until then maintained the existence of the Most Most Holy Sun Absolute, there were required outside of the Sun Absolute corresponding sources in which such forces could arise and from which they could flow into the presence of the Most Most Holy Sun Absolute, our ALMIGHTY ENDLESSNESS was just then compelled to create our now existing Megalocosmos with all the cosmoses of different scales and relatively independent cosmic formations present in it, and from then on the system which maintained the existence of the Sun Absolute began to be called Trogoautoegocrat.

"Our COMMON FATHER OMNI-BEING ENDLESSNESS, having decided to change the principle of the maintenance of the existence of this then still unique cosmic concentration and sole place of HIS most glorious Being, first of all altered the process itself of the functioning of these two primordial fundamental sacred laws, and HE actualized the greater change in the law of the sacred Heptaparaparshinokh.

"These changes in the functioning of the sacred Heptaparaparshinokh consisted in this, that in three of its Stopinders HE altered the what are called 'subjective actions' which had been until then in the Stopinders, in this respect, that in one HE lengthened the law-conformable successiveness; shortened it in another; and in a third, disharmonized it.

"And, namely, with the purpose of providing the 'requisite inherency' for receiving, for its functioning, the automatic affluence of all forces which were near, HE lengthened the Stopinder between its third and fourth deflections.

"This same Stopinder of the sacred Heptaparaparshinokh is just that one, which is still called the 'mechano-coinciding-Mdnel-In.'

"And the Stopinder which HE shortened is between its last deflection and the beginning of a new cycle of its completing process; by this same shortening, for the purpose of facilitating the commencement of a new cycle of its completing process, HE predetermined the functioning of the given Stopinder to be dependent only upon the affluence of forces, obtained from outside through that Stopinder from the results of the action of that cosmic concentration itself in which the completing process of this primordial fundamental sacred law flows.

"And this Stopinder of the sacred Heptaparaparshinokh is just that one, which is still called the 'intentionally-actualized-Mdnel-In.'

"As regards the third Stopinder, then changed in its 'subjective action' and which is fifth in the general successiveness and is called 'Harnel-Aoot,' its disharmony flowed by itself from the change of the two aforementioned Stopinders.

"This disharmony in its subjective functioning, flowing from its asymmetry so to say in relation to the whole entire completing process of the sacred Heptaparaparshinokh, consists in the following:

"If the completing process of this sacred law flows in conditions, where during its process there are many 'extraneously-caused-vibrations,' then all its functioning gives only external results.

"But if this same process proceeds in absolute quiet without any external 'extraneously-caused-vibrations' whatsoever, then all the results of the action of its functioning remain within that concentration in which it completes its process, and for the outside, these results only become evident on direct and immediate contact with it.

"And if however during its functioning there are neither of these two sharply opposite conditions, then the results of the action of its process usually divide themselves into the external and the internal.

"Thus, from that time, the process of actualization began to proceed in the greatest as well as in the smallest cosmic concentrations with these Stopinders of this primordial sacred law of Heptaparaparshinokh changed in this way in their subjective actions.

"I repeat, my boy: Try very hard to understand everything that will relate to both these fundamental cosmic sacred laws, since knowledge of these sacred laws, particularly knowledge relating to the particularities of the sacred Heptaparaparshinokh, will help you in the future to understand very easily and very well all the second-grade and third-grade laws of World-creation and World-existence. Likewise, an all-round awareness of everything concerning these sacred laws also conduces, in general, to this, that three-brained beings irrespective of the form of their exterior coating, by becoming capable in the presence of all cosmic factors not depending on them and arising round about them—both the personally favorable as well as the unfavorable—of pondering on the sense of existence, acquire data for the elucidation and reconciliation in themselves of that, what is called, 'individual collision' which often arises, in general, in three-brained beings from the contradiction between the concrete results flowing from the processes of all the cosmic laws and the results presupposed and even quite surely expected by their what is called 'sane-logic'; and thus, correctly evaluating the essential significance of their own presence, they become capable of becoming aware of the genuine corresponding place for themselves in these common-cosmic actualizations.

"In short, the transmutation in themselves of an all-round understanding of the functioning of both these fundamental sacred laws conduces to this, that in the common presences of three-brained beings, data are crystallized for engendering that Divine property which it is indispensable for every normal three-brained being to have and which exists under the name of 'Semooniranoos'; of this your favorites have also an approximate representation, and they call it 'impartiality.'

"And so, my dear boy, our COMMON FATHER CREATOR ALMIGHTY, having then in the beginning changed the functioning of both these primordial sacred laws, directed the action of their forces from within the Most Holy Sun Absolute into the space of the Universe, whereupon there was obtained the what is called 'Emanation-of-the-Sun-Absolute' and now called, 'Theomertmalogos' or 'Word-God.'

"For the clarity of certain of my future explanations it must here be remarked that, in the process of the creation of the now existing World, the Divine 'Will Power' of our ENDLESSNESS participated only at the beginning.

"The subsequent creation went on automatically, of its own accord, entirely without the participation of His Own Divine Will Power, thanks only to these two changed fundamental primordial cosmic laws.

"And the process itself of creation proceeded then in the following successiveness:

"Thanks to the new particularity of the fifth Stopinder of the sacred Heptaparaparshinokh, these emanations issuing from the Sun Absolute began to act at certain definite points of the space of the Universe upon the prime-source cosmic substance Etherokrilno from which, owing to the totality of the former and the new particularities of the sacred primordial laws, certain definite concentrations began to be concentrated.

"Further, thanks to these factors and also to their own laws of Heptaparaparshinokh and Triamazikamno which had already begun to arise in these definite concentrations with their action upon each other, everything which had to be gradually began to be crystallized in these concentrations, and as a result of all this, those large concentrations were obtained which exist also until now and which we now call 'Second-order-Suns.'

"When these newly arisen Suns had been completely actualized and their own functionings of both the fundamental laws had been finally established in them, then in them also, similarly to the Most Most Holy Sun Absolute, their own results began to be transformed and to be radiated, which, together with the emanations issuing from the Most Most Holy Sun Absolute into the space of the Universe, became the factors for the actualization of the common-cosmic fundamental process of the sacred law of Triamazikamno, and that is to say:

"The Most Most Holy Theomertmalogos began to manifest itself in the quality of the third holy force of the sacred Triamazikamno; the results of any one of the newly arisen Second-order-Suns began to serve as the first holy force; and the results of all the other newly arisen Second-order-Suns in relation to this mentioned one newly arisen Sun, as the second holy force of this sacred law.

"Thanks to the process of the common-cosmic sacred Triamazikamno thus established in the space of the Universe, crystallizations of different what is called 'density' gradually began to be formed around each of the Second-order-Suns out of that same prime-source Etherokrilno, and grouping themselves around these newly arisen Suns, new concentrations began to take form, as a result of which more new Suns were obtained, but this time 'Third-order-Suns.'

"These third-order concentrations are just those cosmic concentrations which at the present time are called planets.

"At this very place in the process of the first outer cycle of the fundamental sacred Heptaparaparshinokh, namely, after the formation of the Third-order-Suns or planets, just here, owing to the changed fifth deflection of the sacred Heptaparaparshinokh, which as I have already said is now called Harnel-Aoot, the initially given momentum for the fundamental completing process, having lost half the force of its vivifyingness, began in its further functioning to have only half of the manifestation of its action outside itself, and the other half for itself, i.e., for its very own functioning, the consequences of which were that on these last big results, i.e., on these said Third-order-Suns or planets, there began to arise what are called, 'similarities-to-the-already-arisen.'

"And as after this, surrounding conditions of actualizations were everywhere established corresponding to the manifestation of the second particularity of the fifth Stopinder of the fundamental sacred Heptaparaparshinokh, therefore from then on the actualization of the fundamental outer cycle of the sacred Heptaparaparshinokh ceased, and all the action of its functioning entered forever into the results already manifested by it, and in them there began to proceed its inherent permanent processes of transformation, called 'evolution' and 'involution.'

"And then, thanks this time to a second-grade cosmic law which is called 'Litsvrtsi' or the 'aggregation of the homogeneous,' there began to be grouped on the planets themselves, from the mentioned 'relatively independent' new formations named 'similarities-to-the-already-arisen,' yet other also 'relatively independent' formations.

"Thanks just to these processes of 'evolution' and 'involution' inherent in the sacred Heptaparaparshinokh, there also began to be crystallized and decrystallized in the presences of all the greatest and smallest cosmic concentrations, all kinds of definite cosmic substances with their own inherent subjective properties, and which objective science calls 'active elements.'

"And all the results of the 'evolution' and 'involution' of these active elements, actualizing the Trogoautoegocratic principle of existence of everything existing in the Universe by means of reciprocal feeding and maintaining each other's existence, produce the said common-cosmic process 'Iraniranumange,' or, as I have already said, what objective science calls 'common-cosmic-exchange-of-substances.'

"And so, my boy, thanks to this new system of the reciprocal feeding of everything existing in the Universe, in which our Most Most Holy Sun Absolute Itself participated, there was established in it that equilibrium which at the present time no longer gives the merciless Heropass any possibility of bringing about anything unforeseen whatsoever to our Most Great and Most Most Holy Sun Absolute; and thus, the motive for the Divine anxiety of our ALMIGHTY UNI-BEING ENDLESSNESS concerning the wholeness of HIS eternal place of dwelling, disappeared forever.

"Here it is necessary to tell you that when this most wise Divine actualization was finished, our triumphant cherubim and seraphim then gave, for the first time, to all the newly arisen actualizations those names which exist even until today. Every 'relatively independent concentration' in general they then defined by the word 'cosmos,' and to distinguish the different orders of arising of these 'cosmoses,' they added to this definition 'cosmos' a separate corresponding name.

"And, namely, they named the Most Most Holy Prime-Source Sun Absolute itself—'Protocosmos.'

"Each newly arisen 'Second-order-Sun' with all its consequent definite results they called 'Defterocosmos.'

"'Third-order-Suns,' i.e., those we now call 'planets,' they called 'Tritocosmos.'

"The smallest 'relatively independent formation' on the planets, which arose thanks to the new inherency of the fifth Stopinder of the sacred Heptaparaparshinokh and which is the very smallest similarity to the Whole, was called 'Microcosmos,' and, finally, those formations of the 'Microcosmos' and which also became concentrated on the planets, this time thanks to the second-order cosmic law called 'mutual attraction of the similar,' were named 'Tetartocosmoses.'

"And all those cosmoses, which together compose our present World, began to be called the 'Megalocosmos.'

"And then also our cherubim gave names, also existing until now, to the emanations and radiations issuing from all these cosmoses of different scales, by means of which the process of the most great cosmic Trogoautoegocrat proceeds.

(1) The emanation of the Most Most Holy Sun Absolute Itself they called, as I have already told you, 'Theomertmalogos' or 'Word-God.'
(2) The radiation of each separate Second-order-Sun, 'Mentekithzoin.'
(3) The radiation of each planet separately they called 'Dynamoumzoin.'
(4) That given off from the Microcosmoses they called 'Photoinzoin.'
(5) The radiations issuing from the 'Tetartocosmoses' they called 'Hanbledzoin.'

(6) The radiations of all the planets together of any solar system they called 'Astroluolucizoin.'

(7) The common radiations of all the 'Newly-arisen-second-order-Suns taken together they called 'Polorotheoparl.'

"And all the results issuing from all the cosmic sources, great and small, taken together, were also then named by them the 'common-cosmic Ansanbaluiazar.'

"It is interesting to remark that concerning this 'common-cosmic Ansanbaluiazar,' present-day objective science has also the formula: 'Everything issuing from everything and again entering into everything.'

"Independent names were then given also to all the, as they are called, 'temporarily independent crystallizations' arising in each of the innumerable cosmoses by the evolutionary and involutionary processes of these fundamental sacred laws.

"I shall not enumerate the names of the large number of these independent 'centers of gravity' which become crystallized in all separate cosmoses, but shall indicate only the names of those definite 'center-of-gravity active elements' which become crystallized in each separate cosmos, and which have a direct relation with my following elucidations and, namely, those which are crystallized in the presences of Tetartocosmoses and have such a 'temporarily independent center of gravity.'

"In Tetartocosmoses the following names were given to these independent arisings:

(1) Protoëhary
(2) Defteroëhary
(3) Tritoëhary
(4) Tetartoëhary
(5) Piandjoëhary
(6) Exioëhary
(7) Resulzarion

"And now, my boy, after everything that I have elucidated to you we can return to the question why and how 'higher-being-bodies' or, as your favorites name them, souls, began to arise in our Universe, and why our UNI-BEING COMMON FATHER turned HIS Divine attention particularly to just these cosmic arisings.

"The point is that when the 'common-cosmic-harmonious-equilibrium' had become regularized and established in all those cosmoses of different scales, then in each of these Tetartocosmoses, i.e., in each separate 'relatively-independent-formation-of-the-aggregation-of-microcosmoses' which had its arising on the surface of the planets—the surrounding conditions on the surface of which accidentally began to correspond to certain data present in these cosmoses, owing to which they could exist for a certain period of time without what is called 'Seccruano,' i.e., without constant 'individual tension'—the possibility appeared of independent automatic moving from one place to another on the surface of the given planets.

"And thereupon, when our COMMON FATHER ENDLESSNESS ascertained this automatic moving of theirs, there then arose for the first time in HIM the Divine Idea of making use of it as a help for HIMSELF in the administration of the enlarging World.

"From that time on HE began to actualize everything further for these cosmoses in such a direction that the inevitable what is called, 'Okrualno'—i.e., the periodic repetition in them of the completing process of the sacred Heptaparaparshinokh—might be accomplished in such a way that, under conditions of a certain kind of change in the functioning of the common presences of some of these Tetartocosmoses, there might be transformed and crystallized, besides the crystallizations which had to be transformed for the purpose of the new common-cosmic exchange of substances, also those active elements from which new independent formations might be coated in them themselves with the inherent possibility of acquiring 'individual Reason.'

"That this idea first arose just then in our ENDLESSNESS, we can also see from the words of that sacred canticle with which at the present time, at all divine solemnities, our cherubim and seraphim extol the marvelous works of our CREATOR.

"Before continuing to relate further how this was actualized, it is necessary to tell you that the functioning of the mentioned common-cosmic Iraniranumange is harmonized in such a way that all the results obtained from transformations in different cosmoses localize themselves together according to what is called 'qualitativeness of vibrations,' and these localizations penetrate everywhere throughout the Universe and take a corresponding part in planetary as well as in surplanetary formations, and generally have as the temporary place of their free concentration the what are called atmospheres, with which all the planets of our Megalocosmos are surrounded and through which connection is established for the common-cosmic Iraniranumange.

"And so, the further results of this Divine attention in respect of the mentioned Tetartocosmoses consisted in this, that during their serving as apparatuses for the most great cosmic Trogoautoegocrat, the possibility was obtained in them that from among the cosmic substances transformed through them, both for the needs of the Most Most Great common-cosmic Sacred Trogoautoegocrat, as well as for the supply of substances expended by them for the process of their own existence, and composed exclusively of cosmic crystallizations which are derived from the transformations of that planet itself on which the given Tetartocosmoses arose, such results began to be obtained in their common presences under the mentioned conditions as proceed from cosmic sources of a higher order and, consequently, composed of what are called vibrations of 'greater vivifyingness.'

"Now from such cosmic results, exactly similar forms began to be coated in their common presences, at first from the cosmic substances Mentekithzoin, i.e., from the substances transformed by the sun and by other planets of that solar system within the limits of which the given Tetartocosmoses had the place of their arising, and which cosmic substances reach every planet through the radiations of the said cosmic concentrations.

"In this way, the common presences of certain Tetartocosmoses began beforehand to be composed of two different independent formations arisen from two entirely different cosmic sources, and these began to have a joint existence, as if one were placed within the other.

"And so, my boy, when similar coatings of previously coated Tetartocosmoses were completed and began to function correspondingly, then from that time on they ceased calling them Tetartocosmoses and began to call them 'beings,' which then meant 'two-natured,' and these same second coatings alone began to be called 'bodies-Kesdjan.'

"Now when in this new part of these 'two-natured-formations' everything corresponding was acquired, and when all that functioning which it is proper to such cosmic arisings to have was finally established, then these same new formations in their turn on exactly the same basis as in the first case and also under the conditions of a certain kind of change of functioning, began to absorb and assimilate into themselves such cosmic substances as had their arising immediately from the Most Most Holy Theomertmalogos, and similarities of a third kind began to be coated in them which are the 'higher sacred-parts' of beings and which we now call 'higher being-bodies.'

"Further, when their 'higher being-bodies' were finally coated and all the corresponding functions had been acquired in them, and chiefly when it became possible for the data for engendering the sacred function, named 'objective Reason,' to become crystallized in them, which data can become crystallized exclusively only in the presences of those cosmic arisings, and when what is called 'Rascooarno' occurred to these 'Tetartocosmoses' or 'beings,' i.e., the separation of these diverse-natured 'three-in-one' formations from each other, only then did this 'higher-being-part' receive the possibility of uniting itself with the Cause-of-Causes of everything now existing, i.e., with our Most Most Holy Sun Absolute, and began to fulfill the purpose on which our ALL-EMBRACING ENDLESSNESS had placed HIS hope.

"Now it is necessary to explain to you in more detail in what successiveness this first sacred Rascooarno then occurred to these first Tetartocosmoses and how it occurs also now, to the as they are called 'three-brained beings.'

"At first on the planet itself the 'second-being-body,' i.e., the body-Kesdjan, together with the 'third-being-body' separate themselves from the 'fundamental-planetary-body' and, leaving this planetary body on the planet, rise both together to that sphere where those cosmic substances—from the localizations of which the body-Kesdjan of a being arises—have their place of concentration.

"And only there, at the end of a certain time, does the principal and final sacred Rascooarno occur to this two-natured arising, after which such a 'higher being-part' indeed becomes an independent individual with its own individual Reason. Previously—i.e., before the Choot-God-Litanical period—this sacred cosmic actualization was, only after this second process of the sacred Rascooarno, either thought worthy of uniting with the presence of our Most Most Holy Sun Absolute or went into other cosmic concentrations where such independent holy Individuals were needed.

"And if at the moment of the approach of the final process of the sacred Rascooarno these cosmic arisings had not yet attained to the required gradation of Reason of the sacred scale of Reason, then this higher being-part had to exist in the said sphere until it had perfected its Reason to the required degree.

"It is impossible not to take notice here of that objective terror which occurs to the already risen higher-being-parts, who, owing to all results in new cosmic processes unforeseen from Above, have not yet perfected themselves up to the necessary gradations of Reason.

"The point is, that according to various second-grade cosmic laws, the 'being-body-Kesdjan' cannot exist long in this sphere, and at the end of a certain time this second being-part must decompose, irrespective of whether the higher being-part existing within it had by that time attained the requisite degree of Reason; and in view of the fact that as long as this higher being-part does not perfect its Reason to the requisite degree, it must always be dependent upon some Kesdjanian arising or other, therefore immediately after the second sacred Rascooarno every such still unperfected higher being-body gets into a state called 'Techgekdnel' or 'searching-for-some-other-similar-two-natured-arising-corresponding-to-itself' so that when the higher part of this other two-natured arising perfects itself to the required degree of Reason and the final process of the sacred Rascooarno occurs to it, and the speedy disintegration of its Kesdjan body is not yet clearly sensed, this higher being-body might instantly enter this other body Kesdjan and continue to exist in it for its further perfection, which perfection must sooner or later be inevitably accomplished by every arisen higher being-body.

"And that is why, in that sphere to where the higher being-part goes after the first sacred Rascooarno, that process proceeds called 'Okipkhalevnian-exchange-of-the external-part-of-the-soul' or 'exchange-of-the-former-being-body-Kesdjan.'

"Here, you might as well be told that your favorites also have, as it were, a similar representation about the 'Okipkhalevnian exchange' and they have even invented a very clever name for it, namely, 'metempsychosis' or 'reincarnation'; and that branch of their famous science which in recent centuries has been created around this question also gradually became, and at the present already is, one of those minor maleficent factors, the totality of which is gradually making their Reason, already strange enough without this, always more and more, as our dear Mullah Nassr Eddin would say: 'Shooroomooroomnian.'

"According to the fantastic branch of this theory of their 'science,' now called spiritualism, they suppose among other things that each of them already has a higher being-part or, as they call it, a soul, and that a transmigration must be occurring the whole time to this soul, i.e., something of the kind of this same 'Okipkhalevnian exchange' of which I have just spoken.

"Of course, if these unfortunates would only take into consideration that according to the second-grade cosmic law called 'Tenikdoa' or 'law of gravity,' this same being-part—if in rare cases it does happen that it arises in them—instantly rises after the first Rascooarno of the being, or, as they express it, after the death of the being, from the surface of their planet; and if they understood that the explanations and proofs, given by this branch of their 'science,' of all sorts of phenomena which proceed as it were among them there thanks to those fantastic souls of theirs, were only the fruits of their idle fancy—then they would already realize that everything else proved by this science of theirs is also nothing else but Mullah Nassr Eddin's 'twaddle.'

"Now as regards the first two lower being-bodies, namely the planetary-body and the body-Kesdjan, then, after the first sacred Rascooarno of a being, his planetary body, being formed of Microcosmoses or of crystallizations transformed on that planet itself, gradually decomposes and disintegrates there on that same planet, according to a certain second-grade cosmic law called 'Again-Tarnotoltoor,' into its own primordial substances from which it obtained its arising.

"As regards the second-being-body, namely, the body-Kesdjan, this body, being formed of radiations of other concentrations of Tritocosmoses and of the Sun itself of the given solar system, and having entered after the second process of the sacred Rascooarno into the sphere just mentioned, also begins gradually to decompose, and the crystallizations of which it is composed go in various ways into the sphere of its own primordial arisings.

"But the higher being-body itself, being formed of crystallizations received directly from the sacred Theomertmalogos into the solar system within the limits of which the being arises and where his existence proceeds, can never decompose; and this 'higher part' must exist in the given solar system as long as it does not perfect itself to the required Reason, to just that Reason which makes similar cosmic formations what are called 'Irankipaekh,' i.e., such formations of the mentioned Most Most Sacred substances as can exist and be independent of Kesdjanian arisings and at the same time not be subject to what are called 'painful' influences from any external cosmic factors whatsoever.

"And so, my boy, as I have already told you, after these cosmic arisings had perfected their Reason to the necessary gradation of the sacred scale of Reason, they were in the beginning taken onto the Sun Absolute for the fulfillment of roles predestined for them by our CREATOR ENDLESSNESS.

"It is necessary to tell you that concerning the determination of the degrees of individuality, our cherubim and seraphim also then at the very beginning established that still now existing sacred 'Determinator-of-Reason' which is applied for the determination of the gradations of Reason or, more exactly, the 'totality-of-self-awareness' of all separate large and small cosmic concentrations, and by which not only are the gradations of their Reason measured, but there is also determined their, as it is called, 'degree-of-justification-of-the-sense-and-aim-of their-existence,' and also the further role of each separate Individual in relation to everything existing in our great Megalocosmos.

"This sacred determinator of 'pure Reason' is nothing else than a kind of measure, i.e., a line divided into equal parts; one end of this line is marked as the total absence of any Reason, i.e., absolute 'firm-calm,' and at the other end there is indicated absolute Reason, i.e., the Reason of our INCOMPARABLE CREATOR ENDLESSNESS.

"In this place I think it might as well be explained to you further about the various kinds of sources, present in the common presences of all three-brained beings for the manifestation of being-Reason.

"In every three-brained being in general, irrespective of the place of his arising and the form of his exterior coating, there can be crystallized data for three independent kinds of being-mentation, the totality of the engendered results of which expresses the gradation of his Reason.

"Data for these three kinds of being-Reason are crystallized in the presence of each three-brained being depending upon how much—by means of the 'being-Partkdolg-duty'—the corresponding higher-being-parts are coated and perfected in them, which should without fail compose their common presences as a whole.

"The first highest kind of being-Reason is the 'pure' or objective Reason which is proper only to the presence of a higher being-body or to the common presences of the bodies themselves of those three-brained beings in whom this higher part has already arisen and perfected itself, and then only when it is the, what is called, 'center-of-gravity-initiator-of-the-individual-functioning' of the whole presence of the being.

"The second being-Reason, which is named 'Okiarta-aitokhsa,' can be in the presences of those three-brained beings, in whom their second-being-body-Kesdjan' is already completely coated and functions independently.

"As regards the third kind of being-Reason, this is nothing else but only the action of the automatic functioning which proceeds in the common presences of all beings in general and also in the presences of all surplanetary definite formations, thanks to repeated shocks coming from outside, which evoke habitual reactions from the data crystallized in them corresponding to previous accidentally perceived impressions.

"Now, my boy, in my opinion, before going on to a more detailed explanation of how their higher-parts were then coated and perfected in the common presences of the first Tetartocosmoses, as well as in the common presences of those who were afterwards named 'beings,' it is necessary to give you more information about the fact that we, beings arisen on the planet Karatas, and also the beings arisen on your planet called Earth, are already no longer such 'Polormedekhtic' beings as were the first beings who were transformed directly from the Tetartocosmoses, that is to say, beings called Polormedekhtic or, as it is still now said, 'Monoenithits' but are beings called 'Keschapmartnian,' i.e., nearly half-beings, owing to which the completing process of the sacred Heptaparaparshinokh does not proceed at the present time through us or through your favorites, the three-brained beings of the planet Earth, exactly as it proceeded in them. And we are such Keschapmartnian beings because the last fundamental Stopinder of the sacred Heptaparaparshinokh, which at the present time almost all the beings of the Megalocosmos call the sacred 'Ashagiprotoëhary,' is not in the centers of those planets upon which we arise—as it occurs in general in the majority of the planets of our great Megalocosmos—but is in the centers of their satellites, which for our planet Karatas is the little planet of our solar system which we call 'Prnokhpaïoch,' and for the planet Earth, its former fragments now called the Moon and Anulios.

"Thanks to this, the completing process of the Sacred Heptaparaparshinokh for the continuation of the species, for instance, proceeds not through one being, as it proceeded with the Tetartocosmoses, but through two beings of different sexes, called by us 'Actavus' and 'Passavus,' and on the planet Earth, 'man' and 'woman.'

"I might say here, that there even exists in our Great Megalocosmos a planet on which this sacred law Heptaparaparshinokh carries out its completing process for the continuation of the species of the three-brained beings, through three independent individuals. You might as well be acquainted somewhat in detail with this uncommon planet.

"This planet is called Modiktheo and belongs to the system of the 'Protocosmos.'

"Beings arising on this planet are three-brained, like all other three-brained beings arising on all the planets of our Great Megalocosmos, and in their exterior appearance are almost similar to us, and at the same time are—and are also so considered by all others—the most ideal and perfect of all the innumerable various-formed exterior coatings of three-brained beings in all our Great Universe; and all our now existing angels, archangels, and most of the Sacred Individuals nearest to our COMMON FATHER ENDLESSNESS arise just upon this marvelous planet.

"The transformation through them of the cosmic substances required for the common-cosmic Trogoautoegocratic process, according to the sacred law of Heptaparaparshinokh, proceeds on these same principles on which it proceeds through our common presences and also through the presences of your favorites, the three-brained beings breeding on the planet Earth. For the continuation of their species alone does this sacred law effect its completing process through three kinds of beings, wherefore such three-brained beings are called 'Triakrkomnian'; separately, however, just as among us beings of different sexes are called Actavus and Passavus or are called on your planet man and woman, so there on the planet Modiktheo they call the beings of the different sexes 'Martna,' 'Spirna,' and 'Okina,' and although externally they are all alike, yet in their inner construction they are very different from each other.

"The process of the continuation of their species proceeds among them in the following manner:

"All three beings of different sexes simultaneously receive the 'sacred Elmooarno,' or as your favorites say 'conception,' through a special action, and for a certain period they exist with this sacred Elmooarno or 'conception' apart from one another, entirely independently, but each of them exists with very definite intentional perceptions and conscious manifestations.

"And later, when the time approaches for the manifestation of the results of these conceptions, or when, as your favorites say, the time of birth approaches, there becomes evident in all these three uncommon beings, as it is called, an 'Aklonoatistitchian' longing for each other, or as your favorites would say, there appears in them a 'physico-organic-attraction.' And the nearer the time of this being-manifestation or birth approaches, the more they press close to each other and ultimately almost grow onto each other; and thereupon at one and the same time, they actualize in a certain way these conceptions of theirs.

"And so, during their actualization of their conceptions, all these three conceptions merge one with another, and in this way there appears in our Megalocosmos a new three-brained being of such an uncommon construction.

"And three-centered beings of this kind are ideal in our Megalocosmos, because at their very arising they already have all the being-bodies.

"And they have all three being-bodies because the producers of such a being, namely, Martna, Spirna, and Okina, each separately conceives the arising of one of the three being-bodies, and owing to their special corresponding being-existences they aid the Sacred Heptaparaparshinokh to form the given being-body in themselves to perfection and afterwards, at the moment of appearance, merge it with the other bodies into one.

"Note, by the way, my boy, that the beings arising on that incomparable and marvelous planet have no need, like the three-brained beings arising on other ordinary planets of our Megalocosmos, to coat their higher-being-bodies with the help of those factors which our CREATOR designed as means of perfecting—namely, those factors which we now call 'conscious labors' and 'intentional suffering.'

"Now, my boy, to continue the further, more detailed elucidation concerning the process of the transformation of cosmic substances through beings in general, we shall take as an elucidatory example the common presences of your favorites.

"Although the process of the transformation of substances

for the continuation of the species by means of us or by means of the common presences of your favorites does not proceed exactly as it proceeded in the first Tetartocosmoses who were transformed into beings, nevertheless we shall take them as an example, since the process itself of the transformation of cosmic substances for the needs of the Most Great common-cosmic Trogoautoegocrat proceeds through their common presences exactly as it proceeded through the first Tetartocosmoses; at the same time you will acquire information concerning several other small details of the strange particularities of their psyche, and also gain information relating to how they in general understand, and how they regard, their being-duty in the sense of serving the common-cosmic process of Iraniranumange, destroying for the beatification of their own belly every kind of law-conformable foreseeing actualization for the welfare of the whole Megalocosmos.

"As for those particularities of the transformation of cosmic substances, thanks to which the continuation of the species of different beings at the present time proceeds differently, for the present I will say only this, that the cause depends on the place of concentration of the sacred Ashagiprotoëhary, i.e., on the place of concentration of those cosmic substances, which are the results of the last Stopinder in the common-cosmic Ansanbaluiazar.

"Now, my boy, I shall begin by repeating: all your favorites, even the contemporary, are—like us and like all the other three-centered beings of our Megalocosmos—such apparatuses for the Great cosmic Trogoautoegocrat just as the Tetartocosmoses were, from whom arose the first ancestors of the now existing beings as well as the beings now existing everywhere. And through each of them the cosmic substances arising in all seven Stopinders of the Sacred Heptaparaparshinokh could be transformed, and all of them, again even the contemporary, besides serving as apparatuses for the Most Great cosmic Trogoautoegocrat, could have all possibilities for absorbing from those cosmic substances which are transformed through them what is corresponding for the coating and for the perfecting in them of both higher-being-bodies; because each three-brained being arisen on this planet of yours represents in himself also, in all respects, just like every three-brained being in all our Universe, an exact similarity of the whole Megalocosmos.

"The difference between each of them and our common great Megalocosmos is only in scale.

"Here you should know that your contemporary favorites very often use a notion taken by them from somewhere, I do not know whether instinctively, emotionally, or automatically, and expressed by them in the following words: 'We are the images of God.'

"These unfortunates do not even suspect that, of everything known to most of them concerning cosmic truths, this expression of theirs is the only true one of them all.

"And indeed, each of them is the image of God, not of that 'God' which they have in their bobtailed picturings, but of the real God, by which word we sometimes still call our common Megalocosmos.

"Each of them to the smallest detail is exactly similar, but of course in miniature, to the whole of our Megalocosmos, and in each of them there are all of those separate functionings, which in our common Megalocosmos actualize the cosmic harmonious Iraniranumange or 'exchange of substances,' maintaining the existence of everything existing in the Megalocosmos as one whole.

"This same expression of theirs—'We are the images of God'—can here serve us as a very good additional illustration in explanation of how far what is called 'perceptible logic,' or, as it is sometimes still said, 'Aimnophnian mentation,' is already distorted in them.

"Although this expression corresponding to the truth exists there among them, yet concerning the consideration of its exact sense, as in general concerning every short verbal formulation, they at best always express with their strange shortsighted mentation—even if they should wish with their whole common presence actively and sincerely to reveal their inner representation and essential understanding of this expression of theirs—something as follows:

"'Good . . . if we are "images of God" . . . that means . . . means . . . "God" is like us and has an appearance also like us . . . and that means, our "God" has the same moustache, beard, nose, as we have, and he dresses also as we do. He dresses as we do, doubtless because like us he is also very fond of modesty; it was not for nothing that he expelled Adam and Eve from Paradise, only because they lost their modesty and began to cover themselves with clothes.'

"In certain of the beings there, particularly of recent times, their being-Aimnophnian-mentation or perceptible logic has already become such that they can very clearly see this same 'God' of theirs in their picturings, almost with a comb sticking out of his left vest pocket, with which he sometimes combs his famous beard.

"Such a superpeculiar being-Aimnophnian-mentation about their 'God' proceeded in your favorites chiefly from the Hasnamussian manifestations of those 'learned' beings who, you remember, I have already told you, assembled in the city of Babylon and collectively began to invent various maleficent fictions concerning their 'God,' which were afterwards by chance widely spread everywhere on that ill-fated planet. And in view of the fact that that period coincided with the time when the three-brained beings there began to exist particularly 'Selzelnualno,' i.e., particularly 'passively,' in the sense of the being-efforts proper to three-centered beings, therefore these maleficent inventions were thoroughly absorbed and appropriated by the beings.

"And afterwards, in their transmission from generation to generation by inheritance, they gradually began to be crystallized into such monstrous 'logicnestarian-materials,' with the result that in the psyche of the contemporary three-brained beings there, there began to proceed such an already exceptionally distorted being-Aimnophnian-mentation.

"And the reason that they picture their 'God' to themselves just with a long beard was due to the fact that then, among the maleficent inventions of the Babylonian 'learned,' it was said among other things that that famous 'God' of theirs had, as it were, the appearance of a very old man, just with a heavy beard.

"But concerning the appearance of their 'God,' your favorites have gone still further. Namely, they picture this famous 'God' of theirs exactly as an 'Old Jew,' since in their bobtailed notions, all sacred personages originated from that race.

"At any rate, my little Hassein, each of your favorites, separately, is, in his whole presence, exactly similar in every respect to our Megalocosmos.

"I once told you that there is localized in the head of each one of them as well as in us a concentration of corresponding cosmic substances, all the functioning of which exactly corresponds to all those functions and purposes which our Most Most Holy Protocosmos has, and fulfills, for the whole of the Megalocosmos.

"This localization, which is concentrated in their head, they call the 'head-brain.' The separate, what are called 'Okaniaki' or 'protoplasts' of this localization in their head, or, as the terrestrial learned call them, the 'cells-of-the-head-brain,' actualize for the whole presence of each of them exactly such a purpose as is fulfilled at the present time by the 'higher-perfected-bodies' of three-brained beings from the whole of our Great Universe, who have already united themselves with the Most Most Holy Sun Absolute or Protocosmos.

"When these higher parts of three-brained beings, who are perfected to the corresponding gradation of objective Reason, get there, they fulfill precisely that function of the Okaniaki or 'cells-of-the-head-brain,' for which function, as I have already said, our UNI-BEING COMMON FATHER ENDLESSNESS condescended at the creation of the now existing World, to decide to use for the future those coatings who obtain independent Individuality in the Tetartocosmoses, as an aid for Himself in the administration of the enlarging world.

"Further, in each of them, in their what is called 'vertebral column,' another concentration was localized, called there the 'spinal marrow,' in which there are precisely those what are called denying sources, which actualize in their functionings in relation to the parts of the head-brain just such fulfillments as the 'second-order newly arisen Suns' of the Megalocosmos actualize in relation to the Most Most Holy Protocosmos.

"It must without fail be noticed that in former epochs there on your planet, your favorites knew something about the separate particular functionings of the parts of their spinal marrow and they even knew and adopted various 'mechanical means' for action upon corresponding parts of this spinal marrow of theirs, during those periods when some disharmony or other appeared in their, as they express it, 'psychic state'; but the information relating also to this kind of knowledge gradually 'evaporated' and although your contemporary favorites know that certain particular concentrations are in this spinal marrow of theirs, yet of course they have not the slightest notion for what function they were designed by Great Nature, and in most cases simply name them 'brain nodes' of their spinal marrow.

"Well, then, just these separate brain nodes of their spinal marrow are the sources of denial in relation to the separate shades of affirmation in their head-brain, precisely as the separate 'second-order-Suns' are the sources of the various shades of denial in relation to the various shades of affirmation of the Most Most Holy Protocosmos.

"And, finally, just as in the Megalocosmos, all the results obtained by the flow of the fundamental process of the Sacred Heptaparaparshinokh from the 'affirmation' of the Most Most Holy Protocosmos and from the various shades of 'denial' of the newly created 'Suns' began to serve thereafter as a 'reconciling principle' for everything newly arising and already existing, so in them also, there is a corresponding localization for the concentration of all results obtained from the affirmation of the head-brain and from all the shades of denial of the spinal marrow, which results afterwards serve as a regularizing or reconciling principle for the functionings of the whole common presence of each of them.

"Concerning the place of concentration of this localization which serves the common presences of terrestrial three-brained beings as a regularizing or reconciling principle, it must be noticed that in the beginning these three-brained beings of the planet Earth who have taken your fancy, also had this third concentration, similarly to us, in the form of an independent brain localized in the region of their what is called 'breast.'

"But from the time when the process of their ordinary being-existence began particularly sharply to change for the worse, then Nature there, by certain causes flowing from the common-cosmic Trogoautoegocratic process, was compelled, without destroying the functioning itself of this brain of theirs, to change the system of its localization.

"That is to say, she gradually dispersed the localization of this organ, which had had its concentration in one place in them, into small localizations over the whole of their common presence, but chiefly in the region of what is called the 'pit of the stomach.' The totality of these small localizations in this region they themselves at the present time call the solar plexus or the 'complex of the nodes of the sympathetic nervous system.'

"And in those nervous nodes scattered over the whole of the planetary body, there are accumulated at the present time all the results obtained from the affirming and denying manifestations of their head-brain and spinal marrow, and these results, having become fixed in these 'nervous nodes' scattered over the whole of their common presence, are later also such a neutralizing principle, in the further process of 'affirmation and denial' between the head-brain and spinal marrow, just as the totality of everything arising in the Megalocosmos is the neutralizing force in the process of the affirmation of the Protocosmos and the various shades of denials of all the newly arisen Suns.

"And so, the three-brained beings of the planet Earth are not only, as we also are, apparatuses for the transformation of the cosmic substances required for the Most Great Trogoautoegocrat with the qualities of all the three forces of the fundamental common-cosmic Triamazikamno, but also, themselves absorbing these substances for transformation from three different sources of independent arisings, have all the possibilities of assimilating besides the substances necessary for the maintenance of their own existence, also those substances which go for the coating and perfecting of their own higher-being-bodies.

"In this manner those three-sourced substances entering their common presences for transformation are, just as for us, a threefold kind of being-food.

"That is to say, those substances which, on the path of their returning evolutionary ascent from the sacred 'Ashagiprotoëhary'—i.e., from the last Stopinder of the fundamental Sacred Heptaparaparshinokh toward the Most Most Holy Protocosmos—were transmitted with the aid of their own planet itself into definite higher corresponding surplanetary formations, and enter into them for further transformation as their 'first being-food,' which is their ordinary 'food' and 'drink.'

"But those second-sourced substances which, being obtained from the transformations of their own sun and of all the other planets of their own solar system and which entered the atmosphere of their planet through the radiations of the latter, enter into them again, just as into us, also for further evolutionary transformation as the 'second being-food,' which is their, as they there say, 'air,' by which they breathe, and these substances in their air just serve for the coating and maintenance of the existence of their 'second being-bodies.'

"And, finally, the first-sourced substances which for them as well as for us, are a third kind of being-food, serve both for the coating and for the perfecting of the higher being-body itself.

"Well then, it was in relation to those sacred cosmic substances that those sorrowful results occurred among your unfortunate favorites which flowed and still continue to flow from all the abnormalities established by them themselves in the ordinary process of their being-existence.

"Although the substances also of this higher-being-food continue to enter into them also until now, yet they enter, particularly into the beings of the present time, already only spontaneously quite without the participation of their cognized intention, and only as much as is required for the transformations proceeding through them necessary for the purposes of the common-cosmic Trogoautoegocratic harmony and for the automatic continuation of their species demanded by Nature.

"When the abnormal conditions of ordinary being-existence were finally fixed there—in consequence of which there disappeared from their essence both the instinctive and the intentional striving for perfecting—there not only disappeared in them the need of conscious absorption of cosmic substances, but even also the very knowledge and understanding of the existence and significance of higher being-foods.

"At the present time there, your favorites already know only of one, the first being-food, and they know about that only because, in the first place, even without their wish, they could not help knowing about it; and secondly the process of its use there has already become for them also a vice and occupies an equal rightful place alongside other of their weaknesses, which were gradually crystallized in them as consequences of the properties of the, maleficent for them, organ Kundabuffer.

"Up to this time not one of them has yet even become aware that in this first being-food there are substances necessary almost exclusively only for the maintenance of the existence of their coarse planetary body alone—which is a denying-source—and that this first being-food can give almost nothing for the other higher parts of their presence.

"As for those higher cosmic substances of which a certain quantity must, as I have already said, necessarily be transformed through them for the continuation of their species and for the maintenance of the general harmony of the common-cosmic Ansanbaluiazar, your favorites at the present time have no need at all to trouble their inner God self-calming about it, since this is already done in them, as I have already said, quite spontaneously, without the participation of their own cognized intention.

"It is interesting, however, to notice that in the beginning, namely, soon after the destruction of the functioning of the organ Kundabuffer in the three-brained beings breeding on this planet of yours, they also became aware of these two higher being-foods, and then began to use them with cognized intention, and certain beings of the continent Atlantis of its latest period even began to consider these same processes of the absorption of these higher being-foods as the chief aim of their existence.

"The beings of the continent Atlantis then called the second being-food 'Amarloos,' which meant 'help-for-the-moon,' and they called the third being-food the 'sacred Amarhoodan,' and this last word then signified for them 'help-for-God.'

"Concerning the absence in the psyche of your favorites of a cognized need of absorbing these higher sacred cosmic substances, I wish also to draw your attention to one very important for them sorrowful consequence flowing from this.

"And, namely, in view of the fact that in them, together with the cessation of the intentional absorption of these definite cosmic substances necessary for the arising and existence of higher being-parts, there disappeared from their common presences not only the striving itself for perfection but also the possibility of what is called 'intentional contemplativeness,' which is just the principal factor for the assimilation of those sacred cosmic substances, then from that time on, in order to guarantee that the required quantity of those substances might enter into them and be assimilated, Nature gradually had to adapt herself to arrange that for each of them, in the course of their whole process of existence, such 'unexpectednesses' should occur already by themselves as are not at all proper to occur to any three-brained being of our Great Megalocosmos.

"Unfortunately Nature there was compelled to adapt herself to this abnormality, so that, owing to these unexpectednesses, certain intense being-experiencings and active deliberations might proceed in them automatically, independently of them themselves and so that, owing to these 'active deliberations,' the required transformation and assimilation of these necessary sacred particles of the higher being-foods might automatically proceed in them.

"Now, my boy, as for the processes themselves of the transformation in the evolutionary and involutionary movements of all these cosmic substances by means of just such apparatuses of the Most Great common-cosmic Trogoautoegocrat—as all your favorites also are—then those transformations proceed in them as well as in us and in general in all large and small cosmoses of our common Megalocosmos, strictly according to those two same chief fundamental cosmic laws, namely, according to the Sacred Heptaparaparshinokh and the Sacred Triamazikamno.

"Before talking to you about the manner in which the cosmic substances entering into beings as their first being-food are transformed in them for the purposes of the common-cosmic Trogoautoegocratic process, and which enter into three-brained beings—if they have a certain kind of attitude towards this process—also for the coating and the perfecting of their own higher parts, it is necessary for you to bear in mind, for a clear representation of these processes, that in our Megalocosmos—from results which have already flowed from every kind of Trogoautoegocratic process—there are many hundreds of independent 'active elements' with various specific subjective properties which take part in new formations.

"These many hundreds of 'active elements' with various properties wherever they might be, proceeding from the seven Stopinders of the fundamental common-cosmic Sacred Heptaparaparshinokh, are—depending upon the Stopinder from which they received their primordial arising—divided and localized, according to what is called the 'affinity of vibrations,' into seven what are called 'Okhtapanatsakhnian classes.' And all without exception of both the large and small already definite concentrations in all our Megalocosmos are formed from these active elements belonging to seven independent classes, and, as I have already told you, they have their own subjective properties.

"And these subjective properties of theirs and likewise their what are called 'proportions of vivifyingness' are actualized firstly, according to what form of functioning of the fifth Stopinder of the Sacred Heptaparaparshinokh was flowing during their arising, and secondly, whether the given active elements arise owing to the conscious intention on the part of some independent individual, or whether they arose automatically, merely owing to the second-grade law called 'Attraction-and-Fusion-of-Similarities.'

"Well then, these same many hundreds of definite active elements belonging to seven different 'Okhtapanatsakhnian-classes' and having seven different subjective properties—among which the properties of 'vivifyingness' and 'decomposition' have supreme significance—compose in their totality the fundamental common-cosmic Ansanbaluiazar, by which the Most Great cosmic Trogoautoegocrat is actualized—the true Savior from the lawconformable action of the merciless Heropass.

"It is necessary to tell you also that the first appearance of every kind of concentration from the Etherokrilno which is found everywhere in the Universe owing to the second-grade cosmic law, the Attraction-and-Fusion-of-Similarities, proceeds in the following manner:

"If particles of Etherokrilno which are already found

in the different spheres of all seven Stopinders of the fundamental 'common-cosmic Ansanbaluiazar' collide for some reason or another, they begin the arising of all kinds of 'crystallizations' which do not yet have any subjective properties, and furthermore if these particles of Etherokrilno fall for some reason or other into conditions where a process of 'Harnelmiatznel' proceeds, they fuse into one, and owing to the what are called 'complex-vibrations' acquired in them, are transformed into active elements already with definite specific properties.

"And if thereafter these already definite active elements with their own specific-subjective properties enter into other processes of 'Harnelmiatznel' which have other conditions, they again fuse with each other according to the same law of 'affinity of vibrations,' and thus acquiring other properties, are transformed into active elements of another 'Okhtapanatsakhnian class,' and so on and so forth.

"And that is why there are in our Megalocosmos so many independent active elements with their different specific subjective properties.

"And if now, my boy, you satisfactorily grasp the succession of the process of transformation of cosmic substances by means of beings-apparatuses, into which these cosmic substances enter as first being-food, then at the same time you will approximately understand everything concerning the chief particularity of the sacred law of Heptaparaparshinokh as well as the processes of evolution and involution of the other higher being-foods.

"When these evolving active elements, in their returning ascent from the last Stopinder of the fundamental common-cosmic Sacred Heptaparaparshinokh, enter into the common presences of being-apparatuses as their first being-food, they begin already from the mouth itself—with the help of the processes of the second-grade law

Harnelmiatznel, that is, owing to mixture and fusion according to the 'affinity of vibrations,' with the active elements which have already evolved in the presences of the beings and have acquired vibrations corresponding to the subsequent Stopinders of the being-Heptaparaparshinokh—to be gradually changed, and are transmuted this time in the stomach of the beings into definite active elements named 'being-Protoëhary,' which correspond in their vibrations to the ascending fourth Stopinder of the fundamental common-cosmic Heptaparaparshinokh.

"From there, this totality which has the 'gravity-center vibration' of being-Protoëhary, passing—thanks again only to the process Harnelmiatznel—over the whole of what is called the 'intestinal tract' and gradually evolving, completedly acquires in consequence corresponding vibrations, and is this time completely transmuted in what is called the 'duodenum' into 'being-Defteroëhary.'

"Further, a part of these definite substances of 'being-Defteroëhary' go to serve the planetary body itself and also the local Harnelmiatznel in respect of the newly entering food, but the other part, also by means of a process of Harnelmiatznel of local character, continues its independent evolution and is ultimately transmuted in beings into the still higher definite substances which are called, this time, 'being-Tritoëhary.'

"And this totality of cosmic substances, temporarily crystallized in the common presences of 'beings-apparatuses which correspond in their vibrations to 'being-Tritoëhary,' have as the gravity-center place of their concentration in the presences of beings the, what is called, 'liver.'

"It is just in this place of the being-Ansanbaluiazar that the lower 'Mdnel-In' of the Sacred Heptaparaparshinokh is located, called the 'mechano-coinciding-Mdnel-In,' and therefore the substances of the being-Tritoëhary cannot, only owing to the process 'Harnelmiatznel,' independently evolve further.

"Well then, owing to that change in the general functioning of the primordial common-cosmic sacred law of Heptaparaparshinokh, this totality of substances named 'being-Tritoëhary' can in the given case evolve further from this state only with the help of forces coming from outside.

"That is why in this case, if this totality of substances of 'being-Protoëhary' does not receive foreign help from outside for its further evolution in the common presences of the beings, then both this totality and all the definite centers of gravity of the being-Ansanbaluiazar crystallized up to it always involve back again into those definite cosmic crystallizations from which they began their evolution.

"For this help coming from outside, Great Nature in the given case most wisely adapted the inner organization of beings in such a manner that the substances which had to enter into the common presences of beings for the coating and feeding of their second being-bodies Kesdjan, namely, that totality of cosmic substances which your favorites call air, might at the same time serve as just such a help coming from outside for the evolution of the substances of the first being-food.

"The active elements which compose this second being-food or air, and which enter into the presences of beings also for evolution through this second being-food, beginning from the nose of beings, gradually evolve with the co-operation of various processes of Harnelmiatznel of local character, and are also transmuted this time in the what are called 'lungs' of beings into Protoëhary, but into Protoëhary called 'Astralnomonian-Protoëhary.'

"And then the substances of this 'Astralnomonian-Protoëhary,' entering into the presences of beings for their own evolution and having still in themselves, according to the Sacred Heptaparaparshinokh, all the possibilities of evolving from their centers of gravity by the process of Harnelmiatznel alone, mix with the totality of substances of the first being-food which have already evolved up to the third Stopinder of the Sacred being-Heptaparaparshinokh, and further evolve together, and thus help these substances of the first being-food to pass through the lower 'mechano-coinciding-Mdnel-In' and to be transmuted into other definite substances, into 'being-Tetartoëhary,' and the 'Astralnomonian-Protoëhary' itself is transmuted into the substances named 'Astralnomonian-Defteroëhary.'

"At this point in my explanations, you can have one more clarifying example for a full understanding of the difference between Autoegocrat and Trogoautoegocrat, that is, of the difference between the former maintaining system of the existence of the Sun Absolute when that system was Autoegocratic, and the other system now called Trogoautoegocratic which it became after the creation of the Megalocosmos.

"If the transformation of substances through 'beings-apparatuses' proceeded according to the law of the Sacred Heptaparaparshinokh when certain of its Stopinders were not yet changed, that is, as it still functioned before the creation of our now existing Megalocosmos, then the cosmic substances composing the first being-food, entering into such 'apparatuses-cosmoses' for the local process of evolution, would accomplish their ascent up to their completing transmutation into other higher definite active elements without any obstacle and without any help coming from outside—merely by the process of Harnelmiatznel alone, but now since the independent functioning of this primordial sacred law has been changed into a dependent functioning, the evolution or involution in its changed Stopinders must always be dependent upon external 'extraneously caused' manifestations.

"In the given case, this extraneously caused help for

the complete transmutation of cosmic crystallizations through beings into higher crystallizations is the second being-food, which has entirely different causes of its arising and which must actualize entirely different cosmic results.

"I will some time later explain to you in detail how the transformation of the substances of the second and third being-foods proceeds in beings, but meanwhile note only that these higher cosmic substances in beings are transformed according to exactly the same principles as the substances of the first being-food.

"Now we shall continue to investigate just how, according to the Sacred Heptaparaparshinokh, the further completing process of the transformation of the substances of their first being-food proceeds in the presences of 'beings-apparatuses.'

"And so . . . the ordinary first being-food is thus gradually transmuted in beings into definite substances called 'being-Tetartoëhary,' which have in beings, just as of course in your favorites, as the central place of their concentration both of what are called the 'hemispheres of their head-brain.'

"Further, a part of this being-Tetartoëhary from both hemispheres of their head-brain goes unchanged to serve the planetary body of the given being, but the other part having in itself all the possibilities for independent evolution, continues to evolve without any help coming from outside; and mixing again by means of the process Harnelmiatznel with previously formed higher substances already present in the beings, it is gradually transmuted into still higher definite being-active-elements called 'Piandjoëhary.'

"And these substances have as the central place of their concentration in beings the, what is called, 'Sianoorinam' or, as your favorites call this part of their planetary body, the 'cerebellum,' which in beings is also located in the head.

"Just these same substances in beings, according to the fifth deflection of the Sacred Heptaparaparshinokh, have the free possibility of giving, in the manifestations of the common presences of three-brained beings, results not similar but 'opposite to each other.'

"That is why, in respect of these being-substances, the beings themselves must always be very, very much on their guard in order to avoid undesirable consequences for their entire whole.

"From the cerebellum of beings a part of these definite substances also goes to serve the planetary body itself, but the other part, passing in a particular way through the 'nerve nodes' of the spine and the breast, is concentrated in the beings of the male sex, in what are called 'testicles' and in the beings of the female sex in what most of your favorites call 'ovaries,' which are the place of concentration in the common presences of beings of the 'being-Exioëhary,' which is for the beings themselves their most sacred possession. You should know that this particular way mentioned is called 'Trnlva.'

"Only after this are the cosmic substances which enter beings-apparatuses for the purpose of evolution, that is, for the possibility of passing the lower Mdnel-In of the fundamental common-cosmic 'exchange of substances,' transformed into that definite totality of cosmic substances—which transformation is the lot of all beings in general and also of your contemporary three-brained beings who breed on the planet Earth in particular, for the automatic justification of the sense and aim of their existence, and this totality of cosmic substances is everywhere called 'Exioëhary.'

"And so, my boy, this totality of their first being-food which results from the evolution in these beings-apparatuses, corresponds with its vibrations to the last Stopinder of the being-Heptaparaparshinokh, and according to the particularity of this Stopinder, it enters the 'higher-intentionally-actualizing-Mdnel-In' of the law of Heptaparaparshinokh; and in order to transform completedly into new higher substances and in order to acquire vibrations corresponding to the vibrations of the next higher vivifyingness, namely, corresponding to the fifth Stopinder of the fundamental process of the common-cosmic Sacred Heptaparaparshinokh, it inevitably requires just that foreign help which is actualized only in the presences of the three-brained beings exclusively owing to those factors mentioned by me more than once and which are manifested in the 'being-Partkdolg-duty,' that is, owing to just those factors which our COMMON FATHER CREATOR ENDLESSNESS consented to foreordain to be the means by which certain of the Tetartocosmoses—as a final result of their serving the purposes of the common-cosmic Iraniranumange—might become helpers in the ruling of the enlarged World, and which factors also until now serve as the sole possible means for the assimilation of the cosmic substances required for the coating and perfecting of the higher being-bodies and which we at the present time call 'conscious labors' and 'intentional suffering.'

"Here it might as well be noticed and emphasized that of all the definite cosmic substances which are formed and in consequence are always present in the common presences of your favorites, they well know only this 'being-Exioëhary' which they call 'sperm,' and even masterfully perform with it various kinds of their 'manipulations.'

"And by this name 'sperm' they give importance to the totality of the definite substances formed only in the presences of the beings of the 'male sex' and ignore namelessly and with scorn a similar totality of the 'sum-of-the-substances' which arise in beings of the 'female sex.'

"Just this same totality of substances which inevitably always arises as the final sum in the presences of all beings from their first being-food, became one of the chief causes of the fact that later, when they ceased to actualize 'being-Partkdolg-duty' in their common presences, and this totality of cosmic substances in consequence did not receive, according to the Sacred Heptaparaparshinokh, the required foreign help for their completing evolution into other definite higher active elements, it began to involve back in them towards those crystallizations from which their evolution began. And such involutionary processes in them began from this time to serve their common presences as factors which began to engender in their common presences the data for the arising of their innumerable what they call 'illnesses,' and thus on the one hand began to 'de-perfect' their previously established essence-individuality, and on the other hand to shorten the general duration of their existence.

"And your favorites, the beings of the planet Earth, particularly the beings of the present time, do not use these same substances of being-Exioëhary at all consciously, neither for self-perfecting nor for conscious reproduction outside of themselves of new beings similar to themselves.

"And these sacred cosmic substances, formed in them in such a manner, serve either only for the purposes of the Most Great cosmic Trogoautoegocrat entirely without the participation of their own being-consciousness and individual desire, or for the involuntary conception of a new being similar to themselves, who is without their cognized wish a distressing result for them from the mixing of these sacred substances of the two opposite sexes, who actualize in themselves two opposite forces of the Sacred Triamazikamno, during the satisfaction by them of that function of theirs which has become, thanks to the inheritance from the ancient Romans, the chief vice of contemporary three-brained beings.

"I must sadly remark that the mentioned depraved inherency already completely fixed in their common presences is for them, particularly for your contemporary favorites, already an 'automatically acting' means of destroying to their very root even those impulses which sometimes arise in them from manifestations worthy of three-brained beings and which evoke in them the what is called 'thirst-for-Being.'

"I repeat, my boy, besides the fact that these favorites of yours, particularly the contemporary, ceased to use these sacred substances inevitably formed in them, consciously for the coating and perfection of their 'higher-parts' as well as for the fulfillment of their being-duty foreseen by Nature herself, which consists in the continuation of their species, yet even when this latter does accidentally proceed, they already accept it and regard it as a very great misfortune for themselves, chiefly because the consequences which must proceed from it must for a certain time hinder the free gratification of the multitudinous and multiform vices fixed in their essence.

"And in consequence of this, they—particularly the contemporary beings—strive in these cases by every means to prevent with their whole presence the actualization of such an accidental and on their part unintentional sacred manifestation foreseen by Great Nature.

"In the last centuries there, very many among them, in whom data for all kinds of Hasnamussian properties were more strongly crystallized, even became specialists in aiding the destruction of such accidentally actualized sacred being-fulfillments and these specialists they call there 'makers of angels.'

"Whereas, this same 'being-act,' which for your favorites has been turned into their chief vice, constitutes and is considered everywhere in our Great Universe for beings of all kinds of natures, as the most sacred of all sacred Divine sacraments.

"Even many two-brained and one-brained beings of this same planet, such as for instance the beings called there 'hyenas,' 'cats,' 'wolves,' 'lions,' 'tigers,' 'wild dogs,' 'bagooshis,' 'frogs,' and many others who have not in their what are called 'law-conformable-presences' any data at all which give the possibility of 'comparative logic,' at the present time still continue, of course only instinctively, to sense this act as sacred, and manifest it only during those periods which were foredesigned by Great Nature for this sacred sacrament, namely, chiefly at the period of the beginning of a new completing movement of that cosmic concentration on which they have their place of arising and existence, that is, during the period which three-brained beings everywhere call the 'Dionosks-of-the-sacred-sacraments-of-Serooazar,' and which on the planet which has interested you are called 'spring days.'

"Perhaps, my boy, you do not yet know anything about the 'sacred-sacraments-of-the-great-Serooazar'?" Beelzebub asked his grandson.

To this question of Beelzebub's his grandson Hassein replied thus:

"No, dear Grandfather, the details of this I do not yet know; I only know that these Dionosks are regarded among us on the planet Karatas as great holy days and are called 'Helping-God-Dionosks,' and I know that for these great holy days, the Dionosks, all our beings, 'Actavus' as well as 'Passavus,' prepare themselves almost from the end of the previous holy day, and that one 'Loonias' before the beginning of these sacred sacraments, both old and young among us cease to introduce the first being-food into themselves and, by various sacred ceremonies, mentally give thanks to our COMMON CREATOR for their existence.

"I also know that the last two of these solemn Dionosks

are considered and called among us the 'Dionosks-for-the-glorifying-of-the-first-producer-of-each-family.'

"And that is why, my dear Grandfather, every year during these Dionosks we all remembered and talked only of you, and each one of us strove with his whole Being to manifest the sincere wish that your destiny may constantly create for you those conditions of being-existence which might aid you quickly and easily to bring your Reason up to the required sacred gradation and that thereby you might the sooner finish your present 'ordinary-being-existence,' personally burdensome for you."

With these last solemnly pronounced words, Hassein ended his reply.

"Very well, my boy," said Beelzebub. "We will talk about the 'sacred-sacrament-of-the-Serooazar' when we return to our dear Karatas.

"There I will explain to you sometime in detail where and how the sacred sacrament of Serooazar proceeds with the substances being-Exioëhary for the continuation of one's species and on what occasions and in what way the mixing and subsequent results of the two kinds of Exioëhary are obtained; one kind is transformed for the affirming principle in those 'beings-apparatuses' which on our planet Karatas are the beings 'Actavus' and on your planet Earth the beings of the 'male sex'; and the other kind is transformed for the denying principle in those 'beings-apparatuses' which among us on the planet Karatas are the beings 'Passavus' and on the planet Earth the beings of the 'female sex.'

"Come now and let us talk about these 'higher-perfected-being-bodies,' that is about 'souls,' who came onto this holy planet Purgatory to which all my foregoing explanations have referred.

"And so . . . from the very beginning, when these higher being-parts arose in this way and were perfected in beings to the required sacred gradation of Objective Reason, that is to say, when in accordance with the lower Mdnel-In of the Sacred Heptaparaparshinokh, the body-Kesdjan was, thanks to the second being-food formed in beings, and in accordance with the higher Mdnel-In of the same sacred law, the third highest being-body was, thanks to the third being-food, coated and perfected; and when these completely perfected higher being-parts were divided from the lower being-parts, then they were deemed worthy to be immediately united with the Most Most Holy Prime-Source and began to fulfill their Divine foreordained purpose.

"This continued so right up to that time when that terrifying cosmic event occurred which, as I have already told you, is now called the 'Choot-God-Litanical' period.

"Until this common-cosmic misfortune, all the higher being-bodies which arose and were perfected in certain Tetartocosmoses and in their first generations were united immediately with the Most Most Holy Protocosmos itself, because their common presences had already actualized results fully corresponding to it.

"The point is, that before this terrifying cosmic event of which I am speaking, the sacred Theomertmalogos which issued from the Most Most Holy Sun Absolute was still in a pure state without the admixture of any extraneously caused arisings whatsoever with their own subjective properties, and when this sacred Theomertmalogos came into the spheres of those planets on which the sacred crystallizations arose and from the results of the transformations of which higher being-bodies were coated and perfected through beings-apparatuses, then these latter received their presences exactly as they had to, to correspond to the required conditions of existence in the sphere of the Most Most Holy Sun Absolute.

"But afterwards, when the mentioned common-cosmic

misfortune occurred, on account of which the sacred Theomertmalogos began to issue from the Most Most Holy Sun Absolute with the admixture of subjective properties of extraneously caused arisings, then from that time these sacred cosmic arisings ceased to have the possibility of corresponding to the required conditions of existence in the sphere of the Most Most Holy Prime-Source.

"And this admixture of extraneously caused arisings began to be obtained in the sacred Theomertmalogos owing to the following and I must add unforeseen causes.

"When each separate 'higher-perfected-being-body' becomes an independent Individual and acquires in itself its own law of Sacred Triamazikamno, it begins to emanate similarly to the Most Most Holy Sun Absolute but in miniature; and when many of these perfected independent Sacred Individuals had been assembled on the Most Most Holy Sun Absolute, then between the emanations of these Sacred Individuals and the atmosphere of the Most Most Holy Sun Absolute there was established what is called a 'Geneotriamazikamnian contact' and those results were obtained which brought on this terrifying misfortune for the 'higher-being-perfected-parts' of which I have already told you.

"Thereupon although the action of the results of this 'Geneotriamazikamnian contact' soon became harmonized with the already existing actions of our Most Most Holy Sun Absolute itself, nevertheless from that time the sacred Theomertmalogos began to issue changed, and the primary consequences of the results of this contact had time during a certain period to change the harmonious movement of many solar systems and to produce a disharmony in the inner functioning of certain of their planets.

"It was just then that there became separated from the solar system called Khlarfogo that famous planet which exists alone in space and has quite exceptional particularities and which is at the present time called Remorse-of-Conscience.

"This Geneotriamazikamnian contact occurred because, in the atmosphere itself of the Most Most Holy Sun Absolute, various-sourced unusual vibrations began, as I have already said, to issue from these higher being-bodies and to unite with the emanations of the Most Most Holy Sun Absolute, and together with them also to penetrate everywhere in the Megalocosmos and to reach even to those planets on which higher being-bodies were continuing to arise in beings; and these unusual vibrations began to be transformed and crystallized together with the sacred Theomertmalogos and to take part in the coating of the 'higher-parts' in the beings.

"And it was from this time on, that these sacred arisings began to have in their presences special properties which were obtained from this, that certain manifestations of other parts of the given being, in whom these sacred arisings were coated, began to enter and to be assimilated in the composition of the presences of these higher parts and to give also very unusual results which afterwards came to be called and are called until now 'sins-of-the-body-of-the-soul.'

"Just these same various results served as a cause for this, that these cosmic formations, even if they had in their perfecting reached to the required gradation of Objective Reason, yet they had ceased to correspond in their common presences to the conditions of existence in the sphere of the Most Most Holy Protocosmos, and from that time on they lost the possibility of being deemed worthy to unite themselves with it.

"Well, then, when this helpless position of these higher being-bodies who had become 'independent-cosmic Sacred Individuals' perfected in Reason, but who were not corresponding in their presences, first became apparent, our ALL-LOVING CREATOR, being infinitely just and merciful, quickly began to take all corresponding measures concerning such an unforeseen and sorrowful phenomenon.

"This grievous phenomenon of these Sacred Individuals put them indeed in a helpless position, because, although having no possibility on account of those mentioned 'sins' in their presences of uniting with the Bosom of the Prime-Source of the Whole, they at the same time, having attained that gradation of the sacred measure of Reason which brings them into subjection to the second-grade cosmic law named 'Tetetzender,' had lost the possibility of free existence on the surface of ordinary planets.

"Then among the various Divine measures undertaken, there followed HIS Decree, to choose the very best planet in the whole of our Great Megalocosmos, specially to arrange its surface, and to leave it for the free further existence of these higher being-bodies who were perfected in Reason, so that in this way they might receive all the possibilities for self-purification from the undesirable elements which were in their presences.

"So then, from that time on, this holy planet arose with the name of Purgatory, and its chief organization and government was undertaken at His own wish by Our All - Quarters - Maintainer, the Great Arch Cherub Helkgematios, that same Great Helkgematios who after the creation of the World first merited the Sacred Anklad, that is, first acquired that degree of Reason which alone it is in general possible for an independent Individual, whatever his nature, to attain, and which is third in degree after the Absolute Reason of our ENDLESSNESS.

"Although this Holy Planet is indeed the very best in every respect, as you have seen yourself, and everything on its exterior is exclusively of such a kind that it is always perceived by each independent Individual, as I have already said, 'Isklolunitsinernly,' that is 'beautifully-delightfully,' yet to those perfected higher being-bodies existing there this is of no account, since they are always deeply absorbed in their intense work in purifying themselves from those undesirable elements which have entered their presences from causes totally foreign to their individuality.

"In the common presences of these unfortunate higher being-bodies now existing on this holy planet, perfected in Reason to the highest limit attainable by ordinary higher cosmic Individuals, there is only this single datum, which sometimes engenders in them the impulse of hope, and that is that they may at some time purify themselves and obtain the happiness of uniting with and becoming a part of that 'Greatness' which our OMNIPOTENT ALL-JUST COMMON FATHER ENDLESSNESS actualizes for the welfare and happiness of everything existing in our Great Megalocosmos.

"Here it is interesting to notice, that almost all three-brained beings arising on all the various planets of our Great Megalocosmos either know of or instinctively sense the holy planet Purgatory; it is only the three-brained beings arising on your planet who do not know of it, however only most of those who arose towards the end of the existence of the continent Atlantis and after its loss did not and do not know of it.

"As soon as all three-brained beings of our Megalocosmos without distinction of exterior coating acquire any degree of self-awareness, they already begin consciously or instinctively to dream of going on to that holy planet, in order later to have the happiness to become a particle of that Greatness, the blending with which must sooner or later be the lot of every already arisen essence; and three-brained beings who have attained to an already greater self-awareness always eagerly and even joyfully permit during their ordinary-being-existence, for the realization of these dreams of theirs, those unpleasantnesses to their presences which proceed from the accepted privations to their planetary body, because such beings already well understand and instinctively feel that this lower being-body of theirs is, in their own sacred cosmic law of Triamazikamno, the indispensable source for a certain kind of denying manifestation, and as such, of course, always must and will manifest only as denying for their affirming part, that is, that the manifestation of this lower part of theirs must obligatorily be always opposite to what is required for them by their higher being-part.

"In other words, every wish of the planetary body is taken as undesirable for the higher divine part which has to be coated and perfected, and therefore all three-centered beings of our Great Megalocosmos constantly carry on a relentless struggle against the wishes of their planetary bodies so that there should be formed in them in this struggle, from the what is called 'Disputekrialnian-friction,' those sacred crystallizations from which their higher Divine being-part arises and is perfected in them.

"In this constant struggle of theirs, the equilibrating harmonizing principle is their second being-body, which in their own individual law of Triamazikamno represents the neutralizing source; and therefore this second being-part always remains indifferent to their mechanical manifestations, but for all their active manifestations it always tends according to the second-grade cosmic law 'Urdekhplifata' to unite with those desires of which there are more, whether in one or the other of the two mentioned opposite being-parts.

"As I have already said, in the beginning, that is to say before the loss of the continent Atlantis, the three-brained beings of your planet too, also had an approximate understanding of the holy planet Purgatory and there even then existed several Legominisms concerning it, and after the loss of that continent certain partial Legominisms concerning this holy planet Purgatory also survived through learned beings of that time who were by chance saved and began to be transmitted there from generation to generation. But later when, in the psyche of these strange three-brained beings there, that peculiar illness of theirs which I characterized by the words 'to wiseacre' began to arise, then they began their wiseacrings with this partial information which had reached them, and from this partial authentic information concerning the holy planet Purgatory there began to be formed and to be fixed, in the psyche of beings of subsequent generations, data for engendering such representations and understandings as are ideally defined by a certain exclamation of our highly esteemed incomparable Mullah Nassr Eddin, which consists of the following being-consonance 'Chrkhrta-Zoorrt!'

"And as for those partial Legominisms concerning the holy planet, which continued to be transmitted from generation to generation through genuine initiates there, they, having reached unchanged to a very recent epoch, that is, to what is called the 'Babylonian epoch,' also began—owing to what I called the 'agitation of mind,' which then seized everyone and which arose in this Babylon, as I have already related to you, on account of learned beings there of 'new formation' who had various inherencies unbecoming to three-brained beings—to be gradually distorted and ultimately completely, as it is said, 'to wither.'

"The point is that, in spite of the fact that the initiates of that epoch were still relatively normal responsible beings who did not easily change their ideals, as is done there at the present time by the majority of contemporary beings, just as, as they themselves express it, the 'London-Phu-Phu-Klé' change their gloves; yet during this period the psychosis which seized all these strange three-brained beings of finding out at whatever cost whether they had a soul and whether it was immortal, was so strong and widespread, that this unhealthy need of their psyche stirred and infected the minds of even the genuine initiates there and they, having fallen under the influence of this psychosis, mixed into the Legominisms concerning the holy planet Purgatory and handed down such a 'Khaboor-Chooboor' that the tail of our Lucifer from pleasurable emotion turned a shade of what is called the color 'tango.'

"The confusion of the minds of the initiated beings of the planet Earth of that time occurred, in my opinion, chiefly because of that beautiful theory of the Babylonian dualists in which it was said that, in some other world as it were, 'paradise' and 'hell' exist.

"Just these same two expressions, namely, paradise and hell, served, in my opinion, as the cause of all the subsequent 'twaddle.'

"The point is, that in one of the Legominisms about the holy planet Purgatory, both of these words paradise and hell were also used.

"I do not know whether these two words were taken from the Legominism concerning the holy planet or whether they were obtained by a chance coincidence.

"By these same two words the two following conceptions were expressed in the Legominism about the holy planet Purgatory: by the word paradise the magnificence and richness which are on that holy planet were defined, and by the word hell that inner state indeed experienced by the higher being-bodies who dwell there, and, namely, the state of constant anguish, grief, and oppression.

"And in one of the Legominisms the causes for this state of theirs were even explained in detail, that is, that these higher being-parts or souls, having ultimately fallen after inexpressible, consciously suffering labors onto this holy planet, and having seen and understood the reality and significance of everything existing, and chiefly seeing our COMMON FATHER ENDLESSNESS HIMSELF so near and so often, have become aware that on account of the undesirable elements present in them, they are still unable to help HIM in the fulfillment of HIS most sacred tasks for the good of our whole Megalocosmos.

"And so, those two words then, evidently, were just the causes why the poor initiates of that time, when infected by the general psychosis, imagined that the same things were talked of in that fantastic beautiful theory of the Babylonian future Hasnamusses, but only in greater detail; and they began half consciously to insert certain details of this fantastic theory into the Legominisms concerning the holy planet, and afterwards these informations, passing from generation to generation, blossomed out with the additions of these fancies, which again our dear Mullah Nassr Eddin expresses by the one word: 'Kmalkanatonashachermacher.'

"According to what I have just told you, my boy, you can in general judge what kind of understandings and representations they have at the present time there on your planet about the what are called 'questions of the beyond'; it can truly be said that if these understandings and notions of your eccentrics about their questions of the beyond were heard by our hens, they would begin to laugh so hard that the same thing might happen to them from their laughter as happens there among your favorites from what is called castor oil.

"For a better sensing and cognizing and at the same time for a better fairylike illumination of the meaning of these expressions which I just used—hens' laughter and castor oil—I must tell you about some other consequences which flowed from always the same cunning wiseacring of these favorites of yours, in this case concerning the question of the 'being-Exioëhary,' the more so since the knowledge about this will give you additional data for elucidating by a concrete example certain particularities, which I have already explained to you, of the fundamental cosmic sacred law of Heptaparaparshinokh.

"After the loss of the continent Atlantis, certain knowledge concerning the origin and significance of this same 'being-Exioëhary' also survived, and this knowledge also began to pass from generation to generation.

"And so, about thirty or thirty-five of their centuries ago, when after a big process of reciprocal destruction, the majority of them again began—as it usually happens there in general after these terrifying excesses—often to see reality and to be less satisfied with the conditions of their ordinary existence, it so happened that the surviving fragments of the knowledge concerning the significance of being-Exioëhary reached in their authentic form to certain of them who had particularly strongly sensed the emptiness of their existence and who had begun to seek possibilities by which they could somehow fill up this emptiness.

"In these though fragmentary yet nevertheless authentic informations, it was very convincingly indicated that by means of the substances 'Exioëhary' or sperm formed in them, it was possible to perfect oneself, but unfortunately for them there were no indications, in this information which had survived and reached them, what and how precisely this had to be done.

"Then certain of them began to think and to strive persistently somehow to understand what was necessary to be done, in order, by means of these substances inevitably formed in their presences, to struggle for self-perfection.

"The result of these serious ponderings of theirs was

that the conviction at first arose in them that this self-perfection could probably be actualized by itself, by abstaining from the ejection from oneself in the customary manner of these substances formed in them called sperm, and certain of them decided to unite and exist together, in order to convince themselves in practice whether such abstinence could indeed give the supposed results.

"However hard these same beings of your planet who were first interested in this question strove to get clear about this, they arrived at nothing, and it was only the second generation of them who ultimately, after long conscious observations and intensive active mentations, categorically understood that this was indeed possible, exclusively only on condition of a ceaseless fulfillment of being-Partkdolg-duty, and those of them, beings of the said generation as well as certain of the subsequent two generations, who began seriously to actualize this, did indeed attain the expected results.

"But already the fourth generation of those beings who were first interested in this question and who were followers not from essence-conviction but from a property called 'to imitate,' which had by that time also become inherent in these terrestrial three-brained beings, also began to exist together and to do as it were the same thing.

"So from that time it began and until now automatically continues, that such followers organize themselves in separate groups and sometimes form solid sects of various denominations and, putting this same 'abstinence' as the basis of their aim, exist together segregated.

"Just these same places of theirs for segregated common existence together, are called there 'monasteries,' and the separate beings belonging to these sects, 'monks.'

"At the present time, very many of these 'monasteries' exist there, and these innumerable 'monks' who enter them do indeed strictly abstain from the ejection from themselves in the customary way of the being-Exioëhary or sperm formed in them; but of course, no sensible result at all is ever obtained from this abstinence of theirs, and it is not obtained, because the thought has ceased even to enter the heads of these unfortunate 'contemporary' monks that although it is indeed possible, by means of these substances Exioëhary formed in them, to perfect themselves, yet this can proceed exclusively only if the second and third being-foods are intentionally absorbed and consciously digested in one's presence, and this is possible exclusively only if all the parts of one's presence have been accustomed beforehand consciously to fulfill both sacred being-Partkdolg-duties, that is to fulfill 'conscious labors' and 'intentional sufferings.'

"It is however unjust to say that no sensible result at all is obtained among these monks there. There are even obtained among them 'sensible results' of two independent kinds.

"So that you may understand why these mentioned two independent kinds of results are obtained among the contemporary abstaining monks, I must repeat to you once again that, according to the fundamental cosmic sacred law of Heptaparaparshinokh, if everything in general existing in our Megalocosmos, the great as well as the small, does not receive in the process of evolution at the time of its passing through both 'Mdnel-Ins' of the sacred Heptaparaparshinokh corresponding foreign help coming from outside, then it begins to involve back to those definite states from which it began its evolution.

"The same of course proceeds with the definite cosmic substances which are formed in the presences of these same terrestrial abstaining monks.

"And so, my boy, in consequence of the fact that these terrestrial 'monks,' particularly the contemporary, do not intentionally aid the further evolution of these substances inevitably formed in them from the constant use of the first being-food, that is, do not actualize any 'being-Partkdolg-duty' at all in their common presences, either intentionally or even automatically, and at the same time they do not remove these substances from themselves in the normal way foredesigned by Nature, then these substances begin to involve in them themselves, and during this involution of being-Exioëhary or sperm there is worked out, among the many transient definite substances which are in general formed in their common presences by such an involutionary process, a definite transient substance which has the property of having two kinds of action on the general functioning of the planetary body of a being.

"The first kind of action of this definite substance consists in this, that it promotes the depositing of superfluous what is called 'Karatsiag,' or, as they call it there, 'fat.' And its second kind of action promotes the arising and the dispersing over the whole planetary body of what are called 'Poisonioonoskirian-vibrations.'

"The consequence of all this is that in the first case these terrestrial abstaining monks become extraordinarily, as it is usually said there, fat, and sometimes one indeed meets among these fat monks specimens with such an abundant deposit of fat, that they could give many points to that form of being there which they expressly fatten in order to increase this same fat in their planetary bodies, and this form of being they call there 'pig.'

"And in the second case, on the contrary, these abstaining monks become, as it is also usually said there, 'meager-thin'; and the action of the 'Poisonioonoskirian-vibrations' which penetrate through them is chiefly evident in their general psyche which becomes sharply dual and the manifestations of which are divided into two diametrically opposite kinds—the outer, visible and for show, sensed by everyone around them, and the inner and hidden, which the ordinary beings there, especially the contemporary, are entirely incapable of ascertaining or perceiving—namely, in their outer visible manifestations, these 'Poisonioonoskirian-monks' appear to be what your favorites would express as 'bigots' of a high degree; and in their hidden inner manifestations, not shown to others, what your favorites would call 'expert cynics,' also of a high degree.

"As regards the causes why 'Poisonioonoskirian-vibrations' are obtained among certain of the abstaining monks from the involutionary process of the Exioëhary instead of the deposit of fat, there even exists one very detailed theory there about this, worked out by certain, as they are called, 'Catholic monks' who, several centuries ago, proved in great detail that this proceeds because in the first year of their existence these same 'thin monks' very zealously occupied themselves with that occupation from which 'pimples'—known even to medicine there—generally appear on the faces of young beings there.

"For a full representation and understanding concerning the significance of this kind of abstinence among contemporary monks there, it remains for me to add that of which I became convinced during my last sojourn there among them, and, namely, that already, thanks only to these consequences flowing from the involutionary process of the Exioëhary, the fixation of various consequences of the properties of the organ Kundabuffer in the common presences of these unfortunate terrestrial abstaining monks has become greatly facilitated and has in consequence increased."

At this point in his narrative, Beelzebub was interrupted by a ship's servant who gave him a 'Leitoochanbros,' which he put to his ear and began to listen to its contents.

THIRD BOOK

CHAPTER 40

Beelzebub Tells How People Learned and Again Forgot About the Fundamental Cosmic Law of Heptaparaparshinokh

After Beelzebub had listened to what was communicated in the "Leitoochanbros" handed to him, his grandson Hassein again turned to him and said:

"My dear and kind Grandfather! Please help me to clear up for myself one contradiction which I do not understand and which does not accord with my logical confrontations.

"When you began your elucidations about the holy planet Purgatory, you enjoined me to try to take in everything you spoke about, without missing anything, and you also enjoined me constantly to maintain the intensive tension of my 'active mentation,' so that corresponding data for the formation of the notion relating to every question explaining the details of both primordial fundamental sacred cosmic laws should be completely crystallized in me. I did indeed try during all your elucidations to do so, and, it seems to me, I cleared up so much for myself about these cosmic laws that I could perhaps even freely explain them to someone else.

"In any case I can already very well represent to myself the sacred law of Triamazikamno with the particularities of all three of its sacred independent forces and cognize it for my personal essence quite satisfactorily; but as regards the sacred law of Heptaparaparshinokh, then, although I have not yet fully made clear to my reason certain of its, in my opinion, unimportant details, nevertheless I hope that with a little more active pondering I shall understand them as well.

"Now, however, after I had—while trying to assimilate well these sacred laws—clearly sensed and become aware that they are very complicated and in general difficult for a 'complete understanding,' it suddenly greatly astonished me and continues to astonish and interest me how the three-brained beings who arise and exist on the planet Earth could not only understand these sacred cosmic laws, but could even have constated them among the surrounding cosmic results, because, from all your tales about them, I got the full impression that since the second Transapalnian perturbation there, when each of the newly arising results of theirs becomes a responsible being, he becomes, thanks to the abnormal prevailing Oskiano, the possessor of only 'automatic-Reason.'

"And that it is impossible to understand both of these sacred cosmic laws with such a Reason, I became convinced with the whole of my essence when I myself tried to understand them."

Having said this, Hassein looked questioningly and eagerly at his beloved Grandfather.

Having thought a little, Beelzebub began to speak as follows:

"All right, my dear boy, I shall try to elucidate to you also about this natural perplexity which justly arises within you.

"It seems to me I already once told you that although from the period you mentioned on that planet almost all the three-brained beings there became, thanks to the abnormally established conditions of ordinary being-existence, possessors of only an automatic-Reason, nevertheless it does sometimes happen there that certain of them by chance escape this common fate and that instead of that automatic-Reason which has become usual there, a genuine objective 'being-Reason' is formed in certain of them as it is in all three-centered beings of our great Megalocosmos.

"Although such exceptions, especially during recent centuries, are very rare there, yet, I repeat, they nevertheless do occur.

"In order that you may approximately represent to yourself and understand just how such exceptions may occur among them, you must first of all know that, in spite of the fact that from the time when all the consequences of the properties of the organ Kundabuffer began to be crystallized in them and it became proper to them to have automatic-Reason during their responsible existence, yet, nevertheless, always and up to the present time, at the arising and the beginning of the formation of each one of them, there is always in their presence the germs of all possibilities for the crystallization, during their completing formation into responsible beings, of corresponding being-data, which later during responsible existence could serve for the engendering and functioning of objective-Reason, which should be in the common presences of three-brained beings of all natures and of all external forms, and which, in itself, is nothing else but, so to say, the 'representative-of-the-Very-Essence-of-Divinity.'

"Their, in the objective sense, extreme misfortune about that which you yourself already 'perplexedly-instinctively-suspect,' as I discern from the formulation of your question, especially from your having mentioned Oskiano, consists just in this, that they, having indeed at their arising such possibilities in themselves, immediately fall from the very first days after the separation from their mother's womb—only thanks to the abnormalities established in the process of ordinary being-existence of beings around them who have already reached responsible age—under the stubborn influence of that maleficent means, invented by them themselves for themselves, which as I already told you, represents in itself a something of the kind of Oskiano which they call 'education.'

"And in consequence, in this way all possibilities for the free formation of all that which is required for the engendering of objective being-Reason is gradually atrophied and finally disappears in these unfortunate, so to say, 'still-innocent-in-everything' newly arising beings during the period of their what is called 'preparatory age,' and as a result, when these newly arising beings later become responsible beings, they, in their, so to say, 'essence-center-of-gravity,' become the possessors, not of that objective-Reason which they ought to have, but of that strange totality of automatically perceived artificial even deceptive impressions which, having nothing in common with the localization of their spiritualized being-parts, nevertheless acquires a connection with the separate functionings of their common presence. In consequence of this, not only the whole process of their existence flows automatically, but also almost the whole process of the functioning of their planetary body becomes dependent only on chance, automatically perceived, external impressions.

"In very rare cases, certain of these favorites of yours who have reached responsible age become possessors of genuine pure-Reason, proper to three-brained responsible beings. This usually proceeds there thus. For instance, it happens that immediately after the separation from his mother's womb one of the newly arising beings finds himself for the process of his subsequent formation among such surrounding conditions, where for some reason or other all kinds of those abnormalities—with which the entire process of the external being-existence of three-brained beings breeding on this ill-fated planet is already over-filled—do not touch him and do not influence him automatically maleficently, and in consequence of this the germs which are in him for the possibilities of acquiring pure-Reason have not the time during the process of his subsequent formation to become atrophied to the very root. And further, it sometimes also happens that for the subsequent completing formation of such a three-brained being there, newly arisen in the said relatively normal conditions, his responsible guide during his preparatory age for responsible existence is such a three-brained being as had before this, also of course by chance, already been completely formed in the same way, and in the functioning of whose waking consciousness, thanks to the frequent actualization in his presence of being-Partkdolg-duty, there had participated the data which had remained whole in his subconscious for the engendering of the Divine impulse of 'Conscience.'

"And so this same guide, being aware with the whole of his Being of the important significance of this responsibility taken upon himself in relation to this new being who has, in the said manner, only as yet reached his preparatory age, begins according to conscience impartially to create for his Oskiano every kind of what are called 'inner-and-outer-factors' for the perceiving of corresponding impressions in order to crystallize in his common presence all those data, the totality of which alone can give to the three-brained being who has reached responsible age the power to be 'Svolibroonolnian,' or, as your favorites there on Earth would say, the 'potency-not-to-be-identified-with-and-not-to-be-affected-by-externals-through - one's - inevitably - inherent - passions'; and this being-impulse, engendered in the being with these data, can alone help him to acquire the possibility of a free and impartial constatation of all true phenomena appearing in the cosmic results around him.

"Here it is very opportune to repeat once again that on most planets of our Megalocosmos, on which three-brained beings arise and exist, there is an oft-repeated sentence, formulated in the following words:

"'Our COMMON-FATHER-ENDLESSNESS is only the Maker of a three-centered being.' The genuine creator, however, of his essence during the period of his preparatory existence is his 'Oskianotsner,' namely, he whom your favorites call tutor or teacher.

"And so even during the last century, it occasionally happened there that such a one from among your favorites who had already reached responsible age completely formed and prepared in the said manner for external perceptions, constating by chance a certain law-conformable particularity among the cosmic results around him, began to study it in detail and from every aspect and, having ultimately attained after long persevering labors to some objective truth or other, initiated other beings around him and similar to him, into this truth.

"Now, my boy, listen to how these peculiar three-brained beings first became aware of this fundamental cosmic law of the sacred Heptaparaparshinokh and how the totality arose there of all the information concerning its various details thoroughly cognized by previous beings and which had become, after having been transmitted from generation to generation, the possession of every subsequent three-brained being of this planet of yours which could enable them to cognize this information also; and likewise listen to what—and when—thanks to always the same strangeness of their psyche, there resulted from all this.

"I wish to explain to you about this in even as great detail as possible, with all the sequence of the historical course of development both as regards the constatation of the cognizance concerning this sacred law, as well as the gradual forgetting about it, because such information relating to all this will greatly help you, first of all, to elucidate those, as you expressed it, 'unimportant details' of this sacred law, which you have not yet completely transubstantiated in your Reason; and secondly, thanks to these elucidations of mine, you will likewise learn that among the number of your favorites, even the contemporary ones, such responsible beings do occasionally appear in the sphere of genuine learned beings; and assuming that the other three-brained beings there existed more or less normally, then thanks to the impartial and modest conscious efforts of these beings, genuine objective learning might arise and gradually develop also on this ill-fated planet, as a result of which that welfare might be obtained also for them, which the three-brained beings of all the other planets of our great Megalocosmos have long ago deservedly enjoyed.

"In the beginning, during the period when the three-brained beings of that planet had in themselves the organ Kundabuffer, it was of course out of the question that the beings of the Earth could have learned about any cosmic truths.

"But afterwards, when the functioning of this maleficent organ which they had in their presences was destroyed, and when in consequence their psyche became free and became, so to say, their own and 'individual,' it was just from then on that all kinds of stories began concerning their 'relatively sane' being-mentation.

"The perceiving and cognizing of the fundamental cosmic law of the sacred Heptaparaparshinokh by the common presences of these three-brained beings who have taken your fancy, began for the first time on the continent Atlantis at that period when, do you remember, I already told you, certain beings there understood by themselves that something 'not-quite-right' proceeded in them and when they themselves discovered that they had certain possibilities of being able to destroy this something 'not-quite-right' and of becoming such as they ought to be.

"It was just at that period of the 'flow-of-time' when certain of them began to observe those, according to sane being-mentation, 'abnormal functionings' which proceeded in their common presences, and to search out the causes of these abnormalities, and to try to find every kind of possibility for removing them from themselves, and when many branches of real science there had reached a high degree of development, that among the number of those who were seriously interested in this, as it was then called, 'most-necessary-functioning-of-Reason,' there was that terrestrial three-brained being by name, Theophany, who was the first to lay a rational foundation for the subsequent development of this branch of genuine science.

"As I later chanced to learn, this same Theophany was once pouring a certain mixture onto a marble slab to dry, consisting of the extract of the plant then called 'Patetook,' pine-resin, and cream of the milk of the then famous what were called 'Khenionian goats,' so that after its hardening a mastic should be obtained, used for chewing after eating; when for the first time he noticed that in whatever way and in whatever quantity this mixture was poured onto that marble slab, it always—concentrating in the same way—assumed after the final cooling a form composed of seven definite plane surfaces.

"This fact, unexpectedly constated by this Theophany, greatly astonished him and the intensive wish arose in his common presence to elucidate to his Reason the radical causes of this law-conformableness still unknown to him, and therefore from that time on he began to repeat the same thing, but already with a conscious aim.

"Shortly after, still at the beginning of the investigations which Theophany undertook, his friends, other learned beings of that time, with whom he shared the beginnings of his various elucidatory experiments on his constatations, having become interested in this, also participated in these further researches of his.

"Well then, after long and detailed researches, this group of learned three-brained beings of your planet first became aware and categorically convinced that almost all the cosmic results observed around them which are actualized in the course of their manifestness in external transitory states perceived by the organs of beings in some or other definite form, always have seven independent aspects.

"As a result of the conscious labors of these several learned three-brained beings of your planet, that branch of almost normal science then arose and began to grow on the continent Atlantis under the name of 'Tazaloorinono,' the sense of which meant 'the-seven-aspectness-of-every-whole-phenomenon.'

"But when that continent perished and absolutely nothing survived from this branch of genuine science, then again during the course of very many centuries the beings of this planet knew nothing about this sacred cosmic law.

"Evidently this branch of science on the continent Atlantis was so widely known that it was not found necessary to include anything about it in a Legominism, as was usually done, as I have already told you, by the learned beings of the continent Atlantis for all those notions, the knowledge of which they wished to transmit unchanged to beings of future generations.

"If a Legominism concerning this branch of science had also existed, then something or other would certainly have survived of this knowledge, as had survived of other knowledge attained by the beings of Atlantis, through those who were by chance saved after the loss of that continent.

"The knowledge concerning the sacred Heptaparaparshinokh was again known only after many, many of their centuries, thanks to two great terrestrial learned beings, the brothers 'Choon-Kil-Tez' and 'Choon-Tro-Pel,' who later became Saints and who are now on that holy planet Purgatory where we recently were.

"Do you remember, I already told you that on the continent of Asia there was a country Maralpleicie and that a king existed there by name Konuzion, a descendant of that learned member of the Society of Akhaldans who had gone there from Atlantis for the observation of all kinds of natural phenomena of their planet, just that same king who had invented for his subjects the 'wise tale' already mentioned by me in order to save them from the pernicious habit of chewing the seeds of the flower 'Goolgoolian.'

"Well then, to the grandson of this King Konuzion, after the arising of an heir who later also became king over the beings of this group, there arose just these same two results of the male sex, twins, the elder of whom was called 'Choon-Kil-Tez' and the younger 'Choon-Tro-Pel.' The word 'Choon' then in the country Maralpleicie meant 'prince.'

"Owing on the one hand to the fact that the environment of these two brothers, direct descendants of one of the chief members of the great learned society, happened to be arranged correspondingly for their 'preparatory age,' and on the other hand that they themselves tried not to allow the atrophy of the hereditary inherency—which they as in general all newly arising three-brained beings of this planet have—to crystallize the data for engendering in themselves the power to actualize 'being-Partkdolg-duty,' and also in consequence of the fact that the 'affirming-source' of the causes of their arising, that is, their, as is called, father, decided to destine their responsible existence for the field of learning and took all corresponding measures for their preparation for this, then already from the very beginning of their responsible age they almost became such as three-brained beings everywhere on the planets of our great Megalocosmos become who choose the same Aim, that is to say, those who carry out all their studied researches not for the satisfaction of their, what are called 'vainglorious,' 'proud,' and 'self-loving' weaknesses—as is done by the beings there, particularly the contemporary ones who choose the same field for themselves—but for the attainment of a higher gradation of Being.

"At the outset they became, as is said there, learned 'specialists in medicine,' and afterwards, learned in general.

"The period of their preparatory age and the early years of their responsible existence were spent in the town Gob, in the country Maralpleicie, but when this part of the surface of your planet began to be buried under sand, they were both among the number of those refugees who went East.

"This group of three-brained beings, refugees from the country Maralpleicie, among whom were also these two twin brothers, later great learned beings, crossed the Eastern heights of Maralpleicie and then settled on the shores of a great water-space.

"There was afterwards formed from them a settled group of these terrestrial three-brained beings still existing today, which, as well as the country which it inhabits, is now called 'China.'

"Well then, in this new place of their permanent existence called China, these same two brothers were the first to constate and to cognize, after the loss of the continent Atlantis, the fundamental cosmic law of the sacred Heptaparaparshinokh.

"It is in the highest degree an interesting and curious

circumstance that the initial source for this constatation of theirs was the totality of cosmic substances localized in just that same surplanetary formation which is now called there 'Papaveroon' or, as it is still called, poppy; and owing to the implanting of the habit of chewing the seeds of this poppy, their great grandfather, the great King Konuzion, first invented his, as already mentioned by me, 'religious teaching.'

"There were evidently transmitted by inheritance to these two great terrestrial learned beings from their great grandfather, the great King Konuzion, in addition to the ability of well considering and cognizing their being-duty in relation to beings around them similar to themselves, also an interest in and a passion for the study of this product, which has always been for your favorites one of the innumerable harmful means which have brought their psyche, already enfeebled without this, to its ultimate degeneracy.

"In order that you may better represent to yourself and well understand why just such a small planetary formation as I mentioned, named Papaveroon or poppy, was the cause of the constatation by these great terrestrial learned beings of that most great cosmic law, you must first of all know, that on all planets, for the purposes of the transformation of common-cosmic substances during the process of 'Iraniranumange,' there arise, among all kinds of surplanetary and intraplanetary formations in general as well as among formations called 'flora' in particular, three classes of formations.

"The formations belonging to the first class are called 'Oonastralnian-arisings'; those belonging to the second class, 'Okhtatralnian-arisings'; and those belonging to the third class, 'Polormedekhtian-arisings.'

"Through the Oonastralnian-arisings there are transformed in their evolutionary or involutionary processes those cosmic crystallizations or 'active elements' which obtain their arising only from the substances transformed by that planet itself, on which that kind of surplanetary or intraplanetary formation is formed for the purposes of the common-cosmic Iraniranumange.

"Through the Okhtatralnian-arisings there are transformed, besides what I have mentioned, also those active elements which obtain their primary arisings from the substances transformed by the sun itself and the other planets of the given solar system.

"And through the arisings of the third class, namely, the Polormedekhtian, there are transformed besides the first two classes also all those active elements which primarily arise from the transformations of the substances of various cosmic concentrations belonging to other 'Solar-systems' of our common Megalocosmos.

"The surplanetary flora-formation mentioned by me, named on your planet the plant Papaveroon, belongs to the class of Polormedekhtian-arisings and through it there evolves or involves what is called the 'totality-of-the-results-of-the-transformation' of all other cosmic 'gravity-center-concentrations,' which come into the atmosphere of this planet of yours through the common-cosmic process of what is called 'ubiquitous-diffusion-of-the-radiations-of-all-kinds-of-cosmic-concentrations.'

"Well then, my boy, after these two great terrestrial learned beings Choon-Kil-Tez and Choon-Tro-Pel had more or less arranged the new place of their permanent existence in the then still quite young China, they began to continue the intentional actualization in their common presences of being-Partkdolg-duty, interrupted through no fault of theirs, in the field of the profession chosen by them for their responsible existence, namely, 'scientific-research' in the branch called 'medicine.'

"They then began to investigate that totality of cosmic

substances which still before this your favorites had learned to obtain there from the mentioned Polormedekhtian plant, and which they named opium, which then denoted in the speech of the beings of that group 'dream-maker.'

"These two great brothers then began to investigate this opium in consequence of the fact that they as well as many other three-brained beings of that time noticed that, on the introduction into themselves of a certain species of this mass, every painful sensation temporarily disappeared.

"They first of all set out to elucidate the action of all its properties in order perhaps to find a possibility, by means of one of its properties, to destroy or change for the better that special form of 'psychic illness' which had then become very widely spread among the refugees around them, three-brained beings like themselves.

"During these researches of theirs, they first of all noticed that this same opium consists of seven independent crystallizations with definite subjective properties.

"And on further and more detailed investigations they definitely constated that each of these seven independent crystallizations of this 'one whole,' consists in its turn of seven others, also definite crystallizations with their seven independent subjective properties, and these, in their turn, again of seven, and so on almost to infinity.

"This then so greatly astonished and interested them that they put aside all the problems they had previously set themselves and from then on exclusively and perseveringly occupied themselves with the investigation of this fact which had astonished them, and which they had first constated, and ultimately attained to those results which both before—even at the period of the existence of the continent Atlantis—and at any other period later, were unprecedented for the three-brained beings of your planet.

"Many centuries after the period of the planetary existence of these terrestrial great learned beings, now the Saints Choon-Kil-Tez and Choon-Tro-Pel, when I happened for one of my elucidations to become acquainted in detail with the history of their activities, it appeared that when they had become convinced beyond doubt that such a totality of cosmic substances as is named Opium consists of a whole range of compounds with seven 'diversely-subjectively-propertied-active-elements,' they then began with the same aim to investigate many other 'cosmic results' or, as is said there, 'phenomena,' which proceeded in their environment. But later, in these investigations of theirs, they confined themselves only to three, namely, to this same Opium, to what is called the 'white-ray' and to what is called 'sound.'

"Investigating the mentioned three diversely manifested results of cosmic processes, they then, among other things, categorically made clear and became convinced beyond any doubt that although all these three results in respect of the causes of their arising and outer manifestations have nothing in common with each other, yet their inner construction and functioning are nevertheless exactly alike down to the smallest detail.

"In brief, then, for the second time on your planet, in this still quite young China, after the loss of the continent Atlantis, these two twin brothers again constated and categorically made clear that all the separate and, by their exterior, independent phenomena—if each of them is taken as a unit—are in the totality of their manifestations again seven secondary independent units, having their own subjective properties; that these secondary independent units in their turn, consist of seven tertiary units, and so on to infinity; and that in each of these primary, secondary, tertiary, etc., units, the processes of mutual relation and mutual influence proceed equally in every detail down to the smallest exactitudes and with equal consequences.

"By the way, during their investigations, they then first defined, with separate names, the first seven independent aspects taken by them of the whole result, as well as their secondary and tertiary derivatives.

"Namely, the first seven fundamental aspects of each whole they called:

(1) Erti-Pikan-On
(2) Ori-Pikan-On
(3) Sami-Pikan-On
(4) Okhti-Pikan-On
(5) Khooti-Pikan-On
(6) Epsi-Pikan-On
(7) Shvidi-Pikan-On

"And the secondary:

(1) Erti-Noora-Chaka
(2) Ori-Noora-Chaka
(3) Sami-Noora-Chakoo
(4) Okhti-Noora-Chaka
(5) Khooti-Noora-Chaka
(6) Epsi-Noora-Chaka
(7) Shvidi-Noora-Chakoo

"And in order to distinguish to which of the three mentioned results of cosmic processes the given definition referred, they added after each of these definitions the following:

"For the definition of the nuances of sound they, noting the number of their vibrations, always added to this the word 'Alil.'

"For the definition of the particularities of the composite

of the 'white-ray,' they added the expression 'Nar-Khra-Noora.'

"And for the definition of the active elements of the Polormedekhtian product called opium, they added only the number of their, what is called, 'specific gravity.'

"And to define specific-vibration and specific gravity, these great terrestrial learned beings took as the standard unit the unit of vibrations of sound, then first called by them the 'Nirioonossian-world-sound.'

"I will explain to you a little later about the meaning of the definition Nirioonossian-world-sound first adopted by the then great learned beings of the Earth, but meanwhile for the clarity of the understanding of my subsequent elucidations of the given theme, you must also know that everywhere on the planets genuine scientists take as the standard unit for their confrontative calculations of specific gravity and specific-vibrations that part, established by objective science, of the most most sacred Theomertmalogos which still contains all the fullness of what is called the 'vivifyingness' of all the three holy forces of the sacred Triamazikamno; but on your planet genuine scientists as well as those of new formation of all periods took and until today still take as such, a standard unit what is called the 'atom of Hydrogen,' for the same purpose—namely, for the confrontative calculations of all those diversely propertied definite parts of some or other whole which had become known to them, as for instance, for the specific gravity of various active elements which had become known to them among the number which ought to be present in the spheres surrounding their existence—considering this atom of Hydrogen for some unknown reason to be in general the smallest and also indivisible.

"It must not be overlooked that these sorry scientists from among your favorites do not even suspect that if this atom of Hydrogen of theirs is indeed the smallest and indivisible there in all spheres of their planet, then this does not mean that it cannot be broken up many times more within the limits of other solar systems or even in the spheres of certain other planets of their own solar system.

"By the way, you should know that this same Hydrogen of theirs is just one of those seven cosmic substances which in their general totality actualize specially for the given solar system what is called the 'inner Ansapalnian-octave' of cosmic substances, which independent octave, in its turn, is a one-seventh independent part of the fundamental 'common-cosmic Ansapalnian-octave.'

"Such an inner independent Ansapalnian-octave is likewise present in that solar system to which our dear Karatas belongs, and we call these seven heterogeneous cosmic substances of different properties:

(1) Planekurab—which is just their Hydrogen
(2) Alillonofarab
(3) Krilnomolnifarab
(4) Talkoprafarab
(5) Khritofalmonofarab
(6) Sirioonorifarab
(7) Klananoizufarab

"And on your planet the genuine learned beings at different periods called by various names these same seven relatively independent crystallizations of different properties or, according to their expression, active elements, which compose the inner Ansapalnian-octave of their own solar system; the contemporary, as they are called, learned chemists there, however, who are already 'learned-of-new-formation-of-the-first-water,' call them:

(1) Hydrogen
(2) Fluorine
(3) Chlorine
(4) Bromine
(5) Iodine

"For the last two definite crystallizations they have no names at all because their names did not reach them from their ancestors, and at the present time they even do not suspect the existence on their planet of these two cosmic substances, although these two cosmic substances are the principal necessary factors for their own existence.

"These two latter cosmic substances, which might be quite tangible and quite accessible in all spheres of their planet, were still known only about two centuries ago among the 'scientific beings' there who were then called 'alchemists'—but whom the contemporary 'comic-scientists' simply call 'occult-charlatans,' considering them to be only 'exploiters of human naïveté'—and were called by them 'Hydro-oomiak' and 'Petrkarmak.'

"And so, my boy, these great terrestrial learned beings now Saints, the twin brothers Choon-Kil-Tez and Choon-Tro-Pel, were the first after the loss of Atlantis to lay anew the foundation of this knowledge. They not only laid anew the foundation of this 'totality-of-special-information' but they were even the first there on Earth who also constated two of the three chief law-conformable particularities present in that great law about which I have already spoken to you, and, namely, they were the first to constate two of its Mdnel-Ins; they then called that branch of genuine knowledge, similar to that which on the continent of Atlantis was called the 'seven-aspectness-of-every-whole-phenomenon,' the law of 'ninefoldness,' and they called it thus because they added to the seven obvious 'different-manifestations,' called by them 'Dooczako,' of this great law, these two particularities first constated by them and named by them 'Sooanso-Toorabizo,' which name meant 'obligatory-gap-aspects-of-the-unbroken-flowing-of-the-whole.' And they named this law thus, chiefly because during their detailed researches they became convinced beyond all doubt that in all the cosmic 'transitory results' they investigated, these particularities first constated by them likewise obligatorily always proceed in certain places of the process of this great law.

"These two great terrestrial Chinese learned beings then had recourse for their elucidatory experiments to every kind of what are called 'chemical,' 'physical,' and 'mechanical' experiments and they gradually formed one very complicated and in the highest degree edifying experimental apparatus, which they called 'Alla-attapan.'

"By means of this apparatus Alla-attapan, they then clearly proved to themselves and to others that in the very essence of all these three 'transitory results' of cosmic processes, and, namely, in the Polormedekhtian product called there opium, in the white-ray and in sound there are the same properties, and, namely, there are in all these three outwardly quite different cosmic phenomena precisely the same what are called 'actualizing constructions,' that is to say, for their manifestness there are in them precisely the same 'mutually-acting-law-conformablenesses,' and in all three of these outwardly different apparently independent manifestations the functioning of these 'mutually-acting-law-conformablenesses' have precisely the same action on each other as they have in their own manifestations, that is to say, the Dooczako of any one result acts on the corresponding Dooczako of another, precisely the same as it functions in that Dooczako which is one of the seven aspects of this whole cosmic result.

"This same apparatus, by means of which these great brothers made their elucidatory experiments, I saw with my own eyes many centuries after that period when they existed there, and I became very well acquainted with its construction.

"As the cause of my personal acquaintance with all the details of the construction and action of this remarkable experimental apparatus Alla-attapan was due to accidental circumstances connected with my essence-friend Gornahoor Harharkh, and as it will surely interest you very much and at the same time will be exceedingly instructive for you, I shall describe it to you in somewhat greater detail.

"My personal and exhaustive study of this astonishing apparatus Alla-attapan—which became, thanks to Gornahoor Harharkh, famous among the genuine scientists of almost the whole of our Megalocosmos—proceeded according to the following chance circumstances.

"Just at the time of one of my sojourns on the planet Saturn with my essence-friend, Gornahoor Harharkh, he, having already previously in some way heard about this apparatus, requested me during conversation to bring him one of these experimental apparatuses from the planet Earth if I again happened to be there.

"And when afterwards I again visited the surface of this planet of yours, I procured there one of these apparatuses and took it with me to the planet Mars in order to send it on a convenient occasion to the planet Saturn to Gornahoor Harharkh.

"And so, in consequence of the fact that for a long time our ship *Occasion* did not happen to go to the planet Saturn, this apparatus Alla-attapan remained at my home on the planet Mars and it often came within the sphere of the automatic perception of the organs of my sight; and during a period of rest from active mentation I attentively examined it and ultimately became familiar with all the details of its construction and action.

"This famous experimental apparatus Alla-attapan consisted of three independent parts.

"The fore part was called 'Loosochepana,' the middle part 'Dzendvokh,' and the last, the hind part, was called 'Riank-Pokhortarz.'

"Each of these three parts in their turn consisted of several special and separate adaptations.

"The first part which was named Loosochepana had a special cone-shaped pipe, the wide end of which was hermetically fitted into a frame of the sole window of that room where the experiments were made, and the other end was a small chinklike aperture with what is called a 'collecting-disk,' passing through which what are called the rays of 'daylight' coming from the window were transformed into, as your favorites would say, a 'concentrated-white-ray.'

"This concentrated-white-ray thereupon passing through a crystal of a special form was broken up into seven different 'colored rays' which, as is said, fell upon a small slab made of ivory and called 'Pirinjiel.'

"This slab Pirinjiel was so constructed and regulated that the colored rays falling on it were again concentrated, but this time otherwise, and, proceeding through the second crystal, also of a special form, fell on another but larger slab, also made of ivory and called 'Polorishboorda.'

"Opposite this Polorishboorda was a small apparatus of a special construction through which, on its being shifted in a certain way, any chosen colored ray there could be directed further from this Polorishboorda onto the third part of the Alla-attapan called 'Riank-Pokhortarz.'

"Here, by the way, you might as well also be told that the knowledge relating to the construction of the first crystal of this part of the apparatus Alla-attapan also reached down to your contemporary favorites, and they now call this crystal a 'prism.'

"Through this prism contemporary terrestrial learned beings also obtain seven colored rays from the white-ray and they also fancy that through this they can learn about certain other cosmic phenomena.

"But, of course, from these fancies of theirs and from all kinds of other forms of their 'scientific titillation' nothing is obtained, only because through this prism of theirs they obtain from the white-ray only what are called 'negative colored rays,' and in order to understand any other cosmic phenomena connected with the transitory changes of this white-ray, they must obligatorily have its what are called 'positive colored rays.'

"Your contemporary favorites, however, imagine that the colored rays which they obtain by means of this child's toy of theirs, called by them prism, are just those same 'positive rays' which the great scientists obtained; and according to their naïveté they think that the, as they call it, 'spectrum' which they obtain from the white-ray gives just that order of the arisings of the rays in which they issue from their sources.

"And meanwhile in the given case, concerning these terrestrial sorry scientists of new formation among your favorites one can only utter the expression often used by them themselves, 'To hell with them.'

"It is not for nothing that several of our Sacred Individuals in general do not call your contemporary favorites otherwise than 'freaks.'

"And so, thanks to these two crystals, these great learned beings obtained from the white-ray its positive colored rays and afterwards, with the help of the slab Polorishboorda which was a part of the Loosochepana, any one of these colored rays was directed to the third and principal demonstrating part of this astonishing apparatus, namely, to the Riank-Pokhortarz.

"This principal part however consisted of an ordinary

three-legged stand, on the top of which two balls, also of ivory, were fitted one upon the other in a certain way, the upper ball being much larger than the lower one.

"On the lower, smaller ball just opposite that part of the Loosochepana through which the positive colored rays had already passed, a cavity of a special form was made, into which either the whole of the said Polormedekhtian product named opium or single active elements required for the experiments were placed during the experiments.

"Now the upper ball was bored right through diametrically, horizontal to the Loosochepana, and on this large ball there was also radially perpendicular to this large bore drilled right through, yet another smaller bore, reaching only to the center and which was just opposite the Loosochepana.

"This second bore, drilled halfway through, was made in such a way that the colored rays could be directed as desired either directly from the Loosochepana or reflected from the said cavity of the lower smaller ball.

"Through the open bore of the large ball, a, what is called 'bamboo,' previously prepared in a special manner, could be freely moved.

"A long time before the experiments many of these bamboos were soaked together in absolute darkness, or in, as is said there on the Earth, orange 'light' obtained from the burning of 'Simkalash' which was obtained from a certain kind of what is called 'clay' deposited in the soil of your planet, and the deposits of which are usually found near accumulations of 'Salounilovian acids,' which in their turn are formed from 'Mamzolin' or, as your favorites call it, 'naphtha.'

"These bamboos were soaked in a liquid consisting of:

(1) The white of the eggs of the bird then called 'Amersamarskanapa'
(2) The juice of the plant called 'Chiltoonakh'

(3) The excretion of a quadruped being bearing the name 'Kezmaral'
(4) A specially prepared what is called 'mercury-amalgam'

"When these bamboos had been thoroughly soaked, they were inserted one by one into other thicker bamboos which had not been prepared in the said manner, and the ends of which were hermetically sealed.

"These latter preparations were of course also made in absolute darkness, or in the orange light of Simkalash.

"Later, when these soaked bamboos were necessary for the experiment, one end of the thicker unsoaked bamboo was inserted in a special way into the mentioned bore drilled right through the large ball of the Riank-Pokhortarz and opened by a small hook fixed to a thin stick by means of which the soaked bamboo could be moved at any speed desired.

"Now the action of the said liquid in which the bamboo was soaked was such that the part of the soaked bamboo on which the colored ray coming directly from the Loosochepana or, after being reflected from the cavity of the lower smaller ball, fell, was instantly permanently dyed the same color as that ray which had fallen on to it.

"The uncovered places of these bamboos soaked in the said manner were dyed the colors also corresponding to the sound vibrations which touched them, and which were obtained from what are called strings which were on the middle part of the apparatus called Dzendvokh.

"This Dzendvokh consisted of a very strong frame of special form made from the tusks of 'mammoths,' on which there were stretched many strings of various lengths and thicknesses, made partly from twisted what are called 'goat's intestines,' and partly from the tail-hairs of beings there of various exterior forms."

"Tell me, please, my dear Grandfather, what is a mammoth?" asked Hassein.

"A mammoth," replied Beelzebub, "is a two-brained being; in the beginning it also bred on your planet and had, in comparison with other beings there of all brain systems, a large exterior form.

"This kind of being also became a victim of the consequences of that large piece broken off from the planet Earth and now called Moon, which is now an independent, as I expressed it, 'planetary upstart' of this solar system Ors, and the chief bearer of evil to this ill-fated planet of yours.

"The point is that when the atmosphere of this small planetary upstart began to be formed and became gradually harmonized, great winds arose in the atmosphere of the planet Earth, owing to which several regions of its surface—you remember, I have already spoken about this to you—were buried with sand; moreover, at this time snow constantly fell in what are called the 'north' and 'south' polar regions of its atmosphere, and all the depressions of the surface of these north and south polar terra firma regions were covered by these falls of snow.

"The beings of this exterior form used to breed on the mentioned regions of the terra firma surface of your planet, and during these unprecedented, as is said there, 'snow storms,' they were all also buried by snow, and since then this species of beings has never again been re-established there.

"It is interesting to notice that at the present time there, in these depressions formerly covered with snow, and which were later covered with 'Kashiman,' that is with those substances which in general form on the surface of terra firma regions what is called 'soil,' there are sometimes still found now even well-preserved planetary bodies of these mammoths.

"These planetary bodies of mammoths have been so well preserved for such a long time, because these snows were then very soon after covered with Kashiman and thus there obtained the condition of 'Isoliazsokhlanness,' that is, as your favorites would say, the condition of a hermetically closed sphere, in which these planetary bodies of mammoths have never since been exposed, as is said there, 'to decomposition,' that is to say, the active elements of which these planetary bodies are in general formed have not completely involved back to their prime origin.

"And so, my boy, the astonishing apparatus 'Alla-attapan' which I described, demonstrated that all the three mentioned 'transitory results' of cosmic processes not only manifest themselves alike in their inner manifestations, but that they are also formed from the same factors.

"By means of this apparatus it was possible to verify and be convinced that in each of the mentioned three transitory results ensuing from common-cosmic-processes, and which have nothing in common outwardly with each other, there not only proceeds exactly similar what are called 'mutual-actions-ensuing-one-from-the-other-and-forming-one-common-functioning,' and that, in the sense of the evolutionary and involutionary particularities of the law of Heptaparaparshinokh, the action of each separate intermediary stage in one general functioning influences the action of each separate intermediary stage in another, exactly as in its own, but also that according to the particularities of the properties of the vibrations which compose their aggregate, these transitory cosmic results have complete affinity.

"This complete affinity in the inner mutual relations of these three transitory results which have outwardly nothing in common with each other was proved in the following way.

"For instance, a corresponding colored ray directed upon any active element of opium transformed it into another active element which corresponded in its newly acquired vibrations to the vibrations of the colored ray which had acted on the given active element.

"The same result was obtained if instead of these colored rays, corresponding sound-vibrations of the strings of the Dzendvokh were directed upon this same active element.

"Further, if any colored ray were made to pass through any active element of opium, then, passing through it, this same ray took on another color, namely, that color the vibrations of which corresponded to the vibrations of this active element; or if any colored ray were made to pass through the manifested what are called 'wave-of-sound-vibrations' still acting at that given moment from any corresponding string of the Dzendvokh, then, passing through this wave, it took on another color corresponding to the vibrations manifested by means of the given string.

"Or finally, if a definite colored ray and definite sound-vibrations from the strings were simultaneously directed upon any active element of opium from among those composing this Polormedekhtian product and which had a smaller number of vibrations than the totality of vibrations of the colored ray and of the said sound, then this active element was transformed into such another active element of opium the number of whose vibrations exactly corresponded to the totality of the numbers of the said two differently caused vibrations, and so on and so forth.

"This incomparable experimental apparatus likewise demonstrated that all the higher vibrations of one result always give the direction to all the lower vibrations of other 'transitory-cosmic-results.'

"After all that has just now been related to you, my boy, you can now be given that information thanks to which there might be crystallized in your mentation data for the representation into what general form the results of the tenacious-impartial-conscious-labors of these saints, the twin brothers, the terrestrial-great-scientists were then molded in this China, and in addition also data for the representation concerning the degrees of the successive deterioration of being-Reason in the presences of these unfortunate terrestrial three-brained beings.

"And so, when for the second time, from my observations of the existence of these three-brained beings who have taken your fancy, there arose on this still quite young China thanks to the mentioned two great terrestrial scientists, the twin brothers, an independent branch of genuine science, that is, 'the-totality-of-the-information-concerning-the-special-question-thoroughly-cognized-by-perfected-Reason' of three-brained beings who had existed earlier, in the given case concerning the fundamental cosmic law of the sacred Heptaparaparshinokh then called the law of 'ninefoldness,' then this branch of science was not only handed down almost normally in an unchanged form from generation to generation during the first two to three centuries counting from the time of the sacred Rascooarno of the great twin brothers, but it even gradually became—thanks to their followers, also genuine learned beings of that period—as it is said 'detailized' and became accessible to the perception of even ordinary beings.

"This proceeded then chiefly because the practice—which had been established by the learned beings of the continent Atlantis—of handing down such information to the beings of subsequent generations only through beings who were genuine initiates, still continued among them.

"I must not fail, my boy, to remark and acknowledge with conviction that indeed, if such an already long-established practice had continued, though automatically, in the process of the existence of these unfortunate three-brained beings who have taken your fancy, then in the given case just such a totality of true information already thoroughly cognized by the Reason of their still 'relatively normal' ancestors might have remained intact and might also have become the possession of your contemporary favorites; and those of them who constantly strive not to become ultimate victims of the consequences of the, for them, accursed organ Kundabuffer, might take advantage of this information with the aim of easing their already almost impossible what is called 'inner struggle.'

"To the regret of all more or less conscious 'relatively independent' separate Individuals of our Great Megalocosmos and to the misfortune of all subsequent three-brained beings who arose on this ill-fated planet of yours during the mentioned period, namely, during two to three of their centuries, the gradual distortion and ultimate almost total destruction began of just that blessing which had been created for them by their great ancestors thanks to their conscious labors and intentional sufferings.

"This followed from two causes.

"The first cause was, that thanks to the same abnormal conditions of external being-existence established by them themselves, certain of them were formed into responsible beings with that special 'organic-psychic-need' which in their speech might be formulated thus:

" 'An-irresistible-thirst-to-be-considered-as-learned-by-beings-around-them-similar-to-themselves'; and such a 'psycho-organic-need' began to engender in them that strange inherency about which I have many times spoken and which is called by them 'cunning wiseacring.'

"By the way, my boy, bear in mind once for all that when I used and will use the expression 'learned beings of new formation' I referred and will refer to those of your favorites, the learned beings just mentioned by me, who have this specific inherency.

"The other cause was that thanks at that period to certain external circumstances not depending on them, and which ensue from common-cosmic processes, chiefly owing to the action of the law of Solioonensius, the being-data crystallized in them which engendered the impulses of what are called 'sensing' and 'foreseeing' began to weaken in the common presences of the genuine initiated beings and they began to take such newly formed types as I have just described and to initiate them into some of the totalities of the true information known to them alone, among which was also that totality I mentioned, and from that time on this branch of genuine knowledge, which had already at that time become the possession of most of them, gradually began to be distorted and was ultimately again nearly quite forgotten.

"I employed the word 'almost' when I referred to the ultimate almost total destruction of that blessing because some fragments from the whole totality of this, in the objective sense, important true information nevertheless began—after the lapse of the mentioned period there, when their relatively normal process of being-existence was again re-established—to be again handed down to subsequent generations exclusively only through 'genuine' initiates, and being handed down by succession from generation to generation reached unchanged even to your contemporary favorites, though to a very limited number of them.

"There remained, however, as the possession of most of your contemporary favorites from all this true knowledge which had already been attained and thoroughly cognized by their great remote ancestors, those several practical unimportant fragments which had automatically reached them and which in the mentioned confused period were very widely spread among most of the ordinary beings of this then still quite young China.

"Among those unimportant fragments which automatically reached most of the contemporary favorites of yours there are, firstly, several methods of separating from the Polormedekhtian product named opium certain of its independent active elements; secondly, what is called 'the law of combination of colors'; and thirdly, what is called the 'seven-toned scale of sound.'

"As regards the first of the enumerated three fragments of the practical results attained by the Reason of three-brained beings of this ancient China and which reached to your contemporary favorites, it is necessary to tell you that in consequence of the fact that certain of the constituent parts of this whole product called there opium came from then on—thanks to the special properties of their agreeable action on the abnormal general-psyche of the beings—to be continuously used by them, therefore the knowledge of many methods of getting certain of its independent active elements began to be transmitted from generation to generation and reached down to your contemporary favorites.

"And at the present time they also obtain many of its definite parts and use them very avidly for the satisfaction of always the same consequences of the properties of the organ Kundabuffer crystallized in them.

"These parts extracted by them from the general composition of this Polormedekhtian product have of course already other names among your contemporary favorites.

"A contemporary 'comical learned chemist,' a certain Mendelejeff, even collected the names of all those active elements now obtained and classified them as it were according to their 'atomic weights.'

"Although his classification does not correspond at all to reality, yet nevertheless according to these atomic weights of his it is possible approximately to establish that classification which was then made by the great terrestrial learned beings of the future China.

"Of the number of nearly four hundred active elements of opium which then became known to the great brothers, knowledge of how to obtain only forty-two active elements has reached the contemporary 'chemists of the Earth' and these active elements have now the following names there:

[1] Morphine
[2] Protopine
[3] Lanthopine
[4] Porphiroksine
[5] Opium or narcotine
[6] Paramorphine or thebaine
[7] Phormine or pseudophormine
[8] Metamorphine
[9] Gnoskopine
[10] Oilopine
[11] Atropine
[12] Pirotine
[13] Dephteropine
[14] Tiktoutine
[15] Kolotine
[16] Khaivatine
[17] Zoutine
[18] Trotopine
[19] Laudanine
[20] Laudanosine
[21] Podotorine
[22] Arkhatozine
[23] Tokitozine
[24] Liktonozine

[25] Makanidine
[26] Papaverine
[27] Krintonine
[28] Kodomine
[29] Kolomonine
[30] Koilononine
[31] Katarnine
[32] Hydrokatarnine
[33] Opianine (mekonine)
[34] Mekonoiozine
[35] Pistotorine
[36] Phykhtonozine
[37] Codeine
[38] Nartzeine
[39] Pseudocodeine
[40] Microparaine
[41] Microtebaine
[42] Messaine

"The last time I was on your planet I heard that the contemporary learned beings of the community Germany found, as it were, methods of separating several other independent active elements from opium.

"But as I had already become convinced before this that the contemporary 'scientists' of that community, firstly, for the most part only fantasy, and, secondly, like the beings of ancient Greece, do not prepare anything good or beneficial for future generations, I therefore did not interest myself in these, as it were new, as they also call them 'scientific attainments' and do not know the names of these new active elements of the present day.

"As regards the second fragment of the practical results attained by the Reason of the same beings of ancient China and which has reached down to contemporary beings, namely, the knowledge relating to the 'law of the combination of colors,' then all the information concerning this has been handed down almost all the time from generation to generation, but each year it always underwent a greater change for the worse, and was only two centuries ago ultimately forgotten.

"At the present time some information relating to this law still continues to pass down and to become known only to certain of the three-brained beings there who belong to the group of beings there named 'Persians,' but now that the influence of what is called contemporary 'European paintings' is automatically spreading more and more widely in this group, then one must of course expect there the speedy and also total, as our esteemed teacher says, 'evaporation' of this information.

"And as regards the 'seven-toned scale of sound' which had reached them from the ancient Chinese beings, then you must be informed about this as detailedly as possible, because first of all, thanks to this information, you will better understand about the laws of vibrations in which all the peculiarities of the sacred Heptaparaparshinokh can be constated and cognized; and secondly, because, among those things intentionally reproduced by those same three-brained beings of yours who have taken your fancy, for daily use in their general existence, I brought home from there also one 'sound-producing instrument' named there 'piano' on which the vibration-engendering 'strings' were placed which could be arranged just as on the Dzendvokh, that is, the second special part of the famous experimental apparatus Alla-attapan, which was created by the great twin brothers and on which, when we return on to our dear Karatas, I shall be able to explain to you by demonstration, what is called, the 'successiveness-of-the-processes-of-the-mutual-blending-of-vibrations.' Thanks to these practical explanations of mine you will more easily be able to represent to yourself and approximately to cognize just how and in which successiveness in our great Megalocosmos the process of the Most Great Trogoautoegocrat proceeds and in what way the large and small cosmic concentrations arise.

"Relating about how such a fragment of 'practical result' from the ancient true knowledge survived and automatically reached down to your contemporary favorites, I shall first of all elucidate to you with more accuracy about this same definite law of vibrations which was first formulated by the great brothers as the 'seven-gravity-center-vibrations-of-sound.'

"I already said that in the beginning, while that totality of true information or that fragment of 'genuine knowledge' was handed down from the beings of one generation to the beings of subsequent generations only through the genuine initiates there, it not only underwent no change in the entirety of the exact sense put into it, but it even began, thanks to other also genuine learned beings among their followers of subsequent generations, to be 'detailized' and became accessible then to the perception of even ordinary three-brained terrestrial beings.

"Among these followers a century and a half after the sacred Rascooarno of the saints-brothers, there was a certain genuine learned being, King-Too-Toz by name, who, on the basis of the principles of the construction of the middle part of the apparatus Alla-attapan named Dzendvokh, propounded a very detailed theory under the name 'evolution and involution of vibrations,' and for the confirmation of this theory of his he made a special elucidatory apparatus which he called 'Lav-Merz-Nokh' and which, by the way, later became also widely known among almost all the learned beings of our Great Megalocosmos.

"The said apparatus Lav-Merz-Nokh, like the middle part of the Alla-attapan, consisted of a very strong frame with a great many strings stretched on it made from the intestines and tail-hairs of various quadruped beings there.

"One end of each string was fixed to one edge of this frame, and the other to pegs inserted into another edge.

"These pegs were inserted in such a way that they could be freely turned in their what are called 'peg holes,' and the strings fixed onto them could at will be tightened or loosened as much as was necessary for the required number of vibrations.

"Of the great number of strings stretched on the Lav-Merz-Nokh, forty-nine were colored white and the totality of vibrations, that is to say, the definite sound obtained from the vibrations of each one of them, was called a whole 'center-of-gravity-of-the-octave,' which definite sound corresponded to that which your favorites now call a 'whole note.'

"Each seven strings of these 'gravity-center-sounds' or whole notes were then and are still called an 'octave.'

"In this way there were stretched on the apparatus Lav-Merz-Nokh seven octaves of whole notes, the totality of the general consonance of which gave what is called the 'sacred Hanziano,' that is, just what the two great brothers suspected and which happened almost exactly to coincide with what, as I already said, they then named 'Nirioonossian-World-Sound.'

"Each such an octave of strings on the Lav-Merz-Nokh gave that totality of vibrations which according to the calculations of the great twin brothers corresponds to the totality of the vibrations of all those cosmic substances which, issuing from seven separate independent sources, compose one of the seven-centers-of-gravity of the 'fundamental common-cosmic Ansapalnian-octave.'

"Each white string on the Lav-Merz-Nokh was tuned separately by this Chinese learned being King-Too-Toz in such a way that it gave that average number of vibrations which according to the calculations of the great brothers ought also to be in substances which are one of the seven-centers-of-gravity of the given whole totality of substances, which in its turn is one of the seven centers of gravity of the fundamental cosmic octave of substances.

"On the Lav-Merz-Nokh, each octave as well as each whole note of the octave had names of their own.

"And, namely, the highest octave of the strings was called 'Arachiaplnish,'

The second	highest	'Erkrordiapan'
The third	highest	'Erordiapan'
The fourth	highest	'Chorortdiapan'
The fifth	highest	'Piandjiapan'
The sixth	highest	'Vetserordiapan'
The seventh	highest	'Okhterordiapan'

"And the 'gravity-center-strings' themselves were painted white and were called the same in all octaves, but with the addition of the name of the given octave itself.

"And, namely, these whole notes were called thus:

The first	highest	'Adashtanas'
The second	highest	'Evotanas'
The third	highest	'Govorktanis'
The fourth	highest	'Maikitanis'
The fifth	highest	'Midotanis'
The sixth	highest	'Lookotanas'
The seventh	highest	'Sonitanis'

"The contemporary beings of the Earth now call these same whole notes: 'do,' 'si,' 'la,' 'sol,' 'fa,' 'mi,' 're.'

"By the way, my boy, in order that the greatness of these two saints, brothers, should be still more evident to you, I draw your attention to the fact that the calculations made by them and the qualitativeness established by these calculations of what is called the 'vivifyingness-of-the-vibrations' of sound which corresponded according to their suppositions with the vivifyingness of cosmic sources of substances, appeared to coincide almost exactly with reality.

"This merit of theirs was all the greater, because as terrestrial beings they had no true information about this and were able to make their correct suppositions and almost accurate calculations of many objective cosmic truths exclusively only thanks to their own conscious labors and intentional sufferings.

"Further, on this Lav-Merz-Nokh in each octave between these white strings or whole notes, this learned being King-Too-Toz strung in certain places five further strings, but this time painted black.

"These black strings however he named 'Demisakhsakhsa,' which according to the terminology of the beings of the Earth corresponded to what they call 'half notes,' and these 'half-note strings' on the Lav-Merz-Nokh were not strung between those whole notes between which, according to the indications of the saints Choon-Kil-Tez and Choon-Tro-Pel, there is according to the sacred Heptaparaparshinokh no possibility of the independence of the evolution and involution of the vibrations of sound, and these places they were the first to call 'gaps.' And in the given places of the octave where these gaps ought to be, this learned being King-Too-Toz strung special strings between the whole notes made of the tail-hairs of beings called there 'horse.'

"These hair strings gave vibrations which were not always the same and King-Too-Toz named these vibrations 'chaotic.'

"The number of the vibrations obtained from these hair strings depended not on the stretching of them, as in the case of other strings, but on other causes; chiefly on three causes ensuing from surrounding cosmic results, namely: on the action of the vibrations dispersed around them obtained from other strings of the Lav-Merz-Nokh; on the state of what is called the 'temperature of the atmosphere' at the given moment; and on the radiations of the beings present nearby without distinction of brain system.

"On this Lav-Merz-Nokh between these white, black, and hair strings there were also strung in each octave fourteen strings also from 'twisted intestines,' which were painted red and called 'Keesookesschoor,' and if contemporary beings of the Earth were to use these strings they would call them 'quarter notes.'

"In addition to this, all those 'quarter-note strings' which were stretched on either side of the hair strings were fitted in such a way that the vibrations issuing from them could at any moment be changed as desired by means of tightening or loosening these strings and thus the vibrations they produced could be regulated and by ear blended with the frequently changing vibrations obtained from the hair strings.

"And this was so done because thanks to the frequently changing vibrations of the hair strings, the qualitativeness of which, I already said, depended on the temperature of the atmosphere, on the radiations of the beings present nearby, and on many other causes, the vibrations of these 'red strings' acquired such a property that, if they did not blend with the vibrations of the hair strings, the vibrations issuing from them would act on the beings present very 'cacophonically-harmfully,' even to their possible total destruction.

"With the frequent changing, however, of the stretching of the red strings and with the blending of their vibrations with the general vibrations issuing from the Lav-Merz-Nokh, their harmlessness was obtained, that is to say, owing to this, the general vibrations issuing from the Lav-

Merz-Nokh became for the beings who heard them what is called 'Harmoniously flowing' and not harmfully acting.

"And so, my boy, this apparatus, Lav-Merz-Nokh, and also the detailed theory of this ancient conscientious learned being King-Too-Toz suffered the same fate as the incomparable apparatus Alla-attapan and the whole totality of true information cognized by the brothers.

"Owing to the continuing and even increasing formation in the sense of quantity of certain of your favorites of the mentioned new type with the said inherency of cunning wiseacring, all this totality of information was from that time on altered and its genuine sense and significance gradually forgotten.

"And as regards how the basic principle of the arrangement of the strings of the apparatus Lav-Merz-Nokh and also that part of the Alla-attapan, the Dzendvokh, automatically reached to your contemporary favorites, this proceeded owing to the following reasons:

"When the acuteness of the mentioned 'confused period' had passed and when certain of the surviving fragments from all these great attainments of Reason of the still 'relatively normal' three-brained beings of your planet again began to be transmitted to subsequent generations in that way which before this had already been well established in the process of their ordinary existence, that is to say, the way of transmission only through beings who had already merited to become and to acquire the knowledge of genuine initiates, and when each year from among these latter more and more responsible beings were formed with the inherency just mentioned, then at this same period of time a three-brained being, also a 'scientist of new formation' who arose in this same China under the name of Chai-Yoo, was formed into a responsible being and became the cause of the knowledge and practical adoption of this 'seven-toned scale of sound' becoming generally accessible, and, being transmitted from generation to generation, it automatically reached also to your contemporary favorites.

"In the early years of his responsible existence this Chai-Yoo was destined—thanks to certain of his corresponding subjective merits—for a candidate of what is called 'first-degree-of-initiate' and, in consequence, help was given him without his knowledge, as it had long before been established by custom, by the genuine initiated beings there so that he could obtain every kind of information relating to various true events which took place on their planet in the past.

"And as my latest detailed investigations elucidated to me, he became worthy among other things to be also informed about the great apparatus Lav-Merz-Nokh in all details of its construction.

"And then, only in order that similar beings around him should regard him as a 'scientist,' this Chai-Yoo being one of the first so to say 'ideally formed scientists of new formation' there, that is, a being with a 'completedly formed inherency to wiseacre,' not only 'wiseacred' a new theory of his own on the basis of this information learned by him in the said manner concerning the details of the great apparatus Lav-Merz-Nokh, 'affirming and denying' so to say absolutely nothing relating to the laws of vibration, but he also constructed his new simplified 'sound-producing instrument' named 'King.'

"His simplification consisted in this, that without having at all taken into consideration the red and hair strings on the Lav-Merz-Nokh, he made the basis of his sound-producing instrument only the white and black strings, and moreover, only the number of strings of two octaves, and he placed them so that one whole octave which was found in the middle had for its evolutionary and involutionary continuation half an octave from its next higher octave and half an octave from its preceding lower octave.

"And so, although the theory 'wiseacred' by this Chai-Yoo also did not last very long, yet nevertheless this sound-producing instrument King constructed by him had become generally accessible owing to its simplicity; and in consequence of the fact that the result obtained from it during intentional action turned out to be very good and satisfactory for, so to say, the 'tickling' of many data crystallized in their common presences thanks to the consequences of the properties of the organ Kundabuffer—it began to pass automatically down from generation to generation.

"Although the outer form of this sound-producing instrument together with the construction of its frame, the stretch of the strings and their names were changed many times by the beings of subsequent generations—having been ultimately formed among your contemporary favorites into their heavy sound-producing instruments complicated to the degree of idiocy, and in their power incommensurably degenerated to a 'childish degree,' such as 'clavicymbals,' 'clavichord,' 'organ,' 'grand piano,' 'upright piano,' 'harmonium,' and so on—yet the basic principle of what is called 'the alternation of gravity center sounds' has remained at the present time such as were actualized by the saints-brothers Choon-Kil-Tez and Choon-Tro-Pel on the Dzendvokh, that is, the middle independent part created by them of the incomparable experimental apparatus Alla-attapan.

"That is why, my boy, this, as it is now called there, 'Chinese seven-toned subdivision of the octave of sound' simplified by the mentioned Chai-Yoo, which has reached down to your contemporary favorites and which is used at the present time by them for all their sound-producing instruments enumerated by me, might still, as I have already said, partly serve for, so to say, the 'practical confrontative study' and approximate cognizance of how in the process of the Most Great Trogoautoegocrat, from what is called the 'flowing-of-some-vibrations-from-others,' cosmic substances arise of different 'density' and 'vivifyingness,' and in which way, uniting and disuniting among themselves, they form large and small 'relatively independent' concentrations and thus actualize the common cosmic Iraniranumange.

"Moreover, you will soon clearly convince yourself about this when, on returning to our dear Karatas, I will show you, as I have already promised, and explain practically the significance of the tuning on that contemporary sound-producing instrument, the piano, which was taken by me among a number of other things from the surface of your planet and which I brought in order experimentally to elucidate to myself on being free at home, one of its particularities which I did not have sufficient time to elucidate there on the spot and which is connected with the strange psyche of these three-brained beings who have taken your fancy and with the vibrations of different vivifyingness engendered around them.

"And if besides this I now still add, concerning the strange psyche of your favorites, what I constated during my last sojourn among them, namely, that the contemporary three-brained beings of your planet—in spite of the fact that they, having put this same 'Chinese seven-toned subdivision' as the basis of all their 'sound-producing instruments,' almost daily perceive the results of its consequences—are not only not at all inspired by this as they should be objectively, but on the contrary, under the action of this kind of consonance with the total absence of remorse and even with the impulse of satisfaction, intentionally maintain in themselves the flowing of those associations of all their spiritualized parts which arise in their common presences under the influence of data crystallized in them from the consequences of the properties of the, for them, accursed organ Kundabuffer, then you, I am sure, after such a practical demonstration on this piano, will have not only an approximate representation concerning all what are called 'some-obtained-from-the-other-and-harmoniously-flowing-gravity-center-vibrations,' but likewise you will constate once more with the impulse of astonishment, to what an extent there is weakened in the common presences of these favorites of yours the essence of the action of those being-data, which in general are proper to be crystallized in the presences of all three-brained beings and the totality of which is called 'quickness-of-instinct.'

"And so, my boy, thanks on the one hand to the infallibly continuing deterioration in the common presences of these three-brained beings who have taken your fancy, of the quality of the functioning of the data crystallized in them for healthy being-mentation, and on the other hand to the always increasing number among them being formed into responsible beings of the mentioned new 'types,' namely, of learned beings of new formation, there ultimately reached the contemporary three-brained beings of this ill-fated planet from this detailed 'totality of information' already thoroughly cognized by the Reason of former beings similar to them, and almost unprecedented everywhere in the Universe among ordinary three-brained beings and which had gradually begun to change—namely, the totality of that true information which today is already used for the welfare of ordinary three-brained beings everywhere on the planets of our Great Megalocosmos with the exception of the beings of only that planet on which this totality of information arose—only that which our always esteemed Mullah Nassr Eddin defines by the following words:

"'Glory to Thee, Lord Creator, for having made the teeth of wolves not like the horns of my dear buffalo, for now I can make several excellent combs for my dear wife.'

"And with particular regard to the 'Chinese seven-toned subdivision of the octave' which has reached down to your contemporary favorites, then although as I have already said, they use it widely in the process of their ordinary existence, yet at the same time they do not even suspect that such a subdivision was specially created and constructed on those sound principles on which everything existing in the whole of our Great Megalocosmos is maintained.

"If one does not consider that insignificant number of three-brained beings of certain small groups who existed on the continent Asia and who instinctively sensed the hidden meaning of this 'Chinese division of a whole sound into seven definite centers of gravity' and reproduced it practically, exclusively only during such being-manifestations of theirs as they considered sacred, then one may boldly say that in the presences of almost all three-brained beings who arose on this planet of yours during recent centuries the data for the cognizance of the altitude of thought and meaning put into this subdivision have already entirely ceased to be crystallized; but the contemporary three-brained beings there who breed on this same continent Asia as well as on all other terra firma of the surface of this planet of yours, having already lost every kind of instinctive feeling, all without exception use it for the satisfaction of only certain of their low purposes, unbecoming to three-brained beings.

"What is most interesting, however, of all the history related by me concerning the cognizance of the sacred law of Heptaparaparshinokh by three-brained beings who bred on your planet and which concerns chiefly the contemporary beings, is, that although a great number of all kinds of 'totalities of special information' or, as they themselves express it, 'separate branches of scientific knowledge' again arose among them at the present time and began by them, so to say, to be 'learned by rote,' yet concerning the 'law of vibrations'—which branch is the most important and which gives the possibility, though approximately, of recognizing reality—there is among them absolutely nothing, if, of course, one does not reckon that celebrated what is called 'theory of sound,' which arose comparatively recently, and which is 'seriously' studied and, as it were, 'known' by their contemporary, as they are called, 'learned physicists' and 'learned musicians.'

"In order that you may, so to say, 'illuminatingly project' the essence of your contemporary favorites, and in view of the fact that the causes of the arising of various misunderstandings—widely spread among certain of your favorites—in the sphere of this branch of knowledge there are very characteristic and might serve you as excellent material in general for the representation and valuation of the sense and objective significance of all other contemporary separate independent branches of their what is called 'exact science,' I consider it necessary to explain to you in greater detail which theories concerning the 'vibrations of sound' are studied and, as it were, are known by these mentioned contemporary terrestrial 'sorry scientists.'

"But before speaking about this, my essence again enjoins the whole of my common presence to express my sincere condolence on the fate of all contemporary terrestrial three-brained beings, who thanks to their persevering 'being-Partkdolg-duty' peculiar to them finally attain to the state of that degree of Reason when it becomes inevitable for them to have in their presences also the data of the genuine information relating to the law of vibrations.

"About this, I by association at the present moment remember with the impulse of regret, because at the period of my last sojourn among them I happened more than once to meet those three-brained beings there who according to their state of, so to say, 'psychic perfection' ought of necessity to absorb and transmute in themselves just the true information concerning the law of vibrations and at the same time I clearly understand that they could not extract such information from anywhere.

"There is, indeed, among them at the present time such a 'totality of information' or, as they themselves name it, a 'theory of vibrations'; yet the mentioned unfortunate contemporary beings who are in need of this information cannot in spite of their wishes and efforts obtain anything tolerably satisfactory for their searchings, except various misconceptions and contradictions.

"And so, my boy, the basis for the arising of such terrestrial misunderstandings was that various fragments of information concerning the 'law of vibrations' reached the contemporary beings from two independent sources, namely, from those same ancient Chinese and from those ancient Greeks, about whom, you remember, I have already told you that their community was formed there long ago between the continents of Asia and Europe, by those Asiatic fishermen, who, out of boredom during bad weather, invented various 'sciences' among which was just this 'science of the vibrations of sound.'

"And this science of theirs, later also passing from generation to generation, reached your contemporary favorites almost simultaneously with the said Chinese science.

"All subsequent misunderstandings began with this, that in the information which had reached them from the ancient Chinese it was shown that the 'whole octave of vibrations' has seven 'restorials,' that is to say, that the octave consists of seven 'gravity center sounds'; while in the Greek information it was said that the 'whole octave of vibrations' has five 'restorials,' that is to say, that the octave consists of five centers of gravity or five whole notes.

"And so, only in consequence of the fact that in the presences of your favorites of recent centuries the functioning of every kind of data for 'being-logical-reflection' crystallized in them began to proceed almost, as it is said there, 'topsy-turvy,' and as both of these entirely differently sourced informations which reached them appeared to them, according to their 'bobtailed' logical mentation, equally plausible, then those beings of contemporary civilization who began in a new fashion to bake, like pancakes, all kinds of separate independent branches of their illustrious science, having fallen during several years into a state of what is called 'troubled perplexity,' could not in any way whatsoever decide which of these two contradictory theories to prefer and which of them to accept and include in the number of branches of their 'official science.'

"After a great deal of, as they still sometimes say, 'drying of saliva,' they finally decided, in order that no one should be offended and at the same time in order to have also this branch in their science, to unite into one both of these theories which had reached them from ancient times and which had nothing in common with each other. And a little later when one of them, named Gaidoropoolo, thought out a very long 'mathematical' explanation of this misunderstanding, namely, why in one theory there is mentioned the division of the octave into seven 'whole sounds,' while in the other, into only five 'whole sounds,' and why and how such an important contradiction had occurred, then these mathematical explanations of his entirely pacified all the corresponding representatives of contemporary civilization so that now, with a quiet conscience, they produce all their wiseacring concerning vibrations on the basis of the 'mathematical explanations' of this obliging Gaidoropoolo.

"In these mathematical explanations the following considerations were adduced:

"Now, that is to say, this same obliging Gaidoropoolo, in a certain way known to himself, calculated the number of vibrations of all the Chinese seven whole notes and began to explain that in the Chinese 'seven-toned octave' those whole notes called 'mi' and 'si' are not whole notes at all but only half notes, since the number of vibrations which they have almost coincides with the number of vibrations of those Greek half notes which according to the division of the Greek octave are found just between the Chinese whole notes 'mi' and 'fa' and between 'si' and 'do.'

"He made the further supposition that it was obviously convenient for the Chinese to have the restorial of the voice, that is, the 'center of gravity' of the voice also on these half notes, and therefore they divided their octave not into five whole notes like the Greeks, but into seven, and so on in this way.

"After this explanation of Mr. Gaidoropoolo, as I have already told you, all the other contemporary scientists of new formation were completely pacified, having stuck a label also on this branch of their official science.

"And now among them, this branch under the name of the 'theory of the law of vibrations' exists there, as our wise teacher Mullah Nassr Eddin would say, 'in clover.'

"About the given case I still remember and willy-nilly cannot help expressing aloud that wise formulation of our always esteemed Mullah Nassr Eddin, which expression he has in the following words:

"'Ekh . . . you, Koorfooristanian pantaloons, isn't it all the same to you whether you have a mule or a hare for your farm work? Haven't both of these animals four legs?'

"These contemporary favorites of yours of course do not know and do not even suspect that these two independent divisions of the octave into whole notes which they now have and which they called the Chinese and the Greek have as the basis of their arising two entirely different causes: the first, that is, the Chinese division, is, as I already said, the result of the thorough cognizance by the great learned twin brothers—unprecedented on Earth previously as well as subsequently—of the law of Heptaparaparshinokh; and the second, that is, the Greek division, was made only on the basis of what is called the 'restorials of voice' which were in the voices of the beings-Greeks of that period, when this 'five-tone Greek octave' was composed.

"Almost as many of these restorials of the voice or, as they are still sometimes named, 'light sounds of voice' are formed among your favorites and until today are still formed, as there are independent groups into which they are divided and still continue to be divided, and this proceeds so because these light sounds of voice are in general formed among the beings from many outer as well as inner surrounding conditions not depending on them themselves, as for instance: geographical, hereditary, religious, and even from the 'quality-of-nourishment' and the 'quality-of-reciprocal-influences,' and so on and so forth.

"Your contemporary favorites of course cannot understand that however hard these same ancient Greeks tried, or, so to say, 'however conscientious their attitude toward this matter,' they could not with all their wish find in the division of the octave of sound into definite tones either more or less than these five whole notes, since the totality of all the conditions not depending on them, both inner and outer, gave them the possibility at the reproduction of their chanting to rely only on their five restorials of voice.

"'Restorials' or gravity-center-sounds in the voices of beings are in general and are called those notes which, during the reproductions of different sounds by corresponding organs, the beings manifest according to the properties fixed in them and depending on the general functioning of their presence—which properties in their turn are the result of heredity and of acquired faculties—freely, easily, and for a long time, without evoking any tension whatsoever on the part of other separate functionings of theirs, that is to say, in other words the restorials are obtained when the tempo of the result of such a manifestation of theirs fully harmonizes with other functionings of their common presence, the tempo of which is already fixed in them thanks to all the inner and outer conditions of their common being-existence.

"Thanks to the various conditions there of local character and also to various assimilated hereditary qualities, various 'restorials of voice' or gravity-center notes are formed in beings of almost each group or of each geographical place, and hence the division of the octave into whole notes among beings who breed on each definite part of the surface of this planet of yours is quite different.

"At the present time among your favorites such groups exist as have the capacity to reproduce the gravity-center notes in the octave of sounds not only in five or seven gravity-center sounds but even in thirteen and seventeen whole notes.

"To illustrate what I have just said, the beings of a certain smallish group might serve as a good example who dwell on the continent Asia to whose singing I personally very much liked to listen and who in their physiological possibilities—although they had the data for the manifestation of only three restorials—could nevertheless in their chanting reproduce up to forty separate definite sounds.

"Their chanting was extremely delightful and at the same time, however lustily they might sing, yet the calm and sustained reproductions of the vibrations of sound were obtained among them only on one or other of these three of their 'organic restorials.'

"This physiological particularity of theirs, namely, that whatever number of definite sounds they reproduced the beings of this small group always obtained in the whole octave of their voice only on these three restorials inherent in them what is called the 'unchanging totality of vibrations,' and that all during their manifestation these restorials had the property of evoking what is called 'centralization' and echo in the whole presence of a being, I made very clear to myself when, having become interested in their chanting, I began to investigate this particularity, rare among your contemporary favorites, with the aid of three special what are called there 'tuning forks' which I ordered, and with the aid of several very sensitive what are called 'vibrometers' which I possessed and which were invented for me personally by my essence-friend Gornahoor Harharkh.

"In the Chinese division of the octave into whole notes this being-property was not at all taken into account.

"The basis of the Chinese 'subdivision of the octave into seven whole notes,' as well as the basis of all the information composing the totality of the special branch of knowledge relating to the law of Ninefoldness, consisted of the results of those conscious labors and intentional sufferings of the two great twin brothers for which their higher bodies became beatified, and who now dwell on that holy planet on which we recently had the happiness to be.

"However it might have been there, my boy, yet at the present time I regret very much that it will be impossible for me with the contemporary sound-producing instrument piano which I brought from the surface of your planet, to explain fully to you the laws of vibrations of all sources which actualize the common-cosmic 'Ansanbaluiazar' as this was ideally possible to do on the remarkable Lav-Merz-Nokh, created by the follower of the great twin brothers, himself not less great, also a Chinese learned being, King-Too-Toz.

"On that remarkable 'elucidatory apparatus' Lav-Merz-Nokh, King-Too-Toz arranged and tuned, according to the corresponding calculations made by the great brothers, just as many strings for engendering vibrations as there are consecutive sources in the Universe from any planet up to the Protocosmos, in the presences of which the vibrations of cosmic substances changing according to law during the Trogoautoegocratic processes blend correspondingly for the actualization of everything further.

"However, my boy, although the sound-producing instrument piano which I brought from the surface of your planet is a very typical invention of your contemporary favorites, yet owing to the fact, as I have already told you, that the fundamental tuning of the strings of its whole notes and half notes has not yet been changed, therefore according to the consecutive blending vibrations evoked in a corresponding manner by the strings on it, it might still be possible experimentally to demonstrate at least the laws of vibrations issuing from any one fundamental common-cosmic octave of substances, that is to say, issuing from one of the seven fundamental totalities of sources; and thanks to this, it might be possible to represent to oneself and to cognize all the reciprocally acting vibrations issuing from all other sources, because as I have already told you, all the variously scaled cosmoses as well as the independent seventh parts of these cosmoses are almost exactly similar to the Megalocosmos, and in each of them the sevenfold sources of vibrations have the same reciprocal actions as proceed in the Megalocosmos, and therefore having understood the laws of vibrations for any one center-of-gravity, it is possible to understand approximately also the laws of vibrations for all centers-of-gravity, if, of course, their difference of scale is taken into account.

"I repeat, if the strings of this piano are tuned correctly and the corresponding vibrations are evoked in corresponding strings, then the resulting blending of vibrations almost exactly coincides, even mathematically, with the law-conformable totality of vibrations of substances actualized by corresponding cosmic sources on the basis of the sacred Heptaparaparshinokh.

"On this piano the vibrations of each whole note and half note of any octave pass from one to another exactly according to the law of the sacred Heptaparaparshinokh and thus their vibrations—as this occurs always and everywhere in the Universe exactly similarly—mutually help each other to evolve or involve.

"Here, by the way, it will be very interesting to notice that if the calculations and enumerations obtained by these great terrestrial learned beings were almost exact, then they owed it to the fact that the standard unit which they took for their calculations chanced to be that unit which is taken everywhere in the Megalocosmos, that is, that same small particle of the most sacred substance Theomertmalogos in which there might still be all the fullness of the power of vivifyingness proper to it.

"Well, just here I will explain to you as I promised, about the already mentioned 'Nirioonossian-World-Sound.'

"The Nirioonossian-World-Sound is just that sound the

vibrations of which have been taken from ancient times—and even at the present time there, is still taken, it is true, for a very small number of your favorites, of course, of this same China—for their sound-producing instruments as the 'absolute vibrations' of the note 'do.'

"The history of the constatation of the existence there on your planet of this sound is as follows:

"It was first discovered by that learned member of the society Akhaldan which existed on the continent Atlantis, who was a progenitor of these same learned twin brothers and who, do you remember, I have already told you, chanced to meet the first settlers of the country Maralpleicie and was later elected by them as their chief.

"At that time this same learned member of the society Akhaldan, during his observations of different cosmic phenomena which proceeded on and beyond their planet, constated that in a definite locality of a certain part of this country, just near that locality where the town Gob arose, twice a year after certain meteorological perturbations in the atmosphere, the same definite sound always arose and was heard for a fairly long time.

"And therefore he then on the spot constructed an elevation such as he required, as is said there, for the observation of 'heavenly bodies'; and he constructed this required elevation on this spot because he wished during these observations of his at the same time to observe and investigate also this 'cosmic result' at first entirely incomprehensible to him.

"And afterwards, when the two great brothers, the later saints, constated and began to investigate the sacred cosmic law of Heptaparaparshinokh, as they already had knowledge of this cosmic result they established themselves in the same place, and it is there that they succeeded in elucidating the character and the nature of this strange sound which they made the unit of measurement of all their calculations in general.

"On this piano vibrations of extraneous origin come through different shocks and tremblings and for the greater part from what are called aerial vibrations of inertia, which are generally formed in the atmospheric space by the natural vibrations already referred to.

"It is necessary at this point in connection with the actualization of the fifth Stopinder of the sacred Heptaparaparshinokh to trace a parallel between two processes which externally have nothing in common with one another, namely: in the same manner as the first being-food cannot acquire its vivifying power until after its transformation into being-piandjoëhari, in the same manner on this piano the vibrations of a chord do not acquire a corresponding vivifying power until they have been fused with the preceding vibrations produced, starting from the center of gravity of the totality of the vibrations of the note 'sol.'

"This last particularity of the sacred law of Heptaparaparshinokh is absolutely certain in this given case, that is to say on the piano, but uniquely in consequence of the fact that if the vibrations of 'mi' and 'si' are produced in a hermetically sealed room, these vibrations either cease instantaneously or else the notes 'mi' and 'si' by reason of the momentum obtained from the first shock given for their arising undergo involution and immediately cease, that is to say, as soon as the note 'mi' reaches the note 'do' and the note 'si' the lower 'fa.'

"In conclusion of the explanations that I have already given you relating to the subdivision into seven tones of the octave of sound which exists among your favorites, I must once again, alas, insist on this fact that if anything has remained and reached them of this knowledge, they have forgotten everything that was essential and always for the same reason: the disappearance from their presences of the practice of actualizing being-Partkdolg-duty, the same disappearance which is the very cause of the gradual deterioration in them of the mentation proper to three-brained beings."

At this point in his recital Beelzebub became absorbed once again in his own thoughts and his look was fixed on the tip of his grandson's nose.

There was a rather long silence after which he said to the latter:

"Ekh! my dear child, I must now speak to you willy-nilly about an experiment of which I was a witness on that same planet Earth and which refers to the laws of vibrations. I shall moreover speak to you about it in all possible detail for the two following reasons:

"The first is because I have already said much to you about this first fundamental sacred law of Heptaparaparshinokh. I would therefore be very distressed if for some reason or other you should not succeed in understanding clearly the particularities of this law. This is why I now find myself constrained to hide nothing from you concerning these experiments because I am sure that they will enable you to form for yourself an exhaustive representation.

"And in the second place I wish to impart to you all possible details concerning these experiments, because the terrestrial being who made them, thanks to the knowledge of cosmic vibrations which he had acquired, was the sole and unique being who during the many centuries that I existed upon the Earth recognized and came to know my true nature."

CHAPTER 41

The Bokharian Dervish Hadji-Asvatz-Troov

"As my first meeting with this contemporary terrestrial three-brained being—with whom I saw the said experiments and thanks to whom, in all probability, information about the fundamental sacred cosmic law of Heptaparaparshinokh will again be established there and become accessible to everyone, even from among the ordinary contemporary beings with a thirst for knowledge—may turn out to be extremely interesting and instructive to you, I shall therefore tell you all about this meeting also, in all possible detail.

"This first meeting of mine with him took place three terrestrial years before my final departure from that solar system.

"Once while traveling over the continent Asia in that part of it called 'Bokhara,' I chanced to meet and get on friendly terms with a certain three-brained being belonging to the group inhabiting that part of the surface of your planet, who was by profession what they call there a 'dervish' and whose name was 'Hadji-Zephir-Bogga-Eddin.'

"He was very typical of those contemporary terrestrial three-brained beings who have a tendency to enthuse over, as is said there, 'higher matters' and who always automatize themselves to speak about them without any essential cognition with anyone they meet, on opportune and inopportune occasions. And whenever we met, he also liked to talk only about these matters.

"One day we started talking about what is called there the 'ancient-Chinese-science' named 'Shat-Chai-Mernis.'

"This science is nothing but fragments of the above-mentioned totality of true information concerning the sacred Heptaparaparshinokh cognized by the great Chinese twin brothers and by other genuine ancient scientists and then called by them the 'totality of true information about the law of Ninefoldness.'

"I have already told you that certain fragments of this knowledge remained intact and passed from generation to generation through a very limited number of initiated beings there.

"I must here say that if these fragments, which have by chance remained intact and which have passed and are still passing there from generation to generation through this very limited number of initiated beings, do not fall into the hands of contemporary 'scientists' there, then this will be a great stroke of luck for the future three-brained beings of your planet.

"And it will be a great stroke of luck because, if these surviving fragments of genuine knowledge were to fall into the hands of the contemporary 'scientists' there, then thanks to their inherency of wiseacring, they would without fail cook up all kinds of their 'scientific porridge' about the sense put into these fragments, and thereby the, without this, scarcely smoldering Reason of all the other three-brained beings would be entirely extinguished; and besides, these last remnants of the former great attainments of their ancestors would thereby be also completely 'wiped off' the face of this ill-fated planet.

"And so, my boy, once when I was talking with this dervish Hadji-Zephir-Bogga-Eddin about the ancient Chinese science Shat-Chai-Mernis, he, in the course of conversation, proposed that I should go with him to another dervish, a friend of his, a great authority on this ancient Chinese science, to talk about it with him.

"He told me that his friend resided in 'Upper Bokhara,' far away from everyone, and was there occupied with certain experiments concerning that same science.

"Having no special business in that town where we then happened to be, and as his friend resided just among those mountains the nature of which I had long intended to see, I at once agreed and on the very next day we set off.

"From that town where we were, we walked three days.

"Finally, high up in the mountains of Upper Bokhara, we stopped at a small gorge.

"This part of 'Bokhara' is called 'Upper' because it is very mountainous and much higher than that part of Bokhara which, to distinguish it, is called 'Lower Bokhara.'

"At the said gorge my acquaintance the dervish Hadji-Zephir-Bogga-Eddin asked me to help him move a small stone slab to one side, and when we had moved it a small aperture was revealed underneath it from the edges of which two iron bars projected.

"He put these bars together and began to listen.

"Soon a strange sound was heard coming from them, and to my astonishment Hadji-Zephir-Bogga-Eddin said something into that aperture in a language unknown to me.

"After he had finished speaking, we moved the stone slab back to its old place and went on.

"After having gone a considerable distance we stopped in front of a rock and Hadji-Zephir-Bogga-Eddin began to wait very tensely for something, when suddenly the enormous stone which lay there opened and formed an entrance into a kind of cave.

"We entered this cave and began moving forward when I noticed that our way was lit up alternately by what are called gas and electricity.

"Although this lighting astonished me and several questions about it arose in me, I nevertheless decided not to disturb the serious attentiveness of my fellow traveler.

"When we had again walked a considerable distance further, we saw at one of the turnings coming to meet us another terrestrial three-brained being who met us with the greetings customary there on such occasions and led us further.

"He, as it appeared, was the friend of my first dervish acquaintance.

"He was already according to terrestrial understanding quite elderly, and being tall in comparison with those living round about seemed extraordinarily thin.

"His name was Hadji-Asvatz-Troov.

"While talking with us, he led us to a small section of the cave, where we all sat down on the felt that covered the floor there and, while conversing, began to eat what is called cold Bokharan 'Shila-Plav' out of earthen vessels which this elderly being brought to us from a neighboring section.

"While we were eating, my first dervish acquaintance told him by the way that I was also very interested in the science Shat-Chai-Mernis and explained briefly which questions were already well known to me and what in general we had talked about before.

"After that, the dervish Hadji-Asvatz-Troov began to question me himself and I gave him corresponding answers, but of course in that form already habitual to me by which I could always hide my real nature.

"There on your planet I became in general so skillful in talking in this manner that your favorites always took me for one of their brother scientists.

"From subsequent conversation with him, I understood that this respected Hadji-Asvatz-Troov had already been long interested in the said knowledge and that during the last ten years he had been studying it exclusively only practically.

"I also understood that from this studying he had attained results such as it is no longer proper to terrestrial three-brained beings to attain.

"When I had made all this clear to myself, I was much astonished and became very interested to know how this had come about, because I already very well knew that this knowledge had already long before ceased to exist in the Reason of the three-brained beings of the Earth and that this venerable Hadji could scarcely have heard of it often and thus have had an interest, as happens among them, gradually formed in him.

"And indeed, my boy, it has already long ago become proper there to the three-brained beings who have taken your fancy to become interested only in what they often see or often hear about, and whenever they do become interested in something, then this interest of theirs stifles all other being-necessities in them, and it will always seem obvious to them that what interests them at the given moment is just the very thing that 'makes the world go round.'

"When the relations necessary in such a situation had been established between this sympathetic dervish Hadji-Asvatz-Troov and myself, that is to say, when he had already begun to talk with me more or less normally without the so to say 'mask' which it has already become fully proper to contemporary beings to wear in their relations with other beings like themselves, especially when they meet these others for the first time—then, when these necessary relations had been established between us, I asked him, of course in the corresponding approved manner, why and how he had become interested in this branch of true knowledge.

"Here you might as well know that in general there on the surface of your planet on each separate part, during the process of the ordinary being-existence of these strange three-brained beings, their own special forms of external relationship with each other have gradually been formed and have passed from generation to generation.

"And these various forms of mutual relationship among them were formed of themselves after the being-property of sensing the inner feeling of similar beings in relation to oneself had become quite atrophied in their psyche, which property must infallibly exist in all beings of our Great Universe without distinction of form or place of arising.

"At the present time among them, good or bad mutual relationships are established exclusively only according to outer calculated manifestations, chiefly according to what they call 'amiability,' that is, by empty words in which there is not a single atom of what is called 'the result of an inner benevolent impulse,' such as arises in general in the presences of all beings in direct contact with 'those similar to themselves.'

"There, at present, however, one being may inwardly wish another well, yet if for some reason or other this well-wishing being were in some way to express himself to another in words conventionally regarded as not good, then all is over; in all the different spiritualized localizations of the latter, data are invariably crystallized which always by association engender in his common presence the conviction that the former, who as a matter of fact inwardly wished him very well, only exists to do him always and everywhere every kind of what they call 'vileness.'

"It has become very important there, particularly during recent times, to know every kind of form of 'verbal address' in order to have friends and not to make oneself 'enemies.'

"The abnormal existence of these strange three-brained beings has not only spoiled their own psyche, but this abnormal existence of theirs has by repercussion gradually also spoiled the psyche of almost all the other one-brained and two-brained terrestrial beings.

"Data for engendering the aforesaid inner being-impulse are not yet formed either in the presences of any of those terrestrial one-brained or two-brained beings with whom these strange three-brained beings who have taken your fancy have long had and still have frequent contact and relations.

"Although these being-data are still formed in the presences of certain terrestrial one-brained and two-brained beings of other exterior forms, as for example those named by them 'tigers,' 'lions,' 'bears,' 'hyenas,' 'snakes,' 'phalangas,' 'scorpions,' and so on, who have not had and do not now have in their mode of existence any contact or relation with these biped favorites of yours, nevertheless there is already formed in their common presences, thanks of course to the abnormally established conditions of the ordinary existence of your favorites, one very strange and highly interesting particularity, namely, that the enumerated beings, tigers, lions, bears, hyenas, snakes, phalangas, scorpions, and so on, perceive the inner feeling of fear in other beings before them as enmity towards themselves, and therefore strive to destroy these others in order to avert the 'menace' from themselves.

"And this so happened because your favorites, thanks always to the same abnormal conditions of existence, have gradually become, as they themselves say, 'cowardly' from head to foot, and because at the same time the need of destroying the existence of others has been inculcated in them, also from head to foot. And so, when they, being already cowards 'of the highest degree,' are about to destroy the existence of the beings of these other forms, or when they chance to meet such beings—who it must be said, to their misfortune and to our regret, have become at the present time already much stronger than they, physically as well as in other being-attainments—then they become 'afraid,' as they say there in such case, 'to the point of wetness.'

"At the same time, thanks to the inherent need in their presences to destroy the existence of other beings breeding on their planet, they at such moments contrive with their whole Being how to destroy the existence of these beings of other forms.

"And as a result of all this, from the radiations issuing from these favorites of yours inherent in their peculiar presences there are gradually formed in the common presences of these other beings of the aforementioned forms—side by side with the data which should exist in them for engendering the aforementioned impulse of 'instinctively showing respect and sympathy' to every form of being—other data with a special functioning, thanks to which the feeling of cowardice appearing in the common presences of other beings, chiefly in the presences of your favorites, is perceived as a 'menace' to themselves.

"That is why whenever these other mentioned one-brained and two-brained terrestrial beings meet with your favorites, they, wishing to escape the danger to their own existence, always strive to destroy the existence of these favorites of yours.

"There on your planet also, all beings, in the beginning, in spite of difference of exterior form and brain system, existed together in peace and concord; and even now occasionally, one of these favorites of yours perfects himself firstly to the degree of sensing with all his spiritualized parts that every being or, as is said, 'every breathing creature' is equally near and dear to our COMMON FATHER CREATOR; and secondly, thanks to having actualized in himself being-Partkdolg-duty, he attains the complete destruction in his presence of the data for engendering the impulse of cowardice before beings of other forms, in consequence of which these beings of other forms not only do not attempt to destroy the existence of this perfected being from among your contemporary favorites, but even show him every kind of respect and service, as to a being with greater objective possibilities.

"In short, all this and a multitude of other small factors, also ensuing from the abnormal existence of these favorites of yours, have finally brought about the formation among them, for mutual relationship, of various forms of, as they express it, 'verbal amenity,' and, as I have already told you, each locality there has its own special form.

"The attitude taken towards me by this sympathetic terrestrial three-brained being Hadji-Asvatz-Troov was benevolent chiefly because I was the friend of a good friend of his.

"It must here be remarked by the way, that the three-brained beings of this part of the surface of your planet are the only ones among whom the relationship of true friendship still exists.

"Among them, as it is general everywhere among three-brained beings, and just as it was in the first epochs on that planet also, not only is a friend himself a friend, but his near relatives and his friends are also regarded as friends and are treated just the same as the friend himself.

"Because I then passed for the friend of the dervish Hadji-Zephir-Bogga-Eddin, who was a very good friend of this Hadji-Asvatz-Troov, he then at once treated me in a very friendly manner.

"I wished to make the relationship still better, as I very much wanted to know how he had become interested in this knowledge and how he had attained to such scientific accomplishments as were unsurpassed on the Earth, and therefore throughout our conversation I liberally used those forms of verbal amenity which were customary in that locality.

"When during our conversation which dealt exclusively

with the knowledge now called there Shat-Chai-Mernis, we came to speak of the nature and the significance of vibrations in general, and when we happened to talk about the octave of sound, Hadji-Asvatz-Troov then said that not only had the octave of sound seven aspects of relatively independent whole manifestations, but that the vibrations of any one of these relatively independent manifestations follow, in their arising as well as in their manifestation, the same conformity to law.

"Continuing to speak further about the laws of vibration of sound, he said:

"'I myself became interested in the knowledge Shat-Chai-Mernis through the laws of vibrations of sound; and they were the cause of my devoting the whole of my life subsequently to this knowledge.'

"And, after thinking a little to himself, he related as follows:

"'I must first tell you, my friends, that although I was a very rich man before I entered the brotherhood of the dervishes, yet I was very fond of working at a certain craft, namely, I used to make various stringed musical instruments of the kind called "sayaz," "tar," "kiamancha," "zimbal," and so on.

"'And even after I had entered the brotherhood I devoted all my free time to this profession of making musical instruments chiefly for our dervishes.

"'And the cause of my further serious interest in the laws of vibrations was the following:

"'Once the Sheikh of our monastery called me to him and said:

"'"Hadji! In the monastery where I was still an ordinary dervish, whenever during certain mysteries our musician dervishes played the melodies of the sacred canticles, all of us dervishes always experienced from these melodies of the sacred canticles particular sensations corresponding to the text of the given sacred canticle.

"' "But here during my long and careful observations, I have never yet noticed any particular effect on our brother dervishes from these same sacred canticles.

"' "What is wrong? What is the cause of this? To find out the cause has recently been my aim and I have now called you to speak with you about it, and perhaps you, as an amateur specialist at making musical instruments, can help me to clear up this question which interests me."

"'Thereupon we began to enquire into this question from every aspect.

"'After long deliberations we finally decided that probably the whole cause lay in the nature itself of the vibrations of the sounds. And we came to this conclusion because from our conversation it further became clear that in the monastery in which our Sheikh had been an ordinary dervish, they played, besides the tambour, stringed musical instruments, while here, in our monastery, they played these same sacred melodies exclusively on wind instruments.

"'We further decided to replace immediately all the wind instruments of our monastery by stringed instruments; but then another very serious question arose for us, namely, that it would be impossible to get together from among our dervishes the necessary number of specialists for playing the stringed instruments.

"'Then our Sheikh, having thought a little, said to me:

"' "Hadji, you, as a specialist in stringed instruments, try—perhaps you can manage to make a stringed musical instrument on which any dervish, without being a specialist, can produce the sounds of the necessary melody merely by a mechanical action, such as, for example, turning, striking, pressing, and so on."

"'This proposal of our Sheikh then immediately greatly

interested me, and I undertook the task with great pleasure.

"'After this decision I got up and, having received his blessing, went home.

"'Having returned home, I sat down and thought very seriously for a long time; and the result of all my thinking was that I decided to make an ordinary zimbal and to devise with the help of my friend the dervish Kerbalai-Azis-Nuaran such a mechanism of little hammers that their striking should produce the corresponding sounds.

"'And that same evening I went to this friend of mine, the dervish Kerbalai-Azis-Nuaran.

"'Although this dervish friend of mine was regarded by his comrades and acquaintances as rather a queer sort, nevertheless they all respected and esteemed him, as he was very sensible and learned and often talked of such questions that everyone, willy-nilly, had to ponder about them seriously.

"'Before his initiation into the dervishes, he had been a real professional, namely, a watchmaker.

"'And in the monastery also, he devoted all his free time to this favorite craft of his.

"'My friend this dervish Kerbalai-Azis-Nuaran had by the way recently become much enthused over a certain "freakish idea," namely, he was trying to make a mechanical watch which would show the time very exactly without the aid of any spring whatsoever.

"'This freakish idea of his he explained in the following brief and very simple formulation:

"'"Nothing on the Earth is absolutely still, because the Earth itself moves. On the Earth only gravity is still and then only in half the space occupied by its volume. I wish to get such an absolute equilibrium of levers that their movement, which must necessarily proceed from the tempo of the movement of the Earth, should exactly correspond to the required movement of the hands of a clock, and so on and so forth."

"'When I came to this queer friend of mine and explained to him what I wanted to obtain and what help I expected of him, he also immediately became very much interested in this and promised to help me in every way possible.

"'And the very next day we started work together.

"'From this joint work, the skeleton of this mechanical musical instrument devised by me was soon ready. I myself marked and spaced the places for the corresponding strings, while my queer friend continued to work on the mechanism of the little hammers.

"'And then, when I had finished stretching the strings and had begun to tune them correspondingly, just then that began which aroused that further interest in me which brought me to the experiments concerning the laws of vibrations which I began and am still continuing.

"'It began in this way:

"'I must first tell you that before this I already very well knew that half the length of any string gives twice the number of vibrations of a whole string of equal volume and density, and in accordance with this principle I arranged on the zimbal what are called "bridges" for the strings and then began correspondingly to tune all the strings for a certain ancient sacred melody in "one-eighth-toned" sounds, of course according to my "Perambarrsasidaan" or, as it is called in Europe, "tuning fork," producing the vibrations of the Chinese absolute note "do."

"'It was during this tuning that I first clearly constated that the principle, namely, that the number of the vibrations of a string is inversely proportional to its length, does not always but only sometimes coincide with the obtaining of what is called a "common blending harmonic consonance."

"'And this constatation so greatly interested me that I then gave all my attention to the investigation of this alone and entirely ceased to occupy myself with the said zimbal.

"'Then it so chanced to happen that my queer friend also became very much interested in the same thing, and together we began to investigate this fact which had so astonished us both.

"'Only after several days did my friend and I notice that we were neglecting our main work, and therefore we decided from that day to devote half our time to finishing the zimbal and the other half to the said investigations.

"'And indeed we very soon managed to carry out both of these tasks of ours in such a way that one should not hinder the other.

"'Soon the mechanical zimbal devised by us was ready; it was entirely satisfactory to us and I must say turned out to be something of the kind of the "new Greek hand organ" but with quarter-tone sounds and a little larger in size.

"'It was set in action by turning, by which the little hammers struck the corresponding strings; and this correspondence was obtained by means of bundles of flattened reeds in which we had made dents, into which during the turning the ends of the little hammers fell and set the corresponding strings vibrating.

"'For each separate sacred melody we prepared a separate bundle of these flattened reeds fastened together, and they could be changed at will according to the melody required.

"'When we finally handed over our original zimbal to our Sheikh and told him what interested us most of all at that moment, he not only gave us his blessing to leave the monastery for a while for our purpose to occupy ourselves with the question which interested us, but even put at our disposal a large sum of money from the resources accumulated in the monastery.

"'We then moved here and began to live far from other people and outside of our brotherhood.

"'This friend of mine and I lived here all the time in complete peace and concord, and only recently did I lose forever this never-to-be-forgotten and irreplaceable friend of mine.

"'And I lost him in the following lamentable circumstances:

"'Several weeks ago he went down to the banks of the river Amu Darya to the town X for various materials and instruments.

"'As he was leaving the town to return here, a "stray bullet" from the firing taking place between the Russians and the Anglo-Afghans struck him down on the spot, and I was immediately informed of this calamity by our mutual acquaintance, a Sart, who chanced to be passing there.

"'Several days afterwards I brought his remains here and buried him over there,' he added, pointing to a corner of the cave where a peculiar form of projection could be seen.

"Having said this, Hadji-Asvatz-Troov stood up and, making a gesture of prayer evidently for the repose of the soul of his friend, motioned with his head for us to follow him.

"We went and found ourselves again in the chief passage of the cave where this venerable terrestrial being stopped in front of a projection and pressed something, whereupon the block moved apart and behind it an entrance was formed into another section of the cave.

"This section which we came upon this time was, in addition to its formation by Nature Herself, also artificially constructed so originally—according to the Reason of your contemporary favorites—that I wish to describe its construction to you as detailedly as possible.

"The walls of this section, the ceiling, and even the floor were lined with several layers of very thick felt. As it was afterwards explained to me, this accidentally natural formation was utilized and adapted so that there should not penetrate there, from the other sections or from the outside in general, the slightest vibration from any manifestations whatsoever, either from any movement, rustling, shuffling, or even from vibrations produced by the breathing anywhere nearby of various large or small 'creatures.'

"In this unusual interior were several 'experimental apparatuses' of strange form and among them was a specimen of the sound-producing instrument which I brought with me from the surface of your planet, the type of contemporary terrestrial sound-producing instrument which your favorites call a grand piano.

"The cover of this grand piano was open, and to each series of the strings visible beneath it were fitted independent little apparatuses which served as measures of the 'degree of vivifyingness of the variously sourced vibrations' and were called 'vibrometers.'

"When I saw the large number of these vibrometers, the being-impulse of astonishment in my common presence increased to such an intensity as that which our Mullah Nassr Eddin expresses by the following words: 'The limit of full satiety is bursting.'

"This impulse of astonishment had arisen and progressively increased in me from the moment when I saw, in the passages of the cave, the gas and electric lighting.

"I had already then wondered whence and how all this was present here.

"I already well knew before this, that although these strange three-brained beings there have again learned to utilize such sources from cosmic formations for their, as they say, 'lighting,' yet these means for this lighting of theirs are obtained by them with the aid of very complicated adaptations and these adaptations are accessible only where there is a large group of them.

"And suddenly here was this lighting, so far from any such group, and particularly in the absence around the place of any signs by which, among contemporary beings, such possibilities are in general accompanied.

"And when I saw the aforementioned vibrometer for measuring the 'degree of the vivifyingness of vibrations,' the impulse of astonishment in me, as I have already said, increased to the highest degree.

"I was yet the more astonished because concerning this I also already knew very well that at that period there, nowhere did there exist such apparatuses by means of which it is possible to count any vibrations whatever, and therefore I again wondered—from where could this venerable old man dwelling in these wild mountains so far from the beings composing contemporary civilization, have obtained such apparatuses?

"Notwithstanding this interest of mine, I did not venture to ask the venerable Hadji-Asvatz-Troov for an explanation just then; I did not venture to ask him, because it was to be feared that such a digressive question might change the course of the conversation which had begun and from which I expected the elucidation of the chief question which interested me.

"In this section of the cave were many other apparatuses as yet unknown to me, among which stood one very strange apparatus to which were attached several what are called 'masks,' from which something like pipes, made of the throats of cows, went somewhere up to the ceiling of the cave.

"Through these pipes, as I also afterwards learned, the air necessary for the breathing of the beings present during the experiments could flow in from outside, because this interior was then closed hermetically on all sides.

"The beings who were present during the experiments wore over their faces those masks which were on this strange apparatus.

"When we were all seated on the floor in the said section of the cave, the venerable Hadji-Asvatz-Troov said among other things that during the period of his investigations he and his friend the dervish Kerbalai-Azis-Nuaran had also occasion to study very thoroughly all the theories existing on the Earth about vibrations made at any time by serious terrestrial scientists.

"He said: 'We studied the Assyrian theory of the great Malmanash, and the Arabian theory of the famous Selneh-eh-Avaz, and the Greek—of the philosopher Pythagoras—and of course all the Chinese theories.

"'And we made apparatuses exactly similar to those with which all these ancient sages made their experiments, and we even made an addition to one of their apparatuses, which is now the chief one for my experiments.

"'With this apparatus Pythagoras made his experiments, and it was then called a "monochord," but now that I have altered it, I call it a "vibrosho."'

"Having said this, he pressed something on the floor with one hand, and with the other he pointed to a very strangely shaped apparatus standing there and added that it was the same altered 'monochord.'

"The apparatus he pointed to consisted of a two-meter board, the whole front half of which was divided into sections called 'frets,' like the neck of the sound-producing instrument called 'guitar,' and on it was stretched only one string.

"To the other half of this board were fastened a great number of vibrometers like those on the strings of the grand piano, and they were affixed in such a way that their indicating needles came just over the mentioned frets on the front side of the board.

"To the back half of this board was fastened a whole network of various small glass and metal pipes, which also served to produce sounds, but this time sounds obtained from vibrations arising from certain movements and currents of ordinary or of artificially compressed or rarefied air; and for measuring the vibrations of these sounds the same vibrometers served as were used for measuring the vibrations arising from the string.

"The venerable Hadji-Asvatz-Troov was about to say something, but just then from another section of the cave a small boy of the type called Uzbek entered, carrying on a tray a tea service and some green tea.

"When the boy had set the tray before us and had left, the venerable Hadji began to pour out the tea into the cups and turning to us jokingly uttered the following sentence used on such occasions in that locality:

"'Let us imbibe this gift of Nature in the devout hope that it may redound to her glory!'

"Having uttered this, he continued further:

"'I already feel that my sustaining forces are abating within me and hence I must imbibe the due quantity of what can aid the animation of the whole of myself until the next dose.'

"And with a gentle smile he began to drink his tea. While he was drinking it, I decided to take the opportunity to ask him about several questions which were all the time worrying me.

"First of all I asked him the following. I said:

"'Highly esteemed Hadji! Until now I have been fully convinced that nowhere on the Earth does there exist an apparatus for the exact measurement of vibrations. Yet here I see so many of these measuring apparatuses.

"'How am I to understand this?

"'Where did you get them?'

"To this the venerable Hadji-Asvatz-Troov replied as follows:

"'These apparatuses for our experiments were made by my deceased friend Kerbalai-Azis-Nuaran, and it is chiefly to them that I am indebted for all my attainments in the knowledge of the laws of vibrations.

"'Indeed,' he continued, 'there once existed on the Earth at the time of the flourishing of the great Tikliamish, all kinds of similar apparatuses, but at the present time there are none of these apparatuses, unless of course one reckons that, so to say, "childish bauble" now existing there in Europe by means of which vibrations can, as it were, be counted, and which there in Europe is called a "siren." I even had such a siren when I began my elucidatory experiments.

"'This siren was invented two centuries ago by a certain learned physician named Zehbek and it was so to say perfected in the middle of the last century, by a certain Cagniard-de-la-Tour.

"'The construction of this childish bauble consists in this, that a current of condensed air is directed from a pipe on to a revolving disc drilled with little holes, each hole exactly coinciding in size with the opening of the main air pipe; and as this disc revolves, the passage for the current of air, entering these holes from the main pipe, is alternately opened and closed.

"'And thus during the rapid revolution of this disc, successive shocks of air are obtained in the holes, and these produce an even-pitched tone of sound, and the number of revolutions recorded by the clock mechanism, multiplied by the number of the holes of the disc, should give the number of the vibrations of that sound made in the given interval of time.

"'Unfortunately for the Europeans, neither the first inventor nor the perfecter of that siren knew that sound can be obtained not only from the action of genuine vibrations but also from the simple flow of air; and as this siren of theirs sounds only from the flow of air and not at all from natural vibrations, therefore the determination of the exact number of vibrations by the indications of that siren is out of the question. . . .

"'And, that sound can be produced from two causes, namely, from natural world-vibrations themselves and simply from the flow of air, is a very satisfying and interesting fact, and I shall now demonstrate it to you practically.'

"Having said this, the venerable Hadji stood up and brought from another section of the cave a pot of flowers in bloom, placed it in the center of that section of the cave, and then seated himself at the former monochord of the famous Pythagoras.

"Turning to us he said:

"'I will now produce from these combined pipes only five different tones of sound, and you please look attentively at this pot of flowers and look at your watches and notice how long I continue to produce these sounds and also remember the numbers indicated by the hands of the vibrometers for these sounds.'

"Then with a pair of small bellows he began to blow air into the corresponding pipes, which then began a monotonous melody of five tones.

"This monotonous melody continued for ten minutes and not only did we remember the numbers indicated by the hands of the vibrometers but all these five tones of sound were even very well impressed on our organs of hearing.

"When Hadji had finished his monotonous music, the flowers in the pot were in the same state of bloom as before.

"Then Hadji moved from the former monochord to the sound-producing instrument grand piano, and having again directed our attention to the hands of the vibrometers, he began to strike successively the corresponding keys of the grand piano, which gave out the same monotonous melody of the same five tones of sound.

"And this time also, the hands of the vibrometers indicated the same figures.

"Five minutes had barely passed when at a nod from Hadji, we looked at the pot of flowers and saw that the flowers in the pot had begun very definitely to fade, and when after ten minutes, the venerable Hadji again ceased his music, there were then in the pot only the quite faded and withered stalks of the former flowering plants.

"Hadji then again sat down by us and said:

"'As my investigations of long years have convinced me and as the science of Shat-Chai-Mernis states, there do indeed exist in the world two kinds of vibrations: namely, so to say, "creative vibrations" and "momentum vibrations."

"'As I have made clear by experiment, the best strings for the production of the said creative vibrations are those made of a certain definite metal or of goat gut.

"'But strings made of other materials do not have this property.

"'Vibrations issuing from the latter kind of strings, and also the vibrations obtained from the flow of air, are purely momentum vibrations. In this case the sounds are obtained from those vibrations which arise from the mechanical action of the momentum evoked by them and from the friction of the air flowing from it.'

"Hadji-Asvatz-Troov continued:

"'At first we made our experiments with the aid of this vibrosho alone, but one day when my friend Kerbalai-Azis-Nuaran was in the Bokharan town of X on business, he happened to see a grand piano there at an auction sale of a number of things belonging to a Russian general who had left, and noticing by chance that its strings were made of just the metal needed for our experiments, he bought it and afterwards, of course with great difficulty, brought it up here into the mountains.

"'When we had placed this grand piano here, we tuned its strings exactly according to those laws of vibrations indicated in the ancient Chinese science Shat-Chai-Mernis.

"'For the correct tuning of the strings we then not only took the absolute sound of the ancient Chinese note "do," but also, as that same science recommended, took into account the local geographical conditions, the pressure of the atmosphere, the form and dimensions of the interior, and the mean temperature of the surrounding space as well as of the interior itself and so on, and we even took into consideration from how many people human radiations might issue in this interior during our proposed experiments.

"'And when we had thus exactly tuned this grand piano, then from that moment indeed, the vibrations issuing from it immediately acquired all those properties mentioned in the said great science.

"'I will now demonstrate what it is possible to do with a knowledge of the laws of vibration attained by man, and with the vibrations issuing from this ordinary grand piano.'

"Having said this, he again stood up.

"This time he brought from another section of the cave an envelope, paper, and a pencil.

"On the paper he brought he wrote something, placed what he had written in the envelope, attached the envelope to a hook that hung from the ceiling in the center of the room, again sat down at the grand piano, and without saying a word began just as before to strike definite keys, from which there was again produced a certain monotonous melody.

"But this time, in the melody, two sounds of the lowest octave of the grand piano were evenly and constantly repeated.

"After a little I noticed that it was becoming uncomfortable for my friend the dervish Hadji-Bogga-Eddin to sit still, for he began to fidget with his left leg.

"A little later he began to stroke his left leg and it was evident from the grimaces he made that his leg was paining him.

"The venerable Hadji-Asvatz-Troov paid no attention to this and continued to strike the designated keys.

"When at last he had finished, he turned to us and, addressing me, said:

"'Friend of my friend, will you please get up, take the envelope off the hook and read what is written inside.'

"I stood up, took the envelope, opened it and read as follows:

"'On each of you, from the vibrations issuing from the grand piano, there must be formed on the left leg an inch below the knee and half an inch to the left of the middle of the leg what is called a "boil."'

"When I had read this, the venerable Hadji requested us both to bare the indicated places on our left legs.

"When we had bared them, there was to be seen a real boil precisely on that place of the left leg of the dervish Bogga-Eddin; but to the extreme amazement of the venerable

Hadji-Asvatz-Troov, there was nothing whatsoever to be seen on my leg.

"When Hadji-Asvatz-Troov ascertained this, he immediately leaped from his place like a young man and cried out very excitedly, 'It cannot be!' and began to stare fixedly at my left leg with the eyes of a madman.

"Almost five minutes passed in this manner. I confess that for the first time on that planet I was at a loss and could not immediately hit upon a way out of the situation.

"At last he came closely up to me and was about to speak, but just then, from his agitation, his legs began to tremble very violently, and he therefore sat down on the floor and motioned me to sit down also.

"And when we were seated he gazed at me with very sorrowful eyes and in a penetrating manner spoke to me as follows:

"'Friend of my friend! In my youth I was a very rich man, so rich that no fewer than ten of my caravans, each with no fewer than a thousand camels, were constantly moving in all directions over our great Asia.

"'My harem was considered by all who knew it to be the richest and best on the Earth, and everything else was on the same scale; in short, I had in superabundance everything that our ordinary life can give.

"'But all this gradually so wearied and surfeited me that when at night I lay down to sleep, I thought with horror that the same would be repeated on the next day and that I would again have to drag along the same wearisome "burden."

"'Finally it became unendurable for me to live with such an inner state.

"'And then, once, when I felt the emptiness of ordinary life particularly strongly, the idea first arose in me of ending my life by suicide.

"'For several days, I thought quite cold-bloodedly and as a result categorically decided to do this.

"'On the last evening as I entered the room where I intended to actualize this decision of mine, I suddenly remembered that I had not taken a last look at her who was half the cause of the creation and formation of my life.

"'I remembered, namely, my own mother who was then still alive. And this recollection of her reversed everything within me.

"'I suddenly pictured to myself how she would suffer when she learned of my end, and moreover by such a means.

"'When I remembered her I pictured to myself, as if in reality, how she, my dear old mother, would break down in utter loneliness with resigned sighs and inconsolable sufferings, and from all this there arose in me such pity for her that the sobbing evoked by this pity almost choked me.

"'And it was only just then that I cognized with my whole Being what my mother meant to me and what an inextinguishable feeling towards her ought to exist in me.

"'From that time my mother became for me the source of my life.

"'Thereafter whenever it may have been, day or night, no sooner did I remember her dear face than I became animated with new strength, and the desire to live, and to do everything only that her life might flow agreeably for her, was renewed in me.

"'Thus it continued for ten years, until from one of those pitiless diseases she passed away and I was again left alone.

"'After her death my inner emptiness again began to weigh me down more and more, day by day.'

"At this point of his narrative, when the glance of the

venerable Hadji-Asvatz-Troov happened to light upon the dervish Bogga-Eddin, he again jumped up from his place and, addressing him, said:

"'My dear friend! In the name of our friendship pardon me, an old man, that I have forgotten to put an end to the pain caused you from the evil-carrying vibrations of the grand piano.'

"Having said this, he sat down at the grand piano and again began to strike the keys; this time he produced the sounds of two notes only, one from among those of the higher octaves of the grand piano, and the other from among the lower, always alternately, and as he began he almost shouted:

"'Now thanks again to the vibrations engendered by means of the sounds of the grand piano, but this time good-carrying ones, let the pain of my faithful old friend cease.'

"And indeed five minutes had scarcely passed before the face of the dervish Bogga-Eddin again cleared up, and of the enormous horrible boil which until that time had continued to ornament his left leg, not a trace remained.

"Then the dervish Hadji-Asvatz-Troov again sat down beside us and, externally completely calm, continued to talk:

"'On the fourth day after the death of my dear mother, I happened to be sitting in my room thinking in despair what was to become of me.

"'Just then in the street near my window, a wandering dervish began to chant his sacred canticles.

"'Looking out of the window and seeing that the singing dervish was old and had a very benign face, I suddenly decided to ask his advice and immediately sent my servant to invite him in.

"'And when he had entered and, after the usual salutations,

was seated on the "Mindari," I told him of my soul-state without withholding anything at all.

"'When I finished, the wandering dervish became intensely thoughtful and only after some time, looking at me steadily, he said as he rose from his place:

"' "There is only one way out for you—devote yourself to religion."

"'Having said this, he walked away uttering some prayer and left my house forever.

"'After his departure, I again became thoughtful.

"'This time the result of my thinking was that I decided the same day irrevocably to enter some "brotherhood of dervishes," but only not in my native country but somewhere further away.

"'The next day I began to divide and distribute all my wealth among my relatives and the poor, and in two weeks I left my native country forever and came here to Bokhara.

"'Once here in Bokhara, I chose one of the numerous brotherhoods of dervishes and entered it, selecting just that brotherhood whose dervishes were known among the people for the severity of their mode of life.

"'But unfortunately, the dervishes of this brotherhood soon produced a disillusioning effect on me, and I therefore transferred to another brotherhood; but there again the same thing happened, until finally I was enrolled as a dervish of the brotherhood of the monastery, the Sheikh of which set me the task of devising that mechanical stringed musical instrument of which I have already spoken to you.

"'And after that, as I have also already told you, I became very much absorbed in the science of the laws of vibrations and have been occupied with it up to the present day.

"'But today this science has compelled me to experience the same inner state as I experienced for the first time on the eve of the death of my mother, whose love had been my sole hearth of warmth which for so many years had sustained my empty and wearisome life.

"'To this day I cannot recall without a shudder that moment when our physicians told me that my mother could not live more than one day.

"'Then in that terrible state of mind, the first question that arose in me was: How shall I go on living?

"'What further happened to me afterwards and what occurred I have also more or less told you.

"'In a word, when I became absorbed in the science of vibrations, I gradually found for myself a new divinity.

"'This science took the place of my mother for me and in the course of many years has proved just as sustaining, true, and faithful as my own mother had been to me, and until today I have lived and been animated only by its truths alone.

"'Until now there has not yet been a single instance in which in their manifestations, the truths I have discovered concerning the laws of vibrations have failed to yield those precise results I expected.

"'But today for the first time it has happened that the results I confidently expected were not obtained.

"'My chief terror is that today I was more than ever careful in the calculations of the vibrations required for the given case, that is to say, I accurately calculated that the proposed boil should be formed on your body in just that place and in no other.

"'And here the unprecedented has happened. Not only is it not in the designated place, but it has not even been formed on any part of your body at all.

"'This science which until now has taken the place of my faithful mother, has today for the first time failed me, and in me at the present moment, there is indescribable grief.

"'For today, I can still reconcile myself to this exceedingly great misfortune of mine, but what will be tomorrow—I cannot even picture to myself.

"'And if I can still somehow reconcile myself today, it is only because I very well remember the words of our ancient great prophet "Issi-Noora" who said that "an individual is not responsible for his manifestations only when in death agony."

"'Evidently my science, my divinity, my second mother—is also in its "death agony," if it has betrayed me today.

"'I know very well that death agony is always followed by death.

"'And you, dear friend of my friend, have today involuntarily become for me like those physicians who then on the eve of the death of my dear mother announced to me that my mother could not live more than another day.

"'You are for me today just such a newsbearer, that this new hearth of mine will tomorrow also be extinguished.

"'The same terrible feelings and sensations which I experienced then, from the moment when our physicians announced to me the imminent death of my mother until her death, are now being repeated in me.

"'Just as then, in the midst of those terrible feelings and sensations, there was still a hope that perhaps she would not die, so also at this moment, something like that hope also still flickers in me.

"'Ekh! Friend of my friend! Now that you already know my soul state, I earnestly ask you, can you explain to me what supernatural force was involved in this, that the anticipated boil which should infallibly have been formed was not formed on your left leg?

"'For the faith that it must infallibly be formed long ago became in me as firm as the "Tookloonian-stone."

"'And it has become so firm and unshakable because for almost forty years, day and night, I have persistently studied these great laws of world vibrations until the understanding of their meaning and actualization has become for me, as it were, my second nature.'

"Having said these last words, this perhaps last great sage of the Earth looked into my eyes with an expression full of anticipation.

"Can you picture to yourself, my dear boy, my situation then? What could I reply to him?

"For the second time that day, I could not on account of this terrestrial being see any way out of the situation that had arisen.

"This time there was mixed in this state, so unusual for me, my 'being-Hikhdjnapar,' or, as your favorites say there, 'pity,' for that terrestrial three-brained being, chiefly because he was suffering through me.

"And this was because I was then clearly aware that if I spoke a few words to him, not only would he be calmed, but thanks to them, he would even understand that the fact that no boil was formed on my left leg proved the truth and precision of his adored science still more.

"I had full moral right to tell him the truth about myself, because by his attainments he was already 'Kalmanuior,' that is, a three-brained being of that planet with whom it is not forbidden us from Above to be frank.

"But at that moment I could in no way do this, because there was also present there the dervish Hadji-Bogga-Eddin who was still an ordinary terrestrial three-brained being, concerning whom, already long before, it was forbidden under oath from Above to the beings of our tribe to communicate true information to any one of them on any occasion whatsoever.

"This interdiction upon the beings of our tribe was made it seems on the initiative of the Very Saintly Ashiata Shiemash.

"This interdiction on the beings of our tribe was made

chiefly because it is necessary for the three-brained beings of your planet to have 'knowledge-of-being.'

"And any information, even if true, gives to beings in general only 'mental knowledge,' and this mental knowledge, as I have already once told you, always serves beings only as a means to diminish their possibilities of acquiring this knowledge-of-being.

"And since the sole means left to these unfortunate three-brained beings of your planet for their complete liberation from the consequences of the properties of the organ Kundabuffer are just this knowledge-of-being, therefore this command was given to the beings of our tribe under oath concerning the beings of the Earth.

"And that is why, my boy, I did not just then in front of the dervish Bogga-Eddin decide to explain to this worthy terrestrial sage Hadji-Asvatz-Troov the real reason of his failure.

"But as both dervishes were waiting for my reply, I had in any case to tell them something, and therefore, addressing Hadji-Asvatz-Troov, I then told him only as follows:

"'Venerable Hadji-Asvatz-Troov! If you agree to have my answer not now but a little later, then I swear by the cause of my arising that I will give you an answer which will fully satisfy you. You will be convinced not only that your beloved science is the truest of all sciences, but also that since the great scientists, the saints Choon-Kil-Tez and Choon-Tro-Pel, you are the greatest scientist of the Earth.'

"At this reply of mine, that venerable dervish Hadji-Asvatz-Troov merely placed his right hand on the place where the heart is located in terrestrial beings—and in that locality this gesture means 'I believe and hope without doubt.'

"Then, as if nothing had happened, he turned to the dervish Bogga-Eddin and began again to speak about the science Shat-Chai-Mernis.

"In order completely to smooth over the previous embarrassment, I spoke to him again, and pointing to a niche in the cave where many colored silk materials were hanging in strips, I asked him:

"'Most estimable Hadji! What is all that material over there in that niche?'

"To this question of mine he replied that those colored materials were also used for his experiments on vibrations, and he continued further: 'I recently made it clear for myself which colors of the materials—and to what extent—act by their vibrations harmfully on people and on animals.

"'If you wish I will show you this highly interesting experiment also.'

"Having said this, he again stood up and again went into the neighboring section from where he soon led in, this time with the help of the boy, three quadruped terrestrial beings called 'dog,' 'sheep,' and 'goat'; he also brought in several strangely shaped apparatuses resembling bracelets.

"He put one of these special bracelets on the arm of the dervish Bogga-Eddin, and another on his own arm, meanwhile saying to me by the way as he did so:

"'I do not put one of these apparatuses on you . . . as I have certain rather weighty reasons.'

"One of these strange collar-like apparatuses he then put on to the necks of the aforesaid goat, sheep, and dog, and indicating the vibrometers on these strange apparatuses, he asked us to remember or to note down all the figures which would be indicated by the hands of the vibrometers on each of these externally different beings.

"We looked at the figures shown by all the five vibrometers, and wrote these down in the 'block notes' or, as they are usually called there, 'writing pads,' which were given to us by the boy.

"After this, the dervish Asvatz-Troov again sat down on the felt and told us as follows:

"'Every form of "life" has its own "total" of vibrations proper to it, which represents the totality of all the vibrations engendered from the various definite organs of the given form of life; and this total varies at different times in each form of life and depends on how intensely these variously caused vibrations are transformed by the corresponding sources or organs.

"'Now all these heterogenous and variously caused vibrations always blend within the limits of the whole life in the general subjective what is called "chord of vibrations" of the given life.

"'Just take as an example my friend Bogga-Eddin and myself.

"'You see . . .' and showing me the figures on the vibrometer that he had on his arm, he continued:

"'I have in general so many vibrations, and my friend Bogga-Eddin has so many more.

"'This is because he is much younger than I and several of his organs function much more intensely than mine, and the corresponding vibrations in him thus "result" more intensely than mine.

"'Look at the figures on the vibrometers of the dog, the sheep, and the goat. The sum total of the vibrations of the dog is three times greater than that of the sheep and half as much again as that of the goat, and in number of vibrations of his general chord of vibrations, this dog has a trifle less than myself and my friend.

"'It must be remarked that among men, especially men of recent times, very many are to be met with who have not even as great a number of vibrations in the subjective chord of vibrations of their common presence as the number shown by the presence of this dog.

"'This has come about because in most of these people I have just mentioned, one function for instance, and, namely, the function of emotion, which actualizes the main quantity of subjective vibrations, is already almost completely atrophied, and therefore the sum total of vibrations in them proves to be less than in this dog.'

"Having said this, the venerable Hadji-Asvatz-Troov again stood up and went to the place where the materials of different colors lay.

"Then he began to unroll these colored materials consisting of what is called 'Bokharan-silk,' color by color; and with each piece of material, all of one color, he covered by means of specially constructed rollers not only all the walls and the ceiling but even the floor of this section of the cave, owing to which it appeared that the whole interior was draped with the material of that given color. And each of the colored materials changed the vibration number of all the forms of 'life.'

"After experiments with the colored materials, this great terrestrial scientist of recent times asked us to follow him, and, going out of this section of the cave back again into its main passage, we went into another small passage leading off to the side.

"Behind us trailed along the goat, the sheep, and the dog with their improvised collars.

"We walked a fairly long time until we finally came to the most important section of these underground spaces.

"There the venerable dervish Hadji-Asvatz-Troov again went to one of the niches of that big underground space and, pointing to a big pile lying there of some material of a very strange color, said:

"'This material is woven specially from the fibers of the plant "Chaltandr" and has its natural color.

"'This plant Chaltandr is one of the rare formations on the Earth, the color of which not only does not have the ability to change the vibrations of other nearby sources, but is itself completely indifferent to all other vibrations.

"'That is why for my experiments concerning vibrations

arising not from color but from other causes, I especially ordered just this material and made out of it, for the whole of this underground space, something like a large "tent" and so adapted it that it could be moved in any direction and given any form desired.

"'And with this peculiar tent I am now carrying out my experiments, namely, those experiments which I call "architectural." And these architectural experiments are now making clear to me just which interiors—and to what extent—act harmfully upon people and upon animals.

"'These architectural experiments have already fully convinced me not only that the size and the general interior form of a place have indeed an enormous influence on people and animals, but also that all interior what are called "curves," "angles," "projections," "breaks" in the walls, and many other things producing a change in the vibrations proceeding in the atmosphere of the place, always contribute to change for better or for worse the subjective vibrations of the people and animals there.'

"When he began to make his experiments with that large tent, I also noticed among other things that the surrounding vibrations which changed owing to various causes nearby, act much more strongly on the common presences of these three-brained beings who have taken your fancy than on the terrestrial one-brained and two-brained beings.

"This also evidently proceeds in consequence of all the abnormal inner and outer conditions of their ordinary being-existence.

"After these architectural experiments, he led us to still other small sections, where he also showed us many other experiments from which it could easily be seen and understood just which variously caused vibrations, and how, act upon the subjective chords of vibrations of your favorites.

"During these experiments, there were also indicated

the results ensuing from vibrations formed from the radiations of other terrestrial beings of various types of those similar to them as well as of two-brained and one-brained beings, and also the vibrations engendered by their voices and by many other causative actions.

"He demonstrated and explained, among other things, also several experiments proving the harmful action on terrestrial contemporary beings of those causes which they themselves, as if intentionally, produce, especially in recent times, in great quantity—namely, what they call 'works of art.'

"Among these latter were 'pictures,' 'statues,' and of course their famous music.

"From all the experiments demonstrated by this sage, it became clear that the most harmful vibrations, however, for contemporary terrestrial three-brained beings are those formed in them from their what are called 'medical remedies.'

"I stayed in the underground domain of this truly learned being four terrestrial days, after which, with the dervish Bogga-Eddin, I returned again to that Bokharan town from which we had come; and thus ended my first meeting with him.

"During those four days he further demonstrated and explained to us much more concerning the 'laws of vibrations'; but the most interesting thing for me personally was his last explanation about why and how, in that wild place remote from any place of the grouping of contemporary terrestrial beings, in this underground domain of his, there came to be gas and electric lighting.

"During this account of his, while elucidating a certain fact, this highly sympathetic terrestrial three-brained being could not restrain himself, for sincere tears suddenly began to flow, which then so touched me that even now I cannot forget it.

"Information about certain data elucidated by this

account of his can serve for your further existence as good material for corresponding confrontations and for the elucidation of all the results of what are called 'subjective destiny,' that is to say, of those results which in general occur in our Great Megalocosmos where a multitude of relatively independent separate individuals arise and exist together.

"It often happens that while existing together, destiny, for any separate individual in the process of his personal existence, turns out for him personally to be absolutely unjust, but for all the others existing together with him, there are obtained from this in the objective sense, an abundance of just fruits. And that is why I wish to tell you about this in as much detail as possible, and will even try to repeat this account of his to you as verbatim as possible without changing anything.

"It was just before our departure from this underground domain, that is, from that place on your planet, which among other things, convinced me that the results of the attainments of the Reason of the former three-brained beings, their ancestors, have not even there been entirely lost. Even if the subsequent generations of the beings of this strange planet cease to transmute in themselves the cosmic truths discovered by their ancestors, yet although their already discovered truths have not progressed as is everywhere proper because of their abnormal being-existence, they are nevertheless automatically concentrated in that strange underground kingdom of your planet, to await further perfection and elaboration for subsequent three-brained beings.

"And so, when I enquired about the methods of the gas and electric lighting in this underground kingdom of his, he related to me the following:

"'The causes of the origin of these two kinds of lighting are entirely different, and each of these two kinds of lighting has its own independent story.

"'Gas lighting existed here from the very beginning, and was arranged here on the initiative of myself and my old friend the dervish Kerbalai-Azis-Nuaran.

"'As for the electric lighting, it came here only quite recently, and the initiator of its origin was also one of my friends who is still young and who came from among the Europeans.

"'I think it will be better if I tell you the story of each kind of lighting separately.

"'I will begin with the gas lighting.

"'At the time when we first moved here, there was not far from here a certain holy place called the "holy cave" to which various "pilgrims" and "devotees" from all over Turkestan used to throng.

"'The popular belief about this holy place was that once there had lived in this cave, as it were, the famous "Herailaz," who later was taken up "alive" into Heaven.

"'It was further said in this popular belief that he was taken alive into Heaven so unexpectedly that he even had no time to extinguish the fire which lit his cave.

"'This last belief was supported by the fact that in that cave there was indeed an "undying fire."

"'And so, friend of my friend!

"'As neither I nor my friend the dervish Kerbalai-Azis-Nuaran could believe in the verity of this popular belief, we therefore decided to probe into the real cause of that peculiar phenomenon.

"'Having at that time sufficient material possibilities and having at our disposal the conditions necessary for the investigation of this phenomenon without any hindrance from anyone whatsoever, we began to seek the source of its arising.

"'It turned out that not far from that cave there flowed under the ground a stream which washed a medium composed of minerals, the totality of the action of which, on the water, resulted in the separation of an inflammable gas which through chance crevices in the ground found its way into that cave.

"'And the chance inflammation somehow of this gas must obviously have been the cause of the display there of that undying fire.

"'When my friend and I had made this cause definitely clear to ourselves and had at the same time discovered that the said spring was located not far from our cave, we decided to give an artificial outlet to that gas into these caves of ours.

"'And so, from then on this gas flowed through the pipes of clay we laid, here into the main section of our cave, and from there we distributed it by means of "bamboos" according to our needs.

"'As for the appearance in our caves of electric lighting, the history of its origin is as follows:

"'Soon after we had settled in these caves, there once came to see me through a very old friend of mine also a dervish, a still very young European traveler who sought my acquaintance on account of always this same action of the laws of vibrations which interested me.

"'We were soon close friends, as he turned out to be firstly, very serious in the search for truth, and secondly, very kind and "susceptible regarding the weaknesses of all others without exception."

"'He was studying the laws of vibrations in general; but his studies were primarily of those "laws of vibrations" which cause the formation of various diseases in people.

"'During these studies of his, he among other things made clear the causes of the arising in people of the disease existing there under the name of "cancer," and the possibility of destroying in people this malignant arising.

"'He then constated and could already actualize in practice the possibility that, by a certain mode of life and a certain preparation, any man can consciously elaborate in himself vibrations by means of which, if he saturates the person infected with this terrible disease with those vibrations in a certain way and in a certain successiveness of the flow of time, it is possible to destroy it entirely.

"'Although afterwards, when we parted, we did not meet again for a long time, we always had news of one another.

"'I knew that this young friend of mine, soon after we parted, married in his native country and lived with his wife during the following years in full, as we say here in Asia, "family love and mutual moral support."

"'I was particularly interested in news of him which concerned his attainments in respect of the discovery of a cure for destroying in people just the aforesaid curse, because the causes of the arising of just those vibrations, owing to which data for that disease are crystallized, were closely related to the causes the elucidation of the vibrations of which were lately the chief interest in my life.

"'I already knew that although he had not yet discovered any commonly accessible means of bringing about the destruction of that disease, yet according to trustworthy reports which frequently reached me, he employed for those who fell ill with this disease the not commonly accessible practicable cures which he had first constated, and their actualization in practice which he had attained, and he had always achieved the complete destruction of this terrible human scourge.

"'I received very authentic information about these favorable results achieved by him in some tens of cases during that time.

"'Then it happened that for reasons not dependent on either of us, I had no information about that young European, for about ten years.

"'I was already beginning to forget his existence entirely when once, while I was specially absorbed in my occupations, I heard someone give our secret signal, and when I called and asked who was there, I at once recognized his voice; he asked me to make the way accessible for him to enter our underground domain.

"'Needless to say, we were both glad to meet again and once more to exchange views on our beloved science of the "laws of vibrations."

"'When the excitement aroused by our new meeting had abated, and when we had unpacked all the things my young friend had brought on camels—among which by the way were some of the famous contemporary European what are called "Roentgen apparatus," almost fifty "elements of Bunsen," several "accumulators," and several bales of different materials for "electric wiring"—we began to talk quietly and from what he related about himself I learned with great grief the following:

"'Several years before, when on account of higher World-laws surrounding conditions and circumstances became such that scarcely anywhere on the Earth did people have any security for the morrow or any settled dwelling place, he suddenly noticed the appearance in his beloved wife of just that terrible disease, the search for a cure for which had lately been one of the chief aims of his existence.

"'He was particularly horrified because, in view of the surrounding conditions which had arisen, he had no possibility of employing, for the destruction of that terrible disease, that cure he had obtained and which only he alone so far could actualize.

"'And when he had calmed down somewhat after this terrible constatation, he then made the only possible decision—to wait patiently for a corresponding time, and meanwhile to try to create for his wife such conditions of life that the progressive process of that terrible disease should flow as slowly as possible.

"'More than two years passed, during which time the

surrounding conditions changed for the better; and this young friend of mine had the possibility of then preparing himself, at last, to employ that cure known only by him, against that terrible disease.

"'And when he had begun to prepare himself to employ that cure, then on one sorrowful day for him, in one of the large European cities, in the jostling caused by some demonstration, he fell under an "automobile," and although not quite killed, he received very serious bodily injuries.

"'Owing to these injuries, firstly, his own life flowed for several months under a "lapse of memory," and secondly, because of the absence of conscious and intentional direction on his part of the ordinary life of his wife, the process of the terrible disease flowed in her at an accelerated tempo, chiefly because during his illness she took constant and anxious care of him without sparing herself.

"'And so, when this poor friend of mine finally regained consciousness, he soon saw to his horror that the disease process in his wife was already in its last stages.

"'What could he do? What could be done . . . since owing to the consequences of the injuries he had received he was bereft of every possibility of preparing himself and of elaborating in himself the vibrations of the quality needed for the cure he had learned, of destroying in man that terrible disease.

"'Thereupon and in view of all this and seeing no other way, he resolved to have recourse to that means of curing this illness which the representatives of contemporary European medicine employ and thanks to which, they allege, it is possible, as it were, to destroy in man that disease.

"'Namely, he decided to have recourse to what are called X rays.

"'The treatment with the said rays was begun.

"'During the process of that treatment he noticed that, although the principal "concentration" or "gravitational center" of the disease in the body of his wife became, as it were, "atrophied," yet at the same time a similar "concentration" was beginning, this time in an entirely different part of her body.

"'After several months of repeated what they call in Europe "seances," a similar independent concentration made its appearance in her and this time in still a new place—the third.

"'And as a result of it all, it transpired one sad day that the days of the invalid were numbered.

"'Having constated this horror, my young friend decided to throw aside all the wiseacring of contemporary European medicine and without consideration for his own state, he began to elaborate in himself the necessary vibrations and to saturate the body of the invalid with them.

"'Although, in spite of difficulties almost insurmountable to him personally, he succeeded in prolonging the existence of his wife for almost two years, yet nevertheless she finally died from just that terrible human disease.

"'It must be noticed further that during the last period of the illness, when he had already ceased to employ the wiseacring of European medicine, two further similar independent concentrations were noticed in the body of his wife.

"'When my young friend had more or less calmed down after that terrible issue, and again devoted part of his time to his beloved studies and researches of the great World-laws, then, among other things, he became much interested to know why, during the treatment of the cancer by X rays there had arisen in the body of his wife those independent concentrations he had constated which usually do not develop in this disease and which during his long years of previous observations he had never noticed.

"'In view of the fact that the elucidation of this question which interested him turned out to be complicated and in the surrounding conditions of the places of habitation there, impracticable, he decided to come to me and with my help clear them up by experiment.

"'And that was why he had brought with him all the necessary materials for these elucidatory experiments.

"'The next day I put at his disposal one of the sections of the underground domain and several what are called "Salkamourskian" goats and everything else required for his elucidatory experiments.

"'Among other preparations he, with the help of the Bunsen elements, first put into operation the action of the Roentgen apparatus.

"'And already three days after his arrival, that began which was the cause of the arising of permanent electric lighting in our caves.

"'And it began in the following way: As we were making certain experiments by means of my vibrometers and calculating the vibrations of the electric current which produces X rays in the Roentgen apparatus, we noticed that the number of vibrations of the electric current obtained by means of these Bunsen elements all the time either increased or diminished; and because the number of vibrations in a certain length of time were most important for our elucidations during the flowing of the electric current, it then became clear to us that that kind of electric current was absolutely useless for the elucidations we required.

"'This constatation of ours very much discouraged and depressed my young friend.

"'He immediately ceased the experiments he had begun and began to think.

"'The following two days he thought unceasingly even during meals.

"'At the end of the third day, as we were going together to the section where we usually had our repasts and were crossing the little bridge in the main section of our caves built over an underground stream, he suddenly stopped and striking his forehead, cried out excitedly "Eureka!"

"'The outcome of that exclamation, then, was that on the next day, with the help of several hired Tadjiks, there were removed from various ancient and deserted mines lying near by, "lumps" of three kinds of "ore" as large as could be removed; and these were placed in a certain order in the bed of our underground stream.

"'Then after laying that ore in the bed of the stream, he very simply connected from the stream two what are called terminals to the slightly charged accumulators which he himself had brought, and owing to this, the electric current of the famous what is called "amperage" began to flow into these accumulators.

"'And when after twenty-four hours we passed the electric current thus obtained into the said accumulators through our vibrometers, then it turned out that although its amperage was not sufficient, yet the number of vibrations obtained from that electric current remained unchanged and absolutely uniform during all the time of its flow through my vibrometers.

"'To increase the force of the electric current obtained in this peculiar way, he made "condensers" of various materials, namely, from goatskins, from a certain kind of "clay," crushed "zinc ore" and "pine resin," and in this way there was obtained the electric current required for the amperage and voltage for the Roentgen apparatus he had brought.

"'By means of this peculiar source of electric current, we ultimately clearly proved to ourselves the following:

"'Although by the employment of this contemporary

device for the treatment of the said terrible disease in the whole body of man the place of the gravitational center becomes atrophied, yet it greatly facilitates the so to say "Metastases" in other glands and helps the sowing and successful flourishing of it in these new places.

"'And so, friend of my friend! When my young friend had become satisfied after this elucidation, he ceased to be interested in the question in which he had then been absorbed, and when he returned home to Europe he left for our use that source which he had created and which required neither attention nor any outside material; and thereafter we gradually installed electric lamps where we needed them in our caves.

"'Although that peculiar source of ours could not generate sufficient energy for all the lamps we had in our caves, yet by making switches everywhere and using the energy only when necessary, it was not wasted at other times but was gradually stored in accumulators, sometimes even in such a quantity that there was a surplus for various domestic purposes.'"

At this place of Beelzebub's tale, all the passengers of the transsystem ship *Karnak* experienced something like a sweet-sour taste in the region of the inner part of their mouths.

This signified that the ship *Karnak* was now approaching some planet, namely, a place of unforeseen stopping.

And this planet was the planet Deskaldino.

Whereupon Beelzebub ceased his narration and, with Ahoon and Hassein, all three went to their "Kesshahs" to get ready for the descent to the planet Deskaldino.

Note: *If anyone is very interested in the ideas presented in this chapter, I advise him to read, without fail, my proposed book entitled* The Opiumists, *if, of course, for the writing of this book there will be sufficient French armagnac and Khaizarian bastourma.*

THE AUTHOR

CHAPTER 42

Beelzebub in America

Two "Dionosks" later, when the intersystem ship *Karnak* had resumed its falling, and the confirmed followers of our respected Mullah Nassr Eddin had again sat down in their usual seats, Hassein once more turned to Beelzebub with the following words:

"My dear Grandfather! May I remind you, as you bade me, about . . . the three-brained beings . . . of the planet Earth . . . about those . . . how are they called? . . . about the beings who breed and exist just on the diametrically opposite side of the place where contemporary terrestrial civilization is flourishing . . . About those three-brained beings there, who, as you were saying, are very great devotees of the 'fox trot.'"

"Ah! About those Americans?"

"Yes, that's it, about those Americans," joyously exclaimed Hassein.

"Of course, I remember. I did, indeed, promise to tell you a little also about those contemporary queer ducks there."

And Beelzebub began thus:

"I happened to visit that part of the surface of your planet now called 'North America,' just before my final departure from that solar system.

"I went there from my last place of existence on that planet, namely, from the city Paris of the continent of Europe.

"From the continent of Europe I sailed there on a steamship, according to the custom of all contemporary what are called 'dollar holders,' and arrived in the capital of 'North America,' in the city of New York, or as it is sometimes called there, the 'city of the melting pot of the races of the Earth.'

"From the pier I went straight to a hotel called the 'Majestic' which had been recommended to me by one of my Paris acquaintances and which for some reason or other was additionally, though not officially, called 'Jewish.'

"Having settled in this Majestic hotel, I went the same day to look up a certain 'Mister' there, who also had been recommended to me by still another of my Paris acquaintances.

"By this word 'Mister' every being of the male sex is called on that continent who does not wear what is called a 'skirt.'

"When I found this Mister, to whom I had a letter of introduction, he, as is proper to every genuine American businessman, was up to his eyes in innumerable, as is said there, 'dollar businesses.'

"I think I might as well remark now at the very beginning of my elucidations about these Americans, that those three-brained beings there, especially the contemporary ones, who constitute the root population on this part of the surface of your planet, are in general almost all occupied only with these dollar businesses.

"On the other hand, with the trades and 'professions' indispensable in the process of being-existence, exclusively only those beings are occupied among them, who have gone there from other continents temporarily, and for the purpose, as is said, of 'earning money.'

"Even in this respect, the surrounding conditions of ordinary being-existence among your contemporary favorites, chiefly among those breeding on this continent, have been transformed so to say, into 'Tralalaooalalalala,' or, as our respected teacher Mullah Nassr Eddin would define it, 'a soap bubble that lasts a long time only in a quiet medium.'

"Among them there at the present time, these surrounding conditions of ordinary collective existence have already become such, that if, for some reason or other, the specialist professionals of all the kinds necessary for their ordinary collective existence should cease to come to them from the other continents to 'earn money,' then it is safe to say that within a month the whole established order of their ordinary existence would completely break down, since there would be none among them who could even so much as bake bread.

"The chief cause of the gradual resulting of such an abnormality there among them is, on the one side, the law established by them themselves in respect of the rights of parents over their children and on the other hand the institution in schools for children of what is called a 'dollar savings bank' together with the principle of implanting in children a love of such dollars.

"Thanks to this, and to still various other peculiar external conditions of ordinary existence also established by them, themselves, just this love of 'dollar business' and of dollars themselves, has become, in the common presence of each of the native inhabitants of this continent who reaches responsible age, the predominant urge during his responsible what is called 'feverish existence.'

"That is why each one of them is always doing 'dollar business,' and, moreover, always several of them at once.

"Although the aforesaid 'Mister' to whom I had a letter of introduction was also very busy with these 'dollar businesses,' he nevertheless received me very cordially. When he read the letter of introduction I presented to him, a strange process immediately began in him which has already been noticed even by certain of your favorites—it having also become inherent in your contemporary favorites in general—and which they call 'unconscious preening.'

"And this same process proceeded in him because, in the letter I presented, the name of a certain other acquaintance of mine, also a Mister, was mentioned, who in the opinion of many, and of this 'Mister' also, was considered, as they call him behind his back, 'a damn clever fellow,' that is to say, a 'dollar expert.'

"In spite of his having been entirely seized with this inherency, proper to your contemporary favorites, he nevertheless, as he talked with me, gradually calmed down, and eventually he informed me, that he was 'ready to place himself entirely at my disposal.' Suddenly, however, he remembered something, whereupon he added that to his profound regret, owing to circumstances over which he had absolutely no control, he could not possibly oblige me that day, but not until the following day, because he was extremely busy with important affairs.

"And, indeed, with the best will in the world, he could not have done so, for these unfortunate Americans, who are always governed by these dollar businesses of theirs, can do what they please only on Sundays, whereas it just happened that the day I went to see him was not a Sunday.

"There on that continent, all dollar and other businesses depend never upon the beings themselves; on the contrary, your favorites there always themselves depend entirely on these 'businesses' of theirs.

"In short, the day not being a Sunday, this genuine American Mister was unable to do as he pleased, namely, go along with me and introduce me to the people necessary to me, and we had therefore to agree to meet the following morning at a defined place on the famous street there called 'Broadway.'

"This street Broadway is the foremost and principal street not only in this New York, but, as is said there, is the longest street in any of the large contemporary cities of your planet.

"So I set off there on the next day.

"As the 'automobile taxi' in which I drove to this place happened not to come from one of Mr. Ford's factories, I arrived too soon, and consequently this 'Mister' was not yet there.

"While awaiting him, I began strolling about, but as all the New York what are called 'brokers' take their 'constitutional' before their famous 'quick lunch' just in this part of the street Broadway, the jostling in this crowded place became so great that, in order to escape it, I decided to go and sit down somewhere in some spot from where I could see the Mister I was awaiting arrive.

"A suitable spot seemed to be a neighboring typical restaurant there, from the windows of which all the passers-by could be seen.

"I must say, by the way, that there, on all that planet of yours, there are not so many restaurants in the places of existence of any other group of your favorites as there are in that New York.

"They particularly abound in the main section, and moreover, the proprietors of these restaurants there are chiefly 'Armenians,' 'Greeks,' and 'Russian Jews.'

"Now, my boy, in order that you may rest a little from active mentation, I wish for a while to confine myself entirely to the form of mentation of our dear teacher Mullah Nassr Eddin and to talk about a certain in the highest degree original custom which has prevailed during the last few years in these contemporary New York restaurants.

"Inasmuch as the production, importation, and consumption of what are called 'alcoholic liquids' have recently been strictly prohibited to the ordinary beings by the power-possessing beings of this group, and corresponding injunctions have also been given to those beings there upon whom the power-possessing beings rest their hope for their own welfare, it is now supposed to be almost impossible for the ordinary beings there to obtain such liquids. At the same time, in these New York restaurants, various alcoholic liquids called 'Arrack,' 'Doosico,' 'Scotch whisky,' 'Benedictine,' 'Vodka,' 'Grand Marnier,' and many other different liquids, under every possible kind of label, and made exclusively only on what are called 'old barges' lying at sea off the shores of that continent, are to be had in any quantity you please.

"The very 'Tzimus' of the said practice lies in this, that if you point your fourth finger and, covering one half of your mouth with your right palm, utter the name of any liquid you fancy, then immediately, without more words, that liquid is served at table—only in a bottle purporting to be lemonade or the famous 'French Vichy.'

"Now try with all your might to exert your will and to actualize in your presence a general mobilization of your 'perceptive organs' so that, without missing anything at all, you may absorb and transubstantiate in yourself everything relating to just how these alcoholic liquids I have enumerated are prepared at sea on old barges off the shores of that continent.

"I regret very much that I missed making myself thoroughly familiar with all the details of this contemporary terrestrial 'science.'

"All I managed to learn was that into all the recipes for these preparations the following acids enter—'sulphuric,' 'nitric,' and 'muriatic' acids, and most important of all, the 'incantation' of the famous contemporary German 'Professor Kishmenhof.'

"This last ingredient, namely, Professor Kishmenhof's incantation for alcoholic liquids, is delightfully intriguing; and it is concocted, so it is said, as follows:

"First of all, there must be prepared, according to any old recipe, already familiar to specialists in the business, a thousand bottles of liquid; precisely one thousand bottles must be prepared, because if there should be merely one bottle more or one bottle less, the incantation will not work.

"These thousand bottles must be placed on the floor and then, quietly beside them, a single bottle of any genuine alcoholic liquid existing anywhere there, must be placed and kept there for a period of ten minutes; at the end of which time, very slowly and quite indispensably, while scratching the right ear with the left hand, one must utter with certain pauses this said alcoholic incantation.

"Upon this, not only are the contents of all the thousand bottles instantly transformed into precisely that alcoholic liquid contained in the said single bottle, but every bottle of the thousand even acquires the same label borne by that one bottle of genuine alcoholic liquid.

"Among the conjuries of this unprecedented German Professor Kishmenhof, there are, as I learned, several indeed most amazing ones.

"This famous German professor, a specialist in this branch, started, as is said, 'inventing' these remarkable conjuries of his quite recently, that is to say, in the early years of the last great general European process of reciprocal-destruction there.

"When a food crisis supervened in his fatherland Germany, he, sympathizing with the plight of his compatriots, invented his first conjury, which consisted in the preparation of a very cheap and economical 'chicken soup.'

"This first conjury of his is called German chicken soup, and its execution is likewise extremely interesting, namely, as follows:

"Into a very commodious pot, set on the hearth, common

water is poured, and then a few very finely chopped leaves of parsley are strewn into it.

"Then both doors of the kitchen must be opened wide, or, if there is only one door, a window must be opened wide, and, while the incantation is very loudly pronounced, a chicken must be chased through the kitchen at full speed.

"Upon this, a most delicious 'chicken soup' is ready hot in the pot.

"I heard further that during the years of that great process of reciprocal-destruction, the beings of Germany made use of this conjury on a colossal scale, this method of preparing chicken soup having proved in practice to be, as it were, good, or at least extremely economical.

"The reason is that a single chicken could do duty for quite a long time, because it could be chased and chased and chased, until for some reason or other the chicken all by itself, as is said there, 'went on strike' and declined to breathe the air any longer.

"And in the event that the chicken resisted the infection of hypocrisy, in spite of its having existed among your favorites, and indeed did cease to wish to breathe the air any longer, then for this eventuality, as I afterwards learned, a common custom was established there among the beings of that group called Germany.

"Namely, when the chicken went on strike, its owners would very solemnly roast it in the oven, and for this solemn occasion would unfailingly invite all their relatives to dinner.

"It is interesting to notice also, that another professor of theirs, also famous, named Steiner, in the course of his what are called 'scientific investigations of supernatural phenomena,' mathematically established that on the occasions when these chickens were served at these 'invitation dinners,' always their owners would recite the same thing.

"Namely, every hostess, rolling her eyes to heaven and pointing to the chicken, would say with great feeling that it was the 'famous Pamir pheasant' and that it had been specially sent to them from Pamir by their dear nephew who resided there as consul for their great 'fatherland.'

"On that planet there exist in general conjuries for every possible kind of purpose.

"These conjuries began multiplying particularly after many of the beings of this peculiar planet had become specialists in supernatural phenomena and came to be called 'occultists,' 'spiritualists,' 'theosophists,' 'violet magicians,' 'chiromants,' and so forth.

"Besides being able to create 'supernatural phenomena,' these 'specialists' also knew very well how to make the opaque look transparent.

"This same American prohibition of the consumption of alcohol can serve us yet again as an excellently illuminating example for understanding to what degree the possibilities for the crystallization of data for being-reflection are atrophied in these contemporary responsible power-possessing beings, in respect of the fact that such an absurdity is being actually repeated there.

"There on that continent, everybody without exception, thanks to this prohibition, now consumes this same alcohol—even those who in other circumstances would probably never have consumed it.

"There on the continent America, the very same is occurring with the consumption of alcohol as occurred with the chewing of the seeds of the poppy by the beings of the country Maralpleicie.

"The difference is that in the country of Maralpleicie the beings were then addicted to the use of at least genuine poppy seeds, whereas in America the beings now consume any liquid that comes their way, provided only that it bears the name of some alcoholic liquid existing somewhere on their planet.

"And another difference is, that in respect of concealing their consumption of the prohibited product from government eyes, the contemporary beings now breeding on the continent America are not by any means so naïve as were the beings of the Maralpleicie epoch.

"To what lengths your contemporary favorites have gone in this respect, you can understand very well from the following examples.

"At the present time there in that place, every young man with his 'mother's milk' scarcely dry on his lips, infallibly carries with him what seems to be a perfectly ordinary harmless cigarette case or cigar case; and, sitting in a restaurant or in one of their famous dance halls, he casually produces this cigarette case or cigar case from his pocket and everybody around imagines of course that he is about to smoke.

"But not a bit of it! He just gives a peculiar little twist to this cigarette case or cigar case of his, when, presto, a diminutive tumbler appears in his left hand, whereupon with his right hand he s-l-o-w-l-y and q-u-i-e-t-l-y pours out for himself from this cigarette case or cigar case into this diminutive tumbler of his some kind of liquid—probably Scotch whisky, but concocted as I have already told you, on some barge off the American coast.

"During my observations there at that time, I once witnessed still another picture.

"In one of the said restaurants sat two young American women not far from my table.

"An attendant of this restaurant, or, as they say, a 'waiter,' served them with a bottle of some mineral water and a couple of glasses.

"One of the women gave a certain little twist to the handle of her fashionable umbrella, whereupon a liquid, obviously also Scotch whisky or something of the kind, began likewise to flow very q-u-i-e-t-l-y and very s-l-o-w-l-y from the handle into their glasses.

"In short, my boy, the same is being repeated on this continent America as also took place quite recently in the large community called Russia. There the power-possessing responsible beings also prohibited the consumption of the famous 'Russian vodka' with the consequence that these beings very soon adapted themselves to consume, instead of this 'vodka,' the no less famous 'Hanja,' from the effects of which thousands of these unfortunate beings are still dying there daily.

"But in the present case, we must certainly give the contemporary American beings their due. In their skill at concealing their consumption of this famous alcohol from the authorities, they are infinitely more 'civilized' than the beings of the community Russia.

"Well then, my boy, to avoid the bustle of the street, I entered a typical New York restaurant, and having taken a seat at one of the tables there, began gazing out of the window at the crowd.

"As it is the common custom there on your planet, when people sit in a restaurant or any other such public place, always and without fail to pay what they call 'money' for something for the profit of the proprietor of the establishment, I did the same and also ordered for myself a glass of their famous what is called 'orangeade.'

"This famous American drink consists of the juice squeezed from oranges or from the famous what is called there 'grapefruit,' and the beings of that continent drink it always and everywhere in incredible quantities.

"It must be admitted that this famous orangeade of theirs does occasionally refresh them in hot weather, but, on the other hand, in its action upon what are called the 'mucous membranes' of the stomach and intestines this drink of theirs is still another of the many factors there, which, taken together, are gradually bringing about—although slowly yet inexorably certainly—the destruction of that 'unnecessary' and 'negligible' function called the 'digestive function of the stomach.'

"Well then, sitting in the said restaurant with this famous orangeade and watching the passers-by in the hope of seeing among them the Mister I awaited, I began casually looking around at the objects in the restaurant also.

"On the table at which I was sitting, I saw among other things also what is called the 'menu' of the restaurant.

"'Menu,' there on your planet, is the name given to a sheet of paper on which are written the names of all the varieties of food and drink available in the said restaurant.

"Reading the contents of this paper, I found among other things that no fewer than seventy-eight different dishes could be ordered there that day.

"This staggered me, and I wondered what on earth kind of a stove these Americans must have in their kitchens to be able to prepare seventy-eight dishes on it for just one day.

"I ought to add that I had been on every one of the continents there and had been the guest of a great many beings of different castes.

"And I had seen food prepared innumerable times, and also in my own house. So I already more or less knew that to prepare a single dish, at least two or three saucepans were required; and I reckoned that as these Americans prepared seventy-eight dishes in one kitchen they would certainly need about three hundred pots and pans.

"I had the fancy to see for myself how it was possible to accommodate on one stove three hundred saucepans, so I decided to offer what is called there a 'good tip' to the waiter who served me with the orangeade, to let me see the kitchen of the restaurant with my own eyes.

"The waiter somehow arranged it, and I went into the kitchen.

"When I got there, what do you think? . . . What kind of picture did I see? . . . A stove with a hundred pots and pans?

"Not on your life!! . . .

"I saw there only a small what is called there 'midget gas stove,' such as what are called 'old bachelors' and 'man-haters,' that is to say, 'worthless spinsters,' usually have in their rooms.

"By the side of this 'pimple of a stove' sat an extremely fat-necked cook of 'Scotch origin' reading the newspaper inseparable from every American; he was reading, it seems, the newspaper *The Times*.

"I looked around in amazement and also at the neck of this cook.

"While I was thus looking round in astonishment, a waiter came into the kitchen from the restaurant and, in peculiar English, ordered a certain very elaborate dish from this fat-necked cook.

"I think I may as well tell you that I then also noticed from his accent that the waiter who ordered this dish with a fancy name had only recently arrived there from the continent of Europe, obviously with the dream of filling his pockets there with American dollars—with that dream in fact about these American dollars which indeed every European has who has never been to America and which now allows no one in Europe to sleep in peace.

"When this aspirant to an 'American multimillionaire-dom' had ordered the said fancy dish from the fat-necked cook, the latter got up from his place without haste and very heavily, and first of all took down from the wall a small what is called there 'bachelor's frying pan.'

"Then having lighted his 'dwarf stove' he put the frying pan on it; and still moving ponderously, he then went over to one of the many cupboards, took from it a tin of some canned food, opened it, and emptied its contents into the said frying pan.

"Then in the same way he went over to another cupboard and again took out a tin of some canned food, but this time he put only a little of the contents into the frying pan and, having stirred the resulting mixture, he put the whole lot with precision on a plate which he set on the table and again sat down in his former place and resumed the interrupted reading of his newspaper.

"The waiter who had ordered this 'fancy dish' soon returned to the kitchen bearing a very large what is called 'copper' tray on which were a vast quantity of hollow metal what is called fashionable cutlery and, having placed the dish with this strange food on the said tray, he carried the whole into the restaurant.

"When I returned and resumed my seat at my table, I saw that at another table quite near, a Mister was sitting who was smacking his lips while eating the dish which I had chanced to see prepared in the kitchen.

"Looking again out of the window into the street, I eventually discerned the Mister I expected in the crowd, so, settling my bill at once, I left the restaurant.

"And now, my boy, maintaining the form of mentation of our dear teacher, I might as well tell you also a little about the 'speech' of these American beings.

"You must know that before my arrival on that continent I could already speak the 'tongue' of the beings of that continent, namely, what is called the 'English tongue.'

"But from the very first day of my arrival in the capital of this North America, I already experienced great inconvenience in my 'verbal intercourse' because, as it turned out, although these beings use this English tongue for verbal intercourse among themselves, this English tongue of theirs is rather special and in fact quite peculiar.

"So, having felt the inconvenience, I made up my mind to learn this peculiar 'conversational English' of theirs also.

"On the third day after my arrival there, as I was on my way to my newly acquainted Mister specially to ask him to recommend me a teacher for this 'English tongue,' I suddenly saw reflected on the sky, by projectors, an 'American advertisement' with the words:

'SCHOOL OF LANGUAGES BY THE SYSTEM
OF MR. CHATTERLITZ
13 North 293rd Street'

"The languages and the times when they were taught were set forth and, of the 'American English language' in particular, it was stated, among other things, that it could be learned in from five minutes to twenty-four hours.

"At first I could not make head or tail of it, but I decided all the same to go the next morning to the address indicated.

"When the next day I found this Mr. Chatterlitz, he received me himself in person, and when he heard that I wished to learn the 'American English language' by his system, he explained to me first of all that this conversational language could be learned by his system in three forms, each form corresponding to some special requirement.

"'The first form,' he said, 'is the conversational language for a man who is obliged to earn here among us our American dollars.

"'The second form is required for a man who, although not in need of our dollars, nevertheless likes to do dollar business and, furthermore, in order that in his social relations with our Americans everybody will think that he is not "just a nobody" but a real "gentleman" with an English upbringing.

"'As for the third form of the English language, this form is required by anybody who wishes to be able to procure here, there, and everywhere and at any hour—Scotch whisky.'

"As the time for learning the second form of the English language by this system suited me best, I decided to pay him immediately the dollars he charged in order to know the secret of his system.

"When I had paid him the dollars he charged and he had, seemingly quite casually, but in reality not without that avidity which has also already become proper to all the beings of your planet, placed my dollars in an inside pocket, he explained to me that in order to learn this second form, only five words had to be memorized, namely:

1. Maybe
2. Perhaps
3. Tomorrow
4. Oh, I see
5. All right

"He added that if I had occasion to converse with one or more of their misters, I should only need to utter any one of these five words every now and then.

"'That will be quite enough,' he added, 'to convince everybody that in the first place you know the English language very well, and secondly that you are an old hand at doing dollar business.'

"Although the system of this highly esteemed Chatterlitz was very original and meritorious, yet I never had occasion to put it into practice.

"And the occasion did not arise, because the next day I met by chance in the street an old acquaintance, an, as he is called, 'editor,' from the continent of Europe who in conversation confided to me an even more ideal secret for the American language.

"When I told him, among other things, that I had been the day before to Mister Chatterlitz about the local language and had told him a little about the system, he replied:

"'Do you know what, my dear doctor? As you are a subscriber to our paper over there, I cannot help revealing to you a certain secret of the language here.'

"And he said further:

"'Knowing several of our European languages, you can by employing this secret of mine be master of the language here to perfection, and indeed converse about anything you wish, and not simply make others think that you know the English language—for which purpose, I do not deny, the system of this Chatterlitz is indeed excellent.'

"He explained further that if, when pronouncing any word taken from any European language, you imagine that you have a hot potato in your mouth, then some word of the English language is in general bound to result.

"And if you imagine that this same hot potato is furthermore well sprinkled with ground 'red pepper,' then you will already have the pronunciation of the local American English language to a tee.

"He advised me moreover not to be timid in choosing words from the European languages, since the English language in general consisted of a fortuitous concourse of almost all the European languages, and hence that the language contained several words for every ordinary idea, with the consequence that 'you almost always hit on the right word.'

"'And suppose that, without knowing it, you use a word entirely absent from this language, no great harm is done; at worst your hearer will only think that he himself is ignorant of it.

"'All you have to do is just to bear in mind the said hot potato and . . . no more "boloney" about it.

"'I guarantee this secret, and I can safely say that if, on exactly following my advice, your "language" here does not prove to be ideal, then you may stop your subscription.'

"Several days later, I had to go to the city of Chicago.

"This city is the second in size on that continent and is, as it were, a second capital of 'North America.'

"On seeing me off for Chicago, that Mister, my New York acquaintance, gave me a letter of introduction to a certain Mister there.

"As soon as I arrived in this city Chicago, I went straight to this said Mister.

"This Chicago Mister turned out to be very amiable and most obliging.

"His name was 'Mister Bellybutton.'

"For the evening of the first day, this amiable and obliging Mr. Bellybutton suggested my accompanying him to the house of some of his friends so that, as he expressed it, I should 'not be bored' in a quite strange city.

"I, of course, agreed.

"When we arrived, we found there a fair number of young American beings, guests like ourselves.

"All the guests were exceedingly gay and very 'merry.'

"They were telling 'funny stories' in turn and the laughter from these stories of theirs lingered in the room like the smoke on a day when the wind is south over the chimneys of the American factories where the American sausages called 'hot dogs' are prepared.

"As I also find funny stories amusing, that first evening of mine in the city of Chicago passed very gaily indeed.

"All this would have been quite sensible and very delightful, if it had not been for one 'feature' of the stories told that first evening, which greatly astonished and perplexed me.

"And that is, I was astonished by their what is called 'ambiguity' and 'obscenity.'

"The ambiguity and obscenity of these stories were such that any single one of these American storytellers could have given a dozen points to 'Boccaccio,' famous there on the planet Earth.

"Boccaccio is the name of a certain writer who wrote for the beings of the Earth a very instructive book called the *Decameron*; it is very widely read there at the present time and is the favorite of contemporary beings breeding there on all continents and belonging to almost all communities there.

"The following day, also in the evening, this kind Mr. Bellybutton took me again to some still other friends of his.

"Here also were a large number of young American beings, both male and female, sitting in various corners of a very large room conversing quietly and very placidly.

"When we were seated, a pretty young American girl soon came and sat down beside me, and began chatting with me.

"As is usual there, I took up the conversation, and we chatted about anything and everything, she asking me among other things many questions about the city of Paris.

"In the midst of the conversation, this American as they say 'young lady' suddenly, for no earthly reason at all, began stroking my neck.

"I immediately thought, How kind of her! She must certainly have noticed a 'flea' on my neck and is now stroking the place to allay the irritation.

"But when I soon noticed that all the young American

beings present were also stroking each other, I was much astonished and could not understand what it was all about.

"My first supposition concerning the 'fleas' no longer held good because it was impossible to suppose that everybody had a flea on his neck.

"I began speculating what it was all about, but try as I might, I could give myself no explanation whatever.

"Only afterwards, when we had left the house and were in the street, I asked Mr. Bellybutton for an explanation of it all. He immediately burst into unrestrained laughter and called me 'simpleton' and a 'hick.' Then, calming down a bit, he said:

"'What a queer guy you are; why, we have just been to a "petting party."' And still laughing at my naïveté, he explained that the day before we had also been to a party, but to a 'story party,' and tomorrow, he continued, 'I was planning to take you to a "swimming party" where young people bathe together but of course all dressed in special costumes.'

"When he saw that the same look of perplexed astonishment still remained on my face, he asked, 'But if for some reason or other you don't like such "tame affairs," we can go to others that are not open to everybody. There are lots of such "parties" here and I am a member of several of them.

"'At these parties which are not open to everybody, we can, if you like, have something more "substantial."'

"But I did not take advantage of this kindness of this obliging and exceedingly 'amiable' Mr. Bellybutton, because the next morning I received a telegram which made it necessary for me to return to New York."

At this point of his tales Beelzebub suddenly became thoughtful and, after a rather protracted pause, sighing deeply, he continued to speak thus:

"The next day I did not go by the morning train as I had

decided on receiving the telegram, but delayed my departure until the night train.

"As the cause of the delay of my departure may well illustrate for you the evil resulting from a certain invention of these American beings which is very widely spread over the whole of your planet, and which is one of the chief causes of the continued, so to say 'dwindling of the psyche' of all the other three-brained beings of your unfortunate planet, I shall tell you about it a little more in detail.

"Just this maleficent invention of the beings of this continent, which I now intend to explain to you, has not only been the cause of the acceleration of the tempo of the still greater 'dwindling' of the psyche of all the three-brained beings breeding on that unfortunate planet of yours, but it was and still is the cause also that in the beings of all the other continents of recent times there is already completely destroyed that being-function which it is proper for all three-brained beings to have, and which was the one single function which even until the last century arose in their presence of its own accord, namely, that being-function which is everywhere called the 'sane instinct to believe in reality.'

"In the place of this function, very necessary for every three-brained being, another special very definite function gradually crystallized, whose action induces in its bearer a continuous doubt about everything.

"This maleficent invention of theirs they call 'advertising.'

"Better to understand what follows, I must first tell you that several years before this trip of mine to America, once when traveling on the continent of Europe, I bought myself some books to read in the train to pass away the prospective long and tedious railway journey. In one of these books, written by a very famous writer there, I read an article about this America in which a great deal was said about what is called 'the slaughterhouses' existing in that same city Chicago.

"Slaughterhouse is the name there for a special place where three-brained terrestrial beings carry on the destruction of the existence of those beings of various other forms whose planetary bodies they are addicted to using for their first being-food, again owing to those abnormally established conditions of ordinary being-existence.

"Moreover, executing this manifestation of theirs in these special establishments, they even say and imagine that they do it from necessity and, as it were, in a perfectly what they call 'humane way.'

"This said terrestrial contemporary very famous writer, the author of this book, rapturously described, as an 'eyewitness,' a, in his opinion, superlatively well-organized slaughterhouse of this same city Chicago.

"He described the perfection of its machines of every possible kind and its marvelous cleanliness. Not only, he wrote, does humaneness to the beings of other forms reach in this slaughterhouse the degree of 'divinity,' but even the machines are so perfected that it is almost as if a live ox is driven through a door at one end and some ten minutes later out of a door at the other end you could get, if you wished, hot sausages ready to eat. Finally, he specially emphasized that it was all done entirely by the 'perfected' machines alone, without the touch of a human hand, as a consequence of which, as he said, everything was so clean and neat there that nothing could possibly be imagined cleaner and neater.

"Several years after reading that book, I chanced to read again almost the same thing about this Chicago slaughterhouse in a certain also serious Russian magazine, in which this slaughterhouse was lauded in the same way.

"And thereafter, I heard of this Chicago slaughterhouse

from a thousand different beings, many of whom had been, presumably, eyewitnesses to the marvels they described.

"In short, before my arrival in the city of Chicago, I was already fully convinced that a 'marvel' unprecedented on the Earth existed there.

"I must mention here that I had always been greatly interested in these establishments of theirs, namely, those places where your favorites destroy the existence of various forms of terrestrial beings; and furthermore, from the time when I began organizing my observatory on the planet Mars and had to do with various machines for it, I took always and everywhere a great interest in every other sort of machine as well.

"So, when I happened to be in this same city of Chicago, I thought it would be inexcusable on my part not to use the opportunity to see this famous 'Chicago slaughterhouse.' So, in the morning on the day of my departure from there, I decided to go, accompanied by one of my new Chicago acquaintances, to inspect this rare construction of your favorites.

"Having arrived there, we took as our guide, on the advice of one of the assistants of the chief director, an employee of a branch of some bank there which was connected with this slaughterhouse, and together with him we set off to inspect the place.

"Accompanied by him, we first of all went through the places where the unfortunate quadruped beings are driven and where they remain until their slaughter.

"This place was in no way different from that of all establishments of the kind on your planet, except that this particular place was on a considerably larger scale. On the other hand, it was very much dirtier than any of the slaughterhouses I had previously seen in other countries.

"Afterwards we went through several more what are

called 'annexes.' One of them was the 'cold storage' for the meat that was ready; in another they destroyed the existence of quadruped beings simply with hammers and also stripped off their hide—again in the manner usual in other slaughterhouses.

"By the way, in passing through this last annex I remember I then thought: this place here is in all probability for the slaughter of cattle intended especially for the Jews, who, as I already knew, in accordance with the code of their religion, destroy quadruped beings in a special way.

"Walking through the said annexes took rather a long time, and all the while I was waiting for the moment when we should eventually arrive at the section about which I had heard so much and which I was determined to see without fail.

"But when I expressed my wish to our guide to hasten on to that section, I learned that we had already seen everything there was to see in this famous Chicago slaughterhouse, and that no other sections existed. I had not, my dear boy, seen there anywhere a single machine, unless one includes the rollers on rails which are in all slaughterhouses for moving the heavy carcasses; and as for the dirt in this Chicago slaughterhouse, you could see as much as you liked.

"In cleanliness and general organization, the slaughterhouse of the city Tiflis, which I had seen two years before, could have given many points to this slaughterhouse of the city Chicago.

"In the Tiflis slaughterhouse, for example, you would not find anywhere on the floor a single drop of blood, whereas, in the Chicago slaughterhouse, everywhere, at every step, there were pools of it.

"Obviously some company of American businessmen, inevitably resorting to 'advertising' for every business in general, had to advertise the Chicago slaughterhouse also, in order to spread a false notion about it, totally unrelated to reality, over the whole planet.

"As is in general the rule there, they certainly did not spare their dollars in this case either, and since the sacred being-function of 'conscience' is completely atrophied among contemporary terrestrial what are called 'journalists' and 'reporters,' the result is that in all your favorites breeding on all the continents there is crystallized just that definite, monstrously exaggerated notion of the slaughterhouses of the city of Chicago.

"And it can be said, indeed, that they did so in true American fashion.

"On the continent America, the three-brained beings have become so expert in this advertising of theirs, that it is quite possible to apply to them the saying of our dear Mullah Nassr Eddin which declares that 'that man will become a friend of the cloven-hoofed who perfects himself to such Reason and such being that he can make an elephant out of a fly.'

"They have indeed become so skillful at 'making elephants out of flies' and they do it so often that already at the present time, on seeing a genuine American elephant, one has to 'remember oneself with the whole of one's being' not to get the impression that it is only a fly.

"From Chicago I returned again to New York and, as all my projects for the fulfillment of which I had come to this continent were then unexpectedly rapidly and rather successfully actualized, and seeing that the surrounding circumstances and conditions of the ordinary existence of the three-brained beings of that city turned out to be corresponding to what was required for my periodic complete rest which had already become customary for me during my last personal sojourn on the surface of your planet, I decided to stay there longer and exist with the beings there merely according to the being-associations inevitably flowing in me.

"Existing in the said way in this central point of the beings of this big contemporary group and rubbing shoulders on various occasions with the various types among them, I just then—without any premeditation but thanks only to my acquired habit of collating material, so to say 'by the way,' for those statistics of mine, which, as I have already told you, I gathered during the whole of my last personal sojourn among your favorites for the purpose chiefly of comparing the extent to which all the illnesses and all the strange what are called 'being subjective vices' existing among the beings of the different groups are spread—constated a fact which greatly interested me, namely, the fact that in the common presences of almost half of all the three-brained beings I met there, the proceeding functioning of the transformation of the first being-food is disharmonized, that is, as they themselves would say, their digestive organs are spoiled; and that almost a quarter of them have or are candidates for that form of disease specific to beings there, which they call 'impotence,' thanks just to which disease a great many of the contemporary beings of your planet are forever deprived of the possibility of continuing their species.

"When I chanced to constate this, a great interest in the beings of just this new group arose in me, and I thereupon changed my previously determined mode of existence among them and allotted half my time from my personal rest to special observation and investigation of the causes of this fact—for me so strange and for them so deplorable. In pursuit of this aim I even took occasion to visit various other provincial points of the beings of this new contemporary group, though I stayed nowhere more than one or two days with the exception of the city 'Boston,' or, as it is sometimes called, 'the city of the people who escaped race degeneration.' There I existed for a whole week.

"And so, as a result of these observations and statistical investigations of mine, it became clear that both these aforesaid diseases, which to a certain extent are prevalent among the contemporary beings in general who breed on all continents, are on this continent so inordinately widespread that its proximate consequences were immediately patent to me, namely, that if it continues among them at the present rate, then just the same fate will befall this contemporary large independent group of three-brained beings who have taken your fancy as recently befell that large community there which was called 'monarchic Russia,' that is to say, this group also will be destroyed.

"The difference will be only in the process of the destruction itself. The process of the destruction of the large community 'monarchic Russia' proceeded in consequence of the abnormalities of, so to say, the Reason of the power-possessing beings there, whereas the process of the destruction of this community America will proceed in consequence of organic abnormalities. In other words, the 'death' of the first community came from, as they say, the 'mind' whereas the death of the second community will come from the 'stomach and sex' of its beings.

"The point is, that it has long ago been determined that in general the possibility of long existence for a three-brained being of your planet depends at the present time exclusively only on the normal action of these two aforementioned being-functions, namely, upon the state of their as they say 'digestion' and upon the functioning of their 'sex organs.'

"But it is precisely these two functionings necessary to their common presence, which are now both going in the direction of complete atrophy; and moreover, at a highly accelerated tempo.

"This community America is at the present time still quite young; it is still, as they say there on your planet, like an infant, all 'peaches and cream.'

"And so, if while still so young its beings have in respect of the two chief motors of their existence thus deviated retrogressively, then, in my opinion, in this case also—as it in general occurs to everything in the Megalocosmos—the degree of the further movement for the purpose of blending again with the Infinite will depend on the direction and degree of the forces obtained from the initial impetus.

"In our Great Megalocosmos, there is even established for all beings with Reason a law, as it were, according to which one must always and in everything guard just against the initial impetus, because on acquiring momentum, it becomes a force which is the fundamental mover of everything existing in the Universe, and which leads everything back to Prime Being."

In this place of his tales Beelzebub was handed a 'Leitoochanbros,' and when he had finished listening to the contents of the communication he turned again to Hassein and said:

"I think, my boy, that it will be very useful to you for your more detailed representation and understanding of the strangeness of the psyche in general of these three-brained beings who have taken your fancy and who arise on the planet Earth if I explain to you in somewhat greater detail the causes which, in the common presences of these American three-brained beings, produce disharmony in both of these fundamental functionings of theirs.

"For convenience of exposition I shall explain to you separately the causes of the disharmony of each of these two fundamental functionings, and I shall begin with the explanation of the causes of the disharmony in the functioning of the transformation of their first being-food, or as they themselves would say, with the causes of the spoiling of their stomachs.

"For the disharmony of this function of theirs, there were and now still are several definite causes, comprehensible even to the Reason of ordinary normal three-brained beings, but the chief and fundamental cause is that from the very beginning of the formation of their community, they gradually got accustomed—owing to all kinds of established surrounding conditions and influences proceeding from authority which happened to be formed of itself abnormally—and they are now already thoroughly accustomed, never to use for their first being-food anything fresh whatsoever, but to use exclusively only products already decomposed.

"At the present time the beings of this group almost never consume for their first being-food any edible product which still retains all those active elements put into every being by Great Nature Herself as an indispensable requisite for taking in power for normal existence; but they 'preserve,' 'freeze,' and 'essensify' beforehand all those products of theirs and use them only when most of these active elements required for normal existence are already volatilized out of them.

"And this abnormality proceeded in the ordinary process of being-existence of the three-brained beings who have taken your fancy—in this instance, in the case of this new group—and continues to be spread and to be fixed everywhere there, also of course in consequence of the fact that, subsequent to the time, when they—that is to say, when all the three-brained beings in general of that planet of yours—had ceased to actualize in themselves the indispensable being-efforts, there was then gradually destroyed in them the possibility for the crystallization in their common presences of those being-data thanks to which, even in the absence of the guidance of true knowledge, the maleficence for themselves of any of their manifestations can be sensed instinctively.

"In the present case, if only a few of these unfortunates possessed this instinct proper to three-brained beings, they might then—if only thanks merely to habitual accidental being-associations and confrontations—first, themselves become aware, and afterwards inform all the rest, that as soon as the prime connection with common Nature of any product in general serviceable as a first being-food is severed, then no matter if this product be kept completely isolated, that is to say 'hermetically sealed,' 'frozen,' or 'essensified,' it must like everything else in the Universe change its form and decompose according to the same principle and in the same order in which it was formed.

"Here you should know concerning the active elements from which all cosmic formations are in general formed by Nature—both those subject to transformation through the Tetartocosmoses and which are the products for the first food of beings as well as in general all other completely spiritualized and half-spiritualized arisings—that, as soon as the corresponding time arrives, these active elements, in whatever conditions they may be found, obligatorily begin separating in a certain order of succession from those masses in which they were fused during the Trogoautoegocratic process.

"And the same, of course, proceeds with those products, so dear to the American beings, which they preserve in what are called 'hermetically sealed cans.'

"However 'hermetically' these cans of products may be sealed, as soon as the time of, so to say, 'disintegration' arrives, the corresponding active elements infallibly begin to separate from the whole mass. And these active elements, thus separated from the whole mass, group themselves as a rule according to their origin in these hermetically sealed cans in the form of 'drops' or small 'bubbles' which, so to say, dissolve immediately the cans are opened for the consumption of these products, and, volatilizing into space, are dispersed to their corresponding places.

"The beings of this continent do sometimes consume fresh fruit; but as for these fruits of theirs—they cannot be said to be fruits, but simply and solely as our dear teacher would say, 'freaks.'

"By means of the trees, existing in abundance on this continent, little by little various scientists of 'new format' have succeeded with their 'wiseacrings' in making of these American fruits at the present time, just, so to say, a 'feast for the eye,' and not a form of being-nourishment.

"The fruits there are now already so formed as to have within them scarcely anything of what was foreordained by Great Nature to be consumed for the normal being-existence of beings.

"These scientists of new format there are of course very far from apprehending that when any surplanetary formation is artificially grafted or manipulated in any such fashion it arrives in a state defined by objective science as 'Absoizomosa,' in which it absorbs from its surrounding medium cosmic substances serviceable only for the coating of what is called its 'automatically self-reproducing subjective presence.'

"The point is, that from the very beginning of this latest contemporary civilization of theirs, it somehow so fell out among the beings of all the innumerable separate groups there, that, of the seven aspects of the fundamental commandment given to three-brained beings from Above, namely, 'strive to acquire inner and outer purity,' the single aspect they selected and in a distorted form have made their ideal, is that aspect which is conveyed in the following words:

"'Help everything around you, both the animate and the still inanimate, to acquire a beautiful appearance.'

"And indeed, and especially in the last two centuries there, they have striven simply to attain a 'beautiful exterior'—but, of course, only in regard to those various objects external to them themselves, which chanced in the given period to become as they expressed it 'fashionable.'

"During this said period, it has been of no concern to them whether any object external to them themselves had any substance whatsoever—all that was necessary was that it should have what they call 'a striking appearance.'

"As regards the achievements of the contemporary beings of this continent in respect of actualizing the 'external beauty' of these fruits of theirs, then indeed, my boy, I have nowhere seen, not only on the other continents of the same planet but even on the other planets of that solar system, fruits so beautiful in appearance as those of the present time on this continent America; on the other hand, as regards the inner substance of these fruits, one can only use that favorite expression of our dear Teacher, which consists of the following words:

"'The greatest of all being-blessings for man is the action of castor oil.'

"And to what height they have carried their skill in making their famous preserves out of these fruits—as for this, as is said, 'neither tongue can tell nor pen describe.' You have to see them for yourself to experience in your common presence the degree of the impulse of 'rapture' to which one can be carried on perceiving with the organ of sight the external beauty of these American fruit preserves.

"Walking down the main streets of the cities of the

beings of this continent, especially of the city New York, and seeing the display in any fruit store, it is hard to say at once just what it is the eyes behold. Is it an exhibition of pictures by the futurists of the city Berlin of the continent Europe, or is it a display of the famous perfumery stores for foreigners of the 'world capital,' that is, the city Paris?

"Only after a while, when you have finally managed to take in various details of the appearance of these displays and somehow start reflecting again, can you clearly constate how much greater is the variety of color and shape of the jars in these American displays of fruit preserves than in the mentioned displays of the continent of Europe; and this is evidently due to the fact that, in the common psyche of the beings of this new group, the combination resulting from the intermixture of former independent races happens to correspond more completely to a better perception and a thorough cognition of the sense and beneficence of the achievements of the Reason both of the beings of the contemporary community of Germany in respect of the chemical substances they have invented, called there 'aniline' and 'alizarin,' as well as of the beings of the community France in respect of 'perfumery.'

"I myself when I first saw there such an exhibition could not refrain from entering one of these stores and buying about forty jars of all shapes containing fruit preserves of every shade of color.

"I bought them to please the beings then accompanying me, and who came from the continents of Asia and Europe where fruits so rarely beautiful to look at did not as yet exist. When I brought my purchases home and distributed them these beings were at first, indeed, not a whit less astonished and delighted than I had been by their appearance, but, afterwards, when they had consumed them for their first being-food, all that was needed was to see their grimaces and the change of color on their faces to understand what effect these fruits in general have upon the organism of beings.

"The case is still worse on that continent with that product which, for them as well as for almost all the three-brained beings of the Universe, is the most important product for first being-food, and, namely, that product called 'prosphora,' which they themselves name 'bread.'

"Before I describe the fate of this American bread I must tell you that this terra firma part of the surface of your planet called 'North and South America' was formed thanks to various accidental combinations ensuing, in the first place, from the second great 'cataclysm not according to law' which occurred to that ill-fated planet and, secondly, from the position that terra firma occupies in relation to the process of the 'common systematic movement' having a stratum of what is called 'soil' which was and still is suited for the production of that 'divine grain' of which this same 'prosphora' is made. With conscious knowledge of how to use it, the soil surface of these continents is capable of yielding in a single what is called 'good season' the 'fullness of a complete process of the sacred Heptaparaparshinokh,' or in other words, a 'forty-nine-fold harvest,' and even by its semiconscious use, as is now the case, the soil there yields of this 'divine grain' a considerable abundance in comparison with the other continents.

"Well then, my boy, when the beings of that continent began to have, thanks to various fortuitous circumstances, many of those objects which, for this strange psyche of the contemporary three-brained beings who have taken your fancy, are a subject for their dreams and are everywhere called there 'dollars,' thanks to which fact, according to long established usage there, they acquired in their 'picturings' of the beings of all the other continents, what is called a 'sense of superiority,' with the result, also now usual among them, that they began to wiseacre with everything to achieve that said contemporary ideal of theirs, then they also began wiseacring with all their might with this divine grain out of which prosphora is made.

"They began employing every possible means to, so to say, deform this divine grain in order to give to its product a 'beautiful and striking appearance.'

"For this purpose they invented a variety of machines by means of which they 'scrape,' 'comb,' 'smooth,' and 'polish' this wheat, which has the misfortune to arise on their continent, until they accomplish the complete destruction of all those active elements concentrated on the surface of the grains just underneath what is called the 'husk' and precisely which are appointed by Great Nature for renewing in the common presences of beings what they have expended in worthily serving her.

"Hence, it is, my boy, that the prosphora or bread now produced there from this wheat which arises in such abundance on this continent contains nothing useful to the beings who consume it, and from its consumption there is produced in their presences nothing but noxious gases and what are called there 'worms.'

"However, it must in all fairness be remarked that if they got for themselves from this wheat nothing that enables them to serve Great Nature better or more consciously, nevertheless, by producing in themselves the said 'worms,' they do unconsciously very very greatly assist their planet in honorable service to the Most Great common-cosmic Trogoautoegocrat—for are not these worms also beings through whom cosmic substances are also transformed?

"At any rate, the beings breeding on this continent have already achieved by these wiseacrings of theirs with this bread what they have greatly desired and striven to obtain, and, namely, that the beings of all the other continents should never fail to say of them, as, for instance, in the given case, something as follows:

"'Astonishingly smart fellows, these Americans; even their bread is something extraordinary; so "superb," so "white" and simply charming—really the splendor of splendors of contemporary civilization.'

"But that from this deformity of wheat, their bread results in being 'worthless' and, furthermore, constitutes another of the innumerable factors in the spoiling of their stomachs—what is that to them? Are they not also in the front rank of contemporary what is called 'European civilization'?

"The most curious thing in all this naïveté of theirs is that they give the best and most useful of what Nature forms in this divine grain for their normal existence, to the pigs, or simply burn it, while for themselves they consume that substance which is formed by Nature in the wheat only for connecting and maintaining those active elements which are localized chiefly, as I have already said, just under the husk of the grain.

"A second and also rather important factor in the disharmonizing of the digestive function of these unfortunate American three-brained beings is the system which they have recently invented for the elimination from themselves of the waste residue of their first-food; and that is to say, the 'comfortable seats' of what are called their 'water closets.'

"In addition to the fact that this maleficent invention was and still is one of the chief factors in the said disharmonization now proceeding in them themselves and also in almost all the beings of the other continents—who, by the way, have already begun in recent times very jealously imitating them in all their peculiar methods of 'assisting' their transformatory functioning—your favorites, thanks to this invention of theirs, now striving to fulfill even this inevitable being-function of theirs with the greatest possible sensation of pleasant tranquillity, have got, as it were, a new incentive for the jealous service of their god 'self-calming,' which, as I have already said more than once, has been and still is for them almost the chief evil engendering and evoking all the abnormalities of their psyche as well as of their ordinary being-existence.

"A good example, and even, so to say, an 'illuminatingly enlightening picture for your being-representation' of what extraordinary perspectives are opened for the future by just this invention of theirs, is the fact that already certain of these contemporary American beings who have acquired, of course also by a variety of accidents, a quantity of their famous dollars now arrange in their 'water closets with comfortable seats' such accessories as a small table, a telephone and what is called a 'radio apparatus,' so that when so sitting, they may continue their 'correspondence,' discuss over the telephone with their acquaintances all their dollar businesses, quietly read the newspapers which have become indispensable to them, or, finally, listen to those musical compositions, the work of various Hasnamusses there which, because they are, as is said, 'fashionable,' every contemporary American businessman is also obliged to know.

"The main harm in the significance of the resulting disharmony in the digestive functioning of all the contemporary three-brained beings of your planet from this American invention is due to the following causes:

"In former times, when more or less normal data for the engendering of objective Reason were still crystallized in the common presences of your favorites, and they themselves could reflect and understand when other similar and already enlightened beings explained the subject to them, they made the said posture as was required; but subsequently, when the said being data had definitely ceased to crystallize in them, and they also began discharging this function of theirs only automatically, then, thanks to the system prevalent before this American invention, the planetary body could of itself, automatically, by virtue only of what is called 'animal instinct,' adopt the required definite posture. But now that American beings have invented these 'comfortable seats,' and they have all begun using them for this inevitable function of theirs, their planetary body can no longer possibly adapt itself even instinctively to the required posture, with the consequence that not only have certain what are called 'muscles' which actualize this inevitable being-function become gradually atrophied in those of your favorites who use these American comfortable seats, owing to which what are called obstructions are formed in them, but in addition the causes are engendered of several specifically new diseases which, in the whole of our Great Universe, arise exclusively only in the presences of these strange three-brained beings.

"Among the various primary and secondary causes, the totality of which is gradually bringing about the disharmonization of this fundamental function in the common presences of your contemporary favorites breeding on that continent of North America, there is still another exceedingly peculiar cause which, although 'blatantly obvious' among them, nevertheless, owing to their 'chicken reflections,' flourishes with an impulse of egoistic satisfaction, under as it were a 'cap of invisibility.'

"This peculiar cause arose and also began slowly and quietly, but infallibly disharmonizing this function in them, thanks simply to the fact that in the strange presences of the beings of this new large group, a 'ruling passion' prevails to be as often as possible on the continent of Europe.

"You should also be informed about this peculiar cause, chiefly because you will learn from it of yet another result, harmful for all your favorites, of the 'evil wiseacrings' of their contemporary 'scientists.'

"For your better representation and understanding of this cause of the gradual disharmonizing of this inevitable being-function in the common presences of the American beings, you should first be familiar with a certain detail of just those organs which actualize the said function in their common presences.

"Among their organs for the complete transformation of the first food is one that exists almost everywhere under the name of 'Toospooshokh,' or, as they themselves call it, a 'blind process,' and in their scientific terminology, 'appendix.'

"The action of this organ, as appointed by Great Nature, is that various connective cosmic substances separated by the transformation of the various surplanetary crystallizations which compose the 'first being-food' are gathered in it in the form of what are called 'gases,' in order that later, at the time of the elimination from the common presences of the beings of the already waste residue of the said food, these 'gases' should by their pressure assist this act.

"The gases gathered in this organ actualize by their so to say 'discharge' the mechanical action designed by Nature, independently of the general transformatory functioning proceeding in the beings, and only at definite periods of time established in each being differently according to subjective habit.

"Well then, my boy, thanks to their frequent trips to the continent Europe, the round trip taking from twelve days to a month, conditions are created for a daily change of time for the fulfillment of this established function, with the consequence that a serious factor results for the gradual engendering of disharmony in the process of their common fundamental transformatory functioning. That is to say, when for a period of many days, on account of the change of the established time, they fail to perform this indispensable function of theirs, and the 'gases' thus collected in this organ, not being utilized by them for the automatic action of the purpose indicated, and not fulfilling the design preconceived by Great Nature, gradually escaping from their presences unproductively into space—the totality of these manifestations of theirs, by the way, making existence on these passenger ships of theirs almost intolerable for a being with a normally developed organ for perceiving odors—then, as a result of all this, there often occurs in them what is called a 'mechanical obstruction,' which in its turn also conduces to the said gradual disharmonization of this fundamental transformatory function of theirs.

"When I began to explain to you, my boy, the causes of the disharmony in the presences of these American beings of the function of the transformation of the first being-food and when I mentioned the 'comfortable seats' invented by them, I said among other things, that these strange three-brained beings who have taken your fancy and who breed on the planet Earth were 'again' striving to perform even this indispensable being-function of theirs with the greatest possible sensation of self-satisfaction for themselves. I said 'again' because previously, in various periods of the flow of time, these strange three-brained beings there who have taken your fancy had already several times introduced something similar into the usages of their ordinary existence.

"I remember very clearly one of those periods when the beings of that time, who, by the way, according to the notions of your contemporary favorites, were nothing but ancient 'savages,' invented every possible kind of convenience for performing this same although prosaic yet indispensable being-need, on account of which these contemporary Americans, who in their naïveté consider themselves already civilized to the *ne plus ultra*, have invented these comfortable seats in their water closets.

"This was precisely during the period when the chief center of culture for the whole of your planet was the country Tikliamish and when this country was experiencing the height of its splendor.

"For this being-function, the beings of the country Tikliamish invented something rather like these American comfortable seats, and this maleficent invention also spread widely everywhere among all the other beings of that ill-fated planet.

"If the said invention of the beings of the Tikliamishian civilization were compared with the invention of these contemporary Americans then, according to the expression they sometimes use for comparison, the latter may be called a 'child's toy.'

"The beings of the Tikliamishian civilization invented a certain kind of 'comfortable couch bed' which could be used for sleeping as well as for what is called 'lounging' so that while lying on this 'wonderful contrivance,' and without manifesting the slightest being-effort whatsoever, they could perform this same inevitable being-need for which the contemporary beings of the continent America have invented their 'seats of ease.'

"These 'wonder beds' were so adapted for this purpose that a lever by the side of the bed had only to be touched lightly to enable one instantly, in the bed itself, to perform this same indispensable need freely and of course very 'cosily' and also with the greatest so to say 'chic.'

"It will not be superfluous, my boy, for you to know

also, by the way, that these same famous 'beds' had the effect of causing great and momentous events in the process of their ordinary existence.

"So long as the previous relatively normal system still prevailed among the beings there for the said being-functions, everything went along very peacefully and quietly, but as soon as certain what are called power-possessing and wealth-possessing beings of that time had invented for this purpose the mentioned 'comfortable beds,' which came to be called 'if you wish to enjoy felicity then enjoy it with a bang,' there then began among the ordinary beings of that time that which led to the said serious and deplorable consequences.

"I must tell you that it was just during those years when the beings of Tikliamish were inventing these 'wonder beds,' that this planet of yours underwent a common cosmic process of 'Chirnooanovo,' that is to say, that, concomitantly with the displacement of the gravity center movement of this solar system in the movement of the common-cosmic harmony, the center of gravity of this planet itself was also displaced.

"During such years, as you already know, thanks to this cosmic manifestation, there increases everywhere on planets—in the psyche of the beings inhabiting any planet undergoing 'Chirnooanovo'—a 'Blagonoorarirnian sensation,' or, as it is otherwise called, 'remorse of conscience' for one's past deeds against one's own convictions.

"But there on your planet, thanks to the common presences of your favorites having become so odd, from a variety of causes both proceeding from outside of them and arising through their own fault, the result of the action of this common-cosmic actualization does not proceed in them as it proceeds in the presences of the three-brained beings arising on other planets during 'Chirnooanovo'; that is to say, instead of this remorse of conscience, there usually arise there and become widespread certain specific processes, called the 'reciprocal destruction of Microcosmoses in the Tetartocosmos,' which processes, when proceeding in them, they themselves look upon as what are called among them 'epidemics' and which in ancient times were known by the names 'Kalunom,' 'Morkrokh,' 'Selnoano,' etc., and in present days by the names 'Black Death,' 'cholera,' 'Spanish influenza,' and so on.

"Well then, thanks to the fact that many diseases then called 'Kolbana,' 'Tirdiank,' 'Moyasul,' 'Champarnakh,' and so on, and called by contemporary beings 'tabes,' 'sclerosis disseminata,' 'hemorrhoids,' 'ishias,' 'hemiplegia,' and so on, were widely prevalent among the majority of those using these exceedingly comfortable 'couch beds,' those beings from among them in whose common presences the data for Hasnamussian properties had, thanks to the complete absence of the actualization of being-Partkdolg-duty, already previously begun to be crystallized more intensively than usual, and among whom were those called 'revolutionaries,' observing this particularity, decided to take advantage of it for their own purposes; that is to say, types of this kind invented and circulated broadcast among the masses of beings of that time, that all the aforesaid epidemic contagious diseases resulted from the fact that, thanks to the beds, 'if you wish to enjoy felicity, then enjoy it with a mighty bang,' the 'parasitic bourgeois' contracted various diseases, which diseases afterwards spread by contagion among the masses.

"Thanks to that peculiar inherency of theirs called 'suggestibility,' which I mentioned before and which had been acquired in their common presences, all the surrounding beings, of course, believed this as they call it 'propaganda' of theirs, and, there usually being in these cases a quantity of talk about it, there was gradually crystallized in each of them the periodically arising factor which actualizes in their common presences that strange and relatively prolonged 'psychic state,' which I should call the 'loss of sensation of self'; in consequence of which, as also usually happens there, they set about destroying everywhere, not only these 'wonder beds,' but also the existence of those beings who used them.

"Although the acute stage of this, so to say, obtuseness in the presences of most of the ordinary beings of that period soon passed, nevertheless the 'raging destruction' both of these beds themselves and of the beings who used them continued by momentum during several terrestrial years. Eventually, this maleficent invention went completely out of use, and soon it was even forgotten that such beds had ever existed on the planet.

"At any rate, it can be said with certainty that if the 'civilization' of the beings of the group now breeding on the continent America develops in its present spirit and at its present rate, then they also will unquestionably 'civilize themselves' to the degree of having 'bed couches' as astonishing as were those beds 'if you wish to enjoy felicity, then enjoy it with a bang.'

"It will not be amiss now, my boy, also to remark, by way of illustration, upon the invention of preserved products for the first being-food and their application in the process of being-existence by the beings of this contemporary group, who in recent times have chanced to become for the strange Reason of the beings of all the other continents, so to say, 'objects of imitation,' chiefly on account simply of the fact that they were supposed to be the first on their planet to invent such beneficent and convenient being-usages, namely, in the given case, the device of feeding themselves with preserved products, thanks to which they, as it were, save time.

"The contemporary unfortunate three-brained beings in general who breed on your planet are, of course, not aware, nor for causes already explained to you, have they in themselves the possibility of reflecting, that their remote ancestors of various past ages, who were much more normally formed into responsible beings, must have 'racked their brains,' as is said, 'not a little' to discover means for minimizing the time spent on this inevitable being-necessity of feeding themselves with products; and having found such apparently expedient methods, they every time, after a brief trial of them, eventually became convinced that these products, of whatever kind and however they might be preserved, always deteriorated with time and became worthless for their first-food; and hence they ceased to employ these methods in the process of their ordinary existence.

"As a parallel to this contemporary means of preserving products for one's first being-food in hermetically sealed vessels, let us take as an example that means of preserving which I personally have witnessed in the country Maralpleicie.

"It was just at the time when the beings of the locality of Maralpleicie were vying in everything with the beings of the country Tikliamish and were engaged in a fierce rivalry with them that the beings of all other countries should consider their country the first and foremost 'center of culture.'

"Just then it was that they invented among other things something similar to these American preserves.

"Those beings of Maralpleicie, however, preserved their edible products sealed hermetically not in 'poison-exuding tin cans,' such as the contemporary beings of the continent America use, but in what were then called 'Sikharenenian vessels.'

"Those Sikharenenian vessels in Maralpleicie were prepared from very finely ground, what are called there 'mother-of-pearl,' 'yolks of hen's eggs,' and a glue obtained from the fish named the Choozna sturgeon.

"These vessels had the appearance and quality of the unpolished glass jars now existing there on your planet.

"In spite of all the obvious advantages of preserving products in such vessels, yet nevertheless, when certain beings with Reason in the country Maralpleicie constated that in those beings who habitually used products preserved in this way there was gradually atrophied what is called 'organic shame,' then, having succeeded in widely spreading among the other ordinary beings information about this constatation of theirs, all the other surrounding beings, similar to them, gradually ceased to employ this method, and eventually it was so completely dropped from common use that even the knowledge that such a method had ever existed failed even to reach the fifth or sixth generation after them.

"On this continent Asia there have existed throughout almost all the ages all kinds of methods for preserving edible products for a long time, and even now several of these methods exist there which have come down to the contemporary beings from their very remote ancestors.

"But of all these methods not one was so harmful for the beings themselves as this method invented by these contemporary beings of the continent America, namely, the preserving of products in poison-exuding tin cans.

"Even this device for preserving products 'hermetically sealed' so that without being exposed to the effects of the atmosphere they should, as it were, escape the process of decomposition, exists among certain contemporary Asiatic groups, but they do not all have recourse for this purpose to the aid of these poison-exuding American tin cans.

"At the present time on the continent Asia, only what is called 'sheep's-tail fat' is used for this purpose.

"'Sheep's-tail fat' is a product which is formed in a large quantity around the tail of a certain form of two-brained quadruped being, named there 'sheep,' breeding everywhere on the continent Asia.

"In this 'sheep's-tail fat' there are no cosmic crystallizations harmful for the common presence of a three-brained being, and it is itself one of the chief products for the first-food of the majority of the beings of these general groups on the continent Asia. But as regards the metals from which these contemporary beings of the continent America prepare cans for the preservation of their products, however completely they may be isolated on the inside from the influence of the atmosphere, they also after a definite time, like the contents of the cans, give off from themselves various of their active elements, some of which are very, as they express it, 'poisonous' for the common presences of beings in general.

"These poisonous active elements which issue from tin or similar metal, remaining in hermetically closed cans, are unable to volatilize into space, and in time, meeting among the elements of the products within these cans certain elements which correspond to them by what is called 'kinship of class by number of vibrations,' fuse with them according to the cosmic law named 'Fusion' and remain in them; and together with these products of course afterwards enter into the common organism of the beings who consume them.

"Besides preserving their products in these poison-exuding tin cans so harmful for them, your contemporary favorites grouped on this continent America furthermore preserve them preferably in raw states.

"The beings of the continent Asia always preserve all their food products roasted or boiled, because, according to this custom which reached them from their remote ancestors, products preserved in this way do not decompose so rapidly as when raw.

"The explanation is that when a product is boiled or roasted, there is induced an artificial what is called 'chemical fusion' of the several active elements of which the fundamental mass of the given product consists, thanks to which fusion many active elements useful for beings remain in the products for a comparatively much longer time.

"I again advise you to become thoroughly and particularly well acquainted with all the kinds of fusion proceeding in the Megalocosmos, with the chemical as well as with the mechanical.

"Knowledge of this cosmic law will greatly help you, by the way, to represent to yourself and well understand why and how these numerous and varied formations are in general produced in Nature.

"And how what is called a 'permanent fusion of elements' is obtained in products from boiling or roasting, you will clearly understand if, upon reflection, you grasp merely the process which occurs during the artificial preparation of 'prosphora.'

"Prosphora or bread is in general made everywhere by beings who are aware of its sacred significance. Only your contemporary favorites regard its preparation without any consciousness of its effect, but merely as a practice automatically transmitted to them by inheritance.

"In this bread the crystallization of cosmic substances is also obtained according to the law of Triamazikamno, the substances from the following three relatively independent sources serving as the three holy forces of this sacred law, namely: the holy affirming or active principle is the totality of those cosmic substances composing what your favorites call 'water'; the denying or passive principle is the totality of the substances composing what your favorites call the 'flour' obtained from the divine wheat grain; and the holy reconciling or neutralizing principle is the substance issuing or obtained as the result of burning, or, as your favorites say, from 'fire.'

"For a better elucidation of the thought I have expressed concerning the significance of a permanent fusion of diverse-sourced cosmic substances, let us take as an example the said relatively independent totality of substances which in the formation of this prosphora or bread is the active principle, namely, the relatively independent totality which is called by your favorites 'water.'

"This relatively independent totality of cosmic substances named there on the Earth water, being in itself one might say, a 'natural mechanical mixture,' can be preserved exclusively only in conditions of conjunction with common Nature. If the connection of this water with common Nature is cut, that is to say, if a little of this water is taken out of a river and kept separately in a vessel, then after a certain time the water in this vessel inevitably begins to be gradually destroyed, or as it might otherwise be said, to decompose, and this process, to the perceptive organs of beings, usually smells very 'malodorously,' or, as your favorites would say, this water soon 'stinks.'

"And the same will proceed with the mixture, as in the given case of this said water and flour. Only a temporary mechanical mixture or what is called 'dough' will be obtained, in which this water, after lasting also a relatively short time, will inevitably begin to decompose.

"Further, if this dough, that is, water mixed with flour, is baked over a fire, then, thanks to substances issuing from or formed from this fire—substances which in the given case, as I have already said, serve as the third holy neutralizing force of the sacred law of Triamazikamno—there will result in the given case a chemical fusion, that is, a 'permanent fusion of substances,' as a result of which the new totality of substances obtained from this water and the flour, namely, the prosphora or bread, will now resist the merciless Heropass, that is to say, it will not decompose for a much longer time.

"The bread made in this way can 'dry,' 'crumble,' or even be to all appearances gradually completely destroyed, yet from this process of transformation the elements of the water will, during the said fairly long time, be no further destroyed but will remain active for the said time among what are called the 'enduring prosphorian active elements.'

"And in the given case, my boy, I again repeat that if the contemporary beings breeding on the continent of Asia preserve their products exclusively only in a roasted or boiled state, and not when raw, as the contemporary American beings prefer to do, this also occurs there in consequence of the fact that these usages reached the beings of Asia from their ancestors, the term of whose communities was many centuries, and who in consequence had a long practical experience, whereas the term of the community of those American beings is still, as our wise teacher would say, 'only a day and a half.'

"In order that you may better evaluate the significance of this invention of those contemporary beings breeding on the continent America, and which is, as it were, the real outcome of contemporary civilization, I do not consider it superfluous to inform you also of the methods of preserving several other products for a long time, which methods are now in use among the beings of the continent Asia.

"Such, for instance, is the method of preparing what is called 'Haoorma,' a particularly favorite product of the beings of many groups of the continent Asia.

"This Haoorma on the continent Asia is prepared in

a very simple manner, namely, small pieces of well-roasted meat are tightly packed into 'earthenware jars' or goatskin 'Boordooks.' (A Boordook is the skin stripped in a special manner from the being called 'goat.')

"Melted sheep's-tail fat is then poured over these roasted pieces of meat.

"Although the pieces of roasted meat thus covered with fat do also gradually deteriorate with time, yet over a relatively very long time they do not acquire in themselves any poison.

"The beings of the continent Asia use this Haoorma either cold or heated up.

"In the latter case, it is as if the meat were freshly killed.

"Another very favorite product there preservable for a long time is what is called 'Yagliyemmish,' which consists of nothing else than various fruits.

"For this purpose, fruits freshly gathered from the tree are immediately strung on a cord in the form of what is called a necklace and then thoroughly boiled in water; when these odd necklaces are cooled, they also are dipped several times in melted sheep's-tail fat and, after all this, they are hung up somewhere, where they are exposed to the effects of a current of air.

"However long fruit prepared in this way may hang, it scarcely ever spoils, and when these odd necklaces are to be used for food, they are put into hot water for a little, whereupon all the fat on them being heated entirely disappears, and the fruit itself is as if it had been freshly picked from the tree.

"Even though fruit preserved in this manner differs very little in taste from fresh fruit and will keep a very long time, nevertheless all the well-to-do beings of the continent Asia prefer fresh fruit.

"And this is obviously because in most of them as direct

descendants of the beings of long-existing ancient communities, thanks to the possibilities which have reached them by inheritance, the crystallizing of data for the instinctive sensing of reality proceeds much more intensively in them than in most of your other contemporary favorites.

"I repeat, my boy, that there on your planet, the beings of past epochs, especially those breeding on this continent of Asia, had already many times attempted to use various methods of preserving products for a long time, and it always ended as follows: first of all, certain persons, thanks to their conscious or accidental observations, discovered the undesirable and harmful consequences of this kind of practice both for themselves and for those near them; and then they communicated this to all the other beings, who, having also made observations with as much impartiality as possible towards themselves, also became convinced of the correctness of these deductions; and ultimately they all ceased to employ these practices in the process of their existence.

"Even quite recently on this same continent Asia, certain beings again attempted not only to find a method by which it might indeed be possible to preserve their edible products for a long time without deterioration, but they even tried to find some entirely new means for minimizing as much as possible the time spent on this inevitable being-need of feeding on the first-food; and this time they were almost on the verge of discovering a very suitable method for this purpose.

"I can give you satisfactory details concerning the interesting results of their new investigations in this sphere because I not only personally knew the terrestrial three-brained being who by his conscious labors discovered the said method, but was even present personally at several elucidatory experiments upon the possibilities of applying this method to beings, conducted by the initiator himself of the, so to say, 'new investigations.'

"His name was Asiman and he was a member of a group of contemporary Asiatic three-brained beings, who, having cognized their slavish dependence upon certain causes within themselves, organized a collective existence for the purpose of working upon themselves to deliver themselves from this inner slavery.

"It is interesting to notice that this group of contemporary terrestrial three-brained beings, one of whom was this Brother Asiman, had previously existed in the country formerly Pearl-land, now called Hindustan, but afterwards when beings from the continent of Europe appeared there and began disturbing them and hindering their peaceful work, they all migrated across what are now called there the 'Himalayan Mountains' and settled partly in the country Tibet and partly in what are called the 'valleys of the Hindu Kush.'

"Brother Asiman was one of those who settled in the 'valleys of the Hindu Kush.'

"As time was precious to the members of this brotherhood who were working for their self-perfection, and the process of eating robbed them of a great deal of time, this Brother Asiman, being very well versed in the science then called 'alchemy,' began working very earnestly in the hope of finding what is called a 'chemical preparation' on the introduction of which into himself, a being could exist without spending so much time in the preparation and consumption of all kinds of products for his first-food.

"After long and intensive work, Brother Asiman found for this purpose a combination of chemical substances in the form of a 'powder,' one small thimbleful of which, introduced into a being once in every twenty-four hours, made it possible for him both to exist without consuming anything else except water as food, and to perform all his being-obligations without injury.

"When I chanced to visit this monastery where Brother Asiman existed with the other brethren of the said small group of your contemporary favorites, this preparation had already been used by all the brethren for five months, and Brother Asiman with the participation of others of the brethren who were also very familiar with this question was intensively busy with elucidatory experiments on a large scale.

"And these same experiments showed them that this preparation could not ultimately suffice for normal being-existence.

"After this constatation of theirs, they not only entirely ceased the use of this preparation, but even destroyed the very formula for preparing it, which Brother Asiman had found.

"Several months later I again happened to come upon that monastery and acquainted myself personally with the document of these brethren which had been composed by them on the day when they finally ceased the use of this indeed astonishing preparation.

"This document contained, among other things, several very interesting details about the action of this said preparation of Asiman. It was stated that when this preparation was introduced into the presence of a being, it had besides its nourishing property, a particular action upon what are called the 'wandering nerves of the stomach'; from which action not only did the need for food immediately cease in beings, but furthermore, every desire to introduce into oneself any other edible product whatsoever entirely disappeared. And if something should be forcibly introduced, it took a long time before the disagreeable sensation and state thus provoked would pass.

"It was also stated that at the outset no change was

noticed in the presence of beings who fed on this preparation.

"Even their weight did not diminish. Only after five months did its harmful effect begin to be evident in the common presence of a being in the gradual weakened functioning of certain perceptive organs and of the manifestations of their so to say ableness and sensitiveness. For example, their voices would grow weaker, and their sight, hearing, and so on, worse. Furthermore, in several of them from the beginning of the derangement of these being-functions, changes were observed in their common psychic state.

"In the document composed by these brethren, there was among other things, a lengthy description of the changes in the character of beings after five months' use of this remarkable preparation of Asiman, and, in illustration, some very excellent and apt comparisons were given.

"Although the examples themselves which were given for comparison in this document have not remained in my memory, yet thanks to the so to say 'flavor' of them which I have retained, I shall be able to give you their purport if I use the language of our respected Mullah Nassr Eddin.

"For example, an ordinary good fellow with a character of, as they say, one of 'God's angels,' suddenly became as irritable as those of whom our dear Mullah Nassr Eddin once said:

"'He is as irritable as a man who has just undergone full treatment by a famous European nerve specialist.'

"Or again, beings who one day had been as pacific as the little butter 'lambs' which the pious place on the festal table at their most important religious feasts, would on the next day get as exasperated as a German professor when some Frenchman, also a professor, discovers something new in contemporary science.

"Or again, a being whose love resembled that of a contemporary terrestrial suitor for a rich widow—of course before he has received a single penny from her—would turn just as spiteful as one of those malicious persons who, foaming at the mouth, will hate that poor author who is now writing about you and me, in his work entitled *An Objectively Impartial Criticism of the Life of Man*.

"This poor upstart author, by the way, will be hated both by the 'full-bodied materialists' and by the 'ninety-six carat deists' and even by those of the three-brained beings who have taken your fancy, who, when their stomachs are full and their 'mistresses' are for the moment making 'no scenes,' are 'incorrigible optimists,' but who, quite the contrary, when their stomachs are empty are 'hopeless pessimists.'

"Now, my boy, that we have mentioned this 'queer upstart writer,' there is nothing for it but to inform you here of a certain perplexity which already long ago arose in me in regard to him and which has progressively increased, and that is concerning a naïveté of his.

"I must explain that from the very beginning of his responsible existence, he also became, whether by accident or by the will of Fate I do not know, a follower, and in fact a very devout follower, of our wise and esteemed Mullah Nassr Eddin, and furthermore in the ordinary process of his being-existence he has never lost the smallest opportunity to act entirely according to Mullah Nassr Eddin's unprecedently wise and inimitable sayings. And now, according to the information which has reached me by etherogram, all of a sudden he appears to be constantly acting contrary to one of the very serious and exceptionally practical counsels—certainly not accessible to everybody—of this Teacher above all teachers, which is formulated in the following words:

"'Ekh, Brother! Here on the Earth if you speak the truth you're a great fool, whereas if you wriggle with your soul you are only a "scoundrel," though also a big one. So it is best of all to do nothing, but just recline on your divan and learn to sing like the sparrow that had not yet turned into an American canary.'

"Now, my boy, absorb carefully the information about the causes of the gradual disharmonization—in the presences of these contemporary beings of the continent America—of their second fundamental being-function, namely, the function of sex.

"The disharmony of this function in them is due also to several causes of diverse character, but the fundamental cause, in my opinion, is their negligence 'engendered in their essence and already quite fused with their nature' in keeping their sex organs clean.

"Just like the beings of the continent of Europe, the care they give to their faces and their use of what is called 'facial cosmetics' are only equaled by their neglect of these said organs of theirs; whereas more or less conscious three-brained beings are required to observe the utmost cleanliness in respect to just these organs.

"They cannot, however, be entirely blamed, because in this respect the beings of the continent of Europe are most at fault with their customs existing in the process of their ordinary being-existence.

"The point is that this as yet recently arisen contemporary large group is almost exclusively formed and continues to be supplied with beings from various large and small groups populating the continent of Europe.

"The result is that even if the majority of the three-brained beings now composing this newly formed large group there, are not themselves emigrants from the continent of Europe, their fathers or grandfathers were, who, migrating to this continent of America, took along with them also their European customs, among which were those which brought about this uncleanliness in respect of their sex organs.

"So, my boy, when I now tell you how the matter stands as regards the sex question among the Americans, bear in mind that everything I say will also refer to the beings of the continent Europe.

"The results of this uncleanliness of the contemporary three-brained beings of the planet Earth, who have taken your fancy and who breed on the continents of Europe and America, are very clearly indicated in my statistics.

"Let us take for example what are called there 'venereal diseases.' These diseases are so widespread on the continent of Europe and on this continent of America, that at the present time you will scarcely ever meet a being who has not one or another form of those diseases.

"There is no harm in your knowing among other things, a little more about those interesting and peculiar data, which, in my statistics, indicate in figures how much more of these diseases there is among the beings of the continents America and Europe, than among those of the continent Asia.

"Many of these venereal diseases are entirely absent among the beings of the old communities of the continent of Asia, whereas among the beings populating the continents Europe and America, these diseases are almost epidemical.

"Let us take for example what is called 'clap,' or as scientists there call it 'gonorrhoea.' On the continent of Europe and America almost all the beings both of male and female sex have this disease in one of its different stages, but on the continent Asia it is met with only on the borders where beings frequently mix with the beings of the continent of Europe.

"A good example of what has just been said are the beings belonging to the group existing there under the name Persia, which occupies a relatively large territory on the continent Asia.

"Among the beings dwelling in the central, eastern, southern, and western areas of this relatively large territory, the mentioned diseases are not to be found at all.

"But in the northern part, especially in the locality called 'Azerbaijan,' which comes into direct contact with the large half-European, half-Asiatic community called Russia, the percentage of beings infected with this disease increases more and more in proportion to their proximity to this Russia.

"And exactly the same occurs in other Eastern countries of the continent of Asia: the percentage of this disease increases proportionately to the contact of their beings with the beings of the continent of Europe; for example, in the country called 'India' and partly in China, this disease has in recent times become widespread among the beings there, chiefly in those places where they come into contact with European beings of the community England.

"It can thus be said that the chief disseminators of this disease among the beings of the continent Asia are, from the northwestern side, the beings of the large group Russia, and from the eastern side, the beings of the community England.

"The cause of the absence of this disease as well as of many other evils in the said parts of the continent of Asia is in my opinion that the majority of the beings of the continent Asia have several very good customs for their everyday existence, which have reached them likewise from their ancient ancestors.

"And these customs are so deeply implanted in their everyday existence by their religion that at the present time, observing them mechanically without any wiseacring, beings are thereby more or less ensured against several evils which, owing to the abnormally established conditions of being-existence, have been gradually formed and still continue to be formed in uncountable numbers on that ill-fated planet.

"The beings of most of the groups on the continent Asia are safeguarded against many venereal diseases as well as against any other 'sexual abnormalities' if only, for instance, by such customs known there by the names 'Sooniat' and 'Abdest.'

"The first of these customs, namely, sooniat, or, as it is otherwise called 'circumcision,' not only saves most of the Asiatic beings of responsible age from many venereal diseases there, but also safeguards many of the children and youths of that continent against the 'scourge' mercilessly spread among the children and youths of the continents of Europe and America, namely, that 'scourge' known there under the name 'onanism.'

"According to this custom, the beings of responsible age in most of the contemporary groups of the continent of Asia usually perform on their 'results'—that is to say, on their children—at a certain age, a ritual which consists in this, that in the case of boys they cut what they call the 'frenum' and 'prepuce' of the 'penis.'

"And today those children of your contemporary favorites who of course automatically are subjects of this custom, are almost completely safeguarded against the inevitable result of several evils already definitely fixed in the process of the existence of your favorites.

"For example, according to my statistics, the said 'scourge' that is 'children's onanism,' is scarcely met with among the children of those three-brained beings there who observe this custom of 'circumcision,' whereas all the children and youths of the beings who fail to observe this custom are without exception exposed to this same sexual abnormality.

"The second custom I mentioned, namely, abdest, which by the way is called differently by the beings of different groups on the continent Asia, is nothing else than the obligatory ablution of the sex organs after every visit to what is called the 'toilet.'

"Thanks chiefly to this second custom, most of your favorites breeding on the continent of Asia are safeguarded against many venereal diseases and other sexual abnormalities there."

Having said this, Beelzebub became thoughtful, and after a long pause said:

"The present theme of our conversation has reminded me of a certain very interesting conversation, which I had there during my sojourn in France, with a young sympathetic three-brained being. I think that perhaps it would now be best for your understanding of all that has just been said, if I repeat to you that conversation in full, all the more so as, besides explaining the meaning of the custom abdest or ablution, this conversation will enlighten you on many further questions concerning the peculiar psyche of these favorites of yours.

"This same being, my conversation with whom I recall and now intend to repeat to you, was just that young Persian who, you remember, as I have already told you, was at the request of our mutual acquaintances my 'guide' in the city of Paris, where I happened to be, as I have already told you, just before my departure to this same continent America.

"One day I was waiting for this young Persian in a café in the city of Paris—as always the same Grand Café.

"When he arrived I noticed by his eyes that this time he was, as they say there, more 'drunk' than usual.

"In general he always drank more than enough of the 'alcoholic liquids' existing there; and when we happened to be together in Paris in the restaurants on Montmartre where it was obligatory to order champagne which I neither liked nor drank, he would always drink it all alone with great pleasure.

"Besides always drinking, he was also, as is said there, a great 'petticoat chaser.'

"The moment he saw what they call there the 'pretty face' of a being of the female sex, his whole body and even his breathing suddenly changed.

"When I noticed that he was this time more intoxicated than usual and when, having sat down beside me, he ordered coffee with what is called there an 'apéritif,' I asked him:

"'Explain to me, please, my young friend, why do you always drink this "poison"?'

"To this question of mine he answered:

"'Ekh! My dear Doctor! I drink this "poison," in the first place, because I am so accustomed to it that I cannot now stop drinking without suffering, and secondly I drink it because only thanks to the effect of the alcohol can I calmly look on at the obscenity which goes on here,' he added, waving his hand around.

"'I began drinking this, as you called it, poison because the accidental and for me unlucky and wretched circumstances of my life were so arranged that I had to come and live a long time in this maleficent Europe.

"'I first began to drink because everybody here whom I met also drank, and, unless you drink, you are called a "woman," a "girl," "dolly," "dearie," "sissy," "ninny," and similar derisive names. Not wishing my business acquaintances to call me by these offensive names I also began to drink.

"'And in addition, thanks also to the fact that when I

first came over to Europe, conditions of life here in respect of morality and patriarchality were entirely in contrast with those conditions in which I was born and brought up, I, seeing and perceiving all this, used to experience a painful feeling of shame and an unaccountable embarrassment. At the same time I noticed that from the effect of the alcohol I drank, not only was the depression I experienced alleviated, but I could look upon it all quite calmly, and even have the wish to participate in this abnormal life, so contradictory of my nature and my established views.

"'Thus it came about that every time I began to feel the same unpleasant sensation I began to drink this alcohol, even with a feeling of some self-justification, and in this way became gradually accustomed to this, as you have quite justly called it, poison.'

"Having said this with a perceptive impulse of heartfelt grief, he paused a while to puff at his cigarette mixed with 'Tambak,' and, taking this opportunity, I asked him as follows:

"'Well, all right . . . let us assume I have more or less understood your explanation of your inexcusable drunkenness, and can put myself in your position, but what do you say about your other, and, from my point of view, also inexcusable vice, namely, your "petticoat drooling"?

"'Why! You run after every petticoat if only it hangs about someone with long hair!'

"At this question of mine, he, sighing deeply, resumed his speaking as follows:

"'It seems to me that I got this habit, as well, partly for the reason I mentioned, but I think this weakness of mine can be explained by still another very interesting psychological cause.'

"Of course I expressed the desire to hear him, but first I suggested our going inside that Grand Café into the hall of the restaurant itself, as it was already getting damp out of doors.

"When we were seated in the hall of the restaurant and had ordered their 'famous champagne,' he continued as follows:

"'When you lived among us in Persia, my dear Doctor, you perhaps happened to observe the attitude existing there, very specific for us Persians, of men towards women.

"'Namely, among us in Persia, men have two definite, one can say, "organic attitudes" towards women, in accordance with which women are, for us men, even unconsciously on our part, very sharply divided into two categories.

"'The first attitude is towards the woman, the present or future mother; and the second towards the woman-female.

"'This property of the men of our Persia who have in their nature data for these two independent attitudes and for this instinctive feeling, began to be formed only recently, about two and a half centuries ago.

"'According to the explanations once given me by my "Mullah uncle," whom those around him called behind his back "a Mullah of the old school," it seems that, two or three centuries ago, owing to causes evidently ensuing from certain higher World-laws, men began to make war on each other everywhere on the Earth, and especially among us in Asia, more intensively than usual, and at the same time, somehow, in most of the men, the feeling of piety began very distinctly to decline and in some of them entirely disappeared.

"'And just at that period a certain form of psychic disease spread among men from which many who were infected by it ultimately either became quite insane or committed suicide.

"'Then certain wise people of various independent

groups on the continent of Asia began, with the help of various persons representative of medicine of that time—which, by the way, was then very superior to contemporary medicine—very earnestly to seek the causes of that human misfortune.

"'After long impartial labors they discovered, in the first place, that the men who contracted this disease were exclusively those in whose subconsciousness, for some reason or other, there never arose any impulse of faith in anybody or in anything, and secondly, that those adult men who periodically performed the normal ritual of intercourse with women were not at all subject to this disease.

"'When the news of this conclusion of theirs spread over the continent of Asia, all the rulers and chiefs of the separate Asiatic groups of that time grew alarmed, as almost all the regular troops at their disposal consisted of adult men, and moreover, the constant wars permitted none of them to live normally with his family.

"'In view of the fact that at that period all the governments of the separate Asiatic countries needed and wished to have healthy and strong armies, they were compelled to conclude a truce and either themselves assemble or send their representatives to one place, namely, to the capital of what was then called the "Kilmantooshian Khanate," in order jointly to find a way out of the situation which had arisen.

"'After serious reflections and deliberations, these rulers of the various independent groups of Asiatic peoples, or their representatives, together of course with the representatives of medicine of that time, then came to the conclusion that it was possible to deal with the situation which had arisen, only if what is called prostitution should be established everywhere on the continent of Asia, as is now the case on the continent of Europe, and only if the power-possessing people should deliberately encourage its development and co-operate in its success.

"'Almost all the chiefs of the governments of that time fully agreed with this conclusion of the representatives of all the peoples of the continent of Asia who had gathered together in the capital of the Kilmantooshian Khanate, and, without experiencing any remorse of conscience, they began from then on not only to encourage and aid women in general—except indeed just their own daughters—to engage in this occupation so "abhorrently repulsive" to the nature of every normal person, but also to give, even with a feeling of benevolence, as if this were the most considerate manifestation of man, every possible assistance to women, without distinction of caste or religion, who might wish to leave or to go anywhere for this filthy purpose.

"'Now that we have touched upon this subject, allow me, respected Doctor, to digress, and tell you here the reflections, in my view very interesting and wise, of this same Mullah uncle of mine concerning the causes in general of the arising of this evil and scourge of contemporary civilization.

"'Once, on one of the days of Ramadan, when we were conversing as usual while awaiting the call of the Mullah of our district announcing the meal hour, and we happened to be speaking about this human "scourge," he then, among other things, said:

"'"It is wrong and unjust of you to blame and despise all women of this kind.

"'"Most of them are not themselves personally to blame for their sad lot; one should blame exclusively only their parents, husbands, and guardians.

"'"And precisely their parents, husbands, and guardians should be blamed and despised who have allowed the arising in them during their age preparatory to adult being—while as yet they have not their own good sense—of the property called laziness.

"'"Although at this age this laziness is as yet only automatic in them, and young people have not to make very great efforts to overcome it, and are able in consequence, on acquiring their own good sense, not to allow it to gain complete control of them, yet nevertheless, as regards the organization of women's psyche, the active principle must, owing to results not dependent on our will but ensuing from World-laws, unfailingly participate in every initiative and in every good manifestation of theirs.

"'"And it is just precisely in the early years of the adult life of these contemporary unfortunate prospective women-mothers—thanks to the various ideas of the people of contemporary civilization concerning 'equal rights for women' existing there under the catchwords 'equal rights,' 'equal opportunities,' etc. . . . ideas which are now already widespread everywhere on the Earth, which are naïve to the understanding of a man who has lived his life normally, and which are unconsciously accepted also by the majority of contemporary men—that these contemporary not yet completely formed prospective women-mothers, on the one hand, not having around them the law-conformable, requisite sources of the active principle, such as their parents, guardians and husbands, to whom the responsibility for them passes from the moment of marriage, and on the other hand thanks to the intensive process of imagination and enthusiasms which is proper to proceed in them and which is also in this transitional age foreordained by nature according to Law for the purpose of better actualizing the data for the development of their good sense, they, as it were, gradually absorb the said automatic laziness into their very nature, and this laziness remains in their nature, as a progressive and indispensable necessity.

"‘“A woman with such a nature of course does not wish to fulfill the obligations of a genuine woman-mother, and in view of the fact that being a prostitute enables her just to do nothing and to experience great pleasure, there is gradually formed in her both in her nature and in the ‘passive consciousness’ proper to her a factor for the irresistible urge to be a woman-female.

"‘“But in consequence of the fact that in the instinct of each of these women the data proper to all women for the impulse of ‘shame’ are not atrophied suddenly and at once, and none of them, with all her mental wishing, can endure to become such a woman in her own native country, every one of them always instinctively and half consciously tries to get away to some other country where, far from her native land, without any inner discomfort, and also without doing anything, she can abandon herself entirely to this profession personally pleasant for her in almost every respect.

"‘“And as regards the prevalence everywhere on the Earth at the present time of this human misfortune, the cause of this is in my opinion exclusively only those contemporary men in whom, owing to the same reasons, there arises—as in those young women, future prostitutes—a similar what is called ‘organic essential need to do nothing except enjoy oneself,’ and one of the forms of satisfying the criminal need of these ‘ulcers’ among contemporary people consists, in the given case, in enticing and assisting such women to leave their native land for some foreign country.

"‘“It has already been noticed by many contemporary sensible people, that these two different sexes, victims of the same disease, as a rule consciously and instinctively seek and find each other; and in the given case they exemplify the proverb which has existed from olden times, 'One fisherman recognizes another from afar.'"

"'And so, respected Doctor! Thanks just to the aforesaid causes wisely understood by my uncle, many women prostitutes from various other countries then appeared after several years among us in Persia.

"'And owing to the instinctive attitudes which, as I have already said, had been acquired during centuries by the local women of Persia without distinction of religion towards morality and patriarchality in family traditions, these foreign women were unable to mix with the general mass of Persian women, with the consequence that from then on, there began to be among us the two categories of women I have mentioned.

"'Well then, owing to the fact that the majority of these foreign women, living freely among us in Persia and going about everywhere, in the markets and other public places, often became objects for the gaze of our Persian men, there was gradually formed in the latter, of course unconsciously, along with the already existing attitude towards women as mothers, yet another attitude towards women as simply females.

"'The property of having this definite double attitude towards women, being transmitted by inheritance from generation to generation, has even, among us, finally become so rooted that at the present time our men not only distinguish these two categories of women by their appearance as easily as one distinguishes between a man, a sheep, a dog, an ass, etc. . . . but there has even been formed in them a certain something which instinctively prevents them from mistaking a woman of one category for a woman of another.

"'Even I myself could always unmistakably tell, from a distance, what sort of woman was passing. How I could tell this, whether by their walk or by some other sign, with the best will in the world I could not now explain, but it is a fact that I could tell and was never mistaken, although, as I have already told you, both categories of women wore similar veils.

"'And every normal Persian—normal in the sense of not being under the influence of tambak, alcohol, or opium, the consumption of which has in recent times been unfortunately spreading among us ever more and more—can always unmistakedly tell which woman represents a "woman-mother" and which a "woman-female," that is, a prostitute.

"'To every normal Persian among us, a woman-mother, to whatever religion she may belong and regardless of family and personal relationships, is as his own sister, and a woman of the second category simply an animal who infallibly evokes in him a feeling of aversion.

"'This property of instinctive relationship towards women is very strong in our men and is entirely independent of our consciousness.

"'For example, even suppose it should happen somehow or other that the youngest and most beautiful woman of any district should find herself in the same bed with a man of the same district, this Persian man, even with all his willingness, provided, I repeat, that he were not under the influence of opium or alcohol, would be organically unable to treat her as a female.

"'He would treat her as his own sister; and even if she herself should manifest organic actions towards him, he would only pity her the more, and regard her as "possessed by an unclean power" and would try his best to help her free herself from this misfortune.

"'And the same Persian man will, in a normal condition, also treat a woman of the second category, that is, a prostitute, as a woman-female, since, however young and beautiful she may be, he will inevitably experience an organic aversion to her; nor could he treat her as a woman unless there had been introduced into his organism the toxic products, maleficent for people, which I have enumerated.

"'And so, respected Doctor, I lived until my twentieth year in Persia under these morals and traditions, like every ordinary normal Persian.

"'At twenty, on account of shares I had inherited, I happened to become a partner in a certain large firm which exported Persian dried fruits to various European communities.

"'And my position in this firm, thanks to various circumstances independent of me, was such that I had to be its chief local representative in those countries of the continent of Europe to which these fruits were exported.

"'At first, as I have already told you, I went to Russia, then I went to Germany, Italy, and to other European countries, and now, finally, I have lived here in France already seven years.

"'In the life of none of these foreign countries does there exist any such sharply drawn distinction between these two types of women, between the woman-mother and the woman-prostitute, as I saw and felt during the whole of my youth in my native country.

"'Everywhere among them the attitude towards women is purely mental, that is, only thought out, not organic.

"'For instance, a husband here, however unfaithful his wife may be, will never know it, unless he sees or hears of it.

"'But among us in Persia, without any seeing or any gossip, a husband can tell instinctively whether his wife is faithful; and the same thing applies to the woman—a woman among us can feel any infidelity on the part of her husband.

"'As to this special instinctive feeling in people, several

scientists from the continent of Europe have recently even made among us some very serious special investigations.

"'As I happened by chance to learn, they came to the clear conclusion that in general where "polyandry" and "polygamy" prevail—that is to say, where "more than one husband" and "more than one wife" are permitted by the established local morality—there is acquired in people a peculiar "psycho-organic" particularity in their relations as men and women.

"'This psycho-organic particularity exists also in the people of our Persia, in consequence of the fact that, as you know, we, being followers of the Mohammedan religion, have the custom of polygamy, that is to say, each man is permitted by law to have as many as seven wives.

"'And this psycho-organic particularity in our Persian people by the way is that the feeling of the husband's infidelity never arises in any of the lawful wives concerning his other lawful wives.

"'Such a feeling appears in one of the wives only when her husband is unfaithful with a strange woman.

"'It is only now, respected Doctor, that living here in Europe and seeing all that goes on between husbands and wives, I fully appreciate our custom of polygamy, so extremely sensibly established and so beneficial both for men and for women.

"'Although every man among us is permitted several wives and not simply one, as is the case here in Europe where the Christian religion which allows only one wife is predominant, yet the honesty and conscientiousness of our men towards their wives are beyond compare with the honesty and conscientiousness existing among men here towards their one wife and their family in general.

"'Just look around and see what is going on everywhere here.

"'Glance around merely at these rooms of the Grand Café, where besides the ordinary professional prostitutes and "gigolos" who are constantly here, hundreds of men and women are always sitting at the little tables gaily conversing.

"'Looking at these men and women now, you would say they were married couples who have come here together, either to see Paris or on some family business.

"'But as a matter of fact it is practically certain that in all the halls of this Grand Café there is not a single couple among these men and women so gaily chatting and about to go to some hotel together, who are legal man and wife, even though, at the same time, every one of them may be, on paper, a legal husband or wife.

"'The other "legal halves" of the men and women sitting here, who have remained at home in the provinces are probably now thinking and telling their acquaintances positively, that their "legal wife" or "legal husband" has gone to the world capital Paris to make some very "important" purchases for the family or to meet somebody there very important for the family, or something else of the same sort.

"'But in reality, in order to get here, these birds of passage have had to intrigue for a whole year and cook up every kind of story to convince their legal halves of the necessity of their trip; and now here, in the company of deceivers and intriguers like themselves, in the name of and to the glory of the significance of the "epithalamium," aided by that fine art which this great contemporary civilization has attained, they decorate their stay-at-home "legal halves" with the largest possible "fine art horns."

"'In Europe, thanks to the established order of family

life, it has now already come about that if you meet a man and a woman together and notice that while conversing, gay tones are heard in their voices and smiles appear on their faces, you can then be quite sure that very soon, if they have not already done so, they will very effectively and without fail put on some legal half a pair of the largest and most beautiful horns.

"'Hence it is that any one slightly cunning man here may already be accounted a very "honorable man" and the "patriarchal father of a family."

"'To those around him it is of no concern that this "honorable" and "patriarchal father of a family" has perhaps at the same time—if of course his means permit—as many mistresses as he pleases on the side; on the contrary, those around him here usually show even more respect for such a man than for one who is unable to have any "mistresses" at all.

"'Here, these "honorable husbands" who have the means, not only have on the side, in addition to their one legal wife, seven, but sometimes even seven times seven "illegal wives."

"'And those European husbands who have not the means of supporting several illegal wives in addition to their one legal wife, spend almost the whole of their time in what is called "drooling," that is to say, for days on end they stare at and as it were "devour with their eyes" every woman they meet.

"'In other words, in their thoughts or in their feelings, they betray their one legal wife an innumerable number of times.

"'But although among us in Persia, a man can have as many as seven legal wives, yet nevertheless all his thoughts and feelings are occupied day and night how he can best arrange both the inner and the outer life of these legal wives of his; and the latter, in their turn, are absorbed in him and try their utmost, also day and night, to aid him in his life duties.

"'Here, the reciprocal inner relationship between husband and wife is the same; just as almost all the inner life of the husband is spent in being unfaithful to his one legal wife, so also the inner life of this one wife, from the first day of their union, is always straying outside the family.

"'For a European wife, as a rule, as soon as she is married, her husband becomes for her inner life, as they say, her "own property."

"'After the first night, being then secure in her ownership, she begins to devote the whole of her inner life to the pursuit of a certain "something," that is, to the pursuit of that indefinable "ideal," which from early childhood is gradually formed in every European girl thanks to that famous "education" which is ever more and more always being invented for them by various contemporary conscienceless writers.

"'During my stay in these European countries, I have observed that there is never formed in the being of a woman here, that "something" which should—in her as in our women—constantly maintain what is called "organic shame" or at least the disposition to it, upon which feeling, in my opinion, what is called "wifely duty" is based, and which is just what instinctively aids her to refrain from those actions which make a woman immoral.

"'That is why every woman here can very easily, at any favorable opportunity, without either suffering or remorse of conscience, betray her legal husband.

"'It is in my opinion owing to the absence of this shame in them, that here in Europe the line dividing the woman-mother from the woman-prostitute has gradually ceased to exist and that these two categories of women have already long ago been merged into one; so that at the present time there is neither in the mind nor in the feelings of the men here, that division of women into two categories which almost every Persian makes.

"'Here one can now distinguish the woman-mother from the woman-female only if one sees all her manifestations with one's own eyes.

"'In the European conditions of family life, owing to the absence of the beneficent institution of polygamy—an institution which in my opinion should long ago have been introduced here if only for the simple reason that, as statistics show, the women here far outnumber the men—there are thousands of other discomforts and improprieties which need not exist at all.

"'And so, respected Doctor, the fundamental cause of my second vice was that being born and brought up in traditions of morality entirely opposed to those here, I came here at an age when the animal passions in a man are especially strong. The ensuing evils for me personally arose chiefly from the fact that I came here while still very young, and, according to the notions here, handsome; and owing to my genuine southern type, a great many women here for whom I represented a new and original type of male began a regular hunt after me.

"'They hunted me like "big game."

"'And I was big game for them not only on account of my specific type, a genuine southerner, but also on account of my gentleness and courtesy towards women, properties which had been instilled in me from my earliest childhood in my associations with our Persian women-mothers.

"'When I came here and began meeting the women here, I was, of course, even unconsciously on my part, gentle and courteous towards them also.

"'And so, meeting with the women here and at first only talking with them—chiefly on the subject of contemporary civilization and of the backwardness as it were of our Persia in comparison—I then, of course under the influence of alcohol which I was then already consuming in rather large quantities, fell for the first time, that is to say, I, as a prospective father of a family, behaved vilely.

"'Although this cost me at the time much suffering and remorse of conscience, yet the environment together again with the action of this alcohol caused me to fall a second time; and thereafter everything headed so to say down an inclined plane and led to the point where I am now indeed in this respect a most filthy animal.

"'Especially now at times, whenever I happen to be completely free from the influence of alcohol, I suffer moral anguish and loathe myself with the whole of my being, and at such moments I hasten all the more to pour this alcohol into myself again in order to forget myself and thus drown my sufferings.

"'Having lived this ugly life in the countries of Europe I enumerated, I finally settled down here in Paris, in precisely that European city to which women come from every part of Europe and from other continents with the obvious intention of putting "horns" on their other legal halves. And here in Paris I have now become entirely addicted to both these human vices, that is, to alcohol and, as you have said, to petticoat-chasing, and I run left and right, without any sane reasoning at all. And now the satisfaction of both these vices is more necessary to me than the satisfaction of my hunger.

"'That is how it has all gone with me up to the present moment; and what will come next I do not know and do not care to know.

"'I always even try my best and struggle with myself not to think about it.'

"As he said these last words, he sincerely sighed and dejectedly dropped his head. I then asked him:

"'But, tell me, please, are you really not afraid of being infected with those terrible diseases which these women usually suffer from, whom a "petticoat-chaser" like you runs after?'

"At this question of mine he again sighed deeply and after a short pause told me as follows:

"'Ekh! . . . my esteemed and worthy Doctor!

"'In recent years I have thought about this question a great deal. It has even become for me a subject of such interest, that in a certain sense, it has been a blessed means whereby my inner "odious life" has in spite of everything flowed more or less endurably.

"'As a physician you will, I think, probably be greatly interested to know how and why this same question interested me so much several years ago, and to what conclusions I arrived after I had, in a relatively normal state, very seriously observed and studied it.

"'About five years ago I had such a fit of depression that even alcohol scarcely had any effect on me nor pacified my psychic state.

"'And it so happened just then that I often met with certain acquaintances and friends who talked a great deal about filthy diseases and how easily one could be infected with them.

"'From these conversations I myself began thinking rather often about myself, and little by little I began fretting about my health almost like a hysterical woman.

"'I used often to reflect that being almost always drunk and constantly having affairs with such infected women, then evidently, even if for some reason or other I had so far no obvious symptom of these diseases, I must nevertheless in all probability be already infected with one of them.

"'After such reflections I first began consulting various

specialists, in order to find out what were the early symptoms of whatever disease I already may have had.

"'Although none of the local specialists found anything at all in me, I nevertheless continued to doubt, because on the one hand my fretting about my health and on the other hand my own common sense continued to assure me that I must certainly already have been infected with one of these terrible diseases.

"'All this brought me to the point that I decided at any expense to have a consultation here in Paris, but this time with the leading specialists from the whole of Europe. I could afford myself this because, owing to the World War, when transport had everywhere broken down, and all commodities had gone up in price, our firm, having everywhere very large stocks of dried fruit in storage, had that year made considerable profits, a fairly good portion of which fell to my share.

"'When I had called these European celebrities together, they unanimously pronounced after all kinds of very "detailed" investigations and what are called "chemical analyses" known to them themselves, that there was not the slightest sign of any venereal disease in my organism.

"'Although this finding of theirs put an end to the chronic fretting about my health, yet it was the cause of the growth in me of such a strong feeling of inquisitiveness and curiosity to clear up this question, that from then on it became a sort of mania with me, a kind of "idée fixe."

"'And also from then on, the serious observation and study of everything concerning these diseases animated and justified the sense of what I have called "my odious life."

"'During this period of my life I made these observations and studies of mine at all times with my whole inner real "I" while in a drunken, semi-drunken, and also sober state.

"'And then, among other things I also read assiduously every kind of literature existing here in Europe concerning these diseases, and also most of the books on this question in French and German.

"'This I could easily do because, as you see, I have such a command of French that you can scarcely guess that I am not a real French intellectual; and with the German language also I get along very well, because I lived a fairly long time in Germany and always, in my free time, studied their language and their literature for want of something to do.

"'So, when I became interested in this question, I was able to become fully acquainted with all the knowledge that exists in contemporary civilization on the subject of venereal diseases.

"'In this literature there appeared to be hundreds of theories and hundreds of hypotheses concerning the causes of venereal infection, but I could not discover one convincingly categorical explanation how and why some people are infected with these diseases and others not, and I soon became convinced that I could not clear up this for myself with the knowledge existing on this question at the present time here in Europe.

"'From all this literature—putting aside, of course, and not even mentioning the multitude of those thick "scientific books" here, whose contents immediately show every more or less normal person that they were written by people who were as is said "complete ignoramuses" on these questions, that is to say, not specialists in human diseases at all—I got the general impression that people were infected and fall ill with venereal diseases only owing to their own uncleanliness.

"'When I made this categorical deduction, there was

nothing left to me but to concentrate all my attention upon finding out in what my personal cleanliness particularly consisted which had so far protected me against infection.

"'I then began to deliberate with myself as follows:

"'I do not dress any more cleanly than everybody else living here in Europe; I wash my hands and face every morning also like everybody else; once a week I make a point of going to a Turkish bath, also, it seems, like everyone; and in this way I turned over many things in my mind, and with the result I found nothing in which, in this respect, I was exceptional; and yet the fact remained that, from my loathsome life, I of course ran more chances of being infected.

"'From then on my thoughts were guided by two definite convictions already fully established in me: in the first place, that anyone having relations with such women must inevitably sooner or later be infected; and secondly, that only cleanliness protects one from such infection.

"'In this manner I continued to reflect for a whole week, until I suddenly remembered a certain habit of mine which here in Europe I always scrupulously concealed from my acquaintances; I remembered, namely, about that habit of mine which is called among us in Persia, abdest.

"'The custom of abdest which, according to the notions here might be called ablution, is one of the chief customs among us in Persia.

"'Strictly speaking, every follower of the Mohammedan religion must obey this custom, though it is practiced particularly strictly only by Mohammedans of the Shiite sect; and as almost the whole of Persia is composed of Shiites, the custom is nowhere so widely spread as among us in Persia.

"'This custom is that every adherent of the Shiite sect, male as well as female, must, after every "toilet" unfailingly wash his sex organs. For this purpose, every family has the necessary appurtenances considered among us even as the most important, consisting of a special vessel, a particular kind of bowl called "Ibrkh." And the richer the family the more of these bowls they must have, since such a bowl must at once and without fail be put at the disposal of every newly arrived guest.

"'I myself was from early childhood also personally accustomed to this habit, and it gradually so entered into my daily life that even when I came here to Europe, where this custom does not exist, I could not live a single day without making this ablution.

"'For instance, it is much easier for me to go without washing my face even after a debauch, than not to wash certain parts of my body with cold water after the toilet.

"'At present, living here in Europe, I not only have to put up with a great many inconveniences owing to this habit of mine, but I even have to forego some of the modern comfort which I could easily afford.

"'For instance, I now live in Paris, where owing to my means I could well afford to live at the very best hotel with every modern comfort, but, thanks to this habit of mine, I cannot do this but am obliged to live in some dirty hotel situated far from the "center" and from all those places where I have to be almost every day.

"'In the hotel where I now live, there are no comforts beyond this single comfort which is very important for me; and this is due to the fact that being of old construction, this hotel has "water closets" of the old type and not of the new contemporary American invention, and it is just that old system which is the most convenient and suitable for this habit of mine.

"'It is quite likely that I even half consciously chose

France as my chief dwelling place because it is still possible to find everywhere here, especially in the provinces, water closets of the old system as among us in Persia.

"'In other countries of Europe this, as they now call it, "Asiatic system" scarcely exists. It has almost everywhere been exchanged for the American system with its comfortable, polished "easy chairs" upon which I, personally, could only rest and read the book called the *Decameron*.

"'And so, my honorable Doctor, when I suddenly remembered this habit of mine, I at once understood without any further doubt that if I had hitherto escaped being infected with some filthy disease, it was solely because I frequently wash my sex organs with cold water.'

"Having said these last words, this sympathetic young Persian extended his arms upwards and with his whole being exclaimed:

"'Blessed forever be the memory of those who created for us that beneficial custom.'

"He said nothing further for a long while but looked pensively at a party of Americans sitting nearby who were discussing at that moment whether women dress better in England or in America; and then he suddenly turned to me with the following words:

"'My highly esteemed and honorable Doctor!

"'During my acquaintance with you I have become quite convinced that you are very well educated and, as is said, very well read.

"'Will you be so kind as to give me your weighty opinion, so that I might at last understand and solve one problem which during recent years has aroused my curiosity and which when I am comparatively sober often arises in me and disturbs my thoughts.

"'The point is, that living here in Europe where people profess the religion whose followers compose almost half the world, I have not up to now come across a single good custom in their ordinary life, whereas among us who profess the Mohammedan religion, there are very many.

"'What is wrong? What is the cause of it? Were there no good ordinances foredesigned by the Founder of that great religion for the ordinary life of people, the followers of that religion . . . ?'

"Well, my boy, as this young Persian had become sympathetic to me during our acquaintance, I could not refuse him this request, and I decided to explain the question to him, but also, of course, in such a form that he would not even suspect who I was and what was my genuine nature.

"I told him:

"'You say that in the religion which half the world professes, and you probably mean the "Christian religion," there are not such good customs as in your Mohammedan religion?

"'Are there not? On the contrary; in that religion there were many more good customs than in any of the religions of today; in none of the ancient religious teachings were so many good regulations for ordinary everyday life laid down as in just that teaching on which this same Christian religion was founded.

"'If the followers of this great religion themselves, especially those who are called the "elders of the church" of the Middle Ages, treated this religion, step by step, as "Bluebeard" treated his wives, that is to say, put them into derision and changed all their beauty and charm—that is already quite a different matter.

"'In general you must know that all the great genuine religions which have existed down to the present time, created, as history itself testifies, by men of equal attainment in regard to the perfecting of their Pure Reason, are always based on the same truths. The difference in those religions is only in the definite regulations they lay down for the observance of certain details and of what are called rituals; and this difference is the result of the deliberate adoption by the great founders of these regulations which suited the degree of mental perfection of the people of the given period.

"'At the root of every new doctrine upon which religions are founded, dogmas are always to be found, which have been taken from earlier religions and which had already been well fixed in the life of the people.

"'And in this case, the saying is fully justified which has existed among people from of old—"there is nothing new under the sun."

"'The only things new in these religious teachings, as I have said, are the small details, intentionally adapted by the great founders to the degree of mental perfection of the people of the given epoch. And so as the root of this same doctrine upon which the Christian religion is based there was placed almost the whole of the previously existing great teaching which is now called Judaism, whose followers once also numbered almost, as is said, half the "world."

"'The great founders of the Christian religion, having taken the Judaic doctrine as their basis, changed only its outer details according to the degree of mental development of the contemporaries of Jesus Christ, and in it they effectively provided for everything necessary for the welfare of people.

"'Provision was made in it, as is said, both for the soul and for the body; and it even provided all the necessary regulations for a peaceful and happy existence. And this was all surpassingly wisely provided for in such a way that this religion might be suitable also for people of much later epochs.

"'Had the doctrine of this religion remained unchanged,

it might even perhaps have suited these contemporary people, who, by the way, our Mullah Nassr Eddin defines by his expression, "He will blink only if you poke his eye with a rafter."

"'At its origin there entered into this Christian religion, besides those specially established regulations for ordinary existence which met the needs of the contemporaries of Jesus Christ, also many excellent customs which were already in existence and had become well fixed in the life of the people who were followers of the Judaic religion.

"'Even those good customs which now exist among you in the Mohammedan religion were transmitted to you from the Judaic religion. Take, for example, just that custom of "sooniat" or circumcision which you mentioned. This custom was at first contained in this Christian religion also, and in the beginning was obligatorily and strictly carried out by all its followers. Only subsequently did it very quickly and suddenly entirely disappear from the Christian religion.

"'If you wish, my young friend, I will tell you in detail about the arising of this custom, and you will understand from it why a custom so good for the health and normal life of people was included in the Judaic religion, and since the Judaic doctrine was made the basis of the Christian religion, this custom also could not fail to be taken over and introduced into the process of the ordinary life of the followers of the Christian religion.

"'This custom which you call sooniat was first created and introduced into the Judaic religious doctrine by the Great Moses.

"'And why the Great Moses introduced this custom into the religion of the Judaic people I learned from a very ancient Chaldean manuscript.

"'It was said in this manuscript that when the Great

Moses was the leader of the Judaic people and conducted them from the land of Egypt to the land of Canaan, he constated the fact during the journey that among the youths and children of the people confided to him from Above there was very widely spread the disease then called "Moordoorten," which contemporary people call onanism.

"'It was further said in the manuscript that having constated this fact, the Great Moses was greatly perturbed and from then on began observing very closely in order to discover the causes of this evil and some means of uprooting it.

"'These researches of his led this incomparable sage later to write a book under the title of *Tookha Tes Nalool Pan*, which in contemporary language means "the quintessence of my reflections."

"'With the contents of this remarkable book I also once happened to become acquainted.

"'At the beginning of the explanation about the disease Moordoorten it was said, among other things, that the human organism has been brought by Great Nature to such perfection that each and every organ has been provided with a means of defense against every external contingency; and hence that if any organ should function incorrectly in people, it must always be the people themselves who are to blame owing to their own established conditions of everyday life.

"'And concerning the causes themselves of the appearance of Moordoorten among children, it was said in Chapter VI, Verse xi of this incomparable book that this disease occurs in children for the following reasons:

"'Among the definite substances elaborated by the human organism and constantly thrown off by it as waste, there is a definite substance called "Kulnabo."

"'This substance is in general elaborated in the organism

of beings for the purpose of neutralizing other also definite substances necessary for the functioning of their sex organs, and it is formed and participates in the functioning of the said organs from the very beginning of the arising of the beings of both sexes, that is to say, from their infancy.

"'Great Nature has so arranged it that after its utilization the residue of this substance is discharged from the organism of boys at the place between the "Toolkhtotino" and the "Sarnuonino," and in girls from the places between the "Kartotakhnian hills."

"'The parts of the organism of boys located at the end of what is called the "genital member" and which are named in this incomparable book "Toolkhtotino" and "Sarnuonino" are named by contemporary medicine there "glans penis" and "praeputium penis"; and the "Kartotakhnian hills," covering what is called the "clitoris" of girls, are called "labia majora" and "labia minora" or, as is said in common language, "the large and small obscene lips."

"'For the substance "Kulnabo" contemporary medicine has no name at all, this independent substance being entirely unknown to it.

"'Contemporary terrestrial medicine has a name only for the general mass of those substances among which is also the substance Kulnabo.

"'And this total mass is called "Smegma," a composition of entirely heterogeneous substances secreted by various what are called "glands" which have nothing in common with each other; as, for instance, the "grease" gland, the "Bartholinian" gland, the "Cowperian," "Nolniolnian," and others.

"'The separation and volatilization of these waste substances should in accordance with the providence of Great Nature be induced for the said places by means of all kinds of chance contacts and by various movements occurring in the atmosphere.

"'But, unforeseen by Nature, the clothing which people have invented for themselves prevents the said factors from freely effecting the separation and volatilization of these substances, with the result that this Kulnabo, remaining for a long time on these places, promotes the arising of perspiration; moreover, as this substance is in general the very best medium for the multiplication of what are called "bacteria," which exist in the atmosphere as well as in what are called the "subjective spheres" of all kinds of things coming into direct contact with the children, there occurs from this multiplying there on the given parts of the organism of children a process called "itching."

"'On account of this itching children begin, unconsciously at first, to rub or scratch these places. Later, as there are concentrated in these parts of the organism all the ends of the nerves created by Nature for the special sensation required for the completion of the sacred process Elmooarno, which normally arises in adult people at the end of what is called copulation, and as, especially at a certain period when according to the providence of Great Nature there proceeds in these organs of children a process of preparation for future sex functioning, they experience from this rubbing or scratching a certain peculiar pleasant sensation, they therefore begin intentionally—having instinctively realized from which of their actions this pleasant sensation is evoked in them—to rub these places even when there is no itching; and thus the ranks of the little "Moordoortenists" on the Earth are always increasing by leaps and bounds.

"'As regards just what measures the Great Moses took for eradicating that evil, I learned not from the aforementioned book *Tookha Tes Nalool Pan*, but from the contents of an also very ancient papyrus.

"'From the contents of this papyrus it could be clearly seen that the Great Moses gave practical effect to the thoughts set down on this question in the book *Tookha Tes Nalool Pan*, by creating for his people those two religious rites, one of which is called "Sikt ner chorn" and the other "Tzel putz kann."

"'The sacred "Sikt ner chorn" was specially created for boys and the sacred "Tzel putz kann" for girls, and they were to be obligatorily performed on all children of both sexes.

"'The rite of "Sikt ner chorn," for instance, was identical with your sooniat. By cutting what is called the "Vojiano" or the "frenum penis" of boys, the connection is severed between the head and the skin covering it, and thus there is obtained the free movement of this skin, or, as it is called, "praeputium penis."

"'According to the information which has come down to us from ancient times and also according to our own common sense, it is plain that the Great Moses, who as we learn from another source was a very great authority on medicine, wished by this means to secure that the totality of substances accumulating in the said places might of itself be mechanically removed owing to all kinds of accidental contact and thus cease to become a factor for the arising of the mentioned maleficent itching. Concerning the vast learning of the Great Moses in the province of medicine, many diverse historical sources agree that he obtained his medical knowledge during his stay in Egypt as a pupil of the Egyptian high priests, to whom this knowledge had come down from their ancestors of the continent Atlantis, the first and last genuinely learned beings of the Earth, the members of the society then called Akhaldan.

"'The beneficial results of the customs then created

by the Great Moses even now continue to be fairly visible in practice.

"'Concerning, for instance, the custom of circumcision in particular, I, being a good diagnostician and able to tell from one glance at a man's face what disharmony he has in his organism, can safely say that this terrible children's disease of onanism is scarcely ever found among those children upon whom this rite has been performed, whereas the children of those parents who fail to observe this custom are almost all subject to it.

"'The exceptions in this respect are only the children of those parents who are indeed cultured in the full sense of the word and who clearly understand that the future normal mentation of their children depends exclusively upon whether they do or do not contract this disease in their childhood or youth.

"'Such cultured parents know very well that if even once the sensation of the climax of what is called the "Ooamonvanosinian process" occurs in what is called the "nervous system" of their children before they reach majority, they will already never have the full possibility of normal mentation when they become adult; and hence it is that such cultured parents always consider it their first and chief duty towards their children to educate them in this respect.

"'Unlike most contemporary parents, they do not consider that the education of children consists in badgering them to learn by rote as much poetry as possible, composed by "Moordoortenist psychopaths," or in teaching them to "click their heels well" before their acquaintances, in which accomplishments according to the notions of people of recent times the whole education of children unfortunately consists.

"'And so, my dear friend, and though very depraved yet nevertheless sympathetic young man.

"'These two rites were created by the Great Moses and introduced then into the ordinary life of the Judaic people in order to counteract that maleficent invention of clothes, thanks to which those factors were destroyed which were provided by Nature for the protection of these organs from the harmful action of the substances given off by them; and these two rites were transmitted from generation to generation, both to the followers of this Judaic religion themselves as well as to others who took over these useful rites almost unchanged. And it was only after "the death of the great King Solomon" that the rite "Tzel putz kann" ceased for some reason or other to be performed even by the followers of this Judaic religion, and only the rite "Sikt ner chorn" automatically continued to be performed and reached the contemporary representatives of that race.

"'And this custom together with many other ancient Judaic customs also reached the followers of the Christian religion, who at first observed it very strictly in their everyday life; but very soon, both this custom itself and even the information about its adoption among them similarly quickly disappeared from among the followers of this then still new religion.

"'Yes . . . my dear friend, if only the teaching of the Divine Jesus Christ were carried out in full conformity with its original, then the religion unprecedently wisely founded on it would not only be the best of all existing religions, but even of all religions which may arise and exist in the future.

"'Except for the custom of polygamy, there is nothing in the Mohammedan religion which was not also in the Judaic as well as in the Christian teachings.

"'The custom of polygamy, established on the basis of the scientific deductions of the then famous Arabian learned being 'Naoolan El Aool,' was introduced into the everyday life of people in general after the period of the founding of the Christian religion.

"'Your religion arose much later and its contents were intentionally restricted by its great creators, who had it in mind to lay particular stress on certain everyday customs.

"'They did this because at that time there were clearly manifest both the decline of the Christian religion and the disappearance in ordinary people of the capacity for contemplation, that is, for the state in which alone the truths indicated in the detailedly genuine religious teachings can be understood.

"'Having noticed all this, the great creators of the Mohammedan religion decided on the one hand to simplify the teaching itself and on the other hand to emphasize certain customs, so that the everyday life of the followers of this new teaching—who had lost the capacity for contemplation and consequently the possibility of understanding truths consciously—might at least mechanically flow more or less tolerably.

"'Just at that time, among other customs, they established and laid particular stress on the customs you mentioned of sooniat, abdest and polygamy, the beneficial results of which we can see even now in practice.

"'For example, as you yourself have justly observed, thanks to circumcision and ablution one rarely finds among the followers of this religion either onanism or certain venereal diseases, and thanks to polygamy we see among the followers of this religion such a reciprocal so to say psycho-organic maintenance of the foundation of family life as is almost entirely absent among the followers of the Christian religion.

"'Of the useful customs originally contained in the Christian religion and which were introduced by the creators of that religion into the life of its followers for the preservation of health and for the maintenance of the foundations of morality necessary for a happy life, nothing now remains except the custom of periodic fasting, that is, of abstaining at certain times of the year from the consumption of certain edible products.

"'And even this one surviving good custom is either already fading completely out of the ordinary life of the followers of this religion, or its observance is so changing year by year that no shock is obtained from it for the fasters, though it was just for that shock that this "fast" was established.

"'The changes now taking place in the process of this Christian custom of fasting are very characteristic and provide an excellent example for understanding how in general all the "good Christian customs" have little by little undergone change, until they have finally entirely ceased to exist.

"'A good illustration is the present-day observance of this fast by those called the Russian "Orthodox Christians."

"'These Russian Orthodox Christians took their religion entirely from those called the "Orthodox Greeks," from whom, together with many other Christian customs, this same custom of "fasting" also passed to them.

"'Most of the millions of these Russian Orthodox Christians still continue to fast as is said "rigorously," in conformity with what is called the "orthodox code" now existing there.

"'But as to the manner of their fasting, one cannot help recalling the saying of our dear Mullah Nassr Eddin in such cases:

"'"Isn't it all the same if I sing like a donkey as long as they call me a nightingale."

"'The fasting of these Russian Orthodox Christians is just a case of this kind.

"'As long as they are called Christians and moreover

Orthodox—even though they receive no shock whatever from the fast, is it not all the same?

"'As I have already said, these Russian Orthodox Christians even of the present time very strictly observe the seasons and the days of the fasts indicated in the aforesaid "codes."

"'But as to what should and should not be consumed as food during a fast—just in that question "is buried the left paw of the curly-haired dog of the ex-Emperor Wilhelm."

"'You will clearly understand how these contemporary Russian Orthodox Christians fast, if I repeat to you the exact words of one of these genuine Russian Orthodox Christians, spoken to me not long ago there in Russia.

"'I used to meet this Russian there on certain business and even became somewhat friendly with him and visited him in his home.

"'He was considered by those around him a very good Christian and the patriarchal father of a family; he was descended from what they call the "Old Believers."'

"Here, my boy, you might as well know that certain of the beings who compose this large group, Russia, are called by the rest Old Believers.

"Old Believers is the name given to those Orthodox Christians whose ancestors several centuries ago declined to accept the new rules then laid down by somebody or other for Russian Orthodox Christians, but remained faithful followers of the previously existing rules also laid down by somebody or other, only a century or two before the given 'religious schism' such as usually occurs among them from time to time.

"'And so the said worthy Russian Old Believer'—I continued to the young Persian—'once when we were dining together at his house in the company of several other

Russians, also Orthodox Christians, turned to me and said:

"'"Eh! old dear!"

"'By the way, I must tell you that it is common among the beings of this group there, after the second glass of genuine Russian vodka, to call their acquaintances by various pet names such as "old dear," "my Zapoopoonchik," "my potbellied beauty," "eh, my little brown jug," and so on and so forth.

"'And so this worthy genuine Orthodox Christian, addressing me as "old dear," said:

"'"Never mind, old dear! We shall soon be having Lent and then we shall feast together on real Russian dishes.

"'"To tell the truth, here in Russia we almost always eat the same things during the 'meat' periods.

"'"But it is quite a different story during the fasts, especially during Lent.

"'"Not a day passes but one is privileged to see some of the most tasty dishes.

"'"You know what, old dear?

"'"I made the other day a remarkably interesting 'discovery' on this subject.

"'"This new discovery of mine is miles above the discovery of that old codger Copernicus, who when he was once lying dead-drunk on the ground clearly sensed, it seems, that the Earth goes round.

"'"Ah! What a marvel! What a discovery!

"'"In our own mother Moscow alone, hundreds of thousands of such discoveries are probably made every day.

"'"No! . . . My discovery is a real one and exceedingly instructive and substantial.

"'"This discovery of mine is that we have all been complete fools and hopeless idiots ever to have imagined and been fairly convinced that for the host of good, varied, and most tasty dishes during Lent we are indebted to the famous art of our chefs and cooks.

"'"On the day, peculiarly blessed for those near to me, when I became worthy to understand this truth, that is to say, when our incomparable Doonyasha finally succeeded in placing within the layers of the pie for the 'gromwell fish soup with turbot livers' a series of secondary layers, I understood with my whole being that this had been a great mistake on our part.

"'"First I understood this myself, and afterwards I proved it to the whole of my household, that if we have so many varied and most tasty dishes during Lent, we are indebted only to our blessed and glorious fishes alone.

"'"During fasts and especially during Lent, our homes are made happy by the frequent visits of the:

Most Honorable 'Sturgeon' and the
Estimable 'Sterlet' and the
Respected 'Dried Sturgeon' and the
Ever-memorable 'Turbot' and
Her Illustrious Highness The 'Salmon' and the
Musical 'White Sturgeon' and the
Serenely Plastic 'Mackerel' and the
Eternally Angry 'Pike' and the
Ever-demure 'Gwyniad' and the
Leaping-alive 'Trout' and the
Beauty 'Trioshka' and the
Proud 'Shamai' and that
Worthy Personality 'Bream,' and all our other like benefactors and protectors.

"'"Merely the names alone of these our givers of good and felicity are already for us the greatest gift of God.

"'"When we hear their names, our hearts almost leap within us.

"' "These names of theirs are not just names, but real music. Can one really compare the sounds of the music invented there by various Beethovenings and Chopinings, and other fashionable triflers, with the sounds of the names of these blessed fishes?

"' "Every time we hear the names of these glorious creations, a state of bliss flows within us and courses through our veins and nerves.

"' "Eh, Blessed Fishes, first created by our Creator! Have mercy on us and sustain us also in these 'meat days.' Amen."

"'After this prayer, this worthy Orthodox Russian Christian drained a monster glass of genuine refined Russian vodka and stared fondly at a little statue of "Venus and Psyche" which stood nearby.

"'And indeed, my friend, almost every Russian Orthodox Christian has a similar idea of fasting and a similar attitude towards it.

"'During these "Christian fasts" which passed to them from the Orthodox Greeks, they all eat the flesh of fish.

"'It is not considered a "sin" among them to eat the flesh of fish, and they eat it heartily as a fast dish.

"'I personally find only one thing incomprehensible—from where did these Russian "sorry Orthodox" get the idea that during the Christian fasts, especially during Lent, the flesh of fish may be eaten?

"'I find it incomprehensible because the Orthodox Christians from whom they took this religion, namely, the Greeks, neither in the past nor in the present have ever eaten or do eat the flesh of fish during fasts.

"'Even the Greeks of today eat fish during Lent only on one day, and even then in accordance with the code of the Orthodox Church in memory of a day associated with the Divine Jesus Christ.

"'The result of a fast permitting the consumption of

the flesh of fish not only gives no shock at all to the fasters, but is even directly contrary to what the Divine Jesus Christ himself intended and taught, and for which this custom was established by the great creators of this Christian religion.

"'In confirmation of what I have just told you, you might as well, my young friend, listen to what I once chanced to read about Christian fasting in an ancient Judaic-Essenian manuscript.

"'In this ancient Judaic-Essenian manuscript it was stated that the custom established for the followers of the teaching of Jesus Christ, of fasting at certain times of the year, was instituted long after His death, namely, in the two hundred and fourteenth year after His birth.

"'The custom of fasting was instituted and introduced into the Christian religion by the great secret Kelnuanian Council.

"'This secret Kelnuanian Council was convened by all the followers of the then still new teaching of Jesus Christ in the locality of Kelnuk, lying on the shores of the Dead Sea. Hence it is known in the history of the Christian religion as the Kelnuanian Council.

"'And it was held in secret because the followers of the teaching of Jesus Christ were then everywhere rigorously persecuted by the power-possessing people.

"'The power-possessing people persecuted them because they greatly feared that if people lived according to this teaching, then although they themselves, namely, the power-possessing people, could also live very well, yet all the motives for displaying their power would disappear, and thereby those shocks would cease, the satisfaction of which evoke the tickling of their inner god named "Self-Love."

"'It was just during that Kelnuanian Council that its members first laid down the rule that the followers of the teaching of Jesus Christ should on certain days abstain from consuming certain edible products for food.

"'And the initial cause of the institution of this fast was the dispute at this Kelnuanian Council between two then famous learned men, namely, the great Hertoonano and the great Greek philosopher Veggendiadi.

"'The great Hertoonano was the representative of all the followers of the teaching of Jesus Christ settled on the shores of the Red Sea, while the philosopher Veggendiadi was the representative of all the then followers of that teaching in Greece.

"'The philosopher Veggendiadi was famous for his learning only in his own country, but Hertoonano was famous all over the Earth. He was considered the greatest authority on the laws of the inner organization of man, and also an authority on the science then called alchemy—not of course the alchemic science of which contemporary people have a notion and which they express by the same word.

"'The famous dispute between the great Hertoonano and Veggendiadi arose on the following occasion.

"'The philosopher Veggendiadi, it seems, occupied two days in affirming and proving that it was absolutely necessary to spread among all the followers of the teachings of Jesus the notion that to kill animals for the purpose of consuming their flesh for food was the greatest sin, and moreover that such flesh was very harmful to the health, and so on.

"'After the philosopher Veggendiadi, several other representatives ascended the rostrum and spoke for or against his case.

"'Finally, as this manuscript stated, the great Hertoonano with measured dignity slowly mounted the rostrum and spoke in the manner proper to him, clearly and calmly.

"'According to the text of this manuscript, he then spoke as follows:

"'"I fully concur in all the evidence and arguments set forth here by our Brother in Christ, the philosopher Veggendiadi.

"'"I for my part will even add to all he has said, that to cut short other lives merely to stuff one's own belly is an infamy of infamies such as only man is capable of.

"'"Had I not also been interested in this question for many years and had I not reached certain entirely different definite conclusions, then after all that our Brother in Christ Veggendiadi has said here, I should not hesitate a moment but should urge and conjure you all not to delay until tomorrow, but without looking behind to hasten back to your towns, and there in the public squares to cry aloud: 'Stop! Stop! People! Consume no more meat for food! This practice of yours is not only contrary to all the commandments of God, but is the cause of all your diseases.'

"'"As you see, I do not do this now. And I do not do so only because during my long years of unremitting study of this question I have, as I have already told you, arrived at an entirely different definite conclusion.

"'"Concerning the definite conclusion at which I have arrived I can now tell you only this, that it will never happen on the Earth that all people will profess one and the same religion. Hence, in addition to our Christian religion, other religions will always exist. And it is not possible to be certain that the followers of these other religions will also abstain from consuming meat.

"'"But if we cannot now be certain that at some time or other all people on Earth will abstain from meat, then we must now, as regards the consumption of meat, take quite other more practicable measures, because if one part of mankind consumes meat and the other part does not, then according to the results of my experimental investigations, the greatest of evils—than which nothing could be worse—would befall the people who did not consume meat.

"' "Namely, as my detailed experiments have shown me, among people who do not consume meat but who nevertheless live among those who do, the formation ceases of what is called 'will power.'

"' "My experiments proved to me that although when they abstain from meat people's bodily health improves, nevertheless, when such abstainers find themselves mixing with those who consume meat, their psychic state inevitably grows worse, in spite of the fact that the state of their organism may at the same time sometimes improve.

"' "Thus, a good result for people who abstain from meat can be obtained exclusively only if they live always in complete isolation.

"' "As regards the people who constantly consume meat or those products which contain the element called 'Eknokh,' although the appearance of the state of their organism undergoes no change, nevertheless their psyche, especially its chief feature which is sometimes designated by the general word the 'character' of man, gradually changes in regard to positiveness and morality for the worse, beyond all recognition.

"' "I must tell you that I made all these deductions from the experiments I was enabled to conduct over a period of many years, thanks to two good philanthropic men, namely, to the rich shepherd Alla Ek Linakh and his money, and to the scientist we all respect, El Koona Nassa, with his remarkable invention the apparatus 'Arostodesokh.'

"' "By means of this said remarkable apparatus Arostodesokh I was enabled for several years to register daily the general state of the organism of all those thousands of people who lived under test conditions at the expense of the good shepherd Alla Ek Linakh.

"'"May our CREATOR multiply his flocks!

"'"Well then, when, thanks to these experimental researches of mine, I became clearly convinced that if people continue to consume meat for their food it will be very bad for them, and that on the other hand if only some of them should abstain, no good would come of this either, I thereafter devoted myself entirely for a time to finding out what could nevertheless be done for the future welfare of the majority of the people.

"'"At the outset I then established for myself two categorical propositions: the first, that people accustomed for so many centuries to consuming meat for their food would never, with their weak wills, be able to make themselves cease consuming it in order to overcome this criminal tendency of theirs; and the second, that even if people should decide not to eat meat and should in fact keep their decision for a certain time, and should even lose the habit of eating meat, they would nevertheless never be able to abstain from eating it for a sufficient length of time to acquire a total aversion to it. They would not be able to do so because never on the Earth will it occur that all people will have the same religion or form a single government, without which condition there can never exist common to all, any suggestive, prohibitive, penal, or other kind of compulsory influence, owing to which alone people possessing in general the property of being stimulated by example, aroused by envy, and influenced magnetically, might be enabled to keep forever a resolution once taken.

"'"Notwithstanding these two facts, incontestably clear in my conviction, I nevertheless, with these facts as the basis of my subsequent researches, persevered in my search for some possible way of escape from the unhappy situation confronting people.

"‘"Of course all my further investigations on a large scale proceeded again with the aid of the inexhaustible wealth of the herdsman Alla Ek Linakh and the wonderful apparatus of the wise El Koona Nassa.

"‘"The results of these last researches of mine made it clear to me that although in general people's psyche does indeed deteriorate from the constant introduction into the organism of the substance Eknokh, yet this substance has a particularly harmful effect only at certain times of the year.

"‘"So, my Brethren in Christ . . . from all I have said and chiefly from the experimental observations which I made on people daily during a whole year and which clearly showed me that the intensity of the harmful effect of the substance Eknokh decreases at certain times of the year, I can now confidently express my personal opinion that if the custom would be spread and confirmed, among the followers of the teachings of Jesus Christ, of abstaining during at least certain times of the year from the use of these products in the formations of which that substance Eknokh takes a special part, then if such a measure could conceivably be put into effect, it would bring the people a certain amount of benefit.

"‘"As my numerous alchemic investigations have shown me, the substance Eknokh participates in the formation of the organisms of all lives, without exception, breeding on the surface of the Earth as well as within its different spheres, as, for instance, within the Earth, in the water, in the atmosphere, and so on.

"‘"This substance is present also in everything which exists for the formation of the said organism, as for example in the vascular fluid of every pregnant female of every kind of life, and in such products as milk, eggs, caviar, etc. . . .''

"'The ideas expressed by the great Hertoonano so astounded and agitated all the members of that Kelnuanian council that the commotion made it impossible for the great Hertoonano to continue speaking, and he was compelled to abandon his speech and descend from the rostrum.

"'It was further said in that manuscript that the day's result was a unanimous decision on the part of the members of the Kelnuanian council to fix, with the help of the great Hertoonano, those times of the year when the substance Eknokh had more harmful effects on people, and to spread widely among the followers of Jesus Christ the custom of fasting at these times of the year—that is, of abstaining at certain times of the year from products containing the, for them, harmful substance Eknokh.

"'With this that Judaic-Essenian manuscript ended.

"'As you see from this, the creators of this custom had in view that the followers of that religion should abstain at the fixed times from those products which contain the substance very harmful for their health and particularly to their psyche.

"'But the Russian sorry Orthodox Christians, who consider themselves faithful followers of that great religion, also fast, but during their fast they eat the flesh of fish, that is to say, they eat just those organisms which contain according to the researches of the great Hertoonano that harmful substance Eknokh, precisely to guard them against which that wise and salutary custom was created.'

"And with that, my boy, I then concluded my conversation with that sympathetic young Persian.

"Concerning the destruction and transformation by contemporary beings of these good customs which were handed down from the ancient days of their wise ancestors, our incomparable Mullah Nassr Eddin has also a very apt and wise sentence.

"'Ekh! People, people! Why are you people? If only you were not people, you might perhaps be clever.'

"A favorite saying of the American Uncle Sam also does very well to define the same idea.

"It is said that when Uncle Sam from America happens to have drunk a little more gin than usual, he always says during a pause: 'When nothing's right—only then, all is right.'

"But for myself I will only say, in this case 'Wicked Moon.'

"At any rate, my dear boy, I must admit that certain customs existing there which have reached the contemporary favorites of yours from remote antiquity are exceedingly good for the ordinary existence of the beings of certain communities there.

"These customs are good because they were invented and introduced into the process of the existence of beings by those three-brained beings there, who brought the perfecting of their Reason up to so high a degree as unfortunately none of your contemporary beings there any longer attains.

"The contemporary people-beings are able to create only such customs as make the quality of their psyche still worse.

"For instance, they have recently made a practice of always, here, there, and everywhere dancing a certain dance called the 'fox trot.'

"At the present time this fox trot is indulged in everywhere at all times of the day and night not only by young and still unformed beings who do not even begin to be aware of the sense and aim of their arising and existence, but also by those whose faces clearly express—as it can be constated by every normal more or less sensible three-brained being—that in respect of their duration of existence, as our teacher would say, 'not only have they one foot in the grave but even both.' The point, however, is that the process of the experience in a being during the said fox trot is exactly similar to that which proceeds during that children's disease which the Great Moses called 'Moordoorten.'

"The disease which the Great Moses devoted half his existence to eradicating from among children, a host of your contemporary favorites of responsible age have, almost deliberately, resurrected again and spread not only among children and the general mass of adults but also even among the aged as well.

"These good customs for ordinary existence reached your contemporary favorites from ancient three-brained beings of your planet, and very many now still exist there among the beings of various communities of the continent Asia.

"Certain of these customs existing there now, appear when first witnessed as absurdly strange and barbaric, but on a close and impartial investigation of the inner meaning of any of these customs, one can see how skillfully there has been incorporated in them for the people who follow them one or another moral or hygienic benefit.

"Take, as an example, one of the most seemingly senseless of the customs there—one existing among a certain tribe of Asiatic beings called 'Kolenian Loors' or 'Kolenian gypsies' dwelling between Persia and Afghanistan, and which other beings there call 'Gypsy self-fumigation.'

"Exactly the same end is served by this seemingly stupid custom as by the Persian custom of ablution or abdest. This gypsy tribe is regarded as the lowest and filthiest of all the tribes existing on the Earth; and indeed they are so filthy that their clothes are always swarming with the insects called lice.

"Their custom of 'self-fumigation' also serves by the way to destroy these insects.

"Although the men-beings of that tribe are indeed exceedingly filthy, yet not only do no venereal diseases exist among them, but they do not even know and have never heard that such diseases can be contracted.

"In my opinion, this is the outcome entirely of that custom of theirs, which some ancient clever being there invented for the welfare of the people of his epoch, and which passing afterwards from generation to generation, chanced to reach these contemporary filthy beings of the tribe of Kolenian gypsies.

"For this rite of self-fumigation every family of gypsies has also what is called an, 'Ateshkain,' that is, a stool of special form which they regard as sacred; and this whole ritual of theirs they perform with the aid of this sacred stool.

"Every family of these gypsies has also what is called a 'Tandoor,' that is, a special kind of earth pit, such as is found in the houses almost everywhere on the continent of Asia and which serves as a hearth on which they usually bake bread and prepare food.

"In these Tandoors in Asia they burn chiefly what is called 'Keeziak'—a fuel composed of the dung of quadruped animals.

"The rite itself consists in this, that when the family of these gypsies returns home in the evening they first remove all their clothing and shake them in this Tandoor.

"It is almost always hot in this Tandoor because the dung burns very slowly and the ashes formed around the Keeziak keep the fire burning for a very long time.

"By the way, it is interesting to remark that when these gypsies shake their clothes in the Tandoor a highly interesting phenomenon results from this action of theirs; namely, the lice in their clothes crawl out and, falling into the fire, explode before burning, and the various sounds of the explosion of these lice, large and small, produces altogether a surprising 'musical symphony.'

"From the said explosion of the lice, a hearer sometimes has the impression that somewhere not far off, firing is going on from several dozen of their what are called machine guns.

"Well then, after these 'worthy gypsies' have shaken their no less worthy clothing, they proceed with the sacred ritual.

"First of all they solemnly and with a certain ceremony lower their sacred family stool into the Tandoor and in turn, according to age, they step into the Tandoor and stand upon it.

"The sacred stool consists simply of a small board to which four iron legs are fixed; and by this means it is possible to stand in the Tandoor without burning one's feet in the hot ashes.

"As each member of the family stands on that sacred stool, all the other members of the family sing their sacred canticle, while the one standing upon this stool slowly and solemnly, bending the knees, lowers and raises himself and at the same time recites prayers. The custom requires that he should do this until every part of his sex organs has been warmed by the Tandoor.

"A second custom, very similar and seemingly just as stupid, I saw among the people of another small tribe, called 'Toosooly Kurds,' dwelling in Transcaucasia not far from Mt. Ararat.

"This tribe is not filthy as is the tribe of the Kolenian gypsies. On the contrary, from their daily bathing in the river Arax and existing mostly in the fresh air—being chiefly shepherds—not only are the people of this tribe very clean but they even do not give off the specific odor which is peculiar to people of almost all the small tribes which populate this great Asia.

"Each family of this tribe has its own what is called 'hut,' which serves as a dwelling and for the reception of guests—as the custom of visiting one another is highly developed among the separate families of this tribe.

"In each hut it is customary for them to have, in the corner of the front section, what is called a 'sacred Mungull,' that is a hearth on which a fire of smoldering charcoal or of the said Keeziak is constantly kept, and near each such sacred Mungull there hangs a small wooden box called 'Ktulnotz' which is always kept supplied with the roots of a certain plant.

"The 'rite of self-fumigation' consists in this, that every member of the family and every guest of either sex, before going into the principal section of the hut, is obliged to enter this sacred Mungull in order as they say to purify himself from the influence of those evil spirits by which man is surrounded when he is busy with honest work.

"And this purification is carried out in the following manner:

"Each person going into the hut must approach and take a few roots out of the hanging box and throw them into the fire, and afterwards, in the smoke from the burning of these roots, fumigate his sex organs. In the case of a woman, she simply spreads her skirt and stands over the Mungull! If it is a man, he either takes off or lets down his trousers and also stands over the said smoke.

"Only after such a purification can they enter the chief room; otherwise, as they affirm, not only will evil influences be brought into the house, but owing to these accumulated influences, a man might contract very evil diseases.

"These sacred Mungulls are usually screened by the

very best 'Djedjims,' that is, by a special fabric woven only by the Kurds.

"I repeat, my boy, there exist at the present time on that continent Asia a great many similar customs.

"I personally saw hundreds of them which seemed at first sight no less strange and barbarous but, upon a serious and impartial study of their hidden meaning, always revealed one and the same aim, namely, either the destruction of the noxious carriers of various diseases, or the strengthening of moral shame.

"But on the continent of Europe I scarcely found a single custom specially created either for purposes of hygiene or for instilling morality among the masses.

"It cannot be denied that various customs also exist on the continent of Europe, even thousands of them, but they are all established only in order that beings may have the possibility of pleasing each other, or to conceal the real state of affairs, that is to say, to disguise the undesirable forms of one's exterior—undesirable of course only according to subjective understanding—and to conceal the nullity of one's own inner significance.

"These customs existing there progressively increase year by year the 'duality' of the personality and mind of the beings there.

"But the principal evil lies in this, that at the present time there, all the 'Oskianotznel' of the rising generation, or the education of the children, is rendered and reduced only to the adoption of these innumerable customs which exist among them and engender only immorality. Hence it is that year by year the data crystallized in them by tens of centuries for the Being 'of an image of God,' and not simply, as they themselves would say, 'of an animal,' are on the one hand decrystallized, and on the other hand their psyche is already becoming almost such as our dear Teacher defines by the words:

"'There is everything in him except himself.'

"And indeed, my boy, owing to the complete absence of good patriarchal customs and to their notorious 'education,' the contemporary beings of that continent have already become completely transformed into what are called 'automatons' or living mechanical puppets.

"At the present time any one of them can become animated and manifest himself outwardly, only when there are accidentally pressed the corresponding what are called 'buttons' of those impressions already present in him, which he mechanically perceived during the whole of his preparatory age.

"But unless these buttons are pressed, the beings there are in themselves only, as again our highly esteemed Mullah Nassr Eddin says, 'pieces of pressed meat.'

"It must without fail be remarked here that one of the principal causes of this state of the beings of contemporary civilization is also that same onanism of theirs, a disease which in recent times has come to be almost epidemic there, and which is in its turn also a consequence again of their education of children, thanks to a certain maleficent idea established among its rulers and which is already, as it were, an inseparable part of the consciousness of everybody, namely, their maleficent idea that 'to speak to children about the sex question is absolutely improper.'

"And further, I again emphasize that just this, for their naïve reason, trifling idea, the significance of which none of them takes into consideration—considering it simply as what they call a question of 'decency' or 'indecency'—is the chief cause of their having come to this phenomenal so to say 'psychic mechanicality.'

"In the totality of definite understandings which they call 'education,' there is even a certain section which elucidates and exactly indicates just what is, as they express it, 'decent' and what is 'indecent' to say to children.

"You must know that at the end of my last sojourn on the surface of your planet, I had to make this maleficent terrestrial question the subject of my special observation and even to study it in great detail.

"To know approximately what results the terrestrial contemporary education of children leads to, I will tell you of just that one occurrence which was the first cause of my subsequent special interest in the question of this terrestrial misunderstanding.

"Although this occurrence took place in the large community of Russia, yet nevertheless this 'story' which I shall now tell you is very characteristic and gives a very good picture in general of the education of the children of their contemporary civilization.

"It is characteristic because in this large community Russia also, the contemporary responsible beings, especially the beings of what is called the upper 'ruling class,' educate their children exactly as the contemporary responsible beings of the other communities breeding on the continents of Europe and America educate theirs.

"My account of this occurrence, which evoked in me an impulse of interest to acquaint myself specially with the question of the terrestrial education of children, I shall preface with a story of something that occurred just previously to this and which admirably illustrates the significance of this education of theirs and was also, so to say, a 'link' in my gradually becoming interested in this question.

"I happened once to exist continuously for several months in the capital of this community—in the city of St. Petersburg.

"During my stay there I became acquainted with an elderly couple.

"The man was what is called a 'senator' and his wife

was a 'society lady' and a patroness of several 'welfare institutions.'

"I used to visit them often at their home and enjoyed playing chess with this senator—as is customary there among what are called 'respectable people.'

"This elderly couple had several daughters.

"All the elder daughters were already settled, that is, married; only their youngest daughter, twelve years old, remained at home.

"As this couple had no further responsibilities concerning their other daughters, they decided to give this youngest daughter of theirs the very best education according to the notions of that time, and for this purpose they placed her in a special 'boarding school,' a higher educational establishment called an 'institute.'

"This youngest daughter of theirs came home only on Sundays and for the chief holidays, and once a week on special days her father and mother used to visit her at the boarding school.

"I was almost always with them during the holidays, and I met this charming as yet unspoiled girl and sometimes even took walks with her in the neighboring what is called 'park.'

"During these walks we either joked or she told me about her lessons and her new impressions.

"During these meetings and conversations, a tie, something like friendship, grew up little by little between us.

"She was very quick in her perceptions and manifestations, or as your favorites themselves define such persons from among themselves, an 'alert and thoughtful' girl.

"My acquaintance, this senator, was sent on a certain as they say there 'inspection,' somewhere far off in Siberia.

"His wife decided to accompany him, for the senator was suffering from what is called 'liver trouble' and constantly needed care; but they could not make this joint trip because of their youngest daughter, since there would be no one to visit her at the institute and to take her home during the holidays.

"So, one morning, the parents—these elderly acquaintances of mine—came to see me at my apartment and asked me if I would agree to take their place with their youngest daughter during their absence, to visit her every week at the institute and to take her home with me for the holidays.

"I, of course, at once agreed to this proposal of theirs and when, very soon after, the senator and his wife left for Siberia I began punctually to fulfill the obligations taken upon myself in regard to their daughter who had by that time become a pet of mine.

"Upon my first visit to this educational establishment which existed specially for the education of children, I noticed a certain strange thing which also served as one of the causes of my subsequent observations and studies of the consequences on your contemporary favorites of that 'maleficence' invented by them themselves.

"On the day of my visit to this, as they call it, 'genteel institution,' there were many visitors in the reception room where the meetings of the parents or guardians with their children or wards actually took place.

"One or two parents or guardians had only just come in, others were already talking with their children or foster children, others were awaiting the arrival of their children and all their attention was fixed on the door through which the pupils of that establishment usually entered. I also, after I had come into this reception room and had explained to the inspectress on duty who it was I wished to see, sat down to wait for my chance foster child. While waiting I looked around. All the pupils of this 'genteel establishment' were dressed alike and all wore their hair similarly braided in two braids, the ends of which, tied with ribbons, hung down their backs.

"What struck my eye was a certain peculiarity in these ribbons and braids. On some of the pupils these ribbons simply hung down the back, but on others, although they also hung down the back, yet the ends of these ribbons were tied together in a certain way.

"On the very next holiday, when I took my foster child home, talking with her over what is called a samovar, I asked her:

"'Tell me, Sonia, please, why, although the pupils of your institute dress alike in everything else, there is that peculiarity in the ends of their braids?' She immediately blushed and without answering this question of mine stared pensively into her tea, and only after a certain time nervously replied:

"'It's not just a simple thing among us. Although this is our big institute secret, yet I cannot help telling it to you, my friend, as I am quite sure that you will not give away this big institute secret of ours to anybody.'

"She proceeded to tell me frankly as follows:

"'The manner of tying our ribbons was intentionally devised by the pupils so that they could recognize one another; that is, know to which club a pupil belongs, and at the same time so that the class teachers and supervisors, and in general anyone not a pupil of the institute, should not know or discover the secret.

"'All the pupils of our institute are divided into two categories, one belongs to what is called the "men's club" and the other to what is called the "women's club," and we recognize one another just by the manner of tying these ribbons.'

"After this she explained to me in detail in just what the difference between these two clubs lies.

"She said that as a rule all new arrivals in the institute

were at first members of the women's club, and only afterwards, if any pupil proved to be daring toward the teachers or in general showed herself very active in some way or other, then by the common consent of all the pupils she was enrolled as a member of the men's club and from that moment tied the ends of the ribbons of her two braids together.

"'We usually make the meeting place of our club a spare classroom or dormitory, but more often the toilets.

"'The members of the men's club have in general the following privileges: they have the right to choose and to command as many as they like and whom they please of the pupils who are members of the women's club; and these latter are obliged always to gratify every wish of the given member of the men's club and do their utmost to make her stay in our boarding school easy for her, as, for example, to make her bed in the morning, copy her lessons, share with her the presents sent from home, and so on and so forth.

"'The chief occupation in the clubs consists of reading together forbidden books procured by one of the pupils. They chiefly read one very rare manuscript, obtained with money raised by a general institute subscription, wherein is expounded in detail the whole of the teaching of the famous poetess Sappho.'

"I must tell you, my boy, that Sappho was the name of a certain Greek poetess who first discovered there on your planet the 'way to real happiness' for many women of the Greek-Roman as well as of the contemporary civilization.

"This great creator of 'women's happiness' had her dwelling place on the island of 'Lesbos,' from which word originated the title of those women who have already become worthy to understand and to actualize during the process of their existence the teaching of this remarkable woman, and who at the present time are called 'Lesbians.'

"This foster child of mine, who had chanced to become my enlightener upon the subtleties of the psyche of the beings of the female sex of your planet, further explained to me that every pupil of the institute who was a member of the men's club could choose for herself as many partners as she wished for the common pastime; this of course proceeding in full accordance with the teachings of the poetess Sappho.

"I think that thanks merely to this one fact which I have related to you out of thousands of other observations of mine, you can already clearly picture to yourself that such a phenomenal ugliness could not exist among the rising generation if the notion was not prevalent there that it is exceedingly 'indecent' to talk to children about the 'sex question.'

"This notion of 'decency' came down to contemporary civilization by inheritance from the beings of the epoch called the 'Middle Ages.'

"These candidates for Hasnamusses of the Middle Ages, having been among the chief agents in the destruction of the real meaning of the teaching of the Divine Teacher Jesus Christ, then also devised and introduced into everyday existence, as a regulation, the maleficent invention which they called 'bon ton.' And this maleficent invention then became so strongly fixed in the psyche of the majority that it became organized for them and began to pass by heredity from generation to generation, so that now your contemporary favorites, who have become completely weak-willed, are unable, however they may try, to overcome such an abnormal psychic fixation as, in the given case, the notion of the indelicacy of talking to their children about the 'sex question.'

"What? Talk to one's children about 'sex'? Is that not indecent?

"At the present time the people of contemporary civilization talk to their children and teach them for their edification only what has been invented or is being invented in the manuals of various candidates for 'Hasnamuss individuals' under the aforesaid title of 'bon ton.'

"And since in all these manuals it seems that it is very indecent to talk about the 'sex question' and in the case of children even 'immoral,' then even if contemporary people see their favorite son or daughter rotting, they simply cannot, and even as I have already told you, with all their mental wish dare not, explain frankly to their children the harm and sin of these criminal habits.

"And so, my boy, when my good acquaintances the senator and his wife had returned from Siberia and I was free of the obligations I had taken upon myself in regard to my pet, their youngest daughter, there just then occurred the aforementioned event which served as the beginning of my special observations and studies of this terrestrial contemporary question, maleficent also to themselves.

"This sorrowful event occurred there in St. Petersburg itself in just such another educational institution and consisted in the following. The headmistress of this institution, finding that one of her pupils had behaved contrary to their famous regulations of 'decency,' reprimanded her so harshly and so unfairly that as a result the accused and her friend, two growing girls with the germs of data for future normal women-mothers, hanged themselves.

"My investigations into this case elicited the following:

"It appeared that among the pupils of the mentioned educational institution was a certain young girl Elizabeth who had been brought by her parents from a distant estate to the capital in order that there, in a special higher educational institution, she might receive this same contemporary 'education.'

"Here in St. Petersburg in this said boarding school, it happened that this thirteen-year-old Elizabeth became great friends with another young girl, Mary, who like herself was not yet developed.

"The same year on the day of the 'spring holiday' or as it is otherwise called there 'May Day,' all the pupils of that higher educational institution were taken according to custom for an excursion into the country, and these two 'bosom friends' happened to be in different groups which were walking at some distance from each other.

"Out in the fields Elizabeth chanced to see a certain 'quadruped animal' called there a 'bull,' and very much wishing for some reason or other that her bosom friend Mary should not miss seeing this dear quadruped animal, she shouted, 'Mary! Mary! Look, there goes a bull!'

"No sooner had she uttered the word 'bull' than all the, as they are called, 'governesses' swarmed round this Elizabeth and flung at her all kinds of cruel preachings.

"How could one utter the word 'bull'!! Does not that quadruped animal occupy itself with what no well-brought-up person would on any account speak of and still less a pupil of such a 'genteel institution'?

"While the governesses were persecuting this poor Elizabeth, all the pupils of the institute gathered around and the headmistress herself came up, who, having learned what it was all about, began in her turn to reproach Elizabeth.

"'Shame on you!' she said. 'To utter such a word which is considered so very, very indecent.'

"At last Elizabeth could contain herself no longer and she asked amid her tears:

"'What then ought I to have called that quadruped animal if it actually was a bull?'

"'The word,' said the headmistress, 'by which you call that animal, any of the scum call it. But you, since you are here in the institute, are not of the scum; so you should always find out how to call indecent things by names which do not sound indecent to the ear.

"'For instance, when you saw that indecent animal and wanted your friend to look at it, you might have shouted, "Mary, look, there goes a beefsteak," or "Mary, look yonder, there goes something that is very good to eat when we are hungry," and so forth.'

"From all this poor Elizabeth became so nervous, especially as this 'reprimanding' took place in the presence of all her friends, that she could not restrain herself and cried out with all her might:

"'Oh, you wretched old maids! Striped hobgoblins! Spawn of deepest hell! Because I called a thing by its name, you immediately begin to suck my blood. Be thrice damned!!!!!'

"Having said these last words, she fell as they say there 'in a faint,' followed in turn by the fainting of the headmistress herself and of several 'class mistresses' and 'governesses.'

"The 'class mistresses' and 'governesses' of this 'genteel institution' who had not fainted then raised such a 'hubbub' as really only occurs at what is called the market where 'Jewesses' from the town of Berdichev exclusively bargain.

"The result of it all was that when the 'class mistresses' and 'governesses' who had fainted, revived, they then and there held in the field under the presidency of this same headmistress of the institution, what is there called a 'teachers' council,' by whose sentence it was decided immediately on return to town to telegraph Elizabeth's father to come for his daughter, as she was expelled from the institute with loss of right to enter any other similar institute in the Russian Empire.

"The same day, an hour after the pupils were sent home, one of what are called the 'porters' of the institute happened to find in the 'woodshed' that two as yet undeveloped growing future mothers were hanging by ropes fastened to the beams.

"In Mary's pocket was found a note with the contents:

"'Together with my dear Elizabeth, I do not wish to live any longer with such nonentities as you, and I am going with her to a better world.'

"This case then so interested me that I began, of course privately, to investigate psychoanalytically from every aspect the psyche of all the parties in this sad story. I partly elucidated among other things that at the moment of the manifestation of her violent outburst, there was in the psyche of poor Elizabeth what is called there 'chaos.'

"And indeed it would have been astonishing if such a 'chaos' had not been in the psyche of this as yet unself-conscious thirteen-year-old girl, who before this miserable event had always lived on her father's big estate, where she had always seen and felt the same richness of nature as on that day in the field near the city of St. Petersburg.

"She had been brought to that stifling noisy city of St. Petersburg and had been kept for a long time in an improvised box. Suddenly she had found herself in an environment where every fresh impression evoked all kinds of memories of former pleasantly perceived sensations.

"On your planet, during what is called 'early spring' there are indeed sometimes pictures to the charm of which it is difficult not to yield.

"Picture to yourself the following: afar, cows are seen at pasture; near, at one's feet snowdrops shyly peep out from the earth; close to one's ear, a little bird flies by;

to the right is heard the twittering of quite an unknown bird; on the left one's sense of smell is quickened by the perfume of some also unknown flower.

"In short, at such moments as these, in the beings there, especially in one so young as Elizabeth, finding themselves, after a long period of oppressive existence in a suffocating city, in the midst of such a rich abundance of all kinds of unaccustomed impressions, the mental associations evoked from a natural being-joy would naturally arise of themselves from every external thing perceived.

"Elizabeth must have felt this especially strongly, having lived, as I have already said, before the institute, on her father's large estate which lay far from the already exceedingly abnormal conditions of city vanities.

"Thanks to this, every impression newly perceived by her would naturally call up previous childhood memories, each connected in its turn with various other pleasant incidents.

"So it is not difficult to picture to yourself that the sudden appearance of that quadruped animal called 'bull,' such as she had seen at home on the farm and which had enjoyed there the affection of all the children, who secretly even took it bread from the table, was to this as yet unformed impressionable young girl a shock for the corresponding associations under the influence of which, she, being full of a feeling of sincere happiness still unspoiled by the abnormally established conditions of being-existence, instantly wished to share her happiness with her bosom friend who was some distance off, and shouted to her to look at that dear bull.

"Now I ask you, how should she have called this quadruped being, since it actually was a bull?

"Really, 'beefsteak'?—as advised by the 'esteemed' headmistress of this 'esteemed higher educational institution,' which existed there specially for the 'education of children' according to the barbarous system of theirs existing there to their misfortune also at the present time.

"As you see, my boy, intending to tell you a little more about the three-brained beings who have interested you and who breed on that continent of North America, I have, by the way, said a great deal in general about the three-brained beings arising and existing on all the continents of that peculiar planet.

"I don't think you will have any grievance against me for this, since you have at the same time managed to learn many more facts elucidating the details of their strange psyche.

"Concerning specially what is called the 'degree of degeneration' of the common presences of those who compose this contemporary large group on the continent America, in respect of the loss of possibilities for the acquisition of Being nearer to the normal Being of three-brained beings in general, I can tell you something somewhat consoling for them, namely, that in my opinion there remains among them the largest percentage of beings in whose presences the said possibility is not entirely lost.

"Although this new group is composed of and still continues to be increased by three-brained beings breeding on the continent of Europe, where for such beings with the aforementioned possibilities it is already necessary, particularly in recent times, as our wise Teacher Mullah Nassr Eddin says on such occasions, 'to look specially with the most powerful electric arc lamps,' nevertheless, I repeat, in this large group there is a larger percentage of such beings than on the continent of Europe.

"It seems to me that this has happened because there have migrated there, and still now migrate from the continent of Europe, beings chiefly from among what are called the 'simple beings' who are not, so to say, the 'hereditary offspring' of the European beings belonging to the 'ruling caste' in whom, thanks to transmission by inheritance from generation to generation during long centuries of predisposition to Hasnamussian properties, there is at the present time so much of what is called 'inner swagger' that it would never permit them to blend with the general mass in order to strive together with common efforts to become such three-brained beings as they should be.

"Thanks only to the fact that among the three-brained beings breeding on that continent there were only very few of the 'offspring of the ruling caste' and that the general mass of beings was in itself a medium in which it was still possible for 'our brother' to exist and not be under the influence of those local radiations which are formed owing to surrounding beings and which act harmfully on what are called the 'subjectively natural inner forces' of every being—I was therefore able during my stay among them to rest as I desired.

"Now, my boy, that I have spent so much of my time explaining the meaning of all the various innovations and all the renewals of former pernicious customs—which had already many times existed on their planet—among the beings of this big new contemporary grouping, and which have already at the present time become, in the objective sense, harmful not only for them themselves, but also for all the other three-brained beings who have interested you and who breed on quite other continents, it is therefore in my opinion already unavoidably necessary for a, so to say, 'closing chord' to initiate you also into those of my thoughts which began in my mentation on the last day of my sojourn among them in the city of New York and which ended on the steamer as it was moving away from that continent toward the East.

"On that day I was sitting in one of the singular cafés

there named 'Childs,' situated at what is called 'Columbus Circle,' awaiting the beings from the continent Europe who had accompanied me to this continent, to go with them to the dock of the outgoing steamer, and I was looking out of the window at the various passing beings from among the inhabitants of that city, who although according to automatized perception were distinguishable on that day in exterior appearance—of course chiefly due to the usage, recently fixed in them more than in any beings of any other continents, of becoming 'slaves' to always that same maleficent terrestrial invention which they call 'fashion'—nevertheless somehow seemed to me, in respect of their inner content, particularly alike.

"Observing them, I thought just about the final deduction I had made the day before, that in the present period of the flow of the Heropass in the common planetary process of the ordinary existence of those in general strange three-brained beings, the source of the intensive manifestation of that already long-established particularity of the general totality of their strange psyche, which one of the highest sacred Individuals once characterized by the words 'the periodic fundamental source of the issuing of new causes of abnormality,' is represented just by the beings of this new grouping.

"The shock for the beginning of associations and for my further active meditations this time, was the constatation I happened to make of the fact that everything constituting what is called the 'totality of the subjective appearance' of each one of them—such as clothes, gestures, manners, and in general all the established usages which all three-brained beings acquire in the ordinary process of their collective existence—is a totally exact imitation exclusively only of all that exists among the beings of various other independent groupings breeding on other continents, an imitation of just that which is considered by the free beings of these other groupings, that is to say, by those beings among them who have already experienced and consequently been disappointed in everything the process of ordinary existence can give, as unworthy of manifestation by beings similar to them.

"This accidental constatation of mine at once very much astonished me, chiefly because I was already informed from every aspect and wholly convinced that in the present period everywhere on this planet the beings of almost all the other groupings, those recently formed as well as those which are at a very advanced stage of their community, imitate to the full all the innovations of the beings of this still quite recently formed grouping and enthusiastically adopt these innovations in the process of their ordinary existence, and at the same time, all the external manifestations of the beings of this new grouping and consequently the 'inner subjective significance' which engenders these external manifestations, consist only of that which, as I have already said, has become to the great grief of the free beings of these other independent groupings fixed and inherent in the common presences of the ordinary beings of these groupings.

"In consequence of this unexpected constatation of mine, there then arose in me a highly intensive impulse of curiosity to make clear to myself the logical causes which had engendered this terrestrial incongruity.

"All that day, while sitting in this Childs awaiting the arrival of the beings from the continent of Europe who had accompanied me, and while riding in the 'motor taxi' and also while on the boat itself, I continued to ponder very actively the solution of this question, of course appearing to strangers as an automatic observer of everything proceeding around me; and in the ability outwardly to appear such, in order to resemble them in this respect, and thus not to be, so to say, conspicuous, or as they say there 'not to strike the eye,' I became there on the Earth ideally or as they would say 'artistically' expert.

"Sitting on the deck looking at the twinkling of the lights on the shore of this continent gradually growing fainter as the steamer moved away towards the East, and pondering over and logically comparing all the facts ensuing one from the other, I, as a result, made it almost entirely clear to myself just why and how the said incongruity could have arisen on this ill-fated planet.

"At the beginning of these ponderings of mine, I established many facts which had enabled this to arise, but afterwards, when I began successively to exclude those which inevitably ensue—as is done in such cases—then as a result one fact became clear to me, which, though at first glance insignificant, astonished even me and which as it turned out was, all the time, and still is, the originating cause of this abnormality there.

"And that is to say, it turned out that owing to the consequences of that same famous 'education' of theirs, so many times mentioned by me, there inevitably arise in the common presence of each of them in general during his age of preparation for responsible existence, to whatever independent group he may belong, data for the definite conviction that in the former epochs on their planet the beings similar to them had never perfected themselves to that Reason to which their contemporaries have attained and in which they can still continue to perfect themselves.

"When my thoughts were concentrated on this and I began to recall my former impressions concerning this question, those consciously and also those incidentally and automatically perceived during my previous observations of them in general, I gradually established that all your favorites, particularly in the last thirty centuries, had indeed become convinced during all their responsible existence that their contemporary what they call 'civilization' is simply the result of the direct continuation of the development of the Reason which began at the very commencement of the arising of three-brained beings on their planet.

"And so when the beings, their contemporaries of any grouping, owing to the formation in them while still in their preparatory age of new data for this false conviction, accidentally became the possessors of something which is accounted in the given period desirable and thereby acquire authority, and at the same time find out, of course also accidentally, about some idea of the beings of past epochs which has already existed many times, and, giving it out as having been thought of by themselves, spread it around, then the beings of other groupings, through the absence in their common presences, due to wrong education, of the data which it is proper to all three-brained beings of responsible age to have in their presences, and which engender what are called 'an instinctive sensing of reality' and 'a broad outlook,' believe in the first place that this idea has arisen on their planet for quite the first time, and secondly that once the practical application of it has been actualized by those who already possess the said 'something desirable,' then it must indeed be very good, and they forthwith begin to imitate everything really good as well as bad, notwithstanding its complete contrariety to everything there is and to everything well fixed in their ordinary existence, merely in order to possess that which for today is considered desirable.

"I then even remembered that I had already once long before very seriously reflected on this matter in the period of my fifth personal sojourn on the surface of your planet, when the city of Babylon was considered the center of culture of these strange three-brained beings, and when I had, on account of some similar question, to make a 'logical analysis' of just this strange feature of the psyche of these peculiar three-brained beings.

"I then, among other things, also reasoned as follows:

"That they think thus may perhaps be possibly justified by taking it into consideration that owing to the abnormal conditions of ordinary existence established in past epochs no exact information has reached them about events which have occurred in the past in the process of the existence of the three-brained beings who existed before them on their planet; but how is it possible to admit that up till now there has not arisen in the mentation of any one of them—in whom it has already been established that even until quite recently there does sometimes proceed a 'something' similar to the process of 'comparative logic'—at least the following simple and almost, as they themselves would call it, 'childish idea'?

"And, namely, if as they themselves say and are even certain, that their planet has already existed many, many centuries with their species on it, beings similar to them—that is to say, beings who could mentate—and that many many millions of them must have also arisen and existed before them, would there really not have been then, from among these many many millions, at least a few beings who could also have invented for the well-being of their contemporaries all kinds of comforts as in the given case these contemporary American beings are now inventing and all the others are uncritically and even rapturously imitating, as, for example, 'comfortable seats' in the water closets, preserves, and so on and so forth.

"This unpardonable lack of thought is all the more strange in that they themselves admit the existence of many, as they now call them, ancient sages, and also do not deny the great amount of most varied information which has come down to them concerning the many objective truths elucidated by these sages, which information, by the way, certain of your favorites at the present time are, without any remorse of conscience, giving out as having been thought of by themselves and exploiting to the full for their various egoistic aims, without at all suspecting that the totality of the results of these wiseacrings of theirs will inevitably lead their descendants sooner or later to total destruction.

"This particularity of their mentation—very complicated for any 'logical analysis' undertaken for the purpose of understanding it—engendering in them this false conviction, was during the whole of my observation of them, beginning with the end of the existence of the continent Atlantis, always, so to say, the 'gravity center cause' of almost all the more or less major events unfavorable for them in the process of their collective existence.

"Thanks to this false conviction, the result of their strange mentation, and in addition, thanks to the effect on the totality of the functioning of their feelings, of the consequences of the properties of the organ Kundabuffer which inevitably arise in their presences at responsible age and which are called 'envy,' 'greed,' and 'jealousy,' it always happens there, that when the beings of any grouping become the possessors of anything which in the given period is considered desirable, in most cases because of that maleficent practice fixed in their everyday existence, which they express by the words 'not to cease progressing,' there immediately arises in the common presences of all the beings of other groupings, on whatever continents they may breed, as soon as the rumor of this reaches them, the desire to have the same, and from that moment, there arises in each of them firstly, the need to imitate them, and secondly, the 'indubitable certainty' that the beings of this other grouping must exist very correctly, since they have been able to acquire just what in the given period is accounted desirable.

"In this connection, the so to say 'piquancy' of the strangeness of the mentation of your favorites is that there never occurs in their mentation the process called 'to ponder' in order to understand if only approximately the true causes of the possession by others of that on account of which there arise in them 'envy,' 'greed,' 'jealousy,' and so on.

"And so, my boy, in spite of the fact that as far as the acquisition and hence the possession of the results attained by the conscious labors and intentional sufferings of the three-brained beings of past epochs of their planet are concerned, the beings of their new group have absolutely nothing at all, but consist as to inner content as well as to exterior manifestations only of everything bad that exists among contemporary beings of other independent groupings—solely because in recent times they have accidentally become the possessors of just that which in the objective sense is most despicable, yet which, owing in general to the fixed abnormal conditions of the ordinary existence of these unfortunates, is considered desirable—nevertheless the beings of all the other groupings now imitate to the full everything they invent.

"Of all the maleficent inventions of the beings of this contemporary grouping which have accidentally acquired authority, the most harmful for their common presences—in respect of the possibility of rectifying in the future the so to say already actualized maleficences—must be considered the practice they have established of passing a great part of the time of their existences in high houses.

"In order that you may clearly picture to yourself the significance of all the harm from just this invention of theirs, I must first of all explain to you the following:

"Do you remember, when I spoke to you about that 'maleficent means' existing there at the present time called 'sport,' I said that the duration of the existence of these favorites of yours was in the beginning also Fulasnitamnian, that is to say, they had to exist until their body Kesdjan was completely coated in them and perfected up to the required gradation of Reason, and that afterwards, when very abnormal conditions of ordinary being-existence began to be established there, Great Nature was constrained to actualize their presences and also the subsequent process of their existence on the principle of Itoklanoz, that is, according to the results of certain surrounding causes.

"Thereafter, one of these causes has also been the 'degree of the density of the vibrations' of their 'second being-food,' that is, as they themselves would say, the 'degree of condensation of the air they breathe.'

"The point is that this cosmic formation which serves as the second food for beings is also composed according to the second fundamental common cosmic law of the Sacred Triamazikamno, and is also actualized by means of its three heterogeneous cosmic substances.

"And, namely, the first is the emanation of the sun of that system in which this same definite cosmic arising serves as the 'second food' for beings.

"The second are the substances transformed on that planet itself on which the beings fed by this food exist.

"And the third are those substances which are transformed through the other planets of this system and which come to the given planet through their radiations.

"And so, the process of fusion of all those substances required for the normal formation and existence of beings, which are transformed by the planet itself and which actualize the second holy force of the Sacred Triamazikamno, can proceed in the correspondingly required definite proportion only within certain limits of the atmosphere from the surface of planets because, owing to the second grade cosmic law called Tenikdoa, or as your favorites would call it, 'law of gravity,' these substances cannot penetrate beyond a definite height of the atmosphere.

"In my opinion you can yourself apprehend all the subsequent ensuing consequences of this question which I have just now brought to light, and compose data in yourself for your own opinion of the significance of this invention of theirs.

"I think, my boy, that I have now already fully satisfied your curiosity concerning these 'dollar fox-trotting' followers of what is called 'Christian Science.'

"In the name of objective justice it now only remains for me to remark that whatever they may turn into in the future, I had however during my existence among them the possibility of inwardly resting, and for this I ought now to express to them my sincere thanks.

"And you, just you, my heir, to whom has already been transmitted and will be transmitted by inheritance everything acquired by me during my long existence—of course only in so far as you yourself will deserve it by your own conscientious being-existence and honorable service to the ALL-COMMON FATHER MAINTAINER, our ENDLESSNESS—I command you, if you happen for some reason or other to be on the planet Earth, to visit without fail the city of New York, or if by that time this city should no longer exist, then at least stop at that place where it was situated and to utter aloud:

"'In this place my beloved grandfather, my just Teacher Beelzebub, pleasantly passed a few moments of his existence.'

"I even charge you—of course again as the heir to whom, as is general, will devolve the fulfillment of the obligations which his predecessor took upon himself and which for some reason or other were left unfulfilled—specially to turn your attention to and to elucidate a question which greatly interested me and which I personally was unable to elucidate as it was still premature to do so; that is to say, I charge you to elucidate for yourself into what a 'maleficent form' for their descendants—if of course by that time their descendants still continue to arise—will the results have become molded of the 'disease' very widespread at that time, which one of their Misters, by name Onanson, called 'writing itch.'

"And indeed, my boy, having then during my stay there a more or less close relationship with many of them, I very soon found out that almost every one of them either had already written a book, or at that time was writing one, or was getting ready quickly to burst into authorship.

"Although this peculiar 'disease' was then, as I have already said, widespread among almost all the beings of this continent and moreover among the beings of both sexes and without distinction of age, yet among the beings at the beginning of responsible age, that is, as they themselves say, among the 'youth,' and particularly among those who had many pimples on their faces, it was for some reason or other, as it is said, 'epidemical.'

"I must further remark in just this connection that there flourished that specific particularity of the strangeness of the common psyche of these peculiar beings who have taken your fancy, which has already long existed in their collective existence and which has been formulated by the following words: 'the concentration of interests on an idea which has accidentally become the question of the day.'

"Here also, many of them who turned out to be a little, as is said there, 'more cunning,' and in whom the data for the being-impulse called 'instinctively to refrain from all manifestations which may lead surrounding beings similar to oneself into error' were more atrophied, organized various what are called 'schools' and composed all kinds of 'manuals,' in which much attention was given to showing in detail just what the sequence of words should be so that all compositions should be better perceived and assimilated by the reader.

"And thus all those attending these 'schools' and all readers of these 'manuals,' being themselves in regard to Being and in regard to information concerning reality exactly such types as our Teacher Mullah Nassr Eddin defined by the words 'nullities with an atmosphere of unendurable vibrations,' began according to these indications to wiseacre; and since in the first place thanks to various other abnormalities fixed in the conditions of the ordinary existence of the beings of this new grouping, the process of reading has previously in general become an organic need of theirs, and secondly, that it was possible to appreciate the contents of any composition exclusively only by reading it through, and all the other beings of this continent, seduced, what is more, by all kinds of, as they say there, 'loud' titles, read and read, then parallel with this it was definitely noticeable how their mentation, which had already, so to say, become 'diluted' without this, continued to become more 'diluted' and still more 'diluted.'

"I did not lightly say that if by that time their descendants still continue to arise, because among other things I then noticed that same extraordinary particularity in respect of the consequences of the new formation of the planetary body of beings of the female sex which I had already once noticed long before in the process of the ordinary existence of these strange three-brained beings, and parallel with this, I minutely constated among other special observations, the consequences ensuing from this particularity.

"This extraordinary fact occurred there before the loss

of the continent Atlantis, in the process of the existence of a small group of three-brained beings who were concentrated from various large groupings of that time and who existed in isolation on the then famous island called 'Balakhanira,' situated on the west of Atlantis and which was engulfed within the planet at the same time as Atlantis itself.

"The continuation of the race of this small group ceased owing to this same strange particularity of the formation of the planetary body of the beings of the female sex, and this form of cessation of the race was then called by the learned members of the society Akhaldan, 'Dezsoopsentoziroso.'

"This extraordinary particularity was that several centuries before the final cessation of their race, there began gradually to narrow in their beings of the female sex what is called the pelvis.

"The progressiveness of this narrowing was such that two centuries before the final cessation of their race, they were already producing all the accidental conceptions in them and the so to say 'haphazard' forming of these conceptions for their appearance, as is said there, 'in God's World' by the means then called 'Sitrik,' namely, by means of what is now called Caesarian operations."

At this point of Beelzebub's tales, what is called a "crosscurrent" or "agitation" began in the ether which penetrated the whole of the ship *Karnak*. This signified that the passengers of the ship *Karnak* were summoned to the "Djamdjampal," that is, that "refectory" of the ship in which all the passengers together periodically fed on the second and first being-foods.

So Beelzebub, Hassein, and Ahoon ceased their conversation and hastily went off to the Djamdjampal.

CHAPTER 43

Beelzebub's Survey of the Process of the Periodic Reciprocal Destruction of Men, or Beelzebub's Opinion of War

When Beelzebub, Hassein, and Ahoon had returned from the "Djamdjampal" and had resumed their usual places, Hassein, again turning to Beelzebub, said:

"Dear Grandfather! Although thanks to your exhaustive explanations relating to different episodes which proceeded on the planet Earth during the process of the existence of the three-brained beings, I obtained a clear conception and convincing understanding of the surprising strangeness of their psyche, nevertheless the question still arises in me about one particularity of this psyche of theirs which I cannot yet understand at all and which, even taking their strange psyche into account, appears to me not logical. My thoughts constantly return to this perplexing question and were even concentrated on it during the sacred sacrament in the Djamdjampal.

"From all of your explanations concerning the process of the existence of these three-brained beings, I very definitely understood that although during all their responsible existence, particularly after the third Transapalnian perturbation there, they began to have chiefly purely automatic Reason, yet even with this automatic Reason they can mentate fairly often and deliberate so well that they are even able to constate all kinds of more of less exact laws of Nature on their planet, according to which they even invent something themselves.

"At the same time, parallel with this, the mention of that particularity of theirs proper to them alone, namely, the need of periodically occupying themselves with the destruction of each other's existence, runs like a crimson thread through all your tales.

"And so, my dear Grandfather, I cannot at all understand how it can happen that in spite of having existed over such a long period, they have not yet become aware and until now continue to be unaware of the horror of this property of theirs.

"Don't they really ever see that these processes of theirs are the most terrible of all the horrors which can possibly exist in the whole of the Universe, and don't they ever ponder on this matter, so that they might become aware of this horror and find a means of eradicating it?

"Please, Grandfather, tell me why it is so, and which aspects, composing the totality of the strangenesses of their psyche, are the causes of this particularity of theirs?"

Having said this, Hassein again looked expectantly, and with a tense desire to know, at his dear grandfather.

In response to this request of his grandson, Beelzebub continued to look at him with, as it is said, a "remorseful smile" and then, sighing deeply, said:

"Ekh! . . . my dear boy. . . .

"This particularity and all the results ensuing from it are chiefly the cause of all their abnormalities and so to say 'muddled logic.'"

And having again paused a little, he continued:

"Good, I will help you to get clear about this question, the more so as I have already once promised to elucidate it to you in detail.

"Of course, in this case, for the sake of the development of your active mentation, I shall not for this reason give you my personal opinion but will tell you about this also in such a way that you should be able to obtain the necessary material for logical confrontation and, in consequence, for the crystallization in you of the data for your own individual opinion about this matter.

"By the way, you have asked whether they really never ponder on this predisposition of theirs—phenomenally terrible and exclusively inherent in them alone.

"Of course they ponder, of course they see . . .

"A number of them do ponder even very often and, in spite of the automaticity of their Reason, they fully understand that this particularity of theirs, namely, their predisposition to periodic reciprocal destruction, is such an unimaginable horror and such a hideousness that no name can even be found for it.

"Yet, unfortunately, from this pondering of these three-brained beings there, no sense at all is ever obtained.

"And no sense is ever obtained, partly because only isolated beings there ponder over this matter, and partly thanks to the absence there, as is usual, of one common-planetary organization for a single line of action; and therefore, if even the mentioned isolated beings ponder over this question and constate something sensible about this horror, then this constating of theirs is never widely spread and fails to penetrate into the consciousness of other beings. And in addition, it is very sad about this 'sincere pondering' of the beings upon similar questions. I must tell you that thanks to the abnormally established conditions of being-existence there, the 'waking psyche' as it is expressed there, of each one of them gradually becomes from the very beginning of responsible existence such that he can 'think sincerely' and see things in the true light exclusively only if his stomach is so full of first being-food that it is impossible for what are called 'wandering nerves' in it to move, or, as they themselves say, he is 'stuffed quite full'; and besides, all his needs already inherent in him which are unbecoming to three-brained beings and which have become the dominant factors for the whole of his presence, are fully satisfied, of course, only for that given moment.

"And as, owing to those same wrongly established conditions there, not all the beings have the possibility of becoming thus satisfied, then, on this account and for many other reasons, most of them, even with their full desire, can neither think sincerely nor see and sense reality, and therefore 'sincere thinking' and the 'sensing of reality' have already long ago become a very rare luxury on this planet of yours and inaccessible to most of them.

"Only certain beings there who are called 'important' and power-possessing have the possibility of being satisfied to satiety; in truth, it is precisely these terrible beings who it would seem could, owing to their position, do something for the eradication of this evil, or at least diminish it to a certain extent.

"But just these 'important' and power-possessing beings who have the possibility of filling themselves to satiety and who could perhaps do something toward this end, in reality do nothing at all for still quite other reasons.

"And the fundamental causes of this flow from always the same maleficent means fixed in the process of their ordinary being-existence and called by them 'education.'

"This maleficent means is adopted there for all the young during their preparatory age, but especially adopted everywhere in relation to those young beings who later almost always, as a rule, become power-possessing.

"Well then, when these same young beings, who almost always become power-possessing, become responsible beings and begin to bear responsible obligations, they of course do not have any data at all for manifesting what is called 'logical reflection,' owing to the fact that they have not used the time destined by Great Nature exclusively for the purposes of preparing in themselves being-data for a worthy and responsible existence, but waste it only for developing in themselves the properties which flow from the totality of the results of this celebrated education of theirs, which, as a rule, dictates to them how better to give oneself up to what is called 'self calming.'

"Thanks to this abnormal education of theirs, not only is nothing crystallized in them to enable them to reflect and actualize anything effective in practice, but on the contrary, thanks to this abnormal education those many consequences of the properties of the for them accursed organ Kundabuffer devised by the great Angel, now already Archangel Looisos, are gradually formed in them and become organic functions, and, being transmitted by heredity from one generation to another, are in general crystallized in the psyche of these unfortunates.

"Namely, those consequences of the said organ are formed in them, which exist there today under the names of 'egoism,' 'partiality,' 'vanity,' 'self-love,' and so on.

"For such power-possessing or important beings there, our wise Mullah Nassr Eddin also has a very interesting definition, and, namely, he says:

"'The degree of the importance of these people depends only on the number of their corns.'

"And so, my boy . . .

"When these three-brained beings of your planet, particularly of the present time, who have the means of gorging to satiety and of fully satisfying all their other needs and who perhaps could do something for the struggle against this phenomenal evil prevailing on their planet, are satiated, and their mentioned needs are satisfied, and they are seated on what are called their 'soft English divans' in order, as is said there, 'to digest it all'—they do not profit, even during this time so suitable for sincere thinking, by those favorable conditions, but indulge instead in the maleficent self-calming.

"And since it is impossible for all the three-brained beings of the Universe and therefore also for all the beings of your planet to exist without the process of mentation, and since at the same time your favorites wish to have the possibility of indulging very freely in their inner 'evil god self-calming,' they then gradually and very efficiently accustom themselves that a sort of thinking should proceed in them purely automatically, entirely without the participation of any being-effort of their own.

"One must give them their due; in this they have attained perfection, and at the present time their thoughts flow in all directions without any intentional exertion of any part whatsoever of their presence.

"For instance, when after gorging and satisfying themselves these important and power-possessing beings of the Earth are seated on their said divans, the associative thoughts which ought inevitably to flow in them receive shocks from the reflexes of their stomach and sex organs and wander freely in all directions, as they say there, 'to their heart's content,' and so pleasantly free and easy, as if they, that is these thoughts of theirs, were 'strolling of an evening in Paris along the Boulevard des Capucines.'

"When these power-possessing beings of your planet are seated on their soft divans, subjects like the following a-think in them.

"For instance, how to get his revenge on that acquaintance of his, John Smith, who a few days before looked at a woman he 'liked,' not with his right eye but with his left.

"Or this 'digesting' terrestrial power-possessing or important being thinks: 'Why did not my horse come in first yesterday at the races as I expected, but some other?'

"Or, 'Why do those stocks which are in fact quite worthless, go up every day on the market, higher and higher?'

"Or, finally, he thinks something of this kind: 'If I were in John Smith's shoes who invented a new method of breeding flies for making ivory from their skeletons, then from the profits obtained I would do this, that, and the other, and not as that fool, who, like a dog in the manger, will neither himself eat nor let others eat,' and so on in the same strain.

"Still, it does occasionally happen there, that some power-possessing or important being of the Earth suddenly chances to think not under the influences of the reflexes of his stomach and sex organs, but thinks sincerely and quite seriously about these or other questions, with particular regard to this terrifying terrestrial question.

"But even these sincere reflections of the power-possessors occur for the most part also quite automatically from casual external causes of the following kind. Either someone very near to them has had his existence violently terminated during the last such process of theirs, or someone offends them strongly and painfully, or someone stirs their emotions by doing some great favor for them or giving them something which they did not at all expect, or finally, when they really feel the approach of the end of their own existence.

"And in these cases, when the power-possessing beings there sincerely ponder about this phenomenal horror which proceeds on their planet, they are always greatly agitated by it, and of course in this state of theirs they make a vow to undertake at all costs and to actualize everything necessary to put an end to this increasing evil.

"But here lies the trouble, no sooner do the stomachs of these sincerely agitated beings become empty or no sooner do they recover a little from these externally arisen impressions which had dejected them, than they not only instantly forget their vow, but even they themselves again begin consciously or unconsciously to do precisely everything which is generally the cause of the outbreak of these processes between communities.

"As a rule, in consequence of the fact that these power-possessing or important beings there do not use the time foreseen by Great Nature for preparing themselves to become worthy responsible beings—owing chiefly to which during their responsible existence, even in their waking state, all kinds of associations in their common presences almost always flow automatically—therefore they themselves without any individual intentions and at times even half-intentionally try to do everything in such a way that the next process of reciprocal destruction should occur sooner, and they even hope that this next process should proceed on as large a scale as possible.

"Such a monstrous need arises in their abnormal psyche because they expect certain egoistic profits from these processes, either personally for themselves or for their nearest, and with their degenerated mentation they even hope that the greater the scale of the next process, the greater the extent of the said profits to be obtained, either personally for themselves or for their nearest.

"It even sometimes happens there, my boy, that certain of the power-possessing and important beings among your favorites unite and form a special society with the aim of jointly finding out and actualizing in practice some possible means for the abolition of this archcriminal property of theirs.

"Just as I was leaving that solar system forever, there was again there, on your planet, a great deal of talk about the formation of such a society and it seems that they intended to call their new society the 'League of Nations.'

"I said 'again' because they had already many times formed similar societies which always finally died in the same strange way—namely, they always died without any 'death agony.'

"I very well remember when such a society first arose there in the town of Samoniks in the country Tikliamish just at that period when this country was regarded as the chief center of culture for all the three-brained beings of this peculiar planet of yours.

"Then for the first time, just such important beings from among the ordinary beings of most of the communities of the continent Asia assembled at the mentioned place with the aim of jointly drawing up a common agreement that there should never again arise among the different Asiatic communities any cause whatsoever for such 'processes of reciprocal destruction.'

"This society of beings then had as their motto the following sentence: 'God is where man's blood is not shed.'

"But owing to their various personal egoistic and vainglorious aims, the ordinary terrestrial important and power-possessing beings who had then assembled, very soon quarreled among themselves and went their ways home without accomplishing anything.

"Several centuries after the existence of Tikliamish there again arose a similar society of beings there on the same continent Asia, but this time in the country which was then called 'Mongolplanzura.'

"This society existed there with the motto: 'Love one another and God will love you.'

"And this society, having given no positive results for the same reason, ended its existence also in the same manner.

"Later they again formed such a society, but this time in the country which is today called Egypt, and this society began to exist there under the motto: 'If you learn how to create a flea only then dare you kill a man.'

"Still later, the same arose in the country 'Persia' where the following sentence was taken as the motto for this society of theirs: 'All men are divine, but if only one is violently killed by another, then all will be as nothing.'

"On this last occasion which was quite recent, only

about four or five of their centuries ago, such a society was formed also on the continent Asia, in the city which it seems was called 'Mosulopolis,' and at their arising this society was called, 'The-Earth-Is-Equally-Free-for-All.'

"But when some dispute shortly afterwards arose among the members, they renamed their society and it later ended its existence under the new name of: 'The-Earth-Must-Be-Only-for-Men.'

"The members of this latter society, namely, 'The-Earth-Is-Equally-Free-for-All,' might perhaps have accomplished something effective because, in the first place, they had as the basis of their aims an actualizable program and secondly, because they were all, without exception, old and honorable beings who had already had a great deal of experience during their planetary existence and had in consequence become disillusioned about everything that their ordinary planetary existence could in general give them.

"And, thanks to this, they had fewer egoistic, vain, and other properties, on account of which similar societies there usually break down.

"Above all, from this society something effective might have resulted because there was not a single power-possessing being among them, since on account of their same egoistic and vainglorious aims these beings sooner or later always dispatch all the accomplishments of any society whatsoever of a common planetary character of which they happen to be members—and moreover dispatch them with 'musical accompaniment'—to the famous swine of our Mullah Nassr Eddin, which always gobble up everything, without what are called 'parlor manners.'

"These terrestrial power-possessing and important beings, particularly the contemporary ones, at times do not frustrate such national affairs from which they might expect considerable gain personally for themselves or for the beings of their own caste.

"From the tasks of such a society good results might be obtained for all the beings of their planet without distinction of caste, but then, as soon as the affairs of this society begin to be somewhat difficult, or, as it is said, a crisis arises, these tasks instantly bore the terrestrial power-possessing beings and even at the mention of them or when by association they themselves remember about them, expressions of martyrdom immediately appear on their faces.

"And the reason why also nothing resulted from the labors of those beings who called their society 'The-Earth-Is-Equally-Free-for-All'—although almost everything was done by them for this aim that was possible to do there in the conditions which almost always reign on this incomparable planet—I shall tell you a little later, and even rather in detail, because the information concerning the causes of the fall of just this society, which was formed by your favorites in their attempt to eradicate or at least to diminish this archcriminal property which had been implanted in them, is once again very characteristic for your elucidation of the strangeness of their psyche in general and at the same time this information will serve as material for the understanding to a certain extent of the chief objective causes why these terrifying processes of reciprocal destruction proceed among them.

"And now as regards this contemporary society about which I spoke to you and told you that it was formed by the three-brained beings of your planet with the same aim of jointly elucidating and actualizing in practice corresponding measures for the total cessation on their planet of this terrifying process, and which contemporary society of theirs will be called or is already called the League of Nations, then if you wish to know my sincere opinion,

I am more than sure that this time also nothing effective will come of it for two reasons.

"The first reason will become clear to you at the end of this tale of mine; and the second reason is that this property has already entered into the three-brained beings of that planet Earth, as is said into their 'flesh and blood.' And just as nothing could be accomplished by the beings of their planet of former epochs, who, becoming responsible beings had even attained in respect of Being at least to what is called 'self-remembering,' then all the more, nothing effective can be done, devised, or actualized by beings with that Reason which the beings of this contemporary society possess and who in respect of Being are only perfected to the degree which our dear Mullah Nassr Eddin defines by the notion expressed in the following words: 'Look! Look! He already begins to distinguish mama from papa!'

"Still, I must remark that these contemporary important and power-possessing beings who are or will be members of this contemporary society will achieve personally for themselves by this new contrivance of theirs one 'most formidable' and 'most useful' result, namely, thanks to this 'official society' of theirs, they will have still another as it is said very plausible excuse for drawing wool over the eyes of their what are called 'proprietresses,' who are for these terrestrial contemporary power-possessing beings either their 'wife,' 'mistress,' 'mother-in-law,' or finally, the 'assistant' in some large store, and so on.

"Whereupon, thanks to this new official society of theirs, they will have the opportunity of passing the time tranquilly among their friends, important and power-possessing beings like themselves, and at these official 'five o'clocks' which without doubt will be very often arranged ostensibly for affairs connected as it were with the aims of this important official society of theirs, they will be able to pass the time without the silent though terrifying glances and watchfulness on the part of their 'proprietresses.'

"Such societies of power-possessing beings usually arise there at the beginning of the end of the great processes of reciprocal destruction. And almost each time they arise in the following way:

"A number of them, namely, from among those power-possessors, personally suffered during their last process of reciprocal destruction such 'heavy losses'—the 'momentum of the action' of which had not yet ceased in their common presence and had engendered for the general functioning of their psyche a certain combination—that the data in their subconsciousness for the arising of the being-impulse named 'conscience,' had begun by itself to take part in the functioning of that 'automatic consciousness' of theirs, which had already long ago become habitual to them; that is to say, there was obtained by itself in their general psyche that combination about which the Most Saintly Ashiata Shiemash had dreamed for all the three-brained beings of that ill-fated planet.

"Well then, my boy, owing to this, when the said power-possessing beings meet together and discuss a great deal about this terrible property of theirs, they gradually begin to see it almost in its true light and a genuine sincere desire just begins to appear in them to do everything possible to attain to the abolition of this appalling horror proceeding on their planet.

"And so, if it happens that several such terrestrial power-possessing beings with so to say 'resurrected conscience' should chance to meet, and, thanks to a long mutual influence, see and feel reality almost in its true light, then they unite in order jointly to find some possibility or other of actualizing these sincere wishes of theirs.

"In this manner all such societies formed there usually begin.

"These beings might, perhaps, somehow or other achieve good results, but the evil lies in this, that, as a rule, other of these terrestrial important and power-possessing beings very soon enter such societies and begin to take part in them.

"These latter enter and take part in the tasks of such societies not because their conscience also begins to speak—far from it. They join only because, according to all those same abnormally established conditions of ordinary being-existence, they, being important and power-possessing, must as a matter of course be members of and participate in every 'important' society.

"When these other terrestrial important and power-possessing beings enter such societies and also begin to participate in their affairs, then they, with their personal egoistic and vainglorious aims, as a rule not only very soon send all the tasks of the society and everything that has been done by the beings with 'resurrected consciences' as is said 'flying up the chimney,' but as a rule, they also very soon, as it is also said there, 'put genuine spokes into the wheels of the first founders of these societies.'

"And therefore, these societies of beings which are formed there for common-planetary welfare always quickly die—and die, as I already told you, even without 'death agony.'

"Concerning the effective results obtained from all these good beginnings of the important beings, our worthy Mullah Nassr Eddin has also a very wise saying, namely, he says:

"'Past centuries have shown us that Karabaghian asses will never sing like nightingales, nor will they refrain from indulging their noble taste for real Shooshoonian thistles.'

"Here apropos, it will be opportune for you also to

know that during the long centuries of my attentive observations of the three-brained beings of the planet Earth I never once noticed that in any of the societies formed by them with the aim of jointly devising means for the happy existence of the great masses—which societies there, now and then, also happen to exist—did beings ever participate who had more or less objective Reason, to which, as I have already told you, many there did nevertheless attain by their perseverant efforts in their aim for self-perfection.

"In the course of observations during my last sojourn there I cleared up, among other things, that the beings with objective Reason do not happen to be in these societies for the following reasons:

"The point is that in order to participate in any society whatsoever, a being must always of necessity be important and such a being there among them, thanks once again to the abnormally established conditions of being-existence, can only be one who either has a great deal of money or who becomes what is called 'famous' among the other beings there.

"And since especially during recent times only those beings can become famous and important among them in whom the mentioned sacred function, namely 'being-conscience,' is entirely absent, then in consequence of the fact that this sacred function in the presences of beings is in general always associated with everything that represents and is Objective Reason, then, of course, those three-brained beings with Objective Reason always have conscience as well, and consequently such a being with conscience, will never be 'important' among the other beings.

"That is why the beings with Pure Reason there never have had and never will have the possibility of taking part in the societies of beings who are formed of important and power-possessing beings.

"And regarding the same question it happens there just as our dear Mullah Nassr Eddin has already once said, namely: 'This is the highest punishment: pull at the tail the mane gets stuck, pull at the mane and the tail gets stuck.'

"Whatever might have been, yet as I have already said, your favorites at the present time again wish to find possible ways and means for the abolition of this terrible property of theirs which has become inherent in them and fastened on their psyche as strongly as the consequences of the properties of the organ Kundabuffer.

"And, of course, these members of the contemporary society, the League of Nations, will endeavor to attain this abolition by all kinds of regulations and various agreements devised by them, by which means those ancient beings also endeavored to attain it, that is to say, by those ways and means by which in my opinion it is now already absolutely impossible there to attain anything 'effective.'

"From this contrivance of your contemporary favorites some advantage might be derived, even quite a great one, but only for their inevitable newspapers, for drawing-room conversations, and, of course, for the various Hasnamussian manipulations of the terrestrial as they are called 'stock-jugglers.'

"The state of affairs in regard to this terrifying evil there is at the present time already such that to attain the immediate total destruction on the surface of their planet of this, as I said, hideous property which has already entered their flesh and blood, is not only a meaningless task for their miserable Reason, but is in general almost impossible.

"However, my boy, even these contemporary beings of this contemporary common-planetary society the League of Nations, might perhaps—in spite of the fact that impartial Reason, proper to the presence of all three-brained beings who have already attained responsible age, is absent in them—also achieve positive results in the fundamental aim they have set themselves, if they occupy themselves with the solving and actualizing of only those questions which are in the sphere of their competence and powers.

"Knowing their, so to say, 'ways,' I am quite sure that they will not occupy themselves with those questions which are within the reach of their understanding.

"They would like to do and really do everything in such a direction that these processes of reciprocal destruction should cease immediately and forever.

"If, indeed, with all their Being they were aware of the whole objective terror of these processes and desired sincerely jointly to eradicate this evil from the surface of their planet, then they would willy-nilly penetrate into the essence of this question and would understand that such an inherency which had become fixed in their psyche during hundreds of centuries can never be decrystallized in the course of a few decades.

"If they understood this, they would not attempt to decide or to actualize anything in this respect for the welfare of their contemporaries, but would direct and use all their attention, all their powers, and all their possibilities, having only the beings of future generations in view.

"For instance, if instead of wiseacring now and as is still said there 'Don-Quixoting' with the aim of immediately attaining the total cessation of these processes of theirs, they were to occupy themselves with the eradication of the conviction, which has become fixed in their ordinary process of existence, of the virtue of two notions they have; that is to say, if they would try to attain the abolition of the practice of exalting certain of the participants in these processes to what are called 'heroes' and rewarding them with honors and what are called 'orders,' and also if they would try to attain the abolition even of one of their illustrious 'sciences' from among their many 'Hasnamussian sciences,' invented by certain pimpled beings among them, in which it is nonchalantly proved that the periodic reciprocal destruction on the Earth is very, very necessary, and that if it did not exist an intolerable overpopulation would result on the Earth, and such economic horrors would ensue that men-beings would begin to eat one another.

"If they would attain the abolition of these two practices which have already become firmly fixed in the process of their abnormal ordinary being-existence, then, thanks to the abolition of the first, they would eradicate forever the greater part of those 'automatic factors' which make the psyche of the growing generation also predisposed to be subject to that special property on account of which they always fall into that state into which it has already become without fail habitual for them to fall during these processes; and thanks to the second they would help towards this, that there might not reach to the beings of future times at least one of those idiotic ideas from the number of already without this sufficiently numerous similar ideas constantly arising there, which are transmitted from generation to generation as 'something' lawful and indubitable and which all together are partly the cause of the formation in their presences of those properties not one of which is becoming to three-centered beings of our Great Megalocosmos and among the number of which there belongs also that property inherent in them alone which engenders in them even 'doubt in the existence of Divinity'; and owing chiefly to this doubt there has almost entirely disappeared from their common presences the possibility of the precipitation of those data which should without fail be precipitated in the presences of all three-brained beings, the totality of which data engenders in them the impulse, called the 'instinctive sensing,' of those certain cosmic truths, which are always felt even by all one-centered and two-centered beings, wherever they might breed in the whole of the Universe.

"But the misfortune for all the other ordinary favorites of yours is that these power-possessing and important beings assembled from the whole of the planet do not begin to occupy themselves with these questions, considering them to be beneath their dignity.

"What next! Such 'important' members of such 'important' societies suddenly occupying themselves with such trivial matters!

"In general, in consequence of the fact that every kind of data for individual manifestation have already quite ceased to be crystallized in most of these three-brained beings who have taken your fancy, particularly the contemporary ones, and they manifest themselves only according to the dictates of the consequences of the properties of the organ Kundabuffer, they therefore do not like to occupy themselves with such affairs which are within their Reason and within their power, but occupy themselves always with decisions of such questions which are incomparably higher than their Reason.

"Thanks to this 'feature' of their strange psyche, one other peculiar and in the highest degree strange 'psychic-organic need' had been formed in them during the last twenty centuries.

"The chief manifestation of just this psychic-organic need of theirs consists in this, that each of them must always of necessity as they say 'teach others sense,' or 'put them on the right road.'

"Do you know, my boy, my mentioning this exceptional

feature of their character, inherent in all of them without exception, leads me to the thought of the desirableness of explaining to you at this point about their strange psyche and to give you the advice like that which that good old fellow, our Ahoon, already once gave you, when I ended my explanation about the contemporary terrestrial illustrious 'Art.'

"He then said, among other things, that if for some reason or other you happen to exist there on the planet Earth, and to mix with these strange three-brained beings, then you must always be very careful with those contemporary types there who are called 'representatives of Art' and never offend them, and thus not make 'violent' enemies among them.

"At that time, our dear Ahoon, bearing in mind their numerous weaknesses, such as their self-love, pride, vanity, and still many others, indicated to you in which cases just which of these specific properties of theirs it was necessary, as he expressed it, to 'tickle.'

"He even then explained to you in detail about what and how it was necessary to speak to them so that they should always have good relations with you and so that they should always and everywhere praise you and only speak good about you.

"Concerning this advice of his I can say nothing bad; it cannot be denied, it is ideal for the types he mentioned.

"These contemporary representatives of Art there in fact have in great abundance the specific properties enumerated by our dear Ahoon and if on each occasion you 'tickle' these particular properties of theirs, they will indeed 'worship' you and in everything always behave towards you not worse than those who were called there 'Asklaian-slaves.'

"But though this advice of his is excellent and even indispensable for existence among them, I personally do not consider it practical for you; not practical in the first place, because since not all the beings of the Earth are like representatives of Art, this advice does not apply to all of them in general; and secondly, because it will be inconvenient for you always to have to remember all these numerous particularities and each time to stop and think on which occasion which of these numerous weaknesses of theirs must be 'tickled.'

"I wish to point out to you one great 'secret' of their psyche, namely, I wish to point out to you only one particularity of theirs which, if you know how to profit by it, might create in each one of them the same effect in their manifestations about which Ahoon spoke.

"If you will act upon them through this same particularity, then you will not only be on very good terms with them all, but even, if you wish, you will be able, knowing this 'secret' of their psyche, fully to ensure your tranquil and happy existence there both as regards 'money' necessarily required there, as well as other conveniences, the taste and blissful significance of which our dear Teacher expressed by the words 'Roses, Roses.'

"You, no doubt, my boy, have already guessed that by this secret of their psyche I refer just to this same, as I called it, 'psycho-organic-need' of theirs to 'teach others sense' and 'to put them on the right road.'

"This special property formed in their psyche, thanks of course also always to the same abnormally established conditions of ordinary being-existence, becomes as it were—when each one of them already becomes a responsible being—an obligatory part of his presence.

"Everyone there without exception has this 'psycho-organic need'; old and young, men and women and even those whom they call 'prematurely born.'

"The mentioned 'particular need' of theirs arises in them, in its turn, thanks to another particular property of theirs which is that from the very moment when each of them acquires the capacity of distinguishing between 'wet' and 'dry,' then, carried away by this attainment, he ceases forever to see and observe his own abnormalities and defects, but sees and observes those same abnormalities and defects in others.

"It has already become customary there at the present time that all your favorites always teach others like themselves even things the notion of which they have not even dreamed of, and the joke of it is that if these others do not learn from him, or at least, do not pretend that they wish to learn, then they are not only offended, but even always inwardly very sincerely indignant; and on the contrary, if one of these others should learn 'sense' from them or at least pretend that he is very anxious to learn it, then these beings will not only 'love' and 'respect' him but will feel fully satisfied and greatly delighted.

"It must be remarked here that only in these circumstances can your favorites speak about others without malice and without criticism.

"And so, my boy . . .

"I strongly advise you that if for any reason you have to exist among them, always pretend that you wish to learn something from them. Act in the same way towards their children and then you will not only be on excellent terms with them all, but the whole family will even look on you as the honored friend of the house.

"Always remember that any one of them, however insignificant he himself may be in essence, looks down, owing always to his self-conceit ensuing from this particular property, with contempt upon the conduct and actions of others, especially if their conduct and actions sharply contradict his own subjectively established point of view, and in these cases he, as I have already said, usually becomes inwardly sincerely offended and indignant.

"I might as well here remark that thanks to this property of your favorites always to grow indignant at the defects of others around them, they make their existence, already wretched and abnormal without this, objectively unbearable.

"Thanks to this constant indignation, the ordinary being-existence of these unfortunates flows almost always with unproductive what are called 'moral sufferings,' and these futile moral sufferings of theirs continue, as a rule, by momentum to act for a very long time on their psyche, so to say 'Semzekionally' or, as they would say there on your planet, 'depressingly'; that is, they ultimately become, of course without the participation of their consciousness, 'Instruarian' or, as they would say, 'nervous.'

"And then they become in the process of their ordinary being-existence completely 'uncontrolled,' even in those being-manifestations of theirs, which have nothing in common with the primary causes which have evoked this 'Instruarness' or 'nervousness' of theirs.

"Only thanks to this property of theirs alone, 'to be indignant at the defects of others,' their existence has become gradually even archtragic-comic.

"For instance, at every step there you meet a picture of this sort:

"These freaks lose, so to say, that outer mask which thanks to the same maleficent means existing there, called 'education,' most of them have little by little learned to wear from their childhood and thanks to which they can very well conceal their genuine inner and outer trifling significance from others, and in consequence they automatically become slaves of others to the degree of humiliation; or, as they themselves say there, they fall as regards all their inner experience, under somebody's 'thumb'; for instance, under the 'thumb' of 'wife' or 'mistress,' or of such another who by some means has ferreted out the inner insignificance of the given terrestrial being, and thus the latter ceases to have for them this artificial mask.

"And indeed, it is just such a terrestrial being under somebody's thumb who, as a rule, is more indignant than anyone else at other beings of their planet, as for instance at some king, who for some reason or other is unable to keep in submission tens or hundreds of thousands of his community. And it is just such beings who are under somebody's thumb who usually write various manuals in which they show in detail how and what must be done for the good 'government' of others.

"Or again, when one of the contemporary beings of this peculiar planet, whose heart as they say always 'sinks into his boots' from fright when, for instance, a mouse runs past him, learns that so and so on meeting a tiger felt a little timid, then this 'hero' will be inwardly extremely indignant with him and will, without fail, in conversation with his friends, 'foaming at the mouth' denounce him and prove that he is a vile, criminal 'coward' for having been frightened by such a 'mere' tiger.

"And yet again the various books and manuals concerning also what must be done and how, and what must not be done on meeting a tiger or other similar being, are written by these 'mouse-unflinching-heroes' there.

"Or, further, one of them who has a score of various as it is said there 'chronic diseases,' thanks to which for whole weeks at a time his stomach does not work and his whole body is covered with all kinds of malignant pimples, from which diseases he of course suffers day and night—in short, such a being there who for many years has been a genuine 'walking anatomical museum' of all the diseases existing on that planet—is always more indignant than anyone else when someone has carelessly caught, let us say, a cold.

"And these walking anatomical museums there invariably instruct others with great authority how to get rid of this cold and it is precisely they alone who write various books and manuals concerning all kinds of other diseases there and expound in minute detail how to guard against and get rid of them.

"At every step one might also observe such an absurdity as this: One of them who even does not know in the least what that ordinary tiny being which often bites him, called 'flea,' looks like, writes a 'huge volume' or draws up a special what is called 'popular lecture' that the flea whose bite made the neck of a certain historical King Nokhan swell, had on its left paw an 'abnormal orange-crimson growth of a peculiar strange form.'

"Well then, if this expert in fleas there will write his voluminous work or if he will read for a whole evening his popular lecture on the 'orange-crimson growth' on the mentioned flea, then if anyone will not believe him and will express his doubt to his face, he will not only be offended but even greatly indignant; and he will be indignant chiefly because this somebody is such a what is called 'ignoramus,' that he has even not yet heard anything about the 'truths' communicated to him by this 'expert.'

"Thanks to all the aforementioned, such pictures are met with at every step there on your planet in the existence of these strange three-brained beings, that only from observing and studying them every normal being existing there, if he will indeed take in and study his perceptions, might become fully instructed in all branches of general objective science.

"For the satisfying of your favorites' astonishingly strange need, as is said there, not to suffer, they must always have at least one 'victim' for their teachings, but among a number of them who have acquired for some reason or other in these manifestations of theirs a certain authority over others and who have become in consequence by increasing habit more impudent, the appetite grows to the point of acquiring an always greater number of these 'victims.'

"Yes, my boy, when you will exist among them and will be a witness of these incongruous being-manifestations, then, even in spite of the fact that you know the cause of these incongruities, you will be unable, as they express it, not to 'laugh' inwardly and at the same time with the whole of your Being you will pity these unfortunates, and with your 'inner laughter' there will gradually be mixed by itself what is called 'an-essence-palnassoorian-grief.'

"The same particularity of the psyche of the three-centered beings there is especially strongly developed there among the beings belonging to their caste, called the 'intelligentsia.'

"The word intelligentsia itself almost denotes that notion there which we define by the words 'force-in-oneself.'

"Yet, though by its essence the word intelligentsia has there almost the same sense, nevertheless the beings there, particularly the contemporary ones, for some reason or other call by this word just those beings who are the exact opposite of what this word denotes.

"The word intelligentsia is also taken from the ancient Greek language.

"It is interesting to notice that this same word was used also by the Romans; but having taken it from the Greeks not by its sense but by its sound, they later imagined that the roots of this word belonged to their own language.

"But among the ancient Greeks this word denoted a being so perfected that he was already able to direct his functions as he wished, and not for instance as occurs with every what is called inanimate cosmic formation, every action of which proceeds only as a reaction to external causes.

"Such beings, no doubt, are also still met with there on your planet as approximately answer to this sense of the word, but only among those contemporary beings of the planet Earth who are considered, according to the understanding of most of the beings there, as 'unintelligent.'

"In my opinion, if those beings especially of the most recent times who are called there intelligentsia would simply be called 'mechanogentsia,' then perhaps this would be more correct.

"It would be more correct because the contemporary intelligentsia there can themselves not only give absolutely no direction at all to their being-functions, but there are already finally atrophied in them even those data for impulses of essence-initiative for daily being-existence which in general are always placed by Great Nature herself in all three-centered beings at their arising.

"During their responsible existence these intelligentsia beings there always act or manifest only when they receive corresponding shocks from outside, and it is these same shocks proceeding from outside which give them the possibility of becoming correspondingly animated and of experiencing, only through the unrolling of the series of former corresponding automatic perceptions already present in them and not depending at all on their own wish or will; and these external shocks of theirs for the said kind of experiencing are usually in the first place animate or inanimate things accidentally coming within the sphere of their organs of perception of visibility; secondly, the various beings they meet; thirdly, the sounds or words reverberating where they happen to be; fourthly, scents accidentally perceived by their sense of smell; and finally, unaccustomed sensations that proceed from time to time during the functioning of their planetary body, or as they say, their 'organism,' and so on.

"But never do their outer manifestations in general nor those inner-being-impulses of theirs, which ought to be under the directive of their being-'I,' proceed according to their own wish resulting from the whole of their entire presence.

"I must here tell you further that certain of those terrestrial 'intelligentsics,' in whom during the period of their responsible existence certain already established forms of their inner functioning have, for various reasons, become definitely changed, are no longer called by the other terrestrial beings 'intelligentsics' but are given other names composed of different words, or, more exactly, of the roots of the words of ancient Greek.

"Namely, they name them:

'Bureaucrats'
'Plutocrats'
'Theocrats'
'Democrats'
'Zevrocrats'
'Aristocrats'

and so on. . . .

"The first of the names enumerated, namely, bureaucrats, is given to those intelligentsics in whom the series of their ordinary automatic associations already present in them which engender experiencings are limited, that is to say, however varied the shocks coming from without may be, associations are evoked in these bureaucrats of always the same experiencings which thanks to the frequent repetition acquire their own specific character and manifest quite independently without the participation of any separate spiritualized being-part whatsoever of their common presence.

"And as regards the beings of the second of the enumerated states, that is, those who also after a certain transformation of their psyche are called by other beings plutocrats, then to the beings thus called, those of the intelligentsics there are promoted who previously, during the period of their responsible existence, were able very artistically to get all the honest, that is 'naïve,' fellow countrymen of theirs they came across, into their toils, thanks to which they become the owners of a great quantity of what is called there 'money' and 'slaves.'

"Here, bear in mind that it is just from these terrestrial types that most Hasnamuss-individuals arise.

"When I was there, during my investigations of the questions which interested me, I chanced to learn the secret of the origin of this word plutocrat.

"As I have already told you, during the last twenty-five centuries there every suspicious notion and every suspicious thing has for some reason or other been called by ancient Greek words; likewise these names, as bureaucrats, aristocrats, democrats, and so on, which express in themselves suspicious notions, are also composed of two ancient Greek words.

"For instance, the word bureaucrat consists of two words: 'buro' which means 'chancellery' and 'crat' which means 'to keep' or 'to hold.'

"And both of these words together mean: 'those . . . who manage or keep the whole chancellery.'

"And as regards the word plutocrat, it seems that the history of its origin is somewhat different and does not go very far back.

"This word was formed only seven or eight of their centuries ago.

"Although these types already existed in ancient Greece, also, yet they were then called there 'plusiocrats.'

"Several centuries ago, however, when many of these 'types' were developed there and when it became clear that the other beings of the Earth had somehow to dignify them with a title, then those beings there who at that time were in charge of such questions invented for them this name plutocrat.

"It seems that they then deliberated and pondered a very long time precisely what name to invent for them. They deliberated and pondered a long time because they already very well understood that these types on their planet are scoundrels of the deepest dye, and already so to say, saturated by every kind of Hasnamussness to the marrow of their bones.

"At first in order to dignify them they wished to invent some or other very 'forceful' word corresponding to their inner significance; but later they became afraid of doing so, because these terrestrial types, thanks to what is called 'ill-gotten' gains, had already then acquired 'force and power' far greater perhaps than that of their kings. And they were afraid that if they dignified them by just such a word as would define their real significance, then they might be greatly offended and begin to do still more harm to the other beings; and therefore they ultimately decided to be cunning and invented this word thanks to which they could call them by their real name and at the same time appear to 'dignify' them.

"The mentioned beings of that time achieved this in the following way:

"As the title of these terrestrial types had of course also to be composed of two ancient Greek words and as all such names have the ancient Greek word 'crat' as their second half, then, in order that the new word might not strike anyone's eye, they left in it this same ancient Greek consonance.

"The first half, however, of this word was not taken from the ancient Greek as was usually done, but from the what is called 'Russian language,' namely, they took the Russian word 'plut'—in Russian 'plut' means 'rogue'—and in this way obtained plutocrat.

"These terrestrial beings then indeed attained their aim as perfectly as possible because at the present time there on your planet both these terrestrial parasites themselves and also all the other beings of the Earth are quite content with this 'title.'

"These terrestrial monsters are so satisfied with their title that, out of swagger, they go about in top hats, even on weekdays.

"And the other terrestrial beings are also satisfied, since they call these 'freaks' by their genuine names, not only without making them angry, but even causing them to strut like 'turkey cocks.'

"As regards the third of the names I enumerated—namely, theocrats—by this title those 'intelligentsics' there were then dignified in whose common presences in the psycho-organic sense there proceeded almost the same 'perturbation' as in those who became plutocrats.

"The difference between the plutocrats and the theocrats there is only this, that the first act upon their surroundings for the satisfaction of their Hasnamussian needs through that function which is called among them 'trust'; while the second act through that function which has gradually replaced in your favorites the sacred function that serves all the three-brained beings as one of the three sacred paths for self-perfecting, and this function they call by the name 'faith.'

"In order that you should obtain a more complete notion about these theocrats, it will be sufficient, if I relate to you once more one of the sayings of our highly esteemed Mullah Nassr Eddin. Concerning these theocrats there he once uttered something very strange.

"Namely, he said: 'Isn't it all one to the poor flies how they are killed? By a kick of the hooves of horned devils, or by a stroke of the beautiful wings of divine angels?'

"And concerning those types there whom all others called democrats, it is first of all necessary to tell you that these types there do not always come from the so to say 'hereditary intelligentsics'; for the greater part they in the first place happen to be simple ordinary terrestrial beings and only afterwards when they chance to become intelligentsics and when with functions present in them degenerated also from the sacred function of 'Conscience,' almost the same proceeds in them as among the future plutocrats and theocrats—they are transformed into just these democrats.

"Here it might as well be remarked that when some of these democrats for some reason or other occasionally occupy the places of the power-possessing beings, then a very, very rare cosmic phenomenon sometimes occurs from their actions, namely, as Mullah Nassr Eddin says, 'the very corns turn pedicures.'

"And this rare phenomenon occurs in my opinion because when the democrats there chance to occupy the places of the power-possessing beings, they have in themselves no inherited aptitudes at all for instinctively being able to direct others and in consequence they are quite unable to direct the existence of beings who happen to be in their power.

"Our priceless Teacher Mullah Nassr Eddin has also for these terrestrial types a corresponding sentence; each time he recites it he first raises his arms to Heaven and only then with great reverence pronounces:

"'Thanks be to Thee, Great and Just CREATOR, that by

Thy abundant and just grace it is so ordained that cows do not fly like pretty little birds.'

"Now, my boy, from the various intelligentsics enumerated by me it remains for me to tell you about those terrestrial types whom the other beings call zevrocrats and aristocrats, who are distinguished by the cognomens given to them, such as 'emir,' 'count,' 'khan,' 'prince,' 'melik,' 'baron,' and so on, the consonance of which for some reason or other acts extremely pleasantly on that function of your favorites which is always very strongly expressed in them, which remains in them up to their very death and which is called 'vanity.'

"And I must frankly confess to you, that it is very difficult to explain about these types there not only in ordinary speech but also in the language of our most wise Mullah Nassr Eddin.

"The most we can say of them is that they are simply 'jokes of nature.'

"Still, I must say that although both these types there among your favorites are called differently, yet in fact these same aristocrats and zevrocrats are similar in every respect and have exactly identical inner properties.

"Remember I have already told you that there on your planet, in various communities, there exist two kinds, as is said there, of 'state organization.'

"One is called a 'monarchic' state organization and the other a 'republican.'

"In the communities where a republican state organization exists, these types are called zevrocrats; but where a monarchic state organization exists, they are called aristócrats.

"Trying to give you at least some notion about these two terrestrial types, I think it will be best if I tell you about one of my embarrassments which occurred to me every time when, being on your planet, I accidentally happened to meet these 'misconceptions.' At chance meetings with them, one thing chiefly surprised me—how could this kind of terrestrial three-brained type exist on your peculiar planet almost as long as the other three-brained beings there?

"Such a question was evoked in me by the beings there who belong to the caste of the bureaucrats, yet nevertheless as regards them one might still explain this to you, at least 'more or less.' Although the series of experiencings in them is also very limited, yet at any rate they actually have them; they have them at least for every hour of the day and night.

"All the experiencings, however, of these aristocrats and zevrocrats there, according to my observation, can be reduced to only three series.

"The first concerns the question of food; the second consists of the recollections associated with the former functionings of their sexual organs; and the third relates to the memories of their first nurse.

"And how the beings, who have in all only three series of such experiencings, could have the length of their existence the same as other beings on the surface of your planet, will always be for me an insoluble puzzle.

"It is said that about this same puzzling question, that is, about how these terrestrial types manage to exist on the surface of the planet, even the great cunning Lucifer once grew very thoughtful, and he grew so intensely thoughtful that all the hairs of the tip of his tail turned quite gray.

"About these mentioned so to say 'jokes of nature,' it remains for me only to attempt to explain to you why such a sharp difference exists there in the names of one and the same kind of being.

"I said 'attempt' because I myself do not know exactly the cause of it, yet, knowing the roots of both words from which these names were formed, I think I can presume with great certainty that it was obtained thanks to a certain custom existing there.

"I must tell you that your favorites there for some reason or other delight in sometimes arranging what are called 'puppet shows.'

"For some reason or other it also pleases them that these same zevrocrats or aristocrats should also take part in these 'puppet plays' of theirs, and accordingly they drag them also into these 'puppet shows.'

"As these beings there are in themselves already quite vacuous and consequently feeble, it becomes necessary during these 'puppet shows' for other beings of the given community to support them.

"And simply from the method of their supporting, that is to say, by which arm they are supported, the difference in name was obtained; in the communities, namely, where 'monarchic state organization' exists, it has already long ago been the custom to support them with the right arm, and hence in these communities such types are called aristocrats.

"And in the communities in which a 'republican state organization' exists they are supported with the left arm, and hence they are called zevrocrats.

"Concerning in general a similar difference in the names there of terrestrial beings, another remarkable saying of our wise Mullah Nassr Eddin comes to my mind which he himself once told me personally.

"Once we spoke about the difference in the legal proceedings and in the sentences passed between the Turkish and Persian 'kazi,' that is, magistrates; and concerning the equality of their justice, he then said:

"'Ekh! My dear friend!

"'Is there such a thing anywhere on Earth as a wise legal examination of men's guilt?

"'The kazi are the same everywhere, only their names are different. In Persia they are called Persian, in Turkey, Turkish.

"'And that is just as it is everywhere on Earth; donkeys are alike, they are only differently called.

"'For instance, the species of donkey breeding in the Caucasus is called "Karabaghian"; and precisely the same kind of donkey breeding in Turkestan is called "Khorassanian."'

"And this wise sentence of his was thereafter always imprinted in my brain; and during my existence on your planet I always remembered it when I had any comparison to make.

"May his name be praised forever on that planet where he arose and was formed!

"And so, my boy!

"I repeat once more! If for some reason or other you have to be on their planet, bear always in mind that the weakness about which I have told you is most strongly developed in the most ordinary intelligentsics there and in those who ordinarily spring from them and belong to one or another of the enumerated castes with the names ending in 'crat.'

"Well, now, my boy, after this digression which I have made for your practical benefit, let us return again to the serious question touched upon; I shall begin with the history promised you about how the society of terrestrial beings which had as its motto 'The-Earth-Is-Equally-Free-for-All' arose and fell, because the information about this will give you the possibility to understand well just about that first and chief cause why there on your planet this terrible process of periodic reciprocal destruction by these unfortunate three-brained beings of our Great Megalocosmos must already almost inevitably proceed.

"And likewise you will learn how the, so to say, local

Nature—when something unforeseen hinders its correct functioning for the purposes of the common-cosmic Trogoautoegocrat—adapts itself so that its results should correspondingly blend with the harmony of this most great cosmic law.

"The said society of terrestrial beings-men arose, as I have already told you, six or seven centuries ago on the continent Asia in a town then existing under the name of Mosulopolis.

"And it arose from the following cause:

"Just at that period, the processes I have mentioned were flowing particularly frequently on just that same continent.

"These processes occurred partly between different communities and partly within the limits of these communities themselves; and these latter processes afterwards came to be called 'civil wars.'

"One of the chief causes of these terrible processes which became frequent both between and within communities on the continent Asia was, at that period, a religion, then only just formed, which had been fantastically founded on the teaching of a genuine messenger of our ENDLESSNESS—Saint Mohammed.

"The foundation of the said society was then first laid by the brothers of the fraternity then existing in Central Asia under the name of 'The Assembly of the Enlightened.'

"Here it must be noticed that in those days the brothers of this fraternity were beings who were very much venerated by other three-brained beings around them of almost the whole of that planet, and hence this brotherhood was sometimes also called 'The-Assembly-of-All-the-Living-Saints-of-the-Earth.'

"This brotherhood of the three-brained terrestrial beings had already long before been formed of such beings who had also noticed in themselves the consequences of the properties of the organ Kundabuffer and had banded together to work collectively for their deliverance from these properties.

"And so, when on their continent Asia these terrible processes of reciprocal destruction there became already too frequent, certain brothers of the said fraternity, with the most venerable Brother Olmantaboor at their head, just decided for the first time to try whether it would not be possible to obtain by some means, if not the total abolition of this terrible phenomenon proceeding on their planet, at least the reduction of this crying evil.

"Having devoted themselves to the carrying out of this decision of theirs they then began to visit various countries of the continent Asia and everywhere very movingly preached the colossal criminality and sin of these actions of men and in this way they found many people earnestly with them.

"And as a consequence of all their impartial and truly philanthropic labors, there was formed in the city Mosulopolis the mentioned large and serious society of men-beings under the title, 'The-Earth-Is-Equally-Free-For-All.'

"Already quite from the beginning, the members of this society of men-beings actualized to this end many things which no beings of the Earth, either before or since, were able to actualize.

"And they were able to do this, only because the program itself from the very beginning was very well drawn up in respect of its actualizability in the conditions existing there.

"Among other things, there entered into the fundamental program of this society—gradually to act in such a direction as would enable them to obtain a result—in the first place, the actualization for all the beings of the continent Asia of one common religion which they wished to base upon the teaching of the sect of what are called the 'Parsis,' only changing it a little; secondly, one common language, and for this common language they wished to adopt what is called the 'Turkoman' language, the oldest on the continent Asia and one whose roots had already entered into very many Asiatic languages.

"And thirdly, there entered into the fundamental program of this society finally to bring about the organization in the center of Asia, namely, in the city Margelan, the capital of what was called the 'Ferghanian Khanate,' of a chief and basic government for all the countries of Asia under the name of 'The-Council-of-the-Elders,' the members of which had to be honorable beings from all the Asiatic communities.

"It had to be so named because only the oldest and most deservedly honorable beings could participate in it.

"According to their understanding only such beings of their planet are able to be impartial and just toward other beings of the Earth, irrespective of to what religion or nationality they belong.

"Among the members of this society then in the city Mosulopolis, there were already beings belonging to almost all the Asiatic communities.

"Among them were also those called 'Mongols,' 'Arabs,' 'Kirghizes,' and 'Georgians,' 'Little Russians,' and 'Tamils,' and even the personal representative of the then famous conqueror Tamarlane.

"Thanks to their intensive and indeed impartial and unselfish activities, those increasing wars and civil wars on the continent Asia began to diminish, and it was anticipated that many other good things might still be done for this same end.

"But something just then happened which began the breakup also of this society of effective men-beings of that unparalleled planet.

"And everything subsequent came about through the influence of a then very famous philosopher, Atarnakh, and his theory expounded by him in a treatise under the title: 'Why do Wars Occur on the Earth?'

"When this philosopher made his appearance among the members of this society, all their notions were confounded.

"I know very well the history of this same philosopher Atarnakh also, because during my studies of ever the same consequences of the creations of the Most Saintly Ashiata Shiemash it became necessary for me to learn in detail about his activities also, and of course also about himself.

"This philosopher Atarnakh was born in that same city Mosulopolis in a family of those who are called 'Kurds.'

"He, on attaining responsible age, became for the planet Earth a very great learned being.

"In the very beginning, this same Kurd, Atarnakh, perseveringly studied during many Earth-years every possible question which it seemed to him might give him an answer to the question, 'what in general is the sense of man's existence,' and during his study of these questions it seems that by some means there fell into his hands a very ancient but well-preserved what is called 'Sumerian manuscript.'

"This manuscript was well preserved because it had been inscribed on the skins of being-snakes called 'Kalianjesh' with the blood of the being 'Chirman.'

"As my investigation made clear to me, the contents of this manuscript, inscribed by some ancient being, extremely interested the philosopher Atarnakh who was particularly struck by that place of the manuscript where, as presupposed by this ancient learned being, it was said:

"'In all probability there exists in the World some law of the reciprocal maintenance of everything existing.

"'Obviously our lives serve also for maintaining something great or small in the World.'

"This idea expressed in the ancient manuscript so captivated the philosopher Atarnakh that thereafter he devoted himself wholeheartedly to the study of only this aspect of the question which had interested him.

"This idea served as the basis for his whole further plausible theory, which, after minute researches during several years and elaborate experimental verifications of his own conclusions, he expounded in his chief work under the name 'Why Do Wars Occur on the Earth?'

"I became acquainted also with this theory of his.

"It was indeed near to reality.

"All the suppositions of this Kurd Atarnakh were very similar to the great fundamental cosmic law Trogoautoegocrat existing in our Universe, which law I explained to you in more or less detail when I was speaking about the holy planet Purgatory.

"In this theory of the philosopher Atarnakh it was very definitely proved that there exists in the world, without any doubt, a law of the 'reciprocal-maintenance-of-everything-that-exists' and that for this reciprocal maintenance certain chemical substances also serve, with the help of which the process of the spiritualization of beings, that is to say 'Life,' is carried out, and these chemical substances serve for the maintenance of all that exists only after the given life ceases, that is, when a being dies.

"With the help of very many elucidatory logical confrontations it was also fully proved in the theory of Atarnakh that at certain periods there must infallibly proceed on the Earth such a definite quantity of deaths as in their totality will yield vibrations of a 'definite degree of power.'

"Once, when at a general meeting of the beings-members of this society, 'The-Earth-Is-Equally-Free-for-All,' this anything but ordinary terrestrial three-brained being, who was also the elected representative from the whole population of the country called 'Kurdistan,' expounded this theory of his very eloquently and in great detail at the request of his fellow members, then great confusion and agitation proceeded among the members of this society.

"They were so struck with this theory of his, that at first, as is said there, a 'sepulchral silence' prevailed among them for quite a time, and, plunged into stupor, none of them could even stir, and only after the lapse of rather a long time such a great noise and hullabaloo arose among them as if the saving of each one's life depended on the degree of his excitement and its outer manifestations.

"The result of it all was that late in the evening of the same day they unanimously decided to elect from their midst several learned beings, jointly to investigate thoroughly the details of this theory which had struck them and afterwards to make a detailed report upon it to the general assembly.

"From the very next day, those elected learned members of the society 'The-Earth-Is-Equally-Free-for-All' very earnestly set to work to familiarize themselves with the theory of this Atarnakh.

"But to the misfortune of all three-brained beings of future times, arising on this ill-fated planet, it turned out that although all the elected learned members were also already advanced in years, and those malignant functions which in the beings of the Earth make their Being so to say 'jealous' and 'greedy' were almost atrophied in them, yet for various reasons, chiefly owing to their abnormal education, certain of them it seems had not yet acquired enough ground to be convinced of the nonactualizability of their dreams—which they owed to that notorious abnormal education of theirs—with the result that they were still not yet sufficiently disillusioned to be able to be fully impartial and just.

"In consequence of this, from that very same day, as they gradually became familiar with the details of this astonishing theory, they began to get into the state typical of beings of the Earth, that is to say, they began to forget the extraordinary hypothesis that had struck them, which was mentioned in that theory, and began gradually to return, as is proper to three-brained beings there, to their former typically subjective and therefore always changeable conviction, and immediately split into two opposite parties.

"Some of these began without any logical criticism to take convincingly on faith all the hypotheses made in this theory; others however did not fail, as is in general proper to most of the learned beings of the Earth, to speak and to prove quite the opposite of these hypotheses; and as a result they worked themselves up into a state of enmity not only against the theory of Atarnakh, but even personally against him himself.

"In short, my boy, instead of these learned members, who were elected for the detailed study of the theory of Atarnakh, helping the other members of their society to get out of their confusion and agitation and to unify their disputes among themselves, they brought still more bewilderment into their notions, and gradually in the common presence of each separate member of this earnest society, data began to arise automatically for two totally opposite convictions.

"The first of these convictions was that everything takes place precisely according to the theory of the philosopher Atarnakh, that is to say, that there must necessarily proceed 'wars' and 'civil wars' on the Earth quite independently of the personal consciousness of men; and the second conviction was that which all the members of the society had already previously had, namely, that if they succeeded in carrying out the program which their society had set itself, this evil also which proceeded on their planet might be destroyed root and branch, and everything might proceed in a desirable way.

"It was just from that time that discussions, quarrels, and disturbances arose among all the members of that society; and in this case also the same began to proceed as I already mentioned and as had in general long before become customary there: Those quarrels and disturbances of theirs gradually spread also among the ordinary beings there, in this case to the citizens of the city Mosulopolis, and were the cause of the inflaming of their abnormal psyche.

"And I do not know how all this would have ended, if the brothers of the society, 'The Assembly of the Enlightened,' had not also just then arrived there and had not taken a hand in this affair.

"Thanks to their influence, all the members of this serious society gradually calmed down and started anew peaceably and seriously to ponder and deliberate upon just what to do in the future.

"The result of all their serious deliberations and ponderings was that they unanimously elected Atarnakh as their chief director, and begged him to help them to find an issue from this situation.

"After several meetings, already directed by the Kurd philosopher Atarnakh himself, the following categorical conclusion was unanimously arrived at.

"According to the laws of Nature, there must periodically always proceed on the Earth, independently of the will of men, 'wars' and 'civil wars'; and this is because during certain periods there is required for Nature a greater quantity of deaths. In view of this we are all, with much grief but with inevitable inner resignation, compelled to agree that by no mental decisions of man is it possible to abolish the shedding of blood between states and within states themselves; and we therefore unanimously resolve to wind up current affairs and everything done by our society and perforce disperse for home and there to drag out our inescapable 'burden of life.'

"It was only after this categorical resolution was proposed when all the members without exception of that indeed serious society decided to begin that same day the complete liquidation of all their affairs; only then did that, in the opinion held there, truly learned, though very proud and self-loving Kurd Atarnakh ascend the cathedra and speak as follows:

"'My honorable colleagues:

"'I am very sincerely grieved that I have unintentionally been the cause of the dissolution of this great philanthropic undertaking, into which you, the most honorable and wise of all the countries of the Earth, have for several years put more impartial and unselfish labor than men of the Earth have ever been or ever again will be able to bear for others, that is, for men quite unknown and indifferent to them.

"'You have labored unceasingly for some years to obtain for the masses the most necessary welfare and, although I too have worked upon my theory for many years, also for people unknown to me, nevertheless it has been the cause of the frustration of your indefatigable labors and benevolent aspirations.

"'The consciousness that it seems that I am to blame for all the misunderstandings which have arisen among you has given me no peace during these last days, and I have been thinking and pondering all the time whether it is not possible somehow to repair this involuntary fault of mine.

"'And so, wise colleagues elected from the whole Earth,

I wish to share with you the final conclusion to which these deliberations of mine have brought me.

"'If the universal laws I have discovered are opposed to the means you expected might bring a certain happiness to mankind, then, however strange it may seem to you at first glance, if only these same laws be employed otherwise, they might serve for the attainment of this aim we have set for ourselves.

"'Now listen to what we must do to attain this aim. The results of all my researches clearly prove that Nature requires that at certain periods a certain number of deaths should take place on the Earth; and at the same time I have succeeded in making clear that for the needs of Nature it is indifferent which deaths these are, whether deaths of people themselves or deaths of the lives of other forms of beings.

"'From this it follows that if the number of deaths required by Nature is made up by the deaths of other forms of lives of the Earth, then obviously the need for the number of deaths of men themselves will thus be of itself correspondingly reduced.

"'And it will be quite possible to attain to this if all the members of our society continue to work with the same intensity, only not with the aim of realizing our former program, but of reviving upon the Earth on a larger scale than before the ancient custom among men of offering sacrifices to their gods and saints by destroying the lives of other forms.'

"When this proud Kurd had finished his speech, there arose among the members of the society 'The-Earth-Is-Equally-Free-for-All' an astonishment and agitation not less than on the occasion when he had first expounded his famous theory.

"For nearly three days and three nights following that memorable day they scarcely adjourned, but in the halls that had been put by the citizens of Mosulopolis at the disposal of this all-planetary society of men-beings there was a continuous rumble of discussion and deliberation; at last, on the fourth day, an official general meeting was convened at which by general consent a resolution was carried, to do in the future also everything exactly as should be indicated by the great Kurd, the philosopher Atarnakh.

"And on that same day, the name of that society was changed.

"Some days later, the members of that society now under the new motto, 'The-Earth-Only-for-Men,' dispersed from the city Mosulopolis to their native countries where, under the general instructions issuing from the philosopher Atarnakh, they so acted that among the populations of the continent Asia the idea should be strengthened and again take root of 'making themselves agreeable' to their gods and idols by killing beings of different forms.

"And indeed, afterward, when they began to actualize in practice this new program of theirs, there very soon began to be re-established among the beings all over the continent Asia the custom of offering sacrifices to their fancied 'saints' by the destruction of the existence of various weak and stupid one-brained and two-brained beings there.

"From the beginning the members of this new society, 'The-Earth-Only-for-Men,' began to actualize this task of theirs for the most part through what are called the 'clergy' of that religion which was formed upon the teaching of Saint Mohammed and which at that period was very widely spread over the whole continent Asia.

"And this custom was adopted this time on a larger scale than it had been when at the request of the Angel Looisos I descended there to try to do what I could to destroy that same custom among the three-brained beings there, which seemed at that time to His Conformity very undesirable for cosmic phenomena of a greater scale, because during all this time the number of your favorites had greatly increased and consequently the number also had increased of those anxious to 'give pleasure' to their fantastic idols.

"The destruction of the existence of other forms of beings was resumed there not only privately in houses, among their families, but also publicly in special places.

"But this time these special places were chiefly associated in a certain respect with the memory of Saint Mohammed, or with those around him.

"The number of these slaughters increased there by year to year to such an extent that already only some hundred or so of their years after the time of the arising of the society 'The-Earth-Only-for-Men' the number had amounted during one of their years in one single place alone to a hundred thousand of such beings as they had sacrificed in previous times, namely, 'oxen,' 'sheep,' 'camels,' and so on.

"During the last two centuries such special honored favorite places were the cities Mecca and Medina in Arabia, the city Meshed in the locality called Baghdad, the environs of Yenikishlak in Turkestan, and several others. . . .

"In a word, there on the continent Asia, blood again 'flowed like a river.'

"These sacrificial offerings were most frequent during the Mohammedan feasts called 'Bairam' and 'Goorban,' and likewise during the Christian feasts existing there under the name of 'Shrovetide,' 'Saint George's Day,' and so on.

"In this way, my boy, afterward when thanks to the strenuous efforts of the members of the society 'The-Earth-Only-for-Men' there had again been implanted in three-brained beings there such an abnormality, then these terrible processes of theirs began indeed to proceed there less often and on a smaller scale, and through this the sporadic, relatively great, what is called 'mortality' was diminished, yet the general 'mortality' of the three-brained beings was not only not reduced by this but even increased, since owing to the continued progressive deterioration of their being-existence and in consequence owing to the deterioration of the quality of the radiative vibrations of their presences in the process of their existence required from them by Nature, the length of their existence on the one hand was still further diminished, and on the other hand their what is called 'birth rate' was increased.

"So it continued until that time when a certain famous Assadulla Ibrahim Ogly, a Persian dervish who obtained his arising and who was formed into a responsible being on that same continent, turned all this in another direction.

"The dervish Assadulla Ibrahim Ogly began his activities there only some thirty or forty terrestrial years ago.

"Being simply only a fanatic of the Mohammedan religion without that serious and deeply learned knowledge possessed by the Kurd Atarnakh, he perceived in the custom of sacrificial offerings only horrible injustice on the part of the people toward beings of other forms, and he set as the aim of his existence to obtain, at whatever cost, the destruction on the Earth of this, in his opinion, antireligious custom.

"Having begun from that time to wander on the continent Asia, chiefly in those countries where the greater part of the three-brained beings were the followers of the Mohammedan religion, he began to work mainly through dervishes like himself, who are to be found in almost all the communities there on the continent Asia.

"This ingenious and energetic Persian dervish Assadulla Ibrahim Ogly, here, there, and everywhere, very cleverly persuaded these other dervishes of the 'truth' of his idea, and these in their turn now everywhere persuaded the ordinary beings of the continent Asia that the destruction of the existence of beings of other forms is not only not pleasing to God, but that the destroyers would even be obliged to bear 'in another world,' in hell, a double punishment, one for their own what are called 'sins' and one for the 'sins' of the beings destroyed by them, and so on.

"And thanks to preachings of this kind about the 'other world' by dervishes, considered great authorities on such questions, the beings of Asia did indeed year by year diminish their sacrificial offerings.

"In short, the result of all the activity of this 'good' Persian dervish was precisely the latest great process of reciprocal destruction, or, as your favorites call it, 'The Great World War.'

"And so, my boy, although the hypothesis put forward in the theory of that uncommon learned Kurd Atarnakh very nearly, as I have already told you, approximated to reality, yet nevertheless he failed to understand what was most important, namely, that the vibrations required by Nature, which have to be formed from the radiations issuing from beings both during their existence as well as from the process of their Rascooarno, have no significance quantitatively, but only qualitatively.

"It is possible that the Kurd Atarnakh, being an unusual terrestrial being, would have understood this also if he had known the details of the results that had been obtained after those conditions of being-existence had been already more or less established on this planet, which were especially created for the three-brained beings arising there by the Most Saintly Labors of the 'essence-loving' Very Saintly Ashiata Shiemash.

"During that said period, not only did their rate of 'mortality' begin to decline, but what they call their birth rate also began to decline.

"Their birth rate declined because, when the three-brained beings there were already existing more or less as is becoming to three-centered beings and when the radiations issuing from them were yielding vibrations more akin to the vibrations required from them by Nature both for the Most Great common-cosmic Trogoautoegocrat in general and for the maintenance of the Moon and Anulios in particular, then Great Nature did not fail to adapt herself to the diminishing of their birth rate, the more so as in recent times the need for the said vibrations for the maintenance of the existence of the planet Moon had to be diminished.

"The aspect of this fundamental question regarding the significance of the sense and aim of the existence of your favorites is so important for the understanding of a great deal that proceeds there on the Earth, and by the way also of the question touching the causes of war, that I consider it necessary to refer to it once more.

"I first learned that the destiny of beings arising on this planet of yours is chiefly to elaborate—by means of the process of their existence—the vibrations required by Nature for the maintenance of those former parts of the planet now called Moon and Anulios, when, do you remember, I became worthy personally to converse for the second time with His Conformity the then still Angel, but now Archangel, Looisos.

"His Conformity then told me that although the movements of both former parts of the planet Earth were now already finally regulated with the general harmony of movement and that every kind of apprehension of some or other surprise in the near future had absolutely vanished, yet to avoid any possible complications in the distant future it had been explicitly decided by the Most High, Most Sacred Individuals to actualize the 'corresponding' on the planet for the formation of what is called the Sacred Askokin so that this sacred cosmic substance, required for the maintenance of that planet's former parts, might continuously issue from that planet.

"And further, His Highness also explained that this cosmic substance, the Sacred Askokin, exists in general in the Universe chiefly blended with the sacred substances 'Abrustdonis' and 'Helkdonis,' and hence that this sacred substance Askokin in order to become vivifying for such a maintenance must first be freed from the said sacred substances Abrustdonis and Helkdonis.

"To tell the truth, my boy, I did not at once clearly understand all that he then said, and it was only later that I came to understand it all clearly, when, during my studies of the fundamental cosmic laws, I learned that these sacred substances Abrustdonis and Helkdonis are just those substances by which the higher being-bodies of three-brained beings, namely, the body Kesdjan and the body of the Soul, are in general formed and perfected; and when I learned that the separation of the sacred Askokin from the said sacred substances proceeds in general when the beings on whatever planet it might be transubstantiate the sacred substances Abrustdonis and Helkdonis in themselves for the forming and perfecting of their higher bodies, by means of conscious labors and intentional sufferings.

"And when I had become interested in these favorites of yours and had begun to observe and to study their strange psyche, only then did I finally understand to which end both Great Nature herself and the Most High and Most Saintly Individuals always patiently adapt themselves to everything, and concerning this, the following personal opinion was formed in me.

"That if these favorites of yours would at least properly ponder over this and serve Nature honestly in this respect, then perhaps their being-self-perfecting might as a consequence proceed automatically even without the participation of their consciousness and, in any case, the poor Nature of their ill-fated planet would also not have to 'puff and blow' in order to adapt Herself to remain within the common cosmic harmony.

"But unfortunately for everything existing in the Megalocosmos, there is no honesty in your favorites even in respect of the fulfillment of their duties to Nature, not even to that Nature to which, strictly speaking, they owe their very existence.

"As regards the absence of honesty in your favorites in the fulfillment of their duty towards Nature, I have just now remembered a very wise sentence of our incomparable Teacher Mullah Nassr Eddin which in the present case justifies its hidden meaning.

"He once said:

"'Plague and cholera are, at any rate, less ignoble than human honesty, since people with a conscience can at least live at peace with them.'

"And so, my dear Hassein, when it appeared that the instinctive need for conscious labor and intentional suffering in order to be able to take in and transmute in themselves the sacred substances Abrustdonis and Helkdonis and thereby to liberate the sacred Askokin for the maintenance of the Moon and Anulios had finally disappeared from the psyche of your favorites, then Great Nature Herself was constrained to adapt Herself to extract this sacred substance by other means, one of which is precisely that periodic terrifying process there of reciprocal destruction.

"Here, for the correct valuation of your contemporary favorites it will be apropos to remind you that after the action of the organ Kundabuffer had been destroyed in the three-brained beings of your planet, the first generations very soon learned that a certain cosmic substance had to be transformed through them and that their assistance in this transformation was one of their chief being-duties.

"Do you remember, I have told you that the beings of the continent Atlantis even considered this being-duty of theirs as sacred and called it 'Amarloos,' which in their language means 'Help-to-the-Moon.'

"The three-brained beings of the continent Atlantis of that period, namely, the period then called the 'Samliosian civilization,' even devised and very strictly practiced certain customs that greatly contributed to the fulfillment of those being-duties as productively as possible.

"The beings of the continent Atlantis even very wisely and expediently devised the fulfillment of these two being-duties—namely, the duty of the perfecting of their higher bodies and the duty of serving the Most Great cosmic-Trogoautoegocrat—by uniting them into one and performing them simultaneously.

"And this union they organized in the following way:

"In every populated locality, and even in separate districts of these localities, three very substantial indispensable special buildings were erected there.

"One, for the beings of the male sex, was called 'Agoorokhrostiny.'

"The second building, specially for beings of the female sex, was called 'Gynekokhrostiny.'

"And the third, for such beings as were then called the 'middle sex'; this sacred building was called 'Anoropari-onikima.'

"The first two of these substantial buildings were then considered sacred by the beings of the continent Atlantis, and these buildings were for them the same as their 'temples,' 'churches,' 'chapels,' and other sacred places are for the contemporary beings of the Earth.

"When I descended for the first time on that planet and was on the continent Atlantis, I personally visited certain of these buildings and at that time became very well acquainted with their purpose.

"In the male temples, namely, in the Agoorokhrostiny, beings of the male sex of the given locality or of the given district performed in turn corresponding 'mysteries' while in the special state called 'self-remembering.'

"The beings of the continent Atlantis had a definite notion that beings of the male sex are sources of active manifestation, and hence in their Agoorokhrostiny they gave themselves up to active and conscious contemplation the whole time, and in this state performed these corresponding sacred mysteries, so that there should be transubstantiated in them the sacred substances Abrustdonis and Helkdonis.

"And they did this deliberately and with full consciousness in order that this certain sacred substance, liberated in them, and issuing through their radiations for its further vivifyingness, should become the active part of that sacred law which they call the 'Holy Trinity.'

"In the sacred Gynekokhrostiny, built for the beings of the female sex, each of these beings was obliged at certain periods, namely, at those periods which contemporary beings call 'menstruation,' to stay without leaving. Moreover, the women, acknowledging themselves to be passive beings, had to be, the whole time of their stay there, only passive, in order that the vibrations issuing through their radiations should serve as the passive part of that same sacred law for their further vivifyingness.

"And hence they passed their whole time in these Gynekokhrostiny in a state of complete passivity, trying consciously not to think about anything.

"With this aim in view, they tried to have no active experiencings during their monthly states, and in order that thoughts flowing by association should not hinder them from concentrating, everything was arranged so that their thoughts should be directed the whole time to wishing well to their present or future children.

"And as regards the third kind of the buildings of the beings of that time, which were called Anoroparionikima, as I already told you, the beings then called the 'third sex,' for whom these buildings were erected, our Mullah Nassr Eddin would call 'misconceptions,' or beings who are 'neither one thing nor another.'

"Among these middle-sex beings were beings both of the male sex and the female sex.

"These were beings who, for various reasons, already lacked the possibility either of perfecting themselves or serving Nature; they were, as is said in a saying of our same Mullah Nassr Eddin, 'Neither a candle for the Angel, nor a poker for the devil.'

"Those beings of the male sex were put into these houses for a certain time who, for some reason or other, were already entirely deprived of the possibility of ever consciously contemplating; and of the number of the beings of the female sex, those were placed in them who generally either did not 'menstruate' at all, or in whom 'menstruation' occurred abnormally; likewise those who in the sense of their sexual desires became transformed at certain periods into, as it was said there, 'Knaneomeny,' or, as our dear Mullah would say, 'into veritable mares in the spring.'

"Among the beings then on the continent Atlantis, conceptions of several definite, very peculiar symptoms were current, according to which the given beings were recognized and confined in the Anoroparionikima.

"And these symptoms were as follows:

(1) If a being believed in any kind of 'balderdash'

(2) If a being began to prove to others anything about which he himself knew nothing whatsoever, or was not sure of
(3) If a being failed to keep his word of honor, or took his oath in vain
(4) And finally, if there appeared in any being tendencies to 'spy' upon the others and to be occupied with 'Took-soo-kef'

"But the most conclusive symptom of all was when that property appeared in somebody which was then called 'Moyussool' and which contemporary beings already consider an illness and call 'hemorrhoids.'

"In these Anoroparionikima, beings of this kind were obliged to remain without stirring from them during those periods indicated by the surrounding beings; but they were under no compulsion to do anything, but existed as they liked. In regard to them there was only one aim, that they neither met nor spoke with normal beings of the given locality.

"Such beings were then confined in these buildings because, according to the notions then, they at certain periods of the month, thanks to these various 'taints' of theirs, interfered by their radiations with the quiet and regular existence of the surrounding beings.

"Yes, indeed . . . my dear boy. . . .

"Beings of the later period of the existence of the continent Atlantis had already many very good customs for normal being-existence; but, as regards the contemporary beings of your planet, one can only pity them, because owing to the second great calamity to their ill-fated planet, the said continent with everything upon it entered into the planet, and with it there disappeared also all those good customs for ordinary existence which had gradually during long centuries entered into the process of their ordinary existence.

"After that continent of Atlantis had perished, the custom

was again on the point of being re-established among later three-brained beings there, of having special constructions similar to those of which I have just told you for the process of ordinary existence.

"The need for these special buildings was again understood and they were actualized by a very sensible Hebrew king named Solomon.

"And that special building which this sensible Hebrew king decided first of all to construct and which still continued long afterwards among his subjects, was called 'Tak-tschan-nan.'

"They somewhat resembled the Gynekokhrostiny, such as had existed in Atlantis, and beings also of the female sex were put into them, and they were obliged to remain there during the whole of their menstruation.

"The King Solomon hastened then to establish this custom because, during his wise reign, he had often constated that when beings of the female sex experienced the state of menstruation their character became for the surrounding beings, especially for their husbands, not only intolerable, but in respect of resulting 'inconsistent relations and dealings' with other beings like themselves, even psycho-organically harmful; and he therefore decided without delay to promulgate a severe law for his subjects according to which special isolated buildings were compulsorily constructed near every populated district in which to confine the beings of the female sex for the whole duration of their said state.

"I even chanced to read the law he promulgated.

"In this law it was said, among other things, that women during their menstruation are, in the consecrated sense, unclean; and that during these periods, for others, and especially for their husbands, not only to touch them, but to speak with them, is the highest sacrilege and a crime.

"An unclean force or evil spirit will enter into those husbands or into men in general who touch or even speak with them during this period; in consequence of which there would be among men in their everyday relations and affairs only misunderstandings, quarrels, and enmity.

"This last statement of this great 'Earth-sage,' King Solomon, remains today an unchangeable truth.

"And indeed, at the present time, this also is one of the numerous causes thanks to which, in the general complexity, ordinary existence has already become nonsensical in the extreme for the beings of your planet.

"In the contemporary 'Earth-beings' of the female sex, there is still further increased during these states that specific property of theirs which was acquired in them during recent centuries and which they call 'hysteria,' and during this state of theirs they bring surrounding beings, particularly their husbands, to this, that the latter become like those beings there of whom our great Mullah Nassr Eddin says:

"'The purpose of their existence is to be the victims of leeches.'

"And indeed, it is only because the contemporary beings of the female sex go about freely during 'menstruation' that many contemporary beings of the male sex not only can never have good and kind relations with each other, but on account of this, very frequently become genuine what are called 'later-repenting blasphemers.'

"This favorable custom created by the wise King Solomon existed among the Hebrew people for a considerable time and would certainly have been spread all over the Earth also, had it not been for that specific property of the beings there, about which I have also already once told you.

"Namely, when this Hebrew people, as usually happens there, had fallen from their greatness and were despised and persecuted by the beings of other communities, who on account of the impulses of jealousy and envy of all those higher than themselves, hated her in the days of her greatness and power, which impulses had already become inherent in the three-brained beings of your planet—then these beings of other communities, of course, also despised all the indeed good customs which they had already had.

"That is why this good custom was not only not spread further, but gradually, also owing to their other characteristic properties, which I have already sufficiently explained to you, that is to say, owing to the fact that this Hebrew people had themselves fallen under the influence of other communities which had become great, and had followed their examples—this good custom began to be despised and was ultimately forsaken and forgotten by the very founders themselves.

"At the present time, this custom exists there only among a very small community to be found in the mountains of the Caucasus and bearing the name 'Khevsoory,' just those same Khevsoory who give many scientists there no sleep, because of the problem of the origin of that small community.

"As regards your favorites also destroying the good customs for ordinary existence already existing on their planet and attained by their ancestors, we must, like it or not, again express our condolence with poor Nature there who must always be adapting and readapting Herself.

"And concerning a misfortune of this kind for their Nature, our very dear Teacher, the peerless Mullah Nassr Eddin, has also some very wise sentences.

"Namely, in similar misfortunes he sometimes says:

'Ekh . . . if you're unlucky in life, you may even be infected by your godmother with venereal disease,' or sometimes he also says:

"'Oh, you unfortunate creature! Your mother must have sung an Armenian ballad while you were being born.'

"Even the interpreter of Russian wisdom, Kusma Proutkoff, has good sayings for such a case:

"'The unluckiest among us is the fir cone, because every Makkar stumbles over it.'

"I repeat, this unfortunate Nature of the planet Earth must continuously and without respite adapt Herself to manifest always otherwise, and yet again otherwise, so as to remain within the common-cosmic harmony.

"In order that you may represent to yourself and understand well in what way unfortunate Nature there so adapts Herself that there should be attained what is called the 'equilibrium of vibrations,' required from this planet for the common-cosmic harmony, I shall explain to you only about one fact which is just now being actualized there, that is to say, subsequent to that process of theirs which they called the 'World War.'

"It was plainly owing to the fact that during the said process what is called 'poison gas' was invented by beings called 'Germans,' and what are called special 'rapid-fire machine guns' by beings called 'Englishmen,' that the amount of Rascooarnos or deaths unforeseen by Nature took place on this occasion and in a far greater quantity than was then required by Her, or, as the candidates for Hasnamuss there, namely, the commercial businessmen, would say, 'overproduction' occurred in respect of the deaths of the three-brained beings required there.

"In consequence, Nature there had again to begin from that moment to 'puff and blow,' and, as is said there, 'jump out of Her skin' in order to correct this unforeseeingness and adapt Herself once again in a corresponding manner.

"This time, from what I myself learned for certain during my last stay there, and also from the intimation communicated to me by etherogram, Great Nature there is evidently about to increase, for future times, the birth rate of other forms of beings there.

"I noticed in the cities Petrograd and Tiflis situated in the large community Russia, of which community more beings perished than of any other during that World War of theirs, that that kind of quadruped being which as a rule never appeared there, namely, the quadruped beings which hate people and which are called 'wolves,' were already prowling in the streets.

"In the information communicated to me by etherogram it was said, among other things, that in the same large community Russia the birth rate of beings of the kinds of rodents called 'mice' and 'rats' had increased to such an unprecedented extent that at the present time they are beginning to devour most of the stored provisions of the beings of the said community.

"It was further conveyed in the same etherogram that the power-possessing beings of the community Russia had applied to the beings of another European community to undertake the destruction of the existence of those small beings—mice and rats—which had multiplied among them, in return for which they promised to pay them as much money as it would cost.

"Though a temporary reduction of the numbers of these poor rats and mice may be obtained by the various means at the disposal of those specialists in the destruction of the existences of others, yet the beings of the other communities will possibly not quite consent to do this 'gratis.' To pay in money, however, this the beings of that Russia who promised it will, of course, not be able to do, since it might cost them in money much more than their last war.

"And to get money from the same sources from which they drained it during that great process, as our dear Mullah Nassr Eddin says, 'As to this, nothing doing! Even a donkey can understand that peasant flesh costs nothing in peacetime.' "

Having said this, Beelzebub became silent and began to look expectantly at his grandson who, as if talking to himself, very sadly, in a tone full of despair, said:

"How will it all end? Is there really no way out at all?

"Must these unfortunate souls who were formed on that unfortunate planet really remain eternally unperfected and be endlessly coated into various planetary forms and everlastingly toil and moil on account of the consequences of the properties of that accursed organ Kundabuffer, which, owing to the reasons extraneous to them themselves, was attached to the planetary bodies of the first three-centered beings of that ill-fated planet?

"Where, then, is that pillar upon which, as it were, our whole Megalocosmos rests, and which is called Justice?!!!!

"No! This cannot be! Something is wrong here, because during the whole time of my existence, not once has a single doubt ever crept into me as to the existence of objective Justice.

"All I have to do is just to clarify and understand . . . why! . . . why!

"At any rate, from this present moment, the aim of my existence shall be to understand clearly why the souls arising in these terrestrial three-centered beings are in such an unprecedented, terrifying situation. . . ."

Having said this, poor Hassein, full of melancholy, drooped his head and became sadly thoughtful.

And Beelzebub looked at him with a very strange look; strange because in this look his love for Hassein was very clearly seen, and at the same time it could be sensed that he was nevertheless very glad that his grandson was experiencing such a depression.

This silence continued a fairly long time. At last Beelzebub heaved a deep sigh, with, as it were, the whole of his essence, and spoke to his grandson in the following words:

"Yes, my dear Hassein. . . .

"Certainly there is something not quite right here.

"But if nothing could be done for the beings of that planet by that Being who now already has the Reason of the sacred 'Podkoolad' and is one of the first assistants of our ENDLESSNESS in the government of the World, namely, the Very Saintly Ashiata Shiemash—if He could do nothing, what then can we expect, we, beings with the Reason of almost ordinary beings?

"You remember the Very Saintly Ashiata Shiemash, then in his deliberations, under the title 'The Terror of the Situation' said:

"'If it is still possible to save the beings of the Earth, then Time alone can do it.'

"We can now only repeat the same in regard to this terrible property of theirs, of which we have just been speaking, namely, their periodic processes of the destruction of each other's existence.

"We can only say now, that if this property of terrestrial beings is to disappear from that unfortunate planet, then it will be with Time alone, thanks either to the guidance of a certain Being with very high Reason or to certain exceptional cosmic events."

Having said this, Beelzebub again began to look at Hassein with that same strange look.

CHAPTER 44

In the Opinion of Beelzebub, Man's Understanding of Justice Is for Him in the Objective Sense an Accursed Mirage

Smiling and continuing to look affectionately at his grandson Hassein, Beelzebub said:

"It is only now, my dear future substitute, after all that I have related to you and all that you have in a general way taken in during this time concerning the three-brained beings breeding on the planet Earth, that I find it opportune to tell you about that terrestrial 'question' to which I promised to devote myself at the very end of all my tales.

"Namely, about that maleficent idea widespread among all of them, which, you remember—when I spoke about the chief 'kink' in their psyche, that is about their diverse and peculiar 'Havatvernonis' or, as they themselves call them, 'religions'—I said was made by them the basis of all these religions of theirs, and which maleficent idea was called 'Good and Evil.'

"I then also told you that, on account of this maleficent idea existing among the terrestrial three-brained beings, great events or, as I would express it in the words of your favorites, 'turmoils' recently occurred on the holy planet Purgatory, and the involuntary cause of their arising were certain members of your 'Hernasdjensa' or, according to the expression of your favorites, your 'genealogical tree.'

"In order that you should the better picture to yourself and more easily assimilate all that I intend to explain to you, it is in my opinion necessary first of all to say something about certain of these long-past events which at first glance have nothing in common with this idea.

"And so . . . I have already once told you that when I descended for the fifth time onto the surface of this planet of yours, I remained on it a short time and soon returned home to the planet Mars.

"This happened then because my friends notified me from the Center that in the near future there would appear on the planet Mars one of the Cherubim near to our ALL-EMBRACING ENDLESSNESS, who had some command or other concerning me.

"After my arrival on the planet Mars, the said Cherub did indeed soon make his appearance, and the command given him from Above concerning me was this, that owing to my conscious labors for the attainment of results for the purpose of common-cosmic welfare, that is to say, owing to the fact that I had attained on your planet the abolition of the practice of 'sacrificial offerings' among the three-brained beings who have taken your fancy, and also owing to the personal petition of His Conformity the Angel Looisos before our COMMON FATHER ENDLESSNESS, my punishment for my personal transgression was reduced in this respect that thenceforward it should no longer affect my posterity.

"So it was just from then on that my children, that is your father and your uncle Tooilan, could already, whenever they wished, at their own desire, return to the Center, and there discharge their appropriate obligations to the innumerable actualizations of our UNIVERSAL FATHER.

"After this great event for our family, my children indeed soon left the planet Mars and returned to the Center, where on their arrival, being already great sages in certain spheres of objective knowledge and good actualizers of its laws in practical application, they were soon appointed to appropriate responsible duties.

"Your father, as I have already told you, was immediately assigned to the post of 'Zirlikner' on one of the parts of the surface of our dear Karatas, in which post he gradually became worthy of obtaining the responsibility of chief Zirlikner over all the three-brained beings breeding on our planet, which post he still retains.

"And your uncle Tooilan, as I have also already told you, was then enrolled as one of the assistants to the director of the etherogram station on the holy planet Purgatory, which, then as now, has an 'etherogram connection' with almost all the planets of our Great Universe.

"Later he also merited the post of chief director and this post he still retains at the present time.

"I must explain to you, my boy, also why on their arrival there at the Center, my results or, according to the expression of your favorites, my 'sons,' then became worthy immediately to obtain these responsible posts.

"In order that this should become comprehensible to you, I must tell you that among those exiled with me, at the very beginning of our exile there, was the chief 'Zirlikner' of our planet Karatas, the then still young but already very learned Pooloodjistius, who after the all-gracious pardon, became worthy to be and still is an assistant to the Great Observer of the movements of all the concentrations of the Megalocosmos—His Self-Keepness the Archseraph Ksheltarna.

"And so, when I began there on the planet Mars to organize my observatory, this same learned Pooloodjistius proposed to me that I should take him in the capacity of inspector and manager of this new establishment of mine.

"Of course I then immediately agreed with his proposal, as he was a very great authority on locating all large and small concentrations as well as an authority on the laws of their reciprocal maintenance, and from then on this great learned Pooloodjistius began to exist in my house on the planet Mars.

"Later when the results of my active principle arose

and were formed to corresponding age, I once asked this learned Pooloodjistius to undertake the duty also of 'Oskianotsner,' or, as your favorites would say, 'educator' of my children; and to this proposal of mine he agreed with great readiness, because, existing there under unusual conditions, he had no possibility of using his multifarious learning to his satisfaction, and, thanks to this proposal of mine, what is called a 'wide field of activity' was opened up for him in this respect.

"From then on, apart from the execution of his strict duties which at the beginning were not too much for him, he began to devote himself entirely to the creation of corresponding outer and inner conditions so that my sons should take in impressions for the purpose of crystallizing in themselves the requisite being-data for a responsible existence worthy of three-brained beings.

"My sons soon became so attached to him that they never left his side even during the execution of his strict duties concerning my observatory, and even under these conditions the good Pooloodjistius constantly enlightened their Reason and gave them practical explanations about all the observations on the concentrations, the methods of studying their mutual influence, and the significance of these influences themselves.

"He always explained to them why and for what purpose any definite cosmic concentration occupies just a certain place, and informed them about the particularities of the influence of these concentrations on each other during the common-cosmic Trogoautoegocratic process.

"In this way, under the guidance of this remarkable learned being, there was not only crystallized, in the common presences of my results, data required for every kind of responsible three-brained being, but also numerous data for the thorough cognizance and the sensing of true information about cosmic concentrations and their functions.

"By the way, it was just at this period that their subjectively favorite subjects for observation and study were gradually formed in each of my sons.

"Namely, your father liked to observe and study the mutual influence and maintenance of cosmic concentrations situated in the spheres nearest to the Prime Source, the Most Most Holy Sun Absolute, and your uncle Tooilan manifested an interest in the observations on the planet Earth and in the process which proceeded on it of the being-existence of the three-brained beings who have interested you. When I happened to be occupied with something else, I often commissioned him to keep note of all the changes which proceeded there.

"When my sons were prepared to leave the planet Mars forever, your uncle Tooilan begged me to keep him periodically informed of my observations of the Earth beings, which I of course promised to do; and they flew away from there to the Center nearer to Our Lord.

"When they arrived there and it proved that they were well informed concerning the position of cosmic concentrations and their properties and particularities, and also that they were practically versed in the calculations of the totality of the reciprocal influences, then thanks to all this they were immediately assigned to the said responsible duties.

"And so when I learned of the permanent place of their existence and to which posts they were found worthy, I, from then on, according to my promise, sent every quarter of our year to Tooilan an exact copy of all my written summaries of those observations which I continued to make. Rather many years passed since the time I began to send Tooilan these etherograms and I personally did not know what became of them until I received information about these same turbulent events on the planet Purgatory. It transpired that the great Governor of the holy planet Purgatory, His All-Quarters-Maintainer the Archcherub Helkgematios, having once by chance learned that one of the assistants of the Governor of the etherogram station, Tooilan, periodically received from the solar system Ors very long etherograms from his father, evinced a desire to become acquainted with their contents, and having become acquainted with them, he not only became interested in them himself, but even commanded your uncle Tooilan always to reproduce the contents of these etherograms in the common planetary 'Toolookhterzinek,'* so that some of the 'higher being-bodies' dwelling on the holy planet might, if they wished, for a rest, be informed of the psyche of those peculiar three-brained beings breeding in one of the very remote corners of the Megalocosmos.

"Your uncle Tooilan afterwards always did so. Whenever he received etherograms from me he always reproduced their contents in the common planetary Toolookhterzinek, and in this way all those righteous souls dwelling on the holy planet were kept informed of all my observations and investigations of everything concerning their strange psyches.

"From then on, certain of the righteous higher being-bodies there on the holy planet not only began to follow all my observations very attentively, but they also began to ponder on the strangeness of their psyche.

"The results of the pondering of the blissful higher being-bodies was that they began to understand that something was wrong with the psyche of the three-brained beings of that planet Earth, and they even discerned something suspicious in the cause of this 'something wrong,' and ultimately many of them began to be seriously indignant at what first seemed to them an injustice coming, as it were, from Above.

* Toolookhterzinek is similar—of course to a certain degree—to that which on Earth is called a "radiogram."

"The more these indignant righteous 'souls' shared their impressions with others, the greater their number gradually increased, so that everywhere in the 'Zarooaries'* on the holy planet they thought and deliberated among themselves only about this.

"The result of it all was that all of the inhabitants of the holy planet chose fifty righteous souls from among their number to investigate jointly and to find out the true reason why such an absurdity exists in the psyche of the three-brained beings of that planet Earth, which makes the self-perfecting impossible for that 'higher being-part' which for various reasons sometimes arises also in certain of them.

"These chosen fifty religious 'souls' were just those who were already worthy to be candidates for going to the Most Most Holy Source of Everything Existing.

"Then even His All-Quarters-Maintainer the Archcherub Helkgematios, the Governor of the holy planet, not only sanctioned the choice of these fifty blissful souls but also by His own all-gracious decision expressed a desire to help them in every way in the fulfillment of their undertaking.

"And so, my boy, when these fifty candidates for the Sun Absolute began their investigations, then, after long and complicated researches, it became clear to them that the fundamental cause of the whole abnormality of the psyche of the three-brained beings arising on this planet was that a very definite notion arose and began to exist, that outside the essence of beings, as it were, there are two diametrically opposite factors—the sources of 'Good' and the sources of 'Evil'—which are just the instigators for all their good and bad manifestations.

"It was then established by them that this universally

* Zarooaries on the holy planet correspond approximately to what on the planet Earth are called towns and villages.

disseminated maleficent idea, the data for which gradually became crystallized in each of them during their formation into preparatory age, already dominates their common psyche at their responsible existence and becomes on the one hand a tranquillizer and justifier of all their manifestations and on the other hand the fundamental impeding factor for the possibility which arises in certain of them for the self-perfecting of their higher being-parts.

"When the righteous dwellers on the holy planet had made all this clear to themselves, they began to consider and deliberate among themselves how to find a way out of the situation and what they could do from their side.

"As it was related to me, they began to arrange meetings and conferences everywhere in Zarooaries, to try by collective effort to arrive at some decision, and after long deliberations and complicated what are called 'ballots' by the righteous souls of single Zarooaries as well as by different Zarooaries, the following resolution was ultimately almost unanimously carried:

"'First of all to lay a petition at the feet of our MAKER CREATOR that HE in HIS Providence should send to the three-brained beings of the planet Earth a Messenger from Above with data corresponding to such a Reason as could on the spot find a possibility of uprooting this maleficent idea; and secondly, in view of the fact that the actualization on the surface of this planet of such a maleficent idea was and until now is the fundamental cause of all the terrifying misfortune for the sacred higher being-parts arising there, to venture with contrition to request our COMMON FATHER not to allow the higher being-part of that terrestrial three-brained being who was the cause of the arising there of a maleficent idea to be taken on the holy planet, even if this higher being-body is perfected to the required gradation of Sacred Reason, but to doom it to exist eternally on the planet Remorse-of-Conscience.'

"Well it was just then, my boy, after the dwellers on the holy planet had sanctioned this resolution, that as I expressed it, that 'turmoil' broke out there which, even until now, not one of the Sacred Individuals who knew this epic story can recall without so to say 'shuddering.'

"This turmoil was evoked there in the following way: After the said resolution was carried, it was soon undertaken on the initiative of all those fifty chosen candidates for the Sun Absolute, to elucidate just which terrestrial three-brained being—with perhaps his higher being-part already formed in him—was the cause of the arising on this planet of yours of such a maleficent idea.

"And according to this elucidation, it turned out that that three-brained being who was the first to give the beginning of the crystallizing of that maleficent idea was a certain Makary Kronbernkzion whose higher being-part perfected to the required gradation of Reason had not only become worthy to go to the holy planet, but was even already considered one of the first candidates to be taken onto the Most Most Holy Sun Absolute.

"As was afterwards related to me, when this became known a 'groan,' so to say, hovered over the whole of the holy planet, and there was not a single righteous soul there who could think without remorse about this terrible fact.

"For almost a quarter of a year they only 'judged back and forth' about this unprecedented turmoil, and in each 'Zarooary' commissions and subcommissions of every kind again set to work to resolve such an extraordinary situation as had arisen.

"The result of it all was that the following resolution, again on the same basis, was this time passed:

"'To leave in abeyance the first common-planetary sentence which was passed concerning the higher-part of

Makary Kronbernkzion and to lay at the feet of HIS ALL-MOST-GRACIOUS ENDLESSNESS the request of all the dwellers of the holy planet to mitigate this terrifying sentence.'

"And therefore, at the next appearance on the holy planet of our ALL-MOST-GRACIOUS CREATOR ENDLESSNESS, this request was laid at His feet.

"Our ALL-MOST-GRACIOUS CREATOR then, as it is said, only thought a little and then consented to command that this deserving soul should continue to exist on the holy planet until the future results of his evil deed should be revealed.

"In spite of the fact that this completely formed higher being-part was the fundamental cause of the impossibility for all the higher being-bodies which arise in the presences of certain three-brained beings of this planet to perfect themselves completedly, this gracious command was given by our COMMON FATHER evidently because He hoped that ultimately these three-brained beings themselves might perhaps cognize their errors and begin to exist as is becoming to three-centered beings to exist. And in that case there would be no need to punish so terribly the higher-part of that being who, without yielding to adverse conditions not depending on himself and much stronger than his possibilities, and mercilessly struggling with his own inevitable denying principle, was able to perfect himself to such a gradation thanks to which he had acquired the possibility of reaching the threshold of the basis of everything existing in the Universe.

"Owing to the said command of our ALL-MOST-GRACIOUS CREATOR, the higher-part of this poor Makary Kronbernkzion now still exists on the holy planet and his future now depends exclusively only on the three-brained beings who have taken your fancy."

After rather a long pause Beelzebub continued thus: "The information concerning these events proceeding on the holy planet first reached me just during my sixth personal descent on the surface of your planet, and I, of course having become very interested in it all, began on my part also to investigate in detail on the spot this distressing story connected with the three-brained beings who have taken your fancy.

"First of all, my boy, I consider it necessary to tell you sincerely, just to you, my direct substitute, that although all the righteous dwellers on the holy planet, with the help of various and at the same time very elaborate means, made it clear that the fundamental cause of all the abnormalities of the psyche of these three-brained beings who have taken your fancy was and until now still is only this maleficent idea, yet nevertheless I cannot myself confirm this categorically.

"Of course it cannot be denied that this fantastic idea played a big part in respect of the gradual so to say 'dilution' of the psyche of these unfortunates.

"Many impressions were a-taken in me and data crystallized for a subjective opinion, when having become interested in this story, I began among other things to make my researches and to make clear to myself also the story of the arising and formation of this same Makary Kronbernkzion.

"It was just these same special investigations of mine which clearly showed me that although he indeed first used the words 'Good' and 'Evil,' yet he was not to blame that these words later acquired there in the process of the existence of the beings of all subsequent generations such a maleficent sense for your favorites.

"If, my boy, I now initiate you into the information I learned concerning the history of the arising and process of the existence there of this Makary Kronbernkzion, then perhaps corresponding data would be crystallized in you for an approximate representation concerning this terrestrial fact.

"I shall begin by saying that when I decided to occupy myself there with this, I then began from that time on, whenever I met any corresponding individual, to inquire about everything which in totality might throw some light on one or other aspect of the individuality of this Makary Kronbernkzion.

"You will probably be interested to learn that among the first individuals I met who could give me some information about what I have said, a very aged being of our tribe turned out to be very useful. In conversation he cleared up many things for me and indicated to me several very good sources from which I later drew very useful and detailed information.

"This elderly being about whom I now speak was none other than the uncle of that young being of our tribe on whose account I had to descend to this planet of yours the first time and who afterwards became the chief over all the beings of our tribe who were exiled to that system Ors.

"This mentioned elderly being of your planet existed just on the continent Atlantis and just at that period when that Makary Kronbernkzion existed there also.

"According to all the information I learned and also according to every other special method of my investigation, it transpired that this terrestrial three-brained being named Makary Kronbernkzion arose and began to exist there on the continent Atlantis from the sacred process of 'Elmooarno' which proceeded between two terrestrial beings there of different sex who had just reached responsible age.

"Owing to the fact that this couple had a healthy heredity in every respect, and that the external conditions of ordinary being-existence in general there were still relatively normal and for this couple happened to be specially favorable, hence the result of this sacred process, that is to say, this same, according to them, 'son' of theirs who was later called Makary Kronbernkzion, already received in his presence from the beginning of his arising and during his early existence almost the same data for the Being of a future responsible being as every Keschapmartnian three-brained being should possess at his arising anywhere on any other planet of our Great Megalocosmos, and as a desire happened to arise in his producers, or as it is said there in his 'parents' to prepare their 'result' to become a responsible being with a 'scientific career,' and as they also happened to find successful guides for him, then when this result of theirs became a responsible being, he became a very good 'scientist'—of course, very good for the planet Earth.

"He soon became worthy on account of his scientific merits even to become a full member of the learned society Akhaldan.

"During the process of his responsible existence in the scientific field, he once more clearly saw the real value of his own significance and sincerely realized his 'nullity.'

"From then on he began with sore grief to meditate seriously on these realizations of his, and the result of his meditations was just this, that in every part of his entire presence, the hope gradually began to arise and ultimately even the conviction became definitely fixed that conscious labors and intentional sufferings might transform him from a nothing into a 'something.'

"And then he began to labor consciously with a complete mercilessness towards his denying-part and to create intentionally disturbing conditions for this denying-part of his. Moreover he began to actualize these conscious labors of his and intentionally created conditions of his exclusively only in the manifestations and perceptions in the sphere of those duties of a responsible being which he had taken upon himself, that is to say, in the matter of scientific investigations.

"It was just during that period of his existence that he understood certain cosmic truths.

"And in consequence of the fact that data for the engendering of the being-impulse called 'love-of-kind' were still crystallized in him as in most of the three-brained beings of that period, then in order that other beings of his planet around him similar to him should also know about these truths which he had learned, he created out of marble a 'Boolmarshano' under the title of 'The Affirming and Denying Influences on Man.'

"A Boolmarshano on the continent Atlantis was what the contemporary beings there have replaced by what they call 'books.'

"An exact copy of the mentioned Boolmarshano, made from the tusks of what are called 'Chirniano,' I happened to see personally later, namely, at my sixth descent there, and to decipher it rather in detail.

"As the information I learned concerning the question—in what way the said copy of the Boolmarshano incised with his own hand by Makary Kronbernkzion and which I happened to decipher during my last sojourn on your planet, remained intact and reached to the contemporary epoch—will be very instructive and interesting to you, I will briefly tell you about it.

"When the original of that Boolmarshano was created and sincerely admired and approved by the other learned members of the society Akhaldan, it was placed in the middle of the central what is called 'cathedral' of the beings belonging to that society.

"In consequence of the fact that the contents of the said Boolmarshano then began to interest a greater and greater number of the beings of that period, then the leaders of the mentioned society decided to make several copies of it in order to place them in the same way in all the branches of the Church in other cities of that same continent Atlantis as well as on other continents.

"Seven very exact copies were made of it just for this purpose from the said tusks of the Chirniano.

"One of these mentioned copies, as my what is called 'Spipsychoonalian investigations' cleared up for me, was then assigned to that branch of the Church which was situated on the small continent then existing named 'Sinndraga,' which lay not far from the still existing continent Africa.

"During the second Transapalnian perturbation to that ill-fated planet, this small continent Sinndraga, also just like the continent Atlantis, entered with all that was on it within the planet.

"And as regards the continent Grabontzi or, as it is now called, 'Africa,' you must notice that although this continent did not then enter wholly within the planet, yet nevertheless the same happened to it as happened to other still existing continents, as for instance to the continent Asia; namely, certain parts of it entered within and in their place, from beneath the water, others arose, which having become joined to its remaining parts, became formed as it is now at the present time.

"When, as it seems, the said copy was brought to the continent Grabontzi in order from there to send it further, then, just at that time, that second great catastrophe befell to this ill-fated planet, and owing to that fact that that part of the surface of the continent Grabontzi on which this copy was found happened to remain intact, this copy did not enter within the planet.

"After this terrifying event, this production of the pending Saint Makary Kronbernkzion lay for a long time beneath the ruins and was gradually covered with

'Kashiman,' and only after about thirty centuries, when the three-brained beings who have taken your fancy again multiplied and their process of reciprocal destruction proceeded near this place between the communities of that time named 'Filnooanzi' and 'Plitazoorali,' the beings belonging to the community Filnooanzi, when digging holes to obtain drinking water for themselves and their camels, came across this copy and dug it out.

"And when soon after that, the beings belonging to both of the mentioned communities concluded among themselves, as it has already become usual there, what they call a 'friendly peace,' and began to divide everything acquired during this process of theirs by various means which have also already become usual there and which they express as 'conquest,' 'pillage,' 'commandeering,' 'indemnities,' and so on—then this discovery also, which according to the understanding of the beings of the Earth of that period was valued only as rare material, was divided into halves, and the beings of each separate community took for themselves one half of the said great creation.

"One of the halves of this copy, passing for various reasons from one group to another, finally fell, after seven centuries, into the hands of what are called the 'Egyptian high priests.'

"That strange and peculiar combination of several tusks, already incomprehensible to them, became a sacred relic to them, and in this character it existed there until the period when that Persian king, about whom I once already told you, went there with his hordes, and made, as is said there, a 'clean sweep' of that same unfortunate Egypt.

"Further, that same half of the copy of the Boolmarshano happened to get this time to the continent of Asia and, again passing from hand to hand, passed in the middle of my sixth descent there, by inheritance from his grandfather, just to that Aisorian priest by whom I saw it for the first time.

"As for the second half of that unprecedented work which cannot be made again there, passing also from hand to hand owing to reasons of every kind, it finally also happened to get into one of the central communities of Asia, and during one of what they call 'earthquakes' there it entered within the planet, though not very deep beneath its surface.

"Here I must tell you by the way also how during that sixth descent of mine, I learned about all the aforesaid events—as well as about in general certain other similar information—which had happened long before.

"I have already told you that during that sixth descent of mine there, I became a professional, namely, a 'physician-hypnotist,' and that I studied the strange psyche of your favorites with the help among other things of 'hypnotism' also, that is, through the special specific inherency acquired in their psyche.

"During the period of these activities of mine among them, I specially prepared some of them in a certain way, and made from these subjects what they themselves in former epochs called 'Pythias' and what contemporary beings call 'mediums.'

"Into Pythias or mediums those three-brained beings are converted there in whom, either spontaneously only owing to accidentally arranged surrounding conditions, or intentionally on the part of another consciousness, the inner functioning of the planetary body gets well accustomed to every change of the inner general psyche during sudden changes of their blood circulation, in consequence of which in such subjects there is not hindered the free functioning of various peculiarities of their general psyche which are consciously or unconsciously directed from outside and of the chief automatic data still present in them for genuine being-consciousness, which totality of functioning proceeding in them they call 'subconsciousness.'

"In this same subconsciousness of theirs, owing to many causes formed in them, that particularity of the common psyche of the three-brained beings also accidentally survived which, in general, might function under certain conditions and which is called the 'seeing-and-sensing-of-what-has-occurred-in-the-remote-past.'

"And so, my boy, when during that sixth descent of mine I learned about the beginning of that sad common-cosmic history which came about there on your planet, and when I began to investigate it on the spot during my sojourn there, and also to make clear to myself the individuality of this Makary Kronbernkzion, then, because a very long time had already elapsed since that event, and even every 'Kalzanooarnian' trace concerning the Being who was to blame for it all had absolutely vanished there, I decided to have recourse, in addition to the ordinary forms of investigation, also to this Spipsychoonalian means.

"Among these Spipsychoonalian means of mine, I had recourse also to what is called 'mediumism,' that is to say, I had recourse to the mentioned special property of the said mediums specially prepared by me.

"When, during my investigations concerning the actions and personality of this Makary Kronbernkzion, it seemed probable that there still existed on the surface of that planet 'something' which had a close connection with him, I just began to look for that 'something' also in the said manner.

"Having learned in this way that the aforesaid Aisorian priest possessed the half I referred to of the copy of the original Boolmarshano created personally by Makary Kronbernkzion, and likewise having learned that the same Aisorian priest existed on the continent Asia in the locality called 'Urmia,' I went there and, having found him, soon made it clear that indeed he had a very ancient and, as he expressed it, 'shapeless large ivory mass' which he himself considered very antique and valuable.

"Although after brief negotiations he agreed to show it to me, yet he did not wish to sell it for any money at all; nevertheless, as a result of my talks and persuasions of several days, he allowed me to make an alabaster copy of it which I took away with me.

"As for the second half, although owing to the same method of searching I soon found out where it was, yet it cost very much trouble and bother to obtain it for the immediate deciphering of its contents.

"Although I said that the second half had not yet had time during that period to enter deeply into that planet, yet nevertheless it did enter so deep that it was impossible to obtain it by ordinary methods.

"But my chief trouble was caused then by this, that the place where it existed was near a center populated by your favorites, and I had to prepare everything in advance and to take all suitable measures in order that none of them should either learn nor even suspect anything about it at all.

"Among the measures I took, for instance, was even the purchase of parts of the outskirts of the given place from various large and small proprietors, and I had it dug by workmen exclusively of foreign origin, under the guise of preparing a shaft for what are called copper mines.

"And so, my boy! After I had found both of these halves of the copy of the creation of the pending Saint Makary Kronbernkzion by the aforesaid means, and took them to the city of the country now called 'Turkestan' in which at that period I had the chief place of my existence, I began to decipher the inscriptions and incisions on the Boolmarshano of the scientific thesis by Makary Kronbernkzion under the title of 'The Affirming and Denying Influences on Man.'

"When we return home, I shall without fail try to recall

and tell you as nearly as possible word for word the whole contents of this great production of the Reason and, as is said, of the 'hand' of a three-brained being, but meanwhile I will expound to you only that part of it in which Makary Kronbernkzion first employed the notion of 'Good and Evil,' signifying by these words those forces which are just the basis for the formation of the presence as well as of the flowing state of every separate relatively independent cosmic arising, and also of course of every being.

"If the notions recorded on this Boolmarshano were put into ordinary language, they could be stated in the following words:

"'Evidently we men, also like all the existing units of the World, are formed and always consist of the same three independent forces, by means of which the process of reciprocal maintenance of everything existing proceeds; namely, of the following three independent World forces:

"'The first of these forces constantly arises from the causes which proceed in the Prime Source itself and from the pressure of the newly arisen, and issuing from it by momentum, flows out of that Prime Source.

"'The second World force is what this first force becomes, when, after having spent the momentum which it has received, it strives to reblend with the source of its arising, according to the fundamental World law called "The effects of a cause must always re-enter the cause."

"'Both of these forces in the general process of reciprocally maintaining forces are entirely independent, and in their manifestations have always and in everything their own properties and particularities.

"'The first of these two fundamental forces, namely, that one which for compelling reasons always manifests outside the source of its arising, must constantly involve; and the second one, on the contrary, striving to blend with the cause of its arising, must always and in everything evolve.

"'Owing to the fact that the first of the mentioned three independent forces arises from vivifying actions proceeding in the very foundation of the cause of everything existing and thus receives in its presence the germ of the possibility of manifesting vivifyingness, it may be considered as "Good," that is, as a factor for the actualizing of the backward-flowing effects which in relation to this first force can and must be considered as "Evil."

"'Moreover, the first of these forces, which is manifested from inevitable and compelling causes arising in the Prime Source itself, can from this point of view be considered as passive. And the second backward-flowing force, because it must constantly resist in order to have the possibility of penetrating backward or at least the possibility of withstanding the opposite-flowing first passive force which has received its momentum from the Prime Source causes, must be regarded as active.

"'And as for the third independent World force, this force is nothing else but only the result of the clash everywhere and in everything of these two fundamental descending and ascending independent forces.

"'Although this third independent force is only the result of both first fundamental forces, it is nevertheless the spiritualizing and reconciling source of every World formation.

"'And it is the spiritualizing source of every World formation because it arises and must exist in them as a presence all the time while the given results exist which arise from various unusual mutual resistances occurring between the said two fundamental forces flowing in entirely opposite directions.'

"And so, my boy, it was in this sense and in this

meaning that the words 'Good' and 'Evil' were first used by this unfortunate Makary Kronbernkzion.

"Thanks to the aforesaid Boolmarshano of his and according to other data elucidated by me there on the spot, there was crystallized in me, both concerning Makary Kronbernkzion himself and everything else, my own special opinion, entirely different from the one which the righteous dwellers of the holy planet expressed as a result of all their researches, which although wise were not direct.

"I repeat, although the idea of 'external Good and Evil' first arose there thanks to the individuality of that Makary Kronbernkzion, yet he was, in my opinion, not to blame for it having taken such a maleficent form.

"However it might have been, my boy, indeed according to the detailed and impartial researches I made there on the spot concerning all this, the following then became very definitely clear to me:

"When this maleficent idea there gradually took on such a definite form and began to be for the psyche of your favorites what is called an 'actualizing factor' for the crystallization in their common presences of data for the fantastic notion, namely, that outside of them there exist, as it were, objective sources of 'Good and Evil' acting upon their essence; then from that time on, other peculiar data—at first spontaneously and later through their strange consciousness—began to be crystallized in the general psyche of each of them, which data, owing to automatic being-associations, engender the conviction that the causes of all their manifestations, both good and bad, are not they themselves personally nor their own criminal essence-egoism, but some or other external foreign influences not depending on them at all.

"The fundamental evil, for all these unfortunates, from this fantastic idea resulted there chiefly because, even before this—of course thanks always to the same conditions of ordinary being-existence established by them themselves—data ceased to be crystallized in them for the engendering of what is called 'various being-aspects of a world view,' and instead of this a 'world view' is formed in them based exclusively on that maleficent idea about external Good and Evil.

"And indeed at the present time there, your favorites have already based all questions without exception, questions concerning ordinary being-existence as well as questions about self-perfecting and also about various 'philosophies' and every kind of 'science' existing there, and of course also about their innumerable 'religious teachings' and even their notorious what are called 'morality,' 'politics,' 'laws,' 'morals,' and so on, exclusively on that fantastic but for themselves in an objective sense very maleficent idea.

"If now, my boy, in addition to all I have told you concerning this maleficent idea, I shall tell you only about how the beings of our tribe who were exiled on this peculiar planet involuntarily became the participants of the arising of a certain comical story; then, I am sure, you will obtain almost a real conception of the weird notion of your favorites about 'Good' and 'Evil.'

"The beings of our tribe were in the following way the involuntary cause of the complete fixing of this comical story in the process of the ordinary existence of these strange three-brained beings.

"I have already told you once that many beings of our tribe happened in the beginning to exist there and to mix with the ancestors of these favorites of yours, and even to have friendly relations with certain of them.

"It is necessary to remark that when our tribe indeed existed there among them, there was absolutely nothing at all concerning this tragicomic story about which I shall now tell you, unless we exclude the fact that before our tribe left that planet the last time a notion arose and began to exist among certain beings there—but only among those particularly naïve—that the beings of our tribe are, as it were, 'immortal.'

"And this notion then arose there evidently because the beings of our tribe had an incommensurably longer duration of existence than theirs, and hence the cases of the sacred 'Rascooarno' among our tribe were rare, and perhaps it happened that in those periods this sacred process did not even occur to any of our tribe.

"I repeat that besides the aforesaid, there was nothing else there at that period when our tribe existed among them.

"Only afterwards when for certain considerations the desire was expressed from Above that as few as possible of the beings of our tribe should exist on that planet, and when therefore the majority of us emigrated to exist on other planets of this same system, in consequence of which scarcely any of our beings remained among them, just from that time on began that aforementioned comical story in which, even until now, the real names of certain beings of our tribe are involuntarily involved.

"The events which gave rise there to this peculiar coincidence, namely, that these strange three-brained beings connected the names of many beings of our tribe with this fantastic idea of theirs, came about owing to the following:

"Soon after our beings departed from this planet, a certain Armanatoora who had belonged to the epoch of the blossoming of the Tikliamishian civilization, and who was by profession a priest—but from among those of this profession whom others regarded as 'learned priests'—was the first who built up a whole 'religious teaching' based on this maleficent idea.

"It was just in that same 'religious teaching' that he,

among other things, explained for the first time that certain invisible spirits existing among them spread 'external Good and Evil,' and compelled men to take in and manifest this 'Good and Evil'; and that these 'spirits,' the spreaders of 'Good,' were called 'Angels,' and those 'spirits,' the spreaders of 'Evil,' were called 'Devils.'

"The Angels, the bearers and spreaders of 'Good,' that is, of the most high and most divine, being themselves high and divine, could never be seen or sensed by men.

"But as regards the Devils, they, having the lowest origin, that is to say, coming from 'below' itself, can on the contrary be seen by men.

"And if sometimes men do not actually see Devils, then this is only because of their 'suggestion,' and hence the visibility of Devils for the perception of human sight increases in proportion to the increase of the 'righteousness' of people.

"When this new religious teaching was widely spread, certain of them, according to the tales of your ancestors, had information about the existence in former times among them of those beings who, as it were, were immortal and who suddenly disappeared; and it was just these beings who decided to spread the supposition that evidently they were just these same Devils who, foreseeing the arising of a true religious teaching and fearing that people in consequence would perhaps 'find them out,' made themselves invisible but continued in reality to exist among them.

"It was then that the real names of many beings of our tribe, which also chanced to reach in the said manner to the beings of the period when this mentioned religious teaching appeared, acquired a greater special meaning and, passing from generation to generation, these names even reached to your contemporary favorites.

"To these names they have, up till now, continued to attribute all kinds of fantastic 'roles,' which, according to their imagination, must be present in those 'corps' of beings-devils, which have been, as it were, specially organized by our CREATOR HIMSELF and sent to their planet to mock them.

"In short, to the imagination of these three-brained freaks of our Megalocosmos, a Devil is that invisible 'somebody' existing, as it were, among them, who on the command of our CREATOR ALL-MAINTAINER dwells on their planet for certain of HIS ALL-MAINTAINER'S aims.

"These Devils, as it were, suggest by every truth and falsehood to men-beings and compel them to manifest at every step those innumerable 'villainies' which have already become, as it were, a property of their essence.

"Of course, none of them even suspects that if every kind of villainy proceeds among them in general, then they do these villainies exclusively only because, existing wrongly, they thus permit to be formed in them their inner 'evil-God,' which I once called 'self-calming' and which has absolute dominion over the whole of their psyche and for which only this idea of 'external Good and Evil' is necessary.

"At all events, from this fantastic idea of theirs, very great publicity was obtained there for the praising and glorifying of the name of our Incomparable Lucifer, because nowhere in the Universe are his capabilities so praised and glorified as they are praised and glorified by these favorites of yours."

At this point of Beelzebub's tales, there entered that part of the cosmic ship *Karnak* where the conversations took place one of the servants of the ship, who gave Beelzebub a newly received 'Leitoochanbros' addressed to him; and on leaving he turned to everybody and joyfully exclaimed that the reflections of the sphere of the planet Karatas could already be seen.

CHAPTER 45

In the Opinion of Beelzebub, Man's Extraction of Electricity from Nature and Its Destruction During Its Use, Is One of the Chief Causes of the Shortening of the Life of Man

After Beelzebub had listened to the contents of the Leitoochanbros and had put it by the side of the "Sinooa" near him, that is, something similar to our étagère, he again deeply sighed and continued to speak as follows:

"It would be only half a calamity for our common Megalocosmos, if the abnormalities of the ordinary existence of the three-brained beings of this planet of yours had all kinds of bad consequences only for them themselves, that is, for the three-brained beings, which they are, and also for the possibilities of completely perfecting themselves with those higher being-bodies which have already had the extreme misfortune to arise within them or which will arise within them in the future.

"But now the whole terror lies in this, that their abnormal existence already begins to have a repercussion and a harmful influence on the normal existence of the three-brained beings who breed on quite different planets, though, it is true, belonging to the same solar system, and also have a harmful influence on the possibilities of the normal self-perfecting of their higher being-parts coated in their common presences.

"I happened to learn about this distressing fact of common-cosmic character only just before my departure forever from that solar system Ors.

"The most interesting information for you, of all the events which have given cause for a clear constating and completed crystallizing in my common presence of the 'imperishable' being-data for the indubitable conviction of precisely such a common-cosmic distressing fact, might be the information that in this I was greatly helped by none other than the result, or as your favorites would say the son, of my essence-friend Gornahoor Harharkh, the young conscious individual Gornahoor Rakhoorkh, who also, like his producer, devoted the whole of his existence to the study of all the details of the properties of the cosmic Omnipresent-Okidanokh and also, little by little, became worthy of being considered one of the what are called 'higher-degree' common-cosmic learned three-brained beings.

"Do you know, my boy? In consequence of the fact that all the events and conversations which served as the cause of the gradual elucidation and crystallization in me of the data for the indubitable conviction of such a common-cosmic distressing fact are in general very interesting, and might be for you very instructive, and, as only the reflections of the sphere of our dear Karatas are meanwhile visible, I will tell you also about this in somewhat greater detail.

"In order to give you a fuller representation about why in my Being the data has been crystallized for the constating and thorough cognizing of this, I shall tell you, in its order, about what proceeded and shall begin from the moment when, while still on this planet of yours, I first heard about my full pardon.

"As soon as I heard about this special most glorious act of grace toward me, I, of course, decided at that very moment to return at the first opportunity to the dear essence-place of my arising.

"And for this it was necessary for me first of all to ascend to the planet Mars in order thoroughly to prepare for such a long journey.

"Several days after having left your planet forever, I,

as always, returned on our same *Occasion* to the planet Mars.

"Arriving there on the planet Mars we soon received a command from Above that I and all other beings of our tribe who wished to return to the place of their arising should assemble on the planet Saturn, using the ship *Occasion*, on which planet that large intersystem ship *Omnipresent* would land which would bring us all to our destination.

"I nevertheless had to exist on the planet Mars for a certain time in order to liquidate all my personal affairs there and to give various orders concerning the beings of our tribe. And it was just at this time that I was told that the 'Toof-Nef-Tef' there very much wished to see me.

"Toof-Nef-Tef on the planet Mars is the name given to the being who is the head of all the three-brained beings breeding on this planet, and he is like that being who in the same position on your planet is called 'king.'

"I knew this Toof-Nef-Tef or king in his youth when he was only a 'Plef-Perf-Noof,' and a Plef-Perf-Noof is almost the same as our Zirlikners or, on your planet Earth, 'physicians.'

"Apropos, I must also tell you that on almost all the planets of our Great Universe and likewise on the other planets of this solar system also, a being becomes the head of beings by merit, just from among these former Plef-Perf-Noofs, or physicians.

"My first meeting with the Martian Toof-Nef-Tef took place when we first arrived in this solar system and settled on this planet Mars. He was then a Plef-Perf-Noof just on that part of the surface of this planet where I and all who came with me had the place of our residence.

"Since then, existing on various parts of the surface of the planet Mars in the capacity of Plef-Perf-Noof, he merited becoming the head over all the beings breeding on the planet Mars; and when he neared the state of the sacred 'Ischmetch,' he desired to return to just that part of the surface of his planet where he had spent his youth. That is why this former Plef-Perf-Noof, now Toof-Nef-Tef, happened at that time to be near the place of my residence on Mars.

"This Martian Toof-Nef-Tef was, according to the notions of your favorites, already an extremely old being: he was by the time-calculation of the planet Mars about twelve thousand Martian years old, which is only a little less than the time-calculation of the Earth.

"Here you must be told that on the planet Mars the duration of the existence of beings in general is almost the same as that of the three-centered beings of all the other planets of our Megalocosmos, excepting of course those beings who are directly formed from the first 'Tetartocosmoses,' and whose duration of existence may be three times as long.

"The three-brained beings arising and existing on the planet Mars as well as the three-centered beings of all those planets of our Megalocosmos on which an existence normal for three-centered beings proceeds, also have full possibility of reaching the state of the sacred Ischmetch, namely, that being-state when the existence of a being already becomes dependent, as regards the Most Great cosmic Iraniranumange, only on those substances which arise directly from the manifestations of the Most Most Holy Prime Source Itself, and not as it proceeds in the other beings whose existence depends on cosmic substances arising through the results of all corresponding gravity-center concentrations of the common-cosmic fundamental Ansanbaluiazar.

"And when they reach this state of the sacred Ischmetch and the Reason of their highest part is already perfected up to the required gradation of the sacred measure of Reason, then in the first place, the process of the sacred

Rascooarno may also proceed with them, but only by their own wish; and secondly, their highest being-body is taken directly to the holy planet Purgatory.

"And so, when I returned to the planet Mars from the planet Earth, and while I was hurriedly finishing the liquidation of my affairs there, I was informed that the Toof-Nef-Tef of the planet wished to see me personally.

"This request of the honorable Toof-Nef-Tef was translated to me through our Ahoon by means of what is there called a 'Kelli-E-Ofoo.'*

"The text of this Kelli-E-Ofoo was as follows:

"'I have heard that you, your Right Reverence, have become worthy of receiving from our COMMON FATHER CREATOR full pardon for the transgressions of your youth, and that you are now leaving my native land forever. And therefore, I, an old being, very much wish to see you and to bless you personally for the last time, and at the same time to thank, through your person, all the beings of your tribe for their constant good relations with the beings of my native land during so many years.'

"At the end of this Kelli-E-Ofoo was the postscript:

"'I personally would present myself at your house, but as you know, the size of my planetary body does not permit me in any way to do so, and hence I am compelled to beg you not to refuse to come to my "Fal-Fe-Foof."†

"I must say that the three-brained beings of the planet Mars knew our genuine nature from the very beginning, and also the true reason why we were compelled to dwell on their planet.

"They were not like the three-brained beings of your planet who never knew anything and never even suspected who we were and why we existed on their planet.

* Kelli-E-Ofoo on the planet Mars is the same thing which on the Earth is called a "note."

† Fal-Fe-Foof in Martian speech signifies a dwelling.

"And so, my boy, when I received the said invitation from the honorable Toof-Nef-Tef, I of course immediately decided to go to him without delay, and when I arrived there, this, in the full sense of the word, great Toof-Nef-Tef, after all the prescribed ceremonies and exchange of courtesies, turned to me as we were talking, with his request, which was just the cause for the subsequent crystallization in me of corresponding data for the indubitable conviction that the results ensuing from the abnormal existence of the three-brained beings of your planet had already begun to act harmfully also on the ordinary existence of the three-brained beings arising and existing on the planet Mars, in respect of their 'potency' to perfect themselves as is proper to all three-brained beings.

"I shall try to give you in our speech the contents of this request of the Great Toof-Nef-Tef almost literally.

"He then said as follows:

"'Your Right Reverence!

"'Thanks to the most gracious pardon granted to you from Above, you have again acquired the right freely to actualize your justly merited wishes. And thanks to this all-embracing grace, you have again all the possibilities of becoming what you might long ago have been owing to your formerly acquired merits as regards Reason, and of course from now on, you, your Right Reverence, will undoubtedly meet various Individuals corresponding to your Reason who have already reached the higher gradations of Reason.

"'And so, I take the liberty of applying to you, as my old friend, with the request which consists in this, that on meeting these Individuals you should remember about me, an old being, and not forget to ask their opinion about that fact which during recent years has almost all the time been a shock for the arising of disturbing associations in all my spiritualized parts, and that when you will have learned their opinion, not to refuse to communicate it to me somehow or other at a suitable occasion.'

"And he continued further:

"'The point is that during the last few "Ftofoos" I constated very definitely that, among the beings of our planet, the "Noorfooftafaf"* increases each "Ftofoo," and parallel with this, I observed in them a proportional diminishing of the intensity of their potency for the possibility of active mentation.

"'When I first discovered this fact, so deplorable for the beings of our planet, and began from then on intensively to ponder and to seek the cause of it, in order to be able to give corresponding indications to those beings who have entrusted themselves to me to help them in their struggle to uproot this lamentable factor that has newly arisen in their common presences, then in spite of the fact that I meditated very often and long on this question which constantly agitates me, I have up till now not been able even approximately to elucidate for myself where the trouble lies and what corresponding measures must be taken to destroy this evil.'

"Thus ended the request of the honorable Toof-Nef-Tef of the planet Mars, and I, my boy, of course, there and then promised this oldest friend of mine to inquire about all this and at my first meeting with a corresponding Individual to communicate the reply to him without fail.

"Several Martian days after the interview of which I have told you, we left this hospitable planet forever and ascended to the planet Saturn.

"No sooner had we arrived on the planet Saturn than the chief of our tribe there at once came and announced

* The expression "Noorfooftafaf" signifies on this planet something like what is called on the Earth "will-lessness."

to us the contents of the etherogram he had just received, in which it was stated that the big intersystem ship *Omnipresent* would land on the planet Saturn only early in the 'Hre-Hree-Hra.'

"Hre-Hree-Hra means there one of those periods of time determined by a certain position occupied by this planet in relation, on the one hand to the sun of its system, and on the other, to another planet of this same system called Neptune.

"There are in one year seven of these definitely established periods there on the planet Saturn, and each of them has its own name.

"As by the time-calculations of the planet Mars there yet remained to this Hre-Hree-Hra almost half a 'Foos,' or by the time-calculation of your favorites, about one and a half months, we decided to organize our ordinary being-existence there during this waiting in a more or less suitable manner.

"One part of our beings remained on the ship *Occasion* itself, another found accommodation in the places offered us by the amiable beings of the planet Saturn, and I with Ahoon went to Rirkh, that is, to just that large populated center of beings there where my friend Gornahoor Harharkh existed.

"In the evening of our arrival there I, by the way, asked this essence-friend of mine during friendly conversation how the existence of his heir proceeded, that is, my dear 'Kesdjanian-result-outside-of-me,' or as your favorites would say my godson, Gornahoor Rakhoorkh.

"He thanked me and said that Rakhoorkh existed quite well, that he had already become his heir in all respects, and that he had made the aim of his existence also the study of the details of the Omnipresent substance Okidanokh which had previously been for himself also the aim of all his responsible existence.

"After having paused a little, he added that in respect of the knowledge attained of the question of the cosmic substance Okidanokh his heir had already, as he expressed himself, 'smelled-out-its-very-essence.'

"He said further that owing to the results of the scientific attainments of his heir, all the data for every conviction that had been previously crystallized in his essence, thanks to persevering labors during long years, had by that time not only been totally decrystallized, but that he had even entirely destroyed all his inventions relating to the investigations of this omnipresent cosmic substance, among which was also his famous 'non-radiating lamp'; and sighing deeply, he ended by saying:

"'I am now in full agreement with the opinion of the "result-of-my-all," that it was the greatest misfortune for me to have been occupied so long with this, in the objective sense, absolutely "unredeemable sin."'

"Talking further on various incidental topics, we began, in accordance with the flowing of associations of being-mentation, to talk also of the three-brained beings breeding on the planet Earth.

"You remember, I have already told you that my friend Gornahoor Harharkh was always kept informed of my observations on their strange psyche which I sent to him as well as to your uncle Tooilan, even with duplicates of certain of my notes.

"So, as we were talking of these three-brained beings who have taken your fancy, Gornahoor Harharkh happened by the way to ask me:

"'Tell me, please, my friend, is it possible that the general duration of existence of these unfortunates still continues to diminish?'

"When I began to explain to him the state of affairs there at the present time on this question, and the new data I had elicited concerning that abnormality there, just at that moment, the 'result' of Gornahoor Harharkh, Gornahoor Rakhoorkh himself, entered the room where we were.

"Though the newcomer had exactly the same exterior as his 'producer' he had the appearance of being very virile and full of fiery youth.

"When he had taken his place on his perch, as is proper to the three-brained beings of that planet, he began, as is usual to them, to welcome me in an 'angelically musical voice' with kind and self-satisfying wishes of being-feeling.

"And in conclusion he said, with a certain pathos:

"'Although you are only my "Kesdjanian father," yet, in view of the fact that during my "Hirr-Hirr"* you assuredly fulfilled with the feeling of full and thorough cognizance the divine obligations taken upon yourself in respect of me, there have been crystallized in my common presence in respect of you data equivalent to those which should be in the common presence of each three-brained being in respect of his own producer, and it is, without doubt, just because of this that I very often remember you and each time in my thoughts I wish for you such ensuing circumstances at all times as can lead in general to, in the objective sense, a good and happy future.'

"You probably, my boy, did not understand what I meant when I told you that Gornahoor Rakhoorkh took his place on his perch.

"The point is that the three-brained beings of this planet according to their outer coating gradually acquire the habit of resting only in that posture, when after having stooped in a special way they let the whole weight of their planetary body rest on their lower extremities, and for these means of resting it gradually became necessary

* Hirr-Hirr on the planet Saturn is the name given to that sacred ceremony which is similar to what is called on the planet Earth "baptism."

for them to be at a certain height; hence it is that the three-brained beings there have established the practice of fixing at a certain height, in the rooms where they exist, special sticks for resting, which they call perches.

"I may as well say also that these perches of theirs are usually embellished with various knick-knacks or carved with all kinds of figures, just as is done by your favorites also, when they manifest the same weakness in regard to what they call their 'furniture.'

"And so, after having taken his place on his perch and expressed his welcome, my dear 'Kesdjanian-result-outside-of-me,' or my godson, Gornahoor Rakhoorkh, began to take part in my conversation with Gornahoor Harharkh.

"And so, my boy, when during our general conversation on various topics, I, by the way, became interested to learn from my godson what was the reason which led to the crystallizing in his presence of data for the engendering of the impulse to interest himself seriously in the sphere of the elucidating of the details of the Omnipresent cosmic-substance Okidanokh, thanks to which he also, like his producer, had become worthy to make certain great cosmic discoveries; then after young Rakhoorkh's reply with explanatory details to this question of mine, the fact became clear to me that the abnormal existence of your favorites already began to act harmfully on the normal existence and on the conscious self-perfecting of beings breeding on the planet Mars, and at the same time, thanks to this detailed reply of his, which was based on scientific foundations, I drew also data for the elucidating of that question for the solution of which my old Martian friend, the Great Toof-Nef-Tef had applied to me with his request.

"I will try, my boy, to reproduce to you in our speech all the thoughts of this reply of his, also as exactly as possible.

"After having thought a little at the question which I had put to him, Gornahoor Rakhoorkh replied with deep seriousness:

"'At the beginning of my existence, namely, at the age when I was still preparing to be a responsible being, I—as is proper to all three-brained beings at this age—devoted the greater part of my time to practicing for the potency "to-deliberate-actively-and-long"; and of itself it so happened that during the interval of time for necessary rest, I used to be occupied with the various experimental apparatuses of my producer.

"'And it was just then at that period of my existence that I began to notice more than once, that on certain days the forces and degree of my active mentation grew particularly worse.

"'What I thus constated aroused in me a subjective interest which served as the source for the engendering in my presence of the requisite impulse for the thorough cognizance of the cause of this fact, and from then on I began to pay attention both to myself as well as to what proceeded around me and to seek out the causes for it; and after one "Rkhee" I became convinced beyond doubt that this undesirable state proceeded with me each time, on the day when our large "Lifechakan"* was in action.

"'It was just this fact which I then first constated which was the cause that I have, since then, become seriously interested in this omnipresent cosmic substance and deeply absorbed in the study of its details.

"'As a result, from the very beginning of my subsequent experimental elucidations, I came to possess an immeasurable number of every kind of proof for the elucidation, both for myself and for others, of the fact that the

* Lifechakan approximately corresponds to what on Earth is called a "dynamo."

Omnipresent substance Okidanokh is such a particle of the common presence of the atmosphere of our planet, and evidently of the presence of the atmosphere of other planets, as takes part both in the arising of every planetary and surplanetary formation—among which of course there is also the "Hraprkhabeekhrokhnian" part of every being—as well as in the maintenance of their existence.

"'Upon my further experimental elucidations I also became aware, beyond all doubt, that although our solar system like all the other solar systems of the Great Universe has its own Ansanbaluiazar, and each planet with its atmosphere is a special place of concentration of one or another class of cosmic substances of the given "Systematic-Ansanbaluiazar," yet nevertheless the cosmic-substance Okidanokh is an indispensable and predominant part of the presence of each planet.

"'And later, also thanks to my experiments, it became clear to me that this cosmic substance is, owing to the common universal equilibrium, concentrated in every system in a strictly corresponding proportion and is distributed also in a strictly definite proportion between the atmospheres of each planet of the given solar system, and that when this universal substance is used up by accident or design in any one place of atmospheric space, it must without fail be replenished for the equilibrium of its common proportionalness in the atmosphere, and this proceeds by its flowing in from other places, and thereby this balancing transposition of Okidanokh must proceed not only from one space to another in the atmosphere of any planet, but also from the atmosphere of one planet to the atmosphere of another planet, if in this other planet for some reason or other more than its established norm is used up.

"'Finally, I still further very definitely and from every aspect made clear to my reason and proved to others that the Omnipresent cosmic-substance Okidanokh present in our atmosphere and which is constantly being replenished, is for the common presence of our planet not only necessary and most important for every kind of arising and maintaining of existence, but also that the essence of every "relatively independent" intraplanetary and surplanetary formation as well as of the beings of every system of brains and external coating depends on this substance, and likewise that the possibilities for three-brained beings to perfect themselves and ultimately to blend with the Prime Cause of everything existing depend exclusively also on it.

"'I repeat, as a result of all my experimental elucidations, I very definitely cognized for myself and acquired indubitable data for the possibilities of proving from every aspect to all those around me, beings like myself, that the destruction in the presences of the planet and of its atmosphere, of the Omnipresent cosmic-substance Okidanokh is almost equivalent to the conscious destruction of all the labors and results of the First-Sacred-Cause of everything that exists.'

"With these words, captivated by the theme of this exposition, my dear godson, the young high-spirited Gornahoor Rakhoorkh, finished his talk.

"In the middle of Gornahoor Rakhoorkh's explanations concerning the mentioned properties of the Omnipresent cosmic-substance Okidanokh and the inevitable consequences of its extraction and destruction from the common presence of your planet, the suspicion arose in me, and in my memory there gradually began to be restored all kinds of general pictures—previously perceived during my personal sojourn among your favorites just during the period of my close observations on their existence from the planet Mars of the impressions from their ordinary being-existence—of how they at different periods repeatedly obtained this substance or its separate parts from the nature of their planet and used them for their different, naïvely egoistic aims.

"And when during the further explanations of Gornahoor Rakhoorkh, I, by association, remembered the request of the great Toof-Nef-Tef of the planet Mars, I then with all my being became aware without any doubt of all the maleficent consequences of just this manifestation of the three-brained beings of your planet.

"They named the totality or the separate parts of this substance, sacred just for them, differently at different periods, and at the present time they name the result of the blending and the mutual destruction of two parts of this omnipresent substance 'Electricity.'

"And, indeed, although there they had already several times in earlier epochs found out, of course thanks always to accidentally successive circumstances, how to extract by various means from the nature of their planet, and to use for every kind of their, as I already said, 'naïvely egoistic' aims, various parts of this omnipresent substance absolutely necessary for normal cosmic processes, yet never have they destroyed so much of it as in recent times.

"So in this way, thanks to the explanations of my 'Kesdjanian-result-outside-of-me,' in the first place it became indubitably clear to me concerning the maleficent action, already begun, of the results of the ordinary abnormal being-existence of the three-brained beings who have taken your fancy; and secondly, the disturbing question of my old friend was solved of itself, namely, why during recent times it had become more and more difficult for the three-brained beings of the planet Mars to perfect themselves.

"As regards the solution in this manner of this question, I might say that it was obtained, just as is said about similar cases, in one rarely used saying of our esteemed

Mullah Nassr Eddin, who formulated it in the following words:

"'One can never know who might help you to get out of galoshes.'

"And the solution of this question was thus obtained, because my very old friend had in view individuals with quite other data and possibilities than these Saturn friends of mine possessed, who were only ordinary three-brained beings; my friend probably did not suspect that in most cases concerning these questions, just these ordinary three-brained beings, who acquire information about every kind of genuine cosmic fact exclusively only thanks to their being-Partkdolg-duty, are more competent than any of the Angels or Cherubim with their prepared Being, who, though perfected in Reason to high gradations, yet as regards practical confrontation may appear to be only such Individuals as our always respected Mullah Nassr Eddin defines in the following words:

"'Never will he understand the sufferings of another who has not experienced them himself though he may have divine Reason and the nature of a genuine Devil.'"

At this point of Beelzebub's tales, there were diffused all along the intersystem ship *Karnak* artificially produced vibrations which had the property of penetrating into the common presences of all the passengers of the ship and which acted on what are called the "wandering nerves" of the stomach.

This artificially produced manifestation was an announcement to the passengers about their assembling in the common what is called "Djameechoonatra," a kind of terrestrial "monasterial refectory" in which the second being-food is collectively taken.

CHAPTER 46

Beelzebub Explains to His Grandson the Significance of the Form and Sequence Which He Chose for Expounding the Information Concerning Man

After the process of taking in the second being-food, Beelzebub did not immediately return from the "Djamee-choonatra" where they usually spent their time in conversation, but first went to his "Kesshah."

Kesshah is the name given to those compartments on space-ships which on terrestrial steamers are called "cabins."

Beelzebub first entered his Kesshah in order to cool his already extremely decrepit tail a little in a certain liquid, to which he was compelled to have recourse from time to time on account of his old age.

When on returning from his Kesshah he silently entered that section of the ship *Karnak* where they usually spent their time, he unexpectedly saw the following picture, unusual for him:

His beloved grandson Hassein was standing with his face to the corner, his hands covering his eyes, weeping. Beelzebub, deeply moved, quickly approached Hassein and in a voice full of anxiety, asked him:

"What is the matter, my dear boy? Are you really weeping?"

Hassein wished to answer, but it could be seen that the sobbing of his planetary body prevented him from speaking.

Only after a rather long time, when the planetary body of Hassein was a little calmed did he, gazing at his grandfather with very sad eyes, but yet with a smile of affection, say:

"Do not worry about me, my dear Grandfather, this state of mine will soon pass. Evidently during the last 'dianosk' I actively pondered a great deal and in all probability, from this unaccustomed 'newly tempoed' functioning, the general tempo of the functioning of the whole of my common presence has changed.

"And now, until this new tempo of my mentation harmonizes with the other tempos of my common functioning already established in me, such abnormalities as this weeping will probably proceed in me.

"I must confess, my dear Grandfather, that the fundamental cause for the arising in my common presence of such a state was the arising by association in my mentation of the picture of the situation and destiny of those ill-fated higher being-bodies which, owing to various chance happenings, arise and are half-formed in the common presences of the terrestrial three-brained beings.

"These associative thoughts, with a proportionately increasing impulse in me of sadness, began still in the Djameechoonatra during the sacred feeding of the second being-food; the thought about them arose in my mentation by association when I was overfilled with happiness from all that took place there.

"In me it began to think, concerning these ill-fated three-brained beings about whom you have given me so much information during recent times, that only thanks to the consequences of the properties of that 'something' accursed for them—which, through causes not depending on their essences at all but exclusively only on the unforeseeingness of certain Most High Sacred Individuals, was implanted in the common presences of their ancestors—not only their 'higher being-bodies' which are coated in them but also they themselves as ordinary beings are forever deprived of the possibility of experiencing that bliss, which is actualized in the presences of all kinds of relatively independent individuals, during such a sacred feeding of the second being-food in which we have just participated."

When Hassein finished speaking Beelzebub looked long and fixedly into his eyes, and then, with a smile which revealed a being-impulse of love, he said:

"Now I see that during the last dianosk you indeed actively pondered a great deal, or, as certain of your contemporary favorites would express themselves, 'during this time you did not inwardly sleep.' Now let us take our usual places and speak about that theme to which I already once promised you to refer, and which will be wholly appropriate to the present occurrence."

When they were already seated and when Ahoon had also arrived, Beelzebub began to speak as follows:

"First of all I shall begin by expressing outwardly in words the impulse of joy concerning you which proceeds from within my common presence. I personally am very, very glad for this crisis which has occurred and still continues in you. I am glad chiefly because your sincere sobbing which I saw and which was manifested just at this present period of your existence, when you, according to the laws of the Great Heropass, are on the threshold of the Being of a responsible being—that is, at just that age when every kind of data for those functionings which during the responsible existence of each three-brained being compose his individuality is crystallized and acquires a harmonious tempo in the common functioning—gives me the assurance that the approximate cognizance or even only the sensing of so to say the 'taste' of this being-joy of mine which is at the first glance not logical, is very desirable and even necessary for you at the period of your responsible existence, as well as for all three-brained beings who have reached responsible age. I shall therefore first of all explain to you about it.

"Your weeping gives me the assurance also that in your future responsible existence there will also be in your common presence those being-data which are the foundation of the essence of every bearer of Divine Reason and which are even formulated by our COMMON FATHER in words placed over the chief entrance of the holy planet Purgatory decreeing the following:

"'ONLY - HE - MAY - ENTER - HERE - WHO - PUTS - HIMSELF - IN - THE - POSITION - OF - THE - OTHER - RESULTS - OF - MY - LABORS.'

"This is what your essence manifested in this present case when, personally experiencing bliss and accidentally remembering by association that others were deprived of it, you sincerely sobbed with the whole of your presence.

"I am glad for you more particularly because the said data, necessary for a being, begin to function in you just at the time when there are crystallized and formed in you all those being-data, the crystallization of which does not at all depend upon a being's own Reason but depends exclusively only upon surrounding beings, external conditions, and the Most Great common-cosmic Iraniranumange.

"Well, then, now we can return to my intended theme, that is, why during the whole of our journey on this space-ship I have told you so much and in such a sequence about the three-brained beings breeding on the planet Earth.

"The point is, that when I returned to our dear Karatas, I, being free from any other being-duties whatsoever, voluntarily took upon myself the responsible guidance of your finishing Oskiano for the Being of a responsible being, or, as your favorites would say, 'your education.' And, in view of the fact that the present period of your existence is for you just that period when in general, in three-brained beings, all those functions present in them are harmonized, which in totality during the period of responsible existence just actualize in them that form of mentation which is called 'sane-mentation'; I, in consequence of this, when we set out on this journey in the space-ship *Karnak*, thought of profiting by this time to help you so that the harmonizing of the functions of yours and the formation of your future active mentation which depends on them should proceed precisely in that order, of the correctness of which I became convinced with the whole of my presence during the process of my long personal existence.

"When at the beginning of our journey I noticed that you were very interested in the three-brained beings of the planet Earth, I then decided, under the aspect of gratifying that interest of yours, to tell you everything about them in such a way that there should be crystallized in you for your future being-associations the required what are called 'Egoplastikoori,' without any admixture of doubt.

"For this, I have in almost all my tales strictly held to the two following principles:

"The first: not to say anything as if it were my own personal opinion, in order that data necessary for your own convictions should not be crystallized in you in a prepared form according to the opinions of another.

"And in accordance with the second principle: to relate to you in just such an order and in such a premeditated and selected sequence about all the events which proceeded on this planet Earth connected with the arising among these three-brained beings who have taken your fancy, of various gradually progressing inner and outer abnormalities in the process of their ordinary being-existence, the total of which has given them their present desolate and almost inescapable state—in order that you should be able to marshal your own subjective reasoning concerning all causes, only on the basis of certain facts which I have told you.

"I decided to do this in order that many diversely

essenced 'Egoplastikoori' for your future logical confrontation should be crystallized in corresponding localizations in your common presence, and also in order that from active mentation the proper elaboration in you of the sacred substances of Abrustdonis and Helkdonis for the purpose of coating and perfecting both of your higher being-parts should proceed more intensively.

"And now, my boy, in order that what I am saying at this moment should become still more comprehensible to you, I find it necessary to repeat in another and more definite form about the difference already mentioned by me many times for different motives, between what are called 'knowledge' and 'understanding' present in three-brained beings in general.

"In order that this difference should stand out more clearly, I shall again take as an example the ordinary Reason of your favorites.

"If one makes an analogy between this as they themselves call it 'conscious Reason' of theirs which is completely fixed in contemporary beings, and that Reason of three-brained beings in general who breed on other planets of our Great Megalocosmos, then the former which they have in them might be called the 'Reason-of-knowing' and the latter the 'Reason-of-understanding.'

"The conscious Reason-of-understanding, which in general it is proper for three-brained beings to have, is a 'something' which blends with their common presence, and therefore information of every kind perceived with this Reason becomes forever their inseparable part.

"The information perceived with this Reason, or results obtained thanks to being-contemplation of the totality of formerly perceived information—however a being himself may change and whatever changes may proceed in the spheres around him—will be forever a part of his essence.

"And as for that Reason which for most of your contemporary favorites has become habitual and which I called the Reason-of-knowing, every kind of new impression perceived through this Reason, and likewise every kind of intentionally or simply automatically obtained result from formerly perceived impressions is only a temporary part of the being, and might result in them exclusively only in certain surrounding circumstances, and on the definite condition that the information which constitutes all his foundation and entirety should without fail be from time to time so to say 'freshened' or 'repeated'; otherwise these formerly perceived impressions change of themselves, or even entirely, so to say, 'evaporate' out of the common presence of the three-brained being.

"Although in respect of the Sacred Triamazikamno the process of the arising of both kinds of being-Reason flows equally, yet the fulfilling factors for the actualization of its three separate holy forces are different. Namely, for the formation of the Reason-of-knowing the formerly perceived contradictory impressions crystallized in any one of the three localizations which three-brained beings have, serve as the affirming and denying factors and the new impressions proceeding from without serve in this case as the third factor.

"And for the Reason-of-understanding these factors are as follows: the first, that is the 'sacred-affirming,' is the newly perceived impressions of any localization which has at the given moment what is called 'the-center-of-gravity-functioning'; the second or 'sacred-denying' is the corresponding data present in another of his localizations; and the third factor is what is called the 'being-Autokolizikners,' or as they otherwise call it 'Hoodazbabognari,' the sense of which name signifies, 'the results of the persevering actualizing of the striving towards the manifestation of one's own individuality.'

"By the way, you might as well hear still once more even if you do know it, that the said being-Autokolizikners are formed in the presences of three-brained beings in general in all three localizations exclusively only from the results of the actualization of 'being-Partkdolg-duty,' that is to say, thanks to those factors which, from the very beginning of the arising of the three-brained beings, our UNI-BEING COMMON FATHER designed to be the means for self-perfection.

"It is these same formations in the common presences of three-brained beings which are actualized as the third holy force of the Sacred Triamazikamno for the arising of the Reason-of-understanding.

"Only thanks to this factor, in the process of the blending of newly perceived impressions of every kind in the presences of three-brained beings, are there crystallized on the basis of the Sacred Triamazikamno data for one's own cognizance and understanding proper to the being alone; and likewise exclusively only during such processes of the crystallization of the data for consciousness in the presences of three-brained beings does there proceed what is called 'Zernofookalnian-friction' thanks to which the sacred substances Abrustdonis and Helkdonis are chiefly formed in them for the coating and perfecting of their higher parts.

"I must tell you here that only the newly perceived impressions which are crystallized in the said order and which newly arise in beings from conscious mentation, settle in the localizations of beings, just in those series of formerly fixed data which are similar to these impressions and which correspond to those already present in them.

"And new impressions, crystallized in another order, that is, through the Reason-of-knowing, settle in the being-localizations at random, quite without any kind of, so to say, 'classification.' All these new impressions settle in the series of those former impressions which almost always have nothing in common with them.

"Well then, it is chiefly for this reason that everything

which has been newly learned settles in the presences of three-brained beings who have only the Reason-of-knowing and always remains only simply as information without any kind of cognizance by the whole of their Being.

"And therefore new data of every kind, formed and fixed in this way for the three-brained beings who have the Reason-of-knowing, have in respect of their use no significance at all for the welfare of their own subsequent existence. Moreover, the duration of the decrystallization of this kind of fixed impressions depends on the quantity and the quality of the impulses engendered in the given being. As regards this latter fact ensuing from the already degenerated functioning of the Reason proper to the three-brained beings and which most of your contemporary favorites today already have, one also very rarely used saying of our respected teacher Mullah Nassr Eddin is remembered in me by association and is expressed by the following words:

"'As soon as anything is needed, it seems that it is filthy and eaten by mice.'

"Although every kind of what your favorites call 'knowledge' which they have and which has been acquired in the common presences of beings in the said manner, is also subjective, yet it has absolutely nothing in common with what is called 'Objective Knowledge.'

"Well then, my boy, in order that the mentioned Zernofookalnian-friction should be obtained in beings, and that at the same time the crystallization of the new perceptions should proceed for the Reason-of-understanding, I—already knowing very well what are called the 'laws-of-the-fixing-and-unfixing-of-ideas-in-localizations,' the details of which laws, to mention it, by the way, I learned also, thanks to the three-brained beings who have taken your fancy, during my sojourn among them as 'professional hypnotist'—had in view during my tales, among many other necessary principles in respect of the current perception of new information through guidance from without, always to keep also to the same inevitable rule, so that the gradualness of the enlarging of, as is said, the 'quintessence of the information' should proceed in you with the entire absence of the being-impulses of 'indignation,' 'offense,' 'vexation,' and so forth.

"In respect of the sequence of my information to you and of the results of your essence-understanding, I must still tell you that if, when I first noticed your interest in the three-brained beings who arise on the planet Earth, I would have given from the very beginning, concerning every event, only my personal conviction and the opinions which had become fixed in me about them during the period of my observations, and only afterwards would have begun to give you the abundant and many-sided 'totality of information' already related by me, then all these facts I related would have been taken in by you without your own being-logical confrontation, and the data which had been crystallized for this information would have settled in your corresponding localizations only simply as information without any genuine being-understanding of them.

"That is why in all my tales about the three-brained beings who breed on the planet Earth I was guided by this, that on the one hand there should be crystallized in the corresponding localizations of your common presence many diversely formed data for your future being-association concerning all the 'totalities' or 'branches' of Objective Knowledge; and on the other hand that the process of Zernofookalnian-friction should proceed intensively in your common presence, and that that result should be obtained which I have just witnessed in the way you answered my question, 'Why are you weeping?'

"Now, my boy, as I have already become more or less convinced that the time I have spent has not been in vain, and that my tales about the three-brained beings of your planet who have taken your fancy have brought you the benefit I expected, then, I think we might stop talking about them so as not to evoke the process of active mentation in you any longer; besides, time is short, for we shall soon be on our dear planet.

"Nevertheless I must now briefly explain and strictly command you that as long as our journey lasts, that is to say, as long as we speak about the three-brained beings of the planet Earth, you should try with the Reason you have in your presence so to arrange that certain of those functions which flow in you and which in general give three-brained beings the possibility of active mentation, should remain inactive, or as is said, should 'rest'; that is to say, those functions should rest in you which during this time participated more intensively than usual in your active mentation, the functionings of which do not depend on the essence of beings but depend exclusively on what is called the 'harmony of the common-cosmic tempo.'

"By the way, you should always remember that the Reason of any being and the intensity of the action of this Reason depend on the correct functioning of all the separate parts of his whole presence.

"For instance, all the functionings of the 'planetary body' and the body itself are the chief parts of a being, but the separate functionings as well as the whole of this body itself without other of the spiritualized parts of the being are only a dependent cosmic formation, conscious of nothing, and therefore, on the basis of what you once called the 'common universal pillar of Justice,' each spiritualized part of a being must always be just towards this dependent and unconscious part and not require of it more than it is able to give.

"Just like everything else in the Megalocosmos, in order that the 'planetary body of a being' may correctly serve its chief part, that is to say, in order that this auxiliary part of the whole being should properly serve his essence itself, this essence must always be just and make demands on it only according to its inherent possibilities.

"Besides this question of Justice, it is necessary to act toward the unconscious part of a being in such a way as to make it possible for certain functions to remain inactive from time to time, in order that it might be always possible for this unconscious part gradually and in its time to blend its newly acquired subjective 'tempos' with the objective 'tempos' of our common Megalocosmos.

"One must notice that in the Megalocosmos the blending of tempos proceeds only 'Kaznookizkernian,' that is, as your favorites would say, with 'law-conformable gradualness.'

"And so, if you wish that your 'active mentation' during your future responsible existence should proceed correctly and productively, you must now, if such a mentation has already begun in you and if such an inner process has undesirable consequences for your planetary body, not occupy yourself at all for a while with such mentation, however much you may like it and however greatly it may interest you, otherwise 'Dezonakooasanz' will result in you, that is to say, only one part of your whole presence will acquire another tempo, and in consequence you will become again, as your favorites would say, 'lopsided.'

"By the way, most of your favorites, particularly the contemporary ones, when they become responsible, become just such lopsided beings.

"In short, only by a gradual change of the tempo of one part of the whole is it possible to change the tempo of all this whole without injuring it.

"I find it necessary to repeat that the 'active mentation' in a being and the useful results of such active mentation are in reality actualized exclusively only with the equal-degree functionings of all his three localizations of the results spiritualized in his presence, called 'thinking-center,' 'feeling-center,' and 'moving-motor-center.'"

CHAPTER 47

The Inevitable Result of Impartial Mentation

Beelzebub intended to say more, but just then everything was suddenly lit up with a "pale blue something." From that moment the falling of the ship *Karnak* began to diminish perceptibly in speed.

All this meant that one of the great Cosmic Egolionopties was about to come alongside the space-ship *Karnak*.

And indeed through the transparent outer parts of the ship *Karnak* the source of that "pale blue something" soon became visible, which lit up not only the whole of the interior of the ship *Karnak* but also all the space of the Universe surrounding this great cosmic Egolionopty as far as the ordinary vision of beings could reach.

Of these great Egolionopties there are only four in the Universe and each of them is under the jurisdiction of one of the four All-Quarters-Maintainers of the Universe.

A hurried and anxious commotion began among all of the beings aboard, and in a short time all the passengers and the crew assembled in the main hall situated in the center of the ship.

Each of them bore a branch of myrtle in one hand and a Devd'el Kascho in the other.

When the great cosmic Egolionopty had come alongside the ship *Karnak*, certain parts of the latter were moved apart in a special way and there passed from the Egolionopty into the main hall of the ship a procession composed of several archangels and a multitude of angels, cherubim, and seraphim, and they all too bore branches in their hands, but of palm.

At the head of this procession walked a venerable archangel and immediately after him two cherubim followed solemnly, bearing a casket from which something also radiated, but this time something orange.

In front of everyone in the main hall of the ship *Karnak* stood Beelzebub and behind him were ranged his kinsmen and the captain of the ship, and all the others stood behind them at a respectful distance.

When the said procession from the Egolionopty neared the beings of Beelzebub's nature who were assembled in expectation, they halted and all of both forces, differently natured three-brained beings, joined together in singing the "Hymn to our ENDLESSNESS," which Hymn is always sung on such occasions everywhere in the Universe, by beings of all natures and all forms of exterior coating.

This Hymn consists of the following words:

Thou Long Patient CREATOR *Of All That Breathes,*
Thou Abundantly LOVING CAUSE *Of All That Exists,*
Thou Unique VANQUISHER *Of The Merciless Heropass,*
Now To The Sounds Of Our Glorifying
Only Rejoice And Abide In Beatitude.
By Thy Unprecedented Labors Thou Hast Given Us
The Beginning Of Our Arisings,
By Thy Vanquishing Of The Heropass Have We
Obtained The Possibility
Of Perfecting Ourselves To The Sacred Anklad.
And Now Only Rest, As Merited,
And We, In Gratitude, Will Maintain All That Thou
Hast Created
And Always And In All Things Will Extol Thee Forever,
Extol Thee MAKER-CREATOR
Thou, The Beginning Of All Ends,
Thou, Proceeding From Infinity,
Thou, Having The End Of All Things Within Thyself,
Thou, Our ENDLESS ENDLESSNESS.

When the Hymn had been sung, the venerable archangel approached Beelzebub and solemnly proclaimed:

"By the decree of his All-Quarters-Maintainer, the Arch-cherub Peshtvogner, and bearing his own sacred rod, we appear before you, your Right Reverence, in order to restore to you, in accord with the pardon granted you from Above and for certain of your merits, what you lost during your exile—your horns."

Having said this, the venerable archangel turned toward the casket borne by the cherubim and with profound reverence carefully took from it the sacred rod.

Meanwhile all those present knelt down on one knee, while the angels and cherubim began to sing the appropriate sacred canticles.

Taking the sacred rod in his hand, the archangel turned again towards Beelzebub and spoke thus to the beings of Beelzebub's nature:

"Beings created by our same UNI-BEING ENDLESSNESS Who has pardoned this once erring being Beelzebub, who by the infinite grace of our CREATOR will again exist among you, beings like Himself. . . .

"As the virility and degree of Reason of beings of your nature are defined and manifested by the horns on your head, we must with the permission of our All-Quarters-Maintainer, and with your help, restore the horns lost by Beelzebub.

"Beings created by our ONE COMMON FATHER, your aid will consist in this, that each of you should consent to renounce for Beelzebub's merited pardon certain particles of your own horns.

"Whosoever therefore consents and wishes to do so, let him approach the sacred rod and touch its handle, and on the length of time the handle of the sacred rod is held will depend the amount of active elements passing from your own horns for the formation of the corresponding horns on this pardoned being of your nature."

Having said this, the venerable archangel, holding the chief end of the sacred rod, that is, the ball, over the kneeling Beelzebub, turned the handle towards those there assembled in such a way that whoever wished might touch it.

As soon as the venerable archangel had finished speaking, a very great commotion began among the beings of Beelzebub's nature, each desiring to approach nearer and to be the first to touch the sacred rod with their hands as long as possible.

Order, however, was soon established and each then in turn approached and held the handle for as long as was indicated by the captain of the ship, who had taken upon himself the necessary direction.

During the solemn, sacred action, horns little by little began to grow upon the head of Beelzebub.

At first, while just the bare horns were being formed, only a concentrated quiet gravely prevailed among those assembled. But from the moment that forks began to appear upon the horns a tense interest and rapt attention began to be manifested among them. This latter state proceeded among them, because everybody was agitated by the wish to learn how many forks would make their appearance on Beelzebub, since by their number the gradation of Reason to which Beelzebub had attained according to the sacred measure of Reason would be defined.

First one fork formed, then another, and then a third, and as each fork made its appearance a clearly perceptible thrill of joy and unconcealed satisfaction proceeded among all those present.

As the fourth fork began to be formed on the horns, the tension among those assembled reached its height, since the formation of the fourth fork on the horns signified that the Reason of Beelzebub had already been perfected to the sacred Ternoonald and hence that there remained for Beelzebub only two gradations before attaining to the sacred Anklad.

When the whole of this unusual ceremony neared its end and before all those assembled had had time to recover their self-possession from their earlier joyful agitation, there suddenly and unexpectedly appeared on the horns of Beelzebub quite independently a fifth fork of a special form known to them all.

Thereupon all without exception, even the venerable archangel himself, fell prostrate before Beelzebub, who had now risen to his feet and stood transfigured with a majestic appearance, owing to the truly majestic horns which had arisen on his head.

All fell prostrate before Beelzebub because by the fifth fork on his horns it was indicated that He had attained the Reason of the sacred Podkoolad, i.e., the last gradation before the Reason of the sacred Anklad.

The Reason of the sacred Anklad is the highest to which in general any being can attain, being the third in degree from the Absolute Reason of HIS ENDLESSNESS HIMSELF.

But the Reason of the sacred Podkoolad, to which Beelzebub had already perfected himself, is also very rare in the Universe, hence even the venerable archangel prostrated himself before Beelzebub because his own degree of Reason was as yet only that of the sacred Degindad, i.e., wanting three degrees to the Reason of the sacred Anklad.

When all had arisen to their feet, the venerable archangel, addressing this time all the assembled beings of various natures, proclaimed:

"Beings created by One CREATOR, we have all just become worthy to be the first to behold the final formation of the appearance of that which is the dream both of all those present and of the beings in general of the whole of our great Megalocosmos.

"And now let us all together exult and rejoice over such a worthiness, which is for us such a revivifying shock for our ability to struggle against our own denying source, which ability alone can lead us to that sacred Podkoolad attained by one of the sons of our COMMON FATHER, who although he first transgressed on account of his youth, yet afterwards was able by his conscious labors and intentional sufferings to become worthy with his essence to be one of the very rare Sacred Individuals of the whole of our Great Universe."

After this proclamation of the archangel all the beings without exception present on the space-ship *Karnak* then began to sing the prescribed sacred canticle entitled "I Rejoice."

And when this last sacred canticle also had been sung, all the angels and cherubim, with the venerable archangel at their head, returned to the cosmic Egolionopty which then left the ship *Karnak* and disappeared gradually into space, whereupon the passengers and crew began to disperse to their places and the *Karnak* resumed its falling toward its destination.

After the termination of the Most Great Universal Solemnity just described, Beelzebub with His grandson and His old servant Ahoon, deeply moved like all of the other passengers of the space-ship *Karnak* by this unexpected event, returned to that part of the ship where all their talks proceeded concerning the men-beings arising and existing on the Earth.

When Beelzebub, now with a transfigured appearance corresponding to His merits and visible to all, had occupied His usual place, Ahoon, His old servant who had been close to Him during almost the whole of His existence, unexpectedly fell prostrate before Him and in a sincerely entreating voice began to speak:

"Sacred Podkoolad of our Great Megalocosmos! Have mercy upon me and pardon me, an unfortunate ordinary three-centered being, for my past disrespectful manifestations, voluntary and involuntary, towards Your Sacred Essence.

"Have mercy and pardon me: just this three-centered being, who, though he has existed a very long time, yet to his misfortune—only because in his preparatory age nobody aided the crystallization in him of the data for the ability of intensively actualizing being-Partkdolg-duty—had until now been so shortsighted that he had been unable to sense the reality present beneath an exterior with which, according to the common-cosmic Trogoautoegocrat, all those existing and newly arising units of the Megalocosmos are coated, who ought to have in their presence that sacred 'something' which is called Reason."

Having said this, Ahoon stood as if sunk in a stupor of silent expectancy.

And Beelzebub, also in silence, gazed at him with a look which, though perceived externally from without was full of love and forgiveness, yet there could be felt in it also His Essence-grief and inevitable resignation.

During this afore-described scene, Hassein stood apart in the posture everywhere called the 'posture-of-the-all-famous-universal-hermit,' Harnatoolkpararana of the planet Kirmankshana.

And when a little bit later Beelzebub cast His eyes around and noticed His grandson in the said posture, He turned to him and said:

"What, my boy! Can it be that the same proceeds in your presence as in our old Ahoon's?"

To this question of Beelzebub's, Hassein, also in an uncertain tone unusual for him, timidly replied:

"Almost . . . yes . . . Sacred Podkoolad of our Great Megalocosmos. Only with this difference, that at this moment the impulse of love both for our Ahoon and for the three-brained beings of the planet Earth now functions still more strongly in me.

"This impulse of love has become stronger in me, evidently because, as it seems to me, both Ahoon and the three-brained beings of the planet Earth have greatly aided me in becoming worthy to be a recent eyewitness of the Great Solemnity of Him who is the cause of the cause of my arising and Whom hitherto I have called my dear grandfather and Who has already visibly become one of the sacred Podkoolads of our Great Megalocosmos, before Whom all will bow and before Whom I have at this moment the happiness to stand."

"Eh, eh, eh!" exclaimed Beelzebub, and having given his features the usual expression He was wont to assume during his sojourn on the Earth, said:

"First of all I wish to remark and in the speech of Mullah Nassr Eddin, whom I particularly honor, to voice the thought which arises by association concerning Ahoon's words which were not peculiar to him and his assumed posture quite unusual for him.

"Our dear teacher in such a case would say, 'Don't shed tears in vain like that crocodile which snapped at the fisherman and missed biting off his lower left half.'

"And now first take your usual places and then let us talk a little more.

"Although our ship is now entering the spheres of our planet Karatas, yet as usually happens with space-ships, in order to exhaust the momentum they have acquired, a fairly long time will elapse before it stops at its destined mooring place."

Hassein and Ahoon immediately and silently proceeded to follow the suggestion of Beelzebub, though by their movements and the translucency of their inner psyche, it was evident that there had been a marked change in their attitude toward the person of Beelzebub since the above-described Common Universal Event.

When they had taken their places they sat down, this time not with the unconstraint they had formerly shown.

Then Beelzebub, turning to Hassein, said, "First of all, my boy, I give you my word that when we return home—unless any event from external causes independent of our Essence will prevent this—I shall explain to you everything relating to the three-brained beings who have taken your fancy, concerning that which during this journey of ours on the ship *Karnak* I promised to explain, but which I have for some reason or other left unexplained.

"But meanwhile, if you have any question in mind that now needs explanation, ask.

"I warn you, however, that we have not enough time to reply in the manner that has become proper to our talks during all this time and hence try to formulate your question in such a way that my answer also may be brief.

"By such a question you can even, apropos, once more show me to what extent your logical mentation has increased during my tales concerning the strange psyche of the three-centered beings arising and existing on the planet Earth."

At this proposal of his grandfather, Hassein deeply thought rather a long time, and then, in an exalted mood, spoke as follows:

"Sacred Podkoolad and fundamental cause of the cause of my arising!

"Since the solemnity which has just taken place, when Your Sacred Essence became coated with a corresponding visible exterior and when thereby the whole of its significance which cannot be perceived nor understood by all three-brained beings became clear and even sensible to me as well as to every other cosmic unit, save Yourself, every word spoken by You and every counsel of Yours is taken by me as law.

"I must therefore strive with the whole of my presence to carry out the suggestion You have just made to me and try as well and as briefly as possible to formulate my question.

"Sacred Podkoolad, and cause of the cause of my arising.

"In order that the convictions formed in me during this time, owing to Your explanation of the abnormalities proceeding on the Earth, may become definitely crystallized in me, I still wish very much to have this time Your personal and frank opinion as to the following: How You would reply if, let us suppose, our ALL-EMBRACING CREATOR ENDLESSNESS HIMSELF, were to summon You before HIM and ask You this:

"'Beelzebub! ! ! !

"'You, as one of the anticipated, accelerated results of all My actualizations, manifest briefly the sum of your long-centuried impartial observations and studies of the psyche of the three-centered beings arising on the planet Earth and state in words whether it is still possible by some means or other to save them and to direct them into the becoming path?'"

Having said this, Hassein arose and, standing in a posture of reverence, began to look expectantly at Beelzebub.

And Ahoon also rose.

Beelzebub, smiling lovingly at this question of Hassein's, first said that He was now quite convinced that His tales had brought Hassein the desired results; and then in a serious tone He continued that if our ALL-EMBRACING UNI-BEING-CREATOR should indeed summon Him before HIM and ask Him thus, He would answer.

Thereupon Beelzebub suddenly also arose unexpectedly and having stretched His right hand forward and His left hand back, He directed His vision somewhere afar off, and it seemed that with His sight He was, as it were, piercing the very depths of space.

Simultaneously 'something' pale yellow began little by little to arise around Beelzebub and to envelop Him, and it was in no way possible to understand or to discern whence this something issued—whether it issued from Beelzebub Himself or proceeded to Him from space from sources outside of Him.

Finding Himself in these cosmic actualizations incomprehensible for all three-brained beings, Beelzebub in a loud voice unusual for Him very penetratingly intoned the following words:

"THOU ALL and the ALLNESS of my WHOLENESS!

"The sole means now for the saving of the beings of the planet Earth would be to implant again into their presences a new organ, an organ like Kundabuffer, but this time of such properties that every one of these unfortunates during the process of existence should constantly sense and be cognizant of the inevitability of his own death as well as of the death of everyone upon whom his eyes or attention rests.

"Only such a sensation and such a cognizance can now destroy the egoism completely crystallized in them that has swallowed up the whole of their Essence and also that tendency to hate others which flows from it—the tendency, namely, which engenders all those mutual relationships existing there, which serve as the chief cause of all their abnormalities unbecoming to three-brained beings and maleficent for them themselves and for the whole of the Universe."

CHAPTER 48

From the Author

After six years of work, merciless toward myself and with almost continuously tense mentation, I yesterday at last completed the setting down on paper, in a form, I think, accessible to everybody, the first of the three series of books I had previously thought out and six years ago begun—just those three series in which I planned to actualize by means of the totality of the ideas to be developed, at first in theory and afterwards in practice, also by a means I had foreseen and prepared, three essential tasks I had set myself: namely, by means of the first series, to destroy in people everything which, in their false representations, as it were, exists in reality, or in other words "to corrode without mercy all the rubbish accumulated during the ages in human mentation"; by means of the second series, to prepare so to say "new constructional material"; and by means of the third, "to build a new world."

Having now finished the first series of books, and, following the practice already long ago established on the Earth—never to conclude any great, as is said, "undertaking" without what some call an epilogue, others an afterword, and still others "from the author," and so on—I also now propose to write something of the same kind for them.

With this end in view I very attentively read over this morning the "preface" I wrote six years ago entitled "The Arousing of Thought" in order to take corresponding ideas from it for a corresponding so to say "logical fusion" of that beginning with this conclusion which I now intend to write. While I was reading that first chapter, which I wrote only six years ago, but which seems to me by my present sensing to have been written long long ago, a sensing which is now in my common presence obviously because during that time I had to think intensely and even as might be said, to "experience" all the suitable material required for eight thick volumes—not for nothing is it stated in that branch of genuine science entitled "the laws of association of human mentation," which has come down from very ancient times and is known to only a few contemporary people, that the "sensing of the flow of time is directly proportional to the quality and quantity of the flow of thoughts"—well then, while I was reading just that first chapter, about which, as I said, I thought deeply from every aspect and which I experienced under the most exclusive action of my own willed self-mortification, and which, moreover, I wrote at a time when the functioning of my entire whole—a functioning which engenders in a man what is called "the-power-to-manifest-by-his-own-initiative"—was utterly disharmonized, that is to say, when I was still extremely ill owing to an accident that had not long before occurred to me, and which consisted of a "charge-and-crash" with my automobile at full speed into a tree standing silently, like an observer and reckoner of the passage of centuries at a disorderly tempo, on the historic road between the world capital of Paris and the town of Fontainebleau—a "charge" which according to any sane human understanding should have put an end to my life—there arose in me from the reading of that chapter a quite definite decision.

Recalling my state during the period of the writing of that first chapter, I cannot help adding here—owing to still another certain small weakness in me which consists of my always experiencing an inner satisfaction whenever I see appear on the faces of our estimable contemporary as they are called "representatives of exact science," that very specific smile peculiar to them alone—that although my body after this accident was, as is said, "so battered and everything in it so mixed up" that for months it looked like a fragment of a general picture which might be described as "a bit of live meat in a clean bed," nevertheless, and for all that, my correctly disciplined what is usually called "spirit," even in that physical state of my body, was not in the least depressed, as it should have been according to their notions, but, on the contrary, its power was even intensified by the heightened excitation which had arisen in it just before the accident owing to my repeated disappointment in people, particularly in such people as are devoted, as they say to "science," and also to my disappointment in those ideals which until then had been in me, and which had gradually been formed in my common presence, thanks chiefly to the commandment inculcated in me in my childhood, enjoining that "the highest aim and sense of human life is the striving to attain the welfare of one's neighbor," and that this is possible exclusively only by the conscious renunciation of one's own.

And so, after I had very attentively read over that opening chapter of the first series, which I had written in the said conditions, and when in my memory by association there had been recalled the texts of those many succeeding chapters, which, according to my conviction, ought to produce in the consciousness of the readers unusual impressions which in turn always, as is said, "engender substantial results," I—or rather, this time, that dominant something in my common presence which now represents the sum of the results obtained from the data crystallized during my life, data which engender, among other things, in a man who has in general set himself the aim, so to say "to mentate actively impartially" during the process of responsible existence, the ability to penetrate and understand the psyche of people of various types—I decided, urged by the impulse called "love of kind" which simultaneously arose in me, not to write in this conclusion anything additional and correspondent to the general aim of this first series, but to confine myself simply to appending the first of a considerable number of lectures, copies of which now are in my possession and which were publicly read during the existence of the institution I had founded under the name of the "Institute-for-the-Harmonious-Development-of-Man."

That institution by the way no longer exists, and I find it both necessary and opportune, chiefly for the purpose of pacifying certain types from various countries, to make the categorical declaration here and now that I have liquidated it completely and forever.

I was constrained with an inexpressible impulse of grief and despondency to make this decision to liquidate this institution and everything organized and carefully prepared for the opening the following year of eighteen sections in different countries, in short, of everything I had previously created with almost superhuman labor, chiefly because, soon after the said accident occurred, that is, three months afterwards, when the former usual functioning of my mentation had been more or less reestablished in me—I being still utterly powerless in body—I then reflected that the attempt to preserve the existence of this institution, would, in the absence of real people around me and owing to the impossibility of procuring without me the great material means required for it, inevitably lead to a catastrophe the result of which, among other things for me in my old age as well as for numerous others wholly dependent on me, would be, so to say, a "vegetation."

The lecture which I propose to append as a conclusion to this first series was more than once read by my, as they were then called, "pupils of the first rank" during the existence of the mentioned institution. Certain of them, by the way, turned out subsequently, to my personal sincere regret, to have in their essence a predisposition to the speedy transformation of their psyche into the psyche called Hasnamussian—a predisposition which appeared and became fully visible and clearly sensible to all more or less normal persons around them, when, at the moment of desperate crisis for everything I had previously actualized, due to the said accident, they, as is said, "quaking for their skins," that is to say, fearing to lose their personal welfare which, by the way, I had created for them, deserted the common work and with their tails between their legs took themselves off to their kennels, where, profiting by the crumbs fallen from my so to say "ideatable" they opened their, as I would say, "Shachermacher-workshop-booths," and with a secret feeling of hope and perhaps even joy at their speedy and complete release from my vigilant control, began manufacturing out of various unfortunate naïve people, "candidates for lunatic asylums."

I append just this particular lecture, in the first place, because, at the very beginning of the dissemination of the ideas I imported into life, it was specially prepared here on the continent of Europe to serve as the introduction or, as it were, threshold for the whole series of subsequent lectures, by no less than the whole sum of which was it possible both to make clear in a form accessible to everybody the necessity and even the inevitability of a practical actualization of the immutable truths I have elucidated and established in the course of half a century of day-and-night active work and also to prove the actual possibility of employing those truths for the welfare of people; and secondly I append it here, because, while it was last being publicly read, and I happened myself to be present at that numerous gathering, I made an addition which fully corresponds to the hidden thought introduced by Mr. Beelzebub himself into his, so to say, "concluding chord," and which at the same time, illuminating once more this most great objective truth, will in my opinion make it possible for the reader properly to perceive and assimilate this truth as befits a being who claims to be an "image of God."

LECTURE NUMBER ONE

THE VARIETY, ACCORDING TO LAW, OF THE MANIFESTATIONS OF HUMAN INDIVIDUALITY

(Last read in New York in the Neighborhood Playhouse, January, 1924)

According to the investigations of many scientists of past ages and according to the data obtained at the present time by means of the quite exceptionally conducted researches of the Institute-for-the-Harmonious-Development-of-Man according to the system of Mr. Gurdjieff, the whole individuality of every man—according to laws and conditions of the process of life of people which have from the very beginning become established and gradually fixed on the Earth—of whatever heredity he is the result, and whatever be the accidental surrounding conditions in which he arose and developed, must already at the beginning of his responsible life—as a condition of responding in reality to the sense and predestination of his existence as a man and not merely as an animal—indispensably consist of four definite distinct personalities.

The first of these four independent personalities is nothing else than the totality of that automatic functioning which is proper to man as well as to all animals, the data for which are composed in them firstly of the sum total of the results of impressions previously perceived from all the surrounding reality as well as from everything intentionally artificially implanted in them from outside, and, secondly, from the result of the process also inherent in every animal called "daydreaming." And this totality of automatic functioning most people ignorantly name "consciousness," or, at best, "mentation."

The second of the four personalities, functioning in most cases independently of the first, consists of the sum of the results of the data deposited and fixed in the presence of man, like that of all animals, through its six organs called "receivers-of-the-varied-qualitied-vibrations," which organs function in accordance with newly perceived impressions and the sensitiveness of which depends upon transmitted heredity and on the conditions of the preparatory formation of the given individual for responsible existence.

The third independent part of the whole being is the prime functioning of his organism as well as what are called the "motor-reflex-reciprocally-affecting-manifestations-proceeding-in-it," and the quality of these manifestations also depends on those aforesaid results of heredity and of the circumstances during his preparatory formation.

And the fourth, which should also be a separate part of the whole individual, is none other than the manifestation of the totality of the results of the already automatized functioning of all the three enumerated personalities separately formed and independently educated in him, that is to say, it is that part which is called, in a being, "I."

In the common presence of a man, and for the spiritualization and manifestation of each of the enumerated three separately formed parts of his entire whole, there is an independent, as it is called, "gravity-center-localization"; and each of these gravity-center-localizations, each with its own entire system, has, for its general actualization, its own peculiarities and predispositions inherent in it alone. In consequence of this, in order to make possible the rounded perfecting of a man, a special corresponding correct education is indispensably necessary for each of these three parts, and not such a treatment as is given nowadays and also called "education."

Only then can the "I" which should be in a man, be his own "I."

According to the already indicated seriously instituted experimental investigations carried on over many years, or even according merely to the sane and impartial reflection of even every contemporary man, the common presence of every man—particularly of one in whom for some reason or another there arises, so to say, the pretension to be not just an ordinary average man, but what is called "one of the intelligentsia" in the genuine sense of the word—must inevitably consist not only of all the said four fully determined distinct personalities, but each of them must of necessity be exactly correspondingly developed, to ensure that in his general manifestations during the period of his responsible existence all the separate parts should harmonize with each other.

For a comprehensive and visible clarification to oneself of the varied sources of the arising and the varied qualities of the manifested personalities in the general organization of man, and also of the difference between what is called that "I" which should be in the common presence of a "man-without-quotation-marks," that is, a real man; and, as it can be expressed, the pseudo "I" which people today mistake for it, an analogy can be very well made. Though this analogy, as is said, has been "worn threadbare" by contemporary what are called spiritualists, occultists, theosophists, and other specialists in "catching fish in muddy waters," in their cackle about what are called the "mental," "astral," and still other such bodies which are supposed to be in man, nevertheless it is well adapted to throw light on the question we are now considering.

A man as a whole with all his separately concentrated and functioning localizations, that is to say, his formed and independently educated "personalities," is almost exactly comparable to that organization for conveying a passenger, which consists of a carriage, a horse, and a coachman.

It must first of all be remarked that the difference between a real man and a pseudo man, that is, between one who has his own "I" and one who has not, is indicated in the analogy we have taken by the passenger sitting in the carriage. In the first case, that of the real man, the passenger is the owner of the carriage; and in the second case, he is simply the first chance passer-by who, like the fare in a "hackney carriage," is continuously being changed.

The body of a man with all its motor reflex manifestations corresponds simply to the carriage itself; all the functionings and manifestations of feeling of a man correspond to the horse harnessed to the carriage and drawing it; the coachman sitting on the box and directing the horse corresponds to that in a man which people call consciousness or mentation; and finally, the passenger seated in the carriage and commanding the coachman is that which is called "I."

The fundamental evil among contemporary people is chiefly that, owing to the rooted and widespread abnormal methods of education of the rising generation, this fourth personality which should be present in everybody on reaching responsible age is entirely missing in them; and almost all of them consist only of the three enumerated parts, which parts, moreover, are formed arbitrarily of themselves and anyhow. In other words, almost every contemporary man of responsible age consists of nothing more nor less than simply a "hackney carriage," and one moreover, composed as follows: a broken-down carriage "which has long ago seen its day," a crock of a horse, and, on the box, a tatterdemalion, half-sleepy, half-drunken coachman whose time designated by Mother Nature for self-perfection passes while he waits on a corner, fantastically daydreaming, for any old chance passenger. The first passenger who happens along hires him and dismisses him just as he pleases, and not only him but also all the parts subordinate to him.

Continuing this analogy between a typical contemporary man, with his thoughts, feelings, and body, and a hackney carriage, horse, and coachman, we can clearly see that in each of the parts composing both organizations there must have been formed and there must exist its own separate needs, habits, tastes, and so on, proper to it alone. From the varied nature of their arising, and the diverse conditions of their formation, and according to their varying possibilities in each of them there must inevitably have been formed, for instance, its own psyche, its own notions, its own subjective supports, its own viewpoints, and so on.

The whole totality of the manifestations of human mentation, with all the inherencies proper to this functioning and with all its specific particularities, corresponds almost exactly in every respect to the essence and manifestations of a typical hired coachman.

Like all hired coachmen in general, he is a type called "cabby." He is not entirely illiterate because, owing to the regulations existing in his country for the "general compulsory teaching of the three R's," he was obliged in his childhood to put in an occasional attendance at what is called the "parish church school."

Although he himself is from the country and has remained as ignorant as his fellow rustics, yet rubbing shoulders, owing to his profession, with people of various positions and education, picking up from them, by bits here and bits there, a variety of expressions embodying various notions, he has now come to regard everything smacking of the country with superiority and contempt, indignantly dismissing it all as "ignorance."

In short, this is a type to whom applies perfectly the definition, "The crows he raced but by peacocks outpaced."

He considers himself competent even in questions of religion, politics, and sociology; with his equals he likes to argue; those whom he regards as his inferiors, he likes to teach; his superiors he flatters, with them he is servile; before them, as is said, "he stands cap in hand."

One of his chief weaknesses is to dangle after the neighboring cooks and housemaids, but, best of all, he likes a good hearty tuck-in, and to gulp down another glass or two, and then, fully satiated, drowsily to daydream.

To gratify these weaknesses of his, he always steals a part of the money given him by his employer to buy fodder for the horse.

Like every "cabby" he works as is said always "under the lash," and if occasionally he does a job without being made, it is only in the hope of receiving tips.

The desire for tips has gradually taught him to be aware of certain weaknesses in the people with whom he has dealings, and to profit himself by them; he has automatically learned to be cunning, to flatter, so to say, to stroke people the right way, and, in general, to lie.

On every convenient occasion and at every free moment he slips into a saloon or to a bar, where over a glass of beer he daydreams for hours at a time, or talks with a type like himself, or just reads the paper.

He tries to appear imposing, wears a beard, and if he is thin pads himself out to appear more important.

The totality of the manifestations of the feeling-localization in a man and the whole system of its functioning correspond perfectly to the horse of the hackney carriage in our analogy.

Incidentally, this comparison of the horse with the organization of human feeling will serve to show up particularly clearly the error and one-sidedness of the contemporary education of the rising generation.

The horse as a whole, owing to the negligence of those around it during its early years, and to its constant solitude, is as if locked up within itself; that is to say, its so to say "inner life" is driven inside, and for external manifestations it has nothing but inertia.

Thanks to the abnormal conditions around it, the horse has never received any special education, but has been molded exclusively under the influence of constant thrashings and vile abuse.

It has always been kept tied up; and for food, instead of oats and hay, there is given to it merely straw which is utterly worthless for its real needs.

Never having seen in any of the manifestations towards it even the least love or friendliness, the horse is now ready to surrender itself completely to anybody who gives it the slightest caress.

The consequence of all this is that all the inclinations of the horse, deprived of all interests and aspirations, must inevitably be concentrated on food, drink, and the automatic yearning towards the opposite sex; hence it invariably veers in the direction where it can obtain any of these. If, for example, it catches sight of a place where even once or twice it gratified one of the enumerated needs, it waits the chance to run off in that direction.

It must further be added that although the coachman has a very feeble understanding of his duties, he can nevertheless, even though only a little, think logically; and remembering tomorrow, he either from fear of losing his job or from the desire of receiving a reward, does occasionally evince an interest in doing something or other for his employer without being driven to it; but the horse—in consequence of there not having been formed in it at the proper time, owing to the absence of any special and corresponding education, any data at all for manifesting the aspirations requisite for responsible existence—of course fails to understand (and indeed it cannot be expected that it should understand) why in general it must do anything; its obligations are therefore carried out quite inertly and only from fear of further beatings.

As far as the carriage or cart is concerned, which stands in our analogy for the body without any of the other independently formed parts of the common presence of a man, the situation is even worse.

This cart, like most carts, is made of various materials, and furthermore is of a very complicated construction.

It was designed, as is evident to every sane-thinking man, to carry all kinds of burdens, and not for the purpose for which contemporary people employ it, that is, only for carrying passengers.

The chief cause of the various misunderstandings connected with it springs from the fact that those who made the system of this cart intended it for travel on the byroads, and certain inner details of its general construction were in consequence foreseeingly made to answer to this aim.

For example, the principle of its greasing, one of the chief needs of a construction of such different materials, was so devised that the grease should spread over all the metallic parts from the shaking received from the jolts inevitable on such roads, whereas now, this cart that was designed for traveling on the byroads finds itself stationed on a rank in the city and traveling on smooth, level, asphalted roads.

In the absence of any shocks whatsoever while going along such roads, no uniform greasing of all its parts occurs, and some of them consequently must inevitably rust and cease to fulfill the action intended for them.

A cart goes easily as a rule if its moving parts are properly greased. With too little grease, these parts get heated and finally red-hot, and thus the other parts get spoiled; on the other hand, if in some part there is too much grease, the general movement of the cart is impaired, and in either case it becomes more difficult for the horse to draw it.

The contemporary coachman, our cabby, neither knows nor has any suspicion of the necessity of greasing the cart, and even if he does grease it, he does so without proper knowledge, only on hearsay, blindly following the directions of the first comer.

That is why, when this cart, now adapted more or less for travel on smooth roads, has for some reason or other to go along a byroad, something always happens to it; either a nut gives way, or a bolt gets bent or something or other gets loose; and after these attempts at traveling along such roads, the journey rarely ends without more or less considerable repairs.

In any case, to make use of this cart for the purposes for which it was made is already impossible without risk. If repairs are begun, it is necessary to take the cart all to pieces, examine all its parts, and, as is done in such cases, "kerosene" them, clean them, and put them together again; and frequently it becomes clearly necessary immediately and without fail to change a part. This is all very well if it happens to be an inexpensive part, but it may turn out to be more costly than a new cart.

And so, all that has been said about the separate parts of that organization of which, taken as a whole, a hackney carriage consists can be fully applied also to the general organization of the common presence of a man.

Owing to the absence among contemporary people of any knowledge and ability specially to prepare in a corresponding way the rising generation for responsible existence by educating all the separate parts composing their common presences, every person of today is a confused and extremely ludicrous something, that is to say, again using this example we have taken, a something resembling the following picture.

A carriage just out of the factory, made on the latest model, polished by genuine German craftsmen from the town of Barmen, and harnessed to the kind of horse which is called in the locality named Transcaucasia, a "Dglozidzi." ("Dzi" is a horse; "Dgloz" is the name of a certain Armenian specialist in buying utterly worthless horses and skinning them.)

On the box of this stylish carriage sits an unshaven, unkempt, sleepy coachman-cabby, dressed in a shabby cloak which he has retrieved from the rubbish heap where it had been thrown as utterly worthless by the kitchen-maid Maggie. On his head reposes a brand-new top hat, an exact replica of Rockefeller's; and in his buttonhole there is displayed a giant chrysanthemum.

This picture, however ludicrous, of contemporary man, is an inevitable result, chiefly because from the first day of the arising and formation of a contemporary man, all these three parts formed in him—which parts, although diversely caused and with properties of diverse quality, should nevertheless, at the period of his responsible existence for pursuing a single aim, all together represent his entire whole—begin, so to say, to "live" and to become fixed in their specific manifestations separately one from another, never having been trained either to the requisite automatic reciprocal maintenance, reciprocal assistance, or to any, even though only approximate, reciprocal understanding; and thus, when afterward concerted manifestations are required, these concerted manifestations do not appear.

Thanks to what is called the "system of education of the rising generation" which at the present time has already been completely fixed in the life of man and which consists singly and solely in training the pupils, by means of constant repetition to the point of "madness," to sense various almost empty words and expressions and to recognize, only by the difference in their consonance, the reality supposed to be signified by these words and expressions, the coachman is still able to explain after a fashion the various desires arising in him, but only to types similar to his own outside of his common presence, and he is sometimes even able approximately to understand others.

This coachman-cabby of ours, gossiping with other coachmen while waiting for a fare, and sometimes, as is said, "flirting" at the gate with the neighbor's maid, even learns various forms of what is called "savoir-vivre."

He also, by the way, according to the external conditions of the life of coachmen in general, gradually automatizes himself to distinguish one street from the other and to calculate, for instance, during repairs in some street, how to get to the required street from another direction.

But as for the horse, although the maleficent invention of contemporary people which is called education does not extend over the horse's formation, and in consequence its inherited possibilities are not atrophied, yet owing to the fact that this formation proceeds under the conditions of the abnormally established process of the ordinary existence of people, and that the horse grows up ignored like an orphan by everybody, and moreover an ill-treated orphan, it neither acquires anything corresponding to the established psyche of the coachman nor learns anything of what he knows, and hence is quite ignorant of all the forms of reciprocal relationship which have become usual for the coachman, and no contact is established between them for understanding each other.

It is possible, however, that in its locked-in life the horse does nevertheless learn some form of relationship with the coachman and that even, perhaps, it is familiar with some "language"; but the trouble is that the coachman does not know this and does not even suspect its possibility.

Apart from the fact that, owing to the said abnormal conditions, no data for even an approximate understanding of each other are formed between the horse and the coachman, there are also still other and numerous external causes, independent of them, which fail to give them the possibility of together actualizing that one purpose for which they were both destined.

The point is, that just as the separate independent parts of a "hackney" are connected—namely, the carriage to the horse by the shafts and the horse to the coachman by reins—so also are the separate parts of the general organization of man connected with each other; namely, the body is connected to the feeling-organization by the blood, and the feeling-organization is connected to the organization actualizing the functioning of mentation or consciousness by what is called Hanbledzoin, that is, by that substance which arises in the common presence of a man from all intentionally made being-efforts.

The wrong system of education existing at the present

time has led to the coachman's ceasing to have any effect whatever on his horse, unless we allow the fact that he is merely able by means of the reins to engender in the consciousness of the horse just three ideas—right, left, and stop.

Strictly speaking he cannot always do even this, because the reins in general are made of materials that react to various atmospheric phenomena: for example, during a pouring rain they swell and lengthen; and in heat, the contrary; thereby changing their effect upon the horse's automatized sensitiveness of perception.

The same proceeds in the general organization of the average man whenever from some impression or other the so to say "density and tempo" of the Hanbledzoin changes in him, when his thoughts entirely lose all possibility of affecting his feeling-organization.

And so, to resume all that has been said, one must willy-nilly acknowledge that every man should strive to have his own "I"; otherwise he will always represent a hackney carriage in which any fare can sit and which any fare can dispose of just as he pleases.

And here it will not be superfluous to point out that the Institute-for-the-Harmonious-Development-of-Man, organized on the system of Mr. Gurdjieff, has, among its fundamental tasks, also the task of on the one hand correspondingly educating in its pupils each of the enumerated independent personalities separately as well as in their general reciprocal relationship; and on the other hand of begetting and fostering in each of its pupils what every bearer of the name of "man without quotation marks" should have—his own "I."

For a more exact, so to say, scientific definition of the difference between a genuine man, that is, man as he ought to be, and a man whom we have called "man in quotation marks," that is, such men as almost all contemporary people have become, it is fitting to repeat what was said about this by Mr. Gurdjieff himself in one of his personal "lecture talks."

It was as follows:

"For the definition of man, considered from our point of view, neither anatomical, nor physiological, nor psychological contemporary knowledge of his symptoms can assist us, since they are inherent in one degree or another in every man and consequently apply equally to all. Hence they do not enable us to establish the exact difference which we wish to establish between people. This difference can only be formulated in the following terms: 'Man is a being who can do,' and 'to do' means to act consciously and by one's own initiative."

And indeed every more or less sane-thinking man who is able to be if only a little impartial, must admit that hitherto there has not been nor can there be a fuller and more exhaustive definition.

Even suppose that we provisionally accept this definition, the question inevitably arises—can a man who is a product of contemporary education and civilization do anything at all himself, consciously and by his own will?

No . . . we answer at the very beginning, to this question.

Why not? . . .

Solely because, as the Institute-for-the-Harmonious-Development-of-Man experimentally proves and from experiments categorically affirms, everything without exception from beginning to end does itself in contemporary man, and there is nothing which a contemporary man himself does.

In personal, family, and communal life, in politics, science, art, philosophy, and religion, in short, in everything entering into the process of the ordinary life of a contemporary man, everything from beginning to end does itself, and not a single one of these "victims of contemporary civilization" can "do" anything.

This experimentally proved categorical affirmation of the Institute-for-the-Harmonious-Development-of-Man, namely, that the ordinary man can do nothing and that everything does itself in him and through him, coincides with what is said of man by contemporary "exact-positive-science."

Contemporary "exact-positive-science" says that a man is a very complex organism developed by evolution from the simplest organisms, and who has now become capable of reacting in a very complex manner to external impressions. This capability of reacting in man is so complex, and the responsive movements can appear to be so far removed from the causes evoking them and conditioning them, that the actions of man, or at least a part of them, seem to naïve observation quite spontaneous.

But according to the ideas of Mr. Gurdjieff, the average man is indeed incapable of the single smallest independent or spontaneous action or word. All of him is only the result of external effect. Man is a transforming machine, a kind of transmitting station of forces.

Thus from the point of view of the totality of Mr. Gurdjieff's ideas and also according to contemporary "exact-positive-science," man differs from the animals only by the greater complexity of his reactions to external impressions, and by having a more complex construction for perceiving and reacting to them.

And as to that which is attributed to man and named "will," Mr. Gurdjieff completely denies the possibility of its being in the common presence of the average man.

Will is a certain combination obtained from the results of certain properties specially elaborated in themselves by people who can do.

In the presences of average people what they call will is exclusively only the resultant of desires.

Real will is a sign of a very high degree of Being in comparison with the Being of the ordinary man. But only those people who possess such Being can do.

All other people are simply automatons, machines, or mechanical toys set in motion by external forces, acting just in so far as the "spring" placed in them by surrounding accidental conditions acts, and this spring can neither be lengthened or shortened, nor changed in any way on its own initiative.

And so, while admitting great possibilities in man, we deny him any value as an independent unit as long as he remains such as he is at the present time.

For the purpose of confirming the complete absence in the average man of any will whatsoever, I will add here a passage from another of Mr. Gurdjieff's personal lectures, in which the manifestations of this famous assumed will in man are picturesquely described.

Addressing those present, Mr. Gurdjieff then said:

"You have plenty of money, luxurious conditions of existence, and universal esteem and respect. At the head of your well-established concerns are people absolutely reliable and devoted to you; in a word, your life is a bed of roses.

"You dispose of your time as you please, you are a patron of the arts, you settle world questions over a cup of coffee, and you are even interested in the development of the latent spiritual forces of man. You are not unfamiliar with the needs of the spirit, and are well versed in philosophical matters. You are well educated and widely read. Having a great deal of learning on all kinds of questions, you are reputed to be a clever man, being at home in a variety of fields. You are a model of culture.

"All who know you regard you as a man of great will,

and most of them even attribute all your advantages to the results of the manifestations of this will of yours.

"In short, from every point of view, you are fully deserving of imitation, and a man to be envied.

"In the morning you wake up under the impression of some oppressive dream.

"Your slightly depressed state, that dispersed on awakening, has nevertheless left its mark.

"A certain languidness and hesitancy in your movements.

"You go to the mirror to comb your hair and carelessly drop the brush; you have only just picked it up, when you drop it again. You then pick it up with a shade of impatience, and, in consequence, you drop it a third time; you try to catch it as it is falling, but . . . from an unlucky blow of your hand, the brush makes for the mirror; in vain you rush to save it, crack . . . there is a star of cracks on that antique mirror of which you were so proud.

"Damn! Devil take it! And you experience a need to vent your fresh annoyance on some one or other, and not finding the newspaper beside your morning coffee, the servant having forgotten to put it there, the cup of your patience overflows and you decide that you cannot stand the fellow any longer in the house.

"It is time for you to go out. The weather being pleasant, and not having far to go, you decide to walk. Behind you glides your new automobile of the latest model.

"The bright sunshine somewhat calms you, and a crowd which has collected at the corner attracts your attention.

"You go nearer, and in the middle of the crowd you see a man lying unconscious on the pavement. A policeman, with the help of some of the, as they are called, 'idlers' who have collected, puts the man into a 'taxi' to take him to the hospital.

"Thanks merely to the likeness, which has just struck you, between the face of the chauffeur and the face of the drunkard you bumped into last year when you were returning somewhat tipsy yourself from a rowdy birthday party, you notice that the accident on the street-corner is unaccountably connected in your associations with a meringue you ate at that party.

"Ah, what a meringue that was!

"That servant of yours, forgetting your newspaper today, spoiled your morning coffee. Why not make up for it at once?

"Here is a fashionable café where you sometimes go with your friends.

"But why did you recall the servant? Had you not almost entirely forgotten the morning's annoyances? But now . . . how very good this meringue tastes with the coffee.

"Look! There are two ladies at the next table. What a charming blonde!

"You hear her whispering to her companion, glancing at you: 'Now he is the sort of man I like!'

"Do you deny that from these words about you, accidentally overheard and perhaps intentionally said aloud, the whole of you, as is said, 'inwardly rejoices'?

"Suppose that at this moment you were asked whether it had been worth while getting fussed and losing your temper over the morning's annoyances, you would of course answer in the negative and promise yourself that nothing of the kind should ever occur again.

"Need you be told how your mood was transformed while you were making the acquaintance of the blonde in whom you were interested and who was interested in you, and its state during all the time you spent with her?

"You return home humming some air, and even the sight of the broken mirror only elicits a smile from you.

But how about the business on which you had gone out this morning. . . . You only just remember it. Clever . . . well, never mind, you can telephone.

"You go to the phone and the girl connects you with the wrong number.

"You ring again, and get the same number. Some man informs you that you are bothering him, you tell him it is not your fault, and what with one word and another, you learn to your surprise that you are a scoundrel and an idiot and that if you ring him up again . . . then . . .

"A rug slipping under your feet provokes a storm of indignation, and you should hear the tone of voice in which you rebuke the servant who is handing you a letter.

"The letter is from a man you esteem and whose good opinion you value highly.

"The contents of the letter are so flattering to you, that as you read, your irritation gradually passes and changes to the 'pleasant embarrassment' of a man listening to a eulogy of himself. You finish reading the letter in the happiest of moods.

"I could continue this picture of your day—you free man!

"Perhaps you think I am overdrawing?

"No, it is a photographically exact snapshot from nature."

While speaking of the will of man and of the various aspects of its supposedly self-initiated manifestations, which for contemporary what are called "enquiring minds"—but according to our reasoning, "naïve minds"—are matters for wiseacring and self-adulation, it will do no harm to quote what was said by Mr. Gurdjieff in another "conversational lecture," because the totality of what he then said may well throw light on the illusoriness of that will which every man supposedly has.

Mr. Gurdjieff said:

"A man comes into the world like a clean sheet of paper, which immediately all around him begin vying with each other to dirty and fill up with education, morality, the information we call knowledge, and with all kinds of feelings of duty, honor, conscience, and so on and so forth.

"And each and all claim immutability and infallibility for the methods they employ for grafting these branches onto the main trunk, called man's personality.

"The sheet of paper gradually becomes dirty, and the dirtier it becomes, that is to say, the more a man is stuffed with ephemeral information and those notions of duty, honor, and so on which are dinned into him or suggested to him by others, the 'cleverer' and worthier is he considered by those around him.

"And seeing that people look upon his 'dirt' as a merit, he himself inevitably comes to regard this same dirtied sheet of paper in the same light.

"And so you have a model of what we call a man, to which frequently are added such words as 'talent' and 'genius.'

"And the temper of our 'talent' when it wakes up in the morning is spoiled for the whole day if it does not find its slippers beside the bed.

"The ordinary man is not free in his manifestations, in his life, in his moods.

"He cannot be what he would like to be; and what he considers himself to be, he is not that.

"Man—how mighty it sounds! The very name 'man' means 'the acme of Creation'; but . . . how does his title fit contemporary man?

"At the same time, man should indeed be the acme of Creation, since he is formed with and has in himself all the possibilities for acquiring all the data exactly similar to the data in the ACTUALIZER of EVERYTHING EXISTING in the Whole of the Universe."

To possess the right to the name of "man," one must be one.

And to be such, one must first of all, with an indefatigable persistence and an unquenchable impulse of desire, issuing from all the separate independent parts constituting one's entire common presence, that is to say, with a desire issuing simultaneously from thought, feeling, and organic instinct, work on an all-round knowledge of oneself—at the same time struggling unceasingly with one's subjective weaknesses—and then afterwards, taking one's stand upon the results thus obtained by one's consciousness alone, concerning the defects in one's established subjectivity as well as the elucidated means for the possibility of combatting them, strive for their eradication without mercy towards oneself.

Speaking frankly, and wholly without partiality, contemporary man as we know him is nothing more nor less than merely a clockwork mechanism, though of a very complex construction.

About his mechanicality, a man must without fail think deeply from every aspect and with an entire absence of partiality and well understand it, in order fully to appreciate what significance that mechanicality and all its involved consequences and results may have both for his own further life as well as for the justification of the sense and aim of his arising and existence.

For one who desires to study human mechanicality in general and to make it clear to himself, the very best object of study is he himself with his own mechanicality; and to study this practically and to understand it sensibly, with all one's being, and not "psychopathically," that is, with only one part of one's entire presence, is possible only as a result of correctly conducted self-observation.

And as regards this possibility of correctly conducting self-observation and conducting it without the risk of incurring the maleficent consequences which have more than once been observed from people's attempts to do this without proper knowledge, it is necessary that the warning must be given—in order to avoid the possibility of excessive zeal—that our experience, based on the vast exact information we have, has shown that this is not so simple a thing as at first glance it may appear. This is why we make the study of the mechanicality of contemporary man the groundwork of a correctly conducted self-observation.

Before beginning to study this mechanicality and all the principles for a correctly conducted self-observation, a man in the first place must decide, once and forever, that he will be sincere with himself unconditionally, will shut his eyes to nothing, shun no results wherever they may lead him, be afraid of no inferences, and be limited by no previous, self-imposed limits; and secondly, in order that the elucidation of these principles may be properly perceived and transubstantiated in the followers of this new teaching, it is necessary to establish a corresponding form of "language," since we find the established form of language quite unsuitable for such elucidations.

As regards the first condition, it is necessary now at the very outset to give warning that a man unaccustomed to think and act along lines corresponding to the principles of self-observation must have great courage to accept sincerely the inferences obtained and not to lose heart; and submitting to them, to continue those principles further with the crescendo of persistence, obligatorily requisite for this.

These inferences may, as is said, "upset" all the convictions and beliefs previously deep-rooted in a man, as well as also the whole order of his ordinary mentation;

and, in that event, he might be robbed, perhaps forever, of all the pleasant as is said "values dear to his heart," which have hitherto made up his calm and serene life.

Thanks to correctly conducted self-observation, a man will from the first days clearly grasp and indubitably establish his complete powerlessness and helplessness in the face of literally everything around him.

With the whole of his being he will be convinced that everything governs him, everything directs him. He neither governs nor directs anything at all.

He is attracted and repelled not only by everything animate which has in itself the capacity to influence the arising of some or other association in him, but even by entirely inert and inanimate things.

Without any self-imagination or self-calming—impulses which have become inseparable from contemporary men—he will cognize that his whole life is nothing but a blind reacting to the said attractions and repulsions.

He will clearly see how his what are called world-outlooks, views, character, taste, and so on are molded—in short, how his individuality was formed and under what influences its details are liable to change.

And as regards the second indispensable condition, that is, the establishment of a correct language; this is necessary because our still recently established language which has procured, so to say, "rights-of-citizenship," and in which we speak, convey our knowledge and notions to others, and write books, has in our opinion already become such as to be now quite worthless for any more or less exact exchange of opinions.

The words of which our contemporary language consists, convey, owing to the arbitrary thought people put into them, indefinite and relative notions, and are therefore perceived by average people "elastically."

In obtaining just this abnormality in the life of man,

a part was played in our opinion, by always that same established abnormal system of education of the rising generation.

And it played a part because, based, as we have already said, chiefly on compelling the young to "learn by rote" as many words as possible differentiated one from the other only by the impression received from their consonance and not by the real pith of the meaning put into them, this system of education has resulted in the gradual loss in people of the capacity to ponder and reflect upon what they are talking about and upon what is being said to them.

As a result of the loss of this capacity and in view, at the same time, of the necessity to convey thoughts more or less exactly to others, they are obliged, in spite of the endless number of words already existing in all contemporary languages, either to borrow from other languages or to invent always more and more words; which has finally brought it about that when a contemporary man wishes to express an idea for which he knows many apparently suitable words and expresses this idea in a word which seems, according to his mental reflection, to be fitting, he still instinctively feels uncertain whether his choice is correct, and unconsciously gives this word his own subjective meaning.

Owing on the one hand to this already automatized usage, and on the other hand to the gradual disappearance of the capacity to concentrate his active attention for any length of time, the average man on uttering or hearing any word involuntarily emphasizes and dwells upon this or that aspect of the notion conveyed by the word, invariably concentrating the whole meaning of the word upon one feature of the notion indicated by it; that is to say, the word signifies for him not all the implications of the given idea, but merely the first chance significance dependent upon the ideas formed in the link of automatic associations flowing in him. Hence every time that in the course of conversation the contemporary man hears or speaks one and the same word, he gives it another meaning, at times quite contradictory to the sense conveyed by the given word.

For any man who has become aware of this to some degree, and has learned more or less how to observe, this "tragicomic feast of sound" is particularly sharply constated and made evident when others join the conversation of two contemporary people.

Each of them puts his own subjective sense into all the words that have become gravity-center words in the said so to say "symphony of words without content," and to the ear of this impartial observer it is all perceived only as what is called in the ancient Sinokooloopianian tales of *The Thousand and One Nights*, "cacophonous-fantastic-nonsense."

Conversing in this fashion, contemporary people nevertheless imagine they understand one another and are certain that they are conveying their thoughts to each other.

We, on the other hand, relying upon a mass of indisputable data confirmed by psycho-physico-chemical experiments, categorically affirm that as long as contemporary people remain as they are, that is to say "average people," they will never, whatever they may be talking about among themselves, and particularly if the subject be abstract, understand the same notions by the same words nor will they ever actually comprehend one another.

This is why, in the contemporary average man, every inner experience and even every painful experience which engenders mentation and which has obtained logical results which might in other circumstances be very beneficent to those round about, is not manifested outwardly but is only transformed into so to say an "enslaving factor" for him himself.

Thanks to this, even the isolation of the inner life of each individual man is increased, and as a consequence what is called the "mutual instruction" so necessary to people's collective existence is always more and more destroyed.

Owing to the loss of the capacity to ponder and reflect, whenever the contemporary average man hears or employs in conversation any word with which he is familiar only by its consonance, he does not pause to think, nor does there even arise in him any question as to what exactly is meant by this word, he having already decided, once and for all, both that he knows it and that others know it too.

A question, perhaps, does sometimes arise in him when he hears an entirely unfamiliar word the first time; but in this case he is content merely to substitute for the unfamiliar word another suitable word of familiar consonance and then to imagine that he has understood it.

To bring home what has just been said, an excellent example is provided by the word so often used by every contemporary man—"world."

If people knew how to grasp for themselves what passes in their thoughts when they hear or use the word "world," then most of them would have to admit—if of course they intended to be sincere—that the word carries no exact notion whatever for them. Catching by ear simply the accustomed consonance, the meaning of which they assume that they know, it is as if they say to themselves "Ah, world, I know what this is," and serenely go on thinking.

Should one deliberately arrest their attention on this word and know how to probe them to find just what they understand by it, they will at first be plainly as is said "embarrassed," but quickly pulling themselves together, that is to say, quickly deceiving themselves, and recalling the first definition of the word that comes to mind, they will then offer it as their own, although, in fact, they had not thought of it before.

If one has the requisite power and could compel a group of contemporary people, even from among those who have received so to say "a good education," to state exactly how they each understand the word "world," they would all so "beat about the bush" that involuntarily one would recall even castor oil with a certain tenderness. For instance, one of them who among other things had read up a few books on astronomy, would say that the "world" is an enormous number of suns surrounded by planets situated at colossal distances from each other and together forming what we call the "Milky Way"; beyond which, at immeasurable distances and beyond the limits of spaces accessible to our investigation, are presumably other constellations and other worlds.

Another, interested in contemporary physics, would speak of the world as a systematic evolution of matter, beginning with the atom and winding up with the very largest aggregates such as planets and suns; perhaps he would refer to the theory of the similitude of the world of atoms and electrons and the world of suns and planets, and so on in the same strain.

One who, for some reason or other, had made a hobby of philosophy and read all the mishmash on that subject would say that the world is only the product of our subjective picturings and imaginings, and that our Earth, for example, with its mountains and seas, its vegetable and animal kingdoms, is a world of appearances, an illusory world.

A man acquainted with the latest theories of polydimensional space would say that the world is usually looked upon as an infinite three-dimensional sphere, but that in reality a three-dimensional world as such cannot exist and is only an imagined cross section of another four-dimensional world out of which comes and into which goes everything proceeding around us.

A man whose world view is founded on the dogmas of religion would say that the world is everything existing, visible and invisible, created by God and depending on His Will. Our life in the visible world is brief, but in the invisible world, where a man receives reward or punishment for all his acts during his sojourn in the visible world, life is eternal.

One bitten with spiritualism would say that, side by side with the visible world, there exists also another, a world of the "Beyond," and that communication has already been established with the beings populating this world of the "Beyond."

A fanatic of theosophy would go still further and say that seven worlds exist interpenetrating each other and composed of more and more rarefied matter, and so on.

In short, not a single contemporary man would be able to offer a single definite notion, exact for all acceptances, of the real meaning of the word "world."

The whole psychic inner life of the average man is nothing but an "automatized contact" of two or three series of associations previously perceived by him of impressions fixed under the action of some impulse then arisen in him in all the three heterogeneous localizations or "brains" contained in him. When the associations begin to act anew, that is to say, when the repetition of corresponding impressions appears, they begin to constate, under the influence of some inner or outer accidental shock, that in another localization the homogeneous impressions evoked by them begin to be repeated.

All the particularities of the world view of the ordinary

man and the characteristic features of his individuality ensue, and depend on the sequence of the impulse proceeding in him at the moment of the perception of new impressions and also on the automatism established for the arising of the process of the repetition of those impressions.

And it is this that explains the incongruity, always observed even by the average man during his passive state, in the several associations having nothing in common, which simultaneously flow within him.

The said impressions in the common presence of a man are perceived owing to the three, as it were, apparatuses in him—as there are apparatuses in general in the presences of all animals—acting as perceivers for all the seven what are called "planetary-gravity-center-vibrations."

The structure of these perceptive apparatuses is the same in all the parts of the mechanism.

They consist in adaptations recalling clean wax phonograph disks; on these disks, or, as they might otherwise be called, "reels," all the impressions received begin to be recorded from the first days after the appearance of a man in the world, and even before, during the period of his formation in his mother's womb.

And the separate apparatuses constituting this general mechanism possess also a certain automatically acting adaptation, owing to which newly arriving impressions, in addition to being recorded alongside those previously perceived and similar to them, are also recorded alongside those impressions perceived simultaneously with these latter.

Thus every impression experienced is inscribed in several places and on several reels, and there, on these reels, it is preserved unchanged.

These impressed perceptions have such a property that

from contact with homogeneous vibrations of the same quality, they, so to say, "rouse themselves," and there is then repeated in them an action similar to the action which evoked their first arising.

And it is this repetition of previously perceived impressions engendering what is called association, and the parts of this repetition which enter the field of a man's attention, that together condition what is termed "memory."

The memory of the average man, in comparison with the memory of a man harmoniously perfected, is a very very imperfect adaptation for his utilization, during his responsible life, of his previously perceived store of impressions.

With the aid of memory, the average man from among impressions previously perceived can make use of and, so to say, keep track of only a very small part of his whole store of impressions, whereas the memory proper to the real man keeps track of all his impressions without exception, whenever they may have been perceived.

Many experiments have been made, and it has been established with indubitable exactitude, that every man in definite states, as for example in the state of a certain stage of hypnotism, can remember to the most minute particular everything that has ever happened to him; he can remember all the details of the surroundings and the faces and voices of the people around him, even those of the first days of his life, when he was still, according to people's notions, an unconscious being.

When a man is in one of these states, it is possible, artificially, to make even the reels hidden in the most obscure corners of the mechanism start working; but it often happens that these reels begin to unwind of themselves under the influence of some overt or hidden shock evoked by some experiencing, whereupon there suddenly rise up before the man long-forgotten scenes, picturings, faces, and so on.

At this point, I interrupted the lecturer and considered it opportune to make the following addition:

THE ADDITION

Such is the ordinary average man—an unconscious slave entirely at the service of all-universal purposes, which are alien to his own personal individuality.

He may live through all his years as he is, and as such be destroyed for ever.

But at the same time Great Nature has given him the possibility of being not merely a blind tool entirely at the service of these all-universal objective purposes but, while serving Her and actualizing what is foreordained for him—which is the lot of every breathing creature—of working at the same time also for himself, for his own egoistic individuality.

This possibility was given also for service to the common purpose, owing to the fact that, for the equilibrium of these objective laws, such relatively liberated people are necessary.

Although the said liberation is possible, nevertheless whether any particular man has the chance to attain it—this is difficult to say.

There are a mass of reasons which may not permit it; and moreover which in most cases depend neither upon us personally nor upon great laws, but only upon the various accidental conditions of our arising and formation, of which the chief are heredity and the conditions under which the process of our "preparatory age" flows. It is just these uncontrollable conditions which may not permit this liberation.

The chief difficulty in the way of liberation from whole

entire slavery consists in this, that it is necessary, with an intention issuing from one's own initiative and persistence, and sustained by one's own efforts, that is to say, not by another's will but by one's own, to obtain the eradication from one's presence both of the already fixed consequences of certain properties of that something in our forefathers called the organ Kundabuffer, as well as of the predisposition to those consequences which might again arise.

In order that you should have at least an approximate understanding of this strange organ with its properties, and also of the manifestations in ourselves of the consequences of these properties, we must dwell a little longer upon this question and speak about it in somewhat greater detail.

Great Nature, in Her foresight and for many important reasons (about which theoretical explanations will be given in later lectures), was constrained to place within the common presences of our remote ancestors just such an organ, thanks to the engendering properties of which they might be protected from the possibility of seeing and feeling anything as it proceeds in reality.

Although this organ was later "removed" also by Great Nature from their common presences, yet owing to a cosmic law expressed by the words "the assimilation of the results of oft-repeated acts"—according to which law, from the frequent repetition of one and the same act there arises in every "world concentration" under certain conditions a predisposition to produce similar results—this law-conformable predisposition which arose in our forefathers was transmitted by heredity from generation to generation, so that when their descendants in the process of their ordinary existence established numerous conditions which proved to be congenial for the said law-conformableness, from that time on the consequences of the various properties of this organ arose in them, and being assimilated owing to transmission by heredity from generation to generation, they ultimately acquired almost the same manifestations as those of their ancestors.

An approximate understanding of the manifestations in ourselves of these consequences may be derived from a further fact, perfectly intelligible to our Reason and beyond any doubt whatever.

All of us, people, are mortal and every man may die at any moment.

Now the question arises, can a man really picture to himself and so to say "experience" in his consciousness, the process of his own death?

No! His own death and the experiencing of this process, a man can never, however he may wish, picture to himself.

A contemporary ordinary man can picture to himself the death of another, though even this, not fully.

He can picture to himself, for instance, that a certain Mr. Smith leaves the theater and crossing the street, falls beneath an automobile and is crushed to death.

Or that a signboard blown down by the wind falls on the head of Mr. Jones who happened to be passing and kills him on the spot.

Or that Mr. Brown, having eaten bad crayfish, gets poisoned and, no one being able to save him, dies the next day.

Anyone can easily picture all these. But can the average man contemplate the same possibility for himself, as he admits for Mr. Smith, Mr. Jones, and Mr. Brown, and feel and live through all the despair from the fact that those events may happen to him?

Think what would happen to a man who clearly pictures to himself and lives through the inevitability of his own death.

If he seriously ponders and is really able to enter deeply into this and to cognize his own death, what could be more terrifying?

In ordinary life, particularly in recent times, over and above the depressing fact of the inevitability of death which must infallibly occur to them, there are indeed for people a large number of other similar facts, whose real picturing alone of the possibility of experiencing them must evoke in us feelings of inexpressible and intolerable anguish.

Suppose that such contemporary people as have already lost entirely all possibility of having any real objective hope for the future, that is to say, those of them who have never "sown" anything during their responsible life and who in consequence have nothing to "reap" in the future—suppose they should cognize the inevitability of their speedy death, then from only an experiencing in thought alone would they hang themselves.

The particularity of the action of the consequences of the properties of the said organ on the common psyche of people consists just in this that, thanks to it, there does not arise among most contemporary people—these three-brained beings in whom were placed all the hopes and expectations of our CREATOR, as possible servers of higher purposes—the cognition of any of these genuine terrors, and also that it enables them peacefully to carry on their existence in unconscious fulfillment of what was foreordained, but in the service only of Nature's nearest immediate aims, as they have meanwhile lost, on account of their unbecoming abnormal life, any possibility of serving higher purposes.

Thanks to these consequences, not only does the cognition of these terrors not arise in the psyche of these people, but also for the purpose of self-quieting they even invent all kinds of fantastic explanations plausible to their naïve logic for what they really sense and also for what they do not sense at all.

As, for instance, suppose that the solution of the question of our inability really to sense various possible genuine terrors, in particular the terror of one's own death, should become, so to say, a "burning question of the day"—which occurs with certain questions in the contemporary life of people—then in all probability all contemporary people, ordinary mortals as well as those called the "learned," would categorically offer a solution, which they would not doubt for a moment and, as is said, spluttering at the mouth, would set about to prove that what in fact saves people from being able to experience such terrors is just their own "will."

But if this is admitted, then why does not this same presumed will protect us from all the little fears we experience at every step?

In order to sense and understand with your whole being what I am now saying, and not merely to understand with that so to say "mind-fornication" of yours, which to the misfortune of our descendants has become the dominant inherency of contemporary people, picture to yourself now merely the following.

Today, after the lecture, you return home, undress, and get into bed, but just as you are covering yourself with your blanket a mouse jumps out from under the pillow and scuttling across your body ducks into the folds of the blankets.

Admit candidly, does not a shiver actually already run through the whole of your body merely at the bare thought of such a possibility?

Is it not so?

Now please try to make an exception and without the participation of any of that, so to say, "subjective emotionalness," whatsoever, which has become fixed in you, think with your mentation alone about such a possible occurrence to you, and you yourself will then be amazed that you react to this in this way.

What is so terrifying in this?

It is only an ordinary house mouse, the most harmless and inoffensive of beasts.

Now I ask you, how can all that has been said be explained by that will, which is presumed to be in every man?

How is it possible to reconcile the fact that a man is terrified at a small timid mouse, the most frightened of all creatures, and of thousands of other similar trifles which might never even occur, and yet experiences no terror before the inevitability of his own death?

In any case, to explain such an obvious contradiction by the action of the famous human will—is impossible.

When this contradiction is considered openly, without any preconceptions, that is to say, without any of the ready-made notions derived from the wiseacring of various what are called "authorities," who in most cases have become such thanks to the naïveté and "herd instinct" of people, as well as from the results, depending on abnormal education, which arise in our mentation, then it becomes indubitably evident that all these terrors, from which in man there does not arise the impulse, as we said, to hang himself, are permitted by Nature Herself to the extent in which they are necessary for the process of our ordinary existence.

And indeed without them, without all these, in the objective sense, as is said, "fleabites," but which appear to us as "unprecedented terrors," there could not proceed in us any experiencings at all, either of joy, sorrow, hope, disappointment, and so on, nor could we have all those cares, stimuli, strivings, and, in general, all kinds of impulses, which constrain us to act, to attain to something, and to strive for some aim.

It is just this totality of all these automatic, as they might be called, "childish experiencings" arising and flowing in the average man which on the one hand make up and sustain his life, and on the other hand give him neither the possibility nor the time to see and feel reality.

If the average contemporary man were given the possibility to sense or to remember, if only in his thought, that at a definite known date, for instance, tomorrow, a week, or a month, or even a year or two hence, he would die and die for certain, what would then remain, one asks, of all that had until then filled up and constituted his life?

Everything would lose its sense and significance for him. What would be the importance then of the decoration he received yesterday for long service and which had so delighted him, or that glance he recently noticed, so full of promise, from the woman who had long been the object of his constant and unrewarded longing, or the newspaper with his morning coffee, and that deferential greeting from the neighbor on the stairs, and the theater in the evening, and rest and sleep, and all his favorite things—of what account would they all be?

They would no longer have that significance which had been given them before, even if a man knew that death would overtake him only in five or six years.

In short, to look his own death, as is said, "in the face" the average man cannot and must not—he would then, so to say, "get out of his depth" and before him, in clear-cut form, the question would arise: "Why then should we live and toil and suffer?"

Precisely that such a question may not arise, Great Nature, having become convinced that in the common presences of most people there have already ceased to be any factors for meritorious manifestations proper to three-centered beings, had providentially wisely protected them by allowing the arising in them of various consequences of those nonmeritorious properties unbecoming to three-centered beings which, in the absence of a proper actualization, conduce to their not perceiving or sensing reality.

And Great Nature was constrained to adapt Herself to such an, in the objective sense, abnormality, in consequence of the fact that thanks to the conditions of their ordinary life established by people themselves the deteriorating quality of their radiations required for Higher Common Cosmic Purposes insistently demanded, for the maintenance of equilibrium, an increase of the quantity of the arisings and existings of these lives.

Whereupon it follows that life in general is given to people not for themselves, but that this life is necessary for the said Higher Cosmic Purposes, in consequence of which Great Nature watches over this life so that it may flow in a more or less tolerable form, and takes care that it should not prematurely cease.

Do not we, people, ourselves also feed, watch over, look after, and make the lives of our sheep and pigs as comfortable as possible?

Do we do all this because we value their lives for the sake of their lives?

No! We do all this in order to slaughter them one fine day and to obtain the meat we require, with as much fat as possible.

In the same way Nature takes all measures to ensure that we shall live without seeing the terror, and that we should not hang ourselves, but live long; and then, when we are required, She slaughters us.

Under the established conditions of the ordinary life of people, this has now already become an immutable law of Nature.

There is in our life a certain very great purpose and

we must all serve this Great Common Purpose—in this lies the whole sense and predestination of our life.

All people without exception are slaves of this "Greatness," and all are compelled willy-nilly to submit, and to fulfill without condition or compromise what has been predestined for each of us by his transmitted heredity and his acquired Being.

Now, after all that I have said, returning to the chief theme of the lecture read here today, I wish to refresh your memory about what has several times been referred to in defining man—the expressions "real man" and a "man in quotation marks," and in conclusion, to say the following.

Although the real man who has already acquired his own "I" and also the man in quotation marks who has not, are equally slaves of the said "Greatness," yet the difference between them, as I have already said, consists in this, that since the attitude of the former to his slavery is conscious, he acquires the possibility, simultaneously with serving the all-universal Actualizing, of applying a part of his manifestations according to the providence of Great Nature for the purpose of acquiring for himself "imperishable Being," whereas the latter, not cognizing his slavery, serves during the flow of the entire process of his existence exclusively only as a thing, which when no longer needed, disappears forever.

In order to make what I have just said more comprehensible and concrete, it will be useful if we compare human life in general to a large river which rises from various sources and flows on the surface of our planet, and the life of any given man to one of the drops of water composing this river of life.

This river at first flows as a whole along a comparatively level valley, and at that place where Nature has particularly undergone what is called a "cataclysm not according to law," it is divided into two separate streams, or, as it is also said, there occurs in this river a "dividing of the waters."

All the water of one stream, soon after passing this place, flows into a still more level valley, and with no surrounding what is called "majestic and picturesque" scenery to hinder it, ultimately flows into the vast ocean.

The second stream, continuing its flow over places formed by the consequences of the said "cataclysm not according to law," ultimately falls into crevices in the earth, themselves also consequences of the same cataclysm, and seeps into the very depths of the earth.

Although after the branching of the waters the waters of both these streams flow further independently and no longer mingle, yet along the whole extent of their further course, they frequently approach so near each other that all the results engendered from the process of their flowing blend, and even at times during great atmospheric phenomena, such as storms, winds, and so on, splashes of water, or even separate drops pass from one stream into the other.

Individually the life of every man up to his reaching responsible age corresponds to a drop of water in the initial flow of the river, and the place where the dividing of the waters occurs corresponds to the time when he attains adulthood.

After this branching, any considerable subsequent movement, according to law, both of this river as well as of any of the small details of this movement for the actualization of the predetermined destination of the whole river, applies equally to every separate drop, just in so far as the given drop is in the general totality of this river.

For the drop itself, all its own displacements, directions, and states caused by the differences of its position, by its various accidentally arisen surrounding conditions, and by the accelerated or retarded tempo of its movement, have always a totally accidental character.

For the drops, there is not a separate predetermination of their personal fate—a predetermined fate is for the whole river only.

At the beginning of the flow of the river, the lives of drops are here one moment, there the next moment, and a moment later they might not at all be as they are, but splashed out of the river and evaporated.

And so when, on account of the unbecoming life of people, Great Nature was constrained to engender the corresponding in their common presences, then from that time on it was so established for the purposes of the common actualizing of everything existing that human life in general on the Earth should flow in two streams; and Great Nature foresaw and gradually fixed in the details of Her common actualization such a corresponding law-conformableness, that in the drops of the water of the initial flow of the river of life, which have corresponding inner subjective what are called "struggles of one's own self-denial," there might arise or not arise that "something," thanks to which certain properties are acquired giving the possibility, at the place of the branching of the waters of the river of life, of entering one or the other stream.

This something, which in the common presence of a drop of water is a factor actualizing in it the property corresponding to one or another of the streams, is in the common presence of each man who attains responsible age that "I," which was referred to in today's lecture.

A man who has in his common presence his own "I" enters one of the streams of the river of life; and the man who has not, enters the other.

The subsequent fate of any drop in the general river

of life is determined at the dividing of the waters, according to the stream the drop happens to enter.

And it is determined, as has already been said, by the fact that one of these two streams ultimately empties itself into the ocean, that is, into that sphere of general Nature which often has what is called repeated "reciprocal exchange of substances between various great cosmic concentrations" through the process of what is called "Pokhdalissdjancha," a part of which process, by the way, contemporary people name "cyclone": in consequence of which this drop of water has the possibility to evolve, as it is, to the next higher concentration.

And at the end of the flow of the other stream, as has already been said, into the crevices of the Earth's "nether regions," where it participates in the continuous process called "involutionary construction" which proceeds within the planet, it is transformed into steam and distributed into corresponding spheres of new arisings.

After the branching of the waters, great and small successive law-conformablenesses and details for the outer movement for the purpose of actualizing the predetermined destination of both streams also ensue from these same cosmic laws, but only the results ensuing from them are so to say "subjectivized" for both streams correspondingly; and although they begin to function independently, yet all the time they mutually assist and sustain each other. These subjectivized second-grade results, issuing from fundamental cosmic laws, sometimes function side by side, sometimes collide or cross, but never mix. The actions of these subjectivized second-grade results can sometimes under certain surrounding conditions spread also over the separate drops.

For us contemporary people, the chief evil is that we—thanks to the various conditions of our ordinary existence established by us ourselves, chiefly in consequence of the abnormal what is called "education"—attaining responsible age and acquiring presences which correspond only to that stream of the river of life which ultimately empties itself into the "nether regions," enter it and are carried along where and whither it wills, and without pondering about the consequences, we remain passive, and submitting to the flow, drift on and on.

As long as we remain passive, not only shall we have inevitably to serve solely as a means for Nature's "involutionary and evolutionary construction," but also for the rest of our lives we shall have to submit slavishly to every caprice of all sorts of blind events.

As most of the hearers present have already, as is said, "crossed over" into responsible age and frankly cognize that until now they have not acquired their own "I," and at the same time, according to the substance of all I have said here, have not pictured for themselves any particularly agreeable perspectives, then, in order that you—just you who cognize this—should not be greatly, as is said, "disheartened" and should not fall into the usual what is called "pessimism" everywhere prevalent in the contemporary abnormal life of people, I say quite frankly, without any arrière-pensée, that, according to my convictions which have been formed thanks to long years of investigations strengthened by numerous quite exceptionally conducted experiments on the results of which are based the "Institute-for-the-Harmonious-Development-of-Man" founded by me—even for you, it is not yet too late.

The point is that the said investigations and experiments showed me very clearly and very definitely that in everything under the care of Mother Nature the possibility is foreseen for beings to acquire the kernel of their essence, that is to say, their own "I," even after the beginning of their responsible age also.

The foresight of Just Mother Nature consists in the

given case in this, that the possibility is given to us, in certain inner and outer conditions, to cross over from one stream into the other.

The expression which has reached us from ancient times, "the first liberation of man," refers to just this possibility of crossing from the stream which is predestined to disappear into the nether regions into the stream which empties itself into the vast spaces of the boundless ocean.

To cross into the other stream is not so easy—merely to wish and you cross. For this, it is first of all necessary consciously to crystallize in yourselves data for engendering in your common presences a constant unquenchable impulse of desire for such a crossing, and then, afterwards, a long corresponding preparation.

For this crossing it is necessary first of all to renounce all the what seem to you "blessings"—but which are, in reality, automatically and slavishly acquired habits—present in this stream of life.

In other words, it is necessary to become dead to what has become for you your ordinary life.

It is just this death that is spoken of in all religions.

It is defined in the saying which has reached us from remote antiquity, "Without death no resurrection," that is to say, "If you do not die you will not be resurrected."

The death referred to is not the death of the body, since for such a death there is no need of resurrection.

For if there is a soul, and moreover, an immortal soul, it can dispense with a resurrection of the body.

Nor is the necessity of resurrection our appearance before the awful Judgment of the Lord God, as we have been taught by the Fathers of the Church.

No! Even Jesus Christ and all the other prophets sent from Above spoke of the death which might occur even during life, that is to say, of the death of that "Tyrant" from whom proceeds our slavery in this life and whose destruction can alone assure the first chief liberation of man.

Summing up all that has been said, the thoughts set out in the lecture you have heard read, as well as what I have added today, that is, about the two categories of contemporary people who in respect of inner content have nothing in common, and about that grievous fact which has been made clear to a certain degree thanks to the addition I have made, namely, that in the common presences of people in recent times, thanks to progressively deteriorating conditions of ordinary life established by us—particularly owing to the wrong system of education of the rising generation—the various consequences of the organ Kundabuffer have begun to arise much more intensely, I consider it necessary to say and even to emphasize still more that all misunderstandings without exception arising in the process of our collective life, particularly in the sense of reciprocal relationship, and all disagreements, disputes, settling-ups and hasty decisions—just these decisions, after the actualization of which, in practice, there arises in us the lingering process of "Remorse-of-Conscience"—and even such great events as wars, civil wars, and other similar misfortunes of a general character proceed simply on account of a property in the common presences of ordinary people who have never specially worked on themselves, which property I this time would call "the-reflecting-of-reality-in-one's-attention-upside-down."

Every man, if he can even a little seriously think, so to say "without being identified" with his passions, must agree with this if he takes into account merely one single fact often repeated in the process of our inner life, namely, that all our experiencings which at first, just at the moment they are still proceeding in us, seem to be stark terrors, appear, after the lapse of only an insignificant time and when these experiencings have been replaced by others and are recalled by chance, and when according to our logical reasoning we are already in another mood, not worth, as is said, "a brass farthing."

In the average man the results of his mentation and feelings often lead to this, that, as it might be expressed, "a fly becomes an elephant and an elephant a fly."

The manifestations in the common presences of the said people of this maleficent property is particularly intensely actualized just during such events as wars, revolutions, civil wars, and so on.

Just during these events, the state, even constated by them, is particularly sharply manifested, under the action of which they all with few exceptions fall, and which they call "mass psychosis."

The essence of this state consists in this, that average people receiving in their already feeble mentation, which at such times becomes still more feeble, shocks from the maleficent stories of some or another lunatic, and becoming in the full sense of the word victims of these malicious stories, manifest themselves completely automatically.

During the period when they find themselves under the action of such a scourge—a scourge which has already become for contemporary ordinary people their inalienable inherency—there already entirely ceases to exist in their common presences that sacred what is called "conscience," the data for the possibility of the acquisition of which Great Nature endowed them with, as godlike beings in differentiation from mere animals.

Informed people sincerely regret just this inherency in contemporary people, because, according to historical data and also to experimental elucidations of numerous genuine learned beings of past epochs, Great Nature has already long ceased to have need for such a phenomenon as mass psychosis for Her equilibrium. Rather the contrary, such a periodically arising inherency in people compels Her always to new adaptations, as for instance increasing the birth rate, changing the what is called "tempo of the general psyche," and so on and so forth.

After all I have said I consider it necessary to say and even to emphasize further that all the historical data which have reached contemporary people and which have chanced to become known also to me, namely, the historical data concerning what really did occur in the past in the life of people, and not just those data invented by contemporary what are called learned beings, chiefly from among the Germans—with which histories all the rising generation is stuffed almost everywhere on the Earth—clearly show that people of former epochs did not divide into two streams of life, but that all flowed along in a single river.

The general life of mankind has been divided into two streams since the time of what is called the "Tikliamishian civilization," which directly preceded the Babylonian civilization.

It was just from then on that there gradually began to be and ultimately was finally established that organization of the life of mankind which, as every sane-thinking man ought to constate, can now flow more or less tolerably only if people are divided into masters and slaves.

Although to be either masters or slaves in a collective existence among children, like ourselves, of the COMMON FATHER, is unworthy of man, yet thanks at the present time to the conditions existing which have already been thoroughly fixed in the process of the collective life of people, the source of which lies in remote antiquity, we must be reconciled to it and accept a compromise that, according to impartial reasoning, should correspond both to our own personal welfare, and also at the same time not be contrary to the commandments specially issuing to us people from the "Prime-Source-of-Everything-Existing."

Such a compromise, I think, is possible if certain people consciously set themselves, as the chief aim of their existence, to acquire in their presences all the corresponding data to become masters among those around them similar to themselves.

Proceeding from this and acting according to the wise saying of ancient times affirming that "in order to be in reality a just and good altruist it is inevitably required first of all to be an out and out egoist," and also profiting by the good sense given us by Great Nature, each one of us must set for his chief aim to become in the process of our collective life a master.

But not a master in that sense and meaning which this word conveys to contemporary people, namely, one who has many slaves and much money, handed down, in most cases, by inheritance, but in the sense that a given man, thanks to his, in the objective sense, devout acts towards those around him—that is to say, acts manifested by him according to the dictates of his pure Reason alone, without the participation of those impulses which in him as in all people are engendered from the mentioned consequences of the properties of the maleficent organ Kundabuffer—acquires in himself that something which of itself constrains all those about him to bow before him and with reverence carry out his orders.

I now consider this first series of my writings ended and ended in just such a form that satisfies even myself.

In any case, I give my word that from tomorrow I shall not waste even five minutes of my time on this first series.

And now, before beginning work on the second series of my writings, in order to put them, from my point of view, into a generally accessible form, I intend to rest for a whole month, to write positively nothing, and for a stimulus to my organism, fatigued to the extreme limit, s-l-o-w-l-y to drink the still remaining fifteen bottles of "super-most-super-heavenly-nectar" called at the present time on Earth "old Calvados."

This old Calvados, by the way, twenty-seven bottles of it, I was thought worthy to find, accidentally covered over with a mixture of lime, sand, and finely chopped straw, several years ago when I was digging a pit for preserving carrots for the winter in one of the cellars of my now chief dwelling place.

These bottles of this divine liquid were buried in all probability by monks who lived nearby, far from worldly temptations, for the salvation of their souls.

It now seems to me for some reason or other that they buried these bottles there, not without some ulterior motive, and that, thanks to their what is called "intuitive perspicacity," the data for which particularity of theirs, one must assume, was formed in them thanks to their pious lives, they foresaw that the buried divine liquid would fall into hands worthy of understanding the meaning of such things; and now indeed this liquid stimulates the owner of these hands praiseworthily to sustain and assist the better transmission to the next generation of the meaning of the ideals on which the co-operation of these monks was founded.

I wish during this rest of mine, which from any point of view I fully deserve, to drink this splendid liquid, which alone during recent years has given me the possibility of tolerating without suffering the beasts similar to myself around me, and to listen to new anecdotes, and sometimes, for lack of new ones, old ones—of course, if there happen to be competent raconteurs.

It is now still midday, and as I have given my word that I would not, beginning only from tomorrow, write anything further for this first series, I still have time and shall not be breaking my word, if I add with a clean conscience that a year or two ago, I had categorically decided to make only the first series of my published writings generally accessible, and as regards the second and third series, to make them not generally accessible, but to organize their distribution in order, among other things, to actualize through them one of the fundamental tasks I have set myself under essence-oath; a task which consists in this: ultimately also to prove, without fail, theoretically as well as practically, to all my contemporaries, the absurdity of all their inherent ideas concerning the suppositious existences of a certain "other world" with its famous and so beautiful "paradise" and its so repugnant a "hell"; and at the same time to prove theoretically and afterwards without fail to show practically, so that even every "complete victim" of contemporary education should understand without shuddering and know, that Hell and Paradise do indeed exist, but only not there "in that world" but here beside us on Earth.

After the books of the first series have all been published, I intend for the spreading of the contents of the second series to organize in various large centers simultaneous public readings accessible to all.

And as regards the real, indubitably comprehensible, genuine objective truths which will be brought to light by me in the third series, I intend to make them accessible exclusively only to those from among the hearers of the second series of my writings who will be selected from specially prepared people according to my considered instructions.